The
Citizen Action
Encyclopedia

The
Citizen Action
Encyclopedia

GROUPS AND MOVEMENTS
THAT HAVE CHANGED AMERICA

Richard S. Halsey

ORYX PRESS
Westport, Connecticut • London

The rare Arabian Oryx is believed to have inspired the myth of the unicorn. This desert antelope became virtually extinct in the early 1960s. At that time several groups of international conservationists arranged to have 9 animals sent to the Phoenix Zoo to be the nucleus of a captive breeding herd. Today the Oryx population is over 1,000 and nearly 500 have been returned to reserves in the Middle East.

Library of Congress Cataloging-in-Publication Data

Halsey, Richard S.
    The citizen action encyclopedia : groups and movements that have changed America / Richard S. Halsey.
      . p.   cm.
    Includes bibliographical references and index.
    ISBN 1–57356–291–2 (alk. paper)
      1. Citizens' associations—United States—Directories.   2. Civic leaders—United States—Biography.   3. Political participation—United States.   I. Title.
    JS303.5.H35   2002
    322.4'0973—dc21   2001034822

British Library Cataloguing in Publication Data is available.

Library of Congress Catalog Card Number: 2001034822
ISBN: 1–57356–291–2

First published in 2002

Oryx Press, 88 Post Road West, Westport, CT 06881
An imprint of Greenwood Publishing Group, Inc.
www.oryxpress.com

Printed in the United States of America

The paper used in this book complies with the Permanent Paper Standard issued by the National Information Standards Organization (Z39.48–1984).

10 9 8 7 6 5 4 3 2 1

For Gillian

Contents

Preface

In his classic *Democracy in America*, Alexis de Tocqueville described Americans' penchant for organizing to make waves and take corrective political action at a time when the only formalized citizen action group in the United States was the Anti-Saloon League. He noted, "The political activity which pervades the United States must be seen in order to be understood. No sooner do you set foot upon the American soil than you are stunned by a kind of tumult; a confused clamor is heard on every side; and a thousand simultaneous voices demand the immediate satisfaction of their social wants."

This book illustrates Tocqueville's "tumult" in modern dress. It provides access to basic information about the organizations, people, and events that make up the history of citizens' attempts to make political leaders and the general public aware of and responsive to societal, economic, and ideologically based issues prominent in twentieth-century America. Included are 160 organizations that succeeded in effecting changes in the legal system, societal values, or the political landscape.

These groups and their founders were motivated by a need to protect or revise the status quo as defined by the legal system, government, big business, the education establishment, or society in general. The organizations are national only and exclude local, state, and regional groups. Also excluded are organizations such as Amnesty International and the World Federalists because their interests are more global than national and their actions have very little effect on American domestic policies and governance. The eighty-eight citizen activists described in this book include some born before 1900 (e.g., Jane Addams [1860–1935] and Marcus Mosiah Garvey Jr. [1887–1940]) whose influence peaked or remained significant during the twentieth century.

Because of the impossibility of describing the several thousand citizen activist groups that flourished during the twentieth century, filtering criteria were applied. First, the organization had to have developed a formalized identity and been involved in grassroots advocacy. Second, the organization had to be committed to making an impact on legislation, electoral outcomes, social services, or the quality of life in the United States. Finally, the organization should have achieved a modicum of success in attaining its objectives. In many instances, an organization was established without grass roots and only later became a significant citizen activist presence.

To qualify for inclusion, individuals had to achieve prominence in one or more categories of dissent or activism; attain sufficient reference value or public notoriety to receive biographical treatment in reputable biographical directories, books, articles, films, or plays; or be given substantial coverage in major city newspapers.

Not considered in the encyclopedia are professional and trade organizations, and unions that lack a strong commitment to change in society as a whole. The American Medical Association, the American Federation of Labor, the petroleum and dairy industry lobbies; and organizations promoting other products such as liquor, military hardware, and petroleum are also excluded.

All entries appear in alphabetical order, with "See also" references and "For Further Information" listings appended to biographical and organization articles. The "For Further Information" listings include print publications and Web site addresses. In cases where the only accessible documentation was on the Internet and no trustworthy or stable printed sources could be located or made available to the author by an organization or individual, the organization or individual in question was eliminated from consideration. Newspaper and periodical articles are often cited in lieu of monographic material because of the newness, secretiveness, or legally vulnerable status of many of the organizations. Cited membership figures are imprecise because many organizations overstate their size and the data in other sources can be stale or inaccurate.

Being a reference tool, this encyclopedia offers accurate but condensed descriptions, not comprehensive disquisitions on people and organizations. Therefore bibliographies are appended to the vast majority of entries to accommodate readers who wish to pursue further research. The work is internally cross-referenced through the use of small capital letters. Words in this style indicate to the reader that there is a separate entry on that individual, organization, or U.S. Supreme Court case. Additionally, "See also" references direct the reader to one or more of the thirty-six umbrella articles. The latter bring together in one place references and basic information on all people, organizations, and Supreme Court cases represented elsewhere in the work and belonging to the same category.

The umbrella article categories are as follows:

Abortion Policy
Activist Think Tanks
African American Rights
AIDS Crisis
Alcohol and Drug Policies
Animal Welfare and Rights
Anti–Nuclear Power Movement
Antiwar/Anti–Nuclear Weapons Movement
Arab American Rights
Child and Youth-Related Issues
Conservatives (Far Right)
Constitutional Rights and Civil Liberties Protection
Consumer Rights and Safeguards
Death Penalty and Choice in Dying
Disabled Persons' Rights
Environment
Extremists
False Front Organizations
Farmers' Rights
Gun Ownership Rights/Gun Controls
Hispanic American Rights
Homelessness
Human Health and Safety
Jewish American Rights
Labor Issues
Lesbians and Gays
Liberal Activism
Militia Movements
Native American Rights
Religious Right
Senior Movement
Student Activism
Tax Reform and Governmental Expenditures
Term Limits
Veterans' Issues
Women's Issues

In summary, what follows is a celebration of the actions and diversity of those who have dared to grapple with and influence the major social and political trends of a tumultuous century. These citizen activists and organizations shape our public policy, voter opinion, electoral outcomes, and the nation's destiny.

I am most grateful to Henry Rasof, vice president for New Product Development at Oryx Press, for his assistance in developing the concept and design of this book. My thanks also go to students at Texas Woman's University who assisted in documenting entries. Amy Turner, Michelle Altug, and David Black were especially helpful.

Introduction

Citizen action is a fundamental right, built into the American experience and form of government, with its origins in the right of petition, first stated in the Magna Carta in 1215. American colonists, when making their break from King George III, affirmed this prerogative in both the Declaration of Independence and the First Amendment to the Constitution, which specifies that "Congress shall make no law . . . abridging the freedom of speech, or of the press; or the right of the people peaceably to assemble, and to petition the Government for a redress of grievances." It is this clause that validates citizen activism as it exists today. And, as it was in the beginning, the main goal of activism is to influence legislators, the electoral process, laws, and regulations to the advantage of various private and public interests. Citizen action has, indeed, been so deeply woven into the American political fabric that the history of lobbying comes close to being the history of American legislation.

Only after the 1960s was there a stunning expansion of the citizen activist universe, now numbering over 15,000 different organizations. This proliferation can be attributed to six factors that changed the rules of the political game.

First among these was the series of dramatic events of the 1960s and 1970s that jolted Americans' social and political think-ing. The Vietnam War, the effort to impeach President Richard Nixon, the civil rights movement, the women's movement, the assassinations of civil rights leader MARTIN LUTHER KING JR., President John F. Kennedy, and his brother, Robert F. Kennedy, riots, the drug culture, and the discarding of traditional moral codes were all traumatic. Adding to the turmoil was an economic downturn that was hurtful to minorities in the cities and to rural America. All of this bred fear, distrust of political leadership, and the motivation to create organizations that would right social wrongs and improve conditions for the disadvantaged.

A second factor was the displacement of a trusting, acquiescent, party-allegiant electorate by active, watchful, rights-conscious citizens who voted across party lines. The familiar distinctions between Democrats and Republicans that had been in place since 1936 became blurred. No longer were the liberals, the poor and the minorities, the labor unions, proponents of social rehabilitation and federal regulation, and fighters for social equality on one side, and the conservatives, the wealthy, capital interests, proponents of minimal restriction of business, and fighters for maximal personal freedom automatically lined up on the other side. Citizen activists moved in to assume responsibilities and positions vacated by politicians, analyzing critical issues and dispensing data and opinions to the media. The new groups went forth and voted in unprecedented numbers, wrote letters, sent e-mail, demonstrated, contributed money, and became foot soldiers in the big, bruising battles over social, moral, political, and religious issues. Referenda and citizen initiatives became frequent. In California, HOWARD JARVIS led a taxpayer revolt because homeowners had lost faith in the ability of political leaders to protect their solvency by resisting financially draining tax increases. Jarvis's success, the passage of Proposition 13, capped property taxes but devastated California's public services, schools, and libraries. In Proposition 13's wake, many supposedly "safe" veteran incumbents were thrown out of office solely because of their failure to hold the line on taxes.

The third factor, term limitations, soon became popular automatic dumping devices to rid cities and statehouses of political dead wood; such limits were more reliable than depending upon disgruntled constituents to go to the polls, exercise their franchise, and vote the incumbents out of office. Because of the questionable conduct of some public officials and the growing hostility toward government, mandatory limits were placed on the number of consecutive terms legislators may serve in many states. Oklahoma, Colorado, and California passed term-limit initiatives as early as 1990, and by 1999, eighteen states and many major cities (e.g., New York City, Los Angeles, Washington, and Dallas) had followed suit. This changed the rules of activism because powerful senior legislators, those who had been most susceptible to strong-arm lobbying tactics, became political "dead stars," no longer in need of campaign contributions. They were also freed from the obligation to be concerned about their constituents. Term limitations dissuaded many talented individuals from committing themselves to careers as elected public servants, while forcing out experienced and conscientious veterans. One unintended result was lobbyists' transferal of attention from lame duck legislators to experienced aides who, as appointed staff, remained immune to removal.

A fourth factor that has complicated and extended the reach of activists is information technology. Commercial television ensures that the majority of voters receive their political information in ten-second sound bites. At the same time, the Internet has changed the nature of citizen interaction with governmental leaders by opening up more avenues of communication. Activists now have at their command a phalanx of communications devices—e-mail, interactive Web sites, faxes, chat rooms, links to like-minded organizations, and fax machines. These are being used to mobilize membership, send messages to allies, send out legislative alerts to trigger timely assaults on politicians, and pinpoint prospects for new members among mailing lists of people with profiles that indicate affinity with group aims.

Fifth, the old Burkean notion of periodically selecting a few educated and intelligent, ethically motivated, and farsighted individuals—those best qualified to govern—who are socially responsible and can be trusted to act according to conscience, is going out of fashion. The idea of representative democracy as defined by Alexander Hamilton in 1777 is now considered elitist. Hamilton cautioned that "when the deliberative or judicial powers are vested wholly or partly in the collective body of the people, you must expect error, confusion and instability. But a representative democracy, where the right of election is well secured and regulated, and the exercise of the legislative, executive and judicial authorities is vested in select persons, in such a system the will of the people prevails." According to Hamilton, this latter form of democracy would provide continuity and make the society immune to passing fads, irrational policies, and harmful legislative and judicial decisions.

As the twentieth century ended, the country had become reluctant to give politicians mandates to act independently and was moving toward making them mirror, from minute to minute, the views of their constituencies. Given this situation, character in any candidate for public office was becoming a handicap rather than an asset. Participatory democracy, which calls for people's self-governance, was coming into favor not only because of traditional representative democracy's elitist connotations but because of changes in the economy, the greatly enlarged dimensions of the U.S. demography, and rising levels of educational attainment. In 1890 fewer than 2 percent of Americans went on to college; now over 25 percent do so. In the 1990s, citizen activists had more control of the country's destiny than legislators did, and their power was about to be upgraded by the capacity to vote electronically, hastening the onset of direct democracy.

A sixth factor, further weakening old style deliberative democracy and increasing the political impact of activists, was the appearance of mass opinion molders in the media: prominent newspaper editors, television news anchors, and TV-radio sociopolitical talk show hosts such as David Letterman, Rush Limbaugh, Howard Stern, Michael Moore, Chris Matthews, Geraldo Rivera, LAURA SCHLESSINGER, Arianna Huffington, and others. These media pundits and personalities have become popular purveyors of opinion and information who influence the voting decisions of a large and growing portion of the adult population. Because of politicians' lost credibility, their limpness of character, and their unwillingness to take stands on major issues until after consulting public opinion oracles, other forces have moved in to fill the leadership gap. These are the media preachers, the few political figures who can grab the public's attention, and the expanding legions of forceful and assertive citizen activists.

In summary, American democracy, as it now functions, offers unprecedented communication avenues, one-on-one access, and power to those who can muster the financial resources and requisite willpower, organizational skills, and energy to fight for their beliefs. It will also become evident to those who scan the select sampling of organizations and activists described in the following pages that Alexis de Tocqueville was uncannily prescient in his prediction of the decline of central authority in America, saying, "So far is the Federal Government from acquiring strength, and from threatening the sovereignty of the states, as it grows older, that I maintain it to be growing weaker and weaker, and the sovereignty of the Union alone is in danger." The twenty-first century may witness a further dissolution of Americans' shared national purpose through the clamor, rancor, and warring of competing groups, or it may see the flowering of true participatory democracy, *e pluribus unum*—alongside the many, the one—as a wonderful and continually timely idea made real.

Formation of the groups within the thirty-six categories represented in this book was the product of one or more of the following motivations: (1) the desire to make society conform to religious rules of conduct or a particular political philosophy; (2) the need to escape from poverty and gain the prosperity achieved by other groups in the society; (3) the need to rebel against institutional, legally sanctioned, or societal discrimination based on ethnic origin, gender, and age; (4) altruism or the compulsion to "do good," to improve the status of others, and to decrease the negative, life endangering, and brutalizing aspects of society; (5) the need to assist those who lack the means to act on their own behalf; (6) political ambition and greed sufficiently strong to enable group leaders to resort to manipulation and deception in attaining their ends; and (7) hatred, intolerance, and extreme poverty vis-à-vis other segments of society.

1. After 1960, many organizations and their leaders decided to protect and advance their own principles to stop them from being undermined by competing political views and belief systems. Examples of organizations and individuals holding opposing views are AMERICANS FOR TAX REFORM and CITIZENS FOR TAX JUSTICE; OPERATION SAVE AMERICA and the NATIONAL ABORTION AND REPRODUCTIVE RIGHTS ACTION LEAGUE; PEOPLE FOR THE AMERICAN WAY and the CHRISTIAN COALITION; the CUBAN

AMERICAN NATIONAL FOUNDATION and CAMBIO CUBANO; the EAGLE FORUM and NATIONAL ORGANIZATION FOR WOMEN; the NATIONAL RIFLE ASSOCIATION and BRADY CENTER TO PREVENT GUN VIOLENCE, PHYLLIS SCHLAFLY and GLORIA STEINEM; RICHARD A. VIGUERIE and RALPH NADER. The conservatives seek to preserve stability, constancy, and the encouragement of individualism, and insist that social hierarchies are natural and desirable. The liberals endorse and fight for change, humanism, and egalitarianism. The right-to-life groups contend that too much power has been given to humans who are making decisions that should properly remain in the hands of God. Freedom of choice advocates believe that women's unrestricted right to reproductive choice frees them from subordinate social positions.

2. The need to escape from poverty and harsh, inhumane working conditions inspired formation of the AMERICAN AGRICULTURE MOVEMENT, the SENIOR MOVEMENT in its early stages, and the labor movement.

3. Discrimination based on ethnicity, gender, sexual preference, and age has a long history in the United States. Between 1961 and 1965 twenty-one murders of black citizens were recorded in the Deep South, and not one white was convicted of murder in any of the crimes. Lynchings were well-attended public spectacles from 1868 until 1968. Many activists and organizations have fought this enduring evil within American society. W.E.B. DU BOIS, Martin Luther King Jr., the REVEREND FRED SHUTTLESWORTH, the NATIONAL ASSOCIATION FOR THE ADVANCEMENT OF COLORED PEOPLE, the CONGRESS OF RACIAL EQUALITY, and the RAINBOW/PUSH COALITION; the AMERICAN-ARAB ANTI-DISCRIMINATION COMMITTEE; ERNESTO CORTÉS, the NATIONAL COUNCIL OF LA RAZA, and the ANTI-DEFAMATION LEAGUE, the AMERICAN INDIAN MOVEMENT, DENNIS BANKS, and RUSSELL MEANS; the HUMAN RIGHTS CAMPAIGN, FLORENCE KELLEY, BETTY FRIEDAN, and the National Organization for Women; and MAGGIE KUHN and the GRAY PANTHERS are examples of citizens' continuing battle.

4. The desire to help save animals and people from harm and improve the quality of participatory democracy has resulted in the formation of such organizations as the PEOPLE FOR THE ETHICAL TREATMENT OF ANIMALS, the SEA SHEPHERD CONSERVATION SOCIETY, the AMERICAN SOCIETY FOR THE PREVENTION OF CRUELTY TO ANIMALS, the FELLOWSHIP OF RECONCILIATION, the National Birth Control League founded by MARGARET SANGER, MOTHERS AGAINST DRUNK DRIVING, the LEAGUE OF WOMEN VOTERS, and COMMON CAUSE.

5. Organizations and individuals that have helped children and the homeless and those who lack legal standing or the means to help themselves include Boys Town, the CHILDREN'S DEFENSE FUND, the NATIONAL CENTER FOR MISSING AND EXPLOITED CHILDREN, the NATIONAL COALITION FOR THE HOMELESS, MARIAN WRIGHT EDELMAN, FATHER EDWARD JOSEPH FLANAGAN, JOHN WALSH, and MITCH SNYDER.

6. Relatively recent additions to the activist ranks include individuals and groups that often cloak their true agendas in rhetoric that preys upon people's fears, ignorance, and greed. The rise of corporate front groups, disguised as public interest organizations, was a direct response to the many influential consumer and environmental groups that came into existence in the 1960s and 1970s. In the 1980s and 1990s ultraconservatives, corporations, and clever fundraisers teamed up to create dozens of FALSE FRONT ORGANIZATIONS that recruited millions of members. Some organizations downplayed the dangers of acid rain and ozone depletion by implying that proposed regulations would not be sensible, responsible, or economically sound. Other activists were energized by urgent warnings received in the mail that raised fears of imminent financial disaster, loss of privacy, confiscation of personal property, denial of medical benefits, and other kinds of calamity—chimerical threats created by clever propagandists. The frightened recipients of such mes-

sages could be counted upon to urge members of Congress to support or oppose pending or existing legislation, unaware that they were being manipulated. Some groups folded after their members discovered they were being misled; others are still operating. Examples include CITIZENS FOR BETTER MEDICARE, Citizens for the Sensible Control of Acid Rain, Coalition for Vehicle Choice, CONSUMER ALERT, Global Climate Coalition, National Wetlands Coalition, SENIORS COALITION, and 60 PLUS.

7. Extremist groups prospered in twentieth-century America, beginning in the mid-1920s when there was a major expansion of KU KLUX KLAN activity. Anti-Semitism was particularly strident and virulent from the 1930s until the 1970s, with FATHER CHARLES E. COUGHLIN, GERALD L. K. SMITH, and ELIZABETH DILLING excelling in the craft of corrosive bigotry. Later extremist leaders and groups included John Bolivar Depuy and the MINUTEMEN, WILLIS CARTO and the LIBERTY LOBBY, the POSSE COMITATUS, and the SYMBIONESE LIBERATION ARMY. The EARTH LIBERATION FRONT and Sea Shepherd Conservation Society were among the more prominent ecoterrorist and extremist animal rights groups.

Seen in broad perspective, citizen activists have been true to the intent of the U.S. Constitution, guaranteeing that "Congress shall make no law . . . abridging . . . the right of the people to petition government for a redress of grievances." They have made the people separate from government and sustained a one-way conversation between citizens and those who govern. Generally they have held to the rule that citizen and government should retain their separate roles. The most effective leaders and their organizations have not trimmed their desires, pressing for less than the ideal as they envision it. The government inevitably compromises because its duty is to honor and hear divergent petitions, thereby giving strength to the First Amendment concept of government as being responsive to citizens' needs.

It is also Congress's place to compromise because Congress is imperfect. Some members are bought by industry, some are small-minded and inflexible, others are ensnared in a mesh of log rolling, and many are gulled into accepting private interest propaganda and biased readings of public preferences. The most effective citizen activists and organizations (e.g., SAUL DAVID ALINSKY, Martin Luther King Jr., Ralph Nader, Maggie Kuhn, Phyllis Schlafly; the SIERRA CLUB, National Rifle Association, Christian Coalition, Anti-Defamation League, Cuban American National Foundation) do not compromise because they believe that what they want is what the majority of Americans want. The tension and turmoil resulting from the clash of principles and compromise has been repeatedly played out in public demonstrations, rallies, marches, vigils, and other actions that project issues onto the media stage. The winning of women' suffrage and of civil rights for blacks and the nation's awakening to the true meaning of the Vietnam War, environmental degradation, and labor exploitation required nothing less than a jolt to the system.

What follows is a record of what happens when ordinary people graduate from spectator to citizen, deciding to do more than observe. Such people rebel at having to cast their vote for less than the best, playing the part of docile consumer and picking from prepackaged political candidates presented by the media. These are the people who recognize that democracy is a work in progress, a continuing path they must tread if the country is to move ahead.

Citizen action is a lesson in pluralism with its maze of mini publics, organizations concerned with religion, ethnicity, race, labor, poverty, the elderly, gender rights, the environment, gun ownership, and animal welfare. Only when citizens act do they move beyond merely observing elected representatives and assume their proper civic duty. When they don't, the result is a government owned and driven by private interests, the increased bifurcation of the society into the relatively comfortable and abjectly poor, and the dominance of citizenship as a kind of voyeurism, a fascination with the personalities and private lives of leaders and an indifference to their worth as political actors.

Most of the people and groups described in this book exhibit honesty, uncommon courage, self-discipline, and unwavering commitment to their particular causes. They are redefining the context in which public policy is made, and they bring light and care to domains of society that were formerly hidden and untended. Their goal is to make the nation more democratic, to foster public discussion about the principles that guide the nation, and to try to ensure that any compromises that must necessarily occur are based on a shared understanding of the common good.

Guide to Related Topics

ABORTION POLICY

Griswold v. Connecticut (381 U.S. 479) (1965)

National Abortion and Reproductive Rights Action League

National Right to Life Committee

National Women's Political Caucus

Operation Save America

Planned Parenthood Federation of America

Roe v. Wade (410 U.S. 113) (1973)

Sanger, Margaret

Schlafly, Phyllis

Terry, Randall A.

Webster v. Reproductive Health Services (492 U.S. 490) (1989)

ACTIVIST THINK TANKS

American Enterprise Institute for Public Policy Research

*Brookings Institution

Cato Institute

*Center for National Policy

*Center for Policy Alternatives

Coors, Joseph, Sr.

*Economic Policy Institute

Free Congress Research and Education Foundation

Heritage Foundation

(*See ACTIVIST THINK TANKS)

*Hoover Institution on War, Revolution and Peace

*Hudson Institute

*Independent Institute

*Joint Center for Political and Economic Studies

*Manhattan Institute for Policy Research

*Pacific Research Institute for Public Policy

*Progress and Freedom Foundation

*Reason Foundation

*Urban Institute

AFRICAN AMERICAN RIGHTS

Abernathy, Ralph David

Black Panther Party

Brown v. Board of Education of Topeka (347 U.S. 483) (1954)

Carmichael, Stokely

Chavis, Benjamin Franklin, Jr.

Clark, Septima

Congress of Racial Equality

Davis, Angela Y.

Du Bois, William Edward Burghardt (W.E.B.)

Evers, Medgar (Wiley)

Farmer, James

Farrakhan, Louis Abdul

Fonda, Jane

Garvey, Marcus Mosiah, Jr.

Hamer, Fannie Lou

Hoffman, Abbie

Jackson, Jesse

King, Martin Luther, Jr.

Malcolm X

Muhammad, Elijah

National Association for the Advancement of Colored People

National Urban League

Newton, Huey P.

Parks, Rosa

Rainbow/PUSH Coalition

Randolph, A(sa) Philip

Roosevelt, Eleanor

Seale, Robert G. ("Bobby")

Shuttlesworth, Reverend Fred

Southern Christian Leadership Conference

Student Nonviolent Coordinating Committee

AIDS CRISIS

ACT UP (AIDS Coalition to Unleash Power)

AIDS Action Council

Kramer, Larry

ALCOHOL AND DRUG POLICIES

American Council on Alcohol Problems

Mothers Against Drunk Driving

National Organization for the Reform of Marijuana Laws

ANIMAL WELFARE AND RIGHTS

American Anti-Vivisection Society

American Society for the Prevention of Cruelty to Animals

Animal Liberation Front

Humane Society of the United States

People for the Ethical Treatment of Animals

Sea Shepherd Conservation Society

ANTI-NUCLEAR POWER MOVEMENT

Clamshell Alliance

Fonda, Jane

Silkwood, Karen Gay

ANTI-WAR/ANTI-NUCLEAR WEAPONS MOVEMENT

Addams, Jane

Berrigan, Daniel J.

Berrigan, Philip F.

Catholic Worker Movement

Council for a Livable World

Day, Dorothy

Fellowship of Reconciliation

Fonda, Jane

Hayden, Tom

Hoffman, Abbie

Lynd, Staughton

Plowshares Movement

SANE, The National Committee for a Sane Nuclear Policy

20/20 Vision

ARAB AMERICAN RIGHTS

American-Arab Anti-Discrimination Committee

Council on American-Islamic Relations

CHILD AND YOUTH-RELATED ISSUES

Children's Defense Fund

Edelman, Marian Wright

Flanagan, Father Edward Joseph

In re Gault (387 U.S. 1) (1967)

Kelley, Florence

Walsh, John

COMMUNITY ACTION EMPOWERMENT

Alinsky, Saul David

Association of Community Organizations for Reform Now

Campus Outreach Opportunity League

Citizen Action

Clark, Septima

Cortés, Ernesto, Jr.

Highlander Folk School

Horton, Myles

Industrial Areas Foundation

National Civic League

Sliwa, Curtis

CONSERVATIVES (FAR RIGHT)

American Conservative Union

American Enterprise Institute for Public Policy Research

Eagle Forum

Free Congress Research and Education Foundation

Schlafly, Phyllis

Viguerie, Richard A.

CONSTITUTIONAL RIGHTS AND CIVIL LIBERTIES PROTECTION

Addams, Jane

American Civil Liberties Union

Americans United for Separation of Church and State

Buckley v. Valeo (424 U.S. 1) (1976)

Brown v. Board of Education of Topeka (347 U.S. 483) (1954)

People for the American Way

Savio, Mario

CONSUMER RIGHTS AND SAFEGUARDS

Center for Auto Safety

Center for Science in the Public Interest

Consumers Union of the United States

Families USA

FORMULA

INFACT

Kelley, Florence

Nader, Ralph

National Consumers' League

OMB Watch

Public Voice for Food and Health Policy

20/20 Vision

U.S. Public Interest Research Group

DEATH PENALTY AND CHOICE IN DYING

American League to Abolish Capital Punishment

Choice in Dying

Furman v. Georgia (408 U.S. 234) (1972)

Gregg v. Georgia (428 U.S. 153) (1976)

Hemlock Society U.S.A.

Kevorkian, Jack

National Coalition to Abolish the Death Penalty

DISABLED PERSONS' RIGHTS

American Disabled for Attendant Programs Today

Chronic Fatigue Immune Dysfunction Syndrome Association of America (CFIDS)

ENVIRONMENT

Abbey, Edward

Alden v. Maine (98 U.S. 436) (1999)

Brower, David Ross

Carson, Rachel Louise

Center for Health, Environment and Justice

Citizens for a Better Environment

Clean Water Action

Defenders of Wildlife

Ducks Unlimited

Earth First!

Earth Liberation Front

Environmental Action

Environmental Defense

Friends of the Earth

Greenpeace U.S.A.

Hoffman, Abbie

Izaak Walton League of America

League of Conservation Voters

National Audubon Society

National Parks and Conservation Association

GUIDE TO RELATED TOPICS

National Wildlife Federation
Natural Resources Defense Council
Sierra Club
20/20 Vision
U.S. Public Interest Research Group
Wilderness Society

EXTREMISTS

Carmichael, Stokely
Carto, Willis Allison
Coughlin, Father Charles
Dilling, Elizabeth Kirkpatrick
Earth First!
Earth Liberation Front
Farrakhan, Louis Abdul
Jewish Defense League
John Birch Society
Ku Klux Klan
LaRouche, Lyndon Hermyle, Jr.
Liberty Lobby
Militia Movements
Minutemen
Muhammad, Elijah
Nation of Islam
Newton, Huey P.
Posse Comitatus
Rudd, Mark
Seale, Robert G. ("Bobby")
Sea Shepherd Conservation Society
Smith, Gerald L. K.
Students for a Democratic Society
Symbionese Liberation Army
Terry, Randall A.
Weatherman

FALSE FRONT ORGANIZATIONS

Citizens for Excellence in Education
Consumer Alert
Coors, Joseph, Sr.
Seniors Coalition
60 Plus Association
United Seniors Association

FARMERS' RIGHTS

American Agriculture Movement
American Farm Bureau Federation
Chavez, Cesar Estrada
National Farmers Organization
National Farmers Union
United Farm Workers of America

GUN OWNERSHIP RIGHTS/GUN CONTROLS

Coalition to Stop Gun Violence
Gun Owners of America
Handgun Control Inc.
National Rifle Association of America

HISPANIC AMERICAN RIGHTS

Cambio Cubano
Chavez, Cesar Estrada
Cortés, Ernesto, Jr.
Cuban American National Foundation
League of United Latin American Citizens
National Council of La Raza
United Farm Workers of America

HOMELESSNESS

National Coalition for the Homeless
Snyder, Mitchell Darryl

HUMAN HEALTH AND SAFETY

Center for Health, Environment and Justice
Citizens for a Better Environment
Clean Water Action
FORMULA
Gibbs, Lois
INFACT
National Breast Cancer Coalition
National Coalition against Domestic Violence
National Vaccine Information Center
National Women's Health Network
Public Voice for Food and Health Policy
20/20 Vision

JEWISH AMERICAN RIGHTS

American Jewish Committee

American Jewish Congress

Anti-Defamation League of the B'nai B'rith

Jewish Defense League

LABOR ISSUES

Alden v. Maine (98 U.S. 436) (1999)

Bloor, Ella Reeve Ware Cohen Omholt

Chavez, Cesar Estrada

Dubinsky, David

Flynn, Elizabeth Gurley

Foster, William Zebulon

Haywood, William Dudley ("Big Bill")

Hill, Joe

Hillman, Sidney

Jones, Mary Harris

Jordan, Crystal Lee

Kelley, Florence

Lewis, John Llewellyn

National Right to Work Committee

Randolph, A(sa) Philip

Reuther, Walter Philip

Shanker, Albert

Sweeney, John J.

United Farm Workers of America

United Mine Workers of America

LESBIANS AND GAYS

ACT UP (AIDS Coalition to Unleash Power)

Bowers v. Hardwick (478 U.S. 186) (1986)

Gay and Lesbian Alliance Against Defamation

Gay Men's Health Crisis

Human Rights Campaign

Kramer, Larry

LIBERAL ACTIVISM

Abzug, Bella

Americans for Democratic Action

Common Cause

Dubinsky, David

Gardner, John W.

Hayden, Tom

New Left

OMB Watch

Public Citizen

Reuther, Walter Philip

Roosevelt, Eleanor

Student Nonviolent Coordinating Committee

Students for a Democratic Society

U.S. Public Interest Research Group

NATIVE AMERICAN RIGHTS

American Indian Movement

Banks, Dennis

Means, Russell

National Congress of American Indians

RELIGIOUS RIGHT

American Council of Christian Churches

American Family Association

Bryant, Anita

Christian Coalition

Citizens for Excellence in Education

Concerned Women for America

Dobson, James C.

Eagle Forum

Falwell, Jerry

Family Research Council

Focus on the Family (FOCUS)

Home School Legal Defense Association

Operation Save America

Promise Keepers

Reed, Ralph

Robertson, Marion Gordon ("Pat")

Schlafly, Phyllis

Schlessinger, Laura

SENIOR MOVEMENT

American Association of Retired Persons

Gray Panthers

League of Women Voters of the United States

National Coalition Against Domestic Violence

National Consumers' League

National Organization for Women

National Women's Health Network

National Women's Political Caucus

Older Women's League

Paul, Alice

Roe v. Wade (410 U.S. 113) (1973)

Roosevelt, Eleanor

Sanger, Margaret

Schlafly, Phyllis

Steinem, Gloria

Women's Action for New Directions

A

ABBEY, EDWARD (1927–1989). Born January 29, 1927, Edward Abbey was an essayist and novelist who defended the wilderness areas of the American West. A militant conservationist, he waged war in his writings against government agencies, tourists, and companies he considered despoilers of the environment. He inspired, through the pages of his comic novel *The Monkey Wrench Gang* (1975), a whole generation of environmental activists, including those who joined FRIENDS OF THE EARTH, EARTH LIBERATION FRONT, and EARTH FIRST! His book explains how to sabotage logging equipment, dynamite dams, and disable earthmoving machinery. When he died in 1989, the American West lost one of its most eloquent advocates.

Through his novels, essays, letters, and speeches, Edward Abbey voiced the belief that the West was in danger of being developed to death, and that the only solution lay in the defense of the wilderness by all possible means, including violence and subversive activity. Abbey authored twenty-one books, including *Desert Solitaire, The Brave Cowboy*, and *The Fool's Progress.*

Abbey grew up in Home, Pennsylvania, and earned a master's degree at the University of New Mexico. His thesis was titled "Anarchism and the Morality of Violence." After a one-year stint on a Fulbright fellowship at the University of Edinburgh, he served as a park ranger and fire lookout for the National Park Service in the southwestern United States from 1956 until 1971.

Novelist Edward Abbey works at his manual typewriter in his fire tower home in Arizona. © *Buddy Mays/CORBIS.*

Married and divorced four times, he died at his home in Fort Llatikcuf, near Tucson, Arizona. His final request was for bagpipes and "a flood of beer and booze! Lots of singing, dancing, talking, hollering, laughing, and lovemaking" to be on hand to celebrate his wake.

See also: ENVIRONMENT

For Further Information

Abbey, Edward. *Confessions of a Barbarian*. New York: Little, Brown, 1994.
———. *The Monkey Wrench Gang*. New York: Lippincott, 1975.

ABERNATHY, RALPH DAVID (1926–1990).

Ralph Abernathy was an American civil rights leader who served as president of the SOUTHERN CHRISTIAN LEADERSHIP CONFERENCE (SCLC) after MARTIN LUTHER KING JR. was murdered in 1968. He was King's closest confidant and companion during the crucial civil rights battles. In 1956 it was Abernathy who enlisted King to join the protest that he had instigated when ROSA PARKS was arrested in 1955 for refusing to give up her seat to a white person on a Montgomery, Alabama, bus. Together, they led the succeeding landmark bus boycott for 381 days. During this time Abernathy's home was bombed and his church dynamited.

Grandson of a slave, Abernathy was born in Linden, Alabama, on March 11, 1926, the tenth of twelve children and the youngest of seven sons. He earned a B.S. in mathematics at Alabama State College, an M.A. in sociology at Atlanta University (1951), and an LL.D. at Allen University in 1960. He became a Baptist minister in 1948 and served as pastor of the First Baptist Church in Montgomery, Alabama, between 1951 and 1961. Abernathy and King helped to organize the SCLC in 1957. When King was assassinated in Memphis, Abernathy cradled King's head during his final moments. Upon King's death, Abernathy became SCLC president. A unique feature of this organization was its program of nonviolent civil disobedience as practiced by Mahatma Gandhi and first described by Henry David Thoreau. Abernathy firmly believed that violence is the weapon of the weak, nonviolence the weapon of the strong. He was jailed at least forty times along with King in an arduous quest for equality under the law that took them to Selma, Albany, Birmingham, Washington, and Chicago. Their protests and marches led to social and legislative changes that significantly improved blacks' social and economic standing, desegregating formerly restricted restaurants, universities, and public facilities throughout the country.

Abernathy led the Poor People's March on Washington, D.C., in May 1968, to dramatize problems faced by the needy. Caravans of the unemployed converged on the Capitol to create Resurrection City with thousands of plywood huts on the Mall and near the Lincoln Memorial. Abernathy had envisioned a model for the rest of the nation to emulate, with poor people of all races, ethnic backgrounds, and religious beliefs joined in a crusade for food stamps, job training programs, and low-income housing. The campaign failed because of inadequate facilities, unruly behavior, and overextension of the city encampment permit.

Abernathy left the SCLC leadership in 1977 to enter an unsuccessful race for the Atlanta seat in the House of Representatives vacated by Andrew Young. In 1980 Abernathy lost the support of other civil rights leaders because of his endorsement of Ronald Reagan's bid for the presidency. His 1989 autobiography, *And the Walls Came Tumbling Down*, caused further controversy because of its revelation that King had had an adulterous liaison the night before he was killed. Nonetheless, Abernathy's courage, tenacious commitment to civil rights, and the inspiration he gave King earn him enduring praise as a key activist.

See also: AFRICAN AMERICAN RIGHTS

For Further Information

Abernathy, Ralph David. *And the Walls Came Tumbling Down*. New York: Harper, 1989.

ABORTION POLICY. Articles within the abortion policy category describe key U.S. Supreme Court decisions and prominent activists and organizations that have opposed or supported a woman's right to terminate a pregnancy before the fetus she is carrying is capable of survival as an individual.

Throughout the twentieth century, abortion was the most controversial of all issues affecting women. Reproductive rights are universal in application and therefore benefit or seem to threaten the greatest number of people.

Until ratification of the Nineteenth Amendment in 1920, women lacked political rights and were denied the opportunity to achieve economic or social equity with men, remaining bound to the home and subservient to their husbands. Choice of an alternative lifestyle would have plunged most women into immediate poverty and repudiation by society. Control over reproduction, the ability to plan the number and timing of births, had to occur before women could embark on independent careers. Many women, and men, still retain the view that the wife should maintain the home, adhering to the role prescribed in Judeo-Christian teachings. These "family values" traditionalists also believe that premarital sex is immoral and should not be condoned, and that tax dollars should not be used to pay for unwed mothers' abortions.

Prior to women's suffrage, birth control was a controversial subject, with the Comstock Act barring dissemination of birth control information through the mail. Poor women and immigrants had few safe or reliable ways to restrict family size except by refusing to have sex with their husbands or by seeking back alley abortions. When MARGARET SANGER began her clinic and campaign for family planning, only the National Women's Trade Union League would publicly support her. The clergy and prominent suffragists such as CARRIE CHAPMAN CATT disapproved of her actions.

Even as recently as the 1960s, two states, Connecticut and Massachusetts, retained laws that banned the sale and free distribution of birth control devices or information. In 1965, as a result of efforts by the NATIONAL ABORTION AND REPRODUCTIVE RIGHTS ACTION LEAGUE (NARAL), the U.S. Supreme Court ruled the Connecticut statute unconstitutional in *GRISWOLD V. CONNECTICUT*, citing infringement of the First, Third, Fourth, Fifth, and Ninth Amendments to the Constitution. The first formal call for repeal of all state laws restricting abortions was included in the Bill of Rights for Women adopted by the NATIONAL ORGANIZATION FOR WOMEN in 1967. The AMERICAN CIVIL LIBERTIES UNION (ACLU) called for repeal a year later.

On January 22, 1973, *ROE V. WADE*, one of the twentieth century's most controversial Supreme Court decisions, stated that a woman's constitutional right to privacy outweighed the state's right to regulate abortions. The Court divided pregnancy into trimesters and defined different rights in each. Absolute rights to an abortion were reserved for the first; in the second, states may regulate the procedure; and in the third, the state must promote an interest in the potential human life.

In response to *Roe v. Wade*, the NATIONAL RIGHT TO LIFE COMMITTEE was formed and PHYLLIS SCHLAFLY publicly attacked the Court ruling, joining Beverly LaHaye in declaring that women must not abandon their God-given roles as wives and mothers. Schlafly linked the decision to the Equal Rights Amendment and predicted eventual destruction of the family and traditional values. In 1976, as part of a backlash in sentiment, the Hyde Amendment was passed by Congress, prohibiting use of federal funds such as Medicaid for abortions in all but the gravest situations. In response the ACLU and NARAL intensified their activism for "freedom of choice."

George Bush, during his run for the presidency in 1988, coined the phrase "adoption, not abortion" and TERRY RANDALL's Operation Rescue (later renamed OPERATION SAVE AMERICA) began its series of blockades of abortion clinics. By 1992 abortion had become a major presidential campaign issue.

Anti-abortion protestors demonstrate outside the Rocky Mountain Planned Parenthood clinic in Denver in June 2000. *AP Photo/Ed Andrieski.*

The Democrats endorsed adherence to *Roe v. Wade*, while the Republican Party supported a constitutional amendment to ban abortions.

After the 1992 Clinton victory, there followed a resurgence of conservative Republican strength in Congress, and several Supreme Court decisions tended to weaken *Roe v. Wade* so that its eventual reversal seemed likely. However, at century's end, the issue of abortion was becoming less salient as public and legislative attention was being diverted to new ethical dilemmas raised by breakthroughs in cloning and control of the human genome structure.

For Further Information

Garrow, David J. *Liberty and Sexuality: The Right to Privacy and the Making of Roe vs. Wade.* Berkeley: University of California Press, 1998.

ABZUG, BELLA (1920–1998). Born in the Bronx, New York City, on July 24, 1920, feminist, Democratic congresswoman, and social policy activist Bella Abzug was one of the most visible, courageous, and vocal defenders of minorities, tenants, targets of McCarthyism, and protesters against the Vietnam War. She was a pioneer in making women's and gay rights matters of public policy, and her death marked the beginning of the end of a generation of fearless fighters for feminism.

Abzug's father was a Russian immigrant, a "humanist butcher" who operated the Live and Let Live meat market. Early in her life, Abzug exhibited precocity, being able to recite complex Hebrew prayers from memory, a feat expected of boys but not girls. Before reaching her teens, she was out in the streets collecting money and giving speeches in behalf of Zionism. At Hunter College she became president of the student body, and at Columbia University she was law review editor. She graduated in 1947 during a time when only 2 percent of the nation's lawyers were women.

After World War II, she did pro bono work for civil rights and civil liberties litigants, including tenants, minority groups, and targets of Senator Joseph McCarthy's communist-hunting House Committee on Un-American Activities. She started wearing her legendary oversized hats after her mother advised her to do it so that her legal clients and colleagues would not mistake her for a secretary.

In 1950 Abzug served as chief counsel in the celebrated but futile appeal of the death sentence of Willie McGee, a Mississippi black man convicted of raping a white woman. The local papers wrote inflammatory articles about McGee's "white lady lawyer," so she decided to sleep sitting up in a brightly lit bus station to avoid attack by the KU KLUX KLAN. At the time, she was eight months pregnant.

As a labor lawyer, Abzug represented fur workers, auto workers, and longshoremen. Later she defended teachers charged with subversive behavior in New York State. In 1960, angered by the U.S. government's resumption of nuclear testing, she became a founding mother and leader of Women's Strike for Peace (1961) and the NATIONAL WOMEN'S POLITICAL CAUCUS (1971).

Encouraged by friends and admirers in the peace movement, she ran for office in 1971 and won a seat in the House of Representatives. During the campaign, her slogan was "This woman's place is in the House—the House of Representatives." In Congress she was an anomaly, being the first Jew and one of only twelve women to hold office. At the time, many politicians believed that legislative chambers should be limited to men, a view illustrated by New York Mayor John Lindsay's response to a reporter when asked why there were so few women in his administration: "Honey, whatever women do, they do best after dark."

On her first day in Congress, Abzug introduced a resolution calling for total withdrawal of American troops from Indochina. It was easily defeated. Then, in 1975, she introduced the first federal legislation to extend civil rights to gays and lesbians and thereafter vigorously championed welfare and women's rights legislation, earning the nickname "Battling Bella."

She ran for the Senate in 1976 and lost a close race to Daniel Patrick Moynihan for the Democratic Party nomination. After losing her seat in The House in 1977, she ran unsuccessfully for New York City mayor. In 1980 she returned to legal practice but remained concerned with political issues. An ardent liberal and defender of women until the end, she supported President Clinton's reelection in 1996 "because the Republicans are advancing a pre-fascist state." She died on March 31, 1998, after surgery for a heart ailment.

See also: LIBERAL ACTIVISM; WOMEN'S ISSUES

For Further Information

Abzug, Bella, with Mim Kelber. *Gender Gap: Bella Abzug's Guide to Political Power for American Women*. New York: Houghton Mifflin, 1984.

Dworkin, Andrea. "Obituary: Bella Abzug: Loud and Clear Against Oppression." *The Guardian* (London), April 2, 1998, p. 18.

MacPherson, Myra. "Bella Abzug, Champion of Women." *Washington Post*, April 2, 1998, Style section, p. 1.

ACTIVIST THINK TANKS. Think tanks are research institutes or organizations employed to solve complex problems or to predict or plan future developments in the military, political, or social arena. Their books, reports, and advisory documents are consulted and used by government officials, legislators, business executives, journalists, and academics. Until the 1970s, think tank scholars were mostly unknown and had no direct contact with the media viewing/listening public. After that time, think tanks extended their missions to include proactive provision of contributions to the marketplace of ideas and recommitted themselves to increasing citizens' ability to make sensible decisions. Today, they affect citizens' voting patterns by presenting openly biased agendas directly through the media. By 1990 the older institutions (Brookings and Hoover) had adopted this same approach. Today, most of the following think tanks are consulted by candidates for public office, deliver testimony that influences legislative and judicial decisions, and have become integral to the functioning of citizen participatory democracy. Profiles of seventeen activist think tanks, listed in founding year order, follow. For each, the date of formation, title, mission statement, examples of policy recommendations, representative researchers or fellows; publications, and Web site address are provided.

Brookings Institution
Founded 1916
Michael Armacost, President
Location: Washington, D.C.
Web site: *http://www.brook.edu*

"The Brookings Institution, an independent, nonpartisan research organization, seeks to improve the performance of American institutions, the effectiveness of government programs, and the quality of U.S. public policies. It addresses current and emerging policy challenges and offers practical recommendations for dealing with them, expressed in language that is accessible to policy makers and the general public alike." An October 1997 *National Journal* article stated that Michael Armacost, Brookings' president, hoped to "quash the last vestiges of the institution's reputation as a left-leaning think tank, so that it can position itself as a centrist, nonpartisan place." Prominent fellows include Robert Crandall on deregulation, John DiLulio on criminal justice, and Stephen Hess, E. J. Dionne, and Thomas E. Mann on politics.

Brookings Institution has opposed tax cuts proposed by Republicans in Congress, advocates cutting the defense budget by as much as 50 percent, and has stated that "market incentives can never fully solve the twin problems of universal access and cost containment" posed by universal health insurance.

Publications include *Brookings Review* (quarterly); *Brookings Newsletter* (quarterly); Robert Reischauer and Henry Aaron, eds., *Setting National Priorities 2000*; and E. J. Dionne and John Dilulio, eds., *What's God Got to Do with the American Experiment?*

Hoover Institution on War, Revolution and Peace
Founded 1919
John Raisian, Director
Location: Stanford University, Stanford, California
Web site: *www.hoover.stanford.edu*

"The Institution's overarching purposes are to—analyze the effects of government actions relating to public policy; generate, publish, and disseminate ideas that encourage positive policy formation using reasoned arguments and intellectual rigor, converting conceptual insights into practical initiatives judged to be beneficial to society; and convey to the public, the media, lawmakers, and others an understanding of important public policy issues and promote vigorous dialogue."

Reagan administration members George P. Shultz and Edwin Meese III serve as distinguished fellows; President Ronald Reagan and Prime Minister Margaret Thatcher are honorary fellows. Fellow Thomas Sowell, a syndicated columnist and black conservative, advises on reform of American education. Other fellows include Nobel Prize winners economist Milton Friedman and Russian writer Aleksandr Solzhenitsyn.

The Institution has recommended the auctioning off of all public lands (national parks and wilderness areas) over a twenty to forty year period, privatization of the U.S. postal system, and cessation of the federal government's attempts to pursue racial equality through public policy legislation.

Publications include *Hoover Digest: Research and Opinion on Public Policy* (quarterly); *Essays in Public Policy* (monthly); Thomas Gale Moore, *Climate of Fear*; Tom

Bethell, *The Noblest Triumph: Property and Prosperity Through the Ages*, and Thomas Sowell, *The Vision of the Anointed*. It also has produced *Uncommon Knowledge*, a public affairs television series.

American Enterprise Institute for Public Policy Research
Founded 1943
Christopher C. DeMuth, President
Location: Washington, D.C.
Web site: *http://www.aei.org*

The American Enterprise Institute (AEI) was founded to "preserve and to strengthen the foundation of a free society" by promoting "limited government, competitive private enterprise, vital cultural and political institutions, and a vigilant defense." Christopher DeMuth, AEI president, has said that "American politics is being driven by deep disillusionment with government, and activist-government liberalism is largely spent as an intellectual force." AEI researchers include Charles Murray, co-author of *The Bell Curve*; Norman J. Ornstein, election analyst and television personality; social commentator Irving Kristol; former UN Ambassador Jeane Kirkpatrick, and legal scholar Robert Bork.

The AEI has argued that "secular rationalism is a prescription for moral anarchy" and that "federal welfare programs have subsidized illegitimacy, the single most important social problem of our time." Robert Bork stated in his *Slouching Towards Gomorrah* that radical egalitarianism and radical individualism are to blame for dramatic alterations to our moral and cultural life. Staff supports federal subsidies to allow the mandatory purchase of complete health coverage by poor individuals, as well as tax credits for wealthier individuals who purchase more than their mandatory catastrophic coverage. AEI opposes term limits and supports the North American Free Trade Agreement.

AEI publications include *The American Enterprise* (bimonthly journal); Leon Kass, *The Ethics of Human Cloning*; Christina Hoff Sommers, *The War Against Boys*; and Wil-liam Baumol, *Toward Competition in Local Telephony*.

Hudson Institute
Founded 1961
Herbert I. London, President
Location: Indianapolis, Indiana
Web site: *http://www.hudson.org*

The Hudson Institute was founded by Herman Kahn as a "lobby for the future." Its mission is "to help shape the future through research designed to anticipate the political, economic, and cultural trends critical to the success of American public policy today and into the 21st Century." This mission "embodies optimism about solving problems, a commitment to free institutions and individual responsibility, an appreciation of the crucial role of technology in achieving progress, and an abiding respect for the importance of values, culture, and religion in human affairs."

Institute staff includes legal scholar Michael Horowitz and former Secretary of Education William Bennett. Former Vice President Dan Quayle joined the Institute's board of trustees in 1992.

In 1967 the Institute predicted the rise of Japan as a major economic power and the economic boom that the early years of the Reagan presidency would produce. It argues that "impoverishing people by imposing heavy restrictions on economic growth and technological progress harms both people and the environment. On the other hand, technology and economic growth can clean up the environment."

Hudson Institute publications include *American Outlook* (quarterly magazine); *Visions* (quarterly newsletter); *Rethinking America's Health Care Priorities*; *Charter Schools in Action: What Have We Learned?*; and *Workforce 2020: Work and Workers in the 21st Century*.

Urban Institute
Founded 1968
Robert D. Reischauer, President

Location: Washington, D.C.
Web site: *http://www.urban.org*

The Urban Institute's goals are "to sharpen thinking about society's problems and efforts to solve them, improve government decisions and their implementation, and increase citizens' awareness about important public choices." The Institute's overall research agenda includes health care, education, welfare reform, the social safety net, community building and development, the nonprofit sector, and the creation of modeling tools to show how the American population's composition and income change over time.

Researchers affiliated with the Urban Institute include taxation and fiscal policy expert Eric J. Toder, former commissioner of the U.S. Social Security Administration Lawrence H. Thompson, and statistician Fritz Scheuren. The Institute was founded to explore the condition of American cities. It has a politically balanced project staff and aims to prepare nonpartisan, reliable data for all sides to examine.

Publications include *In Brief* (monthly), *Update* (bimonthly), and reports on such topics as homelessness, policies affecting noncitizens, discrimination, and children at risk. Recent books are *Retooling Social Security for the 21st Century: Right and Wrong Approaches to Reform* and *Encyclopedia of Taxation and Tax Policy.*

Joint Center for Political and Economic Studies
Founded 1970
Eddie N. Williams, President
Location: Washington, D.C.
Web site: *http://www.jointctr.org*

"The Joint Center for Political and Economic Studies informs and illuminates the nation's major public policy debates through research, analysis, and information dissemination in order to: improve the socioeconomic status of black Americans and other minorities; expand their effective participation in the political and public policy arenas; and

promote communications and relationships across racial and ethnic lines to strengthen the nation's pluralistic society."

Research staff includes David Bositis, Carrie W. Kendrick, and Katherine McFate. The Joint Center collects and analyzes data on all aspects of black political participation. It researches such issues as welfare reform, minority business development, blacks' economic status, and education.

Publications include *Focus*, a monthly magazine. Recent books include *Job Creation Prospects and Strategies, African American Officers' Role in the Future Army*, and *Redistricting and Minority Representation: Learning from the Past, Preparing for the Future.*

Heritage Foundation
Founded 1973
Edwin J. Feulner, President
Location: Washington, D.C.
Web site: *http://www.heritage.org*

The mission of the Heritage Foundation is "to formulate and promote conservative public policies based on the principles of free enterprise, limited government, individual freedom, traditional American values, and a strong national defense." The Foundation states that its "more than 200,000 contributors make it the most broadly supported think tank in America."

Foundation fellows include former cabinet members William Bennett and Edwin Meese III. The Heritage Foundation influenced adoption of supply-side economics, choice in education, and enterprise zones during the Reagan administration. It guided development of the Strategic Defense Initiative and challenged the validity of welfare entitlement programs, Medicare, and Social Security. It continues to advocate reduction of environmental regulations that it contends impede free enterprise, and it advocates strengthening of the U.S. military.

Publications include *Policy Review* (bimonthly), *Reforming Congress* (monthly), and over 1,500 books, reports, and papers. Examples are *School Choice Programs: What's*

Happening in the States, Why America Needs a Tax Cut, and *Avoiding a Telecom Trade War*.

Center for Policy Alternatives
Founded 1975
Linda Tarr-Whelan, President
Location: Washington, D.C.
Web site: *http://www.cfpa.org*

The Center for Policy Alternatives (CPA) "engages a new generation of leaders across the states to envision and realize progressive solutions for America's future," connecting and empowering people for "secure and healthy families; thriving, energized communities; sustainable development to preserve resources; a fair and flourishing economy; and inclusive and participatory democracy."

CPA senior fellows are Ron David, adjunct lecturer of public policy, JFK School of Government; Chellie Pingree, Maine state senator; and Donna Callejon. The CPA anticipated the new federalism of the 1970s and movement of domestic legislative responsibilities and power from Washington to the states. The Center is progressive, concerned with women's economic issues, and maintains a politically neutral position. It brings together about thirty legislators each year, mostly first and second termers, for leadership training.

Publications include *Alternatives* (monthly) and more than sixty books and reports on such topics as campaign finance, childcare financing, family and work, women and the economy, and health care. The CPA Web site monitors developments, leaders, and events at the state level.

Cato Institute
Founded 1977
Edward H. Crane, President
Location: Washington, D.C.
Web site: *http://www.cato.org*

"The Cato Institute seeks to broaden the parameters of public policy debate to allow consideration of more options that are consistent with the traditional American principles of limited government, individual liberty, and peace." Examined areas include the federal budget, Social Security, monetary policy, natural resource policy, military spending, regulation, and NATO.

Cato fellows include economists Milton Friedman and Arthur Laffer, Congressman Henry Hyde (R-IL), educational psychologist Charles Murray, political commentator George Will, and objectivist philosopher David Kelley. In line with its libertarian position, the Institute promotes free markets, individual liberties, and reduced federal government, including elimination of eight cabinet-level departments, among them Education, Agriculture, and Labor. It favors a national sales tax to replace the income tax and would legalize the sale of marijuana and other controlled substances to adults.

Periodicals published by Cato include *Cato Journal* (3/yr.), *Regulation* (quarterly), *Cato Policy Report* (bimonthly), and *Cato Handbook for Congress* (annual). Books include *The Affirmative Action Fraud: Can We Restore the American Civil Rights Vision?*; *Climate of Fear: Why We Shouldn't Worry about Global Warming*; *School Choice: Why You Need It—How You Get It*; and David Kelley's *A Life of One's Own*.

Manhattan Institute for Policy Research
Founded 1977
Lawrence Mone, President
Location: New York, New York
Web site: *http://www.manhattan-institute.org*

"The Manhattan Institute is a think tank whose mission is to develop and disseminate new ideas that foster greater economic choice and individual responsibility." Institute fellows include Chester E. Finn Jr., David Frum, Peter W. Huber, Walter K. Olson, Kay Hymowitz, and Peter D. Salins.

Stands taken by the Institute include opposition to a universal federal subsidy for prescription drugs, support of voucher programs and home schooling, and endorsement of technology and the free market as better protectors of the environment than government regulations.

Institute publications include *City Journal* (quarterly) and over forty books by its fellows. Representative titles are Charles Murray's *Losing Ground*, Myron Magnet's *The Dream and the Nightmare*, Walter Olson's *The Excuse Factory: How Employment Law Is Paralyzing the American Workplace*, and Tamar Jacoby's *Someone Else's House: America's Unfinished Struggle for Integration*.

Free Congress Foundation
Founded 1977
Paul M. Weyrich, President
Location: Washington, D.C.
Web site: *http://www.freecongress.org*

President Paul Weyrich states that "Free Congress Foundation is politically conservative, but it is more than that; it is also culturally conservative. Most think tanks talk about tax rates or the environment or welfare policy and occasionally we do also. But our main focus is on the Culture War. Will America return to the culture that made it great, our traditional, Judeo-Christian, Western culture? Or will we continue the long slide into the cultural and moral decay of political correctness? If we do, America, once the greatest nation on earth, will become no less than a third world country."

Free Congress Foundation has writers on its staff including attorney Thomas Lee Jipping, Lisa S. Dean, who researches and reports on issues related to technology policy, William S. Lind, and Patrick McGuigan. The Foundation opposes political correctness, contending that it is "one of the forces destroying our culture and freedom." It also opposes activist judges "who don't interpret the law but modify it to fit their left-wing beliefs." The Foundation lobbies against judicial appointees who "fail to observe constitutional principles."

Its publications include *Essays on Our Times* (monthly series), *The Judicial Selection Monitor* (quarterly), *Policy Insights* (monthly), and *The Weyrich Insider* (monthly). Representative books are *Cul-*

tural Conservatism: Toward a New National Agenda, Tom L. Jipping's *Does the First Amendment Violate Itself?*, and *Ninth Justice: The Fight for Bork*.

Reason Foundation
Founded 1978
Robert W. Poole Jr., President
Location: Los Angeles, California
Web site: *www.reason.org*

The Reason Foundation "supports the rule of law, private property, and limited government. It promotes voluntarism and individual responsibility in social and economic interactions, relying on choice and competition to achieve the best outcomes. It seeks to preserve and extend those aspects of an open society that protect property and act as a check on encroachments on liberty. Among these are free trade and private property, immigration, labor and capital mobility, scientific inquiry, and technological innovation."

Reason Foundation writers include Virginia Postrel, Charles Paul Freund, and Jacob Sullum, editors of *Reason* magazine. Consistent with its libertarian position, Reason Foundation advocates privatization of airports and the U.S. air-traffic control system, other public transportation, hospitals, and correctional institutions. It opposes attempts to regulate the tobacco industry and environmental pollution, and it contends that reports on global warming lack scientific validity.

The Foundation's monthly magazine, *Reason*, covers politics, culture, and ideas from a libertarian perspective. Foundation books include William D. Eggers and John O'Leary's *Revolution at the Roots: Making Our Government Smaller, Better, and Closer to Home*, George Passantino's *Exploring the Science of Climate Change*, Jacob Sullum's *For Your Own Good: The Anti-Smoking Crusade and the Tyranny of Public Health*, and Virginia Postrel's *The Future and Its Enemies*.

Pacific Research Institute for Public Policy
Founded 1979

Sally C. Pipes, President and Chief Executive Officer
Location: San Francisco, California
Web site: *http://www.pacificresearch.org*

The Pacific Research Institute "promotes the principles of individual freedom and personal responsibility." The Institute believes "these principles are best encouraged through policies that emphasize a free economy, private initiative, and limited government."

Institute fellows include fiscal policy analyst Alejandra Arguello, political scientist Sonia Arrison, journalist and writer Steve Hayward, government programs analyst Naomi Lopez Bauman, and Pamela Riley, who writes on educational reform. The Institute opposes federal regulations that would ban handguns and the use of cell phones while driving automobiles, restrict smoking, or control encryption technology. It also opposes the split-up of Microsoft as intrusive and inimical to the development of innovative technology, increases in the minimum wage, and federally imposed price controls on pharmaceuticals. It favors chartered schools, development of a retirement system to replace Social Security, and protection of the confidentiality of medical records.

Publications include *Trial and Error: The Government's Case Against Microsoft, Free Markets, Free Choice: Smashing the Wage Gap and Glass Ceiling Myths,* and *Online Privacy: Why New Regulations Fail to Protect Children.* Other publications are the bimonthly newsletter *Pacific Outlook*, the quarterly *Policy Briefing*, and *Action Alert*, posted on the Internet.

Center for National Policy

Founded 1981
Maureen S. Steinbruner, President
Location: Washington, D.C.
Web site: *http://www.cnponline.org/*

The Center for National Policy "is committed to the ideal of a vital public sector." Its mission is "to advance the public policy process and determine how government can best serve American interests both at home and abroad." The Center's four program areas are economic analysis, community studies, equal opportunity, and foreign policy. Center fellows include James L. Medoff, Marc A. Weiss, Howard Shapiro, David Kang, and Eric B. Schnurer. Leon Panetta, former Office of Management and Budget director, is chair of the Center's Board of Directors.

The Center supports a more aggressive federal role in elementary and secondary education funding, has opposed Republican tax cuts "targeted at the best-off 10% of taxpayers," and favors "paying down the $3.6 trillion national debt, pumping up public investment on education, health care, and defense, and cutting the payroll tax."

Center publications include *Adolescence and Poverty, Passing the Test: The National Interest in Good Schools for All, Life in the City, Job Quality Index*, and the monthly "PolicyWires" and "CNPStatelines," focusing on such issues as the economy, community life, and equal opportunity at the federal and state levels.

Economic Policy Institute

Founded 1986
Jeff Faux, President
Location: Washington, D.C.
Web site: *http://www.epinet.org*

"The mission of the Economic Policy Institute is to provide high-quality research and education in order to promote a prosperous, fair, and sustainable economy. EPI works to strengthen democracy by providing people with the tools to participate in the public discussion of the economy, believing that such participation will result in economic policies that better reflect the public interest." Economists and researchers on the EPI staff include Eileen Appelbaum, Dean Baker, James P. Barrett, Jared Bernstein, Max B. Sawicky, John Schmitt, and Robert E. Scott.

EPI is attentive to the interests of low- and middle-income workers. It opposes repeal of the federal estate and gift tax, favors raising the minimum wage, and contends that allowing "a portion of each worker's payroll taxes to be placed in a personal account and invested in stocks and bonds would put core retirement income at risk because benefits would be determined by luck and wisdom of investment choices and the ups and downs of financial markets."

EPI publications include *The State of Working America* (biennial report), *How Much Is Enough?—Basic Family Budgets for Working Families*, *MCI WorldCom's Spring Toward Monopoly*, and *The End of Welfare? Consequences of Federal Devolution for the Nation*.

Independent Institute
Founded 1986
David J. Theroux, Founder and President
Location: Oakland, California
Web site: *http://www.independent.org*

"The mission of The Independent Institute is to transcend the all-too-common politicization and superficiality of public policy research and debate, redefine the debate over public issues, and foster new and effective directions for government reform. The Institute's program is pursued to rigorous standards without regard to any political or social biases." Senior fellows on the Institute staff include Bruce L. Benson, Robert Higgs, and Richard K. Vedder. Its board of advisors includes historian Stephen E. Ambrose, economist James M. Buchanan, George Gilder, Nathan Glaser, Charles Murray, and Thomas Szasz.

Institute writers recommend privatization of public schools and Social Security, deregulatory reforms, and limited government. The Institute subscribes to John Stuart Mill's libertarian view that "there is a limit to the legitimate interference of collective opinion with individual independence."

Publications include *American Health Care*; *The Diversity Myth*; *Freedom, Feminism, and the State*; *Hazardous to Our Health? FDA Regulation of Health Care Products*; *That Every Man Be Armed*; *Winners, Losers and Microsoft*; *Cutting Green Tape: Toxic Pollutants, Environmental Regulation and the Law*; and *Can Teachers Own Their Own Schools? New Strategies for Educational Excellence*. The Institute also publishes *The Independent Review: A Journal of Political Economy* (quarterly), *The Independent* (quarterly newsletter), and *The Lighthouse* (weekly e-mail newsletter).

Progress and Freedom Foundation
Founded 1993
Jeffrey A. Eisenach, President
Location: Washington, D.C.
Web site: *http://www.pff.org*

The Progress and Freedom Foundation is dedicated to the study of "the digital revolution and its implications for public policy" and is "currently conducting a major project aimed at identifying public policies to limit government interference in the market for digital broadband networks." Senior fellows include economists Michael K. Block and Joseph J. Cordes, telecommunications specialist Charles Eldering, and communications law expert Randolph J. May.

The Foundation recommends deregulation of telecommunications policy, abolition of the Federal Communications Commission, and transferal of the Food and Drug Administration's safety and efficacy testing to private organizations.

Four activist think tanks described more fully elsewhere in this encyclopedia, the AMERICAN ENTERPRISE INSTITUTE, CATO INSTITUTE, FREE CONGRESS RESEARCH AND EDUCATION FOUNDATION, and HERITAGE FOUNDATION, influence public opinion by placing their spokespersons on talk shows hosted by Rush Limbaugh, Chris Matthews, and Geraldo Rivera, and on *Nightline*, *Crossfire*, and other news programs. Their views are also widely circulated in the nation's major newspapers. Beginning in 1976, these four think tanks helped produce a conservative groundswell that swept traditional liberal Democrats out of office and created Republican majorities in both houses of Congress.

For Further Information

Callahan, David. "$1 Billion for Conservative Ideas." *Nation* 268, no. 15, (April 26, 1999): 21–23.

McGann, James G. *Think Tanks and Civil Societies: Catalysts for Ideas and Action.* Piscataway, NJ: Transaction Publishers, 2000.

Mundy, Alicia. "*Tanks* for the Quotes." *MediaWeek* 6, no. 27 (July 1, 1996): 16–18.

Stefancic, Jean, and Richard Delgado. *No Mercy: How Conservative Think Tanks and Foundations Changed America's Social Agenda.* Philadelphia: Temple University Press, 1996.

ACT UP (AIDS COALITION TO UNLEASH POWER). ACT UP, founded in February 1987, grew rapidly into one of the most influential, militant, and provocative organizations devoted to arousing what its founders regarded as an indifferent and often hostile public to the AIDS crisis. ACT UP made its name by mounting guerrilla-style demonstrations, disruptions, and unruly public outbursts. The original ACT UP was formed in response to a speech given in New York City by LARRY KRAMER, a playwright and polemicist stricken by AIDS whose highly publicized diatribes did much to spur attempts to deal with the disease. ACT UP's original purpose was to serve individuals who were compelled by anger to take direct action to end the AIDS crisis.

The group has achieved major victories against pharmaceutical companies such as Pharmacia & Upjohn and Burroughs-Wellcome that charged exorbitant prices for AIDS medication. Experimental drugs (e.g., AZT, Delavirdine, and All) are now far more widely available and somewhat less costly than they were before ACT UP's incendiary antics (e.g. taunting police, heckling government speakers, staging "die-ins" by lying in the street to symbolize AIDS deaths) caught the attention of the media.

ACT UP believes that officialdom, out of prejudice, has been responsible for preventing drugs from reaching those infected with the virus. The group has adopted rage as its orthodoxy and employed outrageously disruptive tactics as the best means to achieve its aims. Members have fused their grief and anger, venting political rage that has sustained their energy and hope in the face of crushing personal tragedy.

ACT UP's most visible activity is "zapping" those it regards as its enemies with loud public protests that often qualify as civil disobedience. The Food and Drug Administration, National Institutes of Health, and Roman Catholic Church have all been zapped on the grounds that they have blocked attempts to treat the disease and prevent its spread.

With the availability of life-prolonging treatments and a significant decline in AIDS-related deaths, ACT UP demonstrations have become less frequent and more restrained as other issues, such as gay marriage and employment rights, have displaced AIDS as the primary concerns of the gay community.

Currently, ACT UP offices are located in New York City, Philadelphia, and Paris, France. According to ACT UP spokespersons, the size of its membership is indeterminate and may exceed several thousand, as "all persons who attend meetings or demonstrations are automatically considered members." There are also no leaders per se, only facilitators who are elected to conduct meeting discussions.

See also: AIDS CRISIS; LESBIANS AND GAYS

For Further Information

ACT UP/New York, *http://www.actupny.org*

ACT UP/Paris, *http://www.actupp.org*

ACT UP/Philadelphia, *http://www.critpath.org/actup*

Cohen, Peter F. *Love and Anger: Essays on AIDS, Activism, and Politics.* New York: Haworth Press, 1998.

Epstein, Steven. *Impure Science: AIDS, Activism, and the Politics of Knowledge.* Berkeley: University of California Press, 1996.

Kramer, Larry. *Reports from the Holocaust: The Story of an AIDS Activist.* New York: St. Martin's Press, 1994.

ADDAMS, JANE (1860–1935). Born in Cedarville, Illinois, September 6, 1860, Jane

Addams was one of America's foremost social reformers, campaigners against child labor, and feminists. She founded one of the first U.S. settlement houses and won the Nobel Prize. She graduated from Rockford College (A.B., 1882), attended the Woman's Medical College in Philadelphia, and during her trips to England in 1883 and 1888 became interested in social reform. Toynbee Hall, a settlement in London, inspired her to develop a similar service agency for the immigrant poor in the United States. In 1899 she and Ellen Gates Starr founded Hull House, the most important U.S. settlement house, devoted to improvement of community and civic life in the Chicago slums. The settlement provided kindergarten and daycare facilities for children of working mothers, an employment bureau, an art gallery, library, and music and art classes.

Addams worked to secure social justice by sponsoring legislation on housing reform, factory inspection, women's suffrage, and pacifism. She was closely associated with the first eight-hour law for working women, the first state child labor law, and the first juvenile court. An early and strong proponent of the value of research, she saw it as essential in documenting the causes of poverty and crime. Addams stressed the importance of qualified social workers and of social action to advocate reforms, organizing civic groups to pressure legislatures and officials.

As part of its platform, the Progressive Party adopted many of her initiatives in 1912; she seconded Theodore Roosevelt's nomination for president and was an active campaigner on his behalf. She was the first woman president of the National Conference of Social Work (1910), the founder and president of the National Federation of Settlements (1911–1935), and vice president of the National American Woman Suffrage Association (1911–1914), and also helped to found the AMERICAN CIVIL LIBERTIES UNION in 1920. As president of the Women's International League for Peace and Freedom (1919–1935), she shared the 1931 Nobel Peace Prize, awarded in recognition of her efforts to end hostilities in World War I. Her many books include *Democracy and Social Ethics* (1902), *The Spirit of Youth and the City Streets* (1909), *Twenty Years at Hull-House* (1910), *A New Conscience and an Ancient Evil* (1912), and *Peace and Bread in Time of War* (1922).

See also: ANTIWAR/ANTI–NUCLEAR WEAPONS MOVEMENT; WOMEN'S ISSUES

For Further Information

Davis, Allen F. *American Heroine: The Life and Legend of Jane Addams.* New York: Oxford University Press, 1973.

Meigs, Cornelia L. *Jane Addams, Pioneer for Social Justice: A Biography.* Boston: Little, Brown, 1970.

AFRICAN AMERICAN RIGHTS. Throughout the twentieth century, African Americans waged a war for political, economic, and social justice that still remains unwon. A central figure in this struggle was MARTIN LUTHER KING JR., who, with SAUL DAVID ALINSKY and RALPH NADER, was one of the three most effective liberal citizen activists of the twentieth century. As Gunnar Myrdal pointed out in his classic 1944 book, *An American Dilemma*, unequal justice has prevailed in America, with a majority of whites not supporting the idealized goals of a fully equal and socially just society. It was not until the 1950s and 1960s that blacks' actions awakened an indifferent public to the social blight of segregation, forcing the courts and legislative bodies to take corrective action. Six tools were used to achieve results:

1. Advocacy training provided by the HIGHLANDER FOLK SCHOOL, the churches, the SOUTHERN CHRISTIAN LEADERSHIP CONFERENCE (SCLC), and other organizations.

2. Nonviolent resistance and direct action modeled after the civil disobedience of Mahatma Gandhi.

3. Voter education and registration drives.

4. Consciousness-raising and development of a separate independent identity as ex-

In September 1957, white students at Little Rock (Arkansas) High School shout insults at 16-year-old Elizabeth Eckford as she walks down a line of National Guardsmen who are preventing her from entering the school. *AP Photo/Arkansas Democrat Gazette/Will Counts.*

emplified by ELIJAH MUHAMMAD and the NATION OF ISLAM.

5. Self-defense and retaliatory violence of the kind pioneered by the BLACK PANTHER PARTY

6. Urban rioting.

In 1905 W.E.B. DU BOIS helped form the Niagara Movement, planners of which were forced to convene in Canada because blacks were denied hotel accommodations in the United States. At the meeting twenty-nine black leaders drafted a list of demands. These included equal educational opportunity, an end to segregation, and prohibition of discrimination in public accommodations, trade unions, and the courts.

A second beginning of the long march toward equality was marked by formation of the NATIONAL ASSOCIATION FOR THE ADVANCEMENT OF COLORED PEOPLE (NAACP) in 1909, one hundred years after the birth of Lincoln, the Great Emancipator, and less than a year after a horrendous lynching episode in Springfield, Illinois. Du Bois was an NAACP co-founder.

A chronology of other leading organizations, individuals, and events follows.

1911   The NATIONAL URBAN LEAGUE, primarily a social welfare agency, was formed.

1914   MARCUS GARVEY founds the Universal Negro Improvement Association to foster universal black unity and pride. He calls for a return to Africa and formation of a separate black state.

1924   Liberia rejects Marcus Garvey's plan to resettle blacks in Africa.

1925   A. PHILIP RANDOLPH becomes head of the Brotherhood of Sleeping Car Porters and combats exclusionary policies of Northern "whites only" unions.

1934 W.E.B. Du Bois resigns from the NAACP, finding it too conservative.

1934 Elijah Muhammad founds the Nation of Islam in Chicago

1942 The CONGRESS OF RACIAL EQUALITY (CORE) is formed by JAMES FARMER, race relations secretary of the FELLOWSHIP OF RECONCILIATION.

1954 In BROWN V. BOARD OF EDUCATION OF TOPEKA, the U.S. Supreme Court rules unanimously that separate educational facilities for blacks are inherently unequal and unconstitutional.

1955 ROSA PARKS, trained by Highlander Folk School, overcomes her fear and refuses to relinquish her seat to a white man on a bus in Montgomery, Alabama. Her action provides a test case challenging the constitutionality of segregation laws in the South.

1956 SEPTIMA CLARK develops a teaching process to develop activists' skills and self-confidence.

1957 Martin Luther King Jr. forms the SCLC as the black churches' political arm to work on the issues of segregation, voter registration, and other minority concerns. The SCLC will provide the citizen action needed to supplement NAACP legal tactics.

1959 MALCOLM X becomes chief spokesperson for the Nation of Islam and promotes a revolutionary ideology paralleling the emerging nationalist movements in postcolonial Africa.

1961 James Farmer becomes the leader of CORE and organizes "freedom rides" to expose illegal segregation practices at bus terminals.

1961 FRED SHUTTLESWORTH, president of the Alabama Christian Movement for Human Rights, an affiliate of SCLC, warns of attacks in Birmingham after his confrontations with Commissioner of Public Safety "Bull" Connor.

1961 W.E.B. Du Bois renounces U.S. citizenship and moves to Ghana.

1963 Riot in Birmingham.

1964 Riots in Harlem, Rochester, and Philadelphia.

1965 Malcolm X is assassinated in Harlem after voicing hopes for black-white rapprochement following his pilgrimage to Mecca and conversion to Orthodox Islam.

1965 Riots in Watts, Detroit, and Newark.

1966 STOKELY CARMICHAEL puts forward the concept of "Black Power" as incoming president of the STUDENT NONVIOLENT COORDINATING COMMITTEE (SNCC). The SCLC, NAACP, and National Urban League retain their commitment to nonviolence but support the SNCC drive for racial pride and African American unity.

1966 The Black Panther Party, a militant, armed self-defense group, is founded in Oakland, California, by HUEY P. NEWTON and BOBBY SEALE.

1967 ELDRIDGE CLEAVER, author of Soul on Ice, becomes the Black Panthers' information minister.

1968 Martin Luther King Jr. is assassinated.

1968 Riots in major cities follow King assassination.

1968 RALPH DAVID ABERNATHY, Kings's closest confidant, is selected to lead the SCLC.

1971 JESSE JACKSON founds PUSH-Excel (People United to Save Humanity), a crusade to free inner-city schools from vandalism, drugs, teen pregnancy, and high dropout rates.

1984 Jesse Jackson becomes the first black American to mount an effective campaign for the presidential nomination by forming a "Rainbow Coalition" of liberal and minority groups.

1992 Riot in Watts follows the beating of Rodney King by police officers, viewed on national television.

1993 BENJAMIN CHAVIS serves as controversial executive director of the NAACP for one year.

1994 A new Black Panther Party emerges in Dallas and ten other cities.

1995 Benjamin Chavis leads the Million Man

March in Washington, organized by Nation of Islam leader LOUIS FARRAKHAN.

For Further Information

Dunn, John M. *The Civil Rights Movement*. San Diego: Lucent Books, 1998.

Levy, Peter B. *The Civil Rights Movement*. Westport, CT: Greenwood Press, 1998.

Winters, Paul A., ed. *The Civil Rights Movement*. San Diego: Greenhaven Press, 2000.

AIDS ACTION COUNCIL.

Founded in 1984, the AIDS Action Council limits itself to a single purpose, the advocacy of responsible federal policy for improved AIDS care and services, comprehensive AIDS testing, AIDS educational outreach programs, and medical research and prevention of the disease. The AIDS Action Council is a coalition that includes 3,000 member AIDS service organizations in a dozen major cities, including the Northwest AIDS Foundation (Seattle, Washington) and the GAY MEN'S HEALTH CRISIS, based in New York City. The Council considers itself to be the national voice for approximately 1 million HIV positive Americans represented through its community organization network. The organization bears the subheading "Until It's Over" so will presumably dissolve at such time as the AIDS crisis ceases to afflict tens of millions throughout the world.

The group has become one of the country's more powerful citizen action organizations. In 1996 it convinced Vice President Albert Gore to endorse its Reinventing Medicaid proposal, which would for the first time ensure access to life-saving drug therapies for low-income men, women, and children living with HIV. It also succeeded in expanding Medicaid coverage to persons in the early, asymptomatic stages of infection and helped secure authorization of the largest single annual increase in the federal Ryan White Care Act, which supports numerous AIDS treatment programs.

The AIDS Action Council's campaign for needle exchange programs to reduce the spread of AIDS was supported by the Clinton administration in 1998 but opposed by congressional conservatives who contended that the program would encourage drug use as an acceptable way of life.

Demonstrating its technological savvy, the group has used the Internet to hold "virtual marches" on Washington, which have been more effective than actual marches in making direct contact with government officials. The marches take place on a "virtual" Washington Mall, the usual site for many real marches, replete with speakers' podium placed in front of the Capitol. Daniel Zingale is executive director of the AIDS Action Council, which has its headquarters in Washington, D.C.

See also: AIDS CRISIS

For Further Information

AIDS Action Council, *http://www.aidsaction.org*

Cimons, Marlene. "AIDS Activists Swarm Capital Online." *Los Angeles Times*, December 2, 1997, p. 26.

AIDS CRISIS.

Acquired Immune Deficiency Syndrome, or AIDS, was first reported in mid-1981 in the United States, and within the next five years it had claimed the lives of 24,717 persons, creating a health emergency and an AIDS crisis in this country. In 1998 the Centers for Disease Control and Prevention (CDC) reported that the disease had been diagnosed in 641,084 people in the United States and its territories, and by the end of 1997, of these, 390,692 had died. Initially confined mostly to the gay community, AIDS was an almost invariably fatal disease until preventive vaccines and powerful drug combinations were developed that could decrease the amount of HIV virus in the blood to undetectable levels.

Bodily fluids, usually semen and blood, transmit AIDS. Contaminated needles associated with drug use are an additional source of infection. AIDS may have reached the United States as early as 1960 but did not attract medical attention until 1981. Cases of Pneumocystis carinii pneumonia and Kaposi's sarcoma were reported in August 1981 among a population 90 percent of which was homosexual. By 1982 researchers had identified the virus HIV (human immunodeficiency virus) responsible for making the body vulnerable to other illnesses by compromising the immune system.

Initially the public, news media, and government officials treated the disease as a self-imposed scourge limited to the gay community, while the religious right suggested that it was God's punishment for immoral conduct. The circle of concern widened as the disease spread to Haitians, hemophiliacs, blood transfusion recipients, and a growing number of women and babies.

In 1982 LARRY KRAMER met with a small group of gay men in New York City and co-founded the GAY MEN'S HEALTH CRISIS (GMHC) to assist AIDS victims, educate the public, and lobby for funds to support research and improved care and health facilities. He felt compelled to act because of the failure of the Reagan administration, the medical profession, and the media to respond adequately to the crisis.

Kramer, a playwright, essayist, and novelist, had previously written the screenplay for the award-winning film *Women in Love* (1969) and a controversial novel, *Faggots* (1978). Later he was to describe the birth of AIDS activism in his bitingly sarcastic and moving drama, *The Normal Heart* (1985).

Kramer, described as "one of America's most valuable troublemakers," soon became frustrated by GMHC members' reluctance to engage in hardball lobbying and in 1987 formed ACT UP (AIDS Coalition to Unleash Power), which became celebrated for its zany, ultra-rude "zapping" of perceived enemies by hurling red paint at officials and their property, heckling prominent speakers, and screaming and tossing condoms to the congregation during a mass in St. Patrick's Cathedral. The group has scored major victories, including price reductions for drugs and the shortening of the FDA drug approval process.

The AIDS ACTION COUNCIL, founded in 1984, is a third Washington-based group, exclusively committed to promoting responsi-ble federal policies. AIDS Action Council serves as the national voice of AIDS, representing all Americans affected by HIV/AIDS and 3,200 community-based organizations. It maintains a direct action wing, issues legislative alerts, and lobbies for increases in Center for Communicable Diseases appropriations and creation of an AIDS prevention Web site for teenagers. Alternate strategies for attacking AIDS continue to be offered, including distribution of sterilized needles to drug addicts, provision of condoms in the schools, promotion of teen abstinence, and shortening of the testing approval times for curative drugs.

In 1994 AIDS became a worldwide epidemic, with an estimated 4 million people afflicted. By 1999 there were 33 million people living with HIV in the world, almost 22 million in Africa alone. Although an estimated 16,000 new infections worldwide occurred every day, progress was being reported in reducing the ravages of the disease and mortality rates.

For Further Information

Feldman, Douglas A., and Julia Wanger Miller. *The AIDS Crisis: A Documentary History.* Westport, CT: Greenwood Press, 1998.

Lerner, Eric K., and Mary Ellen Hombs. *AIDS Crisis in America: A Reference Handbook.* 2nd ed. Santa Barbara: ABC-CLIO, 1998.

"White House Sounds Alarm on AIDS Crisis in Africa." Harvard School of Public Health: *World Health News,* September 9, 1999.

ALCOHOL AND DRUG POLICIES. Alcoholism and drug abuse presented threats to Americans' health, economy, and social well-being throughout the twentieth century. In the 1820s and 1830s, temperance crusaders had tried unsuccessfully to ration individual alcohol consumption but later became convinced that alcohol was addictive and must be banned altogether. In 1874 Protestant women formed the Woman's Christian Temperance Union, and in 1895 prohibitionists organized the Anti-Saloon League.

During the early years of the twentieth

century, alcoholism was blamed for family neglect, domestic violence, poverty, absenteeism, and lost productivity. The wave of public opinion favoring prohibition strengthened when abstinence was recommended as a necessary patriotic sacrifice during World War I. In 1917 Congress approved the eighteenth Amendment to the Constitution prohibiting the manufacture, sale, and transportation of intoxicating liquors. The amendment was ratified in 1919, with the Volstead Act (1920) providing federal enforcement provisions.

The unintended results included speakeasies, smuggling, bootlegging, gang warfare, and enormous profits for Al Capone and organized crime. Nonetheless, Herbert Hoover in his run for the presidency in 1928 supported continuation of Prohibition. Only four years later, with the Great Depression in progress and Franklin D. Roosevelt in the White House, the public mood shifted. People recognized that the ban actually increased crime, could be evaded by the wealthy, and gave government too much control over citizens' private lives. The twenty-first (repeal) Amendment in 1933 brought to an end the "great experiment."

With the "drys" and Prohibition routed, the Anti-Saloon League lost its mainspring and momentum. After changing its name to the National Temperance League, it adopted its current name, the AMERICAN COUNCIL ON ALCOHOL PROBLEMS (ACAP) in 1974. ACAP continues to promote temperance and abstinence, while focusing on problems caused by the alcohol industry's encouragement of young people's consumption of alcoholic beverages.

MOTHERS AGAINST DRUNK DRIVING (MADD), founded in 1980, has led a successful crusade against drunk driving. By 1985 MADD had 364 chapters, 600,000 members, and a budget of $12.5 million. The founder, Candy Lightner, and nearly half of the chapter presidents have had a family member killed by a drunk driver. Because of the intensity of members' commitment and their confinement to a single issue, MADD activism has been able to reduce the incidence of drunk driving and highway deaths while increasing the severity and number of convictions for driving while under the influence of alcohol.

Unlike drunk driving, drug abuse has proved seemingly immune to attack. During the 1960s, the hippies hoped to create a new society on the ruins of American materialism and military interventionism gone wrong. The use of marijuana was celebrated in rock music and promoted by Allen Ginsburg and Timothy Leary. Pot smoking became a desirable norm for a significant portion of the under-thirty population. Between 1960 and 1978, eleven states passed laws reducing penalties for the private use of small amounts of marijuana. But after 1980 the nation's political environment became less indulgent. LSD, crack, and ever more sophisticated and potentially lethal drugs devastated poor urban areas and moved into suburban public schools. The "War on Drugs" was launched by the Reagan administration, and stringent laws were adopted in New York and in other states, mandating prison sentences for possession of very small amounts of marijuana and other controlled substances. The jails became packed with petty offenders, but traffic in drugs did not diminish, and the big dealers generally remained at large. Again, as with Prohibition, the solution appeared to be exacerbating the damage because it made the abetting of addiction an enormously profitable business.

In 1999 the nation's mood was mellowing and liberalization was being viewed more positively. The NATIONAL ORGANIZATION FOR THE REFORM OF MARIJUANA LAWS (NORML), formed in 1970, initially concentrated on saving veterans and college students from prison sentences stemming from possession of small amounts of marijuana. Later, in the 1990s, NORML shifted its focus to legalization of the drug for medicinal purposes. By 1999 NORML was again advocating removal of all penalties for private possession of marijuana by adults.

NORML's conservative opponents contend that the easing of drug laws would send a dangerous signal, particularly to young people, and that the evidence on marijuana's effects and on its medicinal value in easing the pain and discomfort of cancer and AIDS victims remains inconclusive.

For Further Information

Jaffe, Jerome H., ed. *Encyclopedia of Drugs and Alcohol*. New York: Macmillan, 1995.

Kleiman, Mark. *Against Excess: Drug Policy for Results*. New York: Basic Books, 1992.

Pegram, Thomas R. *Battling Rum: The Struggle for a Dry America, 1800–1933*. Chicago: Ivan R. Dee, 1998.

ALDEN V. MAINE (98 U.S. 436) (1999). In *Alden v. Maine* and two related cases, the Supreme Court eliminated Americans' right to sue state governments for violating federal laws and inflicting injuries. These decisions dramatically changed basic principles of judicial jurisdiction that had existed during the preceding 212 years and were the Rehnquist Court's most significant change in constitutional law. The *Alden v. Maine* ruling also illustrates the tremendous power a president can wield by nominating judges to the Court who favor his political philosophy, be it liberal or conservative.

Signed by the five justices who were appointed or elevated to the Court by Presidents Reagan and Bush, the *Alden v. Maine* decision boldly asserted states' rights and rejected the validity of federal laws taking precedence over state authority. In this decision, authored by Justice Anthony M. Kennedy and supported by Chief Justice William H. Rehnquist and Justices Sandra Day O'Connor, Antonin Scalia, and Clarence Thomas, it was ruled that state employees could no longer sue states for overtime wages due under the Fair Labor Standards Act. In two related cases, Justices Rehnquist and Scalia wrote opinions stating that companies could not sue states for patent infringements or for engaging in false advertising in violation of federal law.

The decision means that a state laboratory can dump toxic wastes in violation of federal laws and persons poisoned by the waste have no recourse to legal redress. Also, any state university can violate copyright law by making multiple copies of a book in print and selling it to students for less than its purchase price, profiting at the expense of the publisher and author. In *Alden v. Maine*, the Court ruled that state sovereignty is overriding and that Congress cannot make states vulnerable to lawsuits. Because Maine was in the forefront among states resisting federal overtime requirements, other states that had been waiting for the decision were expected to follow Maine's lead in disregarding wage mandates for public workers.

In *Marbury v. Madison* (1 Cranch 137) (1803) Chief Justice John Marshall affirmed, "The very essence of civil liberty certainly consists of the right of every individual to claim the protection of the laws, whenever he receives an injury." Because of the Supreme Court's rulings, states will be able to infringe rights created by federal laws and no court will be able to award a remedy.

See also: ENVIRONMENT; LABOR ISSUES

For Further Information

Biskupic, Joan. "In Three Cases, High Court Shifts Power to States." *Washington Post*, June 24, 1999, p. 1.

Chemerinsky, Erwin. "Permission to Litigate: Sovereign Immunity Lets States Decide Who Can Sue Them." *ABA Journal* 85 (August 1999): 42.

ALINSKY, SAUL DAVID (1909–1972). Saul David Alinsky set this century's standard for grassroots empowerment by advising lower-income, working-class Americans on how to form activist groups, acquire influence in local affairs, become politically literate, and improve their economic and social status. He pioneered in the use of protest tactics, including boycotts, picketing, marches, rent strikes, and sit-ins.

Born in Chicago, the son of Russian Jewish immigrants, Alinsky graduated from the University of Chicago in 1930 with an A.B. in archeology. While doing graduate work in criminology, he studied the formation of in-

An undated photo of Saul David Alinsky, taken on a south side Chicago street where Alinsky was organizing a protest against slum conditions. *AP/Wide World Photos.*

dividual and group interests and ways in which opposing groups can convert confrontation into accommodation. After completing a dissertation involving fieldwork with teenage Italian hoodlums and the Capone gang, Alinsky was employed as a criminologist in the Illinois prison system. During this time, he was inspired by the efforts of JOHN L. LEWIS to unionize the coal miners of southern Illinois and form the Congress of Industrial Organizations. Alinsky adopted Lewis's game plan for winning social justice: the promotion of conflicts with authority followed by negotiated resolutions to win political advantage and concessions.

Alinsky's first community action project, initiated in 1939, was the "Back-of-the-Yards" program based in the stockyards area of Chicago. He persuaded recent Czech, Polish, German, and Irish immigrants to stop feuding and start working together for their common good. Aiding him in this effort was

an unlikely coalition of Catholic Church clergy, meatpackers' unions, and radical students. In 1940 the Marshall Field family, the Roman Catholic hierarchy, and the Democratic Party funded the establishment of the INDUSTRIAL AREAS FOUNDATION (IAF) through which Alinsky expanded his work by setting up training courses for community activists. IAF graduates adopted his techniques to help people in poor, working, and middle-class communities organize themselves on a democratic basis and gain power in matters affecting their own interests in San Antonio, Rochester, Detroit, Buffalo, Brooklyn, Pittsburgh, Los Angeles, and other cities.

Prominent Alinsky apostles ERNESTO CORTÉS, CESAR CHAVEZ, and Arnold Graf targeted problems of slum dwellings, urban renewal, racial discrimination, unresponsive politicians, and overcrowded schools. Alinsky won over converts because of his pungent and sharply focused street language, courage, flamboyance, high intellect, humor, and persistence in dealings with allies and antagonists. One of his better known achievements was the Temporary Woodlawn Organization (TWO), created in 1961 in a predominantly black neighborhood in Chicago to protect tenants against greedy landlords, unscrupulous merchants, and threats of property dispossession through urban renewal.

In the mid 1960s Alinsky found himself at odds with Black Power groups who rebuffed white leadership and with President Johnson's War on Poverty, which displaced local community leadership with social service professionals and "do-gooders." In 1969 Alinsky founded a school in Chicago to train persons "who know how to organize in and for a free society" in urban centers. His third book, *Rules for Radicals: A Practical Primer for Realistic Radicals*, was published in 1971. A year later, he died near his home in Carmel, California.

For Further Information

Alinsky, Saul David. *Reveille for Radicals.* Chicago: University of Chicago Press, 1945.

———. *Rules for Radicals: A Practical Primer for Realistic Radicals.* New York: Vintage Books, 1971.

Finks, P. David. *The Radical Vision of Saul Alinsky.* New York: Paulist Press, 1984.

Horwitt, Sanford D. *Let Them Call Me Rebel: Saul Alinsky—His Life and Legacy.* New York: Alfred A. Knopf, 1989.

AMERICAN AGRICULTURE MOVEMENT. The American Agriculture Movement (AAM) was established in 1977 in Springfield, Colorado, to publicize the economic plight of the nation's farmers, resist intrusive governmental regulations, and fight for increased support while decreasing excise taxes. Co-founders Eugene and Derral Schroder were both farmers and populists angered by federal bureaucrats' seeming inability to correct injustices and combat the grossly uneven distribution of wealth and power in the society. AAM is part of the strong tradition of farm politics beginning with the Populist Party (1892) and extending up to Henry A. Wallace's Progressive Party in 1948. As in 1892, a continuing agricultural depression and mounting farmers' debts precipitated an agrarian protest movement in the 1970s.

The first AAM protest action was a nationwide strike scheduled for December 14, 1977. The 7.8 million people then living on farms in the United States were asked to stop producing and selling livestock, grains, and other commodities and to cease buying farm machinery. Though co-sponsored by the NATIONAL FARMERS UNION, the strike failed to materialize because farmers, not yet attuned to twentieth-century activism, planted their crops despite being asked not to do so by the action instigators.

A second and more inflammatory effort that failed to convince legislators to vote in farmers' favor was the AAM series of "tractorcades" initiated between 1977 and 1979. Long lines of tractors driven by farmers, with banners flying, rode through main streets to publicize their grievances and awaken the nation to the increasing gravity of the farming crisis. They rolled through Washington, D.C., other major cities, and Plains, Georgia, Jimmy Carter's home town, to dramatize the fact that production costs (e.g., seed, fertilizer, herbicides, fuel, equipment, and taxes) had become so onerous that profit was not possible even with long hours in the field.

In 1978 AAM representatives met with President Carter to argue for raising the parity ratio to 100 percent. This would have ensured that farmers could recoup the cost of production plus earn a profit dairy farming and raising livestock and grain. Their plea was rejected because of its inflationary impact.

The AAM then ran five candidates for public office in 1986 who promised to protect U.S. agriculture from debt and foreign imports. During the 1990s, AAM opposed federal subsidies, excise tax increases, and the patenting of genetically engineered farm animals.

Although AAM faded from view after

twenty years of fruitless attempts to change agriculture policy and win higher commodity prices, it did succeed in changing elevator bankruptcy laws and Farm Home Administration procedures. In 1999 co-founder Eugene Schroder resurfaced with a new, successor grass roots organization, the Parity Group, dedicated to resolving the ongoing farming crisis.

See also: FARMERS' RIGHTS

For Further Information

American Agriculture Movement, *http://www. aaminc.org*

Mooney, Patrick H., and Theo J. Majka. *Farmers' and Farm Workers' Movements: Social Protest in American Agriculture*. New York: Twayne, 1995.

AMERICAN ANTI-VIVISECTION SOCIETY.

Founded in Philadelphia in 1883, the American Anti-Vivisection Society (AAVS) is a nonprofit animal advocacy organization that has fought to make use of animals in research, testing, and education illegal. A Quaker who operated an infirmary for dumb animals, a physician, several clergymen, and prominent local socialites founded AAVS.

The group's goal is to eliminate animals' subjection to pain-inducing laboratory experimention. AAVS believes that vivisection harms people as well as animals, and that every sentient creature has inherent value and the right to be free from suffering and mutilation. Their mission is to educate the public, lobby legislators to pass laws protecting animals, and help provide nonanimal alternative methods to scientists and educators.

Membership in AAVS has remained small since its formation, and it currently has approximately 11,000 members. However, the AAVS has enlisted animal lovers at the local, state, and national levels in lobbying campaigns that have resulted in legislation forbidding use of animals for any type of lab experiment in which suffering is incurred. Its educational and mail campaigns have forced medical researchers to modify laboratory

procedures to eliminate unnecessarily cruel treatment of animals, this in the face of opposition by the health sciences professions.

In 1926 the AAVS held its first annual International Anti-Vivisection Convention to extend its crusade beyond the United States. Designation of October 4 as World Day for Animals in some cities and states was an outcome of AAVS activism. The Alternatives Research and Development Foundation (ARDF) is an affiliate of AAVS. ARDF awards annual grants to scientists who develop experimental methodologies that do not use animal, or animal by-products. The AAVS produces several publications, including *ActiVate for Animals*, a bimonthly; *Animalearn: The Magazine for Kids Who Love Animals*; and *AV Magazine*, a quarterly.

AAVS headquarters is in Jenkintown, Pennsylvania. Tina Nelson is executive director.

See also: ANIMAL WELFARE AND RIGHTS

For Further Information

American Anti-Vivisection Society. "Point/Counterpoint" (brochure). Jenkintown, PA: AAVS, n.d.

American Anti-Vivisection Society, *http://www. aavs.org*

Singer, Peter Albert David. *Animal Liberation*. New York: Morrow/Avon, 1991.

AMERICAN-ARAB ANTI-DISCRIMINATION COMMITTEE.

Founded in 1980, the American-Arab Anti-Discrimination Committee (ADC) defends the civil rights of Americans of Arab descent and combats defamation and negative stereotyping of Arab Americans in the media and wherever else they occur. ADC was founded by former Senator James Abourezk, son of a Lebanese peddler, who grew up on the Rosebud Indian reservation in South Dakota in the 1930s. While he was senator, Abourezk toured the Middle East in the 1970s and familiarized himself with the region. In 1977 he decided not to seek reelection and soon thereafter established the ADC.

ADC has media monitoring groups and an

action network to report stereotyping of Arabs in the media and oppose discrimination against Arab Americans in employment, education, and politics. Through its Department of Legal Services, ADC offers counseling to persons victimized by discrimination and defamation. ADC's Media and Publications Department issues a bimonthly newsletter, *ADC Times.*

Films that have been picketed by ADC include *Protocol, Ishtar, Operation Condor, True Lies, Father of the Bride II, The Return of Jafar, Kazaam,* and *The Siege,* all of which include ethnic and religious slurs or descriptions of Arabs as bumbling, bloodthirsty zealots. In the Disney film *Aladdin,* ADC negotiated a change in the lyrics of the opening song "Arabian Nights." An offending reference to Arabs' habit of cutting off ears of strangers they dislike was replaced by words describing Arabia's flat terrain and intense heat, making the adjective "barbaric" apply to the land and not to its people.

In 1986 Coleco Industries, creators of the Cabbage Patch Dolls, marketed a swarthy submachine-gun–wielding Nomad warrior doll sporting a nametag written in Arabic. This was withdrawn from the market as a result of ADC pressure.

The ADC has reported upsurges in hate crimes, including arson, bombings, and physical assaults, after each act of Arab terrorism. The bombing of the ADC office in Santa Ana, California, and the murder of the ADC regional coordinator followed the piracy of the Italian cruise ship *Achille Lauro* in October 1985. And after the Persian Gulf War, the number of hate crimes surged from 39 in 1990 to 119 in 1991.

In 1999 ADC lost the U.S. Supreme Court case *Reno v. American-Arab-Anti-Discrimination Committee,* in which it was determined that First Amendment protections do not apply to illegal immigrants seeking to avoid deportation.

ADC's current membership is approximately 20,000. Its headquarters office is in Washington, D.C.; Hala Maksoud is president.

See also: ARAB AMERICAN RIGHTS

For Further Information

American-Arab Anti-Discrimination Committee, *http://www.adc.org*

Haiek, Joseph R., ed. *Arab-American Almanac,* 5th ed., rev. Glendale, CA: News Circle, 1998.

AMERICAN ASSOCIATION OF RETIRED PERSONS. The American Association of Retired Persons (AARP) is the oldest and largest advocacy group for senior citizens in the United States. Its motto is "To Serve, Not to Be Served." As a private, nonprofit organization, it is committed to helping elderly Americans achieve lives of independence, dignity, and purpose. Founded in 1958 by Dr. Ethel Percy Andrus, the first woman to become a high school principal in California, AARP has its roots in the National Retired Teachers Association (NRTA), started by Andrus in 1947 to provide health insurance for aging teachers who had been rejected as poor risks. AARP was formed as a parallel organization to extend NRTA benefits to all seniors.

By 1982 the NRTA had become a division of AARP. Andrus was assisted by Leonard Davis, president of the Colonial Penn Group, who initiated an aggressive direct mail campaign and succeeded in demonstrating that providing life insurance for the elderly was feasible and profitable, while adding significantly to NRTA and AARP membership.

AARP's success is reflected in the increasing relative wealth of seniors. In the 1960s, the spending power of seventy-year-olds was approximately 71 percent of that of thirty-year-olds; in the 1980s, seniors had 18 percent more spending power than thirty-year-olds. AARP's strength has so impressed lawmakers and other lobbyists that they refer to it as the "warm and fuzzy eight hundred pound gorilla." Run by a professional staff that reports to an elected board of twenty-one volunteers and an unpaid chairman, AARP uses much of its income to support its political clout. The current executive director (1991–), Horace B. Deets, is a soft-spoken visionary and retired Jesuit priest; he is additionally an avid user of information technology.

Whenever AARP takes a position on an issue, legislators listen because seniors vote more than any other age group, read more, and have time at their disposal. They constitute over 20 percent of the vote in presidential elections, and the AARP membership base, now at 33 million, is destined to expand. Upon reaching fifty years of age, all Americans receive solicitations to become members. AARP/VOTE was established in 1986 as the grassroots advocacy/political education arm of AARP, employing volunteer action coordinators at the state and congressional district levels throughout the United States. In 1995 AARP opposition was a key factor in defeating the proposed Balanced Budget Amendment because AARP mustered a strong no vote and developed salable intellectual arguments against the amendment.

AARP's joint ventures with such firms as Scudder, Prudential, Bank One, and Amoco enable it to earn income through sales of insurance policies, mutual funds, discounts on prescription drugs, auto rentals and auto club memberships, credit cards, hotel discount packages, adult education programs, and travel services offered to its members. AARP dues are $8 a year, which include subscriptions to *Modern Maturity* and *AARP Bulletin*. *Modern Maturity* has surpassed *TV Guide* and *Reader's Digest* in circulation. The *AARP Bulletin* is the most powerful lobbying voice for the aged, summarizing legislative and political happenings in Washington of interest to seniors. AARP monitors federal and state legislatures, lobbies for laws beneficial to people living on fixed incomes, and cooperates with other groups (e.g., the GRAY PANTHERS) in modifying mandatory retirement laws and eliminating discrimination against the elderly.

The future promises challenges to AARP as the phalanx of other senior citizen action groups has expanded to include the Gray Panthers, the NATIONAL COUNCIL OF SENIOR CITIZENS, the NATIONAL COMMITTEE TO PRESERVE SOCIAL SECURITY AND MEDI-CARE (NCPSSM), the UNITED SENIORS ASSOCIATION, the SENIORS COALITION, and the Gay and Lesbian Association of Retiring Persons. Some of the newly arrived organizations are ultra conservative, and others are polarized on the left or concerned with single issues, as is the NCPSSM, which has already surpassed AARP in money spent on lobbying. Unlike other groups, AARP has maintained its nonpartisan, middle-class image.

AARP's political profile is rising to prominence in step with the realization that the nation's biggest public policy challenge is adequate financing of income and health security for the aged. AARP will be a key player in resolving that challenge. Its service program not only speaks to the organization's self-perception but says a great deal about the attitudes, values, and preconceptions that it brings to the debate. Executive Director Horace Deets "envisions AARP as the nerve center of a national network of older Americans dedicated to tackling the country's social problems—caring for or protecting the dependent aged; spearheading community improvement initiatives; reaching out to deprived children as mentors, tutors, and caregivers; revivifying the political process." AARP national headquarters is in Washington, D.C., with branches in the fifty states, the District of Columbia, Puerto Rico, and the Virgin Islands.

See also: SENIOR MOVEMENT

For Further Reading

American Association of Retired Persons, *http://www.aarp.org*

Morris, Charles R. *The AARP: America's Most Powerful Lobby and the Clash of Generations*. New York: Random House, 1996.

Peterson, Peter G. *Gray Dawn: How the Coming Age Wave Will Transform Amerca—and the World*. New York: Random House, 1999.

AMERICAN ASSOCIATION OF UNIVERSITY WOMEN. The American Association of University Women (AAUW) was founded in Boston in 1882 by Marion Talbot (Boston University) and Ellen H. Richards (Vassar College) to promote women's representation and status in higher education. During its early years, as the Association of Collegiate Alumnae (ACA), its membership included representatives of eight colleges and universities. In 1921 it became the AAUW after merging with the Southern Association of College Women, and its mission broadened to include the general advancement of women in society. Woman suffrage, elimination of gender bias in hiring and salaries, election of women to political office, and ratification of the Equal Rights Amendment to the Constitution have since been added to the AAUW agenda.

For more than a century, AAUW has influenced legislative debate on key social issues, now including reproductive choice, affirmative action, Title IX prohibiting sex discrimination in federally assisted education programs, welfare reform, vocational education, family and medical leave, health care reform, equity in athletics, managed care, and Social Security reform.

In 1958 the AAUW established the Educational Foundation to enable it to award fellowships to women entering graduate schools. AAUW has succeeded in working with other moderate and progressive organizations to defeat attempts to dismantle affirmative action programs and diminish women's opportunities on college campuses. AAUW now comprises three corporations: the Association, a 160,000-member organization with more than 1,500 branches that lobbies for educational equity; the Educational Foundation; and the AAUW Legal Advocacy Fund, which supports women seeking judicial redress for sex discrimination in higher education.

AAUW publishes voting records for Congress, documenting for its membership positions taken by senators and representatives on federal legislative priorities. These positions are often opposed by radical right organizations (e.g., FAMILY RESEARCH COUNCIL and FOCUS ON THE FAMILY). AAUW's activist agenda is supported by frequent symposia on legislative topics, action alerts, and a network of branch and state Web sites and communication action projects. Members' prestigious institutional affiliations and AAUW's lobbying and legal expertise, along with its strong Washington presence, provide the leverage to affect key votes. An ongoing voter education initiative uses fax and e-mail to mobilize grassroots support and get more women to the polls. *Adelante!*, a new diversity awareness and action program, recommends monthly book titles relevant to membership.

Sandy Bernard, long-term member and past president of the AAUW Legal Advocacy Fund, was elected president in 1997. Amy Swanger is executive director. The organization's national headquarters is in Washington, D.C. Its official journal is *AAUW Journal*. The monthly *Action Alert* newsletter is also available for members who seek involvement in lobbying.

See also: WOMEN'S ISSUES

For Further Information

American Association of University Women, *http://www.aauw.org*

Levine, Susan. *Degrees of Equality: The American Association of University Women and the Challenge of Twentieth Century Feminism*. Philadelphia: Temple University Press, 1995.

AMERICAN BIRTH CONTROL FEDERATION. *See* Planned Parenthood Federation of America

AMERICAN CIVIL LIBERTIES UNION. The American Civil Liberties Union (ACLU), originated in 1917 as the American Civil Liberties Bureau, is the nation's foremost advocate of rights set forth in the Bill of Rights of the U.S. Constitution. These include freedom of speech, press, assembly, and religion; due process; and fair treatment under the law regardless of ethnicity, color, sexual orientation, political opinion, or religious belief.

ACLU was formed during World War I to protect conscientious objectors' rights during a period of strong anti-German sentiment. In 1920 Roger Baldwin and Norman Thomas, the Bureau's founders, were joined by Clarence Darrow, John Dewey, Felix Frankfurter, JANE ADDAMS, several notable liberal religious leaders, James Weldon Johnson, Helen Keller, Jeannette Rankin, and others to form the ACLU.

ACLU has argued more cases before the U.S. Supreme Court than any other entity except the federal government itself. Landmark cases and civil rights litigation with which it has been associated include the Sacco and Vanzetti case (1920), the Scopes trial (1925), extension of the Fourteenth Amendment in *Near v. Minnesota* (1931), reversal of the Scottsboro boys' conviction for rape (1935), *Gideon v. Wainwright* (1963), *Miranda v. Arizona* (1966), *Tinker v. Des Moines Independent School District* (1969), *Miller v. California* (1973), *ROE V. WADE* (1973), and *Reno v. ACLU* (1998). Separation of church and state, drug policy and criminal justice, free speech and censorship, lesbian and gay rights, reproductive rights, prisoners' rights, and voting rights are among areas monitored by the ACLU. This is because these areas are afforded protection by the Bill of Rights and the establishment clause of the U.S. Constitution.

In 1950, after Roger Baldwin's retirement, ACLU sought a wider membership, sensing that its issues would appeal to more than a select group of about 9,000 people, most of whom were attorneys. Its recruitment campaign succeeded, and its structure made a transition from an autonomous self-selecting board to a complex democratized organization. During the 1950s, a turbulent period during which endangerment of civil rights became a prominent and recurrent concern (e.g., McCarthyism; the *BROWN V. BOARD OF EDUCATION OF TOPEKA* Supreme Court decision; the Montgomery, Alabama, bus boycott), ACLU's ties to minority causes intensified. Supreme Court Justice Thurgood Marshall and Roy Wilkins joined the ACLU board, and *amicus* briefs were filed in defense of arrested civil rights demonstrators and litigants in school desegregation cases.

During the Vietnam War, the ACLU returned to its earlier theme, the support of war resisters. In May 1970, after the Kent State University shootings of four students by the Ohio National Guard, ACLU declared that the war in Vietnam and Cambodia was a violation of the war powers clause of the Constitution. This caused a split in ACLU ranks, but the influx of new members outnumbered whose who quit over the policy change. More injurious to the organization's image and membership was its defense of Neo-Nazis' right to march through the predominantly Jewish community of Skokie, Illinois, in 1979. ACLU defended the Neo-Nazis because "keeping them off the streets of Skokie could weaken First Amendment rights for others." Although about 25,000 members left ACLU, its membership subsequently rebounded.

ACLU has become progressively stronger and more open in its defense of such cases as *Roe v. Wade*. When Robert Bork was nominated for a Supreme Court vacancy, ACLU discarded its traditional neutrality on judicial nominations and led the coalition that blocked his confirmation by the Senate in 1987.

A recent victory in *Reno v. ACLU*, in which the Supreme Court unanimously declared cyberspace a free speech domain, has been accompanied by an unbroken winning streak against other attempts by Congress to legislate cyber censorship. ACLU field staff works with grassroots people and has launched campaigns against proposed legislation that would outlaw flag desecration and permit prayers to be incorporated into public school curricula.

ACLU headquarters is in New York City; its legislative office is in Washington, D.C. Ira Glasser is executive director, and Nadine Strossen is president. ACLU has 290,000 members.

For Further Information

American Civil Liberties Union, *http://www.aclu.org*

Donohue, William A. *The Politics of the American Civil Liberties Union.* Princeton, NJ: Transaction Books, 1985.

Garey, Diane. *Defending Everybody: A History of the American Civil Liberties Union.* New York: TV Books, 1998. [Accompanies 1998 PBS special on the history of the ACLU.]

Walker, Samuel. *In Defense of American Liberties: A History of the ACLU.* New York: Oxford University Press, 1990.

AMERICAN CONSERVATIVE UNION.

Formed in 1964, the American Conservative Union (ACU) is the nation's largest and oldest conservative lobbying organization. The ACU Statement of Principles "supports capitalism, the doctrine of original intent of the framers of the Constitution, traditional moral values, and a strong national defense." Founding members included former Congressmen Don Bruce (R–IN) and John Ashbrook (R–OH), and others who participated in the failed presidential campaign of Senator Barry Goldwater of Arizona.

Throughout the late 1960s, ACU promoted conservative views and recruited activists through its newsletter, *Battle Line*, position papers, press releases, and distribution of voting ratings of members of Congress. In 1974 the ACU inaugurated the Conservative Political Action Conference (CPAC), a forum to showcase speeches by prominent conservative leaders and officeholders. Young Americans for Freedom joined the CPAC in 1975 to co-sponsor a conference in Washington that included Senators Barry Goldwater and James F. Buckley, EAGLE FORUM leader PHYLLIS SCHLAFLY, columnist Kevin Phillips, and Ronald Reagan. When Reagan entered the primaries in an effort to win the 1976 Republican presidential nomination, ACU conducted a campaign for him, contributing significantly to his strong showing in Florida and later victories in North Carolina and Texas.

The ACU supported the war in Vietnam, retention of the Panama Canal, nonrecognition of the People's Republic of China, the Reagan era tax cuts, and funding of the resistance movements in Nicaragua and Afghanistan. It also strongly supported the Bush administration's nomination of Clarence Thomas to the U.S. Supreme Court and legislation to outlaw burning of the American flag.

Currently ACU favors repeal of the sixteenth Amendment to the Constitution, which allows a federal income tax, and supports mandatory sentencing, continuation of the death penalty, and legislation to end affirmative action. It opposes restrictions on the purchase and use of guns and ammunition by law-abiding citizens and backs the right of parents to have their tax dollars for education used to support a public, private, or parochial school of their choice. ACU also endorses elimination of the departments of Commerce, Education, Housing and Urban Development, Energy, and Labor, as well as the National Endowment for the Arts, National Endowment for the Humanities, Legal Services Corporation, and Corporation for Public Broadcasting.

In 1994 ACU spearheaded the attack on President Clinton's health proposal with a program of "national town meetings" held across the country by "Citizens Against National Health," supplemented by a cross-country "National Health Care Truth Tour."

The ACU serves as an umbrella for many other conservative causes and organizations. RALPH REED (CHRISTIAN COALITION), Grover Norquist (AMERICANS FOR TAX REFORM), Wayne LaPierre (NATIONAL RIFLE ASSOCIATION), and Lewis K. Uhler (NATIONAL TAX LIMITATION COMMITTEE), and conservative Republican Senator Jesse Helms serve on its board.

ACU's headquarters building is in Alexandria, Virginia. David A. Keene has served as chairman since 1984; Thomas R. Katina is executive director. ACU communicates with its more than 1 million members through its magazine, *Battle Line*, and annual *ACU's Rating of Congress* reports.

See also: CONSERVATIVES (FAR RIGHT)

For Further Information

"American Conservative Union." *Human Events* 50, no. 12 (April 1, 1994): 10.

American Conservative Union, *http://www. conservative.org*

Crawford, Alan. *Thunder on the Right: The "New Right" and the Politics of Resentment.* New York: Pantheon Books, 1980.

AMERICAN COUNCIL OF CHRISTIAN CHURCHES.

The American Council of Christian Churches (ACCC) was founded by Reverend Carl McIntire in 1941 to counteract the continuing advance of religious "modernity and to bear witness to the historic faith of the church," which McIntire charged was being abandoned. An eloquent preacher and a skilled organizer, McIntire led the ACCC into politics, committing it to the anticommunist crusade of the 1950s, singling out the Soviet Union as the principal adversary of America and an agent of Satan. In his book, *Author of Liberty* (1946), McIntire stated that the United States was God's chosen instrument to save the world and blamed communists for many of the nation's problems. McIntire, who had been ejected from the United Presbyterian Church in 1936, remained the leader of the ACCC until 1969.

As a religious fundamentalist, McIntire challenged the right of the National Council of Churches or the National Association of Evangelicals to speak for American Protestantism, contending that the ecumenical movement had compromised the truth of the gospel by attempting to build a "one world church" and advocating pacifism and peaceful coexistence with communism. The 1.5 million members of the ACCC supported states' rights and the use of nuclear weapons, and would accept nothing less than total victory in the Vietnamese conflict. They also opposed diplomatic recognition of the People's Republic of China and détente with the Soviet Union.

After Reverend McIntire's departure from ACCC leadership and the lessening of national concern with the "communist menace," the group shifted its attention from specific political agendas to doctrinal issues. The ACCC churches assign exclusive religious authority to Scripture and urge members of other churches to depart from apostate denominations, including those within the National Council of Churches. In line with its rejection of modern culture and insistence on doctrinal purity, the ACCC went on record in 1989 declaring that AIDS is a judgment of God and that he "will deliver homosexuals from their vile affections if they will to turn to God for deliverance through Jesus Christ and the Holy Scriptures."

Major religious denominations within the ACCC fold include the Bible Presbyterian Churches, Evangelical Methodist Churches, Fellowship of Fundamental Bible Churches, Free Presbyterian Churches of North America, Fundamental Methodist Churches, General Association of Regular Baptist Churches, Independent Baptist Fellowship of North America, and Independent Churches Affiliated.

The organization's headquarters is in Valley Forge, Pennsylvania. The ACCC conducts radio and television missions and promotes lay activity on behalf of forty-nine state affiliates, representing a million and a half members. ACCC publications include the *Fundamental News Service.*

For Further Information

American Council of Christian Churches, *http://www.amcouncilcc.org*

Wald, Kenneth D. *Religion and Politics in the United States.* 3rd ed. Washington, D.C.: Congressional Quarterly, 1996, pp. 249–252.

Wuthnow, Robert, ed. *The Encyclopedia of Politics and Religion.* Washington, D.C.: Congressional Quarterly, 1998, pp. 181–187.

AMERICAN COUNCIL ON ALCOHOL PROBLEMS.

The American Council on Alcohol Problems (ACAP), originally named the Anti-Saloon League of America (ASLA), was a major force in American politics from 1895 until 1933. It influenced the U.S. citizenry through printed word and expert lobbying, converting a moral crusade into a constitutional amendment barring the consumption and sale of alcoholic beverages. Founded by clergymen and prohibitionists,

The American Council on Alcohol Problems, originally named the Anti-Saloon League of America, grew out of the temperance movement of the late nineteenth century. Shown here is Carry Nation, the turn-of-the-century temperance activist who was well known for taking a hatchet to bar fixtures and stock. © *Bettmann/CORBIS.*

the ASLA was formed to act as a nonpartisan, single-issue alternative to the Prohibition Party, which had other social problems in addition to liquor on its political agenda. Reverend Howard Hyde Russell, who became the ASLA's first national superintendent, developed affiliates in most states by 1903. ASLA demonstrated its clout by unseating an uncooperative anti-"dry" Republican governor, Myron P. Herrick of Ohio, in 1905 and soon became respected as one of the most successful activist groups in American history. Its three-way strategy combined agitation, legislation, and law enforcement. Agitation was achieved through its printing press at Westerville, Ohio, which circulated millions of pages of anti-liquor propaganda. In the legislation arena, lobbying techniques and political opportunism were used to advantage. Local-option laws were advocated in the "wet" states while statewide prohibition was pushed in local-option states.

Its organizational structure enabled the group to act locally while thinking globally, with a salaried superintendent in each state appointed by and reporting to the national superintendent. Vast power was wielded by the group because of the support of evangelical Protestant churches in the South and Midwest, foreshadowing the tremendous influence of the RELIGIOUS RIGHT on voting patterns in the 1980s and 1990s. ASLA pressure succeeded in getting prohibition adopted in nineteen states, resulting in passage of the Eighteenth Amendment in 1917, followed by its ratification in 1919. The Volstead Act (1919) and Jones Act (1929) were also attributed to ASLA activism.

The fortunes of the ASLA declined thereafter because of the Depression's severe socioeconomic repercussions, repeal of prohibition (twenty-first Amendment) in 1933, and a scandal associated with Southern Methodist Bishop James Cannon Jr., then ASLA's national superintendent. Two new organizations, the Temperance Education Foundation and the Temperance League of America (TLA), were created. The Foundation maintained ASLA archives until they were moved to the Ohio State Historical Society in 1974. The TLA adopted its current name, the American Council on Alcohol Problems, in 1964. The ACAP seeks long-range solutions to the problems posed by alcohol and employs educational and legislative approaches for the prevention of alcoholism and other alcohol-related problems.

ACAP headquarters is in Birmingham, Alabama. Currently the ACAP is a federation of thirty-six state affiliates and twenty-two denominational councils or judicatories. Its monthly journal, *American Issue,* is distributed to members.

See also: ALCOHOL AND DRUG POLICIES

For Further Information

Odegard, Peter H. *Pressure Politics: The Story of the Anti-Saloon League.* New York: Hippocrene Books, 1967.

Pegram, Thomas R. *Battling Demon Rum: The Struggle for a Dry America, 1800–1933.* Chicago: Ivan R. Dee, 1998.

Westerville, Ohio Public Library Anti-Saloon League archives, *http://www.wpl.lib.oh.us/AntiSaloon/*

AMERICAN DISABLED FOR ATTENDANT PROGRAMS TODAY.

Founded in 1983, American Disabled for Attendant Programs Today (ADAPT) has mounted widely publicized disruptive demonstrations in its ongoing battle for unrestricted access to public transit and facilities and a national program of home-based personal assistance (attendant services) for the disabled. ADAPT argues that attendant services would enable physically handicapped persons to remain at home instead of being "warehoused," at greater cost and with lost dignity and freedom, in socially insulated nursing facilities.

ADAPT originated as a project within the Atlantis Community, an independent living community located in Denver. Here it began a seven-year nationwide campaign for wheelchair lifts on buses and access to public transportation for the disabled. Then called American Disabled for Accessible Public Transit, ADAPT caught the public's attention by blocking buses in major cities to dramatize the need for equal and unimpeded access to public transit. ADAPT played a major role in winning passage of the Americans with Disabilities Act (ADA). After enactment, ADAPT became involved in lawsuits initiated by the American Public Transit Association and the American Bus Association against the Department of Transportation. The DOT contended that complying with ADA specifications would impose prohibitive costs upon the bus companies.

Attendant services became ADAPT's primary concern as of July 1990. The group seeks passage of a Community Attendant Services Act (CASA) that would reallocate one-quarter of federal and state Medicaid dollars from institutional programs to consumer-managed community-based programs.

The national headquarters office of ADAPT is in Denver, Colorado. Mike Auberger, a member of the Atlantis Community, coordinates national activities. ADAPT membership totals about 5,000, represented in chapters in thirty-two cities and twenty-seven states. ADAPT issues a quarterly newsletter, *Incitement*, published by its Austin, Texas chapter.

See also: DISABLED PERSONS' RIGHTS

For Further Information

American Disabled for Attendant Programs Today, *http://www.adapt.org/*

Vitez, Michael. "A Challenge to Where the Disabled May Receive Long-Term Care: The Supreme Court Could Decide if States Must Provide Home or Community-Based Services for Some." *Philadelphia Inquirer*, June 14, 1999, p. A01.

Vogt, Katherine. "ADAPT Protesters Arrested at Greyhound Terminal." *Denver Post*, January 16, 1998, Denver and the West section, p. B02.

AMERICAN ENTERPRISE INSTITUTE FOR PUBLIC POLICY RESEARCH.

The American Enterprise Institute for Public Policy Research (AEI), founded as the American Enterprise Association in 1943, has as its goal "to preserve and to strengthen the foundations of freedom—government, private enterprise, vital cultural and political institutions, and a strong foreign policy and national defense" through scholarly research, open debate, and publications.

A pro-business, influential think tank, AEI has on its staff former Supreme Court nominee Robert Bork, who, in *Slouching Towards Gomorrah*, identified radical egalitarianism as a cause of the decline of American moral and cultural life. Other AEI scholars include former UN Ambassador Jeane Kirkpatrick, conservative columnists Michael Novak, Norman Ornstein, and Ben Wattenberg, Alan Keyes,

Nobel Laureate James Buchanan, Charles Murray, author of *The Bell Curve*, and former Speaker of the House of Representatives Newt Gingrich.

In 1987 incoming and current AEI president Christopher DeMuth developed a star system by bringing in the aforementioned celebrities, supplemented by twenty or more academics. Altogether, the AEI has fifty resident scholars and fellows, as well as more than one hundred adjunct scholars based in universities and other policy institutes. They have gone forth and written books, delivered testimony before Congress, provided expert consultation to government, made speeches, and, most important, drawn a large audience in the media, including popular talk radio. In 1984 John Saloma wrote that "AEI has developed perhaps the most effective public-relations campaign for disseminating political ideas that has ever been mounted" (p. 8).

AEI is constantly asked by the media to contribute sound bites and data to support their stories. Editors and talk show hosts need information quickly in order to meet deadlines, and AEI can oblige by offering its original research and eminent senior scholars. AEI has succeeded in stimulating citizen action, as have other think tanks. It has done this by getting its scholars on high visibility programs such as *Crossfire Sunday*, PBS's *Think Tank*, and CNN's *Capital Gang*, and into editorial sections of key newspapers, thus shaping public opinion and influencing electoral outcomes to conservative advantage.

AEI board members include Steve Forbes, sociologist James Q. Wilson, and representatives of Alcoa, Amoco, AT&T, Dow Chemical, W. R. Grace, Procter & Gamble, and other major corporations. AEI sponsors its annual Public Policy Week in December and a World Forum in June. It conducts an Election Watch during national election years.

AEI is headquartered in Washington, D.C. Members receive its publication, *The American Enterprise*, a bimonthly.

See also: ACTIVIST THINK TANKS

For Further Information

American Enterprise Institute for Public Policy Research, *http://www.aei.org*

Goldwin, Robert A., and William A. Schambra. *The Constitution, the Courts, and the Quest for Justice.* Washington, DC: American Enterprise Institute for Public Policy Research, 1989.

Hellebust, Lynn. *Think Tank Directory: A Guide to Nonprofit Public Policy Research Organizations.* Washington, DC: Government Research Service, 1996.

Kass, Leon R., and James Q. Wilson. *The Ethics of Human Cloning.* Washington, DC: AEI Press, 1998.

McGann, James G. *Think Tanks and Civil Societies: Catalysts for Ideas and Action.* Piscataway, NJ: Transaction, 2000.

Saloma, John, III. *Ominous Politics.* New York: Hill and Wang, 1984.

AMERICAN FAMILY ASSOCIATION.

The American Family Association (AFA), a nonprofit organization founded in 1977 by Donald Wildmon, fosters the biblical ethic of decency in American society and focuses primarily on the influence of television and other media, including pornography, on society. The organization urges its members to write letters to networks and sponsors, protesting shows that it contends promote violence, immorality, profanity, and vulgarity, while encouraging the production of programs that are constructive, wholesome, and family oriented.

Donald E. Wildmon, an ordained United Methodist minister, led various church congregations from 1965 until he founded the National Federation for Decency (NFD) in 1977. The NFD became the American Family Association in 1988. TV programs that the AFA has found offensive include *Cheers, The Johnny Carson Show, Saturday Night Live*, and *NYPD Blue*. In 1994 the AFA spent some $3 million on a newspaper, radio, and direct mail campaign discouraging advertisers from airing commercials during *NYPD Blue* and *Ellen*. More recently, AFA has added radio shock jock Howard Stern, Walt Disney Company, and controversial rock star Marilyn Manson to its list of targets.

The group has urged the closing of PBS and convinced many state legislatures to reduce its funding. AFA succeeded in banning magazines it finds offensive (e.g., *Playboy, Hustler,* and *Spice*) from forty-three federal prison commissaries. The National Endowment for the Arts and liberally oriented public school curricula have been condemned by AFA for supporting antireligious and immoral art, books, and lifestyles. Through boycotts, AFA convinced BumbleBee Tuna, Burger King, Clorox, and other national advertisers to drop sponsorship of TV shows considered offensive. AFA, along with allied religious right groups, has condemned American Airlines for its gay-indulgent policies, requesting that it stop endorsing "a radical movement that seeks to use government and corporate power to impose obligatory acceptance of homosexuality on all of society."

The AFA Law Center is staffed by six full-time attorneys and supported by a network of some 400 affiliated lawyers. AFA's Washington Office of Governmental Affairs monitors proposed federal legislation, federal agencies, and activities of the executive and judiciary branches of government.

Based in Tupelo, Mississippi, AFA has over 500,000 members and over 550 affiliate chapters located throughout the country. Donald Wildmon is executive director. AFA media include a membership publication, the monthly *AFA Journal*; a radio show, the *AFA Report*, a thirty-minute production available on about 1,200 local radio stations; and a broadcast ministry, *American Family Radio*, aired on over 150 stations in twenty-seven states.

See also: RELIGIOUS RIGHT

For Further Information

American Family Association, *http://www.afa.net*
Buss, Dale D. "Holding Corporate America Accountable: Christians Press for Greater Responsibility from Businesses." *Christianity Today* 40, no. 12 (October 28, 1996): 76–79.
Detweiler, John S. "The Religious Right's Battle Plan in the 'Civil War of Values.'" *Public Relations Review*, Special Issue: Public Relations and Religion (Fall 1992): 247–255.
Phair, Judith T. "The Battle for Support: Pro and Anti-NEA Forces Wage Grass-Roots Campaigns." *Public Relations Journal*, vol. 46 (August 1990): 18–26.

AMERICAN FARM BUREAU FEDERATION. The American Farm Bureau Federation (AFBF), founded in Chicago in 1919 by the heads of state farm bureaus and agricultural leaders, is the largest and strongest voice representing farmers in state and federal legislatures. Its registered lobbyists work with members of Congress and regulatory agencies to argue such issues as farm policy, budget and taxes, farm credit, labor, conservation, and the environment. The AFBF's purpose is "to make the business of farming more profitable, and the community a better place to live. Farm Bureau should provide an organization in which members may secure the benefits of unified efforts in a way which could never be accomplished through individual effort."

Henry C. Wallace, editor of *Wallace's Farmer* and secretary of agriculture in the Harding and Coolidge administrations, was the organization's founder, and James R. Howard, president of the Iowa Farm Bureau, was its first national president. County agents had spearheaded the AFBF's formation as a counterfoil to the radicalism of the U.S. rural farm population following World War I and the Russian Revolution.

During the 1920s the AFBF favored federal intervention on behalf of farmers, endorsing the McNary-Haugen Farm Relief bill, twice vetoed by President Calvin Coolidge. The AFBF enhanced its lobbying position by forming a bipartisan bloc in Congress. It was successful in helping to formulate the Agricultural Adjustment Act of 1933, an important New Deal legislative initiative, and was instrumental in winning passage of the Soil Conservation and Domestic Allotment Act (1936) and the Agricultural Adjustment Act (1938).

Being sensitive to the fluctuations in federal farm policy, the AFBF continuously adjusted its lobbying priorities until the

Eisenhower and Nixon administrations. When New Deal fervor cooled in the 1940s, the AFBF retracted its endorsement of high price supports in favor of less government control of commodity production. This conservative stance continues, with AFBF supporting free market economics. This position has placed the AFBF at loggerheads with other more liberal groups such as the AMERICAN AGRICULTURE MOVEMENT that campaigned until the late 1990s for federal subsidies, protectionism, and production controls. The group endorsed the farm export policies of Ezra Taft Benson and Earl Butz during the Nixon and Ford administrations.

The AFBF's impact on congressional decision making has waned as the percentage of farmers in the U.S. labor force has declined from 17.4% in 1940 to only 1.6% in 1990. However, despite the severe shrinkage of its base constituency during this period, AFBF membership expanded from 300,000 in 1921 to 1.8 million by 1980.

In 1999 the AFBF retained a broad and ambitious action agenda which included opposition to corporate average fuel economy (CAFE) standards for trucks, and support for grain-based fuels such as ethanol. It also favored fewer federal regulations governing ergonomics, water quality protection, the use of pesticides and the approval of normal trade relations status for China.

Currently 4.8 million farm family members are represented by AFBF. The organization maintains two offices: its general headquarters in Park Ridge, Illinois, and an office in Washington, D.C. Robert Stallman is president. County and state leaders of AFBF receive the *Farm Bureau News*, a weekly. *The Voice of Agriculture* Web site provides news and commentary over the Internet (*http://www.fb.org*).

See also: FARMERS' RIGHTS

For Further Information

American Farm Bureau Federation, *http://www.fb.org*

Howard, James R. *James R. Howard and the Farm Bureau*. Ames: Iowa State University Press, 1983.

AMERICAN INDIAN MOVEMENT. The American Indian Movement (AIM), founded in 1968 at the Pine Ridge Indian Reservation (South Dakota) by DENNIS BANKS, Clyde Bellecourt, Eddie Benton Banai, and George Mitchell, emerged as the most militant group urging radical reform of federal-Indian relations. AIM riveted public attention on Native American problems by occupying (November 2–8, 1972) the Washington, D.C. offices of the U.S. Bureau of Indian Affairs (BIA), demanding the property and rights guaranteed Indians by treaties with the United States, and forcefully taking over the village of Wounded Knee, South Dakota, challenging the locally elected Oglala Sioux government and demanding reform in Indian tribal government. RUSSELL MEANS, an Oglala Sioux, and Dennis Banks, a Chippewa, later became the most prominent spokespersons for the group.

AIM was involved in various highly publicized protests. In 1969, seventy-eight Indians landed on Alcatraz Island, a federal prison facility abandoned in 1963, and demanded that it be converted into a Native American cultural center. The occupation ended on June 11, 1971, when the remaining fifteen holdouts were removed by federal marshals. In 1971 AIM staged a sit-in at the Bureau of Indian Affairs in Washington to protest BIA policies, specifically objecting to the existence of tribal councils because they led to paternalistic control of Indians by the BIA. The small band of protesters removed files and ransacked the BIA facilities. In 1972 a second occupation of BIA headquarters included delivery of a twenty-point claims statement to President Nixon. Claims included restoration of treaty-making, ended by Congress in 1871; formation of a joint Congressional Committee on Reconstruction of Indian Relations; restoration of 110 million acres of land illegally taken by the United States; abolition of the Bureau of Indian Affairs; creation of a new Office of Federal Indian Relations; and immunity to taxes, trade restrictions, and commerce regulation.

For seventy-one days, from February 27 to May 8, 1972, some 250 members of AIM forcefully held the hamlet of Wounded Knee, on the Pine Ridge Reservation. This is the site where, in 1890, the U.S. Seventh Cavalry plundered an Indian village in revenge for the deaths of General George Custer and his men at the battle of Little Big Horn (1876).

Despite mediation attempts by Senator George S. McGovern (D-SD), violence erupted between AIM occupiers and federal law enforcement officers. Eventually FBI agents and U.S. marshals broke the siege by armed force. Means and Banks were convicted on riot and assault charges but U.S. district court judge Fred Nichol (St. Paul, Minnesota) dismissed all charges, saying that government misconduct had "formed a pattern throughout the course of the trial" and "polluted the waters of justice." In 1977 AIM successfully campaigned for adoption of legislation that recognized states' responsibility for Indian education and culture.

After 1978 internal dissension and imprisonment of many of its leaders weakened AIM. Preservation of "Native Nation" sovereignty and Indian culture remains its primary concern. AIM is headquartered in Minneapolis, Minnesota, with chapters in other cities, in rural areas, and in Indian Nations. Current membership figures are not available.

See also: NATIVE AMERICAN RIGHTS

For Further Information

American Indian Movement, *http://www. aimovement.org*

Peltier, Leonard. *Prison Writings: My Life Is My Sun Dance.* Edited by Harvey Arden. New York: St. Martin's Press, 1999.

Stern, Kenneth S. *Loud Hawk: The United States Versus the American Indian Movement.* Norman: University of Oklahoma Press, 1994.

AMERICAN JEWISH COMMITTEE.

Formed in 1906, the American Jewish Committee (AJC) fights for the civil and religious rights of American Jews, believing that the best way to achieve victory is by safeguarding the civil and religious rights of all Americans. The AJC is the oldest and one of the three most politically active Jewish organizations, the other two being the AMERICAN JEWISH CONGRESS and the ANTI-DEFAMATION LEAGUE. Jacob Henry Schiff, a German-born American financier, and Cyrus Adler, president of the Jewish Theological Seminary in New York (1924–1940), were co-founders. The AJC was called the Wanderers prior to its formal establishment.

AJC was a trailblazer in advocacy, filing its first *amicus curiae* brief in the U.S. Supreme Court in 1923. In that case, *Pierce v. Society of Sisters of the Holy Names of Jesus and Mary*, 268 U.S. 510 (1925), the AJC supported a challenge to a KU KLUX KLAN–inspired Oregon statute hostile to Catholic parochial schools. The statute had required that all parents enroll their children in public school or risk criminal conviction. The Supreme Court ruled that the law was invalid and that parents have a right to determine where and how their children are to be educated.

Since that time, the AJC has been involved in most landmark civil and religious rights cases, embracing issues that include the combating of anti-Semitism and extremism; church-state separation; religion in public schools; tuition tax credits, vouchers, and school choice; affirmative action; welfare reform; and family policy. The American Jewish Committee publishes *Commentary*, a monthly journal, and the *American Jewish Year Book: A Record of Events and Trends in American and Worldwide Jewish Life.* It has approximately 70,000 members. AJC has its headquarters in New York City and maintains thirty-two regional groups.

See also: JEWISH AMERICAN RIGHTS

For Further Information

American Jewish Committee, *http//www.ajc.org*

Svonkin, Stuart. *Jews Against Prejudice: American Jews and the Fight for Civil Liberties.* New York: Columbia University Press, 1997.

AMERICAN JEWISH CONGRESS.

Founded in 1918, the American Jewish Congress (AJC) has played a prominent role since 1920 in fighting anti-Semitism, seeking racial justice, and litigating against discrimination. Its mission is "to ensure the creative survival of the Jewish people, deeply cognizant of the Jewish responsibility to participate fully in public life, inspired by Jewish teachings and values, informed by liberal principles, dedicated to an activist and independent role, and committed to making its decisions through democratic processes."

The initial purpose of the organization was to voice Jewish demands for a homeland in Palestine, as promised in Britain's Balfour Declaration in 1917. Rabbi Stephen Wise, who had founded the Zionist Organization of America in 1898, was selected as the AJC's first director. Other key figures involved in the initial planning (1916) included Supreme Court Justices Louis Brandeis and Felix Frankfurter, lawyer and diplomat Henry Morgenthau, and Golda Meir (then living in Milwaukee), who later became Israeli prime minister (1969–1974). In 1920 the AJC committed itself to safeguarding Jews in the United States, throughout the Diaspora, and in Palestine, and with seeking human rights and justice for all.

In the 1920s anti-Semitism mounted as immigration quotas were imposed, Jews were accused of sedition, and organizations such as the KU KLUX KLAN flourished. In response, the AJC set about the task of establishing programs and legal instruments to fight back. In 1933 AJC staged a mammoth rally in New York City's Madison Square Garden, calling for an international boycott of Germany. AJC's president, Stephen Wise, claimed that he was the "first of the Americans to call attention to the dangers of Nazism."

In later years, AJC developed a reputation as a leader in using legislation and litigation to realize the promise of equality. AJC was the first Jewish organization to join the struggle for racial justice in America, forging an unprecedented alliance of blacks and Jews and playing a central role, as early as the 1940s, in the civil rights movement. AJC developed a grassroots presence that fought discrimination in housing, education, employment, health care, voting, and other areas, initiating test cases and testifying in courts throughout the country. In the 1990s its attorneys were especially active in cases concerning the religion clauses of the First Amendment to the Constitution. Issues included protection of Sabbath observers against discrimination in employment, discriminatory Sunday blue laws, mandated public school prayer, the use of public funds to support parochial education, and placement of religious symbols on public property.

AJC's headquarters office is in New York City, and its current membership is approximately 50,000. AJC produces several publications, including a newsletter for members, the *Boycott Report* on developments and trends affecting the Arab boycott and Arab influence in the United States, the *Congress Monthly*, and *Judaism*.

See also: JEWISH AMERICAN RIGHTS

For Further Information

American Jewish Congress, *http://www.ajcongress.org/*

Svonkin, Stuart. *Jews Against Prejudice: American Jews and the Fight for Civil Liberties*. New York: Columbia University Press, 1997.

AMERICAN LEAGUE TO ABOLISH CAPITAL PUNISHMENT. The American League to Abolish Capital Punishment (ALACP), established in 1927, was the leading organization committed to the elimination of the death penalty in the United States until the group's disbandment in 1972. Preceding it was the American Society for the Abolition of Capital Punishment (1830s–1870s), which numbered among its members the poet Walt Whitman, poet and journalist William Cullen Bryant, and educator Horace Greeley.

The ALACP was established in Boston, Massachusetts, by a group of lawyers, penologists, and intellectual leaders. Herbert Ehrmann, a defense attorney in the Sacco and Vanzetti case, and Sarah Ehrmann, who served as ALACP executive director from 1949 to 1967, were joined by other prominent figures in criminology. Clarence Darrow, the famed criminal lawyer, and Lewis E. Lawes, warden of New York's Sing Sing prison, served as the ALACP's first and second presidents, respectively.

By 1972 ALACP had thirty-seven state chapters and over 8,000 members, mostly lawyers, penologists, legislators, and other professionals concerned with social reform. The ALACP gained the attention of the American judiciary through effective lobbying and publication of compelling empirical studies. The research demonstrated that the death penalty was not an effective deterrent to capital crime, that its implementation cost society more than lifetime imprisonment, and that it was applied more often to minority and poor offenders than to the white and the wealthy. Most telling was the finding that it occasionally resulted in the death of an innocent individual. The goals of the League were seemingly achieved in 1972 when *Furman v. Georgia* (408 U.S. 234), a 5–4 U.S. Supreme Court decision, held unconstitutional the imposition of the death penalty and invalidated it as then imposed, sparing the lives of almost 600 condemned persons. The ALACP dissolved at this point, believing that, at long last, its work was finished. At the time, Hugo Adam Bedau was ALACP president. Four years later, the Supreme Court reinstated the death penalty, ushering in a new era and reversing the nationwide trend favoring abolition. The Court decided that the death penalty was no longer unconstitutional because newly revised legal procedures in the states had eradicated arbitrariness, racial bias, and class discrimination in capital cases.

Thirty-eight states have reinstated the death penalty. However, recent opinion polls indicate that the general public is softening its support for the death penalty because of growing awareness that procedural shortcuts may be resulting in the execution of innocent defendants. Other organizations have been formed to carry on the ALACP's effort, the most prominent of which is the NATIONAL COALITION TO ABOLISH THE DEATH PENALTY.

See also: DEATH PENALTY AND CHOICE IN DYING

For Further Information

Bedau, Hugo Adam. *Death Is Different: Studies in the Morality, Law, and Politics of Capital Punishment.* Boston: Northeastern University Press, 1987.

Haines, Herbert H. *Against Capital Punishment: The Anti–Death Penalty Movement in America, 1972–1994.* New York: Oxford University Press, 1996.

AMERICAN LEGION. Founded in 1919, the American Legion provides facilities and resources for veterans to continue friendships formed during military service, lobbies for legislation benefiting veterans, and advocates maintenance of a strong U.S. military establishment. Lieutenant Colonel Theodore Roosevelt Jr. and other members of the American Expeditionary Force, stationed in France at the end of World War I, created the American Legion "to uphold and defend the Constitution of the United States of America; to maintain law and order; to foster and perpetuate a one hundred percent Americanism; to preserve the memories and incidents of our associations in the great wars; to inculcate a sense of individual obligation to the community, state, and nation; to combat the autocracy of both the classes and masses; to make right the matter of might; to promote peace and good will on earth; to safeguard and transmit to posterity the principles of justice, freedom, and democracy; to consecrate and sanctify our comradeship by our devotion to mutual helpfulness."

Currently nearly 3 million members—men and women—are affiliated with approximately 15,000 American Legion posts worldwide. Membership is limited to persons who were on active duty in World War I, World War II, the Korean War, the Vietnam War, Lebanon/Grenada, Operation Just Cause (Panama), Operation Desert Shield/Storm (Gulf War), or the Kosovo military action. The Legion carries on large-scale promotional programs aimed at the public and legislators through its various committees and commissions on Americanism; children and youth; legislation; national security and foreign relations; national economic policies; and veterans' affairs and rehabilitation. In 1989 a national emergency fund was established in the wake of Hurricane Hugo.

The Legion has been an aggressive advocate of federal legislation on issues pertaining to veterans' affairs, national defense, and protection of the American flag from physical desecration. The Legion assisted in writing the Flag Code adopted by Congress in 1942 and continues to be at the forefront of efforts to pass a constitutional amendment to protect "Old Glory" from physical desecration. The National Defense Act (1920), Soldiers' Bonus Act (1924), GI Bill of Rights (1944), and cabinet-level Department of Veterans Affairs (1989) are all outcomes of Legion activism.

In 1993 the Legion helped to force modification of the National Air and Space Museum's *Enola Gay* exhibition to downplay the horrific slaughter of Japanese civilians because this view allegedly slighted contributions of Pacific War veterans to victory. In the 1930s, when pacifists and isolationists were opposing President Franklin D. Roosevelt, the Legion supported his insistence on national military preparedness. In later threatening encounters (e.g., the Cold War, the Korean and Vietnam conflicts, the Gulf War) the Legion adopted a hard line, viewing détente with the People's Republic of China and the former Soviet Union with suspicion, and criticizing antiwar protesters, civil rights demonstrators, and draft evaders. The Legion has vigorously pursued its study of the effects of Agent Orange on the health of Vietnam veterans and continues to press for improved educational and medical benefits for Gulf War veterans.

The Legion publishes three periodicals: *The American Legion Magazine*, the organization's official journal; *The Dispatch*, a bimonthly that updates members on national security/foreign relations, economic and legislative issues, the GI Bill of Health, and key programs such as American Legion baseball, Americanism, and children and youth

activities; and *Firing Line*, published eleven times a year to inform readers of the dangers of terrorism, illegal immigration, and subversive activities against the United States. The Legion's national headquarters is in Indianapolis, Indiana, and Robert W. Spanogle serves as national adjutant. The Legion has 2.9 million members.

See also: VETERANS' ISSUES

For Further Information

American Legion, *http://www.legion.org/*

Pencak, William. *For God and Country: The American Legion, 1919–1941*. Boston: Northeastern University Press, 1989.

Rumer, Thomas A. *The American Legion: An Official History, 1919–1989*. New York: M. Evans and Co., 1990.

AMERICAN SOCIETY FOR THE PREVENTION OF CRUELTY TO ANIMALS. The American Society for the Prevention of Cruelty to Animals (ASPCA) works to prevent cruelty to animals and to enforce existing laws that protect animals; promotes humane treatment of animals; and maintains shelters for lost, stray, or abandoned animals. Henry Bergh founded the ASPCA in 1866 in New York City and served as its president until 1888. Under his direction, the ASPCA succeeded in winning passage in the New York State legislature of the first tough anticruelty law. It was effective in protecting horses, which were often beaten and forced to pull loads far exceeding their physical capacity.

Because New York State gave the ASPCA legal authority to punish infringements of the law, it added horse whipping, dogfights, cockfights, the shooting of live pigeons for target practice, and use of bird feathers as hat adornments to its list of illegal activities.

As ASPCA branches were established in other states and membership grew, the scope of the organization broadened. ASPCA started operating hospitals (1912), began publishing materials for distribution in schools (1916), initiated dog obedience classes (1944), sponsored an animal port facility at John F. Kennedy International Airport from 1958 until 1993, and in 1962 started adoption services for dogs and cats. It also operates a low-cost spay/neuter clinic and conducts pet therapy programs. In recent years, the ASPCA has handled animal emergency evacuation procedures during natural disasters, lobbied for coverage of rats and birds under the Animal Welfare Act, and urged alternatives to dissection of frogs and other animals in classrooms.

The ASPCA provides free care for more than 125,000 animals annually and maintains two shelters in New York City that care for 70,000 animals each year. The ASPCA's Bergh Memorial Animal Hospital in Manhattan provides low-cost vaccinations, surgery, and other services. In the 1980s and 1990s the ASPCA shifted its primary focus from protecting animals from abuse toward advocacy of animal rights, in common with PEOPLE FOR THE ETHICAL TREATMENT OF ANIMALS and the HUMANE SOCIETY OF THE UNITED STATES. The ASPCA has a strong grassroots arm that lobbies at the local, state, and federal levels for animal welfare legislation. In 1998 the ASPCA monitored 14,000 separate pieces of federal and state legislation.

Organization headquarters is in New York City and current membership exceeds 400,000. The ASPCA's membership publication is *Animal Watch*, which covers animal protection, animal farming, genetic engineering, and experimentation. Roger A. Caras is ASPCA president.

See also: ANIMAL RIGHTS AND WELFARE

For Further Information

American Society for the Prevention of Cruelty to Animals, *http://www.asoca.org*

Loeper, John J. *Crusade for Kindness: Henry Bergh and the ASPCA.* New York: Atheneum Books for Young Readers, 1991.

Oliver, Daniel T. "The ASPCA: From Animal Welfare to Animal Rights." In *Alternatives in Philanthropy.* Washington, DC: Capital Research Center, August 1998.

AMERICAN VETERANS COMMITTEE.

The American Veterans Committee (AVC) was formed in 1943 "to achieve a more democratic and prosperous America and a more stable world." Its motto is "Citizens first, veterans second." The group has favored liberal legislation and social reform over initiatives that specifically deal with veterans' concerns. In addition to lobbying for veterans' benefits, the AVC has advocated racial integration, the improved status of women veterans, U.S. payment of delinquent United Nations dues, reapportionment of congressional districts, and revision of outdated state constitutions. The group has run national conferences on issues within the military such as conscientious objection, privacy, political and social rights, and safeguards under the Uniform Code of Military Justice.

Gilbert A. Harrison, a sergeant in the U.S. Air Force during World War II, conceived the AVC as an association "based not on what one could get as a veteran, but on what one could contribute to the postwar world." The AVC would be an alternative to the AMERICAN LEGION and Veterans of Foreign Wars, organizations concerned with maximizing benefits and bonuses but that had excluded African Americans from membership and held isolationist views. By 1945, 4,000 servicemen had joined AVC. By 1948 AVC had 110,000 members and had become the largest World War II veterans' organization. Because of universal conscription, at the time of AVC's formation, U.S. military personnel included more left-of-center servicemen who later joined the organization. This translated into opposition to censorship and racial discrimination and the group decision to reject charter applications from segregated local units.

During recent years, with armed services duty becoming voluntary, the number of veterans holding liberal views has become minimal, and the group's influence and activities have lessened. Most recently AVC has concentrated its attention on women veterans' health care issues.

AVC's total membership is approximately 15,000, including veterans of World Wars I and II, the Korean conflict, the Vietnam War, and the Persian Gulf conflict. National headquarters is in Bethesda, Maryland, and the current executive director is June A. Willenz.

See also: VETERANS' ISSUES

For Further Information

AVC Bulletin, 1946–

Bolté, Charles G. *The New Veteran: Hero or Problem?* New York: Reynal and Hitchcock, 1945.

AMERICAN VETERANS OF WORLD WAR II, KOREA AND VIETNAM.

Originally named American Veterans of World War II, the organization became officially known as AMVETS after it was given this name by a news reporter. AMVETS was created as an alliance of eighteen small veterans' organizations to promote benefits for men who served in the U.S. armed forces during World War II and to relieve distress in their families. Later its charter was updated to include Korean War, Vietnam War, and Gulf War veterans. In 1946 AMVETS National Auxiliary was formed to accommodate female veterans and relatives of males in the parent organization. Current membership is open to anyone who is serving or who has served in the armed forces, including the National Guard and Reserves, at any time after September 15, 1940.

Living up to its motto, "We Fought Together—Now Let's Build Together," AMVETS maintains a staff to serve its 176,000 members in all matters relating to veterans' affairs. It promotes increased government benefits for veterans in Congress and monitors federal assistance programs. Along with the AMERICAN LEGION, it was instrumental in securing congressional enactment of the Korean G.I. Bill of Rights and the Cold War Bill of Rights so that veterans of those conflicts would be eligible to receive benefits similar to those offered to veterans of World War II. AMVETS monitors all veterans' legislation on Capitol Hill in such areas as medical care, health care reform, provisions for homeless veterans, and rights and benefits, and plays a key role in its enactment. *The National AMVET*, a quarterly

magazine, is included in membership dues. National headquarters is in Lanham, Maryland.

See also: VETERANS' ISSUES

For Further Information

AMVETS, *http://www.amvets.org/*

Flanagan, Richard W. *AMVETS: Fifty Years of Proud Service to America's Veterans.* Lanham, MD: AMVETS (American Veterans of World War II, Korea and Vietnam), 1994.

AMERICANS FOR DEMOCRATIC ACTION.

Americans for Democratic Action (ADA) was formed in Washington, D.C., in 1947. In 1948 ADA efforts resulted in the adoption of a strong civil rights plank in the Democratic Party platform that defined the party's commitment for the next fifty years. ADA founders included ELEANOR ROOSEVELT, labor leader WALTER P. REUTHER, economist John Kenneth Galbraith, historian Arthur Schlesinger Jr., theologian Reinhold Niebuhr, and former Vice President Hubert H. Humphrey. ADA remains dedicated to promoting individual liberty and economic justice for all Americans. Its original six-point statement of principles advocated expansion of New Deal programs, protection of civil liberties, support for the UN, and U.S. aid to freedom-loving peoples the world over.

After John F. Kennedy's election to the presidency in 1960, ADA leaders and members were appointed to key positions in his administration and the group reached its pinnacle of influence as the "official" voice of American liberalism. After initially supporting the domestic legislative agenda of Kennedy's successor, Lyndon B. Johnson, ADA opposed his continuing conduct of the Vietnam War. In 1972 ADA called for the impeachment of President Richard Nixon. It has also supported nuclear arms control, the ending of apartheid in South Africa, increases in the minimum wage, and a more equitable tax policy.

ADA has approximately 65,000 members. *ADA Today* is its quarterly report, and *ADAction News and Notes* is its legislative update, produced every Friday evening that Congress is in session. ADA headquarters is in Washington, D.C. Jim Jontz is president; Amy F. Isaacs is national director.

See also: LIBERAL ACTIVISM

For Further Information

Americans for Democratic Action, *http://www. adaction.org*

Gillon, Steven M. *Politics and Vision: The ADA and American Liberalism, 1947–1985.* New York: Oxford University Press, 1987.

AMERICANS FOR TAX REFORM. Americans for Tax Reform (ATR), founded by Grover Norquist in 1985, is the largest and most influential organization committed to opposing tax increases. Its purpose is "to inform Americans of the full costs of taxation, which include not just the actual revenue collected, but also the costs of tax collection, the economic production lost because of disincentives to producers, the damage done by unnecessary bureaucracy, and the costs of supporting the regulatory bureaucracy with tax dollars."

Before the 1996 elections, voters in 150 congressional districts were inundated with mail and phone calls from ATR, an effort funded by $4.6 million from the Republican National Committee. The campaign was credited with helping to ensure that a Republican majority was reelected in Congress.

Since 1986 ATR has sponsored the Taxpayer Protection Pledge, a written promise by legislators and candidates for office that commits them to oppose any effort to increase the federal income taxes on individuals and businesses. By October 1998, 210 House members and 42 sitting senators had signed pledges along with 143 challengers. In 1999 Governor George W. Bush of Texas, while campaigning in New Hampshire, submitted a letter to ATR promising to veto income tax increases if elected president.

In its mission statement, ATR states that it "leads the fight against the Value-Added Tax (VAT), instrumental in the growth of the European-style welfare state . . . supports the concept of a single rate flat tax, and sponsors the calculation of Cost of Government Day, the day on which Americans stop working to pay the costs of taxation, deficit spending, and regulations by federal and state governments." Liberals contend that ATR's proposed flat tax would weaken the current progressive tax code by shifting more than half of the tax breaks to the wealthiest and widening the gap between rich and poor.

Although recruited from the top down, through corporate contributions and conservative Republican leadership, ATR has developed an effective base of 60,000 active paying members and prior to each national election sends out "nonpartisan" mailings to over a million citizens; it also sponsors over 1,500 taxpayer groups. According to Norquist, ATR is a proud member of the "Leave Us Alone" club, which includes groups as diverse as the NATIONAL RIFLE ASSOCIATION, CATO INSTITUTE, CHRISTIAN COALITION, U.S. TERM LIMITS, Republicans for Choice, and HERITAGE FOUNDATION.

After the 1996 election, when Congress retained a Republican majority despite Bob Dole's failure to unseat Bill Clinton, a five-and-a-half-foot boa constrictor, ATR's office mascot, was fed a jumbo white rat in a strange ATR ritual. Past rats fed to the snake have been named after Senator Ted Kennedy and Bill and Hillary Clinton. In 1996 David Bonior, then House Minority Whip, was chosen meal of the moment. Bonior was selected because he steadfastly defended Clinton against impeachment and had led a crusade against Newt Gingrich, urging Democrats to file over seventy ethics charges against Gingrich, some arguably serious and others entirely without merit.

ATR bestows annual Enemy of the Taxpayer and Friend of the Taxpayer Awards. Its headquarters office is in Washington, D.C. ATR's current executive director is Audrey Mullen, and Grover G. Norquist is president.

See also: TAX REFORM AND GOVERNMENTAL EXPENDITURES

For Further Information

Americans for Tax Reform, *http://www.atr.org*

Berlau, John. "Grover Norquist Takes on the Tyranny of Federal Taxation." *Insight on the News*, January 26, 1998, pp. 20–22.

Ferrara, Peter J., and Michael Tanner. *A New Deal for Social Security*. Washington, DC: Cato Institute, 1998.

Grove, Lloyd. "Sharing Power in Washington: A Parable of Snakes and Rats." *Washington Post*, November 6, 1996, Style section, p. F01.

Wayne, Leslie. "Conservative Advocate and His G.O.P. Ties Come into Focus." *New York Times*, July 8, 1997, p. A12.

AMERICANS UNITED FOR SEPARATION OF CHURCH AND STATE.

Americans United for Separation of Church and State (AUSCS) is the only national organization that works exclusively to protect and defend the constitutional principle of church/state separation. Its mission is to preserve adherence to the first sixteen words of the First Amendment to the U.S. Constitution: "Congress shall make no law respecting an establishment of religion, or prohibiting the free exercise thereof." It seeks to guarantee religious liberty for Americans of every faith as well as for those who affirm no faith at all.

Founded in 1947 by religious leaders, AUSCS was originally called Protestants and Other Americans United for Separation of Church and State. AUSCS adopted its current name in the 1970s after it had derailed Catholics' attempts to divert tax dollars to support parochial education. AUSCS continues to oppose tax aid to private religious schools through voucher plans.

The 106th Congress introduced a constitutional amendment that would open school premises to proselytizers for the NATION OF ISLAM, the Church of Scientology, and Heaven's Gate, as well as the major denominations to which AUSCS objected. Although the group supports voluntary prayer, it strongly opposes institutionally organized prayer and other intrusive activities that force children to be exposed to beliefs that run counter to their own religious beliefs.

AUSCS reached a peak of 125 chapters in the 1960s as courts struck down public school prayers and ruled against state aid to parochial schools. This success was followed by a relatively dormant period, with AUSCS chapters being reduced to only four by 1993. Concerns raised by the 1994 victories of the RELIGIOUS RIGHT suddenly reinvigorated the group and the number of chapters rebounded to 115 by 1998.

AUSCS has an estimated 50,000 members. The current executive director, Barry Lynn, is an ordained United Church of Christ minister. AUSCS is headquartered in Washington, D.C. Its membership journal is *Church and State*.

See also: CONSTITUTIONAL RIGHTS AND CIVIL LIBERTIES PROTECTION

For Further Information

Americans United for Separation of Church and State, *http://www.au.org/*

Church and State (journal published by AUSCS).

Lynn, Barry. *Your Right to Religious Liberty: A Basic Guide to Religious Rights*. Carbondale: Southern Illinois University Press, 1995.

ANIMAL LIBERATION FRONT.

The Animal Liberation Front (ALF), founded in England in 1976, states that its objectives include (1) rescuing animals from sites where they are being abused; (2) ensuring that animals live normal lives in compatible environments; (3) infliction of monetary pain upon those who profit from animals' suffering; and (4) publicizing instances of cruelty and misery. ALF mounted guerrilla warfare against fox hunting in England and then moved to the United States in 1977. Its founders are Ronald Lee and Clifford Goodman. Allied groups include the EARTH LIBERATION FRONT, Animal Rights Militia, and Animal Liberation Front Support Group.

No central headquarters exists because many ALF activities are illegal. Members join primarily to inflict damage on the establishment, which is perceived as being greedy, corrupt, and contemptuous of animal rights and needs. The ALF Web site, *www.animal-*

liberation.net, offers advice on how to carry out raids and attacks, suggests readings for those interested in liberating animals, and reports successful campaigns undertaken by ALF members. Members operate in "cells" and are expected to follow ALF guidelines in performing their tasks while being motivated by individual conscience.

ALF has accomplished its goals through raids and large-scale vandalism. Laboratories that house animals for research experimentation have been preferred targets. The Animal Diagnostic Laboratory at the University of California (Davis) incurred $3.5 million in damages caused by ALF arson in 1987. Animal research labs at Michigan State University (1992) and the University of Minnesota (1999) suffered damages totaling over a million dollars.

Agriculture and fur industries have also been targeted by ALF for the "infliction of monetary pain." Poultry and rabbit farms, veal producers, cattle operations, and meat processing plants have been attacked. McDonald's fast-food restaurants, in the United States and abroad, have been vandalized and spray-painted to protest the chain's selling of meat products. Mink farms have been raided and the animals released to the wild. In Utah a facility producing food for mink farms was bombed in 1988, and ALF claimed responsibility for placing incendiary devices in department stores in downtown Chicago to protest fur coat sales. In 1999 FBI Director Louis Freeh told Congress that "the ALF is among the most recognized single-issue terrorist groups in the U.S. today" and warned that it is being buoyed by an infusion of volunteers, mostly idealistic young people. Because ALF operates beyond legal boundaries, its address, leadership, and size are not available.

See also: ANIMAL WELFARE AND RIGHTS

For Further Information

Amimal Liberation Front, *www.animal-liberation. net*

Guither, Harold D. *Animal Rights: History and Scope of a Radical Social Movement*. Carbondale: Southern Illinois University Press, 1998.

Knickerbocker, Brad. "Some Animals Are More Equal than Others." *Christian Science Monitor*, December 2, 1999, Ideas section, p. 15.

Owen, Marna. *Animal Rights: Yes or No?* Minneapolis: Lerner Publications, 1993.

ANIMAL WELFARE AND RIGHTS.

Concern for animal welfare was born during the Age of Enlightenment, a time when Jean-Jacques Rousseau and Voltaire condemned human mistreatment of animals and urged men to respect animals as they did fellow human beings. As early as the 1770s Europeans were pampering their household pets, and in 1824 William Wilberforce and Sir Thomas Fowell Buxton, two leaders of the British movement to abolish the slave trade, helped found the Royal Society for the Prevention of Cruelty to Animals (RSPCA). This group and allied reformers successfully fought for enactment of laws condemning bear and bull baiting by mastiffs (1822) and pushed through a law permitting vivisection only under license in 1826.

In the United States, 1866 marked the birth of the AMERICAN SOCIETY FOR THE PREVENTION OF CRUELTY TO ANIMALS (ASPCA), founded by Henry Bergh. Its original mission was to monitor slaughterhouse conditions and provide ambulatory service to carriage horses and other animals. Soon the performing of surgery on animals for experimental research came under attack, and the AMERICAN ANTI-VIVISECTION SOCIETY (AAVS) was formed in Philadelphia in 1883. The animal welfare advocates of the time— mostly Eastern, urban, and female—were greeted with condescension and derision by the male-dominated scientific establishment. It was claimed that the women were suffering from zoophil-psychosis, a form of obsessive insanity, or were irrational cranks, fanatics, or perverts.

The antivivisectionists fought back, and by 1908 there were two bills regulating animal experimentation in the New York State legislature. The horrors of animal laboratories were put on display in New York City and other cities, followed with similar conscious-

Members of the Animal Defense League—New Jersey protest outside Huntingdon Life Sciences in Franklin Township, New Jersey, in January 2001. *AP Photo/Daniel Hulshizer.*

raising campaigns. Although ASPCA and the AAVS waged a nationwide campaign, the arguments, superior organization, and clout of the medical community prevailed. By 1925 the early antivivisection movement had become dormant. Progressive and compassionate ideas regarding human mental suffering, poverty, and exploitation were adopted in the 1920s but not applied to animals. Animals were out of sight and out of mind, because no longer needed for transport or hidden in factories and farms. Also, the wonders of science were so astounding and life-enhancing that people became indifferent to what was going on in laboratories.

The HUMANE SOCIETY OF THE UNITED STATES (HSUS), formed in 1954, made headway on the animal welfare front with passage of the Humane Slaughter Act (1958), the Laboratory Animal Welfare Act (1966), its publicity of cruelty in "puppy mills," and its subsequent participation with animal rights organizations in the anti-fur crusade. Suddenly, in the 1960s, "speciesism" made its debut as an argument in Peter Singer's *Animal Liberation*, the book that formed the foundation for the modern animal rights movement. Singer compared animals to babies and the mentally retarded, claiming that innocence or dumbness should not deny them the right to moral treatment and protection from suffering. For example, the suffering of farm animals must be weighed against the benefit conveyed to humans by their consumption. According to Singer, becoming a vegetarian was only the most minimal ethical response to the magnitude of the evil visited upon animals.

Tom Regan, a philosopher based in North Carolina, went even further, claiming that all creatures qualify for rights as individuals and that all exploitation of animals for human purposes should be abolished. Animal rights activists became convinced that what they knew of human suffering applied to animals that could not defend themselves. This latter point became the justification for their objectives. They would halt all research and product testing involving animals; enforce availability of vegetarian meals in all public institutions; outlaw stockyards and ban pesticides, furs, sporting animals, and pets; and prohibit fishing and hunting. The ANIMAL LIBERATION FRONT, active in the United States since 1977, has destroyed research facilities and animal research laboratories, committed acts of arson, and mailed letters booby-trapped with razor blades to university researchers.

To their credit, the moderate animal rights groups have successfully challenged the use of animals in medical and drug tests, the consumption of meat, the use of furs and other animal products, and government efforts to control wild animal populations on federal lands. Allied environmental groups such as GREENPEACE and the SEA SHEPHERD CONSERVATION SOCIETY have brought media attention to the unnecessary slaughter of marine mammals and other endangered species. And the Laboratory Animal Welfare Act of 1966 at least requires scientists to provide adequate food and shelter for certain kinds of lab animals even though it does not restrict the kinds of experiments that can be undertaken.

Steven Wise, currently an adjunct professor of animal law at Harvard University, established the Animal Legal Defense Fund (ALDF) in 1979. ALDF, based in Petaluma, California, has become the country's leading animal rights law organization. Inspired by Peter Singer's *Animal Liberation*, Wise has litigated against animal experimentation, factory farming, hunting, and the fur industry. ALDF victories include revision of U.S. Department of Agriculture guidelines for the treatment of laboratory dogs and primates to improve their protection, enforcement of Animal Welfare Act provisions, development of stronger rules to protect animals who travel by air, and the broadening of rights of pet owners. Wise has argued that "when people lose companion animals to veterinary malpractice, they should be eligible for damages for emotional distress and loss of companionship." Courses on animal rights are now being offered at Harvard Law School, the Georgetown University Law Center, Rutgers University, Cornell University, the University of Illinois at Urbana-Champaign, the University of California at Davis, and on more than twenty other college and university campuses in the U.S. and Canada.

PEOPLE FOR THE ETHICAL TREATMENT OF ANIMALS (PETA), under the dynamic leadership of Ingrid Newkirk, is currently the largest animal rights organization in the world. It operates under the principle that "animals are not ours to eat, wear, experiment on, or use for entertainment." PETA brought the animal rights movement into prominence with its case against monkey researcher Edward Taub, which resulted in his conviction on charges of cruelty to animals. PETA also succeeded in halting most major cosmetics companies' testing of products on animals.

Although animal rightists' goals may have seemed out of reach and unrealistic in the past, that is no longer the case because of the skein of victories achieved by citizen activists. These include the elevation of cruelty to animals from a misdemeanor to a felony in twenty-seven states and the cessation of animal testing in the development of beauty, fabric, home care, and paper products sold by Procter & Gamble, Colgate-Palmolive, Mary Kay, and Gillette. There has also been a 66 percent decline in the number of cats used in laboratory research since 1967. The movement has heightened the public's awareness of the indivisible evil of exploitation of any kind, be it sexism, racism, or speciesism.

For Further Information

Animal Legal Defense Fund, *http://www.aldf.org*

Croke, Vicki. "Furriers, Scientists Best Be Wary of Wise." *Boston Globe*, August 5, 1990, West Weekly section, p. 1.

Hoge, Warren. "British Researchers on Animal Rights Death List." *New York Times*, January 10, 1999, International section, p. 8.

Regan, Tom. *The Case for Animal Rights*. Berkeley: University of California, Press 1983.

Singer, Peter Albert David. *Animal Liberation*, Rev. ed. New York: Morrow/Avon, 1991.

ANTIABORTION MOVEMENT. *See* Abortion Policy; Women's Issues

ANTI-DEFAMATION LEAGUE OF THE B'NAI B'RITH. Established in 1913, the Anti-Defamation League (ADL) combats racial and religious prejudice against Jews. In addition to fighting defamation of the Jewish people, the organization seeks justice and fair treatment for all citizens and an end to unjust, unfair discrimination against, and ridicule of, any sect or body of citizens.

Sigmund Livingston, an attorney from Bloomington, Illinois, served as ADL director until 1946. One of the organization's early objectives was to reduce derogatory stereotyping of Jews by the press, in vaudeville, and in the movies. By 1920 the ADL had succeeded in virtually stopping objectionable and vulgar references to Jews in the major newspapers. Up to that time American dailies had often used the word "Jew" as a derogatory adjective and verb (e.g., Jew boy, Jew banker, Jewing down). Gentiles had been generally described as being "thrifty," "honest," "ambitious," and "decent," while Jews with the same commendable traits became "miserly," "deceitful," "avaricious," and "lecherous." The early movies and vaudeville skits were larded with references to ugly stereotypes, Yids, kikes, and Hebes, and eccentric rabbis.

In 1923 ADL publicly accused the KU KLUX KLAN of bigotry and challenged Henry Ford's circulation of the spurious anti-Semitic document purporting to outline a Jewish conspiracy to enslave the world. This document, *The Protocols of the Learned Elders of Zion*, was published in the *Dearborn Independent*. Several years later, Ford publicly apologized to the Jewish people and in a letter to Sigmund Livingston expressed hope that "anti-Semitism would cease for all times."

The Great Depression and Hitler's rise to power provided the impetus for American fascist groups and agitators, including Fritz Kuhn of the German-American Bund and FATHER CHARLES E. COUGHLIN, hate radio personality and leader of the pro-fascist Christian Front. Post–World War II tensions pointed to the need for new civil rights laws. ADL initiated campaigns against restrictive housing, anti-Jewish discrimination in higher education admissions, and the stringent immigration quotas that had prevented the rescue of many European Jews fleeing from Nazi Germany. The League filed its first church/state–related *amicus curiae* brief in 1948 in *McCollum v. Board of Education*, and ADL has continued to argue for separation of church and state while championing the free exercise of religion. The 1962 case *Engel v. Vitale*, ruling that recitation of prayers in public school settings was unconstitutional, was another court victory for ADL.

In the 1950s, ADL filed an *amicus curiae* brief in the landmark case BROWN V. BOARD OF EDUCATION OF TOPEKA, which nullified the 1896 "separate but equal" *Plessy v. Ferguson* ruling. The ADL actively urged passage of the Civil Rights Acts of 1964 and 1968 and the Voting Rights Act of 1965.

The ADL model (1981) for penalty-enhancement laws as deterrents to hate crimes has been adopted in forty states and the District of Columbia. At the White House Conference on Hate Crimes (November 1997), various preventive and counter measures initiated by ADL were highlighted.

Since 1979 ADL national headquarters has been in the United Nations Plaza in New York City; the group's legislative office is in Washington, D.C. ADL has about 400 staff members, and twenty-eight regional offices are located throughout the United States. Current membership totals nearly 170,000. Abraham H. Foxman is national director. Permanent ADL divisions deal with civil rights; community service; development; intergroup relations; internal affairs; leadership; and marketing and communications. *ADL on the Frontline*, a bimonthly, is ADL's membership newsletter. Other publications in-

About 300 anti-nuclear protestors, including veterans of the Seabrook demonstrations from twenty years earlier, march toward the nuclear power plant in Seabrook, New Hampshire, in April 1997. *AP Photo/ Jim Cole.*

clude *Dimensions, Facts, Latin American Report, Law,* and *Law Enforcement Bulletin.*
See *also:* JEWISH AMERICAN RIGHTS

For Further Information

Anti-Defamation League of the B'nai B'rith, *http:/ /www.adl.org*

Belth, Nathan C. *A Promise to Keep: A Narrative of American Encounters with Anti-Semitism.* New York: Times Books, 1979.

Perlmutter, Nate, and Ruth Ann Perlmutter. *The Real Anti-Semitism in America.* New York: Morrow/Avon, 1982.

Svonkin, Stuart. *Jews Against Prejudice.* New York: Columbia University Press, 1997.

ANTI–NUCLEAR POWER MOVE-MENT. The anti–nuclear power movement grew in the 1960s because it played upon people's fear of imminent disaster and dealt with an area in which local citizen actions to protect the environment could make a difference. The postwar era witnessed the emergence of a top secret national security curtain that shielded U.S. foreign policy from public knowledge to a greater extent than ever before. The atomic bomb, the Soviet Union, and the lurking menace of annihilation provided a rationale for confining questions concerning nuclear weaponry to the province of the national security community. Nuclear weaponry was too large an issue, too well guarded by vested interests, and too abstract a target to generate a mass movement. In contrast, nuclear power was tangible and local. Nuclear power plants posed special dangers for nearby animals and people. It would be easier to halt construction of particular plants than to take on the defense industry and "hawks" in Congress and in the military.

In 1976 the CLAMSHELL ALLIANCE was

formed to prevent the construction of the Seabrook Nuclear Plant in New Hampshire because of its anticipated destruction of the surrounding ecologically rich saltwater marsh or "clam flats." Although the effort failed and the plant became operative in 1989, the "Clams' " peaceful civil disobedience proved contagious, being followed by the Abalone Alliance's demonstrations at San Luis Obispo, California, protests at Three Mile Island, Pennsylvania, and similar actions in at least four other states. The 1979 film *The China Syndrome*, produced by Michael Douglas, increased public awareness of the danger of a nuclear meltdown. It featured Jack Lemmon as a nuclear plant controller who discovers an operational flaw that could lead to disaster. This tense, prophetic thriller was released only a few weeks before the Three Mile Island accident. On June 30, 1979, some 40,000 people came to San Luis Obispo for the largest anti-nuclear power rally ever held in the United States, and in the fall of 1979 sixty teach-ins for prospective demonstrators were held in thirty-five cities throughout the country. In 1983 KAREN SILKWOOD's alleged murder in 1974 for blowing the whistle on slipshod practices at a nuclear power plant was memorialized in the Hollywood film *Silkwood*, featuring Meryl Streep in the title role. On April 26, 1986, the Chernobyl nuclear disaster occurred, greatly intensifying the public distrust of nuclear energy. A short time later, a nationwide halt in nuclear power plant construction was called. Between 1973 and 1996 no U.S. reactor orders were placed and orders for 120 nuclear reactors were canceled. The remaining U.S. nuclear power plants have been gradually phasing out since 1973.

For Further Information

Chanman, Karen. "A Shutdown, Not a Meltdown: Citizen's Awareness Network Stages Protest Against Vermont Yankee Nuclear Plant." *The Progressive* 62, no. 11 (November 1998): p. 14.

Garcia, Raymond. "The Citizen Groups in the Nuclear Power Protest Movement: A Reassessment." Master's thesis, Michigan State University, Department of Sociology, 1993.

Lenssen, Nichola, and Christopher Flavin. "Meltdown," *World Watch* 9 (May/June 1996): 22–31.

Nuclear Information and Resource Service, 1414 16th Street NW, #404, Washington, DC 20036.

ANTI-SALOON LEAGUE OF AMERICA (ASLA). *See* American Council on Alcohol Problems

ANTIWAR/ANTI–NUCLEAR WEAPONS MOVEMENT. The anti-war/anti-nuclear weapons movement includes individuals and groups who have directly affected U.S. government policies, who have dealt with the nuclear threat from an American perspective, and who have attracted significant media coverage during the twentieth century.

JANE ADDAMS, founder of Chicago's Hull House, was a dedicated and prominent pacifist. In 1915 she chaired the newly formed Women's Peace Party, and she remained an outspoken opponent to the war after the United States had become a combatant. In 1919 she was elected president of the Women's International League for Peace and Freedom.

The war stimulated formation in 1914 of the FELLOWSHIP OF RECONCILIATION (FOR), a Christian pacifist group initially committed to keeping the United States out of the European conflict. FOR leaders included Abraham J. Muste, who later reemerged as an uncompromising opponent of the Vietnam War, and JAMES FARMER, who founded the CONGRESS OF RACIAL EQUALITY (CORE) in 1942.

A sister organization for nonreligious pacifists, the War Resisters League, was created in 1923. Antinuclear activists joined the League in the 1950s and spearheaded civil disobedience campaigns. These included urging the public to disregard safety precautions during civil defense alerts in 1955, sailing a boat into a nuclear testing zone (1958), and staging protests at missile and submarine bases.

DOROTHY DAY, a radical socialist and founder of the CATHOLIC WORKER MOVEMENT, wrote articles for *The Masses*, a magazine opposing U.S. involvement in World War I, and much later, during the 1960s, was an ardent supporter of resistance to the Vietnam War. Her antiwar resolve inspired the brothers DANIEL BERRIGAN and PHILIP BERRIGAN, radical Catholic priests, to protest against the Selective Service System by destroying draft registration files in Catonsville, Maryland (1968), and to stage PLOWSHARES' series of destructive raids on nuclear missile and submarine installations.

Other individuals who became embroiled in the antiwar turmoil of the mid-1960s included STAUGHTON LYND, TOM HAYDEN, and MARK RUDD. These three also had connections to various civil rights and extremist groups including STUDENTS FOR A DEMOCRATIC SOCIETY, the STUDENT NONVIOLENT COORDINATING COMMITTEE, and the BLACK PANTHERS PARTY.

The antiwar movement of the Vietnam era (1949–1975), extending from President Truman's funding of the futile French attempt to reconquer its lost colony to President Nixon's resignation following Watergate and the fall of Saigon, was a sprawling and seemingly chaotic mass happening. Amazingly, the movement was able to mobilize sustained public dissent and debate for nearly a decade, and it left an imprint on American culture for the remainder of the century. Transformations included the estrangement of American youth and the rise of black power, the counterculture, and women's liberation. This was made possible because of the antiwar movement's confluence with the civil rights movement and student protest, blending opposition to the war and bombing of civilian populations with criticism of American society's failure to treat blacks, women, students, and the poor equitably. Consequently, the antiwar movement generated a vast assemblage of allied and competing grassroots groups across the entire political spectrum. In 1960 a few dozen groups made up the movement; by 1970 it comprised more than 12,000 associations.

For Further Information

Lunardini, Christine A. *The ABC-CLIO Companion to the American Peace Movement in the Twentieth Century.* Santa Barbara: ABC-CLIO, 1994.

McNeal, Patricia F. *Harder than War: Catholic Peacemaking in Twentieth-Century America.* Trenton, NJ: Rutgers University Press, 1992.

ARAB AMERICAN RIGHTS. Arab-Americans have been subjected to prejudice, negative stereotyping, defamation, and hate crimes, the latter escalating during Middle East crises, the Persian Gulf War, and immediately after confirmed and alleged acts of Arab terrorism. Arab Americans were attacked and offices were set on fire within days after the bombing of the Alfred P. Murrah Federal Building (April 19, 1995) and the TWA Flight 800 explosion and crash (July 17, 1996) even though Arabs were not implicated in either tragedy.

Two organizations, the AMERICAN-ARAB ANTI-DISCRIMINATION COMMITTEE (ADC) and the COUNCIL ON AMERICAN ISLAMIC RELATIONS (CAIR), deal with problems besetting the Arab American community, work to promote pride in Islamic culture, and initiate legal action to protect their members' civil rights from infringement. Former South Dakota Senator James Abourezk, who is of Lebanese descent, established the ADC in 1980. The ADC is the largest Arab American grassroots organization in the United States. It distributes on its Web site the *Arab Daily Chronicle*, a service that provides highlights of news in the Mideast and Arab countries.

The CAIR, the more militant group, was formed in 1994. Using the Internet, it issues periodic calls for citizen action by the faithful, offers online assistance, and posts employment opportunities on its Web site. The CAIR serves as a channel to contact the dozen or more other smaller Muslim groups that currently exist in the United States. It issues periodic reports on discrimination in work sites, police misconduct, and discrimination in the judicial system. CAIR "seeks to empower the Muslim community in America through political and social activism."

For Further Information

American-Arab Anti-Discrimination Committee, *http://www.adc.org/*

Council on American Islamic Relations, *http://www.cair-net.org/*

Naff, Alixa. *The Arab Americans.* Broomall, PA: Chelsea House, 1987.

ASSOCIATION OF COMMUNITY ORGANIZATIONS FOR REFORM NOW.

The Association of Community Organizations for Reform Now (ACORN) is the largest low- and moderate-income organization committed to fighting for better schools, jobs, and neighborhoods and securing fair access to credit for low-income and minority neighborhoods. ACORN, formed in 1970, grew out of the National Welfare Rights Organization (NWRO), which had been led by George Wiley in the mid-1960s. NWRO membership was made up exclusively of low-income people and therefore lacked the membership base needed to influence lawmakers.

Wiley enlisted Wade Rathke, a talented organizer, and sent him to Little Rock, Arkansas, to strengthen the group. Using aggressive, "in your face" tactics pioneered by SAUL DAVID ALINSKY, he initiated a successful drive to collect clothing and furniture for the desperately poor, exploiting an obscure clause in Arkansas's welfare laws. NWRO broadened and became the Arkansas Community Organizations for Reform Now. The new ACORN became a unified network of neighborhood groups; black, white, and Latino members; dishwashers, blacksmiths, unemployed electricians, factory workers, small businessmen, and other middle- and lower-income individuals. In Little Rock, ACORN resolved the problems of block-busting (the illegal practice of inducing homeowners to sell their property by telling them that undesirable minority persons are moving into the neighborhood), redlining, and lack of traffic safety in poor sections of the community. Their successes earned the respect of area politicians.

ACORN then extended its efforts by assisting farmers whose land was being threatened by the pending construction of a sulfur-emitting coal-burning power plant. ACORN prevailed after enlisting the support of Governor Dale Bumpers and Harvard University researchers who pressured the Arkansas Power and Light Company to cancel their construction plans. ACORN later forced companies to renovate, move, or cancel plans for toxic chemical facilities and waste incinerators in Memphis, Ft. Worth, Philadelphia, Des Moines, New Orleans, St. Louis, and a half dozen other cities. It also organized parents of lead poisoning victims to pressure local governments for improved monitoring of unsafe housing in New York, Detroit, Chicago, and Washington, D.C.

ACORN became involved in electoral politics in the early 1970s, running its own slate of candidates for city and county offices in Little Rock. By 1975 ACORN had become a multistate operation with branches in Texas and South Dakota. And by 1980 twenty states had joined. In 1979 ACORN developed a People's Platform that called for fair taxes, jobs for all, adequate housing, national health insurance, and subsidized utility rates for the elderly.

ACORN members have been trained to run for public office in Philadelphia, Bridgeport, New York, Chicago, Tulsa, St. Louis, and Des Moines. In the 1980s ACORN launched a campaign to obtain affordable housing for people of modest means by "squatting" (forcefully and illegally seizing and cleaning up vacant houses and refitting them for comfortable living). In 1981 and 1982, 15,000 ACORN members and allies erected tent cities, referred to as "Reagan Ranches," in over thirty-five cities to protest the government's reduced expenditures on social welfare.

Instrumental to ACORN recruiting and public relations was the development of the

Affiliated Media Foundation Movement (AM/FM radio). Starting with KNON Community Radio in Dallas, ACORN has started to establish its own radio and television programming.

Maude Hurd has been national president since 1990, and Wade Rathke continues as chief organizer. Under Hurd's leadership ACORN has dealt with the major banks to negotiate loan programs for minorities and low-income people and has successfully lobbied for the addition of two community interest directors to serve on each of the nation's twelve Federal Home Loan Bank boards. ACORN has also established charter schools in New York City, St. Paul, Minnesota, and Chicago. During the Clinton administration, ACORN played a key role in passage of the 1993 National Voter Registration Act ("Motor-Voter"). Currently ACORN is fighting utility rate increases, promoting major reform in legislation regulating prescription drug prices, and arguing for minimum wage increases in various cities and states.

ACORN publications include *The Organizer, Vamanos,* and *USA: United States of ACORN,* a bimonthly. Its headquarters is in New Orleans, Louisiana, with a legislative office in Washington, D.C. and branches in twenty-six states. Its membership is approximately 120,000.

For Further Information

Association of Community Organizations for Reform Now, *http://www.acorn.org/*

Delgado, Gary. *Organizing the Movement: The Roots and Growth of ACORN.* Philadelphia: Temple University Press, 1986.

B

BANKS, DENNIS (1937–). One of the founders and leaders of the AMERICAN INDIAN MOVEMENT (AIM), Dennis Banks is best known for being a key participant in the forcible occupations of Alcatraz Island (1969–1971) and Wounded Knee, South Dakota (1973). A Chippewa, born April 12, 1937, on the Leech Lake Indian Reservation in northern Minnesota, Banks established AIM in 1968 to promote Native American self-sufficiency and to enforce treaty rights that Indians believed had been violated by the U.S. government.

Banks was among the 200 Indians who occupied Alcatraz Island in 1969, reclaimed it as Native American territory, and demanded that all federal surplus property be returned to Indian control. One objective of the takeover, not realized, was to have the abandoned prison converted into an Indian educational and cultural center. After the occupation ended in 1971, Richard Oakes, a Mohawk leader of the group, was murdered. Angered by this tragedy, the Indians organized the Trail of Broken Treaties' caravan, timed to reach Washington just before the 1972 presidential election and to awaken politicians to the plight of Native Americans. When government officials refused to meet with the group's delegates to discuss treaty and sovereignty rights, they seized control of the Bureau of Indian Affairs building. They vacated the building after being given money and promises that corrective actions would follow.

The next AIM protest took place in January 1973 after AIM was asked by Sarah Bad Heart Bull to come to Pine Ridge. A white man who had killed her son, Wesley Bad Heart Bull, in a barroom brawl, had been charged with involuntary manslaughter. Angry Lakota Indians demanded the charge be changed to murder. When state authorities refused to negotiate with them, the Indians set fire to two police cars and the Custer, South Dakota, Chamber of Commerce building. A month later, Banks, RUSSELL MEANS, and other armed AIM members took over the town of Wounded Knee, where eighty-three years earlier U.S. troops had slain a band of Lakota women and children.

During the seventy-one-day standoff between federal agents and Indians, tensions escalated and two Indians were killed and a federal marshal severely injured. Banks was acquitted of Wounded Knee charges but convicted of riot and assault in 1975 because of his actions at Custer. He fled on foot to California, where he was granted amnesty by then Governor Edmund Brown. While in California (1976–1983), Banks earned an associate of arts degree at the University of California at Davis and was appointed chancellor of Deganawida Quetzecoatl (DQ)

Native American activist Dennis Banks leads an "unthanksgiving ceremony" held on Alcatraz Island on Thanksgiving Day 1982. *AP Photo/Carl Viti.*

University. When Republican George Deuk-mejian succeeded Brown as California governor in 1983, he immediately issued a warrant for Banks's arrest on Inauguration Day. Anticipating his action, Banks fled to a New York reservation, but soon after turned himself in to authorities in Rapid City, South Dakota, to serve eighteen months in prison.

Dennis Banks remains involved in Native American issues. He is AIM national field director and corporate partner of a foundation that benefits young runners by sponsoring an annual Sacred Run, a multicultural, international event Banks initiated in 1978. He has also has had roles in the movies *War Party, Thunderheart,* and *The Last of the Mohicans.*

See also: NATIVE AMERICAN RIGHTS

For Further Information

Cheatham, Karyn. *Dennis Banks: Native American Activist.* Berkeley Heights, CA: Enslow Publications, 1997.

Grossman, Mark. *The Native American Rights Movement.* Santa Barbara: ABC-CLIO, 1996.

BERRIGAN, DANIEL J. (1921–). Daniel Berrigan, a social activist, radical priest, and celebrity, is the son of a frustrated poet and strong trade union man. He was born in Virginia, Minnesota (brother of PHILIP BERRIGAN), entered the Order of the Society of Jesus in 1939, and was ordained in 1952. He studied in France, where he was influenced by the worker-priest movement, and taught at Catholic preparatory schools until becoming an associate professor of theology at LeMoyne College in Syracuse, New York, from 1957 to 1962. *Time Without Number* (1957), his book of poems, won the Lamont Poetry Award. Between 1963 and 1969, he worked with Jesuit missions in New York City.

Attracted by DOROTHY DAY's Catholic

Workers, Daniel Berrigan became a proponent of Catholicism as "a commitment to prayer and compassion and service" and a way to fight the "filthy, rotten system." The antiwar movement hardened his anti-institutional resolve. He accompanied Professor Howard Zinn of Boston University to Hanoi, North Vietnam, to assist in obtaining the release of three downed American pilots, and the diary he kept during this mission, along with eleven poems, became *Night Flight to Hanoi* (1968). He and his brother Philip captured national attention by destroying draft registration files in Catonsville, Maryland, in 1968. They removed the files and ignited the folders with homemade napalm. In 1970 Daniel was sentenced to three years in prison. He escaped and went underground, but federal authorities apprehended him on Block Island (off Rhode Island). After eighteen months in prison, he was paroled in 1972 and participated with his brother in the first PLOWSHARES action (1980), a protest at the General Electric nuclear missile plant in King of Prussia, Pennsylvania.

During this time, Daniel Berrigan became a cult figure, finding common cause with Che Guevara, the BLACK PANTHER PARTY, and other antiwar/anti–big money activists. Living among Jesuits, writing and conducting retreats, he was periodically arrested for protest actions at weapons manufacturing plants and other sites. A prolific writer, he has over fifty books to his credit, including *The Trial of the Catonsville Nine*, an autobiography, and four films. His actions, whatever form they take, stem from his firm conviction that all human life is sacred, whatever a person's nationality, gender, race, or social status.

See also: ANTIWAR/ANTI–NUCLEAR WEAPONS MOVEMENT

For Further Information

Berrigan, Daniel J. *Daniel: Under the Siege of the Divine.* Farmington, PA: Plough Publishing House, 1998.

———. *To Dwell in Peace: An Autobiography.* San Francisco: Harper, 1987.

Polner, Murray, Jim O'Grady, and J. Anthony Lukas. *Disarmed and Dangerous: The Radical Lives and Times of Daniel and Philip Berrigan, Brothers in Religious Faith and Civil Disobedience.* Boulder, CO: Westview Press, 1998.

BERRIGAN, PHILIP F. (1923–). Philip Berrigan, peace activist and the first Roman Catholic priest to be sentenced to jail in the United States for political crimes, was born October 5, 1923, in Two Harbors, Minnesota. The youngest of six brothers, one of whom was DANIEL BERRIGAN, Philip served in the U.S. Army (1943–1946) in the European Theater of Operations. Ordained in 1955 as a Josephite, he held various jobs between 1955 and 1964: assistant pastor in Washington, D.C.; parochial high school counselor in New Orleans; director of promotion at St. Joseph's Society of the Sacred Heart in New York; and English instructor at Epiphany College in Newburgh, New York.

In the early 1960s he and his brother Daniel became totally immersed in the peace movement and achieved national notoriety by torching Vietnam War draft registration files in Catonsville, Maryland, in 1968. Both brothers were sentenced to three years in prison, but went underground. Two years later, federal authorities in Manhattan apprehended Philip. By this time, the Berrigans had folk hero status as the court-scoffing, church-defying, war-denouncing Berrigan brothers.

In 1969 Philip married Elizabeth McAlister but did not formally leave the priesthood. In 1973 he and his wife founded Jonah House, a religious pacifist community in Baltimore, Maryland, committed to nonviolent resistance against arms manufacturing. He published *Year One*, a newspaper highlighting struggles against nuclear armament. He and his brother founded the PLOWSHARES peace group, a movement inspired by the Bible: "They shall beat their swords into plowshares, and . . . nation shall not lift up sword against nation, neither shall they learn war any more" (Isaiah 2:4). The first Plowshares action (1980) was conducted at the General Electric nuclear plant in King of Prussia, Pennsylvania. Here, eight activists battered nuclear missile warheads with hammers, destroying two of them. Subsequently his community took part in at least fifty other actions at weapons factories and nuclear facilities in the United States, Europe, and Australia.

On Ash Wednesday 1997 Philip and five others broke into the Bath Iron Works shipyard in Maine and boarded a nuclear-armed Aegis destroyer. Two of the six activists slipped past a naval officer and started pounding on missile hatches with hammers. They carried plastic baby bottles of their own blood and splashed control units and other equipment to dramatize the carnage caused by weapons of destruction. Philip was sentenced to a two-year term in a federal penitentiary.

The Berrigan brothers never ceased their peaceful resistance to the nemeses they nicknamed the "war machine" and "Lord Nuke." They remained faithful to the teachings and actions of Mahatma Gandhi, MARTIN LUTHER KING JR., and DOROTHY DAY long after other sixties antiestablishment endeavors had faded and folded. Philip Berrigan suggested during a prison interview in 1977 that the most fitting epitaph for Daniel and himself would be "We didn't quit."

See also: ANTIWAR/ANTI–NUCLEAR WEAPONS MOVEMENT

For Further Information

Berrigan, Philip F. *Fighting the Lamb's War*. Monroe, ME: Common Courage Press, 1997.

Polner, Murray, Jim O'Grady, and Anthony J. Lukas. *Disarmed and Dangerous: The Radical Lives and Times of Daniel and Philip Berrigan, Brothers in Religious Faith and Civil Disobedience*. Boulder, CO: Westview Press, 1998.

BLACK PANTHER PARTY. The Black Panther Party (BPP), a radical urban political organization, was founded in 1966 in Oakland, California, by HUEY NEWTON and BOBBY SEALE. Originally named the Black Panther Party for Self-Defense, the group's initial objective was to act as an independent armed force to protect African Americans from police actions that many residents considered unnecessarily brutal. In 1967 BPP adherents started forming affiliates in urban ghetto neighborhoods in the Midwest and northeastern states.

Inspired by Mao Zedong's writings, the Panthers rapidly evolved into a Marxist group that demanded for all blacks the right to carry weapons, exemption from the draft, immediate release from jails and prisons, and the payment of compensation for past wrongs inflicted by white Americans. At its peak, Panther membership exceeded 3,000 and chapters operated in several major cities.

Conflicts with the police and FBI in the late 1960s and early seventies culminated in shoot-outs in Chicago, California, and New York. Fred Hampton and Mark Clark, BPP leaders, were killed during a police raid in Chicago, and in Oakland, Huey Newton and ELDRIDGE CLEAVER, BPP minister of information, were indicted for allegedly shooting several policemen. Seale was exonerated, but Newton had to serve twenty-two months in prison before his conviction was overturned. In the mid-1970s, the BPP drastically changed its tactics in response to plummeting membership and the revulsion of many prominent members of the black community. The Panthers sponsored public service programs, including health clinics and free breakfasts for children, and developed a behavioral code that called for politeness, respect for women, and avoidance of offensive language. Black self-reliance and pride, community control of schools and police, and the cessation of drug traffic were emphasized.

Although the BPP disbanded in the 1980s, it had succeeded in spreading its message through the media as one of the most visible radical groups within the mix of militant civil rights groups that emerged in the sixties and seventies. Through their rhetoric the Panthers had signaled the depth of their grievances and their sense of exclusion from the American system, while alerting the public to African Americans' need for expanded Medicare, day care facilities, and liberalized court procedures.

See also: AFRICAN AMERICAN RIGHTS

For Further Information

Cleaver, Eldridge. *Soul on Ice*. New York: Dell, 1999.

Newton, Huey P. *To Die for the People: The Writings of Huey P. Newton*. New York: Writers and Readers Publishing, 1995.

Pearson, Hugh. *The Shadow of the Panther: Huey Newton and the Price of Black Power in America*. Reading, MA: Addison Wesley Longman, 1995.

BLOOR, ELLA REEVE WARE COHEN OMHOLT (1862–1951). Radical, labor organizer, and feminist Ella Reeve Bloor was born on Staten Island, New York, in 1862, the oldest of twelve children. Not allowed to attend college because her father deemed it inappropriate for a woman, she became a voracious reader. She met Walt Whitman while living in Camden, New Jersey, was influenced by his writings, along with those of political theorists Karl Marx and Friedrich Engels, and became interested in social reform as a teenager. At age nineteen, she married Lucien Ware, the son of an abolitionist, Unitarian, and freethinker. Early contacts with Quakers and Unitarians awakened her to issues of women's equality. Divorcing Ware in 1896, she married Louis Cohen, a socialist, whom she in turn divorced several years later.

In 1897 Bloor joined the Social Democratic Party, formed that year by Eugene V. Debs and Victor L. Berger. In 1902 she became a labor organizer for the Socialist Party, assisting mine workers, machinists, and garment workers.

After publication of his muckraking novel, *The Jungle*, in 1906, Upton Sinclair persuaded Bloor to infiltrate the Chicago meat-packing industry and document the health endangering conditions cited in the book. Sinclair insisted that Richard Bloor, a fellow socialist, accompany her as protection and that she adopt the alias "Mrs. Richard Bloor" to lend respectability to her findings. Her evidence led to passage of the Meat Inspection Act of 1906, and she continued to use her made-up name for the rest of her life.

Bloor formulated plans for day nurseries and kitchens for working mothers on factory premises and marched with suffragists in mass demonstrations in Washington. She was an unsuccessful candidate for secretary of state of Connecticut in 1908, ran for lieutenant governor of New York on the Socialist Party ticket in 1918, and was the Communist Party candidate for governor of Pennsylvania in 1938. In 1919 she had helped found the American Communist Party and was a member of the Party Central Committee from 1932 until 1948.

Between 1908 and 1920, she organized unions for needleworkers and hatters and rallied support for striking miners in Ohio, West Virginia, Illinois, Colorado, and Michigan. Arrested more than thirty times during her career, she earned the adoration of laborers and became known as "Mother Bloor." At age seventy-two she was arrested for assault and inciting to riot. Her later years were spent on a working apple orchard in Lehigh County, Pennsylvania with her third husband, Andrew Omholt, a farmer, communist organizer, and past candidate for Congress from North Dakota.

See also: LABOR ISSUES; WOMEN'S ISSUES

For Further Information

Bloor, Ella Reeve. *We Are Many: An Autobiography*. New York: International Publishers, 1940.

Whitman, Alden, ed. *American Reformers: An H. W. Wilson Biographical Dictionary*. New York: H. W. Wilson, 1985.

BONUS ARMY. On May 29, 1932, during the Great Depression, World War I veterans formed a "Bonus Army" and marched on Washington to demand immediate cashing of service compensation certificates not scheduled to be paid in full until 1945. About 1,000 ex-servicemen arrived at the capital on May 29 with the avowed purpose of staying

A Theodor Horydczak photograph of one of the Bonus Army camps around Washington, DC, in 1932. *Library of Congress, Prints and Photographs Division, LC-H823–1459.*

until Congress authorized immediate cash payments. Other groups of veterans flowed in from all parts of the country, bringing the total number in the "Bonus Expeditionary Force" to an estimated 17,000. Many camped on the Anacostia Flats, on the edge of the city, while others erected unsightly shacks and tents within sight of the Capitol.

Although the House had passed a bill providing for the issuance of $2.4 billion to pay off the certificates, the Senate defeated the measure. Instead the government appropriated funds for returning veterans to their homes. Most of the campers departed peacefully, but about 2,000 refused to disband. The Washington police tried to forcibly evict them, and violence resulted in the deaths of two veterans and two police officers. President Herbert Hoover then called in federal troops led by Brigadier General Perry L. Miles and General Douglas MacArthur, then U.S. Army chief of staff, who completed the

task with the use of tanks and tear gas. This confrontation received heavy coverage in the press, shocked the public with photographs of soldier versus soldier skirmishes and injuries, and further undermined Hoover's waning popularity. A second, smaller Bonus Army arrived in May 1933, and was greeted by Eleanor Roosevelt, the new first lady, and Louis Howe, Franklin Delano Roosevelt's presidential assistant.

After World War I, the AMERICAN LEGION had lobbied for adjusted compensation certificates, and a bill was passed by Congress but vetoed by President Warren G. Harding. In 1923 the bill reemerged and was vetoed by President Calvin Coolidge. Finally, in 1936, after seventeen years of agitation and four successive presidential vetoes, the bill passed despite President Franklin D. Roosevelt's veto, disbursing almost $2.5 billion in veterans' benefits. Profiting from this precedent, Congress recognized that supportive legislation to ease veterans' transition into civilian life was not only good social policy, but could stave off future embarrassing public demonstrations. Consequently, the G.I. Bill of Rights was developed after World War II as a socially constructive means of administering benefits to deserving veterans.

See also: VETERANS' ISSUES

For Further Information

Daniels, Roger. *The Bonus March: An Episode of the Great Depression.* Westport, CT: Greenwood Press, 1971.

BOWERS V. HARDWICK (478 U.S. 186) (1986). The *Bowers v. Hardwick* Supreme Court decision held that the rights of married and unmarried people to have consensual sex in private (affirmed in the landmark 1965 GRISWOLD V. CONNECTICUT decision striking down the state's ban on the use of contraceptives) do not apply to people of the same sex. In *Bowers v. Hardwick*, the defendant, Michael Hardwick, was interrupted in his own bedroom, in flagrante, by an Atlanta police officer who was enforcing the state's anti-sodomy law. Although the Georgia prohibitions, like those of many other Southern states, apply to any anal or oral sex between consenting adults, the Supreme Court effectively ignored the heterosexual permutations and ruled that there is no constitutional right to practice homosexuality. Gay rights activists regard this case as the twentieth-century version of *Plessy v. Ferguson*, the infamous 1896 "separate but equal" decision used to justify the six following decades of legally endorsed racial segregation.

Legal scholar Laurence H. Tribe, Mr. Hardwick's attorney, in referring to this case, later wrote, "In the kind of society contemplated by our Constitution, government must offer greater justification to police the bedroom than it must to police the streets. Therefore, the relevant question is not what Michael Hardwick was doing in the privacy of his own bedroom, but what the State of Georgia was doing there" (p. 1425). In the

decision, the Court expressed concern that permitting homosexual acts would lead the nation down a slippery slope, and that such behavior was equivalent to incest, adultery, child abuse, and wife battering in its capacity to inflict harm.

The Court also stated that "against a background in which many States have criminalized sodomy and still do, to claim that a right to engage in such conduct is 'deeply rooted in this Nation's history and tradition' or 'implicit in the concept of ordered liberty' is, at best, facetious." Simply put, if the majority of the electorate believe that sodomy is immoral, the Court must support the majority opinion and declare such conduct illegal.

In this 5–4 decision, Justices White, Burger, Powell, Rehnquist, and O'Connor delivered the opinion of the Court; Justices Blackmun, Brennan, Marshall, and Stevens dissented.

See also: LESBIANS AND GAYS

For Further Information

Buchanan, G. Sidney. "Sexual Orientation Classifications and the Ravages of *Bowers v. Hardwick.*" *Wayne Law Review* 43 (Fall 1996): 11.
DeCew, Judith Wagner. *In Pursuit of Privacy: Law, Ethics, and the Rise of Technology.* Ithaca, NY: Cornell University Press, 1997.
Tribe, Laurence H. *American Constitutional Law.* Westbury, NY: Foundation Press, 1988, p. 1425.

BRADY CAMPAIGN TO PREVENT GUN VIOLENCE. On June 14, 2001, Handgun Control Inc. was renamed the Brady Campaign to Prevent Gun Violence. The new organization, originally the National Council to Control Handguns, works with law enforcement, public health, religious, and community groups across the country to strengthen and protect federal, state, and local gun control laws, but does not seek to ban all guns. Handgun Control Inc. was founded in 1974 by Dr. Mark Borinsky, a victim of an armed robbery. A year later, Borinsky was joined by Pete Shields, whose son, Nick, had been shot dead in San

Francisco by a member of the then-famous Zebra Killers, a Muslim extremist group, during a large-scale killing spree in 1974. Shields retired from his position as marketing manager at DuPont in 1976 and became executive director and later chair of the organization in 1978.

Sarah Brady, the Brady campaign's current chair, joined the group in 1985, after her husband, James, was shot in the assassination attempt on President Ronald Reagan in 1981. As signer of direct mail appeals, she has been a successful fundraiser and the Brady campaign's most effective public representative. The organization is a nonpartisan citizens' lobby that advocates legal control and regulation of the manufacture, importation, sale, transfer, and possession of guns.

The Brady Campaign had expected to gain legislative ground during the Jimmy Carter administration but could not do so, as other more urgent problems plagued his presidency. With the election of Ronald Reagan in 1980, the NATIONAL RIFLE ASSOCIATION (NRA) saw an opportunity to weaken the provisions of the federal Firearms Control Act of 1968. The resulting McClure-Volkmer Act (1986), a partial victory for both NRA and gun control advocates, allowed interstate purchases of rifles and shotguns but not handguns, and banned machine-guns entirely. Only in the early years of the Clinton presidency did the campaign achieve two major victories. The first, in 1993, was the Brady Law, imposing background checks and a five-day waiting period on handgun purchasers. The second was the assault weapons ban, limiting the sale of certain types of military-style semiautomatic weapons, which took effect in 1994. Despite public support for the ban, in 1995 the Republican-controlled House of Representatives voted to repeal it. In the wake of the 1995 Oklahoma City Murrah Building bombing, the repeal failed in the Senate.

The Brady Center to Prevent Gun Violence is the educational and research affiliate of the Brady Campaign. It compiles statistics, state-by-state law summaries, and documents on safety strategies, kids and guns, and pending legislation. Brady Campaign headquarters is in Washington, D.C. Former Representative Michael D. Barnes (D-MD) is president. The group's membership is about 500,000. Included with membership dues is *Progress Report*, published three times a year.

See also: GUN OWNERSHIP RIGHTS/GUN CONTROLS

For Further Information

Brady Campaign to Prevent Gun Violence, *http://www.bradycampaign.org*

Dreyfuss, Robert, "Dark Days for Gun Control." *Rolling Stone*, no. 820 (September 9, 1999): 43–45.

Shields, Pete. *Guns Don't Die—People Do: The Pros, the Cons, the Facts*. New York: William Morrow, 1981.

Stone, Peter H. "Plenty of Firepower." *National Journal*, July 22, 2000, p. 2370.

BROWER, DAVID ROSS (1912–2000). Born in Berkeley, California, July 1, 1912, David Brower was a leader of the modern environmental movement and responsible for the creation of nine U.S. national parks. He was instrumental in stopping the U.S. Bureau of Reclamation from building dams in the Grand Canyon, in establishing the national wilderness system, and in the passage of such key legislation as the 1964 Wilderness Act. A nominee for three Nobel Peace Prizes, Brower helped transform the SIERRA CLUB from a small group of nature enthusiasts and weekend hikers into one of the world's most influential environmental advocacy organizations.

Brower enrolled at age sixteen at the University of California at Berkeley. He studied for two years before dropping out as a result of mostly emotional and financial stress. When only fifteen, he discovered the butterfly *Anthocaris sara reakirtis broweri*. For several years he worked for the U.S. Park Service at Yosemite National Park. He was an accomplished mountaineer and was the first person to scale Vazquez Monolith in Pinnacles National Monument.

In 1933 Brower joined the Sierra Club,

David Brower at the time of his forced resignation as executive director of the Sierra Club in 1969. *AP/Wide World Photo.*

serving as its executive director from 1952 to 1969, during which time he employed considerably more politically effective and combative tactics than his predecessors, while expanding the Club's membership from 2,000 to more than 77,000. Under Brower's leadership, the Sierra Club became a powerful force in stopping the construction of numerous dams. It was Brower who directed the successful battle that thwarted the Bureau of Reclamation's attempts to build dams in Dinosaur National Monument by creating a coalition of conservation groups that combined sophisticated political intelligence and inspired propaganda. Unfortunately, an agreement Brower and the Sierra Club signed in January 1956 included the dropping of opposition to the construction of Glen Canyon Dam if, in return, Congress abandoned plans for the Echo Park Dam and flooding of the Dinosaur National Monu-

ment. Later, Brower realized that without the compromise, environmentalists could have defeated the entire Colorado River Storage Project and saved Glen Canyon from being eliminated by the damming of the Colorado River to create Lake Powell. Of all the battles Brower fought and lost, it was the submerging of Glen Canyon, his "sellout" to the U.S. government, that he most regretted.

Following a disagreement with the Sierra Club board of directors for being autocratic and for pushing his conservation projects without regard to cost, failing to collaborate with industry, and adopting an international instead of American point of view, Brower was forced to resign in 1969. After leaving the Sierra Club, Brower went on to found the more militant FRIENDS OF THE EARTH and LEAGUE OF CONSERVATION VOTERS, the John Muir Institute for Environmental Studies, and the Earth Island Institute, which he chaired.

More than anyone else, Brower exemplified citizen activism, writing elected officials, speaking out at public meetings, and taking courageous stands on environmental issues. In John McPhee's book *Encounters with the Archdruid,* Brower is described as "the most militant conservationist in the world." In response to the claim that "dammed rivers permit tourists to come closer to the wonders of nature," Brower replied, "We don't flood the Sistine Chapel so tourists can get closer to the ceiling."

In 1995 Brower was reelected to the Sierra Club board of directors but resigned only five years later. In May 2000 he issued a statement in which he said, "The planet is being trashed, but the board has no real sense of urgency; the world is burning, and all I hear from them is the music of violins." His statement was prompted by the board's support of federal government proposals that he felt would contravene the original Sierra Club mandate to protect the California Sierras.

One of the last organizations Brower helped establish was the Alliance for Sustainable Jobs and the Environment, a coalition of steelworkers and conservationists, based in

Portland, Oregon. David Brower died on November 5, 2000, at his home in Berkeley, California.

See also: ENVIRONMENT

For Further Information

Brower, David Ross. *Let the Mountains Talk, Let the Rivers Run: A Call to Those Who Would Save the Earth.* San Francisco: HarperCollins, 1995.

McPhee, John. *Encounters with the Archdruid: Narratives about a Conservationist and Three of His Natural Enemies.* New York: Farrar, Straus and Giroux, 1971.

Wilkinson, Todd. "A Modern Thoreau with Sharp Elbows." *Christian Science Monitor*, June 7, 2000, p. 3.

BROWN V. BOARD OF EDUCATION OF TOPEKA (347 U.S. 483) (1954).

The historic 1954 Supreme Court case *Brown v. Board of Education of Topeka* gave legal meaning to the idea that segregated education must be unequal education. Until 1954, segregated schools in the United States operated under a ruling made by the Supreme Court in 1896, *Plessy v. Ferguson*, that segregation did not create a badge of inferiority if the facilities were on a par and the law was reasonable. The decision in both cases centered on the meaning of the Fourteenth Amendment to the Constitution. This amendment was ratified in 1868, shortly after the conclusion of the Civil War. One of its purposes was to extend the basic guarantees of the Bill of Rights into the areas of state and local government. The most important and controversial section asserts, "No State shall make or enforce any law which shall abridge the privileges or immunities of citizens . . . nor . . . deprive any person of life, liberty, or property, without due process of law; nor deny to any person within its jurisdiction the equal protection of the laws." In the *Brown v. Topeka* case, involving public elementary education, the Court (Earl Warren, Chief Justice) held unanimously that segregation in public education was a denial of equal protection of the laws. The Court in 1955 directed the lower courts to admit Ne-

groes to public schools on a racially nondiscriminatory basis "with all deliberate speed."

Plessy v. Ferguson had involved Homer Plessy, who was one-eighth African American and seven-eighths white. He was arrested for refusing to ride in the colored coach of a train, as required under Louisiana state law. The Supreme Court's decision in this case, that segregated facilities could exist if they were equal, became known as the "separate but equal" doctrine.

The 1954 decision *Brown v. Board of Education of Topeka* overturned the "separate but equal" doctrine by arguing, on the basis of the findings of social scientists, that segregated education was inferior to integrated education in terms of the academic and social skills imparted to students. Even if teachers, plant, equipment, and all other conditions were identical between two racially segregated schools, the white school would also have an inherent advantage over the black school.

Soon after the decision was handed down, the Alabama and Virginia state legislatures passed nullifying resolutions, and nineteen senators and eighty-one representatives issued a Southern Manifesto declaring their intention to employ all lawful means to reverse the desegregation decisions.

The testing of the case's application to schools and public accommodations followed, with resistance culminating in the heroic actions of the SOUTHERN CHRISTIAN LEADERSHIP CONFERENCE, STUDENT NONVIOLENT COORDINATING COMMITTEE, MARTIN LUTHER KING JR., REVEREND FRED SHUTTLESWORTH, ROSA PARKS, RALPH ABERNATHY, and the many others who participated in the civil rights movement of the 1960s.

BRYANT, ANITA (1940–).

Born on March 25, 1940, in Barnsdall, Oklahoma, Anita Bryant, a popular singer and celebrity in TV advertisements promoting Florida citrus industry products, became nationally known for her antihomosexual advocacy and for firing the opening salvo in the "New Right" antigay movement in 1977.

Bryant's career as an entertainer during the 1960s had been unusual in one respect: the intensity of her ties to her Christian religion. She accompanied Billy Graham on his evangelistic crusades, collaborated with Dr. Norman Vincent Peale, who featured her in one of his books, and campaigned for a proposed constitutional amendment to permit prayer in public schools. During this time, Bryant believed that homosexuality is not inborn and that gays should not be given special privileges because this would confirm community approval of an act that God states is immoral.

Upset by the effort of homosexuals in Dade County, Florida, to advocate laws curbing housing and job discrimination based upon sexual preference, Bryant undertook what she termed the "Save the Children" crusade. She won a broad base of support because of her visibility as a media figure and by pointing out that the Dade County law, enacted in January 1977, would enable homosexuals to be employed as teachers in the Florida schools. She campaigned against the new law with her husband and Ed Rowe, who later became head of the Christian Mandate, a Religious Right group. On June 7, 1977, voters repealed the new law by a two to one margin.

Although Bryant won this particular campaign, despite the opposition of local television humorists and commentators, the Dade County gay and lesbian community claimed that it advanced their cause by bringing the discussion of the issue of sexual orientation into most American households. In 1998 the Miami-Dade County commissioners nullified the 1977 repeal by voting 7–6 for a new ordinance banning discrimination based on sexual orientation in housing and employment.

Bryant's involvement in the controversy resulted in the loss of her contract with the Florida Citrus Commission as TV spokesperson in 1979. She later underwent a conversion to born-again Christianity and repudiated some of her previous antihomo-

sexual statements. Between 1995 and 1998, she owned and sang in the Anita Bryant Theatre in Branson, Missouri, and currently lives with her second husband, Charles Dry, a former NASA official, on a ranch in Berryville, Arkansas.

See also: RELIGIOUS RIGHT

For Further Information

Bryant, Anita. *A New Day*. Nashville: Broadman and Holman, 1992.

Kondracke, Morton. "Anita Bryant Is Mad about Gays." *New Republic*, May 7, 1977, p. 13.

Richards, David. "Anita Bryant, Reconstituted: She's Back, She's Singing a Different Tune, Sort of." *Washington Post*, May 12, 1996, Style section, p. F01.

BUCKLEY V. VALEO (424 U.S. 1) (1976).

In *Buckley v. Valeo* the Supreme Court ruled that while the government has a compelling need to restrict contributions to individual political candidates to avoid the semblance of corruption, the spending of money on behalf of political candidates cannot be restricted, because this would restrict the flow of free speech.

In 1974 the Federal Election Campaign Act (FECA) had placed limits on contributions to, and expenditures for, political campaigns. FECA included authority to establish a commission that would rule on cases brought before it. An equal number of Democrats and Republicans would comprise the commission. U.S. Senator James L. Buckley, who had spent $1.8 million during his successful 1970 race in New York State, immediately challenged the new law. During televised debates he had agreed that campaign spending should be limited, but after Congress passed the 1974 legislation that limited spending, he challenged the law in court.

The Court contended that "the concept that the government may restrict the speech of some elements in our society in order to enhance the relative voice of others is wholly foreign to the First Amendment." In this pronouncement, the Court failed to recognize that it is unfair to permit a few wealthy individuals to control the electoral process to their advantage. In *Buckley*, the Court decided that fair representation is representation according to the amount of influence that one can purchase, thereby denying the value of maintaining justice and ensuring that each citizen, regardless of economic status, has an equally effective voice in elections.

This historic decision set the constitutional contours of debate about campaign finance reform from 1976 until the end of the century. In the wake of *Buckley*, contributions to national and state political parties mushroomed to multimillion dollar figures, and "soft money" became the major tool used by political parties and their candidates to avoid Federal Election Campaign Act restrictions. These political donations in large amounts— $50,000, $100,000 or more—circumvent federal regulations or limits. The money is contributed to purportedly nonpartisan organizations and later funneled to political candidates and their campaign "war chests."

As Senator Bill Bradley noted, "Money in politics is like ants in the kitchen—if you don't close every hole, they'll keep coming back."

Toward the end of the twentieth century, the public was souring on politics and becoming increasingly cynical, resentful, and apathetic because legalized bribery was displacing genuine contests of ideas during election campaigns. Many legal scholars agree that the *Buckley* decision was profoundly dismaying, damaged the electoral process, and should be overturned.

See also: LIBERAL ACTIVISM

For Further Information

Morrison, Alan B. "What If . . . Buckley Were Overturned?" *Constitutional Commentary* 16 (Summer 1999): 347.

Rawls, John. *Political Liberalism*. New York: Columbia University Press, 1993.

Rosenkranz, E. Joshua, and Richard L. Hasen. "Introduction to Symposium on Money, Politics, and Equality." *Texas Law Review* 77 (June 1999): 1603.

C

CAMBIO CUBANO. Cambio Cubano (Cubans for Change), a political party opposed to Fidel Castro's communist government in Cuba, advocates elimination of the U.S. trade embargo against Cuba and restoration of democracy on the island through negotiation. The group's leader, Eloy Gutiérrez Menoyo, is living in exile in Miami.

Menoyo, a former Cuban political prisoner, founded Cambio Cubano in January 1993. He fought in Castro's rebel army in the 1950s and led 3,000 men against the Batista dictatorship. When Castro moved into the Soviet camp, Menoyo defected and led a raid against the Cuban dictator that resulted in his twenty-two-year imprisonment.

Menoyo says that he cannot get Washington's attention because Cambio Cubano lacks the money and political influence of the CUBAN AMERICAN NATIONAL FOUNDATION (CANF). Cambio Cubano favors dialogue with the Castro government, a position opposed by CANF. Recent polls indicate that a majority of Miami-area Cuban Americans favor negotiation with Castro.

The Cambio Cubano Web site implores: "Cubans, don't let others speak for you. Think. Don't let ideas be eradicated. In the face of passion, rage, and vociferous demagoguery, use your intelligence and remember the teachings of José Martí. Do not tolerate pressure or censorship against you in a free country. Express yourself. The time for change has come." This message is directed at Cubans who may feel intimidated by the well-financed CANF anti-Castro clique, which favors continuation of the U.S. trade embargo, considered by many to be a useless relic of earlier Cold War policy. The group supports a peaceful transition to democracy and a free-market economy, and would permit shipments of humanitarian aid by exiles to reach Cuba. Menoyo has been subjected to hate mail and death threats, and vilified by local Spanish-language radio stations that support the CANF's hard-line, anti-Castro policy.

Cambio Cubano's headquarters is in Miami, and Eloy Gutiérrez Menoyo, its founder, is president. Cambio Cubano has approximately 200 members.

See also: HISPANIC AMERICAN RIGHTS

For Further Information

Cambio Cubano, *http://www.cambiocubano.com/*
Rohter, Larry. "In Miami, Talk of Talking with Cuba." *New York Times*, June 27, 1993, p. 16.

CAMPUS OUTREACH OPPORTUNITY LEAGUE. Founded in 1984, the Campus Outreach Opportunity League (COOL) is a compact of colleges and universities, administered by a board of students, representatives of nonprofit organizations, and volunteer professionals that prepares students to deliver voluntary community service for the poor and homeless, participate in adult literacy programs, and encourage activism on campuses, in the community, and worldwide.

Wayne Meisel, a Harvard graduate student, started COOL as an effort to counter the prevailing view that students have become "apathetic couch potatoes, zoned out on MTV." In 1978 Meisel, the son of a liberal Presbyterian minister, was dropped from the Harvard soccer team because of lack of commitment to intramural sports. He then convinced 150 fellow students, including other frustrated former high school athletes, to help set up a local youth soccer league. Meisel's interactions with inner-city youth awakened him to the need to free himself from his insular attitude and indifference to the plight of less privileged young people. He paired the college's residential houses with projects in rundown neighborhoods in Cambridge, Massachusetts, working with local day care centers, boys' clubs, and other local community organizations. In 1984 he decided to take his project nationwide.

Meisel launched COOL with a 1,500-mile "Walk for Action" during which he visited sixty-five colleges from Maine to Washington, D.C. Within a year he had enlisted fraternities, U.S. PUBLIC INTEREST RESEARCH GROUP members, and hundreds of individual students, transforming COOL into a significant multicampus force. In 1984 the first COOL conference drew only sixty attendees, but by 1989 the number had reached 1,700, and several thousand new members were joining each year in the 1990s. In 1990, COOL was given the Bush administration's Presidential Voluntary Action Award in recognition of its participation in the president's "Thousand Points of Light" voluntarism campaign.

Liberal students have faulted COOL because of its willingness to accept financial support from sources they insist are undermining social justice and the quality of life. Grants received from Coors and Exxon were criticized because of the Coors family's affiliation with conservative causes and the *Exxon Valdez* Alaskan oil spill. These same students were unhappy with COOL's acceptance of the Kellogg Foundation's funding of its "Into the Streets" program because of the Foundation's stipulation that prohibited participating students from involving themselves in voter registration drives.

In 2000, an election year, COOL appeared to be changing its policy. The annual conference theme would be "Sit In, Speak Up, Take a Stand: Uniting Activism with Advocacy." Guest speakers would include William Upski Wimsatt, author of *Bomb the Suburbs* and *No More Prisons*, along with speakers on environmental citizenship and nonviolent protest.

Headquarters of the approximately 600-school COOL network is in Washington, D.C. Its current executive director is Melissa Kendrick.

See also: STUDENT ACTIVISM

For Further Information

Campus Outreach Opportunity League, *http://www.cool2serve.org*

Greider, William. "Smells Like Team Spirit." *Rolling Stone*, June 24, 1993, pp. 32, 33, 90, 92.

Loeb, Paul Rogat. *Generation at the Crossroads: Apathy and Action on the American Campus.* New Brunswick, NJ: Rutgers University Press, 1994.

CARMICHAEL, STOKELY (LATER KWAME TURÉ) (1941–1998).

Stokely Carmichael is best known for making "Black Power" the rallying cry of the civil rights movement of the 1960s and for honing a sharp, ultraaggressive edge to African Americans' struggle to achieve social equity. He urged black Americans to grasp political and economic control of their own communities, to form separate standards, and to reject the values of white America.

Carmichael was born June 29, 1941, in Port-of-Spain, Trinidad, and educated in the United States from 1952. At the Bronx High School of Science, a public secondary school for academically advanced students, he excelled and was liked by white students. He later recalled that he was "a good little nigger and everybody was being nice to him" as "part of a phony liberal game." While getting his B.A. in philosophy at Howard University from 1960 to 1963, he participated in the first of the Freedom Rides organized by the CONGRESS OF RACIAL EQUALITY (CORE) to challenge segregated travel in the South. He joined the STUDENT NONVIOLENT COORDINATING COMMITTEE (SNCC) in 1964, and became its president in 1966–1967 after the assassination of MALCOLM X.

Carmichael was radicalized by his experiences in the South, where peaceful protesters were beaten, brutalized, and occasionally killed for seeking their basic civil rights. After James Meredith, the first African American admitted to the University of Mississippi, was wounded by a sniper during a "freedom march" from Memphis to Jackson, Carmichael coined the phrase "Black Power" to incite his listeners to action. He served as prime minister of the BLACK PANTHER PARTY from 1967 to 1969, and then severed his ties to the group, which he considered had become insufficiently militant and too willing to ally itself with white radicals.

In 1969, he emigrated to Guinea as a guest of Sékou Touré, the West African nation's Marxist president. He also became a close friend and admirer of Kwame Nkrumah, the Pan-African nationalist and anticolonialist who had taken refuge in Guinea after being ousted from the presidency of Ghana in 1966. After changing his name to Kwame Turé, Carmichael organized and led the All-African People's Revolutionary Party and dedicated himself to "building a movement that will smash everything that Western Civilization has created."

Carmichael's marriages to Miriam Makeba, the South African singer, and Marlyatou Barry, a Guinean physician, ended in divorce. Never rescinding his extreme beliefs, he continued to campaign for a unified socialist Africa until the end of his life, answering phone calls with the exhortative greeting: "Ready for the revolution!" He succumbed to prostate cancer, in Conakry, Guinea, November 15, 1998.

See also: AFRICAN AMERICAN RIGHTS; EXTREMISTS

For Further Information

Carmichael, Stokely (with Charles V. Hamilton). *Black Power: The Politics of Liberation in America*. New York: Vintage Books, 1992.

Johnson, Jacqueline, and Richard Gallin. *Stokely Carmichael: The Story of Black Power*. Parsippany, NJ: Silver Burdett, 1990.

CARSON, RACHEL LOUISE (1907–1964).

Rachel Carson, a writer, influential marine biologist, and ecologist, has been called the mother of the modern environmental movement. She was born on May 27, 1907, in Springdale, Pennsylvania. By the time she was twelve years old, she had had three of her stories published in *St. Nicholas* magazine's section for young authors. In 1929 she received her B.A. in science from the Pennsylvania College for Women (now known as Chatham College) and subsequently conducted research at the Marine Biological Laboratory in Woods Hole, Massachusetts. She earned her master's degree in biology from Johns Hopkins University in 1932.

Carson worked for the U.S. Fish and Wildlife Service (1936–1949), where she eventually assumed responsibility for all publications. Her first book to achieve popular acclaim, *The Sea Around Us* (1951), warned of the mounting danger of large-scale marine pollution. Her most influential book, *Silent Spring* (1962), eloquently described the devastation caused by spraying toxic chemicals that were decimating the bird population in addition to killing mosquitoes and other pests. She challenged the practices of agricultural scientists and the government and warned that pesticides poison the food supply of animals, kill many birds and fish, and can contaminate human foods. In the book, corporate greed, regulatory negligence, and a public breach of faith were cited as causes of the problem. The chemical industry and

Standing in her library in Silver Spring, Maryland, in March 1963, Rachel Carson holds a copy of her controversial and influential book, *Silent Spring*. *AP/Wide World Photo.*

For Further Information

Carson, Rachel. *The Sea Around Us.* New York: Oxford University Press, 1951.

———. *Silent Spring.* Boston: Houghton Mifflin, 1962.

Freeman, Martha, ed. *Always Rachel: The Letters of Rachel Carson and Dorothy Freeman, 1952–1964.* Boston: Beacon Press, 1995.

Lear, Linda. *Rachel Carson: Witness for Nature.* New York: Henry Holt, 1997.

———, ed. *Lost Woods: The Discovered Writings of Rachel Carson.* Boston: Beacon Press, 1998.

CARTO, WILLIS ALLISON (1926–).

Born in Fort Wayne, Indiana, July 17, 1926, Willis Allison Carto has been a leader on the far right since the 1950s and is generally considered to be the most powerful figure in the Holocaust denial movement in the United States. In the early 1950s, he became involved in a number of right-wing groups and by 1955 had created his own organization, Liberty and Property. He joined the JOHN BIRCH SOCIETY but was expelled by Robert Welch, who feared that his affiliation with the Society could damage its reputation. During the late 1950s, Carto's newsletter, *Right*, was recommending that people join George Lincoln Rockwell's American Nazi Party. In 1981 Washington columnist Jack Anderson quoted an editor of the John Birch Society who had said, "In my opinion, the preservation of anti-Semitism as a movement has occurred because of the activities of Willis Carto."

Carto's considerable wealth enabled him to start up and endow what was destined to become his most successful venture, the LIBERTY LOBBY, in 1955. This group initially focused on four themes: (1) Jewish world domination and the international Jewish conspiracy; (2) preservation of white racial and cultural superiority by segregation and eugenics; (3) anticommunism; and (4) Western cultural decay as described in Oswald Spengler's *The Decline of the West* (1926–1929). In Carto's introduction to *Imperium*, a lengthy racist book written by Francis Parker Yockey, he wrote, "Negro equality . . . is easier to be-

conservative politicians disagreed with her findings but she continued to speak out in favor of increased environmental protection. Soon after, a presidential science advisory committee affirmed the validity of her warnings.

Rachel Carson died of breast cancer in 1964, without knowing the eventual impact of her work. In 1967 the Environmental Defense Fund (now ENVIRONMENTAL DEFENSE) was established in her honor. Environmental Defense finances lawsuits to halt pesticide contamination and resolve other environmental problems. Its first major victory resulted in the federal government's banning of the use of DDT. Environmental Defense has become a powerful force in Washington, successfully pushing for passage of other protective legislation.

See also: ENVIRONMENT

lieve in if there are no Negroes around to destroy the concept." Yockey dedicated his book to Adolf Hitler. He was arrested in San Francisco in 1960 on passport fraud charges and subsequently committed suicide in prison.

Imperium is one of several dozen books published by the Noontide Press, owned by Carto. Other titles include ELIZABETH DILL-ING's *The Plot Against Christianity* (1940), Heinrich Hoffman's *Hitler Was My Friend* (1955), Arthur De Gobineau's *Inequality of the Races* (1966), Robert De Pugh's *Can You Survive?* (1973), and Paul Rassinier's *Debunking the Genocide Myth: A Study of the Nazi Concentration Camps and the Alleged Extermination of European Jewry* (1978).

In 1979 Carto founded the Institute for Historical Review, which publishes the *Journal of Historical Review*, specializing in Holocaust denial propaganda. For example, articles have contended that Franklin Delano Roosevelt and Winston Churchill started World War II in response to pressure from the international Jewish banking community. In 1993 a power struggle within the Institute for Historical Review culminated in Carto's ouster.

Carto's Liberty Lobby, based in Washington, D.C., has won the attention of Congress and continues to supply its members with updated versions of its views on political issues. Liberty Lobby publishes a biennial scorecard, rating legislators' voting records on selected issues. In 1999 the Liberty Lobby opposed hate crimes legislation, the Genocide Convention, forced busing, gun control, federal aid to education, the Equal Rights Amendment, and socialized medicine. It supported states' rights, reduced government spending, lower taxes, protective immigration laws, and repeal of the Sixteenth, Seventeenth, and Twenty-fifth Amendments to the U.S. Constitution.

The lobby's weekly tabloid, *The Spotlight* (subtitled "America's Last Real Newspaper. The Voice of the American Majority"), has a circulation of over 100,000. Its writers are populists and antielitists, opposed the Gulf War, and often cite corruption and conspir-

acies in high places. Conspiracies have been attributed to the Rockefellers, the Trilateral Commission, Bilderberg, and the CIA. Recent contributors have suggested that Arab terrorists shot down TWA Flight 800 and have accused the federal government of sequestering billions of dollars seized from U.S. taxpayers to be handed over to Israel. In the year 2000, *The Spotlight* supported the candidacy of Pat Buchanan for president.

Carto currently resides in the Washington, D.C. area.

See also: EXTREMISTS

For Further Information

Carto, Willis A. Letter to the Editor Regarding *Denying the Holocaust. Washington Post*, August 15, 1993, Book World section, p. 10.

Mintz, Frank P. *The Liberty Lobby and the American Right: Race, Conspiracy, and Culture.* Westport, CT: Greenwood Press, 1985.

The Spotlight, *http://www.spotlight.org*

Winston, Andrew S. *"Science in the Service of the Far Right: Henry E. Garrett, the IAAEE, and the Liberty Lobby." Journal of Social Issues* 54 (Spring 1998): 179–210.

CATHOLIC WORKER MOVEMENT.

Formed during the Great Depression in 1933, the Catholic Worker Movement (CWM) is "the chief means of spreading the radical Gospel ideal of utopian dissent through activism on behalf of social justice, peace, and nuclear disarmament." CWM's aim is to realize "St. Thomas Aquinas' doctrine of the Common Good, a society where the good of each member is bound to the good of the whole in the service of God." The ideal would be brought first into the American Catholic community, and subsequently into mainstream American life.

DOROTHY DAY and Peter Maurin established the CWM in 1933 in New York City. Maurin, a French-born Catholic, proposed that a system of communal farms and urban houses of hospitality be developed. The houses, usually located in run-down urban areas, provide food, clothing, shelter, and welcome and are operated by unpaid volunteers.

In 1933 Day and Maurin inaugurated their journal, *The Catholic Worker*, which advocates pacifism, destruction of all nuclear weapons, and social justice. Circulation of *The Catholic Worker* peaked at about 150,000 in the early 1930s and then plummeted during the Spanish Civil War and World War II because of its pacifist editorial position. Currently the paper's circulation has recovered to 85,000.

CWM members refuse to serve in the armed forces or pay taxes that support any war effort, and practice civil disobedience. The organization has avoided applying for federal tax-exempt status, because such recognition would restrict the movement's freedom as an independent radical entity. CWM remains small, decentralized, and dedicated to upholding the ideal of personal responsibility and concern for the common good. Over 160 communities (farms and houses of hospitality) currently serve the poor in thirty-five states and in seven foreign countries. Each community is autonomous, and since Day's death in 1980 there has been no central governing director.

CWM has inspired many citizen activists including DANIEL and PHILIP BERRIGAN, CESAR CHAVEZ, and Roger LaPorte, a Hunter College student who torched himself in front of the UN building in November 1965 as a personal protest against the Vietnam War. Mahatma Gandhi, MARTIN LUTHER KING JR. and Cesar Chavez are among its models of nonviolent resistance.

CWM headquarters is in New York City. The size of its membership is indeterminate. A year's subscription to *The Catholic Worker* (6 issues per year) costs twenty-five cents.

See also: ANTIWAR/ANTI–NUCLEAR WEAPONS MOVEMENT

For Further Information

Catholic Worker, *http://www.catholicworker.org/*

Coles, Robert, and John Erickson. *A Spectacle unto the World: The Catholic Worker Movement.* New York: Viking, 1974.

Piehl, Mel. *Breaking Bread: The Catholic Worker and the Origin of Catholic Radicalism in America.* Philadelphia: Temple University Press, 1982.

CATO INSTITUTE. The Cato Institute, an internationally recognized public policy research foundation, is an activist think tank staffed by approximately eighty researchers, several of whom are among the country's leading advocates of free markets and limited government. The Cato Institute was founded in 1977 by Edward H. Crane, an activist with the Libertarian Party in California, and Charles G. Koch, owner of an oil, natural gas, and land management firm.

During 1976, while Crane was in Washington working with the Libertarian Party presidential campaign, he was impressed by the influence being wielded by think tanks such as the Brookings Institution and the AMERICAN ENTERPRISE INSTITUTE. Upon returning to San Francisco, he started his own institute, named for "Cato's Letters," libertarian pamphlets that helped provide a philosophical rationale for the American Revolution.

After the Cato Institute moved to Washington in 1981, it began to concentrate on public policy, setting forth options consistent with the principles of limited government, individual liberty, and peace. It projects its stands on key issues through an ambitious program of books and other publications, conferences, and seminars designed to illuminate private sector, voluntary solutions to social and economic problems. Cato supports privatization of the U.S. Postal Service, Social Security, and the World Bank; withdrawal from the United Nations; creation of medical savings accounts; strict term limitations; a national sales tax to replace the personal income tax; and abolition of the U.S. Department of Education. It also endorses the legalization of drugs and the lifting of economic sanctions on Cuba. Cato opposes U.S. entanglements in foreign wars and policing actions, limits on political campaign contributions, and all efforts to control global warming. Cato Institute scholars contend that fear of global warming is unfounded and that American air quality has actually improved because of new technology and not because of federal regulation. Cato recommends abandonment of the Clean Water Act and the Endangered Species Act.

Cato has had an impact on public opinion and congressional decisions. In 1994 Institute scholars were invited to discuss the Clinton health care plan on over a hundred television talk shows, and Cato's proposals on balancing the federal budget and welfare reform were cited and used by the 106th Congress.

Currently Cato has about seventy-five staff, fifty-five adjunct scholars, and fourteen fellows, including Representative Henry Hyde (R-IL), economists Arthur Laffer and Milton Friedman, Charles Murray and Richard Herrnstein (co-authors of *The Bell Curve*, controversial because of its argument for the connection between intelligence and race), and political commentator George Will. The *Cato Forum*, a one-hour public affairs show, is aired weekly on National Empowerment Television.

The Institute publishes *Cato Journal, Regulation* magazine (quarterly), the *Cato Policy Report* (bimonthly), *Policy Analysis* (public policy reports), and the *Cato Handbook for Congress*, an annual published since 1995. Cato maintains seven different Web sites: two main sites, in Spanish and English, and subsidiary sites focusing on Social Security, free trade, libertarianism, individual rights, and Cato University programs. Cato Institute's headquarters building is in Washington, D.C., and Edward H. Crane is president.

See also: ACTIVIST THINK TANKS

For Further Information

Cato Institute, *www.cato.org*; *www.socialsecurity. org*; *www.freetrade.org*; *www.libertarianism. org*; *www.individualrights.org*; *www.elcato.org*; *www.cato-university.org*

Crane, Edward H., and David Boaz, eds. *Cato Handbook for Congress: Policy Recommendations for the 106th Congress*. Washington, DC: Cato Institute, 2001.

Hellebust, Lynn. *Think Tank Directory: A Guide to Nonprofit Public Policy Research Organizations*. Washington, DC: Government Research Service, 1996.

CATT, CARRIE LANE CHAPMAN (1859–1947). Reformer, suffragist leader, pacifist, and feminist Carrie Chapman Catt was born in Ripon, Wisconsin, in 1859. In 1866 the family moved to northern Iowa. A turning point in her life came when she asked why her mother was not voting and was told that this civic duty was too important to be placed in women's hands. Her father opposed her wish to go to college, so Catt paid her own way, graduating with a B.S. from Iowa State College's General Science Course for Women in 1880. She did this in three years and was valedictorian and the only woman in her class. In 1881 she was appointed principal in Mason City, Iowa. Two years later she had become superintendent of schools.

In 1885 Catt married a newspaper publisher who died of typhoid after they had moved to San Francisco. She then married a previous schoolmate, George William Catt, after returning to Iowa, and became active in the National American Woman Suffrage Association (NAWSA). Her new husband supported woman suffrage and signed a prenuptial agreement that stipulated that she would be entirely free to work for suffrage for four months each year.

In 1900 Catt was hand picked by Susan B. Anthony to be her successor as NAWSA president. She resigned in 1904 to care for her ailing husband, who died in 1905. During the next decade, she traveled to Europe and organized the International Woman Suffrage Alliance. In 1915 she was asked to return to lead NAWSA, which had been faltering during her absence. In 1916, at the annual NAWSA convention in Atlantic City, Catt unveiled her "Winning Plan"—a campaign operating simultaneously on the federal and state levels. She refused to let World War I serve as a pretext for sidetracking the suffrage initiative. Although she supported the troops during the war, her singleminded devotion to her cause resulted in her being attacked by antisuffrage groups as lacking patriotism and being pro-German.

After vigorous lobbying, Congress reluctantly passed the suffrage amendment in

1919. Catt spent two months in Tennessee, the last state needed to ratify the amendment. Tennessee approved the Nineteenth Amendment by a margin of one vote, and it was officially adopted on August 26, 1920. Its passage was Catt's major life accomplishment, and it is to her, more than any other single activist, that American women owe their right to vote.

She went on to found the LEAGUE OF WOMEN VOTERS, serving as its honorary president for the rest of her life. In 1923 she published *Woman Suffrage and Politics: The Inner Story of the Suffrage Movement*. In her last years, she supported the League of Nations, fought against child labor, and advocated medical aid for pregnant women. She died of heart failure in New Rochelle, New York, on March 9, 1947. Her life's mission is best stated in her own motto: "To the wrongs that need resistance, / To the right that needs assistance / To the future in the distance, / Give yourselves."

See also: WOMEN'S ISSUES

For Further Information

Fowler, Robert Booth. *Carrie Catt: Feminist Politician*. Boston: Northeastern University Press, 1986.

Library of Congress, Manuscript Division. *The Blackwell Family, Carrie Chapman Catt, and the National American Woman Suffrage Association*. Washington, DC: Library of Congress, Manuscript Division, 1985.

Van Vorris, Jacqueline. *Carrie Chapman Catt: A Public Life*. New York: Feminist Press of the City University of New York, 1987.

CENTER FOR AUTO SAFETY. The Center for Auto Safety (CAS) is an independent nonprofit organization that monitors government agencies charged with regulating the automobile industry. The CAS supports safety standards, takes part in the rule-making procedures of the National Highway Traffic Safety Administration and the Federal Highway Administration, and occasionally takes legal action on behalf of consumers. CAS was formed in 1970 by CONSUMERS UNION and RALPH NADER in conjunction with Nader's attack on the Chevrolet Corvair's faulty design, highlighted in *Unsafe at Any Speed*. CAS provides consumers with a voice in Washington and helps owners of cars with manufacturing defects to seek redress.

Clarence M. Ditlow III has been CAS executive director since 1976. He spearheaded the campaign to impose the first fuel-economy standards on new cars, still an ongoing battle.

The CAS victories of the 1970s were followed by the lean years of the Reagan administration, which opposed federal regulations. Consumer advocates contend that during the 1980s, standards for passive restraints, tire quality grading, and auto recall laws were gutted.

Among the many CAS campaigns, the one for mandated installation of dual airbags took longest to win. Originally proposed by CAS in 1970, this requirement finally took effect in 1994 as a result of former Secretary of Transportation Elizabeth Dole's 1984 ruling. CAS counts among its accomplishments enactment of lemon laws to protect the public in every state, recalls of 7 million Chevrolets with defective engine mounts (1971), and GM's forced admission that Buicks, Oldsmobiles, and Pontiacs had been fitted with Chevrolet engines without their purchasers' knowledge. According to Ditlow, in a declaration delivered on behalf of plaintiffs in a class action suit against Ford Motor Company heard in Superior Court of California Docket #763785–2 (1999), the "CAS played a substantial role in the three largest recalls ever: seven million Chevrolets for defective engine mounts in 1971; 15 million Firestone 500 tires for tread separation in 1978; and 3.7 million Evenflo infant and child seats with defective latch buckles in 1990." In 1992 the CAS petitioned the National Highway Traffic Safety Administration to recall all Renault, Volkswagen, BMW, and Isuzu vehicles because their plastic heater cores allegedly rupture, "sending scalding fluid and vapor over the occupants, often causing severe burns."

The CAS serves as a clearinghouse for consumers who want to obtain information on particular vehicles or who wish to report safety problems. Annually it processes about 40,000 letters and phone calls from consumers.

CAS publishes *The Lemon Book*, a new edition of which is produced about once a decade. It also puts out a *Car Book*, assessing new models each year, formerly published by the Federal Department of Transportation but discontinued during the Reagan years. Other publications include the quarterly *Lemon Times*, a citizen action manual for lemon owners. The Washington, D.C.–based CAS has about 20,000 members.

See also: CONSUMER RIGHTS AND SAFEGUARDS

For Further Information

Raymond Bonner. "Ford Paying Millions in Suits." *New York Times*, February 13, 1983.

Center for Auto Safety, *http://www.autosafety.org*

Hershey, Robert D., Jr. "Center for Auto Safety's Point Man." *New York Times*, February 2, 1991.

Wald, Matthew L. "Detroit May Not Like Him, but He's the Crash Dummy's Friend." *New York Times*, October 16, 1997.

CENTER FOR HEALTH, ENVIRONMENT AND JUSTICE. Begun in 1981, the Center for Health, Environment and Justice (CHEJ), formerly the Citizens Clearinghouse for Hazardous Waste, is the only national environmental organization started and led by grassroots organizers. Its founder, LOIS GIBBS, has been nicknamed the "mother of Superfund," the federal program established in 1980 to clean up hazardous waste sites.

Gibbs, a former homemaker and president of the Love Canal Homeowners Association in Niagara Falls, represented 900 families who won relocation benefits between 1978 and 1980 after learning that their neighborhood was adjacent to 121,000 tons of buried toxic waste. Gibbs coordinated a community health survey that confirmed that 56 percent of children born within the area suffered from birth defects and that families had abnormally high incidences of cancer, miscarriages, and other health problems. Initially, the main focus of CHEJ was on helping community groups suffering from the effects of toxic dumps. Today it works on a broad range of issues, including air pollution, incinerators, medical waste, radioactive waste, pesticides, Dioxin exposure, sewage, and industrial pollution.

The federal Superfund program, established in 1980 to clean up waste sites, was the first direct outgrowth of Gibbs's work at Love Canal. In 1989 her "McToxics" campaign convinced McDonalds to stop using Styrofoam and commit $100 million toward efforts to stop its use in restaurants, schools, and public and private institutions. In its ongoing "Kick Ash" campaigns, CHEJ assists local activists in resisting deregulation of solid waste incinerator ash.

Other efforts include promotion of new right-to-know laws so that people can find out which chemicals are being stored or disposed of in their communities. The group has also widely publicized studies that document the deliberate siting of unsafe facilities in localities with concentrations of low-income, uneducated, minority, or rural populations.

Following the model originated by SAUL DAVID ALINSKY, CHEJ conducts leadership training, assists lobbying group formation, and encourages its members to ally themselves with other community organizations to develop sufficient clout to pressure their elected officials to take action.

CHEJ's headquarters office is in Falls Church, Virginia. Lois Gibbs is executive director. The group has approximately 20,000 individual members. Publications for members include the *Environmental Health Monthly Newsletter* and *Everyone's Backyard*, a bimonthly journal.

See also: ENVIRONMENT

For Further Information

Center for Health, Environment and Justice, *http://www.chej.org/*

Gibbs, Lois Marie. *Dying from Dioxin: A Citizen's*

Guide to Reclaiming Our Health and Rebuilding Democracy. Boston: South End Press, 1995.
———. *Love Canal: The Story Continues.* Stony Creek, CT: New Society, 1998.

CENTER FOR SCIENCE IN THE PUBLIC INTEREST.

The Center for Science in the Public Interest (CSPI), formed in 1971, is the leading organization representing consumers in the area of food safety and nutrition problems at the national level. Three scientists who had been affiliated with RALPH NADER's Center for the Study of Responsive Law were its founders.

The Center for Science in the Public Interest was originally set up as a public interest group that would motivate other scientists to focus their expertise on critical social issues. Initially, CSPI's interests were very broad, including food, toxic chemicals and energy, highways and air pollution, nuclear power, asbestos, mercury, lead, and other potential health hazards. In 1977 CSPI started concentrating exclusively on food and nutrition. Then, in the early 1980s, U.S. governmental policies on alcohol and its marketing, labeling, and taxation were added as a secondary CSPI focus.

Today, CSPI is the most influential nonprofit education and advocacy organization committed to improving the safety and nutritional quality of food sold in the United States. CSPI monitors current research and the federal agencies that oversee food safety, trade, and nutrition. It also educates the public about nutrition, eating habits, food additives, organic additives, and links between diet and disease.

The CSPI was instrumental in winning passage of the landmark Nutrition Labeling and Education Act of 1990, legislation that mandates clear and useful nutrition data on practically all food labels, placement of warning labels on alcoholic beverage containers, and the banning of deceptive food claims. CSPI combines research, education, and advocacy. Since 1980 an in-house legal staff has been actively working to enforce existing laws and for the adoption of new regulations or legislation.

CSPI first won public attention through its book, *Nutrition Scoreboard* (1973), which put into the spotlight the high amounts of fat and sugar in many foods. Its 1983 publication, *The Fast-Food Guide*, exposed the nutritional shortcomings of foods offered by fast-food restaurants, attacking Kung Pao Chicken for being the equivalent of four McDonald's Quarter Pounders and referring to fettuccine Alfredo as a "heart attack on a plate." In response, after considerable prodding and negative publicity, the food chains started offering the public detailed nutritional breakdowns on their menus. More recently, CSPI has opposed the use of Olestra, a synthetic fat manufactured by Procter and Gamble, because of users' adverse reactions, for example, gastrointestinal disorders suffered after ingestion.

Although not originally a grassroots organization, the CSPI has become the key citizens' tool in influencing federal policy on food products and alcoholic beverages and in representing the public interest before legislative, regulatory, and judicial bodies. Through its *Nutrition Action Health Letter*, published ten times a year, it reaches over 950,000 people (more than any other health newsletter) that it can mobilize to contact legislators regarding issues it decides to pursue.

CSPI, headquartered in Washington, D.C., has approximately 1 million members. Michael F. Jacobson, an MIT microbiologist, is current executive director.

See also: CONSUMER RIGHTS & SAFEGUARDS

For Further Information

Burros, Marian. "Heroes of Nutrition or Just Plain Zealots?" *New York Times*, May 29, 1996, p. B1.
Center for Science in the Public Interest, *http://www.cspinet.org*
Heylin, Michael. "Center for Science in the Public Interest: A Watchdog at the Kitchen Door." *Chemical and Engineering News* 7, no. 9 (1996): 25–29.

Jacobson, Michael F., and Sarah Fritschner. *The Fast-Food Guide: What's Good, What's Bad, and How to Tell the Difference.* New York: Workman Publishing, 1991.

——. *Marketing Madness: A Survival Guide for a Consumer Society.* Boulder, CO: Westview Press, 1995.

Rocawich, Linda. "Michael Jacobson." *Progressive*, September 1994, pp. 30–34.

CFIDS ASSOCIATION OF AMERICA.

The CFIDS Association of America, founded in 1987 by Marc M. Iverson in Charlotte, North Carolina, is the nation's leading non-profit organization dedicated to conquering CFIDS (chronic fatigue and immune dysfunction syndrome), also known as chronic fatigue syndrome (CFS), and myalgic encephalomyelitis (ME). The Association supports research, education, and public policy advocacy programs.

CFIDS is a debilitating and serious illness that afflicts over 500,000 adults in the United States. It involves incapacitating fatigue, muscle and joint pain, impaired memory or concentration, sore throat, tender lymph nodes, and sleep that does not refresh. One of several illnesses such as the Gulf War syndrome, Lyme disease, lupus, and postpolio syndrome, it is frequently misunderstood and derogatorily dismissed by much of the general public as being the "Yuppie disease" or, at worst, a minor ailment. With more than 23,000 members and a mailing list of nearly 200,000, the CFIDS Association continuously updates Congress on the status of the disease and lobbies for supportive funding by the National Institutes of Health, the Communicable Disease Center, the Department of Education, the Food and Drug Administration, and other agencies.

In 1993 the group initiated its C-ACT program involving over 2,000 members who walk the halls of Congress, write, or phone in personal requests for legislative support of increased and better-directed research funding. The Association has held annual Lobby Days since 1994 to heighten legislators' awareness and has attracted the attention of the media, including CBS, NBC, CNN, the *Wall Street Journal, Newsweek,* and *USA Today.*

Although eradication of CFIDS remains the Association's top priority, it has a public policy program that has successfully pled for federal dollars, which have quadrupled since the organization's inception. CFIDS members receive a subscription to *The CFIDS Chronicle* and advance notice of major media, political, or medical events.

CFIDS Association headquarters is in Charlotte, North Carolina. K. Kimberley Kenney is executive director; Marc M. Iverson is president.

See also: DISABLED PERSONS' RIGHTS

For Further Information

CFIDS Association of America, *http://www.cfids.org*

Overton, Sharon. "Dance with the Serpent: Chronic Fatigue Syndrome Can't Defeat One Charlotte Man." *News and Observer* (Raleigh, North Carolina), November 25, 1990, pp. E1–4.

CHAVEZ, CESAR ESTRADA (1927–1993).

Born near Yuma, Arizona, the son of Mexican American migrants, Cesar Chavez broke through the bonds of poverty and prejudice to form America's first successful union of farm workers. Blending the nonviolent resistance of Mahatma Gandhi with the organizational skills of his mentor, SAUL DAVID ALINSKY, Chavez led the battle to unionize the fields and orchards of California.

During his early years Chavez lived on the family's farm. When he was ten years old, in the depths of the Great Depression, his parents fell behind on their mortgage payments and lost their farm. They moved to California, where they became migrant workers.

After a two-year service stint in the navy during World War II, Chavez returned to Delano, California. In the early 1950s, Saul Alinsky recruited Chavez to assist him in organizing a Mexican American political bloc by conducting voter registration drives and training workers in how to deal with farm

United Farm Workers president Cesar Chavez speaks at a March 1989 press conference. *AP Photo/Alan Greth.*

owners and governmental agencies. In 1958 Chavez resigned from his position with Alinsky's Community Service Organization because of its dominance by non-Hispanic liberals, returned to Delano, and established the National Farm Workers Association.

In the 1950s and 1960s agricultural workers were not covered by federal labor law. Consequently, the farms that employed them had no legal defense against primary and secondary boycotts. This loophole enabled Chavez to organize effective boycotts of grapes, lettuce, and other farm crops in 1962, and to convert the migrants' battle into a national cause célèbre. By 1965 Chavez had organized 1,700 families and persuaded two growers to increase their wages. The next year, his union merged with another one into the United Farm Workers Organizing Committee (UFWOC). After the merger, California's wine grape growers agreed to accept the UFWOC as the collective bargaining agent for grape pickers. When the table grape growers refused to accept this arrangement, Chavez organized a nationwide boycott of California table grapes. He used strikes, pickets, and a 340-mile march from Delano to Sacramento in the struggle to win contracts from growers. By 1970 most table grape growers had conceded and accepted the union. Later that same year, Chavez called for a nationwide boycott of lettuce produced by growers without union contracts. In 1973 the union became the UNITED FARM WORKERS OF AMERICA (UFW), a member union of the AFL-CIO, with Chavez as its president.

In 1983, with Republican George Deukmejian replacing Democrat Edmund G. Brown Jr. as governor of California, the UFW faced increased resistance from growers who had contributed generously to the incoming governor's election campaign. After this point, the migrant farm workers' movement declined even though Chavez's Fast for Life in 1988, the last in a series beginning in 1968, was shared by such celebrities as JESSE JACKSON, Martin Sheen, Emilio Estevez, Danny Glover, Carly Simon, and Whoopi Goldberg.

Although the 1983 change in the governor's office adversely affected the UFW, it was Chavez's autocratic management that did most to undermine its effectiveness. Officials in the UFW field offices were appointed, not elected, by the UFW executive board and were under the direct control of Chavez. In 1993, in an interview with the *Nation*, Aristeo Zambrano, an active unionist fired after a dispute with Chavez, said, "People . . . could see that the union did not belong to the workers, that it was Chavez's own personal business, and that he would run his business as he pleased. Farmworkers were good for boycotting, or walking the picket lines, or paying union dues, but not for leading our union." Chavez's inability to share power ensured the absence of secondary level leadership in the ranks. Nonetheless, Chavez remains justifiably revered for his heroic commitment to social justice, evidenced in his many personal sacrifices.

Chavez was an omnivorous reader, and his office was lined with biographies and books on philosophy, economics, and unionism. His personal style was austere, patterned after the lives of Saint Francis of Assisi and Gandhi. A vegetarian with a weekly salary of $5, he dedicated himself entirely to bettering the lives of exploited farm workers. He said that the "truest act of courage, the strongest act of manliness, is to sacrifice ourselves for others in a totally nonviolent struggle for justice."

Cesar Chavez died in his sleep on April 23, 1993, while on union business in Arizona. Arturo Rodriguez, who succeeded Chavez in May 1993, is the current UFW president.

See also: HISPANIC AMERICAN RIGHTS

For Further Information

Abbott, Cathryn. *Cesar Chavez: Labor Leader.* New York: Vantage Press, 1997.

Bardacke, Frank. "Cesar's Ghost." *Nation*, July 26–August 2, 1993, pp. 130–135.

Griswold del Castillo, Richard. *Cesar Chavez: A Triumph of Spirit.* Norman: University of Oklahoma Press, 1995.

CHAVIS, BENJAMIN FRANKLIN, JR. (1948–).

Born January 22, 1948, in Oxford, North Carolina, Benjamin Franklin Chavis Jr., an African American civil rights leader, led the United Church of Christ Commission for Racial Justice (1985–1993) and directed the NATIONAL ASSOCIATION FOR THE ADVANCEMENT OF COLORED PEOPLE (NAACP) (1993–1994). His great-great-grandfather, John Chavis (1763–1838), was a freed slave who earned a degree in classics at a seminary in New Jersey that later became Princeton University. He returned to North Carolina to teach white children, some of whom later became prominent legislators. According to his great-grandson Benjamin, he may have been killed for teaching white children, a practice that was illegal in North Carolina at that time.

An activist from the start, Chavis joined the NAACP when he was twelve and the next year challenged the whites-only policy in his hometown public library. He participated in the 1963 March on Washington and joined the SOUTHERN CHRISTIAN LEADERSHIP CONFERENCE. He earned a B.A. in chemistry and taught in a high school for a brief time but found it insufficiently challenging. He then worked as a labor organizer for the American Federation of State, County and Municipal Employees.

In 1971, while Chavis was head of the Washington, D.C., field office of the United Church of Christ's Commission for Racial Justice, protests arose against mandated desegregation of the Wilmington, North Carolina, schools. He was sent to Wilmington to lessen the tension, but a series of demonstrations and marches concluded in the exchange of gunfire and the torching of a white-owned store. Chavis was wrongfully convicted and jailed on conspiracy and arson charges (1976–1980) as one of the "Wilmington 10." While incarcerated, he attended Duke University to study for a divinity degree, being escorted to classes in leg irons and handcuffs. Later he earned a doctorate in theology from Howard University.

As an officer of the Commission for Racial Justice, Chavis agitated against locating hazardous waste dumps in poor black regions of the United States. Then Senator Albert Gore praised a report he prepared in 1987, *Toxic Wastes and Race in the United States*, as a landmark study.

When Benjamin Hooks decided to leave his post as executive director of the NAACP, four finalists were in the running to succeed him, including JESSE JACKSON and Chavis. Chavis was elected and served for eighteen months, in 1993 and 1994. When he took the position, the NAACP was being criticized for becoming middle-aged and middle-class and for distancing itself from the needs of young and poor segments of the black community. Chavis combated this perception by traveling to Los Angeles to ease passions raised by the trial of police officers for beating Rodney King, a black motorist. He also acted as a negotiator with the management of Denny's restaurants following the controversy stemming from the chain's alleged refusal to serve blacks. He worked out an agreement that included Denny's pledge of $1 billion over a seven-year period to assist minorities. He also allied himself with black separatist LOUIS FARRAKHAN, leader of the NATION OF ISLAM. Despite his high-visibility efforts attracting 160,000 new and mostly youthful members to the NAACP, his disregard for established NAACP policy favoring racial integration rankled the board. Chavis was fired after it was discovered that he had committed $332,000 in NAACP funds to settle a sexual harassment and discrimination claim against himself, at a time when the organization was already $4.8 million in debt.

In October 1995, Chavis led the Million Man March to Washington, an event organized by Farrakhan. Some 835,000 blacks peacefully participated to demonstrate solidarity among black males and to bring about a spiritual revival that would instill a sense of personal responsibility for improving African Americans' living conditions.

In 1997 Chavis joined the Nation of Islam and changed his name to Benjamin Chavis Muhammad. The United Church of Christ suspended his ministerial credentials, concluding that he "had left the Christian faith." He is currently minister of Muhammad Mosque No. 7 in Harlem, New York.

See also: AFRICAN AMERICAN RIGHTS

For Further Information

Lewis, Neil. "Man in the News: Benjamin Franklin Chavis Jr.; Seasoned by Civil Rights Struggle." *New York Times*, April 11, 1993, sec. 1, p. 20.

Mercadante, Linda A. "Questioning Chavis Muhammad." *Christian Century*, June 4–11, 1997, pp. 548–550.

CHILD AND YOUTH-RELATED ISSUES.

Child and youth-related issues include children's civil rights, access to sufficient health care and nutrition, maternity care and benefits, education from Project Head Start through high school, family day care for working mothers, orphans' and adoptees' rights, safety from harm in violence-prone neighborhoods, teenage pregnancy prevention, and location and return of missing children. Additional concerns include enforcement of child support obligations; protection and counseling of victims of rape, abuse, and incest; AIDS prevention programs; community-based services for at-risk youth; revision of criminal law to prevent underage offenders from being incarcerated with adult criminals; and effective citizenship education.

There are a very limited number of citizen advocacy groups concerned exclusively with child and youth-related issues because children, being minors, are politically powerless and therefore must depend upon adults to wage political battles on their behalf. Unlike seniors, they cannot vote, lobby, wield the power, or spend the money needed to influence elections, legislative behavior, or the quality of health services, education, and other benefits they will receive as they move toward adulthood. In the United States, society expects even the poorest parents to assume total responsibility for bearing, clothing, sheltering, and feeding their children. The result is that on any given day during 1998, 1,827 babies were born with no health insurance, 81 died because of insufficient medical care, and 14 more were killed by guns. The United States may be the only major democracy that takes better care of its seniors than its children.

Jeannette Rankin, the first woman elected to Congress, introduced a child health bill that extended federal maternity and infancy aid to the states. Conservatives viewed the legislation, the Sheppard-Towner Act of 1921, as interference in state affairs and part of an insidious communist plot to undermine family values. The medical profession joined in the attack, and the legislation was allowed to lapse in 1929.

Throughout the first third of the twentieth century, child labor was a concern of social reformers. Although a child labor amendment to the Constitution passed Congress in 1914, farmers and the southern textile industry lobbied against it. By 1950 only twenty-six of the requisite thirty-six states had ratified the amendment. In its stead, President Roosevelt's New Deal produced the Fair Labor Standards Act of 1938, forbidding labor by children under sixteen.

During the 1960s, the civil rights movement and the War on Poverty reawakened the country to the needs of poor children, and Project Head Start and youth employment programs yielded positive results. The Women, Infants, and Children (WIC) program was authorized to improve destitute mothers' and children's health and nutrition. Conservative and libertarian resistance to governmental assistance remains strong. For example, legislation to fund counselors who would make regular visits to the homes of new parents to teach "parenting skills" and monitor homes for possible child abuse was defeated. Opponents feared that government invasion of family privacy would escalate to unprecedented levels.

The dominant figure in the child advocacy field is MARIAN WRIGHT EDELMAN, president of the CHILDREN'S DEFENSE FUND (CDF). Edelman formerly directed the NATIONAL ASSOCIATION FOR THE ADVANCEMENT OF COLORED PEOPLE's Legal Defense and Education Fund in Mississippi and brings to her post a sense of commitment stemming from her childhood as a black in formerly segregated South Carolina and Georgia. The CDF, formed in 1973, is the leading advocate for children, promoting better child care, health services, Head Start, and family support services. CDF's research reports and *State of America's Children Yearbooks* offer thoroughly documented evidence for public and legislative use.

The National Center for Missing and Exploited Children, founded in 1984 by JOHN WALSH, host of the *America's Most Wanted* television show, has developed a very effective search and rescue system to recover children who have disappeared. Based in Alexandria, Virginia, the Center has succeeded in recovering 90 percent of the children it has attempted to locate.

In 1996 Jonah Edelman, one of Marian Wright Edelman's three sons, organized Stand for Children. In contrast to the Children's Defense Fund, which is primarily a research group, Stand for Children, also based in Washington, D.C., lobbies aggressively for children on the state and local levels.

For Further Information

Children's Defense Fund. *The State of America's Children Yearbook, 2000.* Boston: Beacon Press, 2000.

"Families in Poverty: A Symposium." *Journal of Family Issues* 17 (September 1996): 588–721.

National Conference of State Legislatures. *1997 State Legislative Summary: Children, Youth and Family Issues.* Denver: NCSL, 1998.

CHILDREN'S DEFENSE FUND. The Children's Defense Fund (CDF) is a nonprofit lobbying organization founded in 1973 by MARIAN WRIGHT EDELMAN and designed to get people talking about, voting for, and involved in children's issues. It monitors programs and policies for children and youth, particularly poor and minority children. Its interests include health care, education, child care, job training and employment, and family support. *The State of America's Children*, an annual CDF publication, provides comprehensive, thoroughly researched data on the plight of America's children. CDF advocates free immunization shots, nutrition programs, health insurance for all children, and day care programs for poor children. The organization is committed to the guiding principle that "no child be left behind."

CDF was prominent in a three-year campaign to get a child care bill through Congress. The 1990 enactment was the first such measure passed by Congress since 1971, and researchers have confirmed that, since its inception, American children's math and science proficiency, immunization, and infant survival rates have all increased. CDF has built up a strong Washington-based organization and strategic coalitions, alliances with state and local groups, and service-oriented programs. Leadership training sessions are conducted for the CDF at writer

Alex Haley's former Tennessee farm. Since the 1980s, the CDF has helped focus national attention on the problem of teen pregnancy.

The Democrats lost control of Congress in the 1994 elections, and many were replaced by Republicans determined to dismantle federal welfare programs and transfer to the states guarantees of essential support for children. In response, CDF mobilized 200,000 people to come to the Lincoln Memorial in Washington on June 1, 1996, and stage a "Stand Up for Children" protest against the pending federal actions. Almost 3,000 organizations joined in exhorting President Bill Clinton to hold the liberal line, contending that only the federal government can give necessary assurances to children. CDF lost its battle when the president signed the bill, cutting $54 billion from food stamp and other welfare programs and fulfilling his pledge to "end welfare as we know it."

In response to criticism that CDF had "strong morals but weak muscles" because of its lack of grassroots support, Jonah Martin Edelman, one of Marian Wright Edelman's three sons and a co-organizer of the June 1 protest, formed an affiliate group, Stand for Children. Stand for Children sponsors annual "Stand for Children Days" throughout the country each June 1, to which thousands come to promote CDF issues. Stand for Children hopes to become as effective in promoting children's issues as the NATIONAL RIFLE ASSOCIATION and the AMERICAN ASSOCIATION OF RETIRED PERSONS have been in furthering the interests of their respective constituencies.

CDF's *State of America's Children Yearbook* documents what it characterizes as "the descent of huge numbers of children into extreme poverty, sickness, and ignorance." Both organizations have headquarters offices in Washington, D.C. Marian Wright Edelman is CDF president. Jonah Martin Edelman is executive director of Stand for Children.

See also: CHILD AND YOUTH-RELATED ISSUES

For Further Information

Children's Defense Fund, *http://www. childrensdefense.org*
Frankel, Bruce. "Torch Bearer." *People Weekly* 47 (May 26, 1997): 121–123.
Kosterlitz, Julie. "Not Just Kid Stuff." *National Journal*, November 19, 1988: p. 2934.
Serafini, Marilyn Werber, "Not a Game for Kids." *National Journal*, September 21, 1996, p. 2011.
Stand for Children, *http://www.stand.org*

CHOICE IN DYING. Choice in Dying, formerly the Euthanasia Society of America, devised the first living wills in 1967 and in its mission statement (2000), says that it is dedicated to "fostering communication about complex end-of-life decisions among individuals, their loved ones and health care professionals. The organization provides advance directives, counsels patients and families, trains professionals, advocates for improved laws, and offers a range of publications and services."

Charles Francis Potter founded the Euthanasia Society of America in New York City in 1938. Potter, a clergyman who had been forced to resign from the Unitarian ministry because of his unorthodox views, was also responsible for establishing the first Humanist Society of New York in 1930. An advocate of women's rights and birth control and an opponent of capital punishment, he set as one of the Euthanasia Society's goals the legalization of euthanasia. He believed that euthanasia would improve the quality of the human species as well as hasten the release of critically ill patients from intense suffering.

Euthanasia or "mercy killing" soon became one of the most controversial topics of the century because it involves serious social, medical, legal, religious, ethical, and economic issues. Before World War II, the Euthanasia Society had advocated involuntary as well as voluntary euthanasia. In 1939 the Society's president, Dr. Foster Kennedy, drafted a bill to "legalize painless killing," which failed to pass the New York State legislature. Kennedy explained that the proposal was intended to eventually legalize euthanasia for "born defectives who are doomed to remain defective, rather than for normal persons who have become miserable through incurable illness." Upon learning about Nazi Germany's monstrous ethnic cleansing of Jews during World War II (the Holocaust), the group quickly discarded its interest in corrective eugenics.

During the 1960s and early 1970s, legalization of passive euthanasia, the withholding or withdrawing of life support systems for the terminally ill, became the primary goal of the group. In 1967 the Society drew up the first living will, a document instructing physicians and relatives to refrain from using extraordinary measures to prolong life in the event of a terminal illness. Within a year, over 100,000 of these enabling documents had been distributed. In 1974 the Society changed its name to Society for the Right to Die to reflect its new emphasis. In 1976 the New Jersey Supreme Court in the Karen Quinlan decision established the primacy of the patient's wishes over the state's duty to preserve life.

By 1989 the Society and its affiliate, Concern for Dying, had over 64,000 active members. The two groups merged in 1991 to become Choice in Dying (CID). A decade later, laws in fifty states supported the right to complete advance directives to forego treatment (living wills) largely because of CID's sixty-two years of activism. Having accomplished this goal, the CID board decided in 1999 to sever its ties to physician-assisted suicide as practiced by JACK KEVORKIAN and promoted by the HEMLOCK SOCIETY. In 2000 CID joined the Partnership for Caring: America's Voices for the Dying, a consortium that works to improve care for dying people and their families, and includes such organizations as the AMERICAN ASSOCIATION OF RETIRED PERSONS, the American Bar Association, and the National Hospice Organization.

Partnership for Caring has its national office in Washington, D.C., and a program office in New York City. Karen Orloff Kaplan is president and chief executive officer of the 50,000-member organization.

See also: DEATH PENALTY AND CHOICE IN DYING

For Further Information

Choice in Dying, *http://www.choices.org*

Hendin, Herbert. *Seduced by Death: Doctors, Patients, and Assisted Suicide.* New York: W. W. Norton, 1998.

Partnership for Caring, *http://www.partnershipforcaring.org*

CHRISTIAN COALITION. Religious broadcaster PAT ROBERTSON founded the Christian Coalition (CC) in 1989 to educate and mobilize Christians to involve themselves in politics and promote the election of moral legislators and enactment of laws supporting traditional family values. Authors of its action plan state that the "Christian Coalition is the largest and most effective grassroots political movement of Christian activists in the history of our nation."

In 1993 the CC headed up a $1.4 million grassroots and media campaign to inform the public of the dangers of the Clinton health plan and to mobilize broad based opposition. Included in the campaign were 300 million postcards to Congress distributed to 60,000 churches, radio ads that aired in forty congressional districts, ads in thirty newspapers, and mail and telephone bank contacts that reached over 1 million voters.

The CC supported the "Contract with America" that former Speaker Newt Gingrich championed in 1994 and proposed its own ten-point "Contract with the American Family," calling on Congress to enact the following moral and social reforms:

1) Allow religious expression in public places; 2) Abolish the Department of Education and give greater power to parents and local communities; 3) Promote parental school choice vouchers; 4) Enact a Parents Rights Amendment to the Constitution; 5) Provide families with a $500 tax credit per child, remove the "marriage penalty" in tax laws and enable homemakers to contribute

up to $2,000 to an IRA; 6) End partial-birth abortions, end use of Medicaid funds for abortion, and cut off federal funding to groups such as Planned Parenthood; 7) Turn over welfare programs to private charities; 8) Restrict pornography on cable television and the Internet; 9) End federal funding for the National Endowment for the Arts and Humanities, the Corporation for Public Broadcasting and the Legal Services Corporation; 10) Support work-study programs for prisoners and victim restitution.

Because of its size and success in affecting the outcomes of 1994 Senate and House races, it was assumed that any viable Republican candidate for president would be forced to favor the right on social issues during primaries before veering back toward the center in order to win the general election.

In 1996 the Coalition distributed 34 million voter guides to inform citizens on candidate positions along with 17 million "Congressional Scorecards" quarterly so that pro-family Americans would know where their elected representatives stood on such key issues as term limits, work requirements for welfare recipients, partial birth abortion, and cuts in National Endowment for the Arts funding. Congress approved two items on the Coalition's action agenda, the balanced budget and a family tax credit.

Executive Director RALPH REED stepped down in 1997 and was replaced by former U.S. Representative Randy Tate (R-WA). That same year, donations declined to $17 million, down from $26.5 million in 1996. In 1998, faced with a 36 percent cut in revenue, CC reduced its staff, dropped its minority outreach program (Samaritan Project), and ceased publication of its four-color membership magazine, *Christian American*.

Nine policy and issue areas were on the CC agenda during the year 2000: abortion, education, foreign policy, gambling, homosexuality, national defense, pornography, religious freedom, and same sex partners. CC displays on its Web site media coverage of recent actions taken affecting prayer in schools and public areas, partial birth abor-

tion, school curricula, Internet gambling, HIV workshops for teens, pay-per-view adult films on cable television, religious rights, and same sex partner benefits.

Distribution of voter pamphlets, especially in churches, resulted in the loss of CC's 501(c)(4) tax-exempt status in 1999. This was because voting records of lawmakers were scored according to stands taken on issues important to CC, a procedure not allowed by the IRS. After Ralph Reed left as executive director in 1997, the organization's strategy of working closely with the Republican Party changed. Its new strategy, "Families 2000," included recruitment of 100,000 volunteers to serve as liaisons between their churches and local CC chapters to assist in mobilization of hundreds of thousands of pro-family activists by November 2000. As part of this plan, CC would distribute more than 70 million voter guides before Election Day 2000.

The Coalition represents over 2.1 million members. CC founder Pat Robertson is President. Christian Coalition headquarters is in Chesapeake, Virginia.

See also: RELIGIOUS RIGHT

For Further Information

Christian Coalition, *www.cc.org*
Watson, Justin. *The Christian Coalition*. New York: St. Martin's Press, 1997.
Wilcox, Clyde, Matthew DeBell, and Lee Sigelman. "The Second Coming of the New Christian Right: Patterns of Popular Support in 1984 and 1996." *Social Science Quarterly* 80 (March 1999): 81–192.

CHRONIC FATIGUE IMMUNE DYSFUNCTION SYNDROME ASSOCIATION OF AMERICA. *See* CFIDS Association of America

CITIZEN ACTION. Citizen Action (CA) was founded in 1979 to promote effective citizen participation in the economic, environmental, and political decisions that affect Americans' daily lives. During its eighteen-year life, CA fought for comprehensive health care, reduced public utility rates, fair taxation, consumer protection from toxic chemicals, equal voting rights, and campaign finance reform.

Citizen Action was a product of the Midwest Academy, a national training center for many political foot soldier organizations, including the NATIONAL ORGANIZATION FOR WOMEN, UNITED FARM WORKERS OF AMERICA, and Nuclear Freeze. Based in Chicago, the Midwest Academy had its origins in the INDUSTRIAL AREAS FOUNDATION, a training ground for citizen activists developed by SAUL DAVID ALINSKY in the 1920s.

Ira Arlook, a student civil rights activist during the 1960s, was Citizen Action's first executive director and continued in that capacity until the Washington headquarters office was shut down in 1997. William Winpisinger, head of the Machinists Union, and William Hutton, director of the NATIONAL COUNCIL OF SENIOR CITIZENS, assisted in CA's organization. Its first national headquarters office was in the International Association of Machinists building in Washington.

CA had a three-dimensional operational strategy: (1) building local and state wide citizens' organizations, (2) ensuring members' commitment in campaigns that focused on personally close, intensely felt economic and quality of life issues; and (3) supporting carefully selected electoral candidates at local, state, and federal levels. Originally CA included five state affiliates: Connecticut Citizen Action Group, Illinois Public Action Council, Massachusetts Fair Share, Ohio Public Interest Campaign, and Oregon Fair Share. When the national organization disbanded in 1997, thirty states had independent groups.

Moving into the 1980s, Citizen Action broadened the scope of its activities from legislative lobbying to the national electoral arena. In 1984 it endorsed Walter F. Mondale's candidacy for president, and in 1986 it supported Democratic candidates for the U.S. Senate in seven states. By that time, CA had built up a powerful network of organizations—many of them coalitions of unions, senior groups, churches, environmentalists, and community organizations. Its cadre included some 1,500 full-time organizers, fundraisers, researchers, and lobbyists. Victories claimed by CA included the cleanup of toxic dumpsites, blockage of utility rate hikes, health care practice reform, and occasional successes in halting deregulation of industry in cases where public health was threatened.

In 1992, during the early days of Bill Clinton's presidency, CA assumed new prominence. CA founder Heather Booth moved to the Democratic National Committee to direct its campaign for a universal health care program. An army of canvassers and phone-bank volunteers was enlisted and 1 million postcards were mailed to the Clinton White House. During this same time, CA was crusading for "a responsible U.S. Congress" and raising money from unions and wealthy Democrats for "independent" television ads. These actions were disapproved by CA's Ohio and Indiana affiliates, whose 650,000 members seceded. More defections followed when it was discovered that the Washington office had accepted contributions from the tobacco and nuclear power industries, two traditional CA foes. The distance between Washington lobbying and local organization priorities widened, with state affiliates preferring to battle bank redlining, health maintenance organization mergers, and threats to telecommunications access in rural areas stemming from federal deregulation.

In the summer of 1995, CA captured public attention by using rented steamrollers for a brash demonstration on behalf of the poor and elderly, parking the mammoth machines near homes of House members whom CA accused of trying to drive Medicare cuts through Congress without scrutiny or debate. CA's strategy succeeded, with the plan failing to gain a veto-proof majority after Congress was flooded with frightened constituents' calls and letters.

In 1997 scandal hit CA at the acme of its influence as a national grassroots organization, when it was a thriving federation of fifteen independent state groups, supported by fifteen smaller affiliates and offices with a total membership of 2 million activists. In 1996 JOHN J. SWEENEY, the head of the AFL-CIO, contributed $1.5 million to CA for political ads to be aired in vulnerable Republican-held districts. It was discovered that CA had served as an illegal conduit for contributions that were funneled to Ron Carey in his campaign against James P. Hoffa for the presidency of the Teamsters Union. The resultant loss of credibility led to the closing of six CA state chapters and the severing of ties to the national office by Ohio and Indiana in 1996 and 1997. Dismissal of the twenty-member national staff followed as large contributors reneged because of CA's allegedly illegal actions. Citizen Action, as a national grassroots organization, ceased to exist by 1998.

For Further Information

Boyte, Harry C., Heather Booth, and Steve Max. *Citizen Action and the New American Populism.* Philadelphia: Temple University Press, 1986.

Jacoby, Mary. "The Sins of a Self-Styled Citizen Lobby." *Weekly Standard*, July 28, 1997, p. 20.

Judis, John B. "Activist Trouble." *American Prospect*, January-February 1998, p. 20.

CITIZENS AGAINST GOVERNMENT WASTE.

Citizens Against Government Waste (CAGW), founded in 1984 by the late industrialist J. Peter Grace and syndicated columnist Jack Anderson, is the largest and most visible waste-fighting citizen action group in the United States. CAGW was created to place in citizen activists' hands the responsibility of carrying out the recommendations of the Grace Commission Report prepared in 1983 at the request of President Reagan. CAGW, though allegedly nonpartisan, is conservatively tinted and stresses tax savings and minimization of federal government functions. Its purpose is to inform the public and to urge Congress to eliminate waste, mismanagement, and inefficiency in its spending.

CAGW's lobbying arm, the Council of Citizens Against Government Waste, has members assigned to each of the 435 congressional districts and 100 senators. Their task is to question purportedly wasteful governmental expenditures and grade how their representatives cast their votes on the floor of the House and Senate. The rating system covers cost containment measures as well as pork barrel votes. Examples cited as extravagant spending include White House staffing, student loan defaults, presidential libraries, dairy price supports and agricultural subsidies, overly intrusive social welfare programs, redundant regulations, the Senate's $490,000 yearly expenditure on barbers' and beauticians' salaries, and a $16 million program to fight fire ants in Texas. To qualify as CAGW targets, appropriations must be requested by only one chamber of Congress, not be specifically authorized or competitively awarded, and not be requested by the president. They must also exceed the president's budget request or the previous year's funding, not be the subject of congressional hearings, and serve only a local or special interest.

CAGW has succeeded in derailing the $13 billion Superconductor Supercollider project, stopping creation of a federal office of technology assessment, killing construction of a Lawrence Welk museum in North Dakota, and stopping various agricultural research projects.

Thomas A. Schatz is president of the 600,000-member CAGW; Jack Anderson is chairman. The headquarters office is in Washington, D.C. The group produces numerous publications. *Government Waste Watch* is the organization's quarterly newspaper, distributed to CAGW members, Congress, and the media. The annual *Congressional Pig Book Summary* contains examples of pork barrel spending that CAGW defines as excessive and irresponsible.

See also: TAX REFORM AND GOVERNMENT EXPENDITURES

For Further Information

Citizens Against Government Waste, *http://www.cagw.org*

Cohn, Jonathan. "Roll Out the Barrel: The Case Against the Case Against Pork." *New Republic*, April 20, 1998, pp. 19–23.

Grace, J. Peter. "Burning Money: The Waste of Your Tax Dollars." Speech given before the Commonwealth Club of California, San Francisco, California, March 19, 1993. *Vital Speeches of the Day* 59 (1 July 1993): 566–569.

CITIZENS CLEARINGHOUSE FOR HAZARDOUS WASTE. *See* Center for Health, Environment and Justice

CITIZENS FOR A BETTER ENVIRONMENT. Founded in 1971, Citizens for a Better Environment (CBE), a winner of numerous court battles with corporations and municipalities, works with residents and community-based organizations to reduce people's exposure to toxic substances in air, water, and land. CBE strives to involve citizens in decision making that affects the health of their environment by conducting public education programs and providing information to local residents and community-based organizations, including minority and low-income urban dwellers. CBE attorneys, scientists, policy analysts, engineers, and community organizers collaborate in this endeavor.

In the 1970s CBE fought to close down nuclear power plants and urged states to develop emergency evacuation plans in case of nuclear accidents. CBE succeeded in forcing businesses to reduce the public's exposure to toxic waste conveyed through inadequate sewage systems. In California, the group collaborated with environmental agencies in negotiating a decrease in the use of ozone-depleting chemicals by the defense industry (e.g., Hughes Aircraft, Rockwell International, General Dynamics, Allied-Signal).

Litigation has always played a prominent role in CBE's activities. In 1994 it won a Supreme Court decision that stopped the city of Chicago's mismanagement of toxic incinerator ash and the shallow burial of radioactive waste, and that enabled the general public to participate in enforcement of federally delegated environmental programs. Other CBE legal action resulted in decreased dumping of toxic waste into the Mississippi River and made corporate decisions more accessible through CBE insistence upon compliance with freedom of information and right-to-know legislation. As a direct result of CBE efforts, such companies as Monsanto, Amoco, Olin, and Laclede Steel have reduced their use of the atmosphere as an invisible dumping ground for poisonous chemical residues. CBE staff have written and helped pass landmark waste management laws in Wisconsin and Illinois and halted construction of new medical waste burners in the Midwest.

CBE's regional offices are located in Chicago, Milwaukee, and Minneapolis, and its membership is about 30,000. Martin Wojcik is CBE chairperson. Tim Rudnicki is Minnesota state director, Marilyn Goris is Wisconsin executive director, and Stefan Noe is Illinois state director. CBE publishes the *Environmental Review*, a quarterly.

See also: ENVIRONMENT

For Further Information

Ahmed, Safir. "Chemicals Spew Out by Tons." *St. Louis Post-Dispatch*, March 2, 1989, Illinois Five Star edition, p. 11.

Briggs, Michael. "High Court: Incinerator Ash Must Be Separated. City Loses Fight, Must Dump Toxic Waste in Special Landfills." *Chicago Sun-Times*, May 3, 1994, Late Sports final edition, p. 5.

Citizens for a Better Environment, *http://www.cbemw.org*

Meersman, Tom. "Group Promotes Voluntary Efforts at Cutting Pollution." *Star Tribune* (Minneapolis), December 28, 1995, Metro edition, p. 1B.

Novak, Tim. "State Asks Judge to Change Ruling on Landfills, Dumps; Community Control of Garbage Is at Stake." *St. Louis Post-Dispatch*, September 6, 1993, Five Star edition, p. 1B.

Stammer, Larry B. "Twenty Firms Assailed for Ozone Depletion." *Los Angeles Times*, June 29, 1992, Metro Desk, p. A3.

CITIZENS FOR EXCELLENCE IN ED-UCATION. Citizens for Excellence in Education (CEE), a division of the National Association of Christian Educators, organized by Robert L. Simonds in 1983, aims "to save Christian children in public schools from atheism, homosexuality, the occult, drugs, children having children, abortion, brainwashing and crippling psychology." Simonds holds B.Th., M.A., and Th.D. degrees and has been a high school principal and an adjunct professor in teacher education at UCLA. CEE is an active challenger of books and curricula that reflect an anti-Christian humanist worldview. The teaching of evolution, drug-abuse prevention programs, and self-esteem curricula are opposed by CEE.

CEE has succeeded in getting its preferred members elected to school boards throughout the country. As of 1994, CEE stated that its efforts had been instrumental in getting 12,625 of its candidates placed on boards within a five-year period. More recently Simonds has been urging CEE members to take their children out of the public schools as soon as possible because "the price in human loss, social depravity and the spiritual slaughter of our young Christian children is no longer acceptable (and certainly never was!)." Parents are being urged to transfer their children to Christian academies or opt for home schooling, with the goal of completing the exodus from public education by 2010.

CEE has an estimated 350,000 members in 1,680 chapters and 878 "Public School Awareness" church committees who monitor and advocate change in local schools. The organization's headquarters is in Costa Mesa, California. Robert L. Simonds is president. Publications include a quarterly newsletter, *Education Newsline*; *President's Report*; a monthly letter focusing on issues and solutions, goals, and new CEE resources; and various booklets denigrating whole language instruction, peer counseling, holistic and outcome-based education along with one titled *How to Elect Christians to Public Office.* CEE's *Issues in Education* weekly radio show airs on 155 stations nationwide.

See also: FALSE FRONT ORGANIZATIONS; RELIGIOUS RIGHT

For Further Information

Galst, Liz. "The Right Fight." *Mother Jones* March–April 1994, p. 58.

Impoco, Jim. "Separating Church and School." *U.S. News & World Report*, April 24, 1995, p. 30.

National Association of Christian Education—Citizens for Excellence in Education, *info@nace-cee.org*

CITIZENS FOR TAX JUSTICE. Citizens for Tax Justice (CTJ), established in 1979, plays a leading role in tax reform, focusing on federal, state, and local tax policies as they impact the nation. Its goals include (1) fair taxes for middle- and low-income families; (2) taxation of the wealthy that reflects their ability to pay; (3) elimination of corporate tax loopholes; (4) adequate funding of health, education, and other important government services; and (5) reduction of the federal debt.

CTJ began as a liberal coalition of public interest and labor groups formed in reaction to California's Proposition 13 (1978), which rolled back assessed values of homes and businesses to 1975 levels, capping property taxes at 1 percent of the property's value. An unintended result was the painful degradation of services provided by government, including hospitals, schools, and libraries. In 1981 Robert S. McIntyre, previously director of RALPH NADER's Tax Reform Research Group, became CTJ's director.

The CTJ played a prominent role in the enactment of the Tax Reform Act of 1986—landmark legislation that limited tax shelters for corporations and the rich and cut taxes for poor and middle-income families. Over the years, CTJ has produced carefully documented reports (e.g., *Money for Nothing: The Failure of Corporate Tax Incentives, 1981–1984* [1986], *130 Reasons Why We Need Tax Reform* [1986], *Inequality and the Federal Budget Deficit* [1991], *Who Pays: A Distributive Analysis of the Tax Systems in All Fifty*

States [1996]. CTJ research revealed that 128 corporations, including General Motors, General Electric, IBM, Anheuser-Bush, and Aetna Life and Casualty, had paid no taxes in 1982. When this information was released to the press, the ire of the public and of the many corporations that were paying high taxes set the stage for a complete overhaul of the federal tax code.

In 1998–1999, Congress attempted to undo changes in the code with legislation that would shift tax burdens from upper-income groups and large corporations to average taxpayers. According to CTJ, the Republicans' proposed ten-year tax cut package would shave only $157 a year off the taxes paid by someone earning a $38,200 salary and reduce public services, while giving someone earning $204,000 annually a $7,520 tax break.

Robert S. McIntyre is Citizens for Tax Justice's director. Its headquarters is in Washington, D.C. Its approximately 2,700 members receive a newsletter and discounts on tax policy publications.

See also: TAX REFORM & GOVERNMENTAL EXPENDITURES

For Further Information

Citizens for Tax Justice, *http://www.ctj.org*
McWilliams, Rita. "The Best and Worst of Public Interest Groups." *Washington Monthly*, March 1988, pp. 19–26.

CLAMSHELL ALLIANCE. The Clamshell Alliance's series of protests against construction of the Seabrook Nuclear Plant in New Hampshire has been memorialized by many as "the Little Big Horn of the antinuclear movement." Founded in 1976 by Elizabeth Boardman, a Quaker activist who ran for Congress in 1962 to publicize her opposition to the Vietnam War, the group took its name from the clam flats that they contended would be ruined by construction of the Seabrook Nuclear Plant.

The battle at Seabrook began when Robert Cushing and Guy Chichester led about 2,000 protesters in a peaceful demonstration against construction of the plant on May Day, 1977. In anticipation of the protest, some 1,800 people had gone through training in nonviolent disobedience arranged through the Quaker-affiliated American Friends Service Committee. Strict discipline and commitment to the cause were evident in the restrained behavior of the protesters. They rallied in small "affinity groups" and refrained from using drugs, fighting, or carrying weapons. When removed from the construction site by the police, they simply went limp and let themselves be carried away, 1,414 of them being arrested.

The Seabrook demonstration was the first massive show of civil disobedience against a nuclear power plant in the United States and was viewed as forerunner of a national movement comparable in spirit to the 1960s civil rights and antiwar movements. On the same weekend, seven other demonstrations were staged at other nuclear sites, including those at San Luis Obispo, California, and Three Mile Island, Pennsylvania. Fourteen months later, a larger group, estimated at 9,000, returned to Seabrook, led by Dr. Benjamin Spock, comedian Dick Gregory, and singers Pete Seeger and Arlo Guthrie. SEA (New Jersey), Catfish (Florida), Sunflower (Kansas), and Crabshell (Washington) were other regional, short-lived antinuclear alliances formed in 1979.

In June 1989, the Clamshell Alliance returned for a third three-day anti-Seabrook rally to protest the long-delayed startup of the plant's first nuclear chain reaction. Although the effort failed, the "clams" could claim partial responsibility for a nationwide halt in nuclear plant construction. In the 1980s, activists won hundreds of New England town meeting votes supporting a nuclear freeze, injected the issue into presidential politics, and helped shape national energy policy. Their efforts, combined with the Three Mile Island and Chernobyl nuclear plant accidents, changed public opinion from support to distrust of nuclear utilities, leading to a moratorium on new plant construction after 1986. In 1994, after losing the Seabrook battle but winning their war, the Clamshell Alliance disbanded.

See also: ANTI–NUCLEAR POWER MOVEMENT

For Further Information

Downey, Gary L. "Ideology and the Clamshell Identity: Organizational Dilemmas in the Anti–Nuclear Power Movement." *Social Problems*, June 3, 1986, pp. 357–373.

Epstein, Barbara Leslie. *Political Protest and Cultural Revolution: Nonviolent Direct Action in the 1970s and 1980s.* Berkeley: University of California Press, 1991.

CLARK, SEPTIMA (1898–1987). Septima Poinsette Clark, influential teacher, community activist, and unsung hero of the civil rights movement, was born May 3, 1898, in Charleston, South Carolina. Her father was a former slave and her mother was freeborn. Active in civil rights for seventy years, she gathered 20,000 signatures in 1918 in a petition to have black teachers hired by the Charleston County School District, and in 1927 led a campaign to equalize teacher salaries in Columbia. After marrying Nerie Clark, a sailor, and moving to Ohio, she bore two children who died during infancy. Clark separated from her husband and returned to South Carolina to teach on Johns Island and later in the Charleston schools. She was dismissed by the Charleston district because of her membership in the NATIONAL ASSOCIATION FOR THE ADVANCEMENT OF COLORED PEOPLE and took a teaching position at the HIGHLANDER FOLK SCHOOL in Tennessee.

At Highlander, Clark developed and headed up the Citizenship School movement in the southeastern United States. She traversed the entire region, readying students for participation in the SOUTHERN CHRISTIAN LEADERSHIP CONFERENCE and converting illiterate and passive blacks into voter-activists, armed with a new awareness of their constitutional rights and ability to shape their individual destinies. Her ability to spot potential leaders within the black community and awaken a passionate commitment and the self-empowerment to effect social change became legendary, so much so that she was dubbed the "Mother Conscience" of the SCLC. Those she worked with and taught included RALPH DAVID ABERNATHY, STOKELY CARMICHAEL (Kwame Turé), MARTIN LUTHER KING JR., JOHN L. LEWIS, and Andrew Young.

Clark received the Race Relations Award from the National Education Association and a Living Legacy Award from President Jimmy Carter in 1979. She died December 15, 1987, on Johns Island.

See also: AFRICAN AMERICAN RIGHTS

For Further Information

Clark, Septima. *Echo in My Soul.* New York: Dutton, 1962.

———. *Ready from Within.* Navarro, CA: Wild Tree Press, 1986.

Gyant, LaVerne, and Deborah P. Atwater. "Septima Clark's Rhetorical and Ethnic Legacy." *Journal of Black Studies* vol. 26 (May 1996): 577–593.

CLEAN WATER ACTION. Clean Water Action (CWA) is a leading force in the grassroots movement against toxic pollution of communities' drinking water, playing a major role in development of the Clean Water Act, legislation to create the Superfund for Toxic Cleanup, and other important pieces of protective legislation.

Named Fisherman's Clean Water Action Project from its founding in 1971 until 1975, CWA was organized by RALPH NADER to recruit fishermen to the antipollution cause. Because their livelihood and health were being put at risk by water pollution, which had killed 41 million fish in 1969 (up from 6 million in 1960), they, more than any other group, could be counted on to take corrective action. Today, CWA works at local, state, and federal levels for clean, safe, affordable water, using scientific research, grassroots activism, and legal expertise to achieve its goals. Its agenda includes prevention of health-threatening pollution, creation of environmentally safe businesses, and stimulation of citizen action.

In 1977 CWA negotiated new enforcement and incentive provisions in the Clean Water Act that reduced pollution by setting standards for toxic discharges. And in 1987 it mustered sufficient votes to override President Reagan's veto of the 1987 Clean Water Act reauthorization.

Representative Bud Shuster (R-PA) introduced a "Dirty Water Bill" in 1995 that would have scaled back protections for wetlands and permitted industry to dump more toxins and raw sewage. CWA's public education campaign succeeded in killing the Shuster bill, and members of Congress who had voted for it were singled out for negative publicity, resulting in twenty-one of twenty-three incumbents losing their reelection bids in 1996.

Currently CWA is monitoring bills that deal with beach water quality testing and provisions for notification when waters are unsafe; control of pollution from animal feeding operations; and increased accountability of polluters to citizens through right-to-know legislation and payment for violations. Other issues that concern CWA include EPA energy efficiency programs, under attack because of budgetary caps and congressional hostility to global warming prevention measures; protection of wetlands; and continuation of federal standards for water-saving plumbing fixtures.

At the state level, CWA affiliates have been active from coast to coast. They have fought against use of the ocean as a garbage dump in New Jersey, limited lethal mercury emissions from incinerators and power plants in Massachusetts, saved streams from contamination in Maryland, and worked to stem increases in pollutants released by New England oil-burning power plants.

Clean Water Action national headquarters is in Washington, D.C. The organization has about 700,000 members. David Zwick is CWA president. Members receive the *Clean Water Action News*, a newsletter, and frequent reports on CWA actions.

See also: ENVIRONMENT

For Further Information

Allen, Scott. "Air Pollution Leaps at N.E. Power Plants." *Boston Globe*, April 6, 1999, City edition, Metro/Region section, p. A1.

Clean Water Action, *http://www.cleanwateraction.org*

Narus, Bob. "The Ocean as a Garbage Dump." *New York Times*, February 9, 1986, Late City final edition, sec. 11NJ, p. 1.

Vogel, Mike. "Congress Is Blasted for Deep Cuts in Water-Quality Funds." *Buffalo News*, October 14, 1995, Final edition, p. 14A.

COALITION TO STOP GUN VIOLENCE.

Founded in 1974, the Coalition to Stop Gun Violence (CSGV) is composed of forty-five civic, professional, and religious organizations as well as individual members who "seek to ban handguns and assault weapons from importation, manufacture, sale and transfer by the general American public, with reasonable exceptions made for police, military, security personnel, gun clubs where guns are secured on club premises, [and] gun dealers trading in antique and collectable firearms kept and sold in inoperable condition." Originally called the National Coalition to Ban Handguns, its name change defines its broadened commitment to combat the epidemic of gun violence in the United States.

Exempt from the proposed ban are shotguns and rifles used in hunting. The group would license gun owners and limit handgun purchases to one per month for gun owners, raise the cost of gun dealers' licenses, increase taxes on handguns and ammunition to pay for health costs associated with firearms, and impose strict legal liability on firearms manufacturers and dealers.

Besides its 120,000 individual members, CSGV has enlisted such organizations as the AMERICAN JEWISH CONGRESS, American Psychiatric Association, Child Welfare League of America, Presbyterian Church (U.S.A.), and U.S. Conference of Mayors.

As is the case with other 501(c)(4) organizations, which can lobby individual legislators but cannot accept tax-exempt contributions, CSGV has a 501(c)(3) affiliate that can solicit tax-exempt contributions to support its research and public education programs. This latter organization, the Educational Fund to End Handgun Violence, was established in 1978. The Fund administers a "Hands Without Guns" program for school children and maintains a firearm litigation clearinghouse. CSGV engages in vigorous lobbying at the federal and state levels and provides technical support to allied organizations. It is currently building a Cease-fire Action Network to step up its impact on political decision making. The Coalition's headquarters is in Washington, D.C.; its current president is Michael K. Beard.

See also: GUN OWNERSHIP RIGHTS/GUN CONTROLS

For Further Information

Capital Research Center. *Gun Control: Is the Tide Turning? Battleground Shifts to the States.* Washington, DC: Capital Research Center, 1996.
Coalition to Stop Gun Violence, *http://www.gunfree.org*

COMMON CAUSE. Common Cause, established in 1970 by JOHN W. GARDNER, is an uncommonly successful "nonpartisan citizens' lobby dedicated to fighting for open, honest, and accountable government at the national, state, and local level." Gardner was former secretary of health, education and welfare under the Lyndon B. Johnson administration. The concept for Common Cause grew out of the Urban Coalition Action Council, which Gardner chaired in 1969–1970.

Gardner envisioned a movement empowered by grassroots lobbyists reinforced with professional counterparts on Capitol Hill. Within a year after its formation, Common Cause had recruited over 100,000 citizen activists and its agenda expanded to include cessation of the Vietnam War, reform of the campaign finance system, and espousal of civil rights, ethics, and open government.

Since its founding, Common Cause has played a prominent role in winning passage of legislation enabling eighteen-year-olds to vote, helping to ensure congressional passage of the Equal Rights Amendment, and mandating disclosure of major political campaign contributions. The Freedom of Information Act, enactment of open meetings legislation in many of the states, the strengthening of environmental laws, and scrapping of the congressional seniority system can be credited in large part to Common Cause. The group's major unattained goal remains campaign finance reform. This has proven dauntingly difficult to reach because money paves the way to politicians' victories at the polls. Common Cause is attempting to get elected officials to commit an unnatural act—pass legislation that will benefit opponents and reduce their built-in advantage as incumbents.

Consistent with its commitment to accountability, the entire Common Cause membership annually reviews, votes, and prioritizes needed reforms and legislation in Issue Agenda Polls. Volunteer members handle the telephone network, media relations, resource development, monitoring of legislative activity, and other supportive functions.

Membership, currently about 250,000, peaked at 320,000 during the Watergate scandal when there was public clamor for the impeachment of President Nixon. The organization is headquartered in Washington, D.C. Past chairmen have included John Gardner, Archibald Cox, and Edward Cabot. Derek Bok is current chair; Ann McBride has been president since 1995.

See also: LIBERAL ACTIVISM

For Further Information

Common Cause, *www.commoncause.org*
Gardner, John W. *In Common Cause.* New York: W. W. Norton, 1972.
McFarland, Andrew S. *Common Cause: Lobbying in the Public Interest.* Chatham, NJ: Chatham House, 1984.
Rothenberg, Lawrence S. *Linking Citizens to Government: Interest Group Politics at Common Cause.* Cambridge, England: Cambridge University Press, 1992.

COMMUNITIES ORGANIZED FOR PUBLIC SERVICE (COPS). *See* Cortés, Ernesto, Jr.

CONCERNED WOMEN FOR AMERICA.

Concerned Women for America (CWA) states that it is "the nation's largest pro-family women's organization composed of over 600,000 women nationwide. CWA seeks to preserve and protect Biblical values among all citizens, first through prayer, then education, and finally by influencing society, thereby reversing the decline in moral values in our nation." Beverly LaHaye founded the group in 1979 to combat passage of the Equal Rights Amendment and as an alternative to the politically liberal NATIONAL ORGANIZATION FOR WOMEN. In her summary of the CWA's purpose, LaHaye says that "she knew the feminists' anti-God, anti-family rhetoric did not represent her beliefs, nor those of the vast majority of women."

CWA supports voluntary prayer in schools, has testified on behalf of Supreme Court nominees Robert Bork and Clarence Thomas at Senate Judiciary Committee hearings, and opposes funding of the National Endowment for the Humanities. Grassroots activity in most states is coordinated by a CWA area representative and a steering committee. The group monitors state legislation, organizes Prayer/Action chapters and coordinates the "535" program, CWA's citizens' congressional lobbying program.

During the final months of the ERA campaign in 1982, CWA members prayed weekly and interpreted its failure to achieve ratification as a sign from God. The group has also taken policy positions opposing those taken by the AMERICAN CIVIL LIBERTIES UNION (ACLU) in suits involving freedom of speech, prayer in the schools, and political campaign financing. CWA opposes sex education that is not abstinence-based and antidrug and alcohol abuse programs that center on building self-esteem. CWA's legal team has won a Supreme Court decision upholding the legality of state benefits for religious education and has succeeded in lessening barriers to religious organizations' access to public school facilities. In several cases, CWA has convinced school boards to adopt policies that condemn extended and lesbian/gay families. Consequently, many school districts have altered their policies to ward off the possibility of attack.

CWA publications include *Family Voice*, a monthly, *Issues at a Glance*, and *Family Watch*, a church communication that is distributed to 500,000 church attendees. CWA's weekly radio show, *Beverly LaHaye Live*, reaches over 1 million listeners. CWA headquarters office is in Washington, D.C. Current membership is about 600,000. Beverly LaHaye is currently CWA chairman; Carmen Pate has been president since 1998.

See also: RELIGIOUS RIGHT

For Further Information

Concerned Women for America, *http://www.cwfa.org*

D'Agostino, Joseph A. "Carmen Pate." *Human Events*, February 27, 1998, p. 18.

Marshall, S. E. "Who Speaks for American Women? The Future of Antifeminism." *Annals of the American Academy of Political and Social Science* 515 (May 1991): 50–62.

Rofes, Eric. "The Right Wing and Gay Issues in Schools." *Education Digest* 63, no. 3 (November 1997): 54–59.

CONCORD COALITION.

The Concord Coalition is a nonpartisan, grassroots organization dedicated to eliminating federal budget deficits while ensuring that Social Security, Medicare, and Medicaid remain secure for all generations. In 1992 the late former Senator Paul Tsongas (D-MA), former Senator Warren Rudman (R-NH), and former Secretary of Commerce Peter G. Peterson launched the Coalition. Former Senator Sam Nunn (D-GA) was named a co-chair of the group in 1997.

The Coalition focuses on cultivating grassroots activism. It has chapters in all fifty states and most congressional districts, and on many college campuses. In its early days, it placed highest priority on balancing the federal budget. After 1995, when a strong economy started generating annual surpluses, the Coalition shifted its focus from deficit reduction to the long-term impact of the national debt and spiraling costs of federal entitlement programs such as Social Security, Medicare, Medicaid, and federal civilian and military pensions. More recently the Coalition has been urging Congress to protect the budget surplus, by keeping it in reserve until the long-term insolvency of the Social Security program has been resolved. The Coalition's recommendations include reducing government support for the aged through Social Security and Medicare as their income rises in order to reduce costs and narrow the income gap between working-age taxpayers and seniors.

In 1989 the group started dramatizing its plea for fiscal restraint by erecting an eleven-by-twenty-six-foot national debt clock near Times Square in New York City. The clock showed the rapid escalation of the national debt toward the $6 trillion mark until August 1999, at which point the clock starting ticking down instead of up because the cash-heavy federal government had begun to pay off its debts. The Coalition decided that the clock was sending the wrong message and breeding complacency, so it was stopped in September 2000. At that time it read "Our national debt: $5,676,989,904,887. Your family's share: $73,733." In April 2001, the clock was restarted. By July 2001, the national debt had rebounded to $5,710,643,000,000.

Concord Coalition prepares a *Fiscal Responsibility Scorecard* after each session of Congress, awarding a score to each member and showing how he or she voted on critical budget issues. Legislators win high scores by voting for protection of the budget surplus, reduction or elimination of unnecessary defense or domestic programs, and maintenance of budget enforcement procedures. The Coalition claims that its efforts have resulted in federal spending cuts being favored and formerly sacrosanct entitlement programs being subject to debate and possible restructuring.

Headquarters of the 200,000-member Co-alition is in Washington D.C. The group publishes the *Concord Courier*, a quarterly. Coalition officers are Co-Chairs Sam Nunn and Warren B. Rudman, President Peter G. Peterson, and Executive Director Robert L. Bixby.

See also: TAX REFORM AND GOVERNMENTAL EXPENDITURES

For Further Information

Concord Coalition, *http://www.concordcoalition. org*

Peterson, Peter G. *Gray Dawn: How the Coming Age Wave Will Transform America—and the World*. New York: Random House, 1999.

CONGRESS OF RACIAL EQUALITY.

The Congress of Racial Equality (CORE), founded in 1942 by American civil rights leader JAMES FARMER (1920–1999), states that its aim is "to bring about equality for all people regardless of race, creed, sex, age, disability, sexual orientation, religion or ethnic background. CORE seeks to identify and expose acts of discrimination in the public and private sectors of society. When such an act is uncovered, CORE, with its many multi-service departments, goes into action."

Started under the aegis of the FELLOWSHIP OF RECONCILIATION, CORE originated as the Chicago Committee for Racial Equality, an interracial group of students. In 1942 CORE initiated sit-ins to persuade restaurant owners to cease discrimination against non-white customers. Then it moved the fight for integration of public accommodations to the southern United States. During this period, CORE consisted almost entirely of white middle-class college students from the Midwest.

CORE became the razor's edge of the civil rights movement by forcing the issue of de-segregation in interstate transportation with the Freedom Rides of 1961. The group soon supplemented sit-ins with sing-ins, protest marches, and boycotts. CORE's James Chaney, Andrew Goodman, and Michael Schwerner—a black man and two white men—became the first fatalities of the

Mississippi Freedom Summer of 1964. The three were killed by KU KLUX KLAN members and buried under an earthen dam in retaliation for their investigation of a church burning and promotion of voter registration. CORE's courageous fight for equality in access to accommodations, hiring, housing, and educational opportunity undoubtedly created the public pressure required for enactment of the Civil Rights Act of 1964. By 1965 CORE's membership peaked at 82,000, distributed in 114 chapters coast to coast. Farmer, who was CORE chairman until 1966, advocated nonviolent resistance and action to effect change. The 1963 March on Washington for Jobs and Freedom, sponsored by CORE, exemplified this approach.

After Farmer's retirement, his successors, Floyd B. McKissick (1965–1967) and Roy E. Innis (1968–   ), adopted a more militant policy. During the mid-1960s, CORE's membership became increasingly made up of poorer and less educated African Americans, and McKissick escalated the intensity of the campaign to end racism, discrimination, and police brutality. CORE's frequently violent demonstrations coincided with those of the anti–Vietnam War protesters. Armed self-defense was legitimized as a requisite complement to nonviolent direct action. Under Roy Innis's direction, priorities shifted from civil rights to local quality of life issues and the pursuit of Black Power. The new objectives included improving conditions in black communities, assisting new immigrants, offering job training for welfare recipients, and organizing neighborhood anticrime groups. Innis was an enthusiastic supporter of President Nixon's 1972 reelection campaign, a position abhorrent to many of his group's members. When Innis assumed the presidency, he converted CORE into an advocate of black political, social, and economic independence, which is described on its Web site as a "buffer between blacks and a life of welfare, joblessness and dependency."

CORE membership is now relatively small. Its national headquarters is in New York City. Roy Innis is national chairman and chief executive officer; George Holmes is executive director and chief operating officer.

See also: AFRICAN AMERICAN RIGHTS

For Further Information

Congress of Racial Equality, *http://www.core. online/org*

Meier, August. *CORE: A Study in the Civil Rights Movement, 1942–1968*. Champaign: University of Illinois Press, 1975.

Rogers, Kim Lacy. *Righteous Lives*. New York: New York University Press, 1993.

Umoja, Akinyele O. "The Ballot and the Bullet." *Journal of Black Studies* 29 (March 1999): 558–578.

CONSERVATIVES (FAR RIGHT). Far right conservatives oppose or resist change and wish to reestablish pre-sixties era conditions and policies in the United States. They favor conservation of moral principles, respect for law and order, traditional religious faith, patriotism, capitalism, and free enterprise. They strongly oppose government regulation of the economy, industry, and educational policies. The extreme conservative places a higher value on individual freedom and liberty than on equality of opportunity and the erasure of inherent privilege and discrimination based on color, gender, or economic standing. "Equality of opportunity" is extended to mean "equality of opportunity to become as unequal as one's God-given talents allow." Whenever protection of equal rights, public health, or the environment involves governmental oversight or intervention, the far right conservative strenuously objects. Affirmative action, universal health care, and regulatory agencies such as the Occupational Safety and Health Administration (OSHA), the Equal Employment Opportunity Commission (EEOC) U.S. Department of Education, and Department of Energy are all viewed as being unduly costly, intrusive, and unnecessary.

Preservation of family relationships and respect for elders, the discouragement of alternative lifestyles, commitment to a strong national defense, insistence on limited central government and taxes, and confirmation of conservative justices to the U.S. Supreme Court are all important to the ultraconservative. So too is private control of medical and health services.

In 1998 far right idol Senator Jesse Helms (R-NC) achieved a perfect voting score of 100 from the far right AMERICAN CONSERVATIVE UNION (ACU). Helms voted against U.S. participation in the nuclear test ban treaty, Cuban humanitarian aid, and a proposal to require gun dealers to sell trigger and child safety locks with each handgun. He also voted to override President Clinton's veto of the ban on partial birth abortions, and for vouchers to support children's attendance at private schools. In contrast, Senator Edward Kennedy (D-MA) compiled a score of 0 by opposing Helms's position on each of the preceding issues.

The AMERICAN ENTERPRISE INSTITUTE FOR PUBLIC POLICY RESEARCH (AEI), started in 1943, became an activist think tank in 1986 by getting its speakers time on right-wing radio and high-visibility television shows. There they influenced public opinion by airing AEI research presented with a strong conservative bias.

The American Conservative Union began in 1961 as Young Americans for Freedom (YAF) for the purpose of promoting conservatism as a political philosophy. YAF in turn had its roots in the Student Committee for the Loyalty Oath, established by Youth for Goldwater for Vice-President in 1960. The ACU, with over 1 million members, is currently the nation's strongest far right conservative organization.

RICHARD A. VIGUERIE, acknowledged as the fundraising guru for right-wing causes, masterminded direct mail appeals for Barry Goldwater, George Wallace, and Jesse Helms, and for Mayor Rudolf Giuliani during his health-abbreviated Senate campaign against Hillary Clinton.

The HERITAGE FOUNDATION, founded in 1973, is the most generously funded conservative activist think tank. It influences public opinion through its publications, editorial pieces in major newspapers, and presentations on talk radio.

Paul Weyrich, a founder of the Heritage Foundation, started the FREE CONGRESS RESEARCH AND EDUCATION FOUNDATION in 1977 as a conservative activist think tank concerned with upholding traditional Judeo-Christian culture as well as promoting opposition to liberal initiatives such as gun control, gay rights, and freedom of reproductive choice.

AMERICANS FOR TAX REFORM (ATR), started in 1985, campaigns against tax increases, and before each national election mails out purportedly nonpartisan information to over a million people. Besides being fervently antitax, the ATR under Grover Norquist's leadership heads up a "leave us alone" coalition comprising the NATIONAL RIFLE ASSOCIATION, American Conservative Union, NATIONAL RIGHT TO LIFE COMMITTEE, CHRISTIAN COALITION, CATO INSTITUTE, U.S. TERM LIMITS, and Heritage Foundation that works to fight liberal Democrats' programmatic initiatives.

For Further Information

Edwards, Lee. *The Conservative Revolution: The Movement that Remade America*. New York: The Free Press, 1999.

Heineman, Kenneth J. *God Is a Conservative: Religion, Politics, and Morality in Contemporary America*. New York: New York University Press, 1998.

Thorne, Melvin J. *American Conservative Thought since World War II: The Core Ideas*. New York: Greenwood Press, 1990.

CONSTITUTIONAL RIGHTS AND CIVIL LIBERTIES PROTECTION. Entries within this category include individuals and organizations that were most visible and effective in preserving Bill of Rights provisions during the twentieth century. (Abortion and reproductive issues are excluded because covered under ABORTION POLICY and related articles. The NATIONAL ASSOCIATION FOR THE ADVANCEMENT OF

COLORED PEOPLE and the NATIONAL OR-GANIZATION FOR WOMEN are discussed under AFRICAN AMERICAN RIGHTS and WOMEN'S ISSUES and related articles.) Persons and organizations within this category uphold First Amendment rights to freedom of expression, church/state separation, and protection of privacy under the Fourth Amendment, and regard the U.S. Constitution as an inclusive document amenable to changing interpretation to ensure justice for all in current political and social contexts. Landmark U.S. Supreme Court cases consistent with this perspective include *BROWN V. BOARD OF EDUCATION OF TOPEKA* (1954), *Engel v. Vitale* (1962), *Gideon v. Wainwright* (1964), *New York Times Co. v. Sullivan* (1964), *GRISWOLD V. CONNECTICUT* (1965), *Miranda v. Arizona* (1966), *FURMAN V. GEORGIA* (1972), *ROE V. WADE* (1973), and *Reno v. ACLU* (1997).

The AMERICAN CIVIL LIBERTIES UNION, founded in 1920, has the longest and most illustrious record as a civil liberties champion. Its attorneys have presented arguments in cases extending from the Sacco-Vanzetti case (1920) to *Reno v. ACLU* (1997), which declared that communications on the Internet have the same free speech protections that are applied to traditional print media.

AMERICANS UNITED FOR SEPARATION OF CHURCH AND STATE (AUSCS), formed in 1947, seeks to maintain a healthy distance between the institutions of religion and government. The AUSCS is committed to upholding the separation clause in the First Amendment: "Congress shall make no law respecting an establishment of religion, or prohibiting the free exercise thereof." This guarantee of religious liberty for all Americans, regardless of faith or the lack of it, is the primary concern of this group. It supports the view of Thomas Jefferson and James Madison that it is wrong to tax citizens to support the teaching of religion and that there should be no direct or indirect government funding of parochial educational institutions at any level.

PEOPLE FOR THE AMERICAN WAY (PAW) lobbies for preservation of the separation clause and for freedom of expression. Founded in 1980 by television producer Norman Lear, PAW was created to counterbalance the rising influence of RELIGIOUS RIGHT groups such as JERRY FALWELL's Moral Majority.

MARIO SAVIO (1942–1996) is remembered as the leader of the Free Speech Movement at the University of California at Berkeley. In 1964 he led the student demonstration against arbitrary restrictions on freedom of expression imposed by the university administration, sparking a nationwide epidemic of student activism.

For Further Information

Burns, James MacGregor. *The People's Charter: The Pursuit of Rights in America*. New York: Alfred A. Knopf, 1991.

Foner, Eric. *The Story of American Freedom*. New York: W. W. Norton, 1998.

Sigler, Jay A. *Civil Rights in America: 1500 to the Present*. Detroit: Gale, 1998.

CONSULTATION OF OLDER AND YOUNGER ADULTS FOR SOCIAL CHANGE. *See* Gray Panthers

CONSUMER ALERT. Founded in 1977 by Barbara Keating-Edh, Consumer Alert (CA) states that its mission is to "enhance understanding and appreciation of the consumer benefits of a market economy so that individuals and policymakers rely more on private rather than government approaches to consumer concerns." CA is the only free-market public interest group dedicated to what it argues are sound economic, scientific, and risk data in public policy decisions affecting the consumer.

CA is committed to combating excessive growth of government regulation at the national and state levels. The group rejects as false the definition of consumerism as the protection of the buying public by requiring honest packaging, labeling, and advertising, fair pricing, and improved safety standards. It argues that regulations smother the free market and drive up the cost of goods and services, placing an unjustifiable burden on the average consumer.

Consumer Alert is one of the many FALSE FRONT ORGANIZATIONS that have been developed to counteract liberal citizen action groups and movements that matured in the 1960s and 1970s. Environmental regulations, corporate liability for product defects, tariffs on foreign goods, and delays in the approval of new drugs are fought by CA, as are provision of childproof caps on adult prescription drug bottles, restrictions on ATM fees, and mandatory passenger seat airbags in automobiles.

Former Vice President Dan Quayle received the group's 1991 Consumers First Award for his antiregulatory views, and one of CA's major victories was a court-mandated delay in implementing Corporate Average Fuel Economy (CAFE), higher standards for fuel economy for autos sold in the United States. If the more stringent standards were imposed, CA warned that consumers would be priced out of the market for larger, safer cars and sport utility vehicles (SUVs). Other regulations CA considers excessive include those for hairsprays and deodorants that release ozone, and tests for radon, asbestos, and lead prescribed in real estate transactions. CA has succeeded in convincing many legislators that there is no scientifically valid evidence that human use of fossil fuels contributes to global warming.

A formidable lobbying force with a strong legal team, publications, and media outreach, Consumer Alert has its headquarters in Washington. Frances B. Smith is Executive Director of CA; William MacLeod is chairman. Membership is about 3,000. CA publishes a bimonthly newsletter, *Consumer Comments*, and the *CPSC Monitor*, which reports on the activities of the Consumer Product Safety Commission. CA's *On the Plate* fax newsletter evaluates federal policies and proposals relating to food, and *Consumers' Research Magazine* carries a monthly column contributed by CA.

See also: FALSE FRONT ORGANIZATIONS

For Further Information

Consumer Alert, *http://www.consumeralert.org*
Consumer Comments, January–February 1991–   .
"Conservative Spotlight." *Human Events*, September 23, 1994, p. 11.

CONSUMER RIGHTS AND SAFEGUARDS. Consumer rights and safeguards are the concern of citizen action groups and individuals who seek to protect the rights and health of the buying public by requiring such practices as honest packaging, labeling, and advertising, fair pricing, and improved safety standards. They usually favor the strengthening of U.S. federal regulatory agencies to protect consumers against useless, inferior, or dangerous products and services that occasionally enter the marketplace. In the United States, a free-market and consumer driven economy, consumer advocates were active throughout the twentieth century.

In 1899 FLORENCE KELLEY, a prominent figure in the women's movement, founded the NATIONAL CONSUMERS' LEAGUE and pioneered the concept of consumer advocacy. An early League motto was "To live means to buy, to buy means to have power, to have power means to have duties." The national minimum wage (1938), the outlawing of sweatshops, and the exploitation of child and female labor were successfully pursued by the League. Currently it is focusing on fraud in telemarketing and Internet scams, while continuing to strengthen child labor protections.

CONSUMERS UNION (CU), chartered in 1936 by the state of New York, provides consumers with information on goods, services, health, and personal finance through its *Consumers Reports, On Health*, and *Travel Letter*. CU product evaluations influence sales, especially those of automobiles and expensive appliances. CU's 5 million members vote in the annual election of CU's board of directors but do not actively lobby.

The emperor of consumer advocacy is RALPH NADER, author of the 1965 classic exposé of the American automobile industry, *Unsafe at Any Speed*. In 1970 he and Consumers Union established the CENTER FOR AUTO SAFETY to serve as a citizen action group that would reduce deaths and injuries resulting from unsafe motor vehicles and highways. A year later, Nader founded PUBLIC CITIZEN to fight for consumer rights in the marketplace, safe products, a healthful environment, and safe workplaces.

Founded in 1971, the CENTER FOR SCIENCE IN THE PUBLIC INTEREST (CSPI) has waged war against unhealthy fast-food products, canned soups and processed cheese, theater popcorn, alcoholic beverages, and deceptive labeling and advertising. Liberals have commended CSPI for its success in removing unsafe food additives from the market and for its attempts to decrease deceptive advertising aimed at teenage consumers, while conservatives have accused CSPI of treating consumers like children who have to be protected by a Big Nanny from greedy free-market predators.

INFACT and FORMULA attacked defective and misused infant formula and the tobacco industry in the late 1970s. INFACT publicized corporate disregard of human health by placing offending companies such as Nestlé and Philip Morris in its "Hall of Shame" and by boycotting their products. FORMULA was instrumental in achieving passage of the Infant Formula Act of 1980, which established nutrient standards for all infant formulas for the first time.

In the 1980s, additional consumer/health advocacy groups were formed. FAMILIES USA was launched in 1981 as a voice for health care consumer legislation committed to improving Medicaid and children's health services, and developing a patients' bill of rights. In 1982 parents whose children had died or suffered adverse reactions from diphtheria, measles, whooping cough, tetanus, and other vaccines established Dissatisfied Parents Together (DPT), now known as the NATIONAL VACCINE INFORMATION CENTER. That same year, PUBLIC VOICE FOR FOOD AND HEALTH POLICY was set up to monitor federal food policies and to fight for "a safer, healthier, and more affordable food supply for all Americans." The latter group's formation was inspired by the Reagan administration's cuts in federal food assistance and relaxation of food safety standards.

For Further Information

Brobeck, Stephen, Robert N. Mayer, and Robert O. Herrmann, eds. *Encyclopedia of the Consumer Movement.* Santa Barbara: ABC-CLIO, 1997.

CONSUMERS UNION OF THE UNITED STATES. Consumers Union of the United States (CU), publisher of *Consumer Reports*, is an independent, nonprofit testing and advisory organization that serves the public. It was formed in 1936 during the birth of the consumer movement and has become one of the most reliable and respected staples in American life. CU's founding document was *Your Money's Worth: A Study in the Waste of the Consumer's Dollar*, written by Stuart Chase and F. J. Schlink. This book was inspired by a series of articles that had appeared earlier in *The New Republic*. The book was a best seller, convincing Schlink that he should convert his modest consumers' club in White Plains, New York, into an operation capable of delivering objective, thorough, and reliable reports on the quality and safety of consumer products. The first reports summarizing the results of tests conducted by hired scientists appeared in *Consumers' Research Bulletin*, which evolved into today's *Consumer Reports*.

CU ratings are based on laboratory tests, controlled-use tests, and expert judgments by technicians and researchers. To maintain its independence and impartiality, *Consumer Reports* has never accepted advertising in any of its publications and does not accept free samples from businesses. Consequently, Consumers Union has become a comprehensive source for unbiased advice about products and services, personal finance, health and nutrition, and other concerns that relate to consumers' health care, personal finances, and well-being.

Advocacy offices in Washington, D.C., San Francisco, California, and Austin, Texas, monitor and work with consumer issues. Staff testifies before federal and state legislative and regulatory bodies and files lawsuits on behalf of consumers. Legal action has been initiated by CU in such areas as auto safety, telecommunications, toxic pesticides on fruit and vegetables, intellectual property, insurance and redlining, health maintenance organization pricing and services, and biotechnology.

In addition to *Consumer Reports* with its circulation of 4.5 million and Web site with 310,000 paid subscribers, CU publishes an annual buying guide, *On Health* (monthly), *Travel Letter* (monthly), and *Zillions*, consumer reports for kids. CU headquarters is in Yonkers, New York. Rhoda H. Karpatkin is president.

See also: CONSUMER RIGHTS AND SAFEGUARDS

For Further Information

Consumer Reports, current issues.
Silber, Norman Isaac. *Test and Protest*. New York: Holmes and Meier, 1983.

COORS, JOSEPH, SR. (1917–   ). Joseph Coors, born in Golden, Colorado, on November 17, 1917, is the most influential underwriter of and spokesperson for ultraconservative religious right causes, leaders, and organizations. He is the grandson of Adolph Coors, founder of the Adolph Coors Company.

Joseph Sr. graduated from Cornell University in 1939 with a bachelor's degree in chemical engineering. After working at DuPont and the National Dairy Association, he returned to Coors, where he was vice president, vice chair, president (1977–1985), and chief operating officer (1982–1987).

In 1970, while serving on the Colorado University Board of Regents, Coors became appalled by the actions of the STUDENTS FOR A DEMOCRATIC SOCIETY, urban riots, moral laxity, and the generally leftward tilt of national politics. At that same time, conservative members of Congress were looking for a reliable, fast producer of information to counteract the flow of scholarly data being supplied by the faintly liberal Brookings Institution and used by the media. Coors decided that the best way to involve himself was to contribute money to create a strong conservative think tank, the HERITAGE FOUNDATION, that could quickly produce easily digestible news pellets for media consumption. By 1973 the Heritage Foundation had its headquarters in an eight-story building overlooking Capitol Hill, and very soon it became the most influential conservative think tank in America.

Coors also provided the funding for the FREE CONGRESS RESEARCH AND EDUCATION FOUNDATION, which helped to win election victories for Senator Richard Lugar, Congressman Dan Quayle, and Senators Orrin Hatch, Barry Goldwater, Robert Dole, Jesse Helms, Strom Thurmond, Trent Lott, and Jack Kemp. Other groups created by Coors oppose affirmative action, low-cost legal services for the poor, and increased quotas for immigration. Coors has campaigned for English to be designated as the country's official language and contributed $130,000 to Education Research Analysts, a nonprofit corporation formed by Mel Gabler that reviews textbooks submitted for adoption in Texas from a conservative, Christian perspective. Gabler's approval criteria include respect for Judeo-Christian morality, free-enterprise economics, and exclusion of any unflattering portrayals of American history. Coors also funded PHYLLIS SCHLAFLY's STOP ERA organization.

See also: ACTIVIST THINK TANKS; FALSE FRONT ORGANIZATIONS

For Further Information

Baum, Dan. *Citizen Coors: An American Dynasty*. New York: HarperCollins, 2000.

CORTÉS, ERNESTO, JR. (1943–   ). Born on June 15, 1943, Ernesto Cortés transformed poor neighborhoods in Texas and throughout the Southwest into grassroots organizations that enabled over 500,000 Mexican American families to acquire political influence, escape from poverty and powerlessness, and upgrade the quality of their lives.

A native of San Antonio and a graduate of the city's Central Catholic High School, Cortés attended Texas A&M, where he majored in English and economics and graduated at the age of nineteen. While pursuing graduate studies in economics at the University of Texas at Austin, his passion for social justice, coupled with the death of his father, compelled him to leave the university and become involved in the Hispanic community. He initiated a statewide caravan to support striking farm workers and then went to Chicago to study at SAUL ALINSKY's INDUSTRIAL AREA FOUNDATION (IAF), a training institute for community leaders. After working with the IAF in Wisconsin and Indiana, Cortés returned to San Antonio to establish Communities Organized for Public Service (COPS), the longest-lived and most successful IAF enterprise.

Because of centuries of oppression, language barriers, and cultural roadblocks, Chicano communities in the Southwest have been politically insulated and in need of self-empowerment skills. Cortés trained COPS organizers to help people in poor neighborhoods convert their anger about inequality and lack of opportunity into constructive confrontation with the Anglo power elite. He has observed that "power is such a good thing, everyone should have some." Before launching COPS, Cortés conducted more than a thousand meetings with individuals and several follow-up sessions to pinpoint potential leaders. Currently COPS is a broad-based multiethnic interfaith grouping of 1,200 neighborhoods in San Antonio. It has channeled over $800 million into formerly destitute inner-city communities for new housing, streets, sidewalks, drainage and sewers, parks, and libraries.

Cortés has effectively applied Saul Alinsky's Iron Rule—"Never do for others what they can do for themselves"—and has won victories not by speaking for ordinary people but by teaching them how to speak, act, and engage in politics for themselves. COPS

holds well-attended "accountability nights" with staged confrontations between its members and political leaders.

In addition to his work with COPS, Cortés has helped pass major legislation in Texas affecting education, health care, and farm safety. He and his wife have three children and maintain residences in Austin, Texas, and Los Angeles, California. He serves as Southwest regional director of the Industrial Areas Foundation, comprising twenty-three community-based organizations and over a quarter of a million families, stretching from New Orleans to Des Moines to Los Angeles.

See also: HISPANIC AMERICAN RIGHTS

For Further Information

Rogers, Mary Beth. *Cold Anger: A Story of Faith and Power Politics.* Denton, TX: University of North Texas Press, 1990.

COUGHLIN, FATHER CHARLES (1891–1979). Born in Toronto on October 25, 1891, Father Charles Coughlin was the "radio priest" who during the Depression era captured the attention of a nationwide audience with diatribes against communists, Jews, Wall Street, and the New Deal.

Father Coughlin was brought up in a devout Canadian Roman Catholic family and entered the seminary as a young man. In 1926 he became a parish priest in Royal Oak, Michigan, where he began his broadcasting career over station WJR-Detroit, directly from his office at the Shrine of the Little Flower. The content of Coughlin's early broadcasts was limited to homilies and religious topics, but by 1930, as the Great Depression worsened, his messages became explicitly political, self-righteous, and extremist. His richly resonant voice was soon reaching listeners in some 40 million homes. The novelist, Wallace Stegner, said that he "had a voice of such mellow richness, such manly, heart-warming confidential intimacy, such emotional and ingratiating charm, that anyone tuning past it almost automatically returned to hear it again."

Coughlin's early messages contained primarily leftist social welfare–religious themes, as exemplified by the idea that government should protect the workers against exploitation. In 1931 he attacked international bankers for exploiting the Versailles Treaty to maximize their profits. During Franklin D. Roosevelt's first two years in office (1932–1933) he supported New Deal programs as a vigorous anticapitalist populist. Anti-Semitism began to infiltrate his remarks, and his ideology became a mixture of far left and far right beliefs. Coughlin believed that market capitalism threatened society, and he perceived the fact that Jews figured prominently in high finance and the Russian Revolution as proof positive of the insidious influence of "international Jewry."

In 1934 he founded the National Union for Social Justice and began to denounce the New Deal for being sympathetic to communism and for serving the interests of the rich while the poor suffered. In 1936 he started his weekly newspaper, *Social Justice*, which published extracts of the fraudulent anti-Semitic *Protocols of the Elders of Zion*. Coughlin supported Congressman William Lemke of North Dakota and his Union Party, along with Dr. Francis Townsend of old age insurance fame (*see* SENIOR MOVEMENT). He also formed an alliance with GERALD L.K. SMITH, one of the most infamous racists of the twentieth century. Coughlin's broadcasts had by this time earned him the title "Father of Hate Radio." After Lemke's Union Party presidential candidacy failed in 1936, Coughlin left radio, but only for two months; in January 1937 he resumed broadcasting after dissolving the National Union a month earlier. By this time, Coughlin was advocating an Italian-style fascist system of government for the United States, and in 1938 he founded the Christian Front to promote his ideology. His weekly newspaper, *Social Justice*, was subsequently suppressed by the U.S. Post Office and banned from the mails because of its alleged violation of the Espionage Act.

In 1942 Coughlin's superiors ordered him to cease all public pronouncements, and the U.S. attorney general warned him that he could face indictment for sedition. Coughlin then dutifully returned to the priesthood full-time and retired in 1966. He died in 1979 after a forced silence of thirty-seven years.

See also: EXTREMISTS

For Further Information

Marcus, Sheldon. *Father Coughlin: The Tumultuous Life of the Priest of the Little Flower*. Boston: Little, Brown, 1973.
Rees, John, and Alan Brinkley. *Voices of Protest: Huey Long, Father Coughlin and the Great Depression*. New York: Alfred A. Knopf, 1982.

COUNCIL FOR A LIVABLE WORLD. The Council for a Livable World (CLW), founded in 1962 by physicist Leo Szilard, works to "educate the public on the consequences of chemical, biological, and conventional weapons and nuclear war." CLW has expanded the scope of its concerns to include arms control treaties, reduced military spending, peacekeeping, restrictions on sales of weapons of mass destruction to other governments, and support of United Nations peacekeeping operations.

CLW mobilizes political opinion at the grassroots level on specific issues and endorses candidates for the U.S. Senate who support arms control. PeacePAC, an affiliated committee, endorses and raises funds for candidates for the House of Representatives.

In 1980 CLW established an education fund to inform the public about nuclear weaponry, the dangers of the arms race, NATO expansion, and other issues in a series of thoroughly documented briefing books, fact sheets, and newsletters. The CLW's investigative reports on the arms trade have appeared in major news media and were a factor in the passage of the Comprehensive Test Ban Treaty. The CLW maintains a twenty-four-hour arms control hotline and provides weekly updates and suggestions for citizen activist members.

CLW is headquartered Washington, D.C. It has approximately 100,000 members.

John Isaacs is president/executive director, and Jerome Grossman is chairman.

See also: ANTIWAR/ANTI–NUCLEAR WEAPONS MOVEMENT

For Further Information

Council for a Livable World, *http://www.clw.org*
Danitz, Tiffany. "Defense Budget Still a Cash Cow." *Insight on the News*, April 29, 1996, final edition, p. 44.

COUNCIL ON AMERICAN-ISLAMIC RELATIONS.

The Council on American-Islamic Relations (CAIR) was formed in 1994 to present an Islamic perspective on issues of importance to the American public. In offering that perspective, CAIR seeks to empower the Muslim community in America through political and social activism. It protects and advocates Islamic Americans' civil rights and protests activities and products viewed as exhibiting prejudice against Islam and Moslems. The CAIR Web site includes links to press releases, action alerts, online help, and reports on the results of previous lobbying efforts.

As of June 1997, CAIR was receiving at least one telephone call a day from Muslim employees reporting incidents of discrimination. Beginning in 1996, CAIR began issuing annual reports on events in the workplace, police misconduct, and court bias.

High profile legal victories won by CAIR include Seneca Foods Corporation's agreement to provide a place for Muslim employees to pray at their packing plant in Rochester, Minnesota; Nike's recall of shoes bearing a logo resembling the word "Allah" in Arabic script; and Simon and Schuster's recall of a children's book, *Great Lives: World Religions*, that contained a portrayal of the Prophet Mohammed the group found offensive. In June 1999, CAIR participated in a settlement awarding seven Muslim women back pay to compensate for wages lost because they were sent home for wearing Islamic headscarves at Dulles International Airport while working as security staff.

According to Ibrahim Hooper, CAIR's communications director, CAIR is a grassroots membership organization fighting discrimination. Steve Emerson, an authority on international terrorism, disagrees, saying that CAIR is a "spin-off of a Texas front group of the radical organization Hamas." Steven Pomerantz reported in *Commentary* (January 1999) that CAIR is "in fact tethered to a platform that supports terrorism." On August 28, 1999, Ibrahim Hooper refuted these allegations in the Minneapolis *Star Tribune*, saying that "no references to Hamas (Islamic Resistance Movement) or Osama bin Laden (Islamic fundamentalist terrorist), other than in refutations of this type of extremism, will be found in any document published by CAIR."

CAIR headquarters is in Washington, D.C., and it has regional offices in California, New York, Ohio, and Texas. Nihad Awad is CAIR executive director. The group's publications include the *Newsletter of the Council on American-Islamic Relations* (quarterly), *Faith in Action* (quarterly), and "Hajj and Ramadan Publicity Kits" for Muslim leaders and activists.

For Further Information

Council on American-Islamic Relations, *http://www.cair-net.org*

CUBAN AMERICAN NATIONAL FOUNDATION.

The Cuban American National Foundation (CANF), an anti-Castro group, was founded in 1981 by Cuban Americans and led by the Cuban exile, Bay of Pigs veteran, and millionaire businessman Jorge Mas Canosa until his death in 1997. CANF is firm in its support of the U.S. Cuban embargo, believing that it will eventually bring about the fall of the Castro regime. It was the first exile organization to successfully deploy sophisticated lobbying tactics in the highest political echelons in Washington. CANF's interlocking lobbying affiliate and political action committee are based in Miami.

The group has raised millions of dollars

from over 250,000 families, with an estimated 54,000 individuals making monthly donations during the 1980s. In 1995 CANF claimed over 200,000 members. It was instrumental in establishing Radio Marti (1985) and TV Marti (1990) despite the opposition of the National Association of Broadcasters and initial resistance in Congress that was overcome by generous contributions to candidates' campaigns and key committees. Recipients have included Senators Joseph Lieberman and Connie Mack, Representative Bob Graham, and Presidents George Bush and Bill Clinton.

Because of CANF prodding, Congress started funding Radio Marti, a twenty-four-hour pro-democracy news and entertainment station aired by the U.S. Information Agency, in 1985. In 1993 CANF opposed Clinton's first choice for secretary of state for Inter-American affairs, Mario Baeza, because Miami Cubans suspected him of being soft on Castro. Influential Democrats Senator Bill Bradley, Senator Bob Graham, and Representative Robert Torricelli were contacted, and Clinton retracted the nomination.

CANF also played a major role in the passage of the 1992 Cuba Democracy Act, outlawing trade with Cuba, and the Helms-Burton Act in 1996. Until recently, it has torpedoed all calls for dialogue with Fidel Castro. Since Jorge Mas Canosa's death and the pope's visit to Cuba in January 1998, CANF's influence has been weakening.

CANF's current membership is about 3,000. Francisco Jose "Pepe" Hernandez is president. CANF publishes the *Cuban Monitor*, a newsletter, eight times a year. Its headquarters office is in Miami; other offices are in Washington, D.C., Union City, New Jersey, and San Juan, Puerto Rico.

See also: HISPANIC AMERICANS

For Further Information

Bragg, Rick. "For Cuban-Americans, a Void Lingers Two Years after a Leader's Death." *New York Times*, September 12, 1999, late edition—final, p. 24.

Cuban American National Foundation, *http://www.canfnet.org*

Sleek, Scott. "Mr. Mas Goes to Washington." *Common Cause Magazine* (Winter 1991).

Stone, Peter H. "Cuban Clout." *National Journal* 25 (February 20, 1993): 449.

D

DAUGHTERS OF BILITIS. *See* Lesbians and Gays

DAVIS, ANGELA Y. (1944–   ). Angela Y. Davis is a radical political activist and polemicist, best known for her involvement with the STUDENT NONVIOLENT COORDINATING COMMITTEE, the BLACK PANTHER PARTY, and the Communist Party, and for her alleged collusion in the 1970 Soledad Brothers prison break.

Angela Davis was born on January 26, 1944, in Birmingham, Alabama, and grew up on "Dynamite Hill," an early "mixed" neighborhood where bombs, not welcome wagons, greeted many incoming black families and where arch-segregationist Bull Connor, commissioner of public safety, maintained law and order. Her parents were teachers in the Birmingham public schools.

Davis was educated at Brandeis University (B.A., magna cum laude) and the University of California at San Diego (M.A.). Herbert Marcuse, her political philosophy teacher at Brandeis (1964–1965) and San Diego (1968), impressed upon her the need to challenge the capitalist system and shatter it by committing individual acts of resistance and rebellion. Marcuse considered Davis the best student he had ever taught. Since that time, she has worked ceaselessly and often militantly to eradicate oppression and poverty, taking part in radical protests and demonstrations.

In the late 1960s she joined the Student Nonviolent Coordinating Committee, the Black Panthers, and the Communist Party. The UCLA Philosophy Department hired her in 1969. After an FBI informant leaked her Communist Party affiliation to the university administration, she was ousted from the faculty, and Ronald Reagan, then governor, labeled her a dangerous radical and vowed that she would never again teach in a state university.

Among the reasons the California Board of Regents cited for refusing to renew Davis's appointment were her failure to complete her doctoral dissertation and her presentations of highly emotional speeches outside the classroom in which she defended the jailed Soledad (Prison) Brothers. Davis had grown attached to George Jackson, whose brother, Jonathan, was among four persons killed—including the trial judge—in an abortive escape and kidnapping attempt made from the Hall of Justice in Marin County, California, on August 7, 1970. Suspected of complicity, Davis was posted as a "most wanted" criminal by the FBI. She was arrested in New York City and returned to face charges of kidnapping, murder, and conspiracy. In 1972 a jury acquitted her on all counts. In 1980 Davis ran for vice president on the Communist Party ticket.

She has published six books, including *Women, Race, and Class* (1981) and *Women, Culture, and Politics* (1989) and, ironically, is now a tenured professor at the University of California at Santa Cruz. Currently, Davis is crusading as an advocate of penal reform and abolition of the prison system. She cites a recent study that shows there were five times more African American men in California prisons than in the state university system in 1998. It is her belief that the prisons are being used as a means to control low-income people whom society has labeled uneducable and immune to rehabilitation.

See also: AFRICAN AMERICAN RIGHTS

For Further Information

Davis, Angela Y. *Angela Davis: An Autobiography*. New York: International Publishers, 1988.
James, Joy, ed. *The Angela Y. Davis Reader*. Cambridge, MA: Blackwell, 1998.

DAY, DOROTHY (1897–1980). Born November 8, 1897, in Brooklyn, New York, Dorothy Day was a radical journalist and social activist who created a synthesis of radicalism and orthodox Catholicism that influenced a generation of American priests and laity. After successive moves to San Francisco and Chicago, Day won a scholarship at the University of Illinois. Dropping out of college two years later, she moved to New York and became a reporter for *The Call*, the city's only socialist daily, in 1916. She also worked for *The Masses*, a magazine opposing America's involvement in World War I. In 1917 Day and thirty-nine other women were arrested in front of the White House and sent to a rural workhouse for protesting women's exclusion from suffrage.

Day was converted to Catholicism in 1927 after having survived an abortion, a failed marriage, a common law marriage, and numerous affairs and drinking bouts in Greenwich Village. In 1933 she founded the monthly *Catholic Worker*, the chief vehicle for spreading the radical Gospel ideal of uto-

pian dissent to the American Catholic community and, eventually, into mainstream national life. She came under the influence of the French itinerant priest Peter Maurin (1877–1949), and together they founded the CATHOLIC WORKER MOVEMENT, which established houses of hospitality and farm communities for people ruined by the Depression, as described in her *House of Hospitality* (1939). A pacifist and a fervent supporter of farm worker unionization in the 1960s, she helped turn her church's attention to peace and civil rights issues. Many Catholic Workers were imprisoned during the Vietnam War for refusing to be conscripted. Day's steadfast resistance to war, nuclear arms, social injustice, and poverty paved the way for PLOWSHARES, the UNITED FARM WORKERS, and other radical, antiestablishment movements.

Day's movement is still thriving, and there are now some 130 Catholic Worker communities in the United States. Day's autobiography, *The Long Loneliness*, originally published in 1952, was reprinted in 1982.

See also: ANTIWAR/ANTI–NUCLEAR WEAPONS MOVEMENT

For Further Information

Coles, Robert. *Dorothy Day: A Radical Devotion*. Reading, MA: Addison-Wesley, 1987.
Day, Dorothy. *The Long Loneliness*. Reprint, San Francisco: Harper and Row, 1982.
Miller, William. *Dorothy Day: A Biography*. New York: Harper and Row, 1982.
Piehl, Mel. *Breaking Bread: The Catholic Worker and the Origin of Catholic Radicalism in America*. Philadelphia: Temple University Press, 1982.

DEATH PENALTY AND CHOICE IN DYING. The death penalty, euthanasia, and physician-assisted suicide are emotionally charged and controversial issues because they entail matters of conscience, religious beliefs about the sanctity of life, economic realities, and basic human feelings ranging from vengeance to compassion.

In the United States the legal status of cap-

In February 1996, anti-death penalty protestors hold silent vigil outside San Quentin prior to the execution of "Freeway Killer" William Bonin, the first person in California to die by lethal injection. *AP Photo/Paul Sakuma.*

ital punishment has moved in tandem with fluctuations in public opinion because political leaders' actions are driven more by polls than by informed judgments based on empirical evidence. Prior to a 1972 Supreme Court decision outlawing the death penalty as then imposed, the number of executions had been declining. In 1935, 199 people were put to death, but over the three-year span 1965–1967, only 10 were executed. After reapproval of the constitutionality of the death penalty in 1976, the number of executions increased. Between 1976 and 2000, 598 persons were executed, 240 of them during the last three years of the century.

Proponents of capital punishment believe it prevents crime and provides victims' relatives and the public with essential psychological closure through revenge for the death of the victim. Opponents point out that (1) there is no evidence showing that the death penalty works as a deterrent; (2) it is more costly to kill prisoners than to jail them for life; (3) the state's use of legalized murder as an instrument of social policy is immoral; (4) the death penalty is unfairly administered because only wealthy defendants can afford to hire the legal talent needed to evade execution; and (5) innocent persons have been executed. For these reasons most European and Latin American countries have repealed the death penalty. The United Kingdom permanently abolished it in 1969.

In the United States, opposition to the death penalty began in 1927 with the founding of the AMERICAN LEAGUE TO ABOLISH CAPITAL PUNISHMENT (ALACP) by Herbert Ehrmann, a defense attorney in the celebrated Sacco-Vanzetti case. After the 1972 Supreme Court case declared the death penalty a "cruel and unusual punishment," the ALACP dissolved, believing its mission had been accomplished. In 1976, following the Court's reinstatement of capital punishment, the NATIONAL COALITION TO ABOLISH THE DEATH PENALTY was formed.

The right to choose the manner of one's death has been as controversial an issue as capital punishment. Those who advocate this view cite the right to privacy, contending that this should guarantee the individual the choice to speed death with drugs and other methods prescribed by a doctor. Those who oppose this view cite the sanctity of life, contend that unscrupulous doctors and greedy relatives could abuse the option, and worry about depressed or misguided patients being lured into an irreversible choice. Activism to pass legislation that permits dying patients and their physicians to choose whether life-maintaining treatments should be continued started with formation of the Euthanasia Society of America in 1938. In 1968 the Society devised the first living will, now accepted as a legal document in forty-seven states. The Society adopted its current name, CHOICE IN DYING, in 1997.

The HEMLOCK SOCIETY U.S.A., founded in 1980, also advocates the right of patients who are suffering from terminal diseases to choose to die quickly and as painlessly as possible. But, unlike Choice in Dying, Hemlock would have physicians play an active part by prescribing life-ending medication or using other means to assist patients' legally negotiated suicides. Oregon passed a Death with Dignity Act in 1994, and legislation for physician aid in dying has been introduced in twenty other states.

In 1990, DR. JACK KEVORKIAN assisted in the death of Janet Adkins, a victim of Alzheimer's disease. Despite the illegality of his actions he continued to assist patients' suicides, arguing that the laws against physician intervention are "intrinsically immoral." After helping 120 people to die, Kevorkian was imprisoned for the second degree murder of Thomas Youk in 1999.

The legalized "mercy killing" promoted by Kevorkian and the Hemlock Society inspired creation of Not Dead Yet in 1996. Diane Coleman and Woody Osburn, a civil rights

specialist and a quadriplegic, respectively, were perturbed by Kevorkian's ominous statement that "the voluntary self-elimination of individual and mortally diseased or crippled lives, taken collectively, can only enhance the preservation of public health and welfare." Not Dead Yet, based in Forest Park, Illinois, had an estimated 2,000 members as of 1999.

For Further Information

Costanzo, Mark. *Just Revenge: Costs and Consequences of the Death Penalty.* New York: St. Martin's Press, 1997.

Fox, Elaine. *Come Lovely and Soothing Death: The Right to Die Movement in the United States.* New York: Twayne, 1999.

Grabowski, John F. *The Death Penalty.* San Diego: Lucent Books, 1999.

Haines, Herbert H. *Against Capital Punishment: The Anti–Death Penalty Movement in America, 1972–1994.* New York: Oxford University Press, 1996.

Smith, Wesley J. *Forced Exit: The Slippery Slope from Assisted Suicide to Legalized Murder.* New York: Times Books, 1997.

Wolf, Robert V. *Capital Punishment.* Philadelphia: Chelsea House, 1997.

DEBS, EUGENE VICTOR (1855–1926). An eloquent spokesman for the American labor movement, builder of the American Socialist Party, union organizer, and five-time candidate for the presidency, Eugene Victor Debs was born on November 5, 1855, in Terre Haute, Indiana. During his youth, Debs worked in railroad shops and became a locomotive fireman. He was national secretary and treasurer of the Brotherhood of Locomotive Firemen from 1875 to 1893. He also served in the Indiana legislature in 1885. Although many of his accomplishments, among them formation of the American Railway Union (1893) and leadership of the 1894 Pullman car strike (1894), occurred during the nineteenth century, he made his biggest impact on the labor movement and in politics as a Socialist between 1900 and 1920.

During the Pullman strike hundreds of

railway cars were burned and President Cleveland sent federal troops to restore order, safeguard the mail, and protect interstate commerce. Seven hundred strikers were arrested and thirteen were shot to death. Debs was jailed for contempt and soon became a national hero of the labor movement.

Debs organized the Social Democratic Party, forerunner of the Socialist Party, and ran as Socialist presidential candidate five times, in 1900, 1904, 1908, 1912, and 1920. In 1905 he helped to found the Industrial Workers of the World (known as "the Wobblies") from which he later severed connections because of its violent tactics.

In 1918 Debs publicly denounced the spate of sedition prosecutions stimulated by anti-German sentiment and legally rationalized by the newly passed Espionage Act. He opposed America's involvement in World War I, a conflict he viewed as being between two equally culpable imperialist powers. Because of his inflammatory speeches against the war, he was jailed under the Espionage Act. President Warren Harding commuted his ten-year sentence in 1921. Even though his 1920 campaign for president was waged from prison, he drew nearly a million votes, or over 3 percent of the total turnout; in 1912 he had received 6 percent. At its peak, the Socialist Party had 100,000 members, 1,200 officeholders in 340 municipalities, and a loyal following among farmers, railroad workers, coal miners, and lumberjacks.

While incarcerated Debs wrote *Walls and Bars*, a book on prison environments and problems that was published posthumously, in 1927. After his release he continued working for socialism and for his vision of an egalitarian and democratic America until his death in 1926 in Elmhurst, Illinois.

See also: LABOR ISSUES

For Further Information

Salvatore, Nick. *Eugene V. Debs: Citizen and Socialist*. Champaign: University of Illinois Press, 1982.

DEFENDERS OF WILDLIFE. Defenders of Wildlife seeks to protect all native animals and plants in their natural environment. Founded in 1947 as Defenders of Furbearers, the 1,500-member group formed to campaign against steel-jawed leghold traps, snares, and other devices used to trap, poison, and kill animals. Today the group concentrates on conservation issues such as the loss of biodiversity because of species extinction, and the increasing rates of habitat destruction. Defenders seeks new ways to conserve species and prevent their endangerment.

Wolves are a major conservation focus for the Defenders of Wildlife. Wolves were incorporated into the Defenders' logo in 1993 in order to accentuate the theme of biodiversity. Protection of the wolf population includes preservation of their habitat, along with other species residing within it. Defenders has worked to restore populations in the lower forty-eight states, and opposes wolves' removal in areas where they still exist. Reintroduction of wolves in Yellowstone Park and other regions has created public controversy. A Compensation Trust was created to reduce opposition to restoration by reimbursing ranchers for livestock killed by wolves. In 1997 a judge in Wyoming ruled that Defenders' actions were illegal and that the wolves must be removed. On January 13, 2000, the 10th Circuit Court of Appeal reversed the 1997 decision, thereby enabling the wolf recovery program to continue. Other projects include bringing Mexican wolves back to the American Southwest and restoration of lost populations in New York State. Publicity attendant on the furor caused by the wolf programs has resulted in a doubling of the organization's membership during the mid-1990s.

Other animals' welfare falls within the ambit of the organization. As a result of Defenders' lobbying, Congress passed an amendment to the Marine Mammal Protection Act to encourage fishing that did not harm dolphins, and in 1990 Defenders succeeded in getting "dolphin safe" labels placed on cans of tuna. Defenders also backed the Wild Bird Conservation Act, passed in 1992, to stop the shipping of wild birds into the United States. This procedure had resulted in the deaths of four-fifths of the birds while depleting species in the originating habitats. Another initiative has been conservation of bears through educating the public and restocking animals in Florida and Montana.

Defenders' advocacy focuses on education, legislation, litigation, and research. It sponsors conferences and recommends informational resources. It has sued agencies such as the Fish and Wildlife Service to compel enforcement of Endangered Species Act (1973) provisions. It also monitors the impact of ecological disasters such as the *Exxon Valdez* oil spill.

The GrassRoots Environmental Effectiveness Network (GREEN) was initiated by Defenders in 1995 to work with grassroots activists on the national, regional, and state levels. Its daily and weekly electronic news bulletins and alerts quickly engage members within congressional districts, and its Partner Groups enable GREEN to mobilize a coalition of allies on short notice.

Defenders members, now numbering 200,000, receive the quarterly magazine *Defenders*. The organization's headquarters is in Washington, D.C.; Dr. Rodger Schlickeisen is its executive director.

See also: ENVIRONMENT

For Further Information

Defenders of Wildlife, *http://www.defenders.org*

Libby, Rondal T. *Eco-wars: Political Campaigns and Social Movements*. New York: Columbia University Press, 1998.

Rembert, Tracey C. "Interview with Dr. Rodger Schlickeisen." *E Magazine: The Environmental Magazine*, March/April 1998, pp. 10–13.

DEPUGH, ROBERT BOLIVAR. *See* Minutemen

DILLING, ELIZABETH KIRKPATRICK (1894–1966).

Born April 19, 1894, in Chicago, Elizabeth Dilling led a women's crusade against U.S. intervention in World War II, was a prolific writer of stridently anticommunist publications, and was the first woman to be admitted to the inner circle of anti-Semitic and racist crusaders GERALD L.K. SMITH and FATHER CHARLES COUGHLIN. Dilling was the most influential woman on the far right during the 1930s, with a following that exceeded 5 million women.

Dilling was raised as an Episcopalian but attended Catholic schools. In her teens, she became an avid Christian, composing forty-page letters to friends about scripture. In 1912 she enrolled at the University of Chicago to study music and languages but showed little interest in history, politics, or public speaking. She did not complete her degree, abhorred her academic experience, and developed a lifelong loathing of professors. Her first marriage, to Albert Dilling, lasted from 1918 until 1945, at which time she reported that her "happy home was ruined by 'Organized Jewry' who sent a 'bleached gold digger' to seduce her husband."

In 1923 the Dillings traveled to Britain, France, and Italy and had an audience with the pope. Elizabeth was angered by the anti-American attitudes of the British and French and their complaints about America's tardiness in entering World War I. It was her visit to the Soviet Union in 1931 that hardened her anticommunist resolve because of the country's rejection of Christianity and promotion of women's sexual equality with men.

In 1932 Dilling founded the Paul Reveres, a Chicago-based organization committed to combating and ferreting out communists and promoting Americanism. A year later, she stepped down as executive secretary, and the group folded in 1934, a victim of member apathy. At this time she became convinced that militant Christianity was required and rejected all notions of tolerance and interfaith cooperation.

In the mid-1930s, she began speaking and showing home movies of the USSR at Daughters of the American Revolution and AMERICAN LEGION meetings and became a popular speaker at Kiwanis and Rotary clubs.

She visited Nazi Germany in 1938 and noted that "the Germans were happy, industrious, and efficient under Hitler, who had done a great deal of good for his people and helped Christianity flourish." As a guest of the Nazi Party, she attended various state functions and concluded that Adolf Hitler was a great leader. In Palestine she filmed Jews who she claimed were ruining the Holy Land. And after visiting Spain she became convinced that fascist dictator Francisco Franco should be revered as a brave Christian. Although never as popular a public figure as Gerald L.K. Smith or Father Coughlin, she was able to elicit standing ovations from audiences exceeding a thousand by 1939.

The Daughters of the American Revolution bought 10,000 copies of Dilling's *Red Revolution: Do We Want It Here?* Her next book, *The Red Network: A "Who's Who" and Handbook of Radicalism for Patriots* (1934), with its descriptions of 460 subversive groups and 1,300 communists, became a best seller, going into its eighth printing in 1941. The KU KLUX KLAN and various Neo-Nazi groups bought copies, and the book still remains in print. The FBI and other law enforcement agencies consulted it to monitor the activities of allegedly subversive organizations and individuals, including the AMERICAN CIVIL LIBERTIES UNION, LEAGUE OF WOMEN VOTERS, NATIONAL ASSOCIATION FOR THE ADVANCEMENT OF COLORED PEOPLE, JANE ADDAMS, FLORENCE KELLEY, ELEANOR ROOSEVELT, Theodore Dreiser, and Albert Einstein.

Other Dilling books that continue to be sold, read, and quoted include *The Plot Against Christianity* and *The Roosevelt Red Record and Its Background*, which accuses Franklin Roosevelt of being a devious, manipulative, power-mad communist who lifted his "Jew Deal" from the *Communist Manifesto.*

Dilling's Mothers' Movement peaked after her losing fight to defeat the Lend-Lease bill, which enabled Britain to purchase arms on credit or borrow them for the duration of World War II. Dilling was arrested in 1941 during a mass demonstration against the bill.

She was supported by the America First Committee, Friends of Social Justice, and Daughters of the American Revolution, and over 600 women broke into senators' offices and disrupted congressional deliberations. She generated more mail to Congress on the British aid program than on any other issue since the fight over the Versailles Treaty after World War I.

In 1944 Dilling was one of the primary defendants prosecuted under the Sedition Act of 1917, which outlawed attempts to undermine the morale of the armed services in wartime. The indicted defendants included twenty-eight German agents, members of the German-American Bund (then the largest U.S.-based pro-Nazi organization, with 5,000 uniformed storm troopers), and others accused of printing and distributing pamphlets containing antiwar speeches. The *Chicago Tribune* defended Dilling and the American Women Against Communism by publishing a flyer that accused President Roosevelt of attempting to destroy free speech in what became known as the Great Sedition Trial. Charges were dismissed in 1946 because the defendants had not received a speedy trial and because their pronouncements, however bigoted, were protected by First Amendment freedom of speech guarantees.

In the 1950s and 1960s, Elizabeth Dilling continued to produce her personally published *Bulletin*, in which she inveighed against NATO, foreign aid, the graduated income tax, racial mixing, fluoridation, federal power, and the Peace Corps. She died in Lincoln, Nebraska, on April 29, 1966.

See also: EXTREMISTS

For Further Information

Dilling, Elizabeth Kirkpatrick. *The Red Network: A "Who's Who" and Handbook of Radicalism for Patriots.* Kenilworth, IL: Privately printed, 1934.

———. *The Roosevelt Red Record and Its Background.* Kenilworth, IL: Privately printed, 1936.

Jeansonne, Glen. *Women of the Far Right: The Mothers' Movement and World War II.* Chicago: University of Chicago Press, 1996.

Protesting Greyhound's alleged failure to serve people with disabilities, three demonstrators prevent the entrance of a Greyhound bus into the Denver terminal in August 1997. An unidentified passenger (right) argues with them. *AP Photo/David Zalubowski.*

DISABLED PERSONS' RIGHTS. Disabled persons' rights are a matter of concern for an estimated 44 million Americans who suffer from various impairments that limit their mobility, access to public and private facilities, hearing, eyesight, strength, and capacity to participate fully in society. They also comprise more than one-sixth of the total U.S. population, a large constituency of potential citizen activists.

The group has not been politically potent because of several limiting conditions. Spokespersons for the disabled argue that it is difficult for them to discard feelings of dependency because of the patronizing, paternalistic attitudes they face in society. Consequently many find it difficult, if not impossible, to make the transition from passive recipient to citizen activist. Also, this constituency has rarely found it possible to

adopt a unified legislative action agenda because of its fragmentation by type of disability. Different impairments—blindness, deafness, cerebral palsy, AIDS, cancer, diabetes, quadriplegia, Alzheimer's disease—impose different needs. Therefore most disability groups have developed advocacy organizations that cater to their particular requirements and cannot muster the number of activists and strength of commitment needed to convince legislators to respond to their demands. Even within groups, for example, the blind, rival organizations exist. Also, most of the advocacy organizations are administered for the group by social service professionals and not by the disabled membership.

The main areas of activist concern have been limited to rehabilitation programs, support of independent living, the strengthening of civil rights, and enforcement of public accommodations accessibility laws.

In 1974 an umbrella lobby of forty-two groups, the American Coalition of Citizens with Disabilities, did succeed in getting the Carter administration to enforce Americans with Disabilities Act (ADA) regulations. A series of sit-ins—the most effective one being staged in Berkeley, California—convinced Joseph Califano, secretary of Health, Education and Welfare, to sign implementing regulations to open up a new world of equal opportunity for more than 35 million handicapped Americans. At that time, the San Francisco Bay area held the largest concentration of disabled persons in the nation, and the Coalition drew additional support from people affiliated with the ongoing civil rights, gay rights, and women's rights movements. Later, after the regulations had been signed, the Coalition disbanded and each group went its separate way.

During the 1980s and 1990s two organizations with strong advocacy components were the AMERICAN DISABLED FOR ATTENDANT PROGRAMS TODAY (ADAPT) and CFIDS ASSOCIATION OF AMERICA.

ADAPT, formed in 1983, captured public attention by blocking buses in major cities and seizing political offices across the United States to dramatize the need to enforce bus companies' compliance with ADA. ADAPT's other campaign was to increase the share of federal money spent on home-based care so that the disabled could continue living in their own homes. The CFIDS Association, founded in 1987, successfully enlisted its members in efforts to convince federal agencies and legislators to commit more funding to research the etiology of chronic fatigue syndrome and its cure.

For Further Information

Dell Orto, Arthur E., and Robert P. Marinelli, eds. *Encyclopedia of Disability and Rehabilitation.* New York: Macmillan Library Reference USA, 1995.

Freeman, Jo, ed. *Social Movements of the Sixties and Seventies.* New York: Longman, 1983.

DISSATISFIED PARENTS TOGETHER. *See* National Vaccine Information Center

DOBSON, JAMES C. (1936–). Born April 21, 1936, in Shreveport, Louisiana, James C. Dobson is founder and president of the 5 million member FOCUS ON THE FAMILY and considered by many to be the central figure in contemporary conservative Christianity. The mission of Focus on the Family is "to cooperate with the Holy Spirit in disseminating the Gospel of Jesus Christ to as many people as possible, and, specifically, to accomplish that objective by helping to preserve traditional values and the institution of the family."

Dobson grew up in Texas and Oklahoma. His father, grandparents, and great-grandparents were Nazarene evangelists who instilled in him from an early age an abhorrence of all actions they believed offended God. Unlike JERRY FALWELL and PAT ROBERTSON, he did not move into the ministry, instead earning degrees at the University of California in psychology (1962) and child development (1967). He was an associate professor and later served on the staff of Children's Hospital in Los Angeles. His articles on phenylketonuria (a genetic disorder causing progressive mental retardation) were published in the *New England Journal of Medicine* and other highly respected journals.

While working as a counselor, speaker, and writer, Dobson became aware of a culture that dismayed him because of its distance from the wholesome atmosphere in which he had been raised. He became convinced that a conservative Christian antidote to the indulgent, relativist sexual and cultural mores of the sixties and liberal childrearing advice of pediatrician Dr. Benjamin Spock was needed. He wrote *Dare to Discipline* (1970) in which he advocated spanking, though never in anger and tempered by psychological support. His book was an immediate best seller, winning him frequent speaking engagements. Other successful books followed, for example, *What Wives Wish Their Hus-*

bands Knew about Women (1975) and *Preparing for Adolescence* (1978). He developed a seven-part television series, *Focus on the Family*, and this, in turn, evolved into a powerful ministry comprising radio and television broadcasting; *Focus on the Family*, a magazine with a circulation of 2.5 million; and various films and videos.

Dobson's radio show, aired daily on more than 1,900 radio outlets, is popular among millions of listeners because of his moral certitude and warm, folksy, firmly self-assured speaking style. He believes that his way is God's way and that any compromise with the path of righteousness, traditional values, and the institution of the family is sinful. His loyal followers have become what many consider the most potent secular religious force in the country, exerting continuous pressure on Congress to enact pro-family legislation. They oppose clean needle exchange programs for drug addicts, support vouchers to facilitate children's transferal from public to private schools, and seek the banning of federal assistance to overseas countries with family planning programs.

Dobson also is eager to see *ROE V. WADE* reversed. He has established thirty-five regional Family Councils, grassroots groups that fight abortion, homosexuality, and pornography and endorse prayer in public schools. In the 1990s Dobson became the dominant force in shaping the Republican Party's conservative political agenda, urging it to adopt and remain loyal to its stated pro-family value positions.

See also: RELIGIOUS RIGHT

For Further Information

Alexander-Moegerle, Gil. *James Dobson's War on America*. Amherst, MA: Prometheus Books, 1997.

Dobson, James C. *The New Dare to Discipline*. Wheaton, IL: Tyndale House, 1992.

———. *Parenting Isn't for Cowards*. Nashville, TN: Word Publishing, 1997.

———. *What Wives Wish Their Husbands Knew about Women*. Wheaton, IL: Tyndale House 1975.

Murray Zoba, Wendy. "Daring to Discipline America." *Christianity Today*, March 1, 1999, pp. 30–38.

DU BOIS, WILLIAM EDWARD BURGHARDT (W.E.B.) (1868–1963).

Born in Great Barrington, Massachusetts, on February 23, 1868, William Edward Burghardt Du Bois was an important early advocate of radical black protest in the United States. Being African American, Du Bois was very much aware of the injustices being faced daily by members of his race during the immediate aftermath of the Civil War. New opportunities were opening up for blacks in 1870s, and Du Bois's intellect and ambition enabled him to achieve notable scholarly success. He earned degrees at Fiske University and a doctorate from Harvard, eventually becoming a professor at Atlanta University.

Du Bois's position enabled him to be a prominent force, an activist who was striving to connect African Americans with their heritage. He was militantly pro–social reform, co-founding the Niagara Movement, which called for electoral, economic, educational, and First Amendment rights for African Americans. Internal dissension and attack from the outside, however, lessened the effectiveness of the movement. Du Bois also helped found the NATIONAL ASSOCIATION FOR THE ADVANCEMENT OF COLORED PEOPLE.

Du Bois was never able to see many of the reforms he advocated materialize. He joined the American Communist Party and severed his connections with the United States, eventually renouncing his citizenship and moving to Ghana, where he died in 1963.

See also: AFRICAN-AMERICAN RIGHTS

For Further Information

Du Bois, W.E.B. *The Souls of Black Folk*. New York: Signet Classic, 1995.

Lewis, David Levering. *W.E.B. Du Bois: Biography of a Race, 1868–1919*. New York: Henry Holt, 1993.

———. *W.E.B. Du Bois: The Fight for Equality and the American Century, 1919–1963*. New York: Henry Holt, 2000.

McDaniel, Melissa. *W.E.B. Du Bois: Scholar and*

Civil Rights Activist. New York: Franklin Watts, 1999.

DUBINSKY, DAVID (1892–1982). For almost forty years, David Dubinsky, born February 22, 1892, in Brest Litovsk, Russia, as David Dobnievski, was the most inventive, socially responsible, and influential labor leader in the United States. At age fourteen Dubinsky joined a bakers' union in Lodz, Russia, and was soon elected secretary of his local. Czarist police punished him for his activities and banished him to Siberia. He escaped, finagled his way to New York City, and joined other Jewish immigrants in the apparel industry, beginning as a fabric cutter in a local of the International Ladies Garment Workers Union (ILGWU), established in 1900. In 1918 he was elected to the local's executive board and by 1922 had moved into the vice presidency of the union.

Although Dubinsky became a socialist, he denounced communism when the Bolsheviks overthrew the Kerensky provisional government in Russia in 1916. He successfully waged war against Communist Party attempts to take over the ILGWU, keeping the apparel industry free of its influence during the 1930s. In 1932, coincident with the election of Franklin D. Roosevelt and the advent of the New Deal, Dubinsky was elected ILGWU president. Initially the union was in disarray, with a dwindling membership and piled-up debt, but Roosevelt's National Recovery Act facilitated a flood of money into the union's coffers. Gus Tyler, a later ILGWU leader, in an article in the October 1994 issue of *Monthly Labor Review*, points out that Dubinsky decided to use the surplus funds to build the union into a "way of life,— a center of athletic activity, of artistic expression, of social communion, of political participation, of creative performance, of intellectual engagement."

The ILGWU experienced a fourfold increase in three years and subsequently won greatly increased benefits for its members without resorting to strikes or permitting infiltration of its ranks by racketeers. Earlier, Dubinsky had joined JOHN L. LEWIS in organizing the Committee for Industrial Organizations (1935). After the ILGWU was expelled from the American Federation of Labor (AFL) in 1937 he refused to affiliate it with the new Congress of Industrial Organizations (CIO) and led it back to the AFL in 1940.

The ILGWU promoted political causes, raising money for liberal candidates and reform organizations. Dubinsky helped found the Liberal Party of New York (1944) and AMERICANS FOR DEMOCRATIC ACTION in 1947. He was a leading advocate of greater political participation by labor, including extensive lobbying at the state and federal levels. By 1949 the ILGWU had established health centers in major cities, had its own radio network, was sponsoring a summer camp, ran an educational department, and offered its members scholarships to universities. Dubinsky retired from the ILGWU presidency in 1966, at which time the union had $500 million in assets and 445,000 members. He was awarded the Presidential Medal of Freedom in 1969.

See also: LABOR ISSUES

For Further Information

Dubinsky, David. *David Dubinsky: My Life with Labor.* New York: Simon and Schuster, 1977.
Tyler, Gus. "David Dubinsky: A Life with Social Significance." *Monthly Labor Review* 117 (October 1994): 43–49.

DUCKS UNLIMITED. Founded in 1937 by New York City–based sportsmen and conservationists, Ducks Unlimited (DU) is the world's largest wetland conservation organization. Its mission is to "protect, restore, maintain and improve habitat on National Forests and National Grasslands" by furthering the cooperative efforts by "federal agencies, state fish and wildlife agencies, adjacent landowners, and especially national, regional and local conservation groups."

DU was organized to raise money in the United States for waterfowl conservation throughout North America. It acquired shoreline and wetland habitat that had dried up during the Dust Bowl drought in the 1930s. By 1966 DU had raised a million dollars through membership contributions, auctions, dinners, and raffles; in 1996 DU passed the billion-dollar mark. Auction items include sporting art, rifles, decoys, books, and hunting trips to exotic places. Corporate sponsors (e.g., Budweiser, Chevrolet, Dow Chemical, and Winchester Ammunition) also contribute to DU. Funds from the sales of federally distributed "duck stamps," first issued in 1934, produce considerable income, as they currently cost $7.50 each. Every waterfowl hunter over age sixteen in this nation must purchase them each year.

In 1989 Congress enacted the North American Wetlands Conservation Act in response to DU's lobbying efforts. In cooperation with state governments, corporations, farmers, and individual landowners, the group has restored and enhanced over 6 million acres of habitat in all fifty states. It continues its campaign to restore and enhance breeding grounds for migratory waterfowl in the Canadian prairie provinces, which provide 70 percent of North America's goose and duck nesting and staging areas, as well as in Mexico, where millions of ducks spend their winters. DU leaders contend that "true hunters have undeniably proven to be this country's most effective conservationists." The group draws a large and loyal following because its members are doubly motivated; they are committed to waterfowl preservation, saving the ducks so they can hunt them in addition to appreciating them as wonders of nature.

DU membership exceeds 550,000, and 3,500 regional groups and offices are located in the fifty states, Canada, Mexico, New Zealand, and Australia. Matthew B. Connolly Jr. is executive director of the Memphis, Tennessee–based organization. Its office in Washington, D.C., monitors legislation and regulations, updating members on such issues as funding of the Wetlands Reserve and Conservation Reserve programs, which pay farmers to retire marginal farmland from crop production and convert it into wildlife habitat. Members receive a subscription to *Ducks Unlimited Magazine*.

See also: ENVIRONMENT

For Further Information

Ducks Unlimited, *http://www.ducks.org/*

Farrington, Selwyn Kip. *The Ducks Came Back: The Story of Ducks Unlimited*. New York: Coward-McCann, 1945.

Jendryka, Brian. "Make Way for Ducklings." *Policy Review* no. 68 (Spring 1994): 72–78.

E

EAGLE FORUM. Founded by PHYLLIS SCHLAFLY in 1975, the Eagle Forum advocates traditional family and educational values, a strong national defense, and private enterprise. It was praised by former President Ronald Reagan for setting "a high standard of volunteer participation in the political and legislative process." He praised its members for making "such enormous individual efforts in finding and electing good candidates to office from the courthouse to the White House, and especially in the Senate and Congress. God bless all of you," he continued, "for your dedication to God, Family, and Country." Eagle Forum's name is taken from Isaiah 40:31: "They that wait upon the Lord shall renew their strength; they shall mount up with wings as eagles; they shall run, and not be weary; and they shall walk, and not faint."

The Eagle Forum was born during a time when many conservative American women believed that their way of life was being threatened. Although they considered vulnerability to attack by foreign enemies a danger, they believed that inner moral decay was the foremost peril facing the nation. Most resented was the women's movement as exemplified in the liberal agenda of the NATIONAL ORGANIZATION FOR WOMEN. Phyllis Schlafly denounced the Equal Rights Amendment as a feminist plot to destroy the family and led the successful battle against its ratification in the 1970s. Her STOP ERA citizen action network swamped congressional switchboards with calls from religious conservative homemakers from Maine to California. Victory came in 1982 when the ERA fell short of ratification by the required number of states.

Eagle Forum promotes conservative, pro-family policies at all levels of government. It "opposes and exposes the radical feminists, their attacks on the family and on homemakers, their use of 'Anita Hill'–style tactics against men, their support of Affirmative Action quotas and gender 'norming,' their agitation to put women and open homosexuals in combat assignments, their campaign for the misnamed Equal Rights Amendment with its hidden agenda, and their efforts to put the federal government in the babysitting business."

Eagle Forum believes that public schools should "educate children in factual knowledge and academic skills (reading, writing, arithmetic) with an overall purpose of encouraging excellence—not mediocrity." The group supports parents' right to excuse children from classroom activities that involve alcohol and drug education; topics related to globalism, discussions of organic evolution, death education—including abortion and suicide; curricula on nuclear issues; discussion on Eastern mysticism; and education on human sexuality, parenting, or attitudes toward parents. Eagle Forum says that "schools should not impose on children courses in explicit sex or alternate lifestyles, profane or immoral fiction or videos, New Age practices, anti-Biblical materials, or 'Politically Correct' liberal attitudes about social and economic issues."

Other positions taken by Eagle Forum include opposition to all tax increases and U.S. ties to the United Nations, prohibitions on school prayer, gay rights, and abortion rights. In combination with Schlafly's Republican National Coalition for Life, Eagle Forum was a driving force behind the Republican Party anti-choice platform plank in 1992.

Phyllis Schlafly is Eagle Forum president. The group's headquarters is in Alton, Illinois; its political action committee has an office in Washington, D.C. There are 80,000 members and chapters in all fifty states. Publications include the *Phyllis Schlafly Report* and *Education Reporter*. Schlafly also writes a syndicated column for newspapers across the country, and her radio commentaries, covering education, national defense, politics, feminism and the family, economics, and social, public, and foreign policy, are broadcast daily on 270 stations.

See also: CONSERVATIVES (FAR RIGHT); RELIGIOUS RIGHT

For Further Information

Eagle Forum, *http://www.eagleforum.org*
Jacobson, Louis. "The Eagle Has Landed." *National Journal* 29 (October 25, 1997): 2154–2155.
Marshall, Susan E. "Who Speaks for American Women? The Future of Antifeminism." *Annals of the American Academy of Political and Social Science* 515 (May 1991): 50–64.

EARTH FIRST! Founded in 1980, Earth First! (EF!), according to co-founder, David Foreman, is an "eco-warrior" movement that embraces the slogan "No Compromise in the Defense of Mother Earth!" and believes in "using all the tools in the tool box, ranging from grassroots organizing and involvement in the legal process to civil disobedience and monkeywrenching." Earth First! defines monkeywrenching as the "unlawful sabotage of industrial extraction/development equipment and infrastructure, as a means of striking at the Earth's destroyers at the point where they commit their crimes." It is aimed only at inanimate objects and at the pocketbooks of industrial despoilers. A 1989 Earth First! brochure proclaimed that the "ideas and manifestations of industrial civilization are anti-Earth, anti-woman, and anti-liberty."

EF! came into existence at the end of the Carter administration and the beginning of the Reagan years, during a period when environmental safeguards were being weakened. Its co-founders were David Foreman, Michael Roselle, Howie Wolke, Bart Koehler, Ron Kezar, and Susan Morgan, most of them former staff members of traditional environmental groups. Foreman, who had been a lobbyist on Capitol Hill for the WILDERNESS SOCIETY, deplored the constant compromises, litigation, and genteel professional tactics employed by the established groups; even GREENPEACE U.S.A. had been concentrating more on fundraising than direct action. Because ecologists' archenemy Secretary of the Interior James Watt, worry over global warming, and the hole in the ozone layer were still in the future, a strong stimulus for activism was missing.

It was EDWARD ABBEY's *Monkey Wrench Gang*, a 1975 novel about a crew of eco-saboteurs, that inspired and instructed the new group to "resist much, obey little" and to realize that "sentiment without action is the ruin of the soul." The book's characters insert spikes into tree trunks to sabotage loggers' saw blades, pour sugar in fuel tanks of earthmoving equipment, tree sit, yank out survey stakes, dress up as bears that demand salmon dinners from campers, and perform other acts of disobedience. The initial Earth Firsters believed in deep ecology, a nature-centered philosophy that accords equal standing to all animals, plant life, and natural objects. Co-founder David Foreman views

This May 1998, photo shows Earth First! activist Julia "Butterfly" Hill climbing toward her 180-foot-high shelter in "Luna," the old-growth redwood tree near Elinor, California, in which Hill had lived for the previous six months. *AP Photo/Shaun Walker.*

human beings as "a cancer on nature," and has suggested that nature is attempting to heal itself through such events as AIDS and African famines.

Most Earth First! members abhor modern industrial society, contending that the earth is to be nurtured and protected, not exploited. The first salvo in the EF! offensive was its creation of a 100-yard "crack" in the Arizona Glen Canyon Dam, simulated by using strands of black plastic.

In 1986 EF! co-founder Howie Wolke was jailed for removing survey stakes on a road being built by the Chevron Oil Company in the Bridger-Teton National Forest. Three years later, David Foreman and three other EF! members were charged by the FBI with conspiring to destroy nuclear facilities in Arizona, California, and Colorado. In 1990, the Redwood Summer demonstrations in Northern California were modeled after the

Mississippi Freedom Summer Project of 1964, during which student volunteers from Northern colleges had led a statewide black voter registration campaign. EF! drew upon fresh recruits from college campuses to halt clear-cutting of 1,000-year-old-forests. The newly joining young people believed in nonviolent action and opposed tree spiking. Judy Bari, leader of the Redwood protests, and EF! co-founder Michael Roselle agreed and wrote a memo condemning the practice. Foreman, a conservative and a former supporter of Barry Goldwater, quit EF!, angered by its takeover by leftist humanists and sentimental tree huggers concerned with countercultural causes.

EF! has continued its protests, blocking a four-lane road to the Tennessee Valley Authority Watts Bar nuclear plant in 1994 and resuming its battle to save redwood trees from destruction. In 1999 Julia "Butterfly"

Hill gained national notoriety for living 180 feet from the ground in a 1,000-year-old redwood, Luna, for more than 600 days to save it from the loggers.

EF! is a movement, not a formal organization, so it has no staff or designated leaders. This enables it to conceal its many illegal actions and to frustrate law enforcement agencies. Its estimated membership is 3,000 with contacts in thirty-six states and nineteen foreign countries. It publishes *Earth First! The Radical Environmental Journal* eight times a year, on the solstices, equinoxes, and cross-quarter days. The subscription address is P.O. Box 1415, Eugene, Oregon 97440.

See also: ENVIRONMENT; EXTREMISTS

For Further Information

Lee, Martha F. *Earth First! Environmental Apocalypse*. Syracuse, NY: Syracuse University Press, 1995.
Wall, Derek. *Earth First! and the Anti-Roads Movement: Radical Environmentalism and Comparative Social Movements*. New York: Routledge, 1999.

EARTH LIBERATION FRONT. Earth Liberation Front (ELF) is an underground environmental activist organization that is committed to inflicting financial pain on corporations they feel damage the ecosystem. ELF claims to operate "under a strict code of nonviolence as it pertains to harming human or animal life," while conducting "economic sabotage designed to effect change where it counts in our capitalistic society—in the wallet." ELF has claimed responsibility for over a dozen attacks on food producers, research scientists, loggers, miners, ski facilities, mink farms, construction vehicles, and other targets, causing over $32 million in damages.

ELF was founded in 1992 in Brighton, England, by disgruntled EARTH FIRST! (EF!) members who had refused to renounce criminal, nonviolent economic sabotage as a protest tactic at a time when other Earth Firsters were moving their organization from a confrontational to a more mainstream position.

ELF rejects the possibility of integrating conservation into a broader political context. According to ELF, technological society is rapidly ruining the planet and there is too little time left for nonviolent civil disobedience and traditional lobbying to deter disaster; sabotage is the only way to save the earth's genetic heritage and biological diversity from imminent destruction.

In 1993 the ANIMAL LIBERATION FRONT and Earth Liberation Front issued a joint communiqué declaring their solidarity, while Judy Bari, an EF! leader, defended her group's less extremist policy in *Earth First! Journal* (February 1994).

After inflicting considerable damage on allegedly anti-ecology British businesses, earthmoving equipment, gas stations, and tropical wood importers, and destroying Ireland's first genetically engineered sugar beet crop, ELF infiltrated the United States in 1994. Since then, it has claimed responsibility (shared with the Animal Liberation Front) for burning down an Oregon corral used to round up wild horses for slaughter. It has also torched a U.S. Department of Agriculture building where wild animals were allegedly being euthanized, released mink from a Wisconsin fur farm, destroyed the Oregon headquarters of U.S. Forest Industries, and committed other criminal acts in Massachusetts, Washington, Wyoming, and Michigan. On October 19, 1998, in the costliest act of ecoterrorism to date, ELF claimed responsibility for burning down five buildings and four ski lifts at Vail, Colorado, causing $12 million in damage to the resort, this being done to preserve the lynx habitat.

ELFs are organized into cells for security reasons and see themselves as spokes in the wheel of an international civil dissent movement. Membership in the United States is estimated to be no more than 200; leaders and locations are unknown.

See also: ENVIRONMENT; EXTREMISTS

For Further Information

Markels, Alex. "Backfire." *Mother Jones*, March/April 1999, pp. 60–64.
Sullivan, Robert. "The Face of Eco-Terrorism."

The Earth Liberation Front claimed responsibility for the October 1998 fire that destroyed the Two Elks Restaurant at the Vail Mountain Ski Resort in Colorado. *AP Photo/Jack Affleck.*

New York Times Magazine, December 20, 1998, pp. 46–49.

Wall, Derek. *Earth First! and the Anti-Roads Movement: Radical Environmentalism and Comparative Social Movements.* London and New York: Routledge, 1999.

EDELMAN, MARIAN WRIGHT

(1939–). Marian Wright Edelman's all-consuming passion is improvement of the plight of poor children in American society. Currently president of the CHILDREN'S DE-FENSE FUND (CDF), she has waged an unremitting war on children's behalf since 1964. In her youth, she, like other black children in the South, was excluded from the local parks and drug store counters. In response, her father, a Baptist minister, opened up a playground and canteen behind his church to accommodate neighborhood kids. Edelman's sense of outrage and commitment to correc-

tive reform stemmed from her childhood and is lifelong. She has compiled a vast number of grim statistics documenting the nation's neglect of children, its most precious and potentially fruitful investment in the future. Distressingly high poverty, hunger, lack of health insurance and day care, infant mortality, teenage pregnancy, drug and alcohol abuse, and gun violence figures attest to the country's uncaring attitude.

Marian Wright Edelman was born June 6, 1939, in Bennettsville, South Carolina. Excelling academically, musically talented, and an omnivorous reader, Edelman entered Spelman College in Atlanta and went abroad during her junior year. She anticipated a career in the Foreign Service and studied in Paris, Geneva, and Moscow. Her senior year coincided with the dawn of the civil rights movement and her own maturing social conscience. Returning to the States, she was jailed for participating in a sit-in in Atlanta

Marian Wright Edelman, president of the Children's Defense Fund, holds a news conference in Washington in February 1983 to protest proposed Reagan administration cuts in programs for children. *AP Photo/Dennis Cook.*

City Hall. She then went to Yale Law School and upon graduating became a legal counsel for the NATIONAL ASSOCIATION FOR THE ADVANCEMENT OF COLORED PEOPLE (NAACP). In 1964 she represented wrongfully jailed protesters involved in the Mississippi Freedom Summer Project during which three civil rights workers were murdered.

She met and married Peter B. Edelman, a Harvard Law School graduate, and moved with him to Washington, where he founded the Washington Research Project, a public interest research and advocacy organization, in 1968. In 1973 Edelman spun off the Children's Defense Fund from the Washington Research Project and is CDF's current executive director, serving as champion of the true "silent majority," the nation's voiceless and voteless children.

One of Edelman's three sons, Jonah Martin Edelman, has started Stand for Children, a separate activist group, to aggressively lobby for pro-children legislation as a 501(c)(4) organization after a March for Children, attracting 300,000 people to the Lincoln Memorial in Washington, D.C., failed to produce favorable legislation in 1997. Currently, Marian Wright Edelman continues her battle for federal funds and programs with evangelical fervor while CDF collects supportive data and issues annual reports on the status of children in the United States.

See also: CHILD AND YOUTH-RELATED ISSUES

For Further Information

Edelman, Marian Wright. *The Measure of Our Success: A Letter to My Children and Yours.* Boston: Beacon Press, 1994.
———. "Saving the Children: Taking a Stand." *EMERGE*, June 1996, pp. 58+.

———. *The State of America's Children Yearbook, 1999: A Report from the Children's Defense Fund*. Boston: Beacon Press, 1999.

EMILY'S LIST. Founded in 1985, EMILY's List is a donor network supporting pro-choice Democratic women candidates for governorships and for seats in the U.S. Senate and House of Representatives. Ellen Malcolm and twenty-five other Democratic women started the group in order to give women the credibility and financial backing needed to win elections. EMILY stands for "Early Money Is Like Yeast"—it makes the "dough" rise.

As of 1985, no Democratic woman had ever been elected to the U.S. Senate, no woman had been elected governor of a large state, and the number of Democratic women in the House of Representatives had fallen to twelve. Within a year, EMILY's List raised $350,000, the largest commitment going to help elect Barbara Mikulski, a liberal based in Baltimore, Maryland, and the first Democratic woman elected to the Senate in her own right. In the year 1992, EMILY's List grew 600 percent, from 3,500 to 24,000 members, and collected over $6.2 million to support recommended candidates' campaigns. The extraordinary gain in membership was attributed to television viewers' reaction to the dismissive treatment given Anita Hill during the Senate hearings on Clarence Thomas's Supreme Court nomination. In the elections following its formation, EMILY's List has been instrumental in electing seven pro-choice Democratic women senators, forty-nine congresswomen, and three governors. An advisory committee of twenty-five women reviews and recommends candidates to be backed by the organization.

In 1995 EMILY's List launched WOMEN VOTE. This multiyear initiative's aim is to inform and mobilize women voters throughout the country. It targets five groups: seniors, African Americans, Latinas, professional women, and women without college degrees, using mail and telephone calls to urge their increased turnout in forthcoming elections.

The objective is to counteract the extreme right's organizing efforts and to increase Democratic candidates' likelihood of winning.

EMILY's List is headquartered in Washington, D.C. Ellen Malcolm is president and Wendy Sherman is executive director. Current membership is about 50,000. Members select women from a roster of candidates and contribute $100 or more to at least two of them. Members of the "Majority Council" give $1,000 or more annually. A quarterly newsletter, *Notes from EMILY*, is provided for members.

See Also: WOMEN'S ISSUES

For Further Information

EMILY's List, *http://www.emilyslist.org*
Hirschmann, Susan. "EMILY's List: Chicks with Checks." *American Spectator*, April 1993, pp. 20–23.
Rosin, Hanna. "Working Girls." *New Republic*, May 13, 1996, pp. 11–12.

***ENGEL V. VITALE* (370 U.S. 421) (1962).** In *Engel v. Vitale*, the Supreme Court held that "it is no part of the business of government to compose official prayers to be recited as a part of a religious program carried on by government." The decision denied the right of public schools to conduct prayer services within school buildings during regular school hours. Many religious and conservative groups were outraged, arguing that the ruling made public education godless and that an amendment to the Constitution was needed to permit prayer ceremonies to take place.

The case originated in New York State, where the Board of Regents had approved the following denominationally neutral prayer: "Almighty God, we acknowledge our dependence upon Thee, and we beg Thy blessings upon us, our parents, our teachers and our country." The reading of the prayer was struck down as conflicting with the establishment clause of the First Amendment to the U.S. Constitution, which states that "Congress shall make no law respecting an establishment of religion, or prohibiting the free exercise thereof."

In 1963 the ruling was reinforced in a closely related case, *School District of Abington Township v. Schemp*. The issue in the Abington case was a Pennsylvania law that permitted the reading of ten verses from the Bible during the opening hour of each school day. The verses were to be read without comment, and any child could be excused from reading the passages or attending the reading, upon written request of the parents or guardians. The Court made it clear that it did not reject the idea of using the Bible as a part of the study of comparative religion or the history of religion or as a piece of literature. What the Court objected to was the readings as part of a prescribed religious exercise in the curriculum. Although public and political pressure to pass a "Religious Freedom Amendment" has not diminished, the Court has continued to disallow institutionally prescribed school prayers, Bible readings, and meditation.

For Further Information

Andryszewski, Tricia. *School Prayer: A History of the Debate*. Berkeley Heights, NJ: Enslow, 1997.

Haas, Carol. *Engel v. Vitale: Separation of Church and State*. Hillside, NJ: Enslow, 1994.

Ravitch, Frank S. *School Prayer and Discrimination: The Civil Rights of Religious Minorities and Dissenters*. Boston: Northeastern University Press, 1999.

ENVIRONMENT. The biotic environment includes living plants and animals; the abiotic environment is made up of factors that support life, such as temperature, soil, water, air, and protection from radiation in the atmosphere. In the United States, deterioration in the abiotic environment became a serious problem in the early 1900s as air pollution became common in industrial cities and urban expansion began to disrupt the biosphere. Smoke and soot from steel mills, power plants, steam locomotives, and chimneys filled the air. Logging operations and dams threatened and displaced animal populations and destroyed scenic areas. As the population expanded, the problem worsened, and concerned citizens started seeking remedies to halt the ruination.

In response, the universe of conservationist and environmental organizations has become very large, now exceeding 12,000, and extending from the beginnings of the conservation movement (e.g., John Muir and NATIONAL AUDUBON SOCIETY) in the early twentieth century up to the militant "New Environmentalism" born in the 1970s. The individuals (EDWARD ABBEY, DAVID ROSS BROWER, RACHEL LOUISE CARSON, LOIS GIBBS) and organizations (CENTER FOR HEALTH, ENVIRONMENT AND JUSTICE, CITIZENS FOR A BETTER ENVIRONMENT, CLEAN WATER ACTION, DEFENDERS OF WILDLIFE, DUCKS UNLIMITED, EARTH FIRST!, EARTH LIBERATION FRONT, ENVIRONMENTAL ACTION, ENVIRONMENTAL DEFENSE, FRIENDS OF THE EARTH, GREENPEACE U.S.A., HUMANE SOCIETY OF THE UNITED STATES, IZAAK WALTON LEAGUE OF AMERICA, LEAGUE OF CONSERVATION VOTERS, NATIONAL PARKS AND CONSERVATION ASSOCIATION, NATIONAL WILDLIFE FEDERATION, NATURAL RESOURCES DEFENSE COUNCIL, SEA SHEPHERD CONSERVATION SOCIETY, and WILDERNESS SOCIETY) described in this encyclopedia are only a small selective sampling of the many that have made a lasting and major imprint on laws affecting the environment or on public awareness of ecological crises.

Unlike most other issues that can stir up public concern (e.g., gun control, abortion rights, tax reform), the problems of acid rain, pollution, degradation of natural resources, endangered species, loss of the ozone shield, and global warming affect all humankind. A livable environment is viewed as a common good and a universal need, not as a polarizing issue that can create friction along religious, gender, or political fault lines. Therefore the organizations formed prior to 1969, with mostly middle-aged, wealthy, well-educated, and predominantly white members, worked and rallied quietly for conservation. These early groups include the SI-

ERRA CLUB, National Audubon Society, National Parks and Conservation Association, Izaak Walton League, Defenders of Wildlife, Wilderness Society, National Wildlife Federation, Ducks Unlimited, and Environmental Defense Fund, all established between 1892 and 1967. The Natural Resources Defense Council, founded in 1970, is similarly oriented, being primarily involved in publicity and litigation against polluting industries but more willing to negotiate with industry than the radical groups that started up during this same period.

Before the 1960s, environmental groups had been small, low-visibility organizations with mostly regional constituencies. Publication of Rachel Carson's *Silent Spring* in 1962 created a shock wave that jolted the general public and prompted activism. Carson warned of dead rivers and dying songbirds that would result from the unrestricted use of pesticides. Her book and the restive antiestablishment climate of the sixties set off serious public discussion of recycling, ozone layer depletion, and degradation of the environment. Earth Day 1970 gave an added boost to the new environmental movement by placing pollution problems on the national agenda. David Brower, who during his years as director of the Sierra Club (1952–1969) had transformed the formerly undersized and staid group into an aggressive, muscular "in your face" antagonist to dam construction on public lands, provided further stimulation. In 1970 Brower left the Sierra Club and founded Friends of the Earth. The number of people committed to environmental activism remained high in the 1980s despite energy crises, economic downturns, and tax revolts. Anxiety placed the environmental movement on red alert during the early years of the Reagan administration because of the dismantling or disregard of federal environmental policies. Ecological disasters such as the *Exxon Valdez* oil spill and public concern over such issues as global warming and ozone depletion stimulated surges in membership in the early 1990s.

A new cluster of radical environmental groups was brought to life by individuals committed to direct confrontation with industry and who shared a passion for issues and a vision of what the future world should be. Environmental Action, Citizens for a Better Environment, Greenpeace U.S.A., Clean Water Action, and the Citizens' Clearinghouse for Hazardous Waste are representative of this second wave of activism. Even more extreme were the groups inspired by Edward Abbey, author of *The Monkey Wrench Gang* (1975), a popular novel that detailed and promoted eco-sabotage as a way to halt industry's pillage of the environment. The Sea Shepherd Conservation Society, Earth First!, and Earth Liberation Front are among organizations that have taken destructive and violent steps to protect the environment from fishing interests, lumber companies, land developers, and the recreation industry.

A counterforce of groups calling for "wise use" responded to the radicals and extremists, claiming that they, not the arrogant, overly idealistic pro-environment activists, represent the best interests of a majority of Americans. Citizens for the Sensible Control of Acid Rain, Citizens for the Environment, the Alliance for America, and the National Wetlands Coalition, all established and supported by industry, occupy this bloc of groups that praise and publicize the progressive role industry plays in protecting the environment.

See also: FALSE FRONT ORGANIZATIONS

For Further Information

Bosso, C. "After the Movement: Environmental Activism in the 1960s." In N. J. Vi and M. E. Kraft. *Environmental Policy in the 1990s*. Washington, DC: Congressional Quarterly, 1994.

Byrnes, Patricia. *Environmental Pioneers*. Minneapolis: Oliver Press, 1998.

Pringle, Laurence. *The Environmental Movement: From Its Roots to the Challenges of a New Century*. New York: HarperCollins, 2000.

ENVIRONMENTAL ACTION. In their mission statement, the founders of Environmental Action (EA) said, "EA concentrates on the human environment and the dangerous impact of short-sighted corporate practices on environmental quality and public health. We believe in empowering citizens to work though the political process to win effective environmental protection with full citizen and corporate responsibility." The group received its impetus for formation from Earth Day (April 22, 1970), a nationwide event that included rallies, demonstrations, and teach-ins. Its founder and first coordinator, Denis Hayes, organized the first Earth Day.

EA concentrated its energies on combating the dangerous impact of socially irresponsible corporations that degrade and pollute the environment, thereby threatening public health and welfare. The group avoided wilderness and wildlife conservation issues and focused exclusively on the human environment and on citizen action motivation.

EA's first and most prominent victory followed its "Dirty Dozen" campaign, launched in 1970, in which it listed and publicly displayed on roadside billboards the twelve members of the House of Representatives with the worst voting records on environmental legislation during the previous session of Congress. Six of the "Dirty Dozen" were defeated in the next election. In 1980 EA launched its "Filthy Five" campaign, publicizing the political contributions of the nation's then five biggest polluters: Dow Chemical, International Paper, Republic Steel, Occidental Petroleum, and Standard Oil (Indiana).

During its twenty-six-year lifetime, the group concentrated its efforts in three areas: utilities' modes of energy generation, hazardous waste disposal, and recycling and materials preservation. In the 1980s and 1990s, the group intensified its advocacy of more stringent standards for toxic wastes and the reduced use of fossil fuels to decrease global warming.

In 1994 Environmental Action Foundation (EAF) absorbed EA. Foundation members received *Environmental Action* magazine (published six times a year) until EAF's disbandment in December 1996. *Waste-*

lines, a newsletter reporting on solid waste issues, and *The Power Line*, covering citizen action on energy and electrical utility issues, had been available by subscription.

EAF folded in 1996 due to such factors as fundraising shortfalls, loss of focus, and internal disagreements on organizational priorities. At that time, the group's executive director was Margaret Morgan-Hubbard; its headquarters was in Takoma Park, Maryland.

See also: ENVIRONMENT

For Further Information

Environmental Action 1–28 (1970–1996).
Lundegaard, Karen M. "Environmental Group Folds." *Washington Business Journal*, December 6, 1996, p. 6.

ENVIRONMENTAL DEFENSE. Environmental Defense (ED), named the Environmental Defense Fund until January 2000, is "dedicated to protecting the environmental rights of all people, including future generations. Among these rights are clean air, clean water, healthy, nourishing food, and a flourishing ecosystem. . . . Environmental Defense will work to create solutions that win lasting political, economic, and social support because they are bipartisan, efficient and fair." ED is committed to a multidisciplinary approach to environmental problems, combining the efforts of scientists, economists, and attorneys to devise practical, economically feasible solutions. During its early days, ED was noted for its aggressiveness. Its early informal motto was "Sue the bastards," a reference to its goal of forcing companies to improve their behavior through lawsuits.

ED was originated in 1967 by a group of scientists and naturalists on Long Island who were disturbed by loss of ospreys and other birds resulting from DDT spraying and the insecticide's dangerously high concentrations in human mothers' milk. Founding members Arthur Cooley, Charles Wurster, and Dennis Puleston presented testimony that halted the use of DDT in local mosquito control. Extending their court victory to other states, ED convinced the Environmental Protection

Agency to ban DDT spraying nationwide in 1972. In 1970 ED began a parallel campaign to get the lead out of gasoline in response to evidence that pollution from tailpipe fumes was a major threat to children's health.

ED has grown into a very influential citizen interest and action group. Unlike many peer groups, ED cooperates with utilities and businesses in applying economic analysis to energy alternatives, providing energy conservation computer models that can preserve or increase corporate profit margins while improving the environment. The spectrum of ED concerns has widened to include wetlands preservation, water resources and water marketing, toxic substances, acid rain, tropical rain forests, and protection of the ozone layer.

ED achievements include placement of restrictions on airborne asbestos, mercury, and beryllium; revision of U.S. tuna fishing rules to reduce dolphin deaths; banning of asbestos in hairdryers; and sponsorship of international conferences on climate change. Also, ED was responsible for a market incentive approach to acid rain reduction becoming a key component of the 1990 Clean Air Act.

The Internet is used to communicate with and activate the ED member action network, which currently includes more than 100,000 activists. In 1998 ED launched its Chemical Scorecard Internet service (*www.scorecard. org*). This data-rich Web site enables anybody with a modem to find out who is emitting what and how much into her or his neighborhood, and to protest instantly.

In January 2000, the Environmental Defense Fund shortened its name because "Fund" did not accurately describe ED and had become a source of confusion. The group adopted a new logo, the "e" from its name, as a symbol of the Earth and of recurring themes in ED's work—environment, economy, equity, and empowerment.

Frederick Krupp has served as ED executive director since 1984. ED is headquartered in New York City; field offices are located in Colorado, California, North Carolina, Texas, and Washington, D.C. Membership is about

300,000. *ED Letter*, a bimonthly, is included in membership dues.

See also: ENVIRONMENT

For Further Information

Begley, Sharon, Thomas Hayden, Erika Check, Mary Hager, and Stefan Theil. "The Battle for Planet Earth." *Newsweek*, April 24, 2000, pp. 50–53.

Bruce, Rich. *Mortgaging the Earth; The World Bank, Environmental Impoverishment, and the Crisis of Development*. Boston: Beacon Press, 1995.

Environmental Defense, *http://www. environmentaldefense.org*

Rogers, Marion. *Acorn Days: The Environmental Defense Fund and How It Grew*. New York: EDF, 1990.

ENVIRONMENTAL DEFENSE FUND.
See Environmental Defense

EUTHANASIA SOCIETY OF AMERICA. *See* Choice in Dying

EVERS, MEDGAR (WILEY) (1925–1963).
A black civil rights activist whose murder received national attention and made him a martyr to the cause of the civil rights movement, Medgar Evers was born in Decatur, Mississippi, on July 2, 1925. Evers served in the U.S. Army in Europe during World War II. Afterward he and his elder brother, Charles Evers, graduated from Alcorn Agricultural and Mechanical College (now Alcorn State University) in 1950. They resettled in Philadelphia, Mississippi, and pursued differing careers. Medgar became an insurance salesman, while Charles managed a restaurant, gas station, and other enterprises, while forming local affiliates of the NATIONAL ASSOCIATION FOR THE ADVANCEMENT OF COLORED PEOPLE (NAACP). In 1954 Medgar moved to Jackson to take the newly created position of NAACP field secretary in Mississippi. He traveled throughout the state, recruiting NAACP members and organizing voter registration drives.

During the 1960s, tensions mounted between whites and blacks as the STUDENTS FOR A DEMOCRATIC SOCIETY, STUDENT NONVIOLENT COORDINATING COMMITTEE, and SOUTHERN CHRISTIAN LEADERSHIP COUNCIL started pushing for compliance with the *BROWN V. TOPEKA BOARD OF EDUCATION* Supreme Court decision and related federal laws and regulations mandating integration. On June 12, 1963, shortly after President John F. Kennedy had broadcast a plea for peaceful and constructive revolution as the best means to achieve minority civil rights, Medgar Evers was ambushed and shot in the back as he was exiting his car in front of his home. Until then, Medgar Evers was hardworking and effective, but no celebrity. However, local racists resented him because he had counseled James Meredith during his fight for admission to the University of Mississippi and assisted a man who had testified against white men who had murdered a Northern teenager, Emmett Till, for making flip remarks and whistling at a white woman. Evers's death was the first of the decade's series of political assassinations and the first civil rights murder to draw national attention. He was buried with full military honors in Arlington National Cemetery and awarded the 1963 Spingarn Medal by the NAACP. Upon his death Charles Evers took his place as NAACP field secretary.

Byron de La Beckwith, a white supremacist and KU KLUX KLAN member, was charged with the murder. He was freed in 1964 after two all-white, all-male juries failed to reach a verdict. His third trial in 1994 resulted in his conviction, justice prevailing thirty years after the fact because of the profound reduction in interracial prejudice in the South resulting from the civil rights movement.

For Further Information

Evers, Charles. *Have No Fear.* New York: Wiley, 1997.
Massengill, Reed. *Portrait of a Racist.* New York: St. Martin's Press, 1994.
Vollers, Maryanne. *Ghosts of Mississippi.* Boston: Little, Brown, 1995.

EXTREMISTS. Extremists take political ideas to their limits, regardless of any negative repercussions that may result or of the impracticality of their aims. Their intention is to confront, denigrate, disable, and ultimately destroy individuals, initiatives, groups, and institutions to which they are opposed. Intolerance and disregard of the life, liberty, and rights of others is the trademark of extremists and the organizations to which they belong.

Entries in the extremists category are limited to political and antiethnic forms of extremism. Excluded are various radical political parties that were active before World War II (e.g., Progressive Labor Workers, Communist Party USA, and Socialist Workers Party) because they left no lasting imprint on laws, public perceptions, or elections. Extremist individuals and action groups associated with other categories are described elsewhere in this encyclopedia. Examples are RANDALL TERRY and Operation Rescue (ABORTION POLICY), LARRY KRAMER and ACT UP (AIDS COALITION TO UNLEASH POWER) (AIDS CRISIS), ANIMAL LIBERATION FRONT and SEA SHEPHERD CONSERVATION SOCIETY (ANIMAL WELFARE AND RIGHTS), DANIEL and PHILIP BERRIGAN and PLOWSHARES (ANTIWAR/ANTI–NUCLEAR WEAPONS MOVEMENT), EDWARD ABBEY, EARTH FIRST!, and EARTH LIBERATION FRONT (ENVIRONMENT), and DENNIS BANKS and RUSSELL MEANS (NATIVE AMERICAN RIGHTS). Twentieth-century extremism was perpetrated by both right- and left-wing ideologues, all motivated by feelings of alienation and hopes for a better future as they envisioned it.

Right-wing extremists usually blame scapegoats and imagined conspiracies for their own shortcomings or inability to keep pace economically with gains in wealth achieved by others, and for the moral decay in society and government. President Eisenhower was accused of being a communist dupe, and Franklin Delano Roosevelt was castigated as a pawn of international Jewish bankers eager to launch World War II. Other conspiracy theorists have cited imag-

Aryan Nations leader Richard Butler speaks to reporters from his Idaho headquarters in September 2000. © *Reuters NewMedia Inc./CORBIS.*

ined dangers posed by the New World Order (NOW), the Zionist Occupation Government (ZOG), the "bleached out devil race" (whites), the Trilateral Commission, and the U.S. federal government. Far right extremists are authoritarian, reactionary, religious, and intensely patriotic. They harbor nostalgia for an imagined past when everyone knew their place, including women and minorities, and traditional family values were the norm.

Left-wing extremists can also be authoritarian and often embrace Marxist or radical socialist dogma. Their orientation is usually secular and humanistic, multicultural, inclusive, and egalitarian. Their scapegoats include big business, law enforcement authorities, and conservative political leaders. They believe that gaps in education, wealth, health care, and opportunity within the society should be reduced to a minimum. Right-wing adherents contend that the left-wingers lack restraint and rigor, are weak and sentimental, and would destroy the free enterprise system by placing uniform equality above individual liberty.

Twentieth-century extremism originated during the teens and early twenties with the Red Scare. Bombs were sent through the mail intended to kill Justice Oliver Wendell Holmes, J. P. Morgan, and John D. Rockefeller. A second, much more virulent outbreak of extremism followed the release of the popular D. W. Griffith film *Birth of a Nation in* 1915. The original title was *The Clansman,* and the film depicted Negro villains and KU KLUX KLAN heroes. It rubbed raw old Civil War wounds and aroused interest in the KKK. By 1921 KKK membership exceeded 100,000, and by the mid-twenties it had surpassed the million mark. The KKK became the nation's largest, most violent, and most intolerant extremist group, taking threatening actions against Roman Catholics, Jews, and aliens, and intensifying its terror campaign against blacks.

The Great Depression (1929–1934) was the catalyst for formation of communist, fascist, anti-Semitic, and xenophobic organizations such as the America First Committee. FATHER CHARLES E. COUGHLIN, a demagogic pro-fascist priest, aired his views on national radio from the late 1930s until 1942, and GERALD L.K. SMITH, launcher of the Christian Crusade, became the most strident and blatant anti-Semite in the United States from the thirties until his death in 1976.

Examples of far left extremism during the sixties and seventies included the BLACK PANTHER PARTY and HUEY NEWTON, STUDENTS FOR A DEMOCRATIC SOCIETY, MARK RUDD, the WEATHERMAN, and the SYMBIONESE LIBERATION ARMY. Counterparts on the far right included ELIJAH MUHAMMAD and the NATION OF ISLAM, the JOHN BIRCH SOCIETY, WILLIS CARTO and the LIBERTY LOBBY, the MINUTEMEN and the MILITIA MOVEMENTS, POSSE COMITATUS, the JEWISH DEFENSE LEAGUE, LYNDON LAROUCHE, and LOUIS FARRAKHAN.

For Further Information

George, John, and Laird Wilcox. *American Extremists: Militias, Supremacists, Klansmen, Communists, and Others.* Amherst, NY: Prometheus Books, 1996.

Stewart, Gail B. *Militias.* San Diego: Lucent Books, 1998.

F

FALSE FRONT ORGANIZATIONS. Many corporations have found that the best way to win allies and votes in Congress is to disguise themselves as a citizen action group. Although most of these deceptive and unethical "false front" groups fail, a few have been able to draw in substantial numbers of grassroots members who believe the bogus scare messages they receive in the mail and over the Internet. Incited by fear of intrusive federal interference or of potential loss of benefits or freedom of choice, these duped people join, contribute money, and contact their legislators—all under the umbrella of citizen action.

This activity began as early as 1937 when the Consumer Federation and its publication, *National Consumer News*, were launched as purportedly independent product assessment organizations to serve the public. Hidden from the public was the fact that major corporations such as Sears, Roebuck and Walgreen controlled the organization's funding and editorial content.

After 1980 an epidemic of corporate and far right funded coalitions and citizens' groups broke out. Corporations and extremists woke up to the fact that "all politics is local" and that politicians are most prone to mirror their constituents' support or opposition to issues. Using database marketing techniques, they identified constituents most

likely to agree with their political agendas and started corralling them into legitimate-looking citizen action groups, hiding corporate or far right involvement and presenting the groups as spontaneous expressions of grassroots anger. Such groups do not declare their funding or identify instigating sources in their names, literature, and communications with the public, the media, or politicians.

Examples of such organizations include 60 PLUS, the Alliance for America, American Council on Science and Health, Citizens for Better Medicare, Citizens for the Environment, Citizens for the Sensible Control of Acid Rain, Citizens for a Sound Economy, Coalition for Equal Access to Medicines, Coalition for Vehicle Choice, CONSUMER ALERT, Global Climate Coalition, NATIONAL RIGHT TO WORK COMMITTEE, National Wetlands Coalition, SENIORS COALITION, UNITED SENIORS ASSOCIATION, and Workplace Health and Safety Council.

The area in which false front organizations have become most numerous is environmental pollution. Corporations have formed groups that downplay, or dismiss as irrational, fears concerning ozone layer depletion, wetlands preservation, global warming, and acid rain. A second area is public health. Groups have been formed to argue for the safety of pesticides, genetically modified food products, junk food, and alcohol. The third domain is universal health care. Here the pharmaceutical industry and the medical profession have allied to develop "citizen" opposition to federal plans to equalize health care and drug access. Worker rights is a fourth area that is subject to attack by ersatz citizens' groups. Finally, some groups concentrate on elimination of federal regulations and standards for airbags, fuel-efficient vehicles, and workplace safety.

The American Council on Science and Health, funded by such companies as Dow Chemical U.S.A., Kraft Foundation, PepsiCo Foundation, and Archer Daniels Midland, promotes the view that almost all food, drugs, or chemicals are harmless if consumed in moderation. Asbestos, caffeine, Agent Orange, and PCBs are said to impose a minimal public health threat.

Corporations including Amoco, General Electric, General Motors, Philip Morris, and Union Carbide contribute generously to Citizens for the Environment. The group argues that industry plays a positive role in protecting the environment and deflates the issues of acid rain and global warming as "myths." Citizens for the Sensible Control of Acid Rain, formed in 1983 to oppose the Clean Air Act, was funded by the coal and electric utility industries to resist strict controls on the emission of acid rain causing pollutants.

Citizens for a Sound Economy produces and distributes openly political ads, challenging clean air standards and encouraging citizens to take action and contact their representatives in Congress. In one of these ads, aired in 1996, a son was asked by his father, a doctor, how his new job was going. The son cited problems caused by EPA clean air standards. The father replied that the science behind the new standards was bogus, and that the standards would drive up the price of cars and could lead to the banning of lawn mowers and barbecue grills.

The National Wetlands Coalition is committed to decreasing protection of the streams, swamps, and marshes that are the habitat of a third of America's endangered species so that mining companies and real estate developers can be free to develop wetlands commercially.

These and other groups have sprung up because citizens have distanced themselves from the political process and the public relations industry has moved in to take their place, converting the term "grassroots" to fit their own needs. Evolving high-tech data and communications systems have enabled manipulative politicians and wealthy conservatives to custom design "citizen action" to serve the interest of elite clients. The previously mentioned organizations are a small sampling of the more than 300 groups conceived between 1980 and 2000. Most are the products of conservative illusionists who hire expensive specialists such as RICHARD VIGUERIE who know how to tap people's fear, ignorance, cynicism, and greed and goad them to act in what they believe is their own best interest; none of these organizations is a genuine grassroots action group.

Liberal activists are not entirely guilt free. Within the RALPH NADER empire, there are consumer protection groups that are funded by trial lawyers, not by citizens, whose interest is served by publicizing allegedly defective and dangerous products to generate litigation.

Gun manufacturers and the defense industry have no false front groups because they can rely on firm support from Congress and strong lobbies such as the NATIONAL RIFLE ASSOCIATION to accomplish their objectives.

The false front is a deceptive but effective weapon destined to remain in the activist's arsenal for as long as there are people who don't bother to question the authority, sponsorship, and motivation behind solicitations for their money and votes.

For Further Information

Drinkard, Jim. "Front Groups Keep Voters in Dark about Financial Backers." *Seattle Times*, December 21, 1997.

Hosenball, Mark. "Flo's Big-Dollar Backers." *Newsweek*, September 25, 2000, p. 26.

"Public-Interest Pretenders." *Consumer Reports* 59, no. 5 (May 1994): 316–320.

Shabecoff, Philip. "Washington Talk: Single-Issue

Lobbying; Caustic Debate on Acid Rain Letter." *New York Times*, July 31, 1987, Late City final edition, p. B6.

Stone, Peter H. "Grass-Roots Goliath." *National Journal* 28 (July 13, 1996): 1529–1532.

FALWELL, JERRY (1933–   ). Born August 11, 1933, in Lynchburg, Virginia, Jerry Falwell founded Moral Majority, created *The Old Time Gospel Hour*, a popular radio/television show, and rallied support for conservative Republicans in the 1980 and 1984 presidential election campaigns. Falwell studied engineering at Lynchburg College for several years until a religious conversion compelled him to transfer to Baptist Bible College in Springfield, Missouri. In 1956 he founded and became pastor of the Thomas Road Baptist Church in Lynchburg, which by 1985 had ballooned into a ministry with a 22,000-member congregation. Soon after, he initiated *The Old Time Gospel Hour* and founded Liberty Baptist College. In 1979 he established Moral Majority, Inc.

Falwell's Christian fundamentalism, with its literal interpretation of the Bible and fervent opposition to secular humanism, which promotes reason, scientific inquiry, and human fulfillment without alluding to the importance of God, was compatible with the New Right vision in the 1970s and 1980s. His opposition to abortion and displeasure over decaying family values, gay rights, and the Equal Rights Amendment created a symbiotic relationship with President Ronald Reagan's administration. His anger over the exclusion of God from government and the constitutionally mandated omission of the religious dimension from laws, federal programs, and public education resonated with voters.

Christian conservatives became reliable and indispensable partners in the Republican electoral coalition. Falwell traveled over 300,000 miles during the Carter-Reagan campaign and took partial credit for Reagan's landslide victory in the 1980 election. Falwell's income from church and ministry donations and his skillful mobilization of captive audiences, telemarketing, and communications media enabled him to reach and influence the votes of more than 14 million people. In 1980 all forty political candidates endorsed by Falwell's Moral Majority won, and six senators it opposed were unseated. By the mid-1980s Jerry Falwell Ministries were purportedly attracting a weekly audience exceeding 17 million families.

As the 1980s waned, the public became less accepting of political extremism and religious intolerance. Other television preachers, including Jimmy Swaggart and Jim and Tammy Bakker, became tainted by scandal. In 1988 Falwell replaced Jim Bakker as head of the PTL television ministry, only to resign within a year, and Moral Majority, Inc., lost support and closed down in 1989. Falwell has since concentrated his energy on his ministries, which include Liberty University, *The Old Time Gospel Hour*, the Liberty Godparent Home for Unwed Mothers, the *National Liberty Journal* newspaper, and other enterprises.

See also: RELIGIOUS RIGHT

For Further Information

Falwell, Jerry. *Falwell: An Autobiography*. Lynchburg, Virginia: Liberty House, 1997.

Gateway To Jerry Falwell Ministries, *http://www. falwell.com*

FAMILIES USA. Families USA is a "national, non-partisan organization dedicated to the achievement of high-quality, affordable health and long-term care for all Americans." The group has its roots in the Villers Foundation, established in Cambridge, Massachusetts, in 1981 to aid the elderly by improving their status and public image. Founder and current president Philippe Villers, a refugee from World War II France, an early innovator in computer-aided design (CAD) systems and robotics, and a multimillionaire, set up the Foundation to work toward eliminating the deep-rooted discriminatory attitudes and practices that limit opportunities for elderly people.

Initially the Foundation emphasized research, drawing upon the disciplines of economics, sociology, and political science to produce scholarly reports that promoted reform at the federal, state, and local levels. A liberal, high-tech capitalist, Villers views the women's movement and the civil rights movement as role models. The Foundation serves as a forum for debate, legal assistance, and community education.

In 1983 Ronald Pollack became the first and only executive director of the Villers Foundation. Pollack was already a familiar spokesperson for the elderly poor in legislative circles and a veteran of the 1960s civil rights struggle. As former dean of Antioch Law School, now part of the University of the District of Columbia, he had worked with low-income, minority, and women students.

In 1989 the Foundation changed its name to Families USA and started soliciting contributions from individuals. Its program goals and activities became intergenerational, emphasizing that whatever benefits the elderly benefits younger generations, and vice versa. Within three years, Families USA had an activist base of 12,000 members and had established an Internet/mail/fax/phone legislative alert system. During the dawn of the Clinton administration, Families USA campaigned for a government-run health care system that would cover all Americans, one in which everybody pays and everybody is protected. As of July 1994, Families USA was the de facto manager of the Clinton administration's campaign for comprehensive health care legislation, providing heartrending misery stories for the major television networks and print media.

Although the Clinton plan was defeated, Families USA did achieve passage of a 1988 law requiring Medicaid to pay a greater share of health care for the elderly poor. It also played a major role in enactment of a 1990 law enabling states to tap Medicaid funds to care for frail seniors at home rather than in nursing homes. Families USA publishes data in glossy monthly research reports that catch the attention of the public, media, and legislators. Past reports have highlighted the multimillion dollar salaries of health maintenance organization administrators, prohibitively high prices of prescription drugs, problems in health care, and gaps in health insurance availability. The group has been effective in moving its issues to the top of the political agenda and in framing public debate.

Families USA membership is free and includes the option of belonging to its network, asap!, and its sub–groups, the Medicaid Advocacy Network, Children's Health Campaign, and Medicare Action Campaign.

Families USA headquarters is in Washington, D.C. Philippe Villers is president; Ronald F. Pollack is vice president and executive director. As of 1999, the group had about 9,000 members.

See also: CONSUMER RIGHTS AND SAFEGUARDS

For Further Information

Families USA, *http://www.familiesusa.org*

Lewin, Tamar. "The Health Care Debate: Behind the Scenes." *New York Times*, July 28, 1994, p. 20.

Teltsch, Kathleen. "A New Foundation Will Aid the Aged." *New York Times*, August 15, 1982, p. 31.

FAMILY RESEARCH COUNCIL. Founded in 1981 by longtime conservative family advocate JAMES DOBSON, the Family Research Council (FRC) began as a small, little-known, but determined group of concerned activists dedicated to the preservation of the Judeo-Christian ideal of the family. The FRC slogan is "Family, Faith and Freedom." It was a division of FOCUS ON THE FAMILY from 1988 to 1992. Since the 1994 election and under Gary Bauer's direction, FRC has emerged as a leading conservative think tank lobby opposing women's reproductive freedom, equal legal treatment of gays and heterosexuals, and funding of the National Endowment for the Arts (NEA) and the Corporation for Public Broadcasting.

According to Bauer, partial-birth abortion should be banned and gays can be cured of what is a psychological disorder. FRC contends that "homosexual activity is not a civil right, it is a lethal and immoral behavior, and opposition to homosexual behavior is not a discrimination issue, but a moral one." Bauer, in a letter mailed to FRC members in October 1990, has said that "the NEA has allowed itself to be used by a small cadre of cultural revolutionaries, militant homosexuals and anti-religious bigots who are intent on attacking the average American's most deeply held beliefs while sending them the bill."

Bauer was under secretary of education under President Ronald Reagan and a policy analyst for the Reagan-Bush campaign in 1980. In 1988 he left the Reagan administration to head the FRC. In 1991 he chaired the Citizens Committee to Confirm Clarence Thomas as Supreme Court justice. He went on leave in 1999 to campaign for president on the Republican ticket. Chuck Donovan, FRC executive vice president, led the organization during his absence.

Over the years, the views of the FRC have been closely watched by conservative Republicans and activists as a gauge of grassroots opinion on most matters of domestic economic and social policy. The FRC crafted a bill, the "Federalism Shield," conceived to promote the posting of the Ten Commandments in schools and to safeguard individual religious expression in public spaces. It also lobbied on behalf of a school prayer constitutional amendment and succeeded in convincing Cracker Barrel Restaurant not to hire gays.

FRC's *Washington Watch*, a monthly newsletter, reaches the homes of FRC members, and its radio broadcasts are heard daily on 400 stations across the country. The FRC headquarters building is in Washington, D.C. Current membership exceeds 400,000.

See also: RELIGIOUS RIGHT

For Further Information

Bauer, Gary. *Our Hopes—Our Dreams: A Vision for America*. Colorado Springs: Focus on the Family Publishing, 1996.

Family Research Council, *http://www.frc.org*

Martin, William. *With God on Our Side: The Rise of the Religious Right in America*. New York: Broadway Books, 1996.

FARMER, JAMES (1920–1999). Born in Marshall, Texas on January 12, 1920, James Farmer founded the CONGRESS OF RACIAL EQUALITY (CORE), led the Freedom Rides that helped break the back of segregation in the South, and became one of the most respected and visible national civil rights leaders during the 1960s.

Farmer grew up near black college campuses. His father, James Leonard Farmer, a campus chaplain and professor of philosophy and religion, earned the first Ph.D. awarded to a black person in the state of Texas. The younger Farmer graduated from high school at the age of fourteen, and entered Wiley College. After earning a bachelor's degree in 1938, Farmer went on to obtain a divinity degree from Howard University in 1941. He renounced his goal of becoming an ordained Methodist minister when he learned that the church was to remain segregated.

At an early age, racism shaped Farmer's life. At three years of age, while walking with his mother, he asked permission to go into a drug store to buy a soft drink as he had just seen a white child do. His mother explained that they were not permitted in the store simply because they were not white. Farmer remembered this incident for the remainder of his life as the point at which he decided to dedicate himself to eradicating discrimination.

While studying at Howard University, Farmer was introduced to Mahatma Gandhi's philosophy of nonviolent resistance, used to gain freedom from British colonial rule in India. After graduation, Farmer worked at the FELLOWSHIP OF RECONCILIATION (FOR) as a race relations secretary. FOR encouraged nonviolent methods of protest such as boycotts, pickets, and demonstrations. In addition, FOR welcomed all races to participate in their antidiscrimination events. In 1942 Farmer helped organize the Committee of Racial Equality, later to become the Congress of Racial Equality. Like FOR, CORE recruited all races for membership and implemented Gandhi's nonviolent protest in its public crusades. In 1961 Farmer was named CORE's national director.

Shortly after, Farmer began to plan the Freedom Rides, an attempt to integrate public transportation in the South. The Freedom Riders found themselves at the center of national attention when disrupters of the movement torched and burned a bus in Birmingham, Alabama. Farmer was arrested, along with other riders, in Jackson, Mississippi, in 1961. The Freedom Rides not only helped document the need for the U.S. Supreme Court decision *Boynton v. Virginia*, but also sped removal of the humiliating "white only" and "colored only" signs from public drinking fountains throughout the South.

Farmer left CORE in 1966 to join the faculty of Lincoln University for two years. He ran unsuccessfully for Congress in 1968. President Richard Nixon appointed him assistant secretary of health, education, and welfare in 1969. Here, he worked on affirmative action hiring policies and restored the Head Start program. He resigned in 1970 to resume teaching. While a lecturer at Howard University in the 1970s, Farmer headed a think tank, the Council on Minority Planning and Strategy (COMPAS). He taught at Antioch University in 1983 and 1984. His final faculty appointment was as history professor at Mary Washington College in Virginia from 1985 until 1998, at which time poor health forced him to retire.

Farmer received the Medal of Freedom from President Clinton in 1998. He additionally has been awarded twenty-three honorary degrees. He published *Freedom When?* in 1965 and *Lay Bare the Heart: An Autobiography of the Civil Rights Movement* in 1985. Farmer, a diabetic, suffered from a degenerative eye disease that cost him the vision in his left eye in 1979 and spread to his right eye four years later. He died at the age of seventy-nine, on July 9, 1999, in Fredericksburg, Virginia.

See also: AFRICAN AMERICAN RIGHTS

For Further Information

Farmer, James. *Lay Bare the Heart: An Autobiography of the Civil Rights Movement.* New York: Arbor House, 1985.
Wexler, Sanford. *The Civil Rights Movement: An Eyewitness History.* New York: Facts on File, 1993.

FARMERS' EDUCATIONAL AND CO-OPERATIVE UNION OF AMERICA. *See* National Farmers Union

FARMERS' RIGHTS. In the twentieth century, the ability of farmers to influence Congress declined as their numbers shrank. In 1900 farmers constituted 36 percent of the U.S. work force; in 1990 their share had dipped to a meager 1.6 percent. Adding to their challenge as a citizen action group was their fragmentation. Farmers have always had interests that differ depending upon the size of their operation and the commodities they produce and sell. Dairy, wheat, soybean, peanut, cotton, hog, cattle, and other farmers have separate legislative agendas, and the needs of the small family farm have little in common with those of the large consolidated agribusiness.

The earliest twentieth-century farmers' group began as a consortium of local units that consolidated into the NATIONAL FARMERS UNION (NFU) in 1902. The NFU focuses on helping family farmers and ranchers seek financial relief and representation in Congress and in World Trade Organization deliberations.

By far the largest and most influential farmers' organization is the AMERICAN FARM BUREAU FEDERATION (AFBF), formed in 1919. The AFBF grew out of farm bureaus, the first of which was established in Broome County, New York, in 1911. Today, more than 2,800 county Farm Bureaus exist, made up of farm families. The AFBF campaigns across a broad range of issues including farm policy, trade, budget and taxes, farm credit, labor transportation, conservation and the environment, and the dairy price support

Farmers from all over the country drive their tractors through downtown Washington, DC, during a 1978 protest against the Carter Administration's farm policies. © Leif Skoogfors/CORBIS.

program. It supports a free market economy and is against governmental restrictions on biotechnology as applied to agricultural products, export subsidies, and implementation of the Kyoto Protocols to prevent global warming. It also opposes more stringent fuel economy standards for cars and trucks because of their adverse impact on the performance of farm vehicles.

The NATIONAL FARMERS ORGANIZATION (NFO) was established in 1955 to improve the economic leverage of farmers. The NFO's goal was to be farmers' prime bargaining agent in contracts with wholesalers, meatpackers, and processors. It expected to eventually dictate market prices by bypassing the middleman. A vigorous lobbying group until the late 1970s, the NFO now confines itself to improving agricultural commodity prices as a bargaining agent for its members, who are primarily dairy, grain, and livestock farmers.

In 1962 CESAR CHAVEZ organized underpaid and maltreated Hispanic farm workers in California. In establishing the UNITED FARM WORKERS UNION, he provided inspired leadership and became a Gandhi-like leader to most Mexican Americans.

The AMERICAN AGRICULTURE MOVEMENT (AAM), co-founded in 1977 by Eugene Schroder, became the most well known farmers group because of the tractorcade protest it staged in 1978 that disrupted traffic in Washington, D.C., and other major cities.

The AAM opposes federal subsidies, excise tax increases, and patenting of genetically engineered animals and advocates price supports for farm commodities.

For Further Information

Mooney, Patrick H., and Theo J. Majka. *Farmers' and Farm Workers' Movements: Social Protest in American Agriculture.* New York: Twayne, 1995.

FARRAKHAN, LOUIS ABDUL (1933–). Born on May 11, 1933, in the Bronx, New York, Louis Abdul Farrakhan is U.S. leader of the NATION OF ISLAM. He achieved celebrity status as chief apostle of the late ELIJAH MUHAMMAD, founder of the Nation of Islam, the American Muslim sect that preaches a strict moral code and economic independence for African Americans. Until 1995 Farrakhan had championed black separatism and voiced anti-Semitic views, labeling Judaism a "gutter religion" in an interview with a *Chicago Sun Times* reporter and making statements in which he excoriated homosexuals, called Jews "bloodsuckers," and demonized whites, Asians, and Arabs. More recently, he has publicly displayed an ecumenical attitude and recanted his earlier bigoted pronouncements.

Originally named Louis Eugene Walcott, Farrakhan grew up in the Roxbury section of Boston, Massachusetts. His parents emi-

Nation of Islam leader Louis Farrakhan addresses an audience attending a Saviour's Day convention in Chicago in February 1997. *AP Photo/Michael Conroy.*

grated from the Caribbean. In high school, Farrakhan was an honor student, track star, and talented calypso singer and violinist. MALCOLM X conscripted him into the Nation of Islam. As a religion, Nation of Islam promotes racial unity, self-help, and personal dignity. American inner-city blacks greeted with hope the formally attired, clean-cut, articulate, and polite young members of the Nation of Islam. They were a distinctive black counterculture, at odds with mainstream integrationist groups such as the NATIONAL ASSOCIATION FOR THE ADVANCEMENT OF COLORED PEOPLE (NAACP). Walcott rid himself of his "slave" name and renamed himself Farrakhan.

When Malcolm X converted to Sunni Muslim orthodoxy and endorsed cooperation with whites of good will, he was considered a traitor. Farrakhan wrote that he "was wor-

thy of death," and in 1965 Malcolm X was assassinated. Farrakhan was implicated in the crime because Nation of Islam members were identified as the murderers. Meanwhile, Nation of Islam membership continued to rise along with Farrakhan's popularity. He drew an audience of 25,000 to Madison Square Garden in October 1985.

Beginning with Ronald Reagan's election to the presidency in 1980, Farrakhan's appeal rose as the status of inner-city blacks worsened and civil rights movement initiatives were rolled back in Washington. Despite the prominence of African Americans in sports, entertainment, and recently in high positions in federal government, deep-seated suspicions existed that the government was conspiring to cripple and thwart black Americans. Farrakhan, a spellbinding orator, catered to this feeling, and his popularity increased. In 1989 he conjectured that the U.S. government had seeded the AIDS plague in order to decimate the population of central Africa.

In 1995, when Farrakhan organized what turned out to be the highly successful Million Man March, this event was boycotted by the NAACP leadership, prominent blacks holding moderate views, and women's groups because of Farrakhan's exclusion of females and his hate-filled rhetoric. Nonetheless, even his harshest critics praised him for his public call to responsibility issued to the estimated 400,000 African American participants. He asked for their pledge to refrain from violence, spousal abuse, and drugs, and to take responsibility for bettering their families and communities. He also asked the assemblage to help register 8 million eligible voters by 1996 to help change America. Farrakhan, the sixty-two-year-old patriarch of the Nation of Islam, widely perceived as a publicity-hungry, hate-spouting extremist, had managed to mobilize black Americans when more moderate leaders like JESSE JACKSON could not.

In 1996 Farrakhan began to move toward a more centrist position. He reregistered to vote and formed a coalition of religious and civic organizations to "provide a voice for the disenfranchised on the political landscape."

Three years later, in his first public appearance after a near-death bout with prostate cancer, Farrakhan joined Catholic priests, Jewish rabbis, and Muslim clerics at the Nation of Islam mosque in Chicago. At this interfaith conference, he urged forgiveness and unity among all races and religions and atonement for what he and others had said or done to injure members of other races, religious groups, nations, or ethnic groups.

Farrakhan, named by *Time* magazine in 1996 as one of the twenty-five most influential people in the United States, resides with his wife and nine children in Chicago.

See also: AFRICAN AMERICAN RIGHTS

For Further Information

Magida, Arthur J. *Prophet of Rage: A Life of Louis Farrakhan and His Nation.* New York: Basic Books, 1996.

Singh, Robert. *The Farrakhan Phenomenon: Race, Reaction, and the Paranoid Style in American Politics.* Washington, DC: Georgetown University Press, 1997.

FELLOWSHIP OF RECONCILIATION. Established in 1914, the Fellowship of Reconciliation (FOR) is the largest and oldest interfaith peace and justice organization in the United States. Its aim is "to replace violence, war, racism, and economic injustice with nonviolence, peace, and justice." The group educates, trains, builds coalitions, and engages in nonviolent and compassionate actions locally, nationally, and globally.

FOR originated during an ecumenical conference held in Switzerland by Christian pacifists who hoped to prevent war from breaking out in Europe. War was declared before their meeting ended and delegates returned to their respective countries. Two participants, an English Quaker and a German Lutheran, met in Germany and pledged to find a way to fight for peace. In December 1914, members of the group reconvened in Cambridge and formed the Fellowship of Reconciliation. The American FOR was founded by John Nevin Sayre and other liberal-minded religious pacifists in 1915, and within a year had recruited 15,000 members.

The initial goal of the American FOR was to keep the United States out of World War I. Other leaders of the American FOR included socialist leader Norman Thomas and Abraham J. Muste. Muste, an outspoken opponent of the Vietnam War, was praised as America's Gandhi by MARTIN LUTHER KING JR. Several weeks before his death in 1967, Muste visited Hanoi in an effort to negotiate peace.

FOR has affiliates in over forty countries and has significantly affected Christian pacifism in the United States. It assisted with formation of the AMERICAN CIVIL LIBERTIES UNION, the National Conference of Christians and Jews, and the CONGRESS OF RACIAL EQUALITY (CORE). JAMES FARMER, who was active within FOR, became CORE's leader.

FOR contributed to the isolationist stance of the United States in the 1930s, encouraged nonviolent resistance to World War II, and opposed U.S. involvement in the Korean, Vietnam, and Gulf wars. FOR cosponsored demonstrations with Vietnamese Buddhist pacifist movement leaders and later joined with American antiwar protest groups. It initiated the Brothers Project to send medical aid to both North and South Vietnam. It advised and assisted conscientious objectors and deserters, worked for release of political prisoners in South Vietnam, and aggressively sought amnesty for all war resisters. FOR also conducted nonviolence training sessions in the Philippines prior to the 1986 plebiscite rejecting the Marcos regime.

The Campaign to Save a Generation, an ongoing project centered on saving Iraqi children from malnutrition resulting from economic sanctions, and involving efforts to mitigate disease and starvation among impoverished American children, was started in the 1990s. Bosnian students have been sponsored by FOR in a program enabling them to be temporarily placed in U.S. homes and schools. Other FOR programs have been designed to assist Serbs and Kosovars during and after the war in the former Yugoslavia.

Father John Dear, a Jesuit priest, is FOR's current executive director. In 1993 Father Dear was arrested during a PLOWSHARES protest for pounding a nuclear F-15 fighter with a hammer at an air force base in Goldsboro, North Carolina. Headquarters for the 32,500-member group is in Nyack, New York. FOR publishes a bimonthly magazine, *Fellowship*.

See also: ANTIWAR/ANTI–NUCLEAR WEAPONS MOVEMENT

For Further Information

Gwyn, Douglas. *A Declaration on Peace: In God's People the World's Renewal Has Begun. A Contribution to Ecumenical Dialogue*. Scottdale, PA: Herald Press, 1991.

FEMINIST MAJORITY. Feminist Majority (FM) engages in advocacy, fundraising, research, and public education to empower women so that they can become leaders in business, education, the media, law, medicine, and government. FM was established by Eleanor Smeal, Peg Yorkin, Toni Carabillo, Judith Meuli, and Kathy Spillar in 1987 to find and support feminist candidates—men and women—committed to women's equality and to urge them to run for office in unprecedented numbers at the state, local, and federal levels.

Prior to starting FM, Eleanor Smeal and other women seeking an activist political role had resigned from the NATIONAL ORGANIZATION FOR WOMEN (NOW) because of their frustration with the cautious, incrementalist, consciousness-raising approach taken by it and other mainstream women's organizations in the 1980s. In 1987 women made up 53 percent of the population but accounted for only 16 percent of state legislators and 5 percent of members of Congress. The group was formed during a time when abortion rights, women's rights, civil rights, and workers' rights were all under attack.

As early as 1989, FM began charting the rising number of attacks on abortion clinics and predicted that they would culminate in violence and murder. And indeed, between 1993 and 1998, there were numerous bombings and butyric acid attacks and three clinic physicians were assassinated by right-to-life extremists. In 1991 the entertainment community assisted FM with a "Rock for Choice" show featuring rock bands that raised $150,000 for abortion clinic defense, and FM was able to block several antiabortion measures in Oregon. In 1994 FM and other pro-choice advocates won passage of the federal Freedom of Access to Clinics Entrance Act (FACE), which criminalizes clinic blockades and harassment. That same year, the Violence Against Women Act (VAWA), providing federal assistance and civil rights for women victimized by gender-based violence, was signed into law.

In 1991 FM campaigned successfully for an amendment to the Civil Rights Act of 1964 to provide for monetary damages to women who win sexual harassment and sex discrimination lawsuits in court. As of 1992, six states had adopted measures to ensure that all appointments to state government positions be gender balanced to the extent possible.

FM has sponsored annual Feminist Expositions, beginning with Expo '96, held in Washington, D.C. These three-day conferences feature meetings, exhibits, and networking that bring together a broad range of citizen action groups such as the UNITED FARM WORKERS OF AMERICA, EMILY'S LIST, and NOW. By 1998–1999, FM had shifted its main effort to raising money on behalf of women in Afghanistan who were being deprived of their liberties under the Islamic fundamentalist Taliban regime.

FM has about 110,000 members. Its headquarters is in Arlington, Virginia. Contributors to the Feminist Majority Foundation and members of the Feminist Majority receive a quarterly newsletter, *The Feminist Majority Report*. They also are sent periodic action and information alerts via the Internet. Eleanor Smeal is current Feminist Majority president.

See also: WOMEN'S ISSUES

For Further Information

De Witt, Karen. "Feminists Gather to Affirm Relevancy of Their Movement." *New York Times* February 3, 1996, late edition—final, p. 9.

Feminist Majority, *http://www.feminist.org/*

FEMINISTS FOR LIFE OF AMERICA.

Established in Columbus, Ohio, in 1972 by Pat Goltz and Catherine Callaghan, Feminists for Life of America (FFLA) is a nonsectarian, grassroots organization that is committed to protecting human life from conception to natural death. FFLA seeks to redress economic and social conditions that cause women to choose abortion, while opposing all forms of violence, including abortion, euthanasia, and capital punishment, as being inconsistent with the classic feminist principles of justice, nonviolence, and nondiscrimination.

FFLA founders objected to the NATIONAL ORGANIZATION FOR WOMEN's decision to promote legalization of abortion as a primary goal for feminists. In contrast to other groups that believe women's unrestricted access to abortion is a solution, FFLA sees abortion as a symptom of many problems imposed upon women by men and society. The group's leaders cite Susan B. Anthony, Elizabeth Cady Stanton, and Mary Wollstonecraft as models to emulate because they accepted motherhood and celebrated women's life-giving capacity.

Because it is small and a maverick within the pro-life fold, FFLA allies itself with other antiviolence organizations, such as the NATIONAL COALITION TO ABOLISH THE DEATH PENALTY. As a coalition member, FFLA succeeded in blocking a death penalty measure in the Minnesota legislature, lobbied against child exclusion provisions in federal welfare programs, and pressed for stiff penalties for "deadbeat dads" who fail to pay child support. It also works with right-to-life organizations in select antiabortion campaigns, believing in equal rights for the unborn. Recently, FFLA has concentrated on improving support systems for needy women, pregnant students, and working women.

FFLA is headquartered in Washington, D.C., and has branches in forty-seven states. Serrin M. Foster is executive director of the 5,000-member organization. *The American Feminist*, a quarterly, is included in membership dues.

See also: WOMEN'S ISSUES

For Further Information

Houppert, Karen. "Resisting *Roe*: A Feminist for Life States Her Case." *Village Voice*, January 27, 1998, p. 55.

MacNair, Rachel. *Prolife Feminism: Yesterday and Today*. New York: Sulzburger and Graham, 1995.

Feminists for Life of America, *http://www.feministforlife.org*

FISHERMAN'S CLEAN WATER ACTION PROJECT. *See* Clean Water Action

FLANAGAN, FATHER EDWARD JOSEPH (1886–1948).

Born on July 13, 1886, in Roscommon, Ireland, Father Flanagan won public praise because of his outstanding success in developing Boys Town, a community responsible for rehabilitating thousands of delinquent boys of all races and religions. Flanagan immigrated to the United States in 1904 and two years later graduated from Mount St. Mary's College in Emmitsburg, Maryland. After further studies at St. Joseph's Seminary in Dunwoodie, New York, Flanagan completed his preparation for the priesthood at the Gregorian University (Rome, Italy) and the University of Innsbruck (Austria). Assigned to the archdiocese of Omaha, he was a parish priest in O'Neill, Nebraska, for a year, and in 1913 became assistant pastor of St. Patrick's parish in Omaha. In 1914 he set up a workingmen's hostel in Omaha to care for the poor and homeless, but soon became convinced that the best way to reduce crime, alcoholism, and unemployability was to treat the root causes of these societal problems.

In 1917 he rented a house and with five young boys, three of them delinquents, established a residence for homeless boys. A year later he moved his operation to a small tract of land outside Omaha, where together he and the boys built Father Flanagan's Boys Home. In 1922 the home was incorporated as a municipality, Boys Town, with a city council elected and governed by the boys. By 1939 thousands of residents had passed through and been educated, taught citizenship, and socially rehabilitated under the guidance of Father Flanagan, whose belief that no boy was inherently bad was borne out by the success of his charges in later life. His accomplishment was featured in the popular motion picture *Boys Town* (1938) starring Spencer Tracy as the righteous priest who saved youngsters from a life of crime. Tracy won an Academy Award, which he subsequently handed over to Father Flanagan.

In 1937 Pope Pius XI designated Flanagan a domestic prelate with the title Right Reverend Monsignor. After World War II, Msgr. Flanagan served as a U.S. consultant on youth services in Korea, Japan, and Germany. He died while on assignment in Berlin in 1948.

Currently over 800 youth reside in what is now Girls and Boys Town, a youth-managed community with a post office, fire department, police department, credit union, residential homes, and farm. Girls and Boys Town campuses located throughout the United States prepare over 16,000 youth annually for self-sufficient, productive adulthood.

See also: CHILD AND YOUTH-RELATED ISSUES

For Further Information

Girls and Boys Town, *http://www.girlsand boystown.org*

Graves, Charles Parlin. *Father Flanagan: Founder of Boys Town*. Dallas: Garrard Publishing, 1972.

FLYNN, ELIZABETH GURLEY (1890–1964).

An American labor leader, radical, and feminist, Elizabeth Gurley Flynn was the first woman to chair the American Communist Party (ACP). Born in Concord, New Hampshire, in 1890, she also became a leader in the Industrial Workers of the World (IWW) and began speaking out for workers' rights as a teenager perched on a homemade soapbox near Times Square in 1906. Noted for her oratorical and debating skills, she was urged by Broadway producer David Belasco to pursue a stage career. In response she said, "I'm in the labor movement and I speak my own piece."

In 1906 she joined the IWW, at that time a more inclusive and tolerant union than the AFL, which segregated African Americans by restricting them to "Jim Crow" locals, excluded immigrants and women, and condemned birth control, a practice then endorsed by the IWW. Flynn became the only woman leader of the IWW and assumed responsibility for organizing immigrant factory workers in the East, iron ore miners in Minnesota, and lumberjacks in the Northwest.

A resolute advocate of free speech, Flynn was repeatedly arrested during her trips across the country for making inflammatory speeches. She also participated in major strikes by miners and textile workers occurring from 1912 up until the outbreak of World War I. One of these was the 1912 textile workers' union strike in Lawrence, Massachusetts, in which police clubbed down women and children.

Flynn became a founding member of the AMERICAN CIVIL LIBERTIES UNION in 1920, which expelled her in 1940 in response to anticommunist pressure and the strictures of the Smith Act, only to posthumously reinstate her in 1976. Flynn had been a member of the American Communist Party since 1937, was imprisoned from 1955 to 1957 for her affiliation with the ACP, which supported forcible overthrow of the U.S. government, and in 1961 became national chair of the party.

In common with other party members, Flynn remained unperturbed by the Stalinist regime's ruthless purges and its anti-Semitic policies. Flynn died while visiting the USSR as an honored guest and was given a state funeral in Red Square.

See also: LABOR ISSUES; WOMEN'S ISSUES

For Further Information

Camp, Helen C. *Iron in Her Soul: Elizabeth Gurley Flynn and the American Left*. Pullman: Washington State University Press, 1995.

FOCUS ON THE FAMILY. Founded in 1977 by DR. JAMES C. DOBSON, Focus on the Family (FOTF) is the largest organization committed to promoting Judeo-Christian values, strong family ties, and evangelical Christians' participation in the political process. FOTF uses its radio show and magazine, *Citizen*, to urge pro-family voters to become active in state and local primaries and caucuses.

FOTF has a broad base of operations and a substantial budget (over $100 million) and encompasses thirty-five state organizations and fifteen affiliates in other countries, including the People's Republic of China, Canada, and Nigeria. Its ten monthly magazines include *Focus on the Family, BreakAway* (boys); *Brio* (teenage girls), *Clubhouse* (elementary school children); *Clubhouse, Jr.* (pre-Ks), *Parental Guidance* (commentary on contemporary film, video, music, popular culture), *Single-Parent Family, Teachers in Focus*, and *Focus on the Family Physician*. The magazines reach an estimated 3 million homes.

Although its political activities are not highlighted in its public profile, it has strongly espoused views on legislation affecting social policy. The group is anti-choice and anti–gay and lesbian, and is against sex education curricula other than those that prescribe total abstinence before marriage. Local school boards and administrators frequently use Focus on the Family materials to assist them in challenging controversial books or curricula in libraries and schools. Focus on the Family is a very effective grassroots organization, promoting its principles and then urging its members to write and use

their votes to strengthen and protect their homes and families.

Family News in Focus, a daily radio program, is aired on more than 1,500 stations, and a daily half-hour Focus on the Family telecast reaches about 5 million households each week. FOTF ministries include radio, publications, television, videos, funded research, seminars, and councils. James C. Dobson is president. The group's headquarters is in Colorado Springs, Colorado.

See also: RELIGIOUS RIGHT

For Further Information

Focus on the Family, ephemeral materials in the Wilcox Collection of Contemporary Political Movements, Arcadia, California, 1980.
Focus on the Family, *www.fotf.org*
Minkowitz, Donna. "My Encounter with the Far Right." *Nation*, December 7, 1998, pp. 18–22.
Murray Zorba, Wendy. "Daring to Discipline America." *Christianity Today*, March 1, 1999, pp. 30–38.

FONDA, JANE (1937–). Born December 21, 1937, in New York City, actress Jane Fonda became well known during the 1970s for her much publicized antiwar activities, inflammatory rhetoric, and connections with the radical left. The nickname "Hanoi Jane" was applied to her, expressing veterans' and conservatives' contempt for her pro–North Vietnam protestations and actions.

She attended Vassar College and went to Paris to study art, languages, and music between 1963 and 1968. While in France, she married film director Roger Vadim, who had recently divorced Brigitte Bardot. Their collaboration produced *Barbarella, Queen of the Galaxy* (1968), based on a popular French sci-fi comic strip. Her feminist feelings were awakened by the sexual exploitation in the film, and the 1968 student protests in France alerted her to America's growing entanglement in Vietnam.

In 1969 Fonda divorced Vadim and returned to the United States. She quickly transformed herself into a radical activist while establishing a reputation as a versatile

Seated on an anti-aircraft gun near Hanoi, American actress and activist Jane Fonda sings an anti-war song to reporters and North Vietnamese soldiers in July 1972. *AP Photo.*

dramatic actress of considerable emotional depth and sensitivity in *They Shoot Horses, Don't They?* (1969) and *Klute* (1971).

In 1970 Fonda traveled throughout the United States, supporting the BLACK PANTHER PARTY and American Indian rights advocates. She eulogized HUEY NEWTON, the Black Panthers' minister of defense, as being "the only man I've ever met who approaches sainthood." Her activities elevated her to the top of President Nixon's "enemies list," and she was placed under close surveillance. Her phone was tapped, federal agents examined her bank deposits, and she was falsely arrested for illegal possession of drugs while returning from a trip to Canada. The suspected drugs were vitamin pills and prescribed tranquilizers.

With characteristic intensity, she totally immersed herself in the anti–Vietnam War movement, placing herself at the center of controversy. In 1971 Fonda toured coffeehouses near army bases in the United States and took her antiwar revue, FTA ("Fuck the Army"), to military installations in South Vietnam. In July 1972 she created a major sensation by visiting North Vietnam with greetings from "revolutionary comrades in America." She toured hospitals, schools, and factories and gave ten broadcast speeches on Hanoi Radio urging American airmen to stop bombing the North and inviting U.S. servicemen to desert. Photographs were released showing Fonda perched on an antiaircraft gun, and she appeared at a press conference with U.S. prisoners of war; other POWs were tortured for refusing to appear with her. Her actions infuriated many and disturbed at least a few who were as opposed to the war as she was.

Soon after her return to the United States, resolutions condemning her conduct were introduced in the Maryland and Colorado legislatures, several members of Congress called for her trial for treason, and the *Manchester Union Leader*'s editor opined that she should be shot if convicted. During a *20/20* television interview with Barbara Walters aired in 1988, Fonda apologized for her bad judgment in going to North Vietnam, allowing herself to be used as a propaganda tool, and inflicting psychic damage on Americans held prisoner by North Vietnam or fighting in the South.

In 1973 Fonda married her second husband, TOM HAYDEN, who had been a prominent figure in the 1960s student movement. They established the Campaign for Economic Democracy, a short-lived grassroots organization that aspired to take the lead in developing a free, socially responsible private enterprise system to be spearheaded by middle-class Americans.

In 1991 Fonda divorced Hayden and married her third husband, billionaire media magnate Ted Turner. In January 2000 Fonda's separation from Turner was announced. Apparently, after spending thirty years as an adversary of the RELIGIOUS RIGHT, she had become a born-again Christian. This conversion purportedly rankled Turner, who had called Christianity a "religion of losers."

In four critically acclaimed films Fonda dealt with issues with which she had a close affinity: the impact of Vietnam in *Coming Home* (1978), the danger of nuclear reactor accidents in *The China Syndrome* (1979), reconciliation with her father in *On Golden Pond* (1980), and male chauvinism and working women in *9 to 5* (1980).

See also: AFRICAN AMERICAN RIGHTS; ANTI–NUCLEAR POWER MOVEMENT; ANTI-WAR/ANTI–NUCLEAR WEAPONS MOVEMENT

For Further Information

Andersen, Christopher P. *Citizen Jane: The Turbulent Life of Jane Fonda.* New York: Henry Holt, 1990.

French, Sean. "The Observer Profile: Jane Fonda." *Guardian Newspapers Limited: The Observer*, January 9, 2000.

Shorto, Russell. *Jane Fonda: Political Activist.* New York: Houghton Mifflin, 1992.

FORMULA. FORMULA seeks to ensure the safety and nutritional soundness of all infant formulas on the market by advocating corrective regulatory legislation and gathering data from parents whose children have suffered learning disabilities, gross motor dysfunction, seizures, and other symptoms as a result of having been fed infant formulas. Carol Laskin and Lynne Pilot started the group in the Washington, D.C., metropolitan area in 1979. Both women were parents of children who had suffered severe reactions to infant formulas manufactured without essential chloride by the Syntex Corporation. At the time, 20,000 American babies were being fed Neo-Mull-Soy and Cho-Free formulas, and there was no regulation of infant formula content except for compliance with very general manufacturing stipulations applied to all foods. Food and Drug Administration (FDA) regulations did not require testing of baby formulas to guarantee that the ingredients matched the labels.

Senator Albert Gore (D-TN) criticized the FDA for not assigning top priority to a recall of the formulas even after its Health Hazard Board unanimously ruled that they constituted a "life-threatening" hazard. Soon after, FORMULA's testimony and actions resulted in passage of the Infant Formula Act of 1980, which for the first time established nutrient standards, gave the FDA access to factory records, and required thorough testing of infant formulas prior to release to the public. Dr. Sanford Miller, director of the FDA Bureau of Foods, noted that FORMULA had won power for the agency that it had been trying unsuccessfully to gain since 1938.

Since its formation, approximately 5,000 activists have worked with FORMULA. The organization's headquarters is in Arlington, Virginia. Carol Laskin is executive officer.

See also: CONSUMER RIGHTS AND SAFEGUARDS

For Further Information

Claybrook, Joan. *Retreat from Safety: Reagan's Attack on America's Health.* New York: Pantheon Books, 1984.

Stein, L. J. et al. "Increased Liking for Salty Foods in Adolescents Exposed During Infancy to a Chloride-Deficient Feeding Formula." *Appetite* 27 (1996): 65–77.

Willoughby, Anne et al. "Population-Based Study of the Developmental Outcome of Children Exposed to Chloride-Deficient Infant Formula." *Pediatrics* 85 (1990): 485–490.

FOSTER, WILLIAM ZEBULON (1881–1961). Labor organizer, American Communist Party leader, and three-time Communist Party presidential candidate, William Z. Foster was born on February 25, 1881, in Taunton, Massachusetts, and grew up in the working-class Irish slums of Philadelphia. His father introduced him to Irish revolutionary ideology and a hatred of authority. Traumatized by the Philadelphia railway strike of 1895, Foster discarded the Catholicism of his youth and became an ardent radical, union organizer, and soapbox orator. Moving from job to job, he worked as a merchant seaman and a sheepherder, in lumber camps, and on railroads.

Foster absorbed the literature of socialism, and in 1909, after several years' membership in the Socialist Party, joined the International Workers of the World (IWW) and became an organizer and pamphleteer for the "Wobbly" movement and for the American Federation of Labor, particularly the steel and meat-packing industries. He also became an advocate of syndicalism, a quasi-socialist movement calling for the organization and management of production by the unions. The slogan "An end to wage labor" expressed workers' confidence in an oncoming millennium of labor power that was destined to remain a dream.

After having doubled the size of the AFL, Foster led a large-scale but unsuccessful strike of unionized steelworkers in 1919. Its failure resulted in his abandonment of the mainstream union movement. The following year, he formed the Trade Union Education League, which in 1921 was designated the U.S. branch of the Communist International of Labor Unions, or Profintern. From this time on, Foster was a leading figure in the American Communist Party, serving as its secretary general until 1930, when ill health forced him to resign in favor of Earl Browder, a longtime associate.

Foster ran as the Communist Party candidate for president in 1924, 1928, and 1932, and became a regular delegate to the Communist International conferences. During the late 1930s and 1940s, he criticized Browder's accommodating attitude toward liberal reformists, holding to an outspokenly hard-line position. In 1945, with backing from Moscow, Foster was elected chairman of the U.S. Communist Party. He remained in this position until 1956, when the sudden repudiation of Stalinism in the Soviet Union and the brutal suppression of the Hungarian revolt precipitated a rift in the American Communist Party ranks.

In 1956 Foster was indicted with eleven others under the Alien Registration Act of 1940 (Smith Act) on charges of advocating the violent overthrow of the U.S. government, but was excused from appearing at his trial because of ill health. In 1957 Foster, who had remained steadfastly loyal to the Soviet leadership, was made chairman emeritus at the party's national convention in New York City and subtly removed from power.

Foster was a prolific writer of essays, pamphlets, and books. His books include *The Great Steel Strike and Its Lessons* (1920), *Towards Soviet America* (1932), and *From Bryan to Stalin* (1939). He died in Moscow on September 1, 1961, soon after arriving there to seek medical treatment, and was given a formal state funeral.

See also: LABOR ISSUES

For Further Information

Foster, William Z. *The Great Steel Strike and Its Lessons.* New York: B. W. Huebsch, 1920. Reprint. New York: Da Capo Press, 1971.

———. *Towards Soviet America.* New York: International Publishers, 1932. Reprint. Westport, CT: Hyperion Press, 1975.

Johanningsmeier, Edward P. *Forging American Communism: The Life of William Z. Foster.* Princeton, NJ: Princeton University Press, 1994.

FREE CONGRESS RESEARCH AND EDUCATION FOUNDATION.

Free Congress Foundation (FCF), the largest conservative activist think tank devoted primarily to cultural issues, was founded in 1977 by its current president, Paul Weyrich, who is also a founder of the HERITAGE FOUNDATION. In his description of the FCF's purpose, Weyrich states that its "main focus is on the Culture War. Will America return to the culture that made it great, our traditional, Judeo-Christian, Western culture? Or will we continue the long slide into the cultural and moral decay of political correctness? If we do, America, once the greatest nation on earth, will become no less than a third world country."

The FCF has a political action committee (PAC), the Committee for the Survival of a

Free Congress, to facilitate its direct promotion of candidates for public office. FCF produces books and papers on policy issues, as do other think tanks, and at the same time maintains a significant grassroots base. Unlike economic conservative groups that advocate unfettered markets and oppose government intervention, FCF places family values above economics and favors some regulation of personal behavior, as exemplified by the Communications Decency Act passed by the 104th Congress. It lobbies extensively against state ballots that sanction gun control, decriminalization of drugs, and gay rights while supporting school prayer, traditional Judeo-Christian culture, and right-to-life initiatives.

FCF monitors judicial nominations to federal courts and opposes appointees who "fail to observe constitutional principles," recommends adding a "None of the Above" (NOTA) line to ballots, and supports term limitations. According to FCF, NOTA would enable voters to demand better candidates and issue-oriented campaigns because a new election would have to be held with fresh candidates whenever a plurality of voters selects the NOTA option.

In 1992 FCF launched NET (National Empowerment Television, currently America's Voice—"The Political News Talk Network") so that, according to Weyrich, "never again will people who believe in traditional Western culture, political reform, and individual empowerment have to say, 'If only we could get our message out.'" America's Voice, featuring over sixty-five hours of live interactive programming each week, reaches more than 11 million homes. Regular contributors include political columnists Robert Novak and Cal Thomas, former Secretary of Defense Casper Weinberger, political commentator Mary Matalin, and evangelist JERRY FALWELL.

FCF is based in Washington, D.C., and has 80,000 members. Publications include *Essays on Our Times* (monthly), *The Judicial Selection Monitor, Policy Insights*, and *The Weyrich Insider* (monthly).

See also: ACTIVIST THINK TANKS

For Further Information

Free Congress Research and Education Foundation. *Cultural Conservatism: Toward a New National Agenda*. Washington, DC: The Foundation, 1988.

Free Congress Research on Education Foundation: *http://www.freecongress.org*

Weyrich, Paul, comp. *Future Twenty-One: Directions for America in the Twenty-First Century*. Old Greenwich, CT: Devin-Adair, 1984.

FRIEDAN, BETTY NAOMI GOLDSTEIN (1921–).

Betty Friedan, born on February 4, 1921, in Peoria, Illinois, wrote *The Feminine Mystique*, the book that ignited the women's movement. An academically gifted child, Friedan skipped two grades in elementary school and founded a literary magazine in high school. Graduating summa cum laude from Smith College in 1942, Friedan was granted a fellowship to work toward a doctoral degree at the University of California at Berkeley. Opting out of a career path, she chose instead to follow the traditional social convention that encouraged women to marry and raise families.

Friedan was able to find work as a journalist during World War II because there were insufficient men to accommodate the needs of the marketplace. When the war ended, she and most women who had shown themselves capable of balancing career and family demands during the war years were summarily dismissed and expected to return to their household duties. Friedan rebelled, continuing to seek professional employment and moving through a series of dead-end jobs. This experience exposed her to many of the inequities in the workplace.

In 1947 she married Carl Friedan, a producer of summer stock theater, and they had three children. Her involvement in suburban life and childrearing was an exercise in trying to be the kind of woman she wasn't. This experience, combined with her previous encounters with anti-Semitism and discrimination against women, spurred her to conduct a survey of Smith College classmates. The results revealed general misery and frustration among educated women who were house-wives. She wrote *The Feminine Mystique* to inform a broader readership, and her book immediately struck a sympathetic chord among millions of women worldwide. At the end of World War II, women had moved into the suburbs and produced large families, so large that their offspring became known as baby boomers. In her book, Friedan accused commercial advertisers, educators, sociologists, and psychologists of overselling the idea that fulfillment could be earned only by having children. This book, the first of its kind, catapulted Friedan to the forefront of feminism, making her the leader of the modern women's movement. She helped form the NATIONAL ORGANIZATION FOR WOMEN (NOW) in 1966 and became its first president. In its early stages, NOW focused on job discrimination and on changing women's self-image.

After Friedan left the NOW presidency, she organized a strike to take place on August 26, 1970, the fiftieth anniversary of the states' ratification of the Nineteenth Amendment, granting women suffrage. Women in forty cities took part in the strike, the turnout being the largest since the days preceding suffrage.

In 1981 Friedan published *The Second Stage*, a book that defended the combining of career, home, and family. Flextime, job sharing, and split shifts were offered as ways to preserve the core of a woman's feminine qualities by simultaneously accommodating job and family demands.

In 1997 Friedan's book *Beyond Gender: The New Politics of Work and Family* called for a social policy that would be inclusive and leave behind identity politics that tends to create arbitrary and often warring groups representing women, blacks, gays, the disabled, and other single-issue advocates.

See also: WOMEN'S ISSUES

For Further Information

Friedan, Betty. *Beyond Gender: The New Politics of Work and Family*. Baltimore: Johns Hopkins University Press, 1997.

——. *The Feminine Mystique*. 3d ed., New York: W. W. Norton, 1997.

——. *The Second Stage; With a New Introduction*. Cambridge, MA: Harvard University Press, 1999.

Hennessee, Judith Adler. *Betty Friedan: Her Life*. New York: Random House, 1999.

Horowitz, Daniel. *Betty Friedan and the Making of "The Feminine Mystique": The American Left, the Cold War, and Modern Feminism*. Amherst: University of Massachusetts Press, 1998.

FRIENDS OF THE EARTH. Friends of the Earth (FOE) was formed in 1969 in San Francisco by DAVID ROSS BROWER, a former executive director of the SIERRA CLUB and a staunch, eloquent, and uncompromising environmentalist, to promote conservation of natural resources and preservation of wilderness areas. In 1989 FOE absorbed the Environmental Policy Institute and the Oceanic Society.

Currently FOE is "dedicated to protecting the planet from environmental degradation; preserving biological, cultural, and ethnic diversity; and empowering citizens to have an influential voice in decisions affecting the quality of their environment—and their lives." FOE keeps track of voting records of members of Congress and endorses candidates based on the actions they take on legislation affecting the environment. Protection of groundwater and the ozone layer, toxic waste management, reform of the World Bank, and reduction of overconsumption in the United States are major concerns.

FOE is a small and lean, scrappy, creative, committed, and effective citizen action group. Through its Green Scissors Campaign, FOE has worked with Taxpayers for Common Sense and the U.S. PUBLIC INTEREST RESEARCH GROUP to cut $20 billion in spending and subsidies on programs that hurt the environment (e.g., nuclear research programs and pork barrel water projects). It also lobbied unsuccessfully against the North American Free Trade Agreement but praised President Clinton for his refusal to sign budget bills that would sacrifice wildlife community protection while widening corporate profit margins. Pressure from FOE and its allies forced governments to abandon the Multilateral Agreement on Investment in 1998, which would have enabled secret courts to challenge and repeal environmental laws and lower public health standards worldwide.

In 1999 FOE backed Senator Bill Bradley over Vice President Albert Gore in the Democratic presidential primary campaign because of disappointment over the Clinton administration's inaction on global warming. Finally, FOE has won dozens of suits to protect rivers, forest areas, and wetlands from loss through commercial development and has taken the lead in providing information on the safety, economic, and ecological problems associated with increased use of sport utility vehicles.

FOE headquarters is in Washington, D.C., and its membership is about 20,000. Brent Blackwelder is current president. Publications include *Crude Awakening, The Oil Mess in America: Wasting Energy, Jobs and the Environment,* and *Earth Budget: Making Our Tax Dollars Work for the Environment. Friends of the Earth,* a bimonthly newsletter, is included with membership dues.

See also: ENVIRONMENT

For Further Information

Brower, David Ross. *Let the Mountains Talk, Let the Rivers Run.* New York: HarperCollins, 1995.

Friends of the Earth, *http://www.foe.org/*

FURMAN V. GEORGIA (408 U.S. 234) (1972).
This 5–4 Supreme Court decision held unconstitutional the imposition of the death penalty in the cases that were before the Court and invalidated the death penalty throughout the nation as then imposed, sparing the lives of almost 600 condemned persons. There was a per curiam opinion rendered on behalf of the whole court and separate opinions given by each of the nine justices. Justices Brennan and Marshall argued that executions are per se cruel and unusual punishment and violate the Eighth Amendment. Justice William Douglas stated that the discretionary application of punishment affected the "poor and despised" unequally and therefore violated equal protection under the law. Justices Stewart and White found the system as then operating "so wantonly and freakishly imposed" as to be unconstitutional under the Eighth and Fourteenth Amendments. Chief Justice Burger's dissent emphasized that those capital punishment laws which did not mete death out in a random and unpredictable manner might ultimately be held constitutional.

Opposers of the death penalty rejoiced in the decision, but their jubilation was short-lived. Chief Justice Burger's prediction was accurate, with *GREGG V. GEORGIA* following in 1976, and the ban on capital punishment ended. Between 1976 and 2000, 331 people were executed in the United States, including Troy Leon Gregg, who died in the electric chair, and over 3,000 inmates were awaiting execution on death rows in 1999.

See also: DEATH PENALTY AND CHOICE IN DYING

For Further Information

Henson, Burt M. *Furman v. Georgia: The Death Penalty and the Constitution.* New York: Franklin Watts, 1996.

G

GARDNER, JOHN W. (1912–). John W. Gardner founded COMMON CAUSE in 1970 as a national citizens' organization that would be a nonpartisan but politically oriented "third force," putting its money and voting power behind favored legislation and candidates and counterweighing corporate and partisan political influences in government. He served as its director until 1977.

Gardner hoped for a revitalization of the public process to make political and governmental institutions more responsive to the needs of the nation and the will of its citizens. Within one year, a combination of full-page ads in the major dailies, proclaiming that "everyone is represented but the people," and direct mail solicitations persuaded 230,000 people to join Common Cause.

Gardner was born October 8, 1912, in Los Angeles, and graduated from Stanford University in 1935. After earning his doctorate in psychology from the University of California, he was appointed head of the Latin American section of the Foreign Broadcasting Intelligence Service and served in the U.S. Marine Corps between 1943 and 1946. Joining the Carnegie Corporation in 1946, Gardner became its president in 1955. In 1961 he wrote *Excellence: Can We Be Equal and Excellent Too?*, in which he wrestled with the problem of reconciling the American maxim "All men are created equal" with the reality of varying human intellectual capacity. From 1965 until 1968, during President Johnson's administration, he served as secretary of health, education, and welfare.

Gardner directed the National Urban Coalition from 1968 until 1970, the year he founded Common Cause. He also founded the volunteer coalition Independent Sector. As professor of government at Stanford University, he continues to write and speak eloquently in behalf of citizen involvement and to caution against public apathy and alienation. He contends that Americans' "courage and spirit are there, poorly hidden beneath surface pragmatism and self-indulgence, left somnolent by the moral indifference of modern life, waiting to be called forth when the moment comes," and that that moment has come.

See also: LIBERAL ACTIVISM

For Further Information

Gardner, John W. "The American Experiment." *National Civic Review* 87 (Fall 1998): 193–199.

———. *In Common Cause*. New York: W. W. Norton, 1972.

———. *On Leadership*. New York: Free Press, 1990.

GARVEY, MARCUS MOSIAH, JR. (1887–1940). Marcus Mosiah Garvey Jr.'s

most significant contribution to the advancement of African Americans was his recognition of the need for black economic independence and racial solidarity. He insisted that blacks needed to become entrepreneurs in publishing, shipping, and manufacturing in corporate America. His crusade for racial enterprise in the 1910s was revived during the Black Power movement in the 1960s. The NATION OF ISLAM, the BLACK PANTHERS PARTY, the KU KLUX KLAN, and other groups advocating racial separatism were inspired by Garvey's earlier pursuit of Black Nationalism.

In 1914 he founded the Universal Negro Improvement Association (UNIA) and a separatist organization, the African Communities League. He built the first and one of the largest black-owned multinational businesses, the Black Star Lines, founded and edited newspapers in four countries, and lectured on topics ranging from ethics to theology to history. He set in motion African Americans' search for identity and cultural autonomy. The Father Divine movement and the Rastafarians, a religious sect believing in spiritual transference back to Africa and worship of Ethiopian royalty, were manifestations of this awakened urge. ELIJAH MUHAMMAD, leader of the Black Muslim movement, was one of Garvey's disciples. Later, in the 1960s and 1970s, blacks' search for cultural roots renewed interest in Garvey's ideas.

Born August 17, 1887, in St. Ann's Bay, Jamaica, Garvey left school at age fourteen and worked as a printer until his union went on strike in 1907. As foreman in Kingston's leading printing firm, Garvey led the walkout, which failed through lack of worker resolve, instilling his lifelong contempt toward unionism. Between 1909 and 1911, Garvey traveled in Central and South America and then went to London, where he became involved in the Pan African movement. He believed that his destiny was to lead the black race back to the "Promised Land." The UNIA he founded in Jamaica melded elements of the American Chautauqua movement and Booker T. Washington's Tuskegee Experiment, including sponsorship of self-improvement education and popular lectures, debates, and entertainments. Garvey's African Communities League was established to instill racial pride and to create a black-governed nation in Africa.

After failing to attract a following in Jamaica, Garvey moved to New York City in 1916. Arriving in Harlem, he revived the UNIA, where his eloquence and natural leadership abilities drew thousands of new members. He founded *Negro World*, the UNIA weekly, which was published until 1933 and reached a peak circulation of about 180,000. In 1920 he presided over an international UNIA convention, which promoted African nationalism and adopted a Declaration of the Rights of the Negro People of the World. A year later, he proclaimed himself provisional president of the "Empire of Africa." Garvey's forceful chauvinism held more appeal for many blacks than the cautious and more accommodating policies of organizations such as the NATIONAL ASSOCIATION FOR THE ADVANCEMENT OF COLORED PEOPLE (NAACP). By 1924 the Garvey African Legion and UNIA had over 1 million followers with 725 chapters in the United States and more than 250 in forty-one other countries. His "back to Africa" colonization effort collapsed after failing to win support from Liberia and other targeted African nations.

Other Garvey ventures included the Universal Black Cross Nurses, Negro Factories Corporation (NFC), and a chain of restaurants and grocery stores. In the 1920s NFC firms employed more than a thousand people, and nationwide 35,000 blacks controlled businesses with assets exceeding $1 million. However, Garvey's most ambitious project was the Black Star Line (1919), owned and operated by black people, and aspiring to provide freight and passenger service to Africa, America, and the West Indies. In 1922 the line folded after investigators found that the ships were not seaworthy and that the corporation was being mismanaged. Garvey was convicted and imprisoned for mail fraud. President Coolidge commuted his sentence and ordered his deportation to Jamaica as an undesirable alien in 1927. After failing to revive Black Nationalism in Jamaica, he moved to London, where he died in obscurity, after suffering a stroke, in June 1940.

See also: AFRICAN AMERICAN RIGHTS

For Further Information

Garvey, Amy. *Philosophy and Opinions of Marcus Garvey*. New York: Atheneum, 1992.

Hill, Robert A. *Marcus Garvey: Life and Lessons*. Irvine, CA: University of California Press, 1987.

Stein, Judith. *The World of Marcus Garvey: Race and Class in Modern Society*. Baton Rouge: Louisiana State University Press, 1986.

Van DeBurg, William L., ed. *Modern Black Nationalism: From Marcus Garvey to Louis Farrakhon*. New York: New York University Press, 1996.

GAY AND LESBIAN ALLIANCE AGAINST DEFAMATION.

The Gay and Lesbian Alliance Against Defamation (GLAAD) was established in 1985 by a group of eight gay writers in New York City to act as a watchdog and educator of the city's newspapers and television news programs. The *New York Post*'s sensational coverage of AIDS and the negative imagery that it generated incited the group to take action. GLAAD/NY's first public demonstration in December 1985 outside the *Post*'s headquarters drew over 1,000 protesters.

GLAAD's mission is to "organize the lesbian, gay, bisexual and transgender community to respond to negative and positive portrayals of its constituency in the media." It educates members of the media through seminars that correct stereotypes and emphasizes positive images. GLAAD is dedicated to promoting fair, accurate, inclusive representation of individuals and events in all media as a means of combating homophobia and all forms of discrimination based on sexual orientation and identity.

GLAAD has successfully directed its fire on such well-known media personalities as Bob Hope, Mel Gibson, and Andy Rooney, and pop musicians Buju Banton, Marky Mark, and Shabba Ranks. Buju Banton was taken off the *Tonight* show in 1993 for his pop single urging listeners to shoot gay men, and Marky Mark and Shabba Ranks were forced to perform acts of video contrition for writing inflammatory homophobic lyrics and for stating that gays deserve crucifixion. Bob Hope, as compensation for antigay slurs in a skit, produced a public service plea for viewers to not participate in antigay attacks, and Rooney was suspended from the CBS network for three months in 1990 for his antigay commentary. In response to GLAAD pressure, Nynex added gay and lesbian services as a category under Human and Social Services in its New York City Yellow Pages telephone directory.

In 1989 GLAAD initiated its Annual Media Awards to recognize inclusive and accurate portrayals in the media. Absolut Vodka, Anheuser-Busch, American Airlines, and other corporate sponsors support these widely publicized and well-attended events. Annual Media Awards banquet honorees have included Roseanne, Sir Ian McKellen, Jonathan Demme (director of the film *Philadelphia*), Jerry Seinfeld, Spin City, Chicago Hope, Armistead Maupin, Bob and Harvey Weinstein, Barbara Walters, and Pedro Zamora. Celebrities in attendance have included Beatrice Arthur, Steve Allen, Polly Bergen, Whoopi Goldberg, Sharon Stone, Lily Tomlin, Ed McMahon, Gregory Peck, and Lynn Redgrave.

The group generates hundreds of letters and phone calls and has become the most visible gay organization by capturing headline coverage. In 1997–1998 it claimed partial credit for a 23 percent increase in gay roles on television but lost ground in 1998–1999 as networks responded to increased pressure from the religious right.

GLAAD membership is about 10,000. It has regional offices in Atlanta, Kansas City, Los Angeles, San Francisco, and Washington. Its national headquarters is in Los Angeles. The current executive director is Joan M. Garry. Publications include *GLAAD Notes*, a quarterly; *IMAGES*, a biannual publication; and *Access Denied: The Impact of Internet Filtering on the Lesbian and Gay Community*.

See also: LESBIANS AND GAYS

For Further Information

Clendinen, Dudley, and Adam Nagourney. *Out for Good.* New York: Simon and Schuster, 1999.
Gay and Lesbian Alliance Against Defamation, *http://www.glaad.org*

GAY MEN'S HEALTH CRISIS. Alarmed by the emergence of the AIDS epidemic, six gay men met in author-playwright-activist LARRY KRAMER's New York City apartment in 1982 and founded the Gay Men's Health Crisis (GMHC). The group's mission was "to provide services for people with AIDS; to prevent the spread of AIDS through education; and to advocate for greater government leadership and funding in order to provide better services and work towards both a vaccine and a cure."

The group and its allies won passage of the Ryan White Comprehensive AIDS Resources Emergency (C.A.R.E.) Act authorizing provision of $881 million in emergency aid to sixteen cities hardest hit by the AIDS epidemic in 1990–1991. Congress initially appropriated less than $350 million but increased the total funding to $2.9 billion by 1993. In 1992 GMHC intensified its lobbying for AIDS prevention and cure programs at the federal, state, and city levels. GMHC also helped with passage of the Americans with Disabilities Act. By 1993 GMHC was committing 11 percent of its budget to lobbying and had created a separate political action group, GMHC Action, to exploit opportunities presented by the Clinton administration.

Beginning in the mid-1990s, this oldest AIDS agency became beleaguered by a dwindling budget caused by donor fatigue; the influx of poor, elderly, and minority AIDS victims, including women and drug addicts; and a steep decline in its original constituency of relatively affluent gay white men. These problems were compounded by a misguided executive decision to support a New York State law requiring AIDS patients to report names of their sexual partners, setting GMHC at odds with other gay/lesbian rights groups. In response to these challenges and changes, the GMHC appointed Ana Oliveira, a Latina and lesbian, as new executive director in 1999. The largest and oldest AIDS service organization, GMHC is based in New York City and provides care for 7,400 clients annually.

See also: LESBIANS AND GAYS

For Further Information

Dowd, Maureen. "For Victims of AIDS: Support in a Lonely Siege." *New York Times,* December 5, 1983, late city final edition, p. B1.
Gay Men's Health Crisis, *http://www.gmhc.org*
Richardson, Lynda. "AIDS Is Still Here, but Donors Drift Off; As Disease Lingers, Public Interest Wanes and Service Groups Falter." *New York Times,* January 13, 1999, p. B1.

GENERAL WILDLIFE FEDERATION. *See* National Wildlife Federation

GIBBS, LOIS (1951–). Born on June 25, 1951, in Grand Island, New York, Lois Gibbs is recognized for her critical role in the grassroots environmental justice movement and for drawing the nation's attention to toxic chemicals responsible for poisoning residents in the Love Canal community in upstate New York. On October 1, 1980, former President Jimmy Carter acknowledged Gibbs as "the most important . . . grassroots leader of the Love Canal residents. Without her persistence and dedication there might never have been a Love Canal emergency declaration and the agreement between the federal and New York State governments that permitted the state to purchase the homes of residents of the Love Canal area might never have come to pass."

In 1978, as her own children and those of neighbors started to develop serious health problems, she suspected that chemicals buried in a nearby toxic waste site might be the causative factor. Her house, in the Love Canal section of Niagara Falls, was close to the site. She had read an article in the local paper on the use of the Love Canal for toxic

Lois M. Gibbs (left), head of the Love Canal (New York) Homeowners Association, speaks to a police officer prior to her December 1978 arrest for leading a demonstration to protest the trucking through her community of dioxin-contaminated soil from the Love Canal chemical dump site. *AP/Wide World Photos.*

waste disposal. Between 1942 and 1953, the Hooker Chemicals and Plastic Corporation had deposited 20,000 tons of waste in a trench dug for the abandoned nineteenth-century Love Canal project.

Gibbs complained in vain to school authorities and decided to survey neighbors. She discovered that numerous health problems, including birth defects and cancers, were prevalent. Children were being stricken with liver damage, asthma, urinary tract disorders, immune system dysfunctions, and rare blood diseases. Because authorities were still underplaying the danger, Gibbs formed the Love Canal Homeowners Association. By 1980 Love Canal residents' frustration led to the Association holding hostage two Environmental Protection Agency officials and threatening retaliation if immediate action was not taken. Consequently Congress ordered pur-

chase of the homes of the 7,000 evacuees and President Carter signed into law the Comprehensive Environmental Response, Compensation and Liability Act (Superfund law) authorizing $1.6 billion for cleanup of contaminated sites. Since Love Canal and despite the legality of such facilities, not one new commercial hazardous waste landfill has been built in the United States, a measure of the change in public awareness.

Pressures from Gibbs's expanded activism ended her marriage, and in 1981 she moved to Virginia to start up the Citizens Clearinghouse for Hazardous Waste, later to become the CENTER FOR HEALTH, ENVIRONMENT AND JUSTICE (CHEJ). By 1999 the CHEJ included over 8,000 community groups and was recognized as a strong force for public health and a model of constructive citizen action.

A current focus of Gibbs is dioxin, a carcinogen present in hospital waste, burning tires, and tainted food products such as ice cream, fish, and meat. Gibbs, now author of several books and a citizen action celebrity, has remarried. Her second husband, Stephen Lester, is a toxicologist in charge of CHEJ science and technical assistance programs.

See also: HUMAN HEALTH AND SAFETY

For Further Information

Gibbs, Lois. *Dying from Dioxin: A Citizen's Guide to Reclaiming Our Health and Rebuilding Democracy.* Cambridge, MA: South End Press, 1995.

———. *Love Canal: The Story Continues.* North Kingston, RI: New Society, 1998.

GRAY PANTHERS. Established in 1970 by MAGGIE KUHN, Gray Panthers is committed to an intergenerational approach that calls for an economically just society devoid of ageism, racism, sexism, and other forms of stereotyping and stigmatization. Gray Panthers got its start when the United Presbyterian Church informed Kuhn that she would be forcibly retired from her executive position upon reaching her sixty-fifth birthday, although male administrators had been told they could continue indefinitely. She was affronted by this ruling and called together five other professional women active in other religious and nonprofit organizations, all facing mandatory early retirement. Opposition to the Vietnam War, not the issue of ageism, dominated the thinking of Kuhn's newly formed social action group. Soon, however, their agenda expanded to include universal health coverage, age discrimination in the workplace, access to affordable housing, and the 1972 presidential elections. Ultimately, Gray Panthers became intergenerational in its outlook, deciding to work for the common good and on behalf of the elderly.

The original name of the group was Consultation of Older Persons (COP), soon changed to Consultation of Older and Younger Adults for Social Change. After spokespersons appeared on a New York City talk show, the producer nicknamed the group the Gray Panthers because of their forceful, quick-witted, action-oriented presentations. The name stuck. Their exposure widened when the media drew attention to their co-sponsorship of a Black House Conference on Aging with students for peace in Vietnam to publicize the absence of African Americans at President Nixon's first White House Conference on Aging. This was followed by a march to the White House gates with lists of demands for reducing disparities between blacks and whites in health care to be delivered to the president. Although mounted police fended off the group, their demonstration resulted in the appointment of a larger proportion of minority delegates.

Gray Panthers' next target was the Medicare Act of 1964. Although the existing legislation eased the financial burdens of seniors' health care, it did nothing to help the aged cope with chronic diseases and disability, locate home health care assistance, arrange for transportation to and from medical facilities, or obtain financial help when Medicare and personal funds were exhausted. These shortcomings of Medicare were brought to the attention of the American Medical Association during its 1974 conference in Chicago. Panthers, dressed as doctors and nurses, tried to revive a comatose AMA on the front steps of the hotel. The Panther patient, garbed in a hospital gown and labeled "Sick AMA," lay on a stretcher in the lobby while a team attempted to resuscitate him. Vital signs miraculously improved only after the team had extracted a large wad of $100 bills from AMA's chest cavity.

Maggie Kuhn died in 1995. By that time, her group had stopped forced retirement at age sixty-five in the public sector and in most private sector organizations, exposed nursing home abuse, and mobilized voters to work for social justice and intergenerational equity. Timothy Fuller is the current executive director. Jobs, workers' rights, and universal health care continue as key concerns of Gray Panthers' 40,000 members.

See also: SENIOR MOVEMENT

For Further Information

Gray Panthers, *http://www.graypanthers.org*

Kuhn, Maggie, with Christina Long and Laura Quinn. *No Stone Unturned: The Life and Times of Maggie Kuhn*. New York: Ballantine Books, 1991.

GREENPEACE U.S.A. Greenpeace U.S.A., founded in 1971, has set as its goals establishing Antarctica as a world park, protection of the U.S. coast from damaging oil and gas development, opposition to any attempted revival of the nuclear power industry, and the immediate cessation of the production and use of chlorofluorocarbons and all other ozone-destroying chemicals. Greenpeace U.S.A. and Greenpeace International take part in a worldwide environmental coalition that subscribes to the belief that other species and humans should share an equal status in nature's web.

Founded in British Columbia, Canada, it began as a group opposing nuclear weapons testing by the U.S. military in Alaska. The group adopted the name Greenpeace to convey its expanded mission of combating governmental and industrial policies that threaten the world's natural resources, for example, offshore oil drilling, dumping radioactive wastes into the ocean, and the inhumane killing of animals. Such actions would force solutions that are essential to a green and peaceful future.

Greenpeace members are conservationists who contend that verbal protests against threats to the environment must be supplemented by civil disobedience and direct, nonviolent action in order to achieve their objectives. Until the early 1990s, Greenpeace's strategy was to go and intervene wherever an ecological disaster was in the making. For example, the group has placed inflatable boats between harpooners and whales, positioned themselves between hunters and seal pups, and plugged up industrial pipes that discharged toxic wastes into the ocean.

In 1977 Greenpeace used a grant from the World Wildlife Fund to purchase a trawler that had been a research vessel for the British Ministry of Agriculture, Fisheries, and Food. This ship was overhauled and christened the *Rainbow Warrior*. In the 1970s Greenpeace had used a previous boat, a twelve-meter ketch, the *Vega*, to attempt to prevent the French government's detonation of hydrogen bombs in the South Pacific. Thus began a series of boat rammings and other confrontations between the *Vega* and French authorities. On July 10, 1985, the Greenpeace ship *Rainbow Warrior* was blown up, and the crime was traced to two French agents, who pleaded guilty to manslaughter and willful sabotage. A Greenpeace photographer, Fernando Pereira, was killed and the subsequent negative publicity resulted in the French defense minister's resignation. This event aired Greenpeace's sense of urgency worldwide and generated a dramatically increased membership for the organization.

Today Greenpeace focuses on eight issues: (1) civilian use of nuclear energy, (2) disarmament, (3) chlorinated hydrocarbons contained in pesticides and plastics, (4) ocean ecology, (5) toxic waste, (6) pollution transfer, (7) ozone layer depletion and global warming, and (8) forest preservation. Greenpeace has cut its staff, narrowed its focus, and adopted a more temperate and conciliatory tone, offering solutions in place of adversarial face-offs. It continues to encourage businesses to adopt environmentally friendly practices and lobbies for enactment of protective measures such as conservation of fisheries and incentives for insurance companies to invest in ecologically benign power sources. Recently Greenpeace became involved in prevention of the manufacture and sale of potentially harmful vinyl toys.

Greenpeace U.S.A. national headquarters is in Washington, D.C.; Greenpeace International is based in the Netherlands. John Passacantando is the executive director of Greenpeace U.S.A. The group currently has about 400,000 members in the United States and 4 million individual members worldwide. It publishes *Greenpeace*, a quarterly magazine.

See also: ENVIRONMENT

For Further Information

Greenpeace U.S.A., *http://www.greenpeaceusa.org*

Merchant, Carolyn. *Radical Ecology*. London: Routledge, 1992.

Rowell, Andrew. *Green Backlash: Global Subversion of the Environmental Movement*. London: Routledge, 1996.

Zimmerman, Michael E. *Contesting Earth's Future: Radical Ecology and Postmodernity*. Berkeley: University of California Press, 1994.

GREGG V. GEORGIA (428 U.S. 153) (1976).

In *Gregg. v. Georgia* (1976), the Supreme Court decided that sufficient safeguards against unjust or inadvertent errors in the application of the death penalty had been put in place in the state of Georgia. This landmark decision cleared the way for the resumption of capital punishment in the United States in 1980.

Four years earlier, in *FURMAN V. GEORGIA* (1972), the Supreme Court, by a 5–4 vote, had held that the jury-discretionary system of capital punishment was unconstitutional. In the 1972 decision the Court decided that the death penalty had been applied capriciously and in violation of the Eighth Amendment to the U.S. Constitution, which bans the inflicting of "cruel and unusual punishments." The Court left open the question of whether or not death sentences imposed under a system with sufficient safeguards against a miscarriage of justice would be constitutional. This set the stage for *Gregg v. Georgia*. In this later case, the Court stated that "no longer can a jury wantonly and freakishly impose the death sentence; it is always circumscribed by the legislative guidelines. In addition, the review function of the Supreme Court of Georgia affords additional assurance that the concerns that prompted our decision in Furman are not present to any significant degree in the Georgia procedure."

In his dissenting opinion, Justice William J. Brennan stated:

At bottom the battle has been waged on moral grounds. The country has debated whether a society for which the dignity of the individual is the supreme value can, without a fundamental inconsistency, follow the practice of deliberately putting some of its members to death. In the United States, as in other nations of the western world, the struggle about this punishment has been one between ancient and deeply rooted beliefs in retribution, atonement or vengeance on the one hand, and, on the other, beliefs in the personal value and dignity of the common man that were born of the democratic movement of the eighteenth century, as well as beliefs in the scientific approach to an understanding of the motive forces of human conduct, which are the result of the growth of the sciences of behavior during the nineteenth and twentieth centuries. . . . The punishment of death, like punishments on the rack, the screw, and the wheel, is no longer morally tolerable in our civilized society.

Since restoration of the death penalty in 1980, more than 600 people have been executed and 3,000 inmates placed on death row. Capital punishment is legal in thirty-eight states and so popular (over 80 percent of the public favoring it in various opinion polls) that few politicians dare to question its fairness or effectiveness as a deterrent to crime.

See also: DEATH PENALTY AND CHOICE IN DYING

For Further Information

Acker, James R., Robert M. Bohm, and Charles S. Lanier, eds. *America's Experiment with Capital Punishment: Reflections on the Past, Present, and Future of the Ultimate Penal Sanction*. Durham, NC: Carolina Academic Press, 1998.

GRISWOLD V. CONNECTICUT (381 U.S. 479) (1965).

The women's movement was encouraged by *Griswold v. Connecticut* (1965), a Supreme Court decision which held unconstitutional a Connecticut statute banning the use of contraceptives and the offering of medical advice regarding their use. In its decision, the Court stated that "if a law outlawing voluntary birth control is valid, a law requiring compulsory birth control also would seem valid . . . both types of law would unjustifiably intrude upon rights of marital privacy." In addition the Court concluded that the Constitution upheld a broad right to privacy based on several specific guarantees within the Bill of Rights. These include the First Amendment, protecting freedom of association; the Third Amendment, barring the quartering of soldiers in private homes in peacetime without consent; the Fourth Amendment, protecting Americans from unreasonable searches and the seizure of their homes and property; the Fifth Amendment, guaranteeing freedom from self-incrimination; and the Ninth Amendment, giving to citizens rights not specifically enumerated in the Constitution.

The appellants in the case were Estelle Griswold, executive director of the Planned Parenthood League of Connecticut, and Jack Buxton, a physician and professor at Yale Medical School who served as medical director for the League in its New Haven Center. The League had opened the center in November 1961 for the purpose of inviting arrest and litigation to test the constitutionality of the statute.

In his delivery of the Court opinion Justice William O. Douglas wrote:

> The present case . . . concerns a relationship lying within the zone of privacy created by several fundamental constitutional guarantees. And it concerns a law which, in forbidding the use of contraceptives, rather than regulating their manufacture or sale, seeks to achieve its goals by means having a maximum destructive impact upon that relationship. . . . Would we allow the police to search the sacred precincts of marital bedrooms for telltale signs of the use of contraceptives? The very idea is repulsive to the notions of privacy surrounding the marriage relationship. We deal with a right of privacy older than the Bill of Rights—older than our political parties, older than our school system. Marriage is a coming together for better or for worse, hopefully enduring, and intimate to the degree of being sacred. It is an association that promotes a way of life,

> not causes; a harmony in living, not political faiths; a bilateral loyalty, not commercial or social projects. Yet it is an association for as noble a purpose as any involved in our prior decisions.

See also: ABORTION POLICY; NATIONAL ABORTION AND REPRODUCTIVE RIGHTS ACTION LEAGUE

For Further Information

Goldstein, Leslie Friedman. *Contemporary Cases in Women's Rights.* Madison: University of Wisconsin Press, 1994.

GUN OWNERS OF AMERICA. Founded in 1975 by former California state senator H. L. "Bill" Richardson, Gun Owners of America (GO) calls itself the "no-compromise gun lobby," taking a more militant position than that of the dominant NATIONAL RIFLE ASSOCIATION. GO contends that there should be absolutely no regulations governing the sale or purchase of handguns, no waiting periods, no background checks, no trigger locks, and no restrictions placed on access to automatic weapons. Gun Owners of California, Richardson's original group and an affiliate of GO, characterizes itself as being "attack oriented and the toughest, most hard hitting pro-gun organization in the state of California." Richardson believes that "the anti-gun movement is the creature of the most radical leftist elements of the world wide socialist movement."

In 1976 Gun Owners was among the top contributors to congressional candidates opposing gun controls, and by 1980 it had become one of the nation's top dozen PAC (political action committee) campaign dollar givers. It contributed to nineteen Republican House and Senate campaigns in 1994, the year in which it backed Republican Steve Stockman's successful bid to unseat long-standing House Judiciary Committee Chairman Jack Brooks (D-TX), who was expected to win by a wide margin. Brooks had pushed for passage of the Omnibus Violent Crime

Control and Law Enforcement Act of 1994, which contained restrictions on importation and manufacture of assault weapons.

Although Gun Owners has won no major victories since that time in pursuing its purist agenda, it occasionally scores a policy success through zealous activism. In 1989 Lawrence Pratt, GO's executive director since 1976, stated in testimony before a congressional committee that semiautomatic weapons were best suited for home and personal self-defense. Pratt was one of Patrick J. Buchanan's campaign chairs during his run for the presidency in 1996. Pratt was dismissed after reports emerged regarding his alleged association with KU KLUX KLAN leaders, Aryan Nations pastor Richard Butler, extremists in the militia movement, and groups holding anti-Semitic and racist views.

Gun Owners of America headquarters is in Springfield, Virginia. Its current membership is approximately 125,000. GO's Web site includes state and federal alerts, analyses of bills before Congress, form letters to Congress, and other useful information for citizen activists. Its online journal, *The Gun Owners*, reinforces its pro–gun ownership credo.

See also: GUN OWNERSHIP RIGHTS/GUN CONTROLS

For Further Information

Gun Owners of America, *http://www.gunowners. org*; *http://www.gunownersca.com*
Stern, Kenneth. *A Force upon the Plain: The American Militia Movement and the Politics of Hate.* Norman: University of Oklahoma Press, 1997.

GUN OWNERSHIP RIGHTS/GUN CONTROLS.

The controversy between those who favor gun owners' rights and those who back increased gun controls has affected public policy since 1934. Advocates of gun ownership rights declare that stringent controls violate their right to own guns and that taking defensive weapons from law-abiding citizens would endanger lives without preventing possession of guns by criminals. Backers of more restrictive gun control laws cite accidental shootings and high homicide rates, and contend that guns have little value in self-defense.

In the United States, privately owned guns have killed more people since 1900 than have died in all the wars in the nation's history. About half of the families in the United States own at least one gun, and this country has the highest level of violence among industrialized countries, with the majority of homicides committed with guns. The U.S. murder rate is ten times that of Great Britain and eight times that of Japan.

The NATIONAL RIFLE ASSOCIATION (NRA) and GUN OWNERS OF AMERICA argue that without guns, the United States would still be a violent, bloodshed-prone society. NRA insists that "guns don't kill, people do" and that gun registration and the banning of military weapons would give criminals the advantage over law-abiding citizens, eventually lead to confiscation of all firearms, and violate the Second Amendment to the U.S. Constitution. In response, the BRADY CAMPAIGN TO PREVENT GUN VIOLENCE insists that "guns don't die, people do," pointing to the alarming number of murders, suicides, and accidental deaths and the increasing incidence of teenage killing. Gun control advocates are convinced that easy availability of guns results in high rates of death by gunfire.

The pro-gun groups interpret the Second Amendment as a guarantee of the individual's right to bear arms. Extremist organizations such as the JOHN BIRCH SOCIETY, militia groups, and POSSE COMITATUS support this view because they believe that government is always a threat and that individuals must remain free, not only to hunt and shoot for recreation, but to defend themselves against criminals and governmental despotism. By contrast, anti-gun groups place primary emphasis on the right of the people to keep and bear arms, not as individuals but as members of states' active, organized militias, which are the modern-day National Guard units. The courts have failed to strike down local, state, and federal gun control laws on the basis of the Sec-

Former Reagan press secretary James Brady and his wife Sarah greet reporters after the June 1991, Senate passage of the Brady gun control bill. Brady was seriously wounded during the 1981 assassination attempt on President Ronald Reagan. *AP Photo/John Duricka.*

ond Amendment, recognizing that the eighteenth-century notion of the militia does not make sense in contemporary America.

The NRA began its defense of individual ownership by succeeding in convincing Congress to eliminate the requirement that all handguns be registered from the National Firearms Act of 1934. After the assassination of President John F. Kennedy in 1963, Senator Thomas J. Dodd (D-CT) introduced a bill that would have banned mail order sales of firearms to private citizens, made it mandatory that gun sellers obtain a federal license, and set federal regulations on bazookas, grenades, and other military hardware. The NRA objected, claiming that citizens have the right to possess firearms for purposes of self-protection, security of the nation, hunting, and recognized sporting activities.

In March 1981, John Hinckley's shooting of President Ronald Reagan provided a boost for Handgun Control, Inc. (later renamed the Brady Campaign to Prevent Gun Violence, as did the earlier murder of former Beatle John Lennon in December 1980. Sarah Brady joined HCI in 1985 after her husband, Jim, had been shot in the assassination attempt on President Reagan. Within a three-week period after Sarah Brady became its president, HCI membership rocketed from 5,000 to 80,000. However, HCI lobbying failed, and the NRA was able to ensure that between 1968 and 1988 no gun control bill left committee to be voted on by either chamber of Congress. In 1988 President George Bush's platform included support of the individual's constitutional right to keep and bear arms, but the January 1989 massacre of children in a Stockton, California school playground resulted in a tempering of Bush's position. He announced a temporary ban on the importation of AK-47 assault weapons.

In 1993, President Bill Clinton brokered one bill through Congress that became part of the 1994 Violent Crime Control and Law Enforcement Act banning nineteen different types of assault weapons. This bill became the high water mark for gun control progress. Brady II, the Handgun Control and Violence Protection Act of 1994, was awaiting passage in mid-1994. It would have included a national licensing requirement, registration of all guns with the Bureau of Alcohol, Tobacco, and Firearms, and gun show licensing fees, and would have brought U.S. gun control laws to parity with those enforced in European industrialized democracies. The Republican landslide on November 8, 1994, closed the window of opportunity. Conservative NRA-backed Republican candidates gained control of both houses of Congress. NRA succeeded by campaigning on the issues of family values and ethics, not the gun issue. Eighty percent of NRA-endorsed candidates won, including forty-one conservative Democrats. The incoming Speaker of the House, Newt Gingrich, proclaimed that no gun control legislation would move in committee or on the floor as long as Republicans held a majority.

In April 1995, the Oklahoma City Murrah Federal Building explosion occurred, and a year later HCI membership rose above the 400,000 mark, drawing support from urban residents. HCI also forged ties to the Coalition for Peace Action, GRAY PANTHERS, NATIONAL COALITION AGAINST DOMESTIC VIOLENCE, NATIONAL ASSOCIATION FOR THE ADVANCEMENT OF COLORED PEOPLE (NAACP), LEAGUE OF WOMEN VOTERS, and COALITION TO STOP GUN VIOLENCE (later renamed the Brady Center to Prevent Gun Violence). Meanwhile, the NRA attracted intense loyalty from gun-owning middle class conservatives, hunters, and target shooting enthusiasts who possessed multiple firearms, and people in small town rural America.

The NRA, like the CUBAN AMERICAN NATIONAL FOUNDATION, is an outspoken and united minority that operates superbly well in the interest group milieu and can generally prevail over a larger, apathetic majority. The NRA has the commitment, organizational structure, leadership, breadth of membership, and technological and financial resources to prevail in Washington. Between 1988 and 1994, while the Washington climate was hostile, NRA shifted its target and got right-to-carry-weapons legislation enacted in twenty-eight states and laws passed in forty-two states that prohibit local governments from enacting their own gun control laws.

In 1999 a conservative trend was under way, so gun control legislation appeared to be heading nowhere. The April 1999 massacre at Columbine High School in Colorado ended with fourteen students and one teacher dead, and Congress still failed to enact new gun restrictions. The 2000 presidential election promised a showdown on the issue. Candidate George W. Bush strongly opposed new restrictions on gun ownership, while candidate Albert Gore favored gun restrictions. Conservatives were recommending stiffer fines and longer prison terms for selling, lending, exhibiting to minors a broad range of violent or sexually explicit materials and considering regulation of movies and video games. Liberals were advocating restriction of sales of guns at gun shows. Legislation was stalled.

In 1999, individual and mass shootings took the lives of 676 people in their homes, public schools, offices, and churches. Also, almost two-thirds of the approximately 30,000 Americans who committed suicide shot themselves, usually with handguns. An NRA board member, former Lieutenant Colonel Oliver North, a key figure in the Reagan administration's Iran-Contra scandal, speculated that if some sociopath goes out and slaughters a large number of people with guns, that would get coverage, generate public horror, and probably force Congress to act.

For Further Information

Carter, Gregg Lee. *The Gun Control Movement.* New York: Twayne, 1997.

Dizard, Jan E., Robert Merrill Muth, and Stephen P. Andrews, eds. *Guns in America: A Reader.* New York: New York University Press, 1999.

Utter, Glenn H. *Encyclopedia of Gun Control and Gun Rights.* Phoenix: Oryx Press, 1999.

H

HAMER, FANNIE LOU (1917–1977).
Born in Ruleville, Mississippi, the daughter
and wife of sharecroppers, Fannie Lou
Hamer was best known for her success in securing federally guaranteed voting rights for
African Americans. She picked cotton as a
child and had worked for eighteen years in
the fields when, in 1962, she was suddenly
awakened to her potential voting rights.
This happened at a meeting co-sponsored by
the SOUTHERN CHRISTIAN LEADERSHIP
CONFERENCE (SCLC) and the STUDENT
NONVIOLENT COORDINATING COMMITTEE
(SNCC) in a local church. Her first futile attempt to vote in the county seat of India-
nola, Mississippi, reaped severe economic
reprisals and physical violence. Her commitment to the civil rights movement was
sealed by her experience. In 1961 she had
been sterilized without her consent and was
later dismissed from her job for pursuing her
right to vote.

After being fired, Hamer began participating in voter registration workshops. In
1963, when she and SNCC workers tried to
enter a "whites-only" café in Winona, Mississippi, they were arrested. Hamer was jailed
and beaten, and sustained permanent damage to her arms and kidneys. Undeterred by
this incident, she became a mover in economic and community development initiatives. As a founder and vice chairperson of

the Mississippi Freedom Democratic Party
(MFDP), Hamer gained national attention
during the 1964 Democratic National
Convention when the MFDP demanded
seating along with the formally sanctioned
all-white state delegation. The MFDP was
rejected, but Hamer's eloquent oratory and
leadership turned a momentary defeat into a
media coup. Her description of the violence
and injustice experienced by civil rights activists conveyed to millions of television
viewers the intensity of African Americans'
anger and anguish. In 1968 the MFDP, renamed the Mississippi Loyalist Democratic
Party (MLDP), again fought for representation on the convention floor and won. The
segregationist delegates were ejected and
Hamer received an ovation as she took her
seat.

Hamer was elected to the Central Committee of the NATIONAL WOMEN'S POLITICAL
CAUCUS when it was formed in 1971. After
this her health deteriorated, and in March
1977, she succumbed to a fatal heart attack
complicated by breast cancer, diabetes, and
hypertension.

In 1997 President Clinton proclaimed
February as National African American History Month. Fannie Lou Hamer was cited for
her courage, spirit, and dedication to the
struggle against racism in the 1960s.

See also: AFRICAN AMERICAN RIGHTS

Fannie Lou Hamer testifies on poverty in Mississippi before a Senate subcommittee in April 1967. *AP/Wide World Photos.*

For Further Information

Mills, Kay. *This Little Light of Mine: The Life of Fannie Lou Hamer.* New York: Dutton, 1993.

HANDGUN CONTROL INC. *See* Brady Campaign to Prevent Gun Violence

HAYDEN, TOM (1939–   ). An innovative political strategist, media superstar, prolific writer, and omnipresent radical activist from 1960 until 1975, Tom Hayden was the central figure in the battle waged by the STUDENTS FOR A DEMOCRATIC SOCIETY (SDS) against war and racism in the 1960s. The Port Huron Statement, which he presented at the groundbreaking meeting of the SDS, became the political and philosophical testament of the New Left. It rejected the "tired dogma and empty jargon of the Old Left" and pled for reflective commitment, to be

combined with passion and critical talents. Hayden was a cofounder of the SDS, serving as its president during the 1962–63 academic year.

Thomas Emmett Hayden was born on December 11, 1939, in Royal Oak, Michigan, and attended the University of Michigan. In his junior year, he became aware of student demonstrations against the House Un-American Activities Committee and the southern sit-in protests. As editor of the campus newspaper, he urged support of the STUDENT NONVIOLENT COORDINATING COMMITTEE (SNCC), and upon graduation worked with SNCC in Mississippi and Georgia. In 1961 Hayden and other activists at Ann Arbor founded SDS. Hayden emphasized grassroots, participatory democracy and denigrated top-down government bureaucracy.

In 1964 he established the Economic Research and Action Project (ERAP) as part of an SDS plan to stimulate participatory democracy and organize unemployed youths in northern cities, to replicate the success that SNCC had experienced in the South. Following the Newark riots in 1964, ERAP collapsed and Hayden turned his attention to the antiwar movement. In 1965 he accompanied radical African American historian Herbert Aptheker and civil rights activist/grassroots labor historian STAUGHTON LYND to North Vietnam, hoping to link the North Vietnamese to the American peace movement. After making additional highly publicized and criticized trips to Cambodia and Hanoi, he negotiated the release of three American POWs. In 1968 Hayden was one of the Chicago Seven along with Black Panther BOBBY SEALE and activists Abbie Hoffman and Jerry Rubin. Hayden and the others were charged with complicity in the violence that occurred during the National Democratic Convention, charges later voided by a separate appeals court. When the Saigon government collapsed in 1975, Hayden moved into conformist American electoral politics, running for office as a liberal Democrat. Failing in his bid for a U.S. Senate seat in California, he was later elected to successive terms in the California State Assembly and State Senate between 1982 and 2000.

Hayden is founder of the California Campaign for Economic Democracy, chairman of the California SolarCal Council, and author of seven books and numerous periodical articles. He has had three marriages. He broke up with his first wife, Sandra Cason, a civil rights worker with the Student Nonviolent Coordinating Committee, and married JANE FONDA in 1973. His current wife is Barbara Williams.

See also: LIBERAL ACTIVISM; ANTIWAR/ANTI–NUCLEAR WEAPONS MOVEMENT; STUDENT ACTIVISM

For Further Information

Hayden, Tom. *The Port Huron Statement: The Founding Manifesto of Students for a Democratic Society*. Reprint, Chicago: Charles H. Kerr, 1990.

———. *Tom Hayden: An Activist Life*. Niwot, CO: Roberts Rinehart, 1997.

HAYWOOD, WILLIAM DUDLEY ("BIG BILL") (1869–1928).

Born February 4, 1869, in Salt Lake City, Utah, William Dudley Haywood was a leader in revolutionary labor politics and co-founder of the radical Industrial Workers of the World (IWW). He worked as a miner, homesteader, and cowboy, then joined the Western Federation of Miners (WFM) and was elected secretary-treasurer in 1900. He led the union through several turbulent, strife-ridden years of bloody confrontation with state troopers and Pinkerton detectives. This experience convinced him that capitalism must be overthrown.

In 1905 Haywood chaired the inaugural convention of the IWW, an organization dedicated to emancipating the "unskilled, unorganized, and powerless members of society." As leader of the IWW, known as the Wobblies, Haywood became committed to the goal of organizing all workers into a single international union.

Within a year after starting the IWW, Haywood was accused of collusion in the murder of a former antiunion governor of Idaho, Frank Steunenberg. Clarence Darrow, the eminent labor lawyer, defended him, and when he was acquitted, laborers elevated him to hero status. However, his intense radicalism, endorsement of civil disobedience and sabotage, and harsh criticism of conservative unionism resulted in the WFM's eventual withdrawal from the IWW and Haywood's dismissal.

In 1912 he resurfaced as a public figure in Lawrence, Massachusetts, by transforming a seemingly futile strike by immigrant textile workers into a triumph. Haywood did this by leading marches, organizing rallies, canvassing the city, and convincing people to act without resorting to violence. A tall man, blind in one eye, endowed with plentiful charm, dash, sentimentality, and an impresario's knack for the grand gesture, Haywood was a compelling public speaker. He became head of the IWW in 1914, and by 1917 was undertaking union recruitment drives throughout the western United States. Because of the IWW's growing power and the setbacks to the war effort and private profit that could result from strikes, Haywood was convicted of sedition in 1917 on grounds of his opposition to America's participation in World War I.

Over one hundred IWW union leaders were arrested on charges of conspiracy to overthrow the government. Other federal prosecutions followed, and the IWW was eliminated by 1920. Haywood was sentenced to twenty years in prison, but jumped bail and fled to the Soviet Union in 1919. When he died in Moscow in 1928, half his ashes were placed under the Kremlin Wall and the remainder shipped to Chicago and buried near the graves of anarchists sentenced to death for inciting the 1886 Haymarket Riot.

See also: LABOR ISSUES

For Further Information

Carlson, Peter. *Roughneck: The Life and Times of Big Bill Haywood*. New York: W. W. Norton, 1983.

HEMLOCK SOCIETY U.S.A. Founded in 1980 in Santa Monica, California, by Derek Humphry, the Hemlock Society U.S.A. (HSUSA) is the oldest and largest right-to-die organization in the United States. The Hemlock Society's mission is "to maximize the options for a good death, including legalizing physician aid in dying for terminally ill, mentally competent adults who request it, under careful safeguards." Hemlock opposes suicide as a solution for emotional problems and concerns itself only with voluntary euthanasia for incurably ill people.

Humphry, a British journalist and first director of Hemlock, described his first wife's death in his book, *Jean's Way*, published in 1978. In 1975 he had helped her take her life when the pain and indignity of inoperable bone cancer became too much to bear by administering a lethal mixture of two drugs obtained in advance from a physician friend. Although British authorities prosecuted Humphry for assisting in the suicide, the case was dropped because of insufficient evidence. Meanwhile *Jean's Way* became a best seller in England.

In 1976 Humphry married his second wife, Ann Wickett, an American, and they moved to California. In the United States, Humphry acquired celebrity status after appearing on television talk shows and was urged by viewers to start a right-to-die organization. Royalties from *Jean's Way* provided the funds to establish the Hemlock Society, which derives its name from the poison used by Athenian authorities to carry out philosher Socrates' death sentence.

During the 1960s and early 1970s, Americans had become aware of the emotional, ethical, and economic problems created by medical technology's capacity to extend lives of the critically ill, including those afflicted by intense and prolonged pain and suffering. Rising health care costs and a growing elderly population added further urgency, and living wills became common by 1980 as advocacy of the right to assistance in dying benefited from public awareness of the civil rights movement. The "rights" climate and the proven effectiveness of direct citizen action fueled the growth of Hemlock as a grassroots organization.

In 1989 Humphry divorced Ann Wickett three weeks after she had undergone a lumpectomy for breast cancer. In early 1991 Humphry married Gretchen Crocker. Later that year, Wickett died after ingesting a fatal dose of barbiturates. In 1992 Humphry resigned from the Hemlock Society.

Derek Humphry's book, *Final Exit: The Practicalities of Self-Deliverance and Assisted Suicide for the Dying*, published in 1991, became an immediate best seller despite fears of its potential misuse by depressed people or money-seeking relatives. The clash between believers in the traditional Judeo-Christian sanctity of life and those espousing the right to "pull the plug" whenever the quality of life becomes hopelessly dismal broke into the media. DR. JACK KEVORKIAN's emergence as a controversial champion of physician-assisted suicide generated concern, and "right-to-die" measures were defeated in California, New Hampshire, and Washington. Membership in HSUSA started to decline, from 52,000 in 1993 to 25,000 in 1999. The *Hemlock Quarterly*, which had

Hemlock Society founder Derek Humphry is interviewed at the society's annual meeting in Ann Arbor, Michigan, in June 1998. *AP Photo/Carlos Osorio.*

published recipes for suicide to be used by victims of quadriplegia, dementia, colostomies, and other devastating ailments and indignities, ceased publication in 1994. *TimeLines*, its successor, aimed at physicians, politicians, and academics, concentrates on providing fast-breaking legislative news.

In the 1990s a major and rapid shift in public opinion on the issue of doctor-assisted euthanasia occurred, with 75 percent of the adult population approving the procedure if the patient requests it. This change can be largely ascribed to HSUSA. The group has succeeded in getting legislation for physician aid in dying introduced in more than twenty states and won its campaign to legalize physician-assisted suicide in Oregon in 1994. At least nine spinoff right-to-die groups have been spawned by HSUSA, all focusing on legalizing physician-assisted suicide. Adding further to public awareness was *One True Thing*, a 1998 Hollywood film starring Meryl

Streep, based on the novel by Anna Quindlen, which deals sympathetically with a daughter's assistance in the death of her cancer-stricken mother.

In 1998 HSUSA commended Kevorkian for his persistence over eight years in providing medical assistance in dying and bringing the issue of end-of-life choice into every American home. Currently HSUSA has three objectives: (1) to educate the public and professionals about end-of-life choices, including the physician aid-in-dying option; (2) to help people plan for a peaceful death; and (3) to change laws so that medically assisted dying is a legal option instead of a secretive, random practice.

The group is controversial, facing opposition from the Catholic Church, the RELIGIOUS RIGHT, the medical profession, and Not Dead Yet, an organization of the disabled that fears a "Better Dead than Disabled" pretext could be used to hasten their deaths. In recognition of these concerns, the U.S. Congress introduced the Pain Relief Promotion Act in 1999, legislation that would nullify the Oregon law permitting physician-assisted suicide. In rebuttal, HSUSA aired a *Final Exit* program produced by Humphry on cable television in Oregon to stimulate opposition to the U.S. Senate bill. Kevorkian then disputed the HSUSA position, issuing a statement from his prison cell in which he expressed his fear that the public would take the advice of an unqualified writer instead of seeking professional medical counsel.

Hemlock Society U.S.A. headquarters is in Denver, Colorado. Faye Girsh is executive director of the 25,000-member organization. *TimeLines*, a quarterly newsletter, is included with membership.

See also: DEATH PENALTY AND CHOICE IN DYING

For Further Information

Fox, Elaine. *Come Lovely and Soothing Death: The Right to Die Movement in the United States.* New York: Twayne, 1999.

Hemlock Society U.S.A., *http://www.hemlock.org*

Humphry, Derek. *Final Exit: The Practicalities of Self-Deliverance and Assisted Suicide for the Dying.* Collingdale, PA: DIANE Publishing, 1998.

HERITAGE FOUNDATION. The Heritage Foundation's mission is to "formulate and promote conservative public policies based on the principles of free enterprise, limited government, individual freedom, traditional American values, and a strong national defense." It strives to "provide the Washington policy-making community, the national news media and the general public with the facts and analysis needed to make an informed decision on the important issues of the day." At the instigation of Paul Weyrich, leading strategist of both the secular and RELIGIOUS RIGHT, Colorado brewing executive JOSEPH COORS SR. provided $250,000 in seed money for the establishment of the Heritage Foundation in 1973.

Edwin J. Feulner Jr. has led Heritage since 1977. Weyrich left Heritage in 1974 to form his own FREE CONGRESS RESEARCH AND EDUCATION FOUNDATION. Feulner is a former director of the Republican Study Committee and a member of Congressman Melvin Laird's staff. Heritage was an important shaper of Reagan administration policies, and former House Speaker Newt Gingrich has described it as being the most far-reaching conservative organization in the country in the war of ideas. It advocates supply-side economics, which stresses reduction of taxes for those of higher income to encourage business investment and growth, with anticipated "trickle down" benefits to poor and middle-class members of society. The group also promotes choice in education and provided a blueprint for the Strategic Defense Initiative. In 1994 the first bills to pass the 104th Congress instituted changes that Heritage policy bulletins had been urging for years, and Heritage analysts were responsible for defining the content of the "Contract with America," which proposed ten acts of Congress, to include a balanced budget tax limitation amendment, omnibus anticrime legislation, cutbacks on social welfare to promote individual responsibility, the banning of U.S. troops under UN command, and imposition of term limits to replace career politicians with citizen legislators.

Heritage has over 200,000 contributors supporting its ideas and is the largest and most generously funded think tank, with over $43 million in 1998 income. It influences the public through the media in addition to publishing more than 300 books, monographs, and studies each year. Talk radio host Rush Limbaugh has frequently cited Heritage statements on welfare, poverty, labor, and tax issues—even reading the full text of Heritage op-ed articles over the air. Heritage research has also been used by nationally syndicated radio talk show hosts LAURA SCHLESSINGER and G. Gordon Liddy, who was a key participant in the Watergate break-in scandal, and by the venerable radio journalist Paul Harvey.

Heritage has become the most frequently quoted activist think tank in America, with op-ed and editorial pieces appearing in the

New York Times, Washington Post, Chicago Tribune, and other dailies that reach an estimated 30–50 million people each month.

Heritage does its own research, repackaging it into ideas compressed into crisp, easy-to-read position papers, kept under twenty pages. Legislators prefer these "fast info-food" capsules to the lengthier, longer-to-produce background documents available from the Congressional Research Service. Heritage's media specialists are skilled in linking journalists with research staff and focusing their attention on Heritage studies as they are produced. These studies are considered more credible, scholarly, and objective than material available from lobbyists, designated spokespersons, and individual legislators.

Fellows associated with Heritage include former cabinet members William Bennett, Edwin Meese III, and Jack Kemp. Board members include Governor Jeb Bush of Florida, conservative writer Midge Dector, Amway co-founder Jay Van Andel, and *National Review* president Thomas L. Rhodes. Edwin J. Feulner Jr. is Heritage Foundation president. The Heritage Foundation building is in Washington, D.C. Its flagship journal is the quarterly *Policy Review*.

See also: ACTIVIST THINK TANKS

For Further Information

Edwards, Lee. *The Power of Ideas: The Heritage Foundation at Twenty-five Years*. Ottawa: Jameson Books, 1998.

Conservative News and Information, *http://www.townhall.com*

Hellebust, Lynn. *Think Tank Directory: A Guide to Nonprofit Public Policy Research Organizations*. Washington, DC: Government Research Service, 1996.

Heritage Foundation, *http://www.heritage.org*

HIGHLANDER FOLK SCHOOL. Highlander Folk School was founded by MYLES HORTON at Monteagle, Tennessee, in 1932. Modeled after the Danish folk schools, Highlander is based on the assumption that in order to improve a nation's quality of life, one must begin with local community empowerment and create a corps of knowledgeable individuals committed to action for the greater, common good. The Danish folk schools, established by Danish poet, theologian, and philosopher N. S. Grundtvik in 1844, are noncredit, nondegree institutions in which teachers and students decide on goals, methods, and curricula independently of outside authorization, and serve specific political needs rather than those of society as a whole.

Highlander promotes grassroots activism, peer education, and action research. The school has been a major force in training civil rights leaders, providing adult education programs, and working to improve living conditions in the Appalachian region. School desegregation, voter education, labor rights, and equal justice for minorities and women are promoted through Highlander's resources and programs. Graduates include civil rights activists ROSA PARKS and STOKELY CARMICHAEL, civil rights leaders MARTIN LUTHER KING JR. and Andrew Young, First Lady ELEANOR ROOSEVELT, and other prominent activists and students who formed the STUDENT NONVIOLENT COORDINATING COMMITTEE.

Creation of original art and music is encouraged at Highlander. One of the best known songs associated with the civil rights movement, "We Shall Overcome," was adapted from an older and less accessible hymn tune, "I'll Overcome Someday," and simplified by Zilphia Horton, Myles Horton's first wife.

Highlander's South Carolina Sea Island Citizenship Schools, formed in the 1950s, provided literacy training for blacks so that they could read passages from the state constitution and qualify for voter registration. The schools produced over 50,000 new voters by 1965.

In 1961, at the height of the civil rights movement, Highlander had its charter revoked by the attorney general of Tennessee because of its defiance of segregation laws and for being "just a place for Communists to meet." The school was transferred to New

HILL, JOE

Market, near Knoxville, Tennessee, and resumed operation under its current name, the Highlander Research and Education Center. In 1982 Highlander was nominated for a Nobel Peace Prize because of its role in providing education on behalf of human rights in the region. Only Hull House, established by social reformer and feminist JANE ADDAMS in 1889, and the INDUSTRIAL AREAS FOUNDATION, organized by social activist SAUL DAVID ALINSKY, have played as meaningful a part in combating poverty, ignorance, and exploitation of disadvantaged members of American society.

Currently the Highlander Center coordinates residential workshops and assists local leaders in building their own support networks and resource bases. Limits are imposed upon Center activities because of an ebbing interest in overcoming poverty, bigotry, and economic injustice in Appalachia and the South.

For Further Information

Glen, John. *Highlander: No Ordinary School, 1932–1962.* Lexington: University of Kentucky Press, 1988.

Highlander Research and Education Center, *http://www.hrec.org*

Horton, Aimee Isgrig. *The Highlander Folk School: A History of Its Major Programs, 1932–1961.* Brooklyn: Carlson, 1989.

Horton, Myles, and Paolo Freire. *We Make the Road by Walking: Conversations on Education and Social Change.* Philadelphia: Temple University Press, 1990.

HILL, JOE (1879–1915). A Swedish-born seaman and songwriter, Joe Hill popularized the cause of the American labor movement through his music. Hill's original name was Joel Emmanuel Hägglund and he was born in Gävle, Sweden. In 1902 he migrated to the United States, where he moved from job to job from New York to Hawaii before joining the radical Industrial Workers of the World (IWW) in 1910.

The IWW's revolutionary program called for abolition of the wage system and a society run by the workers of the world. Hill became the songwriter for the IWW, whose members always sang in solidarity "To Fan Flames of Discontent," the motto proclaimed on the covers of their "Little Red Songbooks." Caustic, catchy lines created by Hill were set to popular tunes or hymns urging workers to unionize and fight for human rights and dignity. Joe produced a series of IWW "hit" songs including "Tramp, Tramp, Tramp, the Boys Are Marching," a tribute to tramps, and "The Preacher and the Slave," a parody of the Salvation Army hymn "Sweet Bye and Bye." The opening verse of the latter song, containing the popular expression "pie in the sky," is:

> Long haired preachers come out every
>   night,
> Try to tell you what's wrong and what's
>   right,
> But when asked 'bout something to eat
> They will answer with voices so sweet:
> You will eat, bye and bye,
> In that glorious land above the sky;
> Work and pray, live on hay,
> You'll get pie in the sky when you die.

In 1914 Hill was convicted in Salt Lake City of murdering a grocer and his son and sentenced to death. The verdict was based on circumstantial evidence, and witnesses' testimony was neither consistent nor convincing. Because of strong public sentiment against the IWW, vengeance outweighed evidence in the proceedings, and Hill was executed by a firing squad. Appeals by President Woodrow Wilson, Samuel Gompers, president of the American Federation of Labor, Helen Keller, and the Swedish government proved futile. Hill's laidback lifestyle, musical talents, tributes to workers, and dramatic death earned him American folk hero status. His last words were "I die like a true rebel. Don't waste any time mourning—organize."

See also: LABOR ISSUES

For Further Information

Foner, Philip S. *The Case of Joe Hill.* New York: International Publishers, 1965.

Smith, Gibbs M. *Joe Hill.* Layton, Utah: Privately printed, Gibbs Smith, 1984.

HILLMAN, SIDNEY (1887–1946).

Born in Zagare, Lithuania, in 1887, Sidney Hillman rose to prominence as an innovative labor leader, creator of the country's first political action committee, and a pioneer in establishing constructive cooperation between workers and employers. A pragmatic idealist, Hillman believed that the labor movement had the redemptive power and "generosity of spirit" to rescue society from "selfishness, exploitation and organized violence."

While in Russia, Hillman had received a rabbinical education, worked in a chemical laboratory, and become an advocate of socialism and labor reform. He was jailed by the czarist regime in 1905, and upon his release emigrated from Russia to the United States.

By 1909 Hillman had found work in Chicago as an apprentice cutter at Hart, Schaffner and Marx, the largest men's clothier in the country. It was during this time that he was oriented to progressive thinking by social reformer JANE ADDAMS and civil liberties lawyer Clarence Darrow. The following year, he led the United Garment Workers (UGW) in a strike that resulted in a new contract considered a model of labor-business relations.

In 1914 Hillman moved to New York City, where he led a splinter group from the UGW that became the Amalgamated Clothing Workers of America (ACWA) and was elected its first president, an office held until his death. By 1940 the ACWA had greatly increased its membership, secured unemployment insurance, and set up a housing development for its members. Hillman established two banks to make loans to failing companies that dealt fairly with their employees during the Great Depression.

During President Franklin D. Roosevelt's administration, Hillman served in the National Recovery Administration, the Office of Production Management, and the War Production Board's labor division. Beginning in 1943, he became chairman of the CIO's political action committee (PAC) and a shaper of national politics. When Roosevelt, running for a fourth term, was considering vice presidential running mates from among James Byrnes, a high ranking government official; the incumbent vice-president, Henry Wallace; and Missouri's Senator Harry S. Truman, he made it clear that the final decision would have to be cleared with Sidney Hillman. After Roosevelt's death, Truman, Hillman's choice, became president, and solid CIO PAC support helped him win against Thomas E. Dewey in 1948. In 1946 Hillman suffered a fatal heart attack at his family's summer bungalow at Point Lookout, Long Island, while planning union strategy for the postwar years.

See also: LABOR ISSUES

For Further Information

Fraser, Steven. *Labor Will Rule: Sidney Hillman and the Rise of American Labor*. New York: The Free Press, 1991.

HISPANIC AMERICAN RIGHTS.

During the twentieth century, Hispanic Americans' rights to equal justice, adequate education, upward economic mobility, and release from majority-sanctioned exclusion from mainstream Anglo-American entitlements came about only because of the efforts of various citizen action organizations and their leaders.

The forerunner of later organizations, the LEAGUE OF UNITED LATIN AMERICAN CITIZENS (LULAC), was established in 1929 in Texas, during a time when Mexican Americans in the southern border states experienced prejudice, violence, and extreme poverty. LULAC has remained primarily concerned with upgrading the education, assimilation, political influence, health, and civil rights of Mexican Americans, although it maintains an office in Puerto Rico.

Formed in 1968, the NATIONAL COUNCIL OF LA RAZA was a by-product of the civil rights movement. It quickly became the largest and most influential organization advocating Mexican American interests by adopting community empowerment strategies pioneered by social reformer SAUL

DAVID ALINSKY and his INDUSTRIAL AREAS FOUNDATION.

Two groups, the CUBAN AMERICAN NATIONAL FOUNDATION (CANF) and CAMBIO CUBANO (Cubans for Change), represent Cuban Americans. The CANF, founded in 1981 by Cuban Americans who are unified in their resolve to overthrow the Castro regime, wields legislative leverage in Washington equivalent to that of the NATIONAL RIFLE ASSOCIATION and the AMERICAN ASSOCIATION OF RETIRED PERSONS. Despite its small size, estimated to not exceed 7,000 members, the CANF has dictated U.S. policy regarding Cuba since 1982. It has done so because of its members' intense commitment and CANF's authoritarian organizational structure, substantial budget, generous contributions to political leaders, skill in manipulating the media, and lobbying expertise. In contrast, Cambio Cubano, started up in 1993 by an exiled Cuban who had been imprisoned by President Fidel Castro for twenty-two years, seeks to lift the trade embargo and to negotiate Cuba's democratization. Because it lacks the financial resources, fanatical zeal, large membership base, and key political connections that are at CANF's disposal, its more moderate and reflective views on Cuba and Castro have been disregarded.

ERNESTO CORTÉS JR. is the Southwest Regional Director of the Industrial Areas Foundation, founded in Chicago by Alinsky. Cortés gained national recognition by transforming poor and fragmented Mexican American neighborhoods into organized, upgraded, politically savvy groups respected by the local power structure.

See also: LABOR ISSUES

For Further Information

Didion, Joan. *Miami*. New York: Vintage Books, 1999.

Garcia, Mario T. *Mexican Americans: Leadership, Ideology, and Identity, 1930–1960*. New Haven: Yale University Press, 1990.

HOFFMAN, ABBIE (1936–1989).

Abbie Hoffman, born on November 30, 1936, in Worcester, Massachusetts, was a prominent antiwar activist, self-proclaimed revolutionary, media celebrity, and best-selling author during the 1960s and 1970s. In 1968 he and fellow activist Jerry Rubin founded the Youth International Party or Yippies to represent antiestablishment, politically active hippies.

Hoffman frequently employed theatrical pranks in an attempt to awaken people to what he and other restive middle-class youth found most offensive in American culture: the Cold War, materialism, the Vietnam War, social injustice, and commercial degradation of the environment. Celebrated by the media, Hoffman soon became the period's principal pied piper, leading many young people into the Yippies' counterculture.

In 1959 Hoffman obtained his bachelor's degree from Brandeis University, where he was exposed to the teachings of Marxist philosopher Herbert Marcuse. After graduating, he went on to the University of California at Berkeley, where he earned a master's degree in psychology and became involved in student activist politics. For a brief period, 1963–1966, he worked in his father's medical supply company as a pharmaceuticals sales representative while increasingly devoting his off-hours to the civil rights movement. During the summers of 1964 and 1965, he joined other protesters in Mississippi and Georgia until Black Power militancy began making whites unwelcome. In 1967 he pulled off the first in a series of inventive pranks by tossing dollar bills onto the floor of the New York Stock Exchange to create a chaotic ballet of money-grabbing brokers. This was followed by his and his cohorts' attempt to levitate the Pentagon by surrounding and bombarding it with "positive psychic energy" to exorcise its evil spirits. Hoffman believed that University of Toronto theorist Marshall McLuhan, author of *The Gutenberg Galaxy* (1962) and *The Media Is the Message* (1967), was right in emphasizing the effectiveness of imagery as a means to transmit antiwar messages to the general public on the evening news.

In 1968 Hoffman and his Yippies staged demonstrations at the 1968 Democratic National Convention that escalated into violence. He was indicted by a grand jury along with seven others, on charges of conspiracy and attempting to incite a riot. Later he and five others were acquitted.

In August 1973 he was arrested for participating in the sale of cocaine to undercover agents and subsequently jumped bail, disappearing from view in February 1974. Between 1974 and 1980 he lived in upstate New York as "Barry Freed," a freelance writer. While in New York, he organized a successful campaign to save the St. Lawrence River from environmentally unsound dredging by the U.S. Army Corps of Engineers.

On September 3, 1980, Hoffman appeared on national television as a guest on Barbara Walters' show. The next day, he surrendered to authorities in New York City and served one year of a three-year sentence before being released on parole. Hoffman's autobiography, *Soon to Be a Major Motion Picture*, was published in 1980, and he continued to be a popular speaker on college campuses on such topics as apartheid and the environment. In 1989 he died in New Hope, Pennsylvania, an apparent suicide.

For Further Information

Hoffman, Abbie. *Revolution for the Hell of It.* New York: Pocket Books, 1970.
———. *Soon to Be a Major Motion Picture.* New York: Putnam, 1980.
———. *Steal This Book.* 25th ed. New York: Four Walls Eight Windows, 1995.
Jezer, Marty. *Abbie Hoffman: American Rebel.* Piscataway, NJ: Rutgers University Press, 1993.

HOME SCHOOL LEGAL DEFENSE ASSOCIATION. The Home School Legal Defense Association (HSLDA), founded in 1983 "to defend and protect the constitutional right of parents to direct the education of their children by bringing together a large number of home schooling families so that each can have a low-cost method of obtaining quality legal defense," believes home schooling to be "an education opportunity and spiritual blessing" as well as a legal right.

Michael Farris, a conservative Republican and 1993 nominee for lieutenant governor of Virginia, created HSLDA. The group files lawsuits on behalf of parents who consider that local school and state attendance requirements are excessive and intrusive. Although home schooling is legal in all fifty states, qualification and testing requirements vary widely. During the 1990s, HSLDA membership soared to over 60,000 as parents, especially born-again Christians, sought home schooling to protect their children from a perceived decline in academic quality and escalating drugs, gangs, peer influence, and violence in the public schools. In the home, faith-based education, creationist doctrine, and textbooks incorporating biblical teachings across subject areas would replace inculcation of humanism, the teaching of evolution, and sex education.

In the 1970s, only about 15,000 children were being taught at home nationwide; in 1998 the number exceeded 1.6 million. Allies in Congress include Representative Dick Armey (R-TX) and then Senator John Ashcroft (R-MO). And five of the nine Republicans running for president in 2000 made pro–home schooling declarations.

The HSLDA team of lawyers, all home schooling fathers, has successfully pursued legislative changes in at least three states that have eased regulations on home schooling and permit home-educated students to participate in public school athletic events. The organization has doubled its membership since 1993, and Farris opened Patrick Henry College, the nation's first college for home-educated students, in September 2000. HSLDA headquarters is in Purcellville, Virginia, and Michael Farris is president. Over 60,000 families are current members. *The Home School Court Report*, a bimonthly magazine, is free with membership. Linked to HSLDA is the National Home Education Research Institute (Salem, Oregon), which collects statistics on academic achievement and the demographics of home education.

See also: RELIGIOUS RIGHT

For Further Information

Home School Legal Defense Association, *http://www.hslda.org*

Line, Patricia M. "Homeschooling Comes of Age." *Public Interest*, Summer 2000, pp. 74–85.

Mathews, Jay. "A Home Run for Home Schooling; Movement Can Point to High Test Scores in National Study." *Washington Post*, March 24 1999, final edition, p. A11.

National Home Education Research Institute, *http://www.nheri.org*

HOMELESSNESS. Homelessness, formerly restricted to a small number of unfortunate alcoholics and deranged people rarely encountered on city streets, became a highly visible, embarrassing, politically sensitive, and divisive issue beginning in the 1970s. Suddenly disheveled, destitute people came out into the open and pricked the public's collective conscience. Conservatives insisted that federal programs created during the Johnson administration to redress poverty had hurt the people they were intended to help by replacing self-reliance with dependence on handouts. Liberals blamed a flawed, callous private enterprise system and the scarcity of well-designed, adequately funded social welfare programs.

From 1978 until 1990, the leading spokesperson for the homeless was MITCHELL SNYDER, an ex-convict and radical Christian pacifist. The NATIONAL COALITION FOR THE HOMELESS, founded in 1982, is committed to "end homelessness through the promotion of systemic and attitudinal change that will remove the three primary causes of homelessness—lack of livable incomes, lack of affordable, quality housing, and lack of adequate holistic health care." The Coalition's current executive director is Mary Ann Gleason.

For Further Information

Baumohl, Jim, ed. *Homelessness in America*. Phoenix: Oryx Press, 1996.

Jencks, Christopher. *The Homeless*. Cambridge, MA: Harvard University Press, 1994.

HORTON, MYLES (1905–1990). Myles Horton founded and devoted his life to the HIGHLANDER FOLK SCHOOL, an experimental academy for working people and activists. Highlander trained many prominent leaders of the 1930s labor movement and the civil rights movement of the 1960s.

Myles Horton was born July 5, 1905, in Savannah, Tennessee. After attending Cumberland University, he entered the Union Theological Seminary in New York City, then a center of radical Protestant thinking. He was influenced by liberal theologians Reinhold Niebuhr and Harry Ward, joined the Socialist Party and the FELLOWSHIP OF RECONCILIATION, and read Marx and Lenin. Later he went to Chicago, met JANE ADDAMS to discuss settlement houses, became acquainted with pragmatic philosopher John Dewey's progressivism, and subsequently visited Denmark to study the Danish folk high school movement. Returning to Tennessee in 1932, he committed himself to creating Highlander, at Monteagle, Tennessee, a school that would prepare potential activists to bring about radical social change. Horton believed that education and learning are the best tools for perfecting and protecting democracy. He encouraged his students to question and reject authority wherever it sanctions social injustice and the loss of human dignity. His students developed the capacity and confidence to make independent decisions and overcome the rigidity, complacency, and hard-set prejudice in their surroundings. By instilling Gandhian principles of nonviolence and in awakening his pupils' sense of outrage over the plight of the poor, the laborers, and the blacks in the South, Horton built a cadre of fighters willing to stake their lives to win the battles for civil rights that dominated the 1960s. Horton's high profile as head of Highlander and partial subsidization by the Congress of Industrial Organizations (CIO) led to attacks by Senator James O. Eastland, a Mississippi Democrat, who investigated the school for reported communist ties. The White Citizens' Councils, KU KLUX KLAN, and local vigilantes also threatened Horton. When his school was forced to close by the Tennessee attorney general, he immediately set up a similar school, the Highlander Research and Education Center, in Knoxville, Tennessee. The Center moved to its current site, a 1,000-acre campus in New Market, Tennessee, in 1971.

Horton's first wife, the late Zilphia Horton, is often credited with collaborating with folk singer Pete Seeger, rock guitarist Frank Hamilton, and ethnomusicologist Guy Carawan, in converting an old religious folk tune into "We Shall Overcome," the civil rights theme song. Horton's second marriage, to Aimee Isgrig, ended in divorce. In 1990, Horton died of a brain tumor at his home in New Market, Tennessee.

For Further Information

Horton, Myles, with Judith Kohl and Herbert Kohl. *The Long Haul: An Autobiography.* New York: Teachers College Press, 1998.

HUMAN HEALTH AND SAFETY. De-
spite the large number of environmental organizations already in existence (see ENVIRONMENT), other groups decided to organize in the 1970s and 1980s to deal specifically with problems of human health and safety caused by toxic industrial waste products. The existing organizations were looking primarily at protection of nature or preservation of old neighborhoods and historic sites. Humans' quality of life was being neglected.

One of the earliest health and safety advocacy groups was the Fisherman's Clean Water Action Project, started by consumer advocate RALPH NADER in 1971. In 1975 it adopted its current name, CLEAN WATER ACTION (CWA). CWA monitors and works to prevent health-threatening pollution and to create environmentally safe jobs.

CITIZENS FOR A BETTER ENVIRONMENT (CBE), founded as a citizen action group in 1971, has concentrated on decreasing industrial pollution and has been at the forefront of class action litigation to force companies to decrease the dumping of hazardous and

poisonous waste into the environment. CBE is engaged in an ongoing battle with the federal courts to preserve the right of citizens to sue corporate polluters.

INFACT, originally the Infant Formula Action Coalition, was mobilized in 1977 to stop Nestlé Corporation from marketing potentially life-threatening infant formula to Third World nations. INFACT "Hall of Shame" members that have purportedly endangered the public's health have included Dow Chemical and Waste Management. The CENTER FOR HEALTH, ENVIRONMENT AND JUSTICE (CHEJ) has its roots in the Citizens Clearinghouse for Hazardous Waste, established in 1981 by environmental activist LOIS GIBBS. It was Gibbs who marshaled residents in the Love Canal section of Niagara Falls, New York, to aggressively goad governmental agencies into recognition of the lethal danger posed by corrosive chemicals that had been buried in the vicinity by a chemical and plastics company.

Beyond Pesticides/NCAMP (BY/CAMP) began in 1981 as the National Coalition Against the Misuse of Pesticides. This activist group, based in Washington, D.C., educates the public about the hazards of pesticide use and advocates adoption of alternative pest management strategies. BY/CAMP convinced the Maryland legislature to require elementary schools to inform parents in advance before applying pesticides to the interiors of buildings because of findings linking cancer and birth defects to toxins in pesticides. The group is currently campaigning to eliminate wood utility poles that have been treated by hazardous toxic contaminants and is opposing congressional attempts to weaken provisions of the Food Quality Protection Act. The group's URL is *http://www.ncamp.org*

PUBLIC VOICE FOR FOOD AND HEALTH POLICY was created in 1982 to oppose the Reagan administration's dismantling of meat and poultry inspection standards and food assistance programs. The organization advocated healthy school lunches and improved nutrition labeling of grocery products. The group ceased operations in 1999 after failing to stop New England dairy farmers from boosting milk prices above federal guidelines.

For Further Information

Shaiko, Ronald G. *Voices and Echoes for the Environment: Public Interest Representation in the 1990s and Beyond.* New York: Columbia University Press, 1999.

Wildavsky, Aaron B. *But Is It True? A Citizen's Guide to Environmental Health and Safety Issues.* Cambridge, MA: Harvard University Press, 1995.

HUMAN RIGHTS CAMPAIGN. The Human Rights Campaign Fund (HRC) was organized in 1980 as a nonpartisan political action committee to finance campaigns of candidates for the U.S. House and Senate who pledged to support pro-gay legislation. In 1986 the group absorbed the Gay Rights National Lobby, which had focused exclusively on congressional campaigns. Because of its increased emphasis on lobbying, the HRCF became a political action committee in 1989 and dropped "Fund" from its name.

HRC promotes legislation affirming the rights of lesbians and gays and focuses on their civil rights; funding for AIDS research; lesbian health issues; and discrimination in housing, immigration, employment, and the military. Its full-time lobbying team is the largest legal group committed exclusively to dealing with issues affecting the lesbian and gay American community.

Victories for which the group claims partial credit include passage of the Americans with Disabilities Act, the Hate Crimes Statistics Act, the Ryan White Comprehensive AIDS Resources Emergency (CARE) Act, and programs for breast and cervical cancer research and screening. HRC has also pushed for creation of liberal guidelines for National Endowment for the Arts applicants and immigration law reform. HRC alerted its members to help defeat antigay measures in Oregon and Idaho in 1994, and in Maine in 1995, and was the largest single financial contributor to the legal challenge resulting in the U.S. Supreme Court decision over-

turning Colorado's antigay Amendment 2 in 1996. In 1992 and 1996, the group endorsed Bill Clinton's presidential candidacy.

In the 1998 elections, 91 percent of the 2,000 races in which HRC actively participated were won by HRC-endorsed candidates as compared to 83 percent in 1996. Prior to 1992, HRC's political strategy had focused on campaign fund contributions to the detriment of traditional lobbying tactics such as letter writing, visiting legislators' offices, and using the media to its advantage. After President Clinton's failure to end discrimination against gays in the military and the emergence of religious right, ultraconservative forces in Congress, HRC changed its strategy. Under Elizabeth Birch's direction, the group periodically polls its membership, uses information technology to its advantage, and has become an adept and influential lobbying group. However, criticisms were lodged against HRC's top-down, elitist corporate model when it endorsed Republican Senator Alphonse D'Amato in his 1998 race against Representative Charles Schumer for political reasons not obvious to rank and file. Communications within the organization were improved and HRC membership, gay and nongay, increased from 80,000 in 1995 to 300,000 by 1999.

Elizabeth Birch, former head of worldwide litigation for Apple Computers, is still director. HRC's national office is in Washington, D.C. The *HRC Quarterly, Speak Out ActionGrams* (electronic messaging service), and *Action Alerts* are included in membership dues. An Action Center on the World Wide Web enables concerned users to send instant messages to their representatives in Washington.

See also: LESBIANS AND GAYS

For Further Information

Clendinen, Dudley, and Adam Nagourney. *Out for Good: The Struggle to Build a Gay Rights Movement in America.* New York: Simon and Schuster, 1999.

Human Rights Campaign, *http://www.hrc.org*

Ireland, Doug. "Rebuilding the Gay Movement." *The Nation,* July 12, 1999, pp. 11–15.

HUMANE SOCIETY OF THE UNITED STATES.

Chartered in 1954, the Humane Society of the United States (HSUS) was formed to prevent animal suffering and abuse. The HSUS campaigns to create a humane and sustainable world for all animals, including humans, through educational programs, advocacy, and publications. HSUS's goal is to make enduring changes in human perceptions of animals and their behavior; to relieve domestic animals' suffering and prevent their harm, abuse, neglect, and exploitation; and to protect wild animals and their environments. Key programs focus on companion animals by promoting elimination of puppy mills, supporting spaying and neutering to reduce overpopulation, and protecting pets from abuse and neglect. HSUS calls for the elimination of laboratory research that harms and maims animals and for the protection of farm animals from abuse during transport to slaughterhouses. In 1997 HSUS disclosed to the general public the inhumane treatment of mares used for the production of Premarin, an estrogen-based compound used in hormone replacement therapy. Other HSUS activities include assistance to animal victims of disasters, protection of wildlife habitats, and efforts to eliminate dogfighting and cockfighting events, the unnecessary slaughter of marine animals, and cruel treatment of animals in zoos.

With 1,750,000 members, HSUS is the largest animal welfare organization in the world. It maintains ten regional offices and administers six programs: Companion Animals, Animal Research, Farm Animals, State and Federal Legislation, Wildlife Protection, and Investigations and Training. HSUS has a staff of 250, including veterinarians, biologists, lawyers, and other professionals.

Companion Animals is HSUS's most publicly visible program. Priorities include educating the public about the need to reduce animal overpopulation, advice on dog and cat care, and assistance in adopting animals from shelters. HSUS actively discourages people from purchasing animals from "puppy mills." Pets separated from owners due to natural disasters are eligible to receive aid from the HSUS disaster relief program. Qualifying animals receive shelter, and volunteer HSUS staff work to reunite pets and their owners.

In contrast to other groups such as the ANIMAL LIBERATION FRONT and PEOPLE FOR THE ETHICAL TREATMENT OF ANIMALS, HSUS does not disapprove of food and clothing produced by animals, such as beef and leather. However, HSUS does not sanction the killing of animals strictly for their fur and strives to make those who wear fur feel uncomfortable in public. The HSUS Farm Animals program stresses humane treatment of livestock and encourages less dependency on animal products to discourage the proliferation of factory farms.

HSUS investigates suspected abuse of animals. In 1998 an eighteen-month fact-finding probe determined that the Burlington Coat Factory was using dog and cat furs in garments being sold to an unknowing public. It was found that as many as 2 million dogs and cats had been slaughtered and assembled into fur coats. Circuses' treatment of animals is also being continuously monitored. Ongoing research is focusing on the correlation between animal abuse and domestic violence and relationships between animal abuse and juvenile delinquency.

The HSUS has had successes in the legislative arena. In 1999 it introduced a bill in Congress that would require labels on all fur products and ban the export, import, or sale of dog or cat fur. And in 1975 Congress enacted the Animal Welfare Act, backed by HSUS. Considered a victory for animals, the Act set standards for the treatment of animals in research, circuses and zoos, and pet stores. Ongoing legislative initiatives include the banning of "canned hunting," protection of pets that travel on commercial airlines, and outlawing the transportation of fighting cocks across state lines.

Headquartered in Washington, D.C., the 1,750,000 member HSUS relies on dues, contributions, and gifts for its resource base. Publications include *All Animals*, a quarterly journal, *Animal Activist Alert, HSUS News,* and *Shelter Sense*. Paul G. Irwin is HSUS president.

See also: ANIMAL WELFARE AND RIGHTS; ENVIRONMENT

For Further Information

Bekoff, Marc, ed. *Encyclopedia of Animal Rights.* Westport, CT: Greenwood Press, 1988.

Guither, Harold D. *Animal Rights: History and Scope of a Radical Movement.* Carbondale: Southern Illinois University Press, 1998.

Humane Society of the United States, *www.hsus. org*

Owen, Marna. *Animal Rights: Yes or No?* Minneapolis: Lerner Publications, 1993.

I

IN RE GAULT (387 U.S. 1) (1967). *In re Gault* (1967) struck a blow against prevailing juvenile court procedures by finding that the Arizona Juvenile Court had violated the fourteenth Amendment by failing to provide adequate advance notice of hearings, right to counsel, right to confront accusers, cross-examination of witnesses, and exercise of the privilege against self-incrimination to minors. In 1964, in Globe, Arizona, fifteen-year-old Gerald Gault was arrested with a friend and charged with making lewd remarks over the telephone to a woman. At the time Gault was arrested, his parents were both at work. No notice that he was being taken into custody was left at his home. Gault was placed in police custody for twelve hours before his parents were notified of his confinement. Then he was taken to the Gila County Detention Home for a week before being given a hearing. His mother asked that the woman who had made the complaint be present to identify which boy had done the dirty talking over the phone. Her request was denied, the woman never testified or came to court, and no record was kept of the proceedings.

A second hearing was held for the judge to announce his decision. He ordered Gault to remain in the State Industrial School until he was twenty-one years old—or until such time as officials would determine that he could be released to his parents. The parents,

Paul and Marjorie Gault, were shocked by the ruling and decided to fight the case. They had only $100 and neither of them had completed high school, but they were certain that their son had been mistreated. They found an attorney, Norman Dorsen, who appealed their case all the way up to the U.S. Supreme Court.

In re Gault established the following basic rights for juveniles: (1) notice of the charges being made against them; (2) the right to counsel; (3) the right to confront and cross-examine accusers; (4) the privilege against self-incrimination; (5) the right to a transcript of the proceedings; and (6) the right to appellate review.

Dorsen recently admitted that in 1967 nobody foresaw the explosion of crime, including delinquency, that occurred in subsequent years and that it would be very costly for courts to comply with *In re Gault* strictures under current conditions. He went on to warn that "the alternative is continuing disintegration of the system with appalling consequences to the country as well as the young people enmeshed in the law."

See also: CHILD AND YOUTH-RELATED ISSUES

For Further Information

Dolan, Edward F., Jr. *Protect Your Legal Rights: A Handbook for Teenagers.* Parsippany, NJ: Silver Burdett Press, 1983.

Sampson, Robert J. *Crime in the Making: Pathways and Turning Points Through Life*. Cambridge, MA: Harvard University Press, 1993.

INDUSTRIAL AREAS FOUNDATION.

Conceived by social reformer and activist SAUL DAVID ALINSKY in the 1930s, the Industrial Areas Foundation (IAF) serves as a means for poor people to acquire political power and improve the quality of their lives. In the group's original statement of purpose, Alinsky described the 1930s social context that compelled IAF's creation: "Along with the advantages of industrial progress have arisen forces of so menacing a character that today they threaten the very foundation upon which rests the hope of those committed to the democratic way of life. These destructive forces are unemployment, deterioration, disease and delinquency. From the havoc wrought from these forces issue distrust, bigotry, disorganization, and demoralization." Working with teenage gangs and Chicago's Catholic hierarchy, Alinsky showed common people how to fight apathy and exploitation and to take control of their own lives and neighborhoods.

Today the IAF has become the nation's largest faith-based community organizing network. It supplies technical advice and personnel to help people in low-wealth communities, especially in large urban centers, to organize themselves on a democratic basis so that they have power in matters affecting their own interests. IAF strives to compel local authorities to deal with such problems as slum housing, poor sanitation, inadequate schools, policing, and public transportation. After Alinsky's death in 1972, IAF's current director, Ed Chambers, restructured the organization and developed more than sixty local affiliates nationwide.

IAF has created unique self-funded training programs, "schools of public life," to equip people with political, organizational, and leadership skills so that they can be effective citizen activists in their local communities. Notable among IAF projects is the Communities Organized for Public Service (COPS) effort, started in 1973 under the leadership of ERNESTO CORTÉS JR. COPS has succeeded in moving Mexican and African American candidates into formerly off-limits city government positions and diverting more than $1 billion to rehabilitate streets, libraries, parks, public health clinics, and a community college, in addition to building affordable housing, initiating improved policing, and upgrading schools. Over fifty similar IAF efforts are ongoing in Arizona, California, Tennessee, Maryland, New York City, Boston, and Portland, Oregon.

Industrial Areas Foundation headquarters is in Chicago; Edward T. Chambers is its executive director. IAF has sixty-two affiliates in twenty-six states and Washington, D.C. An estimated 1 million IAF members are represented in more than 1,000 church congregations throughout the United States.

For Further Information

Greider, William. "IAF Hits New Hampshire," *The Nation*, January 31, 2000, pp. 6–7.
Warren, Mark R. "Community Building and Political Power." *American Behavioral Scientist* 42, no. 1 (September 1998): 78–92.

INFACT.

Founded in 1977, INFACT is a loose confederation of church organizations and consumer groups whose purpose is to stop life-threatening abuses by transnational corporations and to increase their accountability to people around the world.

In 1977 INFACT, originally named the Infant Formula Action Coalition, set in motion a seven-year campaign to stop the Switzerland-based transnational Nestlé Company from marketing a potentially deadly infant formula to Third World nations. Women in underdeveloped countries who had used the formula diluted it to save money and lacked sanitary water and nipples needed for safe use, so that many of their babies died from malnutrition and disease. INFACT lobbying and negotiations prompted passage of the World Health Organization's International Code of Marketing for Breast Milk Substitutes in 1981 and resulted in the halting of formula sales to over ten countries in 1984.

INFACT's second significant victory, achieved in 1993, was removal of General Electric from its leadership role in the production and marketing of nuclear weaponry, including the MX missile, B-2 bomber, and Star Wars SP-1000 nuclear reactor–powered satellite motor. INFACT launched its third action in 1993, an attempt to stop the tobacco industry from aggressively marketing tobacco products to children and young people outside the United States.

Product boycotting has been INFACT's primary activist strategy. In Nestlé's case the negative impact on food sales was reinforced by feelings of guilt among company employees as they became labeled "baby killers." In the GE campaign, over 4 million people participated in boycotts, reinforced by a documentary video contrasting GE's "We Bring Good Things to Life" promotional slogan with footage showing people dying from radiation and toxic pollution. The video won the Academy Award in the Best Documentary: Short Subject category in 1992, extending awareness of the boycott to television viewers worldwide. GE's sales of medical equipment plummeted as church-related hospitals stopped buying it, and in 1993 the company bowed out of the nuclear weaponry business. The tobacco industry boycotts are aimed at RJR Nabisco and Philip Morris, especially the latter company's popular Kraft, Post, and Maxwell House products.

Since 1996 INFACT has highlighted corporations whose policies and practices purportedly endanger public health and the environment by inducting them into its "Hall of Shame." To date Philip Morris, Dow Chemical, Waste Management, and Columbia-HCA Healthcare have received this dubious honor in well-publicized ceremonies. INFACT headquarters is in Boston, Massachusetts, and its current director is Kathryn Mulvey. With links to 580 health groups, INFACT membership totals 25,000.

See also: CONSUMER RIGHTS AND SAFE-GUARDS

For Further Information

INFACT. *INFACT Brings GE to Light: General Electric: Shaping Nuclear Weapons Policies for Profits.* Boston: INFACT, 1988.

———. *INFACT's 1998 People's Annual Report.* Boston: INFACT, 1999.

INFACT, *http://www.infact.org/*

IZAAK WALTON LEAGUE OF AMERICA.

The mission of the Izaak Walton League of America (IWLA) is to "conserve, maintain, protect and restore the soil, forest, water and other natural resources of the United States and other lands; [and] to promote means and opportunities for the education of the public with respect to such resources and their enjoyment and wholesome utilization." In 1922, fifty-four sportsmen in Chicago established the IWLA to encourage citizens to become involved in local efforts to protect the environment.

At the time of the IWLA's formation, uncontrolled industrial waste discharges, raw sewage, and soil erosion were threatening many of the nation's waterways; wetlands were being drained, habitat destroyed, and pristine wilderness overrun by commercial development. The founders knew that action was needed "to defend the nation's soil, air, woods, waters, and wildlife." They named the group after Izaak Walton, the seventeenth-century English conservationist who wrote the classic *The Compleat Angler, or the Contemplative Man's Recreation.*

Under its founder and first president, Will Dilg, the IWLA soon became America's most effective centrist action group representing sportsmen and recreationists. In 1927 the IWLA produced the first national water pollution inventory, and its members, generally referred to as the "Ikes," were prime movers for the first federal water pollution control law, enacted in the 1940s. IWLA's Save Our Streams program, begun in 1969, includes stream water quality monitoring and wetlands conservation and restoration.

The IWLA played a pivotal role in the passage of key federal environmental laws, including the Waterways Restoration Act

(1954) and the Forest Biodiversity and Clearcutting Prohibition Act (1993). The National Elk Refuge in Wyoming and the Everglades, Isle Royale, and Voyageurs national parks are among the many public lands created as a result of IWLA action.

Currently, the IWLA is urging restoration of the Mississippi River, which has patches of unfishable and unswimmable water that fail to meet national goals. In addition, IWLA has found that maximal concentrations of toxic pollutants occur near minority and poor on-shore communities. Through its Midwest Energy Efficiency program the IWLA sponsors projects that demonstrate the use of wind, solar, and other environmentally friendly forms of energy; a clean air campaign; and an outdoor ethics program.

The IWLA national office is in Gaithersburg, Maryland. Paul Hansen is executive director; Donald Ferris is the current president. The group has 50,000 members and 370 local chapters. Its publications include the quarterly *Outdoor America* magazine and the newsletters *Outdoor Ethics, Sustainability Communicator,* and *Save Our Streams.*

See also: ENVIRONMENT

For Further Information

Firehock, Karen et al. *Save Our Streams Handbook for Wetlands Conservation and Sustainability.* 2nd ed., rev. Gaithersburg, MD: Izaak Walton League of America, 1998.

Izaak Walton League of America. *Annual Reports,* 1993– .

Izaak Walton League of America, *http://www. iwla.org*

Voigt, William. *Born with Fists Doubled: Defending Outdoor America.* Iowa City: Izaak Walton League of America Endowment, 1992.

J

JACKSON, JESSE (1941–). Civil rights activist, political leader, Baptist minister, and the first African American to mount a serious campaign for the U.S. presidency, Jesse Jackson was born on October 8, 1941, in Greenville, South Carolina. He broke into prominence in the 1960s as a member of MARTIN LUTHER KING JR.'s staff and as president of Operation PUSH (People United to Save Humanity).

Jackson worked at various jobs and represented his Baptist church at Sunday school conventions as a boy. Like his stepfather, he was a quarterback on a state championship team. He won a football scholarship to the University of Illinois but rejected the offer and transferred to North Carolina's Agricultural and Technical State College, an all-black school, after he discovered that blacks at the University of Illinois were expected to be linemen, not quarterbacks.

In 1963 Jackson became a campus civil rights organizer, arranging for sit-ins and picket lines to hasten integration of lunch counters and other business establishments in Greensboro, North Carolina. Subsequently he attended the Chicago Technological Seminary on a scholarship. A semester short of graduation, he left to work full-time for Martin Luther King Jr. at the SOUTHERN CHRISTIAN LEADERSHIP CONFERENCE (SCLC) in Atlanta, Georgia.

In 1966 King sent Jackson to Chicago to lead the city's Operation Breadbasket, an effort to secure more jobs for blacks and to improve services in their communities. At the end of a sixteen-week drive, Jackson induced the A&P supermarket chain to sign an agreement to hire 268 more blacks and to stock brands produced by black-owned manufacturers. In 1967 Jackson took over leadership of the Operation Breadbasket organization.

After King's assassination, RALPH DAVID ABERNATHY was selected as the new head of the SCLC. Jackson left SCLC and in December 1971 founded Operation PUSH. He built it into a thriving national campaign, exhorting blacks to exercise initiative to better their status by combating vandalism, drug abuse, teen pregnancies, truancy, and high dropout rates in inner-city schools.

In 1983 Jackson announced his run for the presidency, because the other Democratic contenders had been silent or passive in opposing President Ronald Reagan's economic and social policies. Jackson promised to represent the poor and to forge a "rainbow coalition" of the "rejected and despised." Ronald Reagan was reelected president, and in 1984 Jackson had to decide whether to make a break with LOUIS FARRAKHAN, who had described Adolf Hitler as a great man, albeit wicked, and made outrageously anti-Semitic remarks. Jackson realized that rejec-

Rev. Jesse Jackson gives a thumbs up during an August 1988, rally in Los Angeles to call for the boycott of pesticide-sprayed California grapes. *AP Photo/Bob Galbraith.*

tion of the Black Muslim leader would make him unpalatable to millions of Farrakhan followers. Finally Jackson made the break, publicly branding Farrakhan's remarks reprehensible and morally indefensible.

Jackson campaigned for Walter Mondale in 1984, and 10 million blacks voted that year, more than in any previous presidential election. In 1988 Jackson ran again in the presidential primaries, backed by a more extensive and professionally managed organization. Although he entered the Democratic National Convention with 1,200 delegates, Michael Dukakis was nominated. However, Jackson's voter registration efforts paid off in the election of forty blacks to the House of Representatives, and African American votes as a bloc contributed the winning margin for Clinton's election in 1992.

In foreign affairs, Jackson has independently served as the U.S. focal black inter-mediary seeking to resolve conflicts on the world stage. From 1979 until the present time, he has served as a highly articulate intermediary, representing U.S. interests in negotiations in El Salvador, Nicaragua, Cuba, the Soviet Union, the Middle East, and Yugoslavia.

Jesse Jackson's enduring contribution as citizen activist is attributable to his unwavering dedication to the Golden Rule, "Do unto others as you would have them do unto you." This dedication has enabled millions of African Americans to enter the mainstream of U.S. society and politics.

See also: AFRICAN AMERICAN RIGHTS

For Further Information

Frady, Marshall. *Jesse: The Life and Pilgrimage of Jesse Jackson.* New York: Random House, 1996.
Haskins, James. *Jesse Jackson: Civil Rights Activist.* Berkley Heights, NJ: Enslow, 2000.

JARVIS, HOWARD (1902–1986).

In 1978 Howard Jarvis was suddenly everywhere in the media because of his success in getting the California electorate to vote for Proposition 13, the biggest antitax citizen action since the Boston Tea Party. At the time, California's housing prices were rapidly inflating, and, despite a rising tide of complaints that higher taxes were threatening to force people to move out of their homes, local officials blocked all efforts to reduce the tax burden. When Proposition 13 won on June 6, 1978, despite the opposition of labor unions, the LEAGUE OF WOMEN VOTERS, and Governor Edmund G. Brown, property taxes were slashed by about 58 percent. The measure had deep and long-lasting effects on California. In national rankings, California schools dropped from eighteenth in spending per pupil in 1977 to forty-first in 1998, and health and other social services rapidly deteriorated. The state assumed a larger share of power and responsibility for financing local services, an unintended consequence of the taxpayer revolt. Jarvis was the first in an entire generation of leaders of lobbying groups and politicians to mouth the mantra "lower taxes and less government." He set the stage for public referenda and successful tax reduction campaigns in a dozen other states. During the 1970s, only twenty-one initiatives appeared on state ballots; in the last decade of the twentieth century, there were sixty-one.

Howard Jarvis was born on September 22, 1902, in Magna, Utah, a copper mining town. After graduating from the University of Utah, Jarvis bought the *Magna Times*, a weekly newspaper, and eventually owned a chain of eleven papers. After working as a public information officer in President Herbert Hoover's 1932 campaign, he moved to California and acquired a small plant that developed into the prosperous Femco Corporation. In 1952, 1956, and 1960 he was regional manager for Dwight D. Eisenhower's and Richard Nixon's presidential campaigns. After retiring in 1962, he joined and then led a small citizens' group in Los Angeles that was monitoring local government expenditures and lobbying for lower taxes. Between 1968 and 1977, he led a futile antitax crusade. He not only fought taxes; he had called for the end of public financing of parks, libraries, refuse collection, schools, Social Security, and Medicare. In 1978 he decided to focus exclusively on taxes, not what they support, and this proved to be a winning strategy. In 1978 the Howard Jarvis Taxpayers Association mailing list included more than 300,000 people. In 1999 the association had 130,000 members.

Jarvis died in a Los Angeles hospital in 1986, the victim of a blood disease that had incapacitated him but had not stopped him from waging a final battle to prevent lawmakers from placing limitations on the impact of Proposition 13.

See also: TAX REFORM AND GOVERNMENTAL EXPENDITURES

For Further Information

Jarvis, Howard. *I'm Mad as Hell*. New York: Times Books, 1979.

Morain, Dan. "Aftershocks of Prop. 13 Are Still Being Felt," *Los Angeles Times*, December 14, 1999, home edition, Metro Section, Part B, p. 6.

JEWISH AMERICAN RIGHTS.

Jewish American rights have been restricted because of anti-Semitic prejudice in America that gained strength during the nineteenth century and became a major blight during the first three decades of the twentieth century. As the influx of immigrants from Eastern Europe to this country increased, newcomers became viewed as unwelcome competitors for American jobs and a threat to the dominant white Anglo-Saxon population. Exclusion of Jews from middle-class civic service clubs, hotels, Ivy League colleges, private preparatory schools, high society, and upper-echelon positions in business became commonplace. In rural America, particularly in the South, the KU KLUX KLAN and other extremist groups employed terrorist tactics against Jews.

In 1920 U.S. car manufacturer Henry

Ford's newspaper, the *Dearborn Independent*, attacked international Zionism with a lead article titled "The International Jew: The World's Problem." Ford accused Jews of coordinating with international insurrectionists in plots to take over the U.S. government and establish a New World Order in Washington.

In the 1930s FATHER CHARLES COUGHLIN, an early master of the art of hate radio, held millions spellbound with Sunday afternoon broadcasts containing crypto-fascist, anti-Semitic propaganda. The German-American Bund (1933–1935), a pro-Nazi, quasi-military organization made up of American citizens of German ancestry, added to the legacy of bigotry. The German government supported the Bund and maintained military camps where self-designated, uniformed storm troopers were trained. Sharing their anti-Semitic activities were such groups as the NATION OF ISLAM, LIBERTY LOBBY, JOHN BIRCH SOCIETY, private militias, and POSSE COMITATUS. White supremacist, ultra-right religious and antigovernment extremist groups continued sporadic anti-Semitic shootings and arson into the 1990s. Lesser-known but equally virulent groups include Aryan Nation, World Church of the Creator, and the National Alliance.

Three organizations that are active in combating bigotry and representing American Jewish interests are the AMERICAN JEWISH COMMITTEE, the ANTI-DEFAMATION LEAGUE (ADL), and the AMERICAN JEWISH CONGRESS. In 1968 the JEWISH DEFENSE LEAGUE (JDL) was founded by Rabbi Meir Kahane to fight anti-Semitism and to demonstrate Jews' ability to be as aggressive as their enemies were in protecting their rights. The violent militancy of the JDL during the 1970s and 1980s led to its condemnation by the moderate mainstream Jewish community.

The contemporary Jewish American condition has become almost totally devoid of bias because of the disappearance of the exclusionary white Protestant elitist groups that dominated American society through the first half of the twentieth century. The few extremist groups that remain active are monitored and exposed by the Anti-Defamation League, the AMERICAN CIVIL LIBERTIES UNION, and allied organizations.

For Further Information

Dinnerstein, Leonard. *Antisemitism in America*. New York: Oxford University Press, 1994.
Svonkin, Stuart. *Jews Against Prejudice*. New York: Columbia University Press, 1997.

JEWISH DEFENSE LEAGUE. Founded in 1968 by Rabbi Meir Kahane, the Jewish Defense League (JDL) places Judaism above any other ideology and applies to all of its actions the criterion "Is it good for Jews?" JDL teaches its members the principles of Hadar—"pride in and knowledge of Jewish tradition, faith, culture, land, history, strength, pain, and peoplehood." This extremist organization embraces a form of theological determinism that expresses faith in the permanence and indestructibility of the Jewish people and calls for their unified struggle against assimilation, secularism, liberalism, and exile from Israel. It justifies the use of force and violence to protect Jewish values.

Rabbi Meir Kahane organized the JDL from among predominantly Orthodox Jews in lower middle and working class sections of Brooklyn in 1968. Kahane, the associate editor of the *Jewish Press*, founded the JDL to fight anti-Semitism and to demonstrate Jewish power, emphasizing concepts which were compatible with the American Jewish traditionalist-oriented inner-city reality of the late 1960s. He wanted his group, initially called the Jewish Defense Corps, to be both tough and dangerous. JDL's slogan is "Never Again," referring to the Holocaust. Within three years, JDL grew to over 10,000 members. The group frequently resorted to violence to achieve its goals. Originally it concentrated on opposing anti-Semitism among blacks and radicals, protected synagogues from vandalism, and supported Israel.

In 1971 the JDL began arming its members with rifles and baseball bats and in Brooklyn and the Bronx established Chaya

In October 1988, Rabbi Meir Kahane, founder of the Jewish Defense League, is carried by supporters outside the Israeli Supreme Court in Jerusalem following the court's refusal to allow his anti-Arab Kach movement to take part in upcoming Israeli elections. *AP/Wide World Photos.*

squads ("beasts") who adopted the slogan "Every Jew a 22" to frighten alleged enemies with threats of armed retaliation. Although the JDL had some success as an antiblack protest group, Rabbi Kahane sensed that the issue of persecuted Soviet Jews could create international headlines and convert the JDL into a more significant force. The JDL aligned itself with hawkish conservatives, supporting Senator Henry Jackson over George McGovern in the 1972 presidential race and backing President Richard Nixon's Vietnam War policy. In its campaign for Soviet Jewry, it attempted to hijack a Soviet plane, harassed Soviet officials, criticized impresario Sol Hurok for bringing Soviet artists to the United States, and set off a bomb in the USSR cultural offices in Washington, D.C.

After Rabbi Kahane emigrated to Israel in 1971, his slogan became "Not One Inch," expressing his stance against returning any land to the Arab nations won during the Arab-Israeli war. As representative of an extreme party, Kahane won one term in the Israeli Knesset. In 1988 his party was banned from the Knesset because of its racist and undemocratic policies. In 1990, while speaking before a Zionist group in New York City, Kahane was assassinated by an Egyptian American gunman.

By 1985 JDL membership had declined from 13,000 to an estimated 2,500 as a result of increased police surveillance and growing opposition from the mainstream Jewish community. Irv Rubin, current JDL national chairman, succeeded Rabbi Kahane in 1985. JDL's main office is in Northridge, California, and there are active chapters in sixteen states and several foreign countries. The size of the current membership is not known.

See also: EXTREMISTS; JEWISH AMERICAN RIGHTS

For Further Information

Baumel, Judith Tydor. "Kahane in America: An Exercise in Right-Wing Urban Terror." *Studies in Conflict and Terrorism* 22 (October–December 1999): 311–329.

George, John, and Laird Wilcox. *American Extremists: Militias, Supremacists, Klansmen, Communists, and Others.* Amherst, NY: Prometheus Books, 1996.

Halevi, Jossi Klein. *Memoirs of a Jewish Extremist: An American Story.* Boston: Little, Brown, 1995.

Jewish Defense League, *http://www.jdl.org*

JOHN BIRCH SOCIETY. The current mission of the John Birch Society, formed in 1958, is to educate and inspire Americans "to restore and preserve freedom under the United States Constitution, expose and rout those forces working to enslave mankind, and then to inspire others throughout the world to follow the example of America's newly recovered freedoms." Founded in In-

A March 1961, photograph of Robert H. W. Welch, Jr., then president of the John Birch Society. *AP Wirephoto*.

dianapolis, Indiana, by Robert H. W. Welch, Jr. (1899–1985), a retired Boston candy manufacturer, the society originally concentrated on exposing communists and mobilizing its regional units against Soviet influences in the United States and Cuban communist leader Fidel Castro. While the group is isolationist, it supported the U.S. military presence in Vietnam and defined itself as the antithesis of the antiwar hippies and Yippies of the 1960s and 1970s. In the post–Cold War world, the group has been focusing on what it views as global conspiracies that threaten U.S. sovereignty and promote global government.

Welch regarded "democracy" as a deceptive word, "a weapon of demagoguery and a perennial fraud, a government of man rather than a government of law." The Society was named after John Birch, a fundamentalist missionary and U.S. Army intelligence officer

who was shot by Chinese communists on August 25, 1945, making him the first hero of World War III, according to Welch. In his action guide, the *Blue Book*, Welch said that the United Nations is part of a vast international conspiracy working to destroy U.S. sovereignty and to enslave citizens under a new one-world order. The Federal Reserve System, World Bank, and North American Free Trade Agreement (NAFTA) are considered subversive entities as well. Welch startled many of his adherents by labeling President Dwight D. Eisenhower an "agent of the Communist conspiracy," along with former U.S. Secretaries of State George Marshall and John Foster Dulles, conservative writer and journalist William F. Buckley, and Presidents Gerald Ford and Jimmy Carter.

At the time of Welch's death in 1985, the Society's membership had fallen from an estimated peak of 100,000 in 1964 to 40,000. In 1989 the Society transferred its headquarters from Belmont, Massachusetts, to Appleton, Wisconsin, the hometown of Senator Joseph McCarthy, the former chair of the U.S. House Un-American Activities Committee.

In 1990 President George Bush spoke of "a New World Order, NWO." His statement was interpreted by the Society as a coded signal to the NWO to move in and occupy the United States. Patriots, gun owners, and militias were put on red alert to organize themselves to save the nation from the impending federally imposed NWO. The "Red menace" had moved from Moscow to Washington. The Society's other enemies include the AMERICAN INDIAN MOVEMENT, the Equal Rights Amendment, federal regulations, sex education, the Trilateral Commission, and the Senate Foreign Relations Committee. Currently the Society is campaigning to get the United States out of the United Nations, reclaim the Panama Canal, and cut federal taxes.

The Society administers action programs, professional leadership training, and a youth program. Since 1970 the group has run a weeklong summer camp program held in various locations across the country as an anti-dote to what it considers to be left-wing disinformation disseminated by the public schools, media, and allied institutions. Camp trainees receive crash courses on such subjects as New Age religions, illegal immigration, the U.S. Constitution, and self-defense.

Between 1994 and 1998, membership in the Society rose on the wave of right wing populism. The John Birch Society is one of the more successful extreme right groups because of its patriotic fervor and authoritarian management and the simplistic appeal of its programs. More than 250,000 Americans have held membership in the Society at one time or another, and it has indirectly affected other extremist groups' actions.

The Society publishes the *John Birch Society Bulletin* and *The New American*, a biweekly magazine. John F. McManus has been president since 1991. Current membership figures are not available.

See also: EXTREMISTS

For Further Information

George, John, and Laird Wilcox. *American Extremists: Militias, Supremacists, Klansmen, Communists, and Others*. Amherst, NY: Prometheus Books, 1996.

Hardisty, Jean. *Mobilizing Resentment: Conservative Resurgence from the John Birch Society to the Promise Keepers*. Boston: Beacon Press, 1999.

John Birch Society, *http://www.jbs.org*

JONES, MARY HARRIS (1837–1930).
The greatest woman labor agitator of the twentieth century, Mary Harris Jones, called "Mother Jones" by most workers, helped organize miners and streetcar, garment, and steel workers and fought the evils of child labor, mostly during the final fifty years of her life. Born in Cork, Ireland, in 1837, Mary Harris grew up in Toronto, Ontario. Her family emigrated to Canada in 1847 to escape the ravages of the potato famine which over the next five years claimed over one million lives.

Mary Harris departed Toronto for a teaching job in Monroe, Michigan and later in Memphis, where she met and married George E. Jones, a member of the Iron Molders' Union, in 1861. In 1867 her husband and her four small children perished in a yellow fever epidemic and she moved to Chicago, to work as a dressmaker. In 1871 her shop was destroyed in the great Chicago fire.

The memory of her former husband's harsh work life and her own experience as a sewer of garments for the wealthy awakened her to the extreme economic and social injustice dominant at the time. She met with the newly formed Knights of Labor and started traveling to industrial sites across the country to observe and speak. A dynamic speaker capable of projecting and arousing intense emotion, Mother Jones mixed humor, invective, pathos, irony, and ridicule in her presentations. Elliott J. Gorn, in his recent biography of Mother Jones, points out that "above all, she gave people hope and told them that their aspirations for change were in the best traditions of patriotism and religion. Hundreds of thousands of American workers fought for and received better wages and working conditions during her years of activism, and they embraced a renewed ideal of democratic citizenship" (p. 302).

Wherever there was labor friction, she would be on hand to inspire and help union members wage their battles. She spoke to union members during the Great Railway Strike (Pittsburgh, 1877), the Haymarket riot (Chicago, 1886), and subsequent coal miners' strikes in Pennsylvania. After 1890 she became an organizer for the UNITED MINE WORKERS and was one of the founders of the Industrial Workers of the World (IWW).

In 1903 she led a caravan of striking child laborers from textile mills in Pennsylvania to President Theodore Roosevelt's home in Long Island, New York, to dramatize the need to abolish child labor. She attracted national attention in 1912–1913 during the frequently violent Paint Creek–Cabin Creek strike in West Virginia and led a march of miners' children through Charleston and was arrested. When the trial and a twenty-year jail sentence created a public furor, the governor felt compelled to free the seventy-six-year-old agitator. She then traveled to Colorado and was again arrested. For several more years she appeared at strikes in New York and Pittsburgh.

Today Mother Jones continues to symbolize labor's struggle for humane treatment and decent wages. Her name and fame were resurrected in the 1970s with the premiere of the liberal *Mother Jones* magazine calling for positive social change. Mary Harris Jones died in Silver Spring, Maryland, in 1930.

See also: LABOR ISSUES; WOMEN'S ISSUES

For Further Information

Fetherling, Dale. *Mother Jones, the Miners' Angel: A Portrait*. Carbondale: Southern Illinois University Press, 1974.

Gorn, Elliott J. *Mother Jones: The Most Dangerous Woman in America*. New York: Hill and Wang, 2001.

JORDAN, CRYSTAL LEE (1940–).

The 1979 Oscar-winning film *Norma Rae* was based on Crystal Lee Jordan's courageous challenge to unjust treatment of labor in the textile mills. In 1973 Jordan was fired from her job while working with union organizers at the J. P. Stevens textile factory in Roanoke Rapids, North Carolina. In a moment immortalized by the movie, Jordan, instead of meekly complying with her boss's request to leave the plant, took a piece of cardboard, wrote "UNION" on it with a felt-tipped marker, climbed onto her bench, and held the sign aloft. A sudden silence followed as machines stopped whirring and her fellow workers raised their fingers in V-for-Victory salutes. A year later, they voted to unionize the factory. Jordan subsequently became a paid organizer for the Amalgamated Clothing and Textile Workers Union (ACTWU), and the movie *Norma Rae* became an effective power tool of the labor movement with its simple saga of good plain poor people winning against the greedy bad-guy establishment.

The real-life *Norma Rae*, Crystal Lee Pulley, was born December 31, 1940, in Roanoke Rapids, a cotton mill town. She began working at age seventeen as a battery filler in a textile plant. Two years later, she married Omar Carlos Wood Jr. and had her first child. At age twenty, she was widowed when her husband was killed in an auto accident; at twenty-one she had an out-of-wedlock second child; at twenty-five she had her third. Her second husband, "Cookie" Jordan, worked in a unionized mill and enjoyed better employee benefits than Crystal Lee.

The real-life Eli Zivkovich, a former coal miner and union organizer from West Virginia, was very unlike the smart young New York City intellectual, Reuben, with whom Norma skinny-dips in the movie. Zivkovich's close relationship to Crystal Lee Jordan strained her marriage, and she divorced Cookie Jordan in 1976. She now lives in Burlington, North Carolina, and is married to Lewis Preston Sutton, who works in a unionized textile plant. The annual Crystal Lee Sutton Awards, named after her, recognize "individuals and organizations whose efforts have contributed to presenting positive images of working people to the American public."

See also: LABOR ISSUES; WOMEN'S ISSUES

For Further Information

Brady, Jim. "Struggles of Crystal Lee: Hard Times Continue for the Real 'Norma Rae.' " *Washington Post*, July 24, 1985, Style section, p. 1.

Leifermann, Henry P. *Crystal Lee: A Woman of Inheritance*. New York: Macmillan, 1975.

K

KELLEY, FLORENCE (1859–1932).
Child welfare advocate, feminist, and general
secretary of the NATIONAL CONSUMERS'
LEAGUE, an important women's agency in
progressive reform, Florence Kelley was born
on September 12, 1859, in Philadelphia. Her
father, William Darrah Kelley, a Republican
congressman, was a strong supporter of
woman suffrage. In 1876, with full support
from her father, she was admitted to Cornell
University, one of the few colleges that provided equal education to women at that time.
She graduated in 1882 with a bachelor's degree in literature.

After being refused entry to the University
of Pennsylvania law school on gender
grounds, she went to Switzerland in 1883,
enrolled in the University of Zurich, and
translated works of social, political, and economic theorists Friedrich Engels and Karl
Marx into English. She married a Russian socialist and medical student, returned to the
United States, and joined the Socialist Labor
Party in New York City. The couple divorced
and Kelley moved to Chicago, where she became a resident of social reformer JANE AD-
DAMS's Hull House. Here she took on the
task of investigating child labor and factory
conditions in Illinois and reported incidents
of child abuse in vivid, compelling prose. She
earned her law degree from Northwestern
University and was admitted to the Illinois

bar. Her work led to an Illinois law limiting
women's working hours and prohibiting
child labor. Between 1893 and 1897, she
monitored enforcement of the law as the
state's chief factory inspector.

In 1899 Kelley moved to New York City
to direct the newly formed National Consumers' League. Under her three-decade
leadership, the League initiated consumer
boycotts of sweatshops and companies employing child labor, and introduced the use
of labels that certified producers' compliance
with safety and work regulations. The laws
she promoted provided precedents for New
Deal labor policies that ultimately guaranteed
most American workers a maximum ten-hour
work day, a minimum wage, and improved
working conditions.

In 1901 Kelley was a co-founder of the
NATIONAL ASSOCIATION FOR THE ADVANCE-
MENT OF COLORED PEOPLE (NAACP) and
served as its vice president. She then collaborated with Lillian Wald in establishing a federal agency to monitor and improve the
status of children in society. Their effort succeeded in 1912 with the establishment of the
United States Children's Bureau by the U.S.
Congress. Kelley also served as vice president
of the National American Woman Suffrage
Association during the early 1900s. A dili-
gent, tenacious crusader who placed public
service above her private life, Florence Kelley

was a major figure in forging a new and more humane social order during the twentieth century.

See also: CHILD AND YOUTH-RELATED ISSUES; CONSUMER RIGHTS AND SAFEGUARDS; LABOR ISSUES; WOMEN'S ISSUES

For Further Information

Goldmark, Josephine. *Impatient Crusader: Florence Kelley's Life Story*. Urbana: University of Illinois Press, 1953.

Sklar, Kathryn Kish. *Florence Kelley and the Nation's Work: The Rise of Women's Political Culture*. New Haven: Yale University Press, 1997.

KENT STATE (MAY 4, 1970). *See* Student Activism

KEVORKIAN, JACK (1928–). Jack Kevorkian, often referred to as "Dr. Death," was a much publicized figure during the 1990s because of his administration of life-ending medication to people who requested physician-assisted suicide as a preferred alternative to extended suffering from a terminal illness. Kevorkian was born May 26, 1928, in Pontiac, Michigan. His parents were Armenian refugees whose relatives were among the 1.5 million Armenians murdered by the Turks during World War I.

In 1952 Kevorkian was graduated with an M.D. and specialization in pathology, the study of the conditions and processes of disease. He became particularly interested in examining corpses and tissue to determine the causes of death. It was during his internship at the Henry Ford Hospital in Detroit that Kevorkian became convinced that doctor-assisted euthanasia and suicide were ethical procedures. Kevorkian's medical research became concentrated on the phenomena associated with death and dying. He sought

Dr. Jack Kevorkian displays his "death machine" in this February 1991 photo. *AP Photo/Richard Sheinwald.*

funding for experiments that could resolve blood plasma shortages through transferal of blood from cadavers and attempted to determine the precise moment of death by photographing the eyes of dying patients. These and other experiments resulted in Kevorkian's repeated dismissal from hospital positions. By 1990 he had to concede that his medical opinions were rejected by most of his peers.

In 1989 Kevorkian designed and built his Thanatron or "death machine." Later, at the request of his lawyer, Kevorkian renamed his machine the Mercitron. In the 1970s and 1980s, Kevorkian continued writing and publishing articles but received no requests from patients for his assistance despite advertising his service. Finally, through the media, he located his first patient, Janet Adkins, a fifty-four-year-old woman in the early stages of Alzheimer's disease. She was put to sleep on June 4, 1990, in a public park in Kevorkian's van. After assisting with approximately 130 additional deaths and winning three acquittals on charges of murder and manslaughter, Kevorkian's luck ran out. On April 13, 1999, he was convicted of the second-degree murder of fifty-two-year-old Thomas Youk and sentenced to ten to twenty-five years in prison. After waging a nine-year scornful and defiant crusade for assisted suicide, Kevorkian remained silent while awaiting the verdict. Despite Kevorkian's efforts and the vast publicity generated by his actions, only one state, Oregon, has legalized physician-assisted suicide.

See also: DEATH PENALTY AND CHOICE IN DYING

For Further Information

Betzold, Michael. *Appointment with Doctor Death*. Troy, MI: Momentum Books, 1996.

Kevorkian, Jack. *Prescription Medicide: The Goodness of Planned Death*. Buffalo, NY: Prometheus Books, 1991.

Marker, Rita, and Kathi Hamlon. "Prisoner Number 284797." *Human Life Review* 25 (Summer 1999): 65–76.

KING, MARTIN LUTHER, JR. (1929–1968). Civil rights leader, clergyman, and Nobel Prize winner Martin Luther King Jr. was born on January 15, 1929, in Atlanta, Georgia. "He stood in that line of saints which goes back from Gandhi to Jesus; his violent end, like theirs, reflects the hostility of mankind to those who annoy it by trying hard to put it one more painful step further up the ladder from the ape to the angel" (p. 93). So said I. F. Stone in capturing the essence of Martin Luther King Jr.'s accomplishments and his contribution to the common good.

King was christened Michael Luther by his father, the popular and eloquent pastor of the Ebenezer Baptist Church, who later changed both their names in honor of the great Protestant reformer. He studied at Morehouse College in Atlanta and at the Crozier Theological Seminary in Chester, Pennsylvania. In 1955 he earned a doctorate of divinity from Boston University after marrying Coretta Scott, a voice major at the New England Conservatory of Music. While completing his degree, he became pastor of the Dexter Avenue Baptist Church in Montgomery, Alabama.

In 1955 the refusal of ROSA PARKS to give up her bus seat to a white led to her arrest and a citywide bus boycott in Montgomery. King, as the newly elected leader of the Montgomery Improvement Association, coordinated the boycott and captured the attention of the national media. In December 1957, after the U.S. Supreme Court declared segregation of public accommodations unconstitutional, the buses were integrated.

In 1957 King founded the SOUTHERN CHRISTIAN LEADERSHIP CONFERENCE and became the principal catalyst of civil rights activism throughout the nation. A spellbinding orator, he energized and broadened the movement and in 1963 led the great march of 250,000 people on Washington, where he delivered the memorable "I have a dream" speech. In this, he drew upon the simple and profound utterances of Abraham Lincoln, biblical writings, and his personal experience.

On August 28, 1963, the day of his "I Have a Dream" speech, Rev. Martin Luther King Jr. acknowledges the crowd at the Lincoln Memorial in Washington, DC. *AP Photo.*

King's insistence upon Gandhian passive resistance resulted in national exposure to the horrific spectacle of unarmed blacks being bludgeoned and attacked by white segregationists, police, and guard dogs. In response to the public's revulsion and King's continuing efforts, Congress passed and President Johnson signed into law the Civil Rights Act of 1964 and the Voting Rights Act of 1965. Among the many honors bestowed on King were the Nobel Peace Prize and the Kennedy Peace Prize.

While on a mission to resuscitate a faltering sanitation workers' strike in Memphis, Tennessee, King was murdered. His assassin, James Earl Ray, was apprehended in London and sentenced to ninety-nine years in prison. His widow, Coretta Scott King, succeeded in convincing Congress to establish a national holiday in her husband's honor. In 1968 she established the Martin Luther King Jr. Center for Nonviolent Social Change to carry forward the legacy of her husband.

See also: AFRICAN AMERICAN RIGHTS

For Further Information

Garrow, David J. *Bearing the Cross: Martin Luther King, Jr. and the Southern Christian Leadership Conference.* New York: Morrow/Avon, 1999.
King, Martin Luther, Jr. *The Autobiography of Martin Luther King, Jr.* Edited by Clayborne Carson. New York: Warner Books, 1998.
Stone, I. F. *Polemics and Prophecies: 1967–1970.* New York: Random House, 1972.

KU KLUX KLAN. The Ku Klux Klan is a secret nativist organization patterned on the rituals of its post–Civil War predecessor, and active against minority groups (blacks, Catholics, Jews, and immigrants) as well as against gun control, civil rights legislation, pacifism, and the teaching of evolution in the schools.

In 1866 the Klan began its first era as a social club, formed by Confederate Army veterans in Pulaski, Pennsylvania. Its first leader, called the Grand Wizard, was General Nathan Bedford Forrest. Titles for other officers included Grand Dragon, Grand Titan, and Grand Cyclops. The Klan's name was derived from the Greek word for circle, *kyklos*, to which was added the word 'Klan.' The organization quickly became a white Southern, "invisible empire," committed to restoring white supremacy by terrorizing newly freed and enfranchised slaves. Klan members wore robes and sheets to hide their identity and frighten superstitious blacks during nighttime raids that included beatings and an occasional murder. Reconstruction (1867–1877) following the Civil War had enabled blacks to gain full access to the political process, move freely, and potentially compete with poor whites for jobs and land. Because the first era Klan catered to whites' desire to drive blacks out of Southern political life, it attracted a mass following that succeeded in achieving restoration of white rule in Geor-

In June 2000, members of the Ku Klux Klan march in Huntsville, Texas, in support of a pending execution at Huntsville prison. *AP Photo/David J. Phillip.*

gia, North Carolina, and Tennessee. The movement died after Radical Republican control of the former Confederate states ended in 1877 and was replaced by white supremacy. By 1880 the need for the Klan was seemingly eliminated.

During the Klan's second era (1915–1925) it attained its zenith of power, drawing membership from relatively unprosperous, minimally educated white Protestants who felt threatened by immigrants, radicals, Catholics, Jews, and changing national mores. This Klan was a product of racism, religious bigotry, and eroding personal wealth. Five million Americans joined it, not only in the South, but also in Indiana, Kansas, Oklahoma, Colorado, and Oregon. Small business owners, professionals, skilled laborers, and farmers signed on to a campaign involving overt racism and violence. This second wave was initiated by Colonel

William Joseph Simmons, who had been inspired by D. W. Griffith's 1915 racist film, *The Birth of a Nation*, which glorified the Klan's rescue of a white Southern woman from a lust-crazed freed slave. In its heyday, the Klan, under D. C. Stephenson, Grand Dragon of the Invisible Empire, controlled activities in twenty-three Northern states. Women were recruited for the first time and the Klan won successes in local and state political contests, influenced Democratic and Republican Party platforms in 1924, and waged an aggressive campaign against third party presidential challenger Robert La Follette. Klan members were elected to public office in Colorado, Indiana, Kansas, Maine, Ohio, and Oregon. However, public reaction to Klan lynchings and violence, along with internal dissension, weakened the group. The 1924 election of President Calvin Coolidge and devastation of the political left resulted in Klan groups' decreased membership and restriction to the South. By 1944 the second era Klan had disappeared.

In the 1960s the Klan's third era began in response to the civil rights movement. Again, it confined its activities mostly to the South. The Klan's resurrection was inspired by the dismantling of Jim Crow laws, passage of federal civil rights legislation, and affirmative action initiatives that took away political power and wealth from whites who had benefited from racial oppression. In the 1960s terrorist attacks, bombings of churches and homes, and the murder of three civil rights activists in Mississippi were attributed to the Klan. The U.S. Supreme Court decision *University of California Regents v. Bakke* (1978) limiting the use of affirmative action procedures in determining college admission eligibility, resistance to busing to achieve integrated public schools, and a conservative shift in public attitudes led to a resurgence in Klan membership and the birth of its fourth era in the mid- to late 1970s.

The Klan's current aim is to build a "nationwide grass-roots movement of white Christian men, women and children who support a return of white Christians to government." Its agenda calls for America's withdrawal from the North American Free Trade Agreement and the World Trade Organization, the use of military force to seal off U.S. borders against illegal immigrants, revocation of antigun laws, participation of its members in helping to clean up the environment, and drug tests for people on welfare.

By 1980 the Klan had more than 10,000 members, and in 1991 former Klansman David Duke was able to draw over 700,000 votes in his run for Louisiana's governorship. As the year 2000 approached, the Klan was apparently gaining new adherents, adding thirty-six new chapters in 1998, and developing a strong presence on the Internet with links to skinheads, neo-Nazis, POSSE COMITATUS, and other extremist groups.

The current national director of the Knights of the Ku Klux Klan is Pastor Tho-

mas Robb. The KKK National Office is in Harrison, Arkansas. The current number of members is estimated to exceed 21,000.

See also: EXTREMISTS

For Further Information

Ku Klux Klan, *http://www.kukluxklan.org; http://www.kkk.com/; http://www.wckkk.com/*

Sandberg, Jared. "Spinning a Web of Hate." *Newsweek*, July 19, 1999, p. 28.

Wade, Wyn Craig. *The Fiery Cross: The Ku Klux Klan in America*. New York: Simon and Schuster, 1987.

KRAMER, LARRY (1935–). Larry Kramer is the generally acknowledged leader and voice of the AIDS movement, having forced governmental agencies to acknowledge and respond to the enormity of the AIDS crisis. Single-handedly he has brought about an unprecedented level of public discussion and debate and created a style of brazenly angry health care activism through the organizations he formed and his polemic writing. A second generation of activists continues the vigilance and debate he initiated.

Born June 25, 1935, in Bridgeport, Connecticut, Kramer spent his youth in Washington, D.C. He was a star pupil at the competitive Woodrow Wilson High School, graduating thirteenth in a class of 300 students. He entered Yale in 1953, felt cut off from other students because of his Jewishness and homosexuality, initially had failing grades, became sick, and attempted suicide. After graduating in 1957 with a B.A. degree in English, he became a reader and scriptwriter for Columbia Pictures, assisting in such productions as *Lawrence of Arabia* (1962) and *Dr. Strangelove* (1964). He wrote the screenplay for the Academy Award nominated film *Women in Love* (1969), based on the D. H. Lawrence 1921 novel.

In 1978, Kramer's highly controversial novel, *Faggots*, was published. It contained graphic descriptions of homosexual relationships, predicted the AIDS epidemic, and became a best-seller. He accused the gay

A November 1989 photo of Larry Kramer, the founder and one of the principal voices of ACT UP, the AIDS Coalition to Unleash Power. *AP Photo/Mark Lennihan.*

community of being self-pitying and cowardly. Because of his notoriety as its author, it was suggested that he work within the gay community to raise money for research. On January 4, 1982, Kramer and five other men established the GAY MEN'S HEALTH CRISIS (GMHC). The mission of GMHC was to alert the gay community to the clear and present danger of AIDS and to mobilize the nation's political and health establishments to come to the victims' aid. Later GMHC became a social welfare organization that addressed the needs of dying AIDS patients, after deciding that it would be self-defeating to attack foot-dragging federal, state, and city authorities. Kramer denounced the gay community for failing to exert political pressure and force the government, medical establishment, and press to become accountable and combat the disease during

the early days of its outbreak. In 1983, Kramer circulated an essay describing the spread of the epidemic, the inadequacies in the health care system, the lack of governmental response, and the apparent indifference of most people in the gay community to the severity of the crisis. GMHC then forced Kramer to resign.

In his play, *The Normal Heart*, which opened in 1985, Kramer chronicled the founding of the GMHC and his own later alienation. It is a play with a message, loaded with scientific, political, and sociological data, and setting forth pointed political and moral challenges. More than any other cultural product, *The Normal Heart* spread the politics of AIDS to a mass audience.

On March 12, 1987, Kramer founded ACT UP (AIDS COALITION TO UNLEASH POWER) as an ad hoc community group to fight for the Federal Drug Administration's (FDA) rapid approval of experimental drugs to combat AIDS. On March 24, several hundred members of the group tied up Wall Street traffic during the rush hour to protest the exorbitant pricing by Burroughs Wellcome for AZT, the antiviral drug used to treat AIDS. Soon after the national media reported the demonstration and arrests, FDA regulators, National Institutes of Health (NIH) advisors, public health officials, and the drug companies started negotiating with ACT UP representatives.

By 1991, Kramer's insistence on resorting to tactics of outrageous confrontation led to his rejection by factions within ACT UP. He describes this period in *Reports from the Holocaust*, published in 1994. Members had chained themselves to people's offices, staged die-ins, carried bodies of comrades in wide-open coffins to the gates of the White House, yelled obscenities at public hearings, and draped a giant sized condom over Senator Jesse Helms's residence in North Carolina. ACT UP's greatest success was in twice forcing pharmaceutical companies to reduce the price of AZT.

Kramer's actions have delivered historic reforms, including accelerated FDA approval of experimental drugs, compassionate use of new drugs and innovative applications of old drugs, development of community-based research models, groundbreaking science in basic immunology, virology, and disease prophylaxis, as well as increased consumer scrutiny and political oversight of NIH appropriations and FDA regulations. Other outcomes include improved confidentiality laws, provision of subsidized housing for AIDS patients, and passage of nondiscrimination laws to protect people diagnosed with HIV. These are changes long overdue that will have a profound impact on lives of all Americans for years to come.

In 1988 Kramer learned that he was HIV positive. He is currently suffering from end-stage liver disease and resides in New York City.

See also: AIDS ACTION COUNCIL; LESBIANS AND GAYS

For Further Information

France, David. "The Angry Prophet Is Dying." *Newsweek*, (Special Report) June 11, 2001, p. 42.

Kramer, Larry. *Reports from the Holocaust: The Story of an AIDS Activist*. New York: St. Martin's Press, 1994.

Mass, Lawrence D., ed. *We Must Love One Another or Die: The Life and Legacies of Larry Kramer*. New York: St. Martin's Press, 1997.

KUHN, MARGARET "MAGGIE" (1905–1995).

Born August 3, 1905, in Buffalo, New York, Margaret E. Kuhn ("Maggie") was a self-proclaimed radical and founder of the GRAY PANTHERS, an activist organization that opposes age discrimination in American society. Social consciousness was a strong force in her life, stemming from the instant she was conceived, her mother journeying from Memphis, Tennessee, to Buffalo so that her baby would not be born in the segregated South.

After graduating from Case-Western Reserve University in 1926 with majors in English and sociology, Kuhn briefly considered a teaching career but rejected this alternative because she found public education too rigid

A 1981, photo of Gray Panthers founder Margaret Kuhn. © *Bettmann/CORBIS*.

and bureaucratized for her taste. While at Case-Western, she helped organize a college chapter of the LEAGUE OF WOMEN VOTERS and soon became a self-proclaimed radical activist. She was ahead of her time on key social issues, including desegregation, women's rights, the need for universal health insurance, open housing, problems of the aged, and the Vietnam War. In the 1920s and 1930s she worked for the Young Women's Christian Association. From 1945 until her forced retirement in 1970, she served as program coordinator of the United Presbyterian Church of the United States of America. She edited and wrote for the church publication, *Social Progress* (later retitled *Journal of Church and Society*) and was the church's alternate observer at the United Nations.

In 1970 Kuhn and four other involuntarily retired women founded the Gray Panthers, believing that mandatory retirement should be made illegal and that "citizenship is not served when seniors take themselves out of the mainstream of society and consign themselves to a life of play." She regarded retirement communities as oversized playpens for wrinkled babies, and her favorite motto was "Learning and Sex until Rigor Mortis." She demonstrated its validity by having an affair with a student fifty years her junior. She also contended that "the young and the old in this society are equally discriminated against. Both groups have identity crises. Both groups can't get credit from banks. Both groups are in the drug scene, although there are different drugs and different pushers."

Kuhn was a member of the national advisory boards for Hospice, Inc., and the *Over Easy* public television series. She received many awards, including the Humanist Award of the Year (1978) and the Peaceseeker Award of the United Presbyterian Peace Fellowship (1977). She died on April 22, 1995, in Philadelphia, Pennsylvania.

See also: SENIOR MOVEMENT

For Further Information

Kuhn, Maggie, with Christina Long and Laura Quinn. *No Stone Unturned: The Life and Times of Maggie Kuhn*. New York: Ballantine Books, 1991.

L

LABOR ISSUES. Labor issues such as inadequate pay, overlong hours, brutal treatment on the job, dangerous working conditions, and lack of benefits did not become middle- and upper-class concerns until the 1880s. In the nineteenth century, before labor unions existed, individual workers had little or no voice in determining their wages, hours, or working conditions. Because labor was plentiful, employers could fire anyone for any reason, and unskilled laborers had no rights and worked in dirty and dangerous environments.

In the United States, President Franklin D. Roosevelt's New Deal legislation and passage of the National Labor Relations Act (1935) upgraded workers' rights by requiring employers to bargain with unions. Only then did unions become able to negotiate higher wages, shorter hours, less hazardous workplaces, and fringe benefits. After World War II, various pieces of legislation and court decisions legitimized and stabilized labor's position. However, passage of the Taft-Hartley Act of 1947 severely limited labor's ability to launch disruptive, high-visibility strikes, and right-to-work laws undermined union solidarity.

Members became complacent as they moved into a middle-class lifestyle. Private interests assumed more importance than concern for the welfare of the group, and union membership declined. Between 1950 and 1980, unions lost more than half of their members. Championship of union causes also declined because workplaces with unionized labor provided the best training grounds for political activists.

Beginning in the 1970s, the labor movement started to return to the activism of its early years, forging alliances with feminists, antiwar groups, environmentalists, minority rights advocates, and neighborhood preservation groups. In 1993 labor unions and gay rights groups joined in promotion of national health care. In 1995 labor activists led by JOHN J. SWEENEY blocked bridges in Washington, D.C., to publicize the organizing difficulties faced by janitors. And in 1999 the Teamsters lobbied against the Clinton administration's effort to grant China permanent normal trade relations, while dockworkers marched in Seattle against removal of tariffs because of their concern that businesses would replace U.S. workers with much cheaper foreign labor.

The UNITED MINE WORKERS OF AMERICA (UMWA), founded in 1890, became the most powerful and progressive union within the American Federation of Labor. JOHN L. LEWIS, the UMWA's leader from 1919 until 1960, was the nation's most powerful labor figure during the 1930s and 1940s.

Pioneering labor agitators who were noted

for their dynamism, courage, and eccentric behavior included MARY HARRIS JONES (1837–1930), the legendary "Mother Jones" after which the popular liberal magazine is named; WILLIAM DUDLEY HAYWOOD ("BIG BILL") (1869–1928), radical head of the Industrial Workers of the World (the "Wobblies"); ELLA BLOOR (1862–1951), a radical and early feminist reverentially referred to as "Mother Bloor" by admiring laborers; and JOE HILL (1879–1915), who was the labor movement's inspirational songwriter and coiner of the popular expression "pie in the sky."

Other prominent figures in the history of the labor movement include SIDNEY HILLMAN (1887–1946), head of the Amalgamated Clothing Workers of America and developer of labor's first political action committee (PAC); ELIZABETH GURLEY FLYNN (1890–1964), a controversial radical and feminist who held leadership positions in the IWW and the American Communist Party; A. PHILIP RANDOLPH (1889–1979), organizer of the first influential black union, the Brotherhood of Sleeping Car Porters, and a key figure in the civil rights movement; DAVID DUBINSKY (1892–1982), innovative and incorruptible head of the International Ladies Garment Workers Union from 1932 until 1966; WALTER REUTHER (1907–1970), social reformer and president of the United Automobile Workers from 1946 until 1970; CESAR CHAVEZ (1927–1993), a migrant worker who blended Gandhi's philosophy of nonviolent resistance with grit and charisma and founded America's first successful union of farm workers, the UNITED FARM WORKERS OF AMERICA; and ALBERT SHANKER (1928–1997), who molded the United Federation of Teachers into one of the nation's most effective and powerful unions while offering weekly dosages of intellectual sinew and inspiration in his column in the *New York Times*.

Currently active is John J. Sweeney, AFL-CIO president since 1995 and responsible for the recent resurgence in labor union membership, pride, and commitment to action. The NATIONAL RIGHT TO WORK COMMITTEE, established in 1955 by a co-sponsor of the Taft-Hartley Act of 1947, is an ally of businesses opposed to "big labor." It seeks to weaken union power through extension of right-to-work laws to all fifty states and by placement of rigid restraints on union lobbying, picketing, and recruiting.

Finally, and on a very different note, *Norma Rae*, the popular 1979 Hollywood film, celebrated the union movement and feminism. It brought to a mass audience's attention CRYSTAL LEE JORDAN's courage in organizing a union chapter in the J. P. Stevens textile mill in Roanoke Rapids, North Carolina, in 1973.

For Further Information

Aronowitz, Stanley. *From the Ashes of the Old: American Labor and America's Future.* Boston: Houghton Mifflin, 1998.

Lynd, Staughton. *Living Inside Our Hope: A Steadfast Radical's Thoughts on Rebuilding the Movement.* Ithaca, NY: Cornell University Press, 1997.

LAROUCHE, LYNDON HERMYLE, JR. (1922–).

Founder of the National Caucus of Labor Committees, U.S. Labor Party, Fusion Energy Foundation, and National Democratic Policy Committee, Lyndon LaRouche has been active on the political fringe since 1948, campaigning seven times for the office of U.S. president, beginning in 1976. In 1999 he filed for candidacy for the nomination in the year 2000.

LaRouche was born on September 8, 1922, in Rochester, New Hampshire, to Quaker parents. A lonely and precocious child, he absorbed the works of philosophers Plato, Aristotle, Gottfried Wilhelm Leibniz, Immanuel Kant, David Hume, John Locke, and Bertrand Russell while in his teens and in later life adopted neo-Platonism blended with Marxism and abstruse conspiracy theories as his personal credo. He attended Northeastern University but withdrew without a degree in 1947. During World War II he served in the Army Medical Corps and joined the Communist Party while stationed in Calcutta. Upon returning to the United States, LaRouche enrolled in the Trotskyite Socialist Workers Party, retaining his membership until 1964. In the mid-sixties, he tried to form leftist groups on college campuses, and in 1969 established the National Caucus of Labor Committees (NCLC) from splinter groups of the STUDENTS FOR A DEMOCRATIC SOCIETY.

LaRouche ran for president in 1976 on his own U.S. Labor Party ticket, predicting a second Great Depression and the overthrow of government, Bolshevik-style, by the end of the 1970s. In 1980 LaRouche created a second NCLC affiliate, the National Democratic Policy Committee (NDPC). By 1984 the NDPC had 26,000 members in forty-three states and had built an impressive electoral machine by enlisting middle-class, well-educated conservative Democrats who supported Reagan's Star Wars initiative and rejected "new age" liberal policies. Many viewers responded positively to LaRouche posters reading "Nuclear Power Is Safer than Sex" and "Feed Jane Fonda to the Whales." NDPC fielded over 2,000 candidates in at least thirty states who were running for public office or Democratic Party posts. Bottom-up recruitment included the hawking of LaRouche materials in airports, including subscriptions to the $399 a year *Executive Intelligence Review.*

In 1988 LaRouche was convicted on eleven counts of mail fraud and one count of conspiring to defraud the Internal Revenue Service by deliberately defaulting on $30 million in loans from backers of his presidential campaign. He ran his 1992 race while in jail. After being released, LaRouche declared his candidacy for the 1996 presidential race.

LaRouche's political philosophy is bizarre. In his view, René Descartes, Immanuel Kant, the British empiricist philosophers from David Hume to Bertrand Russell, and the American pragmatists William James and John Dewey have done irreparable damage to society. His enemies include England from 1288 to the present time because he believes the Magna Carta to be "a work of evil" and that England is an oligarchy. He has accused

Queen Elizabeth II of being a drug trafficker and Tony Blair, Britain's "fascist" prime minister, of plotting to destroy Bill Clinton's presidency. A contentious and prolific writer, LaRouche combines econometric theory, nuclear physics, mathematical equations, the arts, and neo-Augustinianism in a brew calculated to dazzle and lure the insecure into his political fold. He currently resides in Leesburg, Virginia.

See also: EXTREMISTS

For Further Information

King, Dennis. *Lyndon LaRouche and the New American Fascism.* New York: Doubleday, 1989.
LaRouche, Lyndon H., Jr. "Will the U.S.A. Keep Its Sovereignty?" *Executive Intelligence Review* 26 (November 19, 1999): 18–39.
Lyndon LaRouche's Presidential Campaign for 2004, *http://www.larouchein2004.com*

LEAGUE OF CONSERVATION VOTERS. The League of Conservation Voters (LCV), formed in 1969, acts as the nonpartisan political voice for over 9 million members of environmental and conservation groups. LCV is the only national environmental organization dedicated full-time to educating citizens about the environmental voting records of members of Congress. Conservationists, led by SIERRA CLUB ex-director DAVID BROWER, established the LCV as the political arm of FRIENDS OF THE EARTH, also established by Brower. Friends of the Earth continues to be aggressive and noncompromising in its advocacy activities, while the LCV acts as the nonpartisan political arm of the environmental movement.

Marion Edey, LCV's first president, devised a national environmental scorecard in 1970 for members of Congress, rating them according to their votes on energy, the environment, and natural resource issues, as evaluated by a consensus of leaders from twenty-seven major national environmental organizations. During the 1980s, the LCV took over ENVIRONMENTAL ACTION's highly effective strategy of publicizing in the media the records of enviro-hostile legislators, labeling them the "Dirty Dozen" and the "Filthy Five."

In 1997 more than a third of the members of the 104th Congress scored zero on the environment, and in 1998 ratings of the 105th Congress dropped even further. The four top-ranking Republicans, Majority Leader Trent Lott, Majority Whip Don Nickles, Conference Chairman Connie Mack, and Conference Secretary Paul Coverdell, earned a collective zero. Despite the pro-industry, anti-regulatory forces in Congress, LCV has displayed considerable power at the ballot box. In November 1998 all five Senate candidates on the LCV "hit list" lost their seats, while its top enviro-friendly candidates won.

National headquarters of the 60,000 member LCV is in Washington, D.C. Nine million additional citizen activists are represented in LCV's affiliated support groups which include the NATURAL RESOURCES DEFENSE COUNCIL, Friends of the Earth, IZAAK WALTON LEAGUE OF AMERICA, U.S. PUBLIC INTEREST RESEARCH GROUP, WILDERNESS SOCIETY, DEFENDERS OF WILDLIFE, Sierra Club, and various state-based conservation organizations. Publications include the *LCV Insider* (quarterly), *The National Environmental Scorecard* (annual), *Presidential Profiles,* and elections reports every election year. Debra J. Callahan is LCV president.

See also: ENVIRONMENT

For Further Information

Baker, Beth. "The Environment as Election Issue." *BioScience* 46 (September 1996): 574.

Bergman, B. J. "It's Lonelier at the Top." *Sierra* 83 (September/October 1998): 58–59.

Franz, Neil. "Fewer Green Voters in Congress." *Chemical Week*, February 23, 2000, p. 24.

League of Conservation Voters, *http://www.lcv. org/*

LEAGUE OF UNITED LATIN AMERICAN CITIZENS. Founded in 1929, the League of United Latin American Citizens (LULAC) is the oldest Hispanic organization in the United States, committed to the advancement of the economic condition, educational attainment, political influence, health, and civil rights of Hispanic Americans.

In 1927 Ben Garza, leader of the Order of the Sons of America in Corpus Christi, convened a coalition made up of his group, the Knights of America, and other Mexican American organizations in Harlingen, Texas, to found the League of Latin American Citizens. In 1929 three members of the coalition met in Corpus Christi, Texas, and united under the name League of United Latin American Citizens (LULAC). Ben Garza was elected LULAC's first president general. The earliest members were middle-class Mexican Americans who promoted education, patriotism, and assimilation.

At the time of LULAC's formation, during the Great Depression, the average Mexican American's living conditions were wretched, school and public accommodations were segregated, and lynchings were commonplace. The mission of LULAC soon broadened to include improvement of the economic condition, political influence, health, and civil rights of the Hispanic population throughout the United States. By 1932 LULAC had spread into Arizona, Colorado, New Mexico, and California, and it now represents Hispanics in most of the United States, Puerto Rico, and Guam. LULAC's efforts resulted in desegregation of barber shops, restrooms, and restaurants and the integration of school districts in Texas during the first two decades of its existence. In 1946 the group filed and won the *Mendez v. Westminster* lawsuit, ending one hundred years of segregation in California's schools.

During President Lyndon B. Johnson's administration, LULAC sponsored the Little School of the 400, which served as the prototype for the very successful federally funded Head Start Program begun in 1965. Head Start awards grants to nonprofit organizations and local governments for operating community programs for children ages three to five from low income families, manages a limited number of parent-teacher centers for families with children of preschool age, and trains Head Start teachers.

Other LULAC accomplishments include organization of the SER-Jobs for Progress with the American GI Forum in 1966, one of the largest and most productive job training programs in the nation. In 1968 LULAC established the Mexican American Legal Defense and Education Fund to support litigation and education programs for the Latino community.

Concerns to be addressed on LULAC's current action agenda include immigration, school dropout rates, bilingual education, and a reported increase in anti-Hispanic sentiment. LULAC opposes the "English only" movement and endorses the learning and fluent use of both the English and Spanish languages.

Although nonpartisan, the group opposed the Supreme Court nominations of Anthony Kennedy and Clarence Thomas. LULAC also publishes a congressional scorecard showing how representatives and senators voted on such issues as civil rights and environmental justice, education, the federal budget, immigration, income security and family support, and voting rights.

LULAC maintains a permanent national office in Washington, with Brent A. Wilkes serving as executive director, a position created in 1997. Rick Dovalina is national president. LULAC has an estimated 110,000 members affiliated with over 400 local groups in forty-three states, Guam, and Puerto Rico. *LULAC News,* a monthly, is the group's membership publication.

See also: HISPANIC AMERICAN RIGHTS

For Further Information

Garcia, Mario T. *Mexican Americans: Leadership, Ideology, and Identity, 1930–1960.* New Haven: Yale University Press, 1989.

League of United Latin American Citizens, *http://www.lulac.org*

Marquez, Benjamin. *LULAC: The Evolution of a Mexican American Political Organization.* Austin: University of Texas Press, 1993.

LEAGUE OF WOMEN VOTERS OF THE UNITED STATES. Formed in 1920, the League of Women Voters of the United States (LWV-US) has adopted as its primary objective the broadening of the "effectiveness of women's votes in furthering better government." Its membership includes women and men interested in nonpartisan political action and study. The delegates of the final convention of the National American Woman Suffrage Association (NAWSA) founded LWV-US to promote newly enfranchised women's participation in the political process. The NAWSA, having secured passage and ratification of the Nineteenth Amendment to the U.S. Constitution, decided that a new organization with an updated mission was needed.

The driving force behind LWV-US's formation was CARRIE CHAPMAN CATT, who served as its honorary national president from 1920 until her death in 1947. The first elected LWV-US president was Maud Wood Park.

Members of Congress respect the League because of its political impartiality and the well-planned strategies it employs in achieving its objectives. The League has six permanent committees: Environment, Foreign Policy, Human Resources, Government, Congress, and Voters' Service. Although the League never supports political parties or candidates, it advocates open government, protection of the environment, and privacy in reproductive choice. Members decide to support or oppose specific pieces of legislation by consensus, and through its Education Fund, the League provides data and background information on key issues to guide public opinion. LWV-US publishes a bimonthly, *The National Voter,* and numerous reports, generally distributed free of charge.

The following landmark pieces of legislation were championed by the League: Tennessee Valley Authority Act (1933), Social Security Act (1935), Pure Food, Drug, and Cosmetic Act (1938), ratification of the UN Charter (1945), General Agreement on Tariffs and Trade (GATT; 1948), Economic

Opportunity Act (1965), Water Resources Act (1965), District of Columbia Home Rule Act (1973), ERA, and National Voter Registration Act of 1993 (Motor Voter). Election campaign finance reform; equal opportunity in education, employment, and housing; and health insurance for children remain high-priority LWV-US agenda items.

League activities are coordinated and staffed by two distinct, complementary organizations: the League of Women Voters of the United States (LWV-US) and the League of Women Voters Education Fund (1957). LWV-US is the political advocacy and membership organization. The LWV Fund is the citizen education and research arm, producing objective analyses of political issues and summarizing the results in reports for the voting public. The League has sponsored nationally televised debates between presidential candidates Gerald R. Ford and Jimmy Carter (1976), Jimmy Carter and Ronald Reagan (1980), and Ronald Reagan and Walter F. Mondale (1984). Since 1988, general election presidential debates have been sponsored by the Commission on Presidential Debates, founded and controlled by the two national political parties. LWV did not sponsor the 2000 debates.

LWV-US national headquarters is in Washington, D.C. Current membership is 110,000, represented in fifty state leagues and over 1,300 local chapters. Some 3,000 of its members are men. Carolyn Jefferson-Jenkins is LWV-US president. The League publishes *The National Voter*, a quarterly magazine.

See also: WOMEN'S ISSUES

For Further Information

League of Women Voters, *http://www.lwv.org*

Stuhler, Barbara. *For the Public Record: A Documentary History of the League of Women Voters.* Westport, CT: Greenwood Publishing Group, 1999.

Young, Louise M., and Ralph A. Young, Jr. *In the Public Interest: The League of Women Voters, 1920–1970.* Westport, CT: Greenwood Publishing Group, 1989.

LESBIANS AND GAYS. Female homosexuals, often called lesbians, and male homosexuals, sometimes referred to as gays, make up between 5 and 10 percent of the U.S. population. During the years before World War I, suppression of homosexuality of both genders was the norm. Even today, many people in most Western countries consider homosexuality immoral or unnatural. Until the mid-twentieth century, state and city governments censored gay and lesbian expression in the arts and politics, and the medical profession agreed that homosexuality could be cured by repression, surgery, hormone therapy, or castration. The public associated "perverts" with murder, other crimes, and an increasingly decadent society. Even today, employees can be fired for being homosexual in thirty-nine states. Homosexuals cannot actually marry someone of the same sex in any state, and in most places the young cannot become Boy Scouts or form their own groups in schools. And many states prohibit homosexual acts between consenting adults, even within the privacy of the home.

In 1924 an early gay movement group, the Society for Human Rights, was formed in Chicago but shut down by the police within a year. In the 1950s Senator Joseph McCarthy and the U.S. House Un-American Activities Committee cited sexual perversion as being responsible for the purported weakening of the nation's moral fiber and for communist subversion. Suspected "perverts" were accused of espionage and dismissed from government jobs, public opinion turned hostile, and the gay/lesbian movement was temporarily stalled. The Mattachine Society, formed in Los Angeles in 1951 to unify, lead, and assist homosexuals, decided to seek respectable assimilation and postponed its fight for equal treatment under the law. The Daughters of Bilitis, a lesbian group formed in 1955, also softened its stand. Both groups soon disappeared.

The modern gay rights movement began in June 1969 in New York City with the police raid of the Stonewall Inn, a bar in Greenwich Village. For the first time, the bar's gay

Spectators at the 1999 Gay Pride Parade in New York's Greenwich Village stand in front of the Stonewall bar, the site of a 1969 riot that initiated the gay rights movement. © *John-Marshall Mantel/CORBIS.*

patrons resisted instead of passively complying with authority and rioted for several days. Thirteen people were arrested and four police officers injured. In 1970, 10,000 gays marched in New York City to celebrate the Stonewall Riot, and by 1979, 100,000 people participated in a national march in Washington, D.C.

Opposition to the new movement began in 1976 when entertainer and television personality ANITA BRYANT led the first religious campaign against gay rights in Florida and California. In Florida, Bryant conscripted political and religious allies and won voter approval of a referendum to repeal a six-month-old civil rights ordinance that had prohibited discrimination on the grounds of sexual orientation. A nationwide effort to roll back similar permissive legislation got under

way. Ronald Reagan's presidency and rise of the New Right ushered in a traditional family values agenda. And in June 1986, the U.S. Supreme Court ruled in a 5–4 decision, *Bowers v. Hardwick*, that states could retain the right to criminalize private sexual conduct between consenting adults of the same gender.

Beginning in the 1980s, the AIDS crisis offered an additional weapon to use against gays because it occurred mainly among homosexual men, and their conduct could be blamed for the disease by the conservative RELIGIOUS RIGHT. In the 1990s antigay spokespersons assumed that the majority of Americans shared their attitude. Prominent organizations and individuals supporting this conservative view included cultural conservative and current president of the FREE CONGRESS RESEARCH AND EDUCATION FOUNDATION and the former president of HERITAGE FOUNDATION Paul Weyrich; evangelist and founder of the Moral Majority JERRY FALWELL; JAMES DOBSON, president of FOCUS ON THE FAMILY and founder of the FAMILY RESEARCH COUNCIL; PAT ROBERTSON, leader of the CHRISTIAN COALITION; Beverly LaHaye, founder and former president of CONCERNED WOMEN FOR AMERICA; PHYLLIS SCHLAFLY, president of the EAGLE FORUM; conservative mores advocate and media talk show host LAURA SCHLESSINGER; the AMERICAN FAMILY ASSOCIATION; and PROMISE KEEPERS.

Currently three dominant national organizations lead the gay and lesbian rights movement: the NATIONAL GAY AND LESBIAN TASK FORCE, established in 1973; HUMAN RIGHTS CAMPAIGN, founded in 1980 to lobby for enactment of federal civil rights protections; and GAY AND LESBIAN ALLIANCE AGAINST DEFAMATION founded in 1985, which promotes positive portrayals of homosexuals in the media.

For Further Information

Clendinen, Dudley, and Adam Nagourney. *Out for Good: The Struggle to Build a Gay Rights Movement in America.* New York: Simon and Schuster, 1999.

Katz, Jonathan. *Gay American History: Lesbians and Gay Men in the U.S.A. A Documentary.* New York: Harper and Row, 1985.

LEWIS, JOHN LLEWELLYN (1880–1969).

A stirring and occasionally pugnacious public speaker, John Llewellyn Lewis was the most powerful labor leader in the United States during the 1930s and 1940s. Born near Lucas, Iowa, on February 12, 1880, of Welsh immigrant parents, Lewis dropped out of school after completing the seventh grade. He then worked in the mines, wandered throughout the western United States, and returned to Lucas to serve as a delegate to the national convention of the UNITED MINE WORKERS OF AMERICA (UMWA) in 1906.

Mostly self-educated, Lewis read and became skilled in drawing upon biblical writings, American history, and English literature in his public utterances. Because of his persuasiveness in recruiting legislators and citizens to mine workers' causes, the UMWA selected him as its Illinois lobbyist and the American Federation of Labor (AFL) appointed him as its chief field agent. He became UMWA president in 1920 and during the next decade saw his union's membership fall from 500,000 to 100,000 due to massive unemployment in the North and resistance to unionization in the South.

The National Industrial Recovery Act (1933) was welcomed by Lewis because it guaranteed unions' right to bargain collectively and spurred a resurgence in membership. In 1935 Lewis formed the Committee for Industrial Organization, combining eight AFL unions representing the mass-production industries. Enmity between the AFL and CIO followed, with clashes between Lewis and William Green, the AFL president, who would not accept the division between industrial and traditional trade and craft unionism. Lewis renamed the CIO the Congress of Industrial Organizations, which by 1936 expanded to include thirteen labor unions representing 1.5 million workers.

Lewis used radio broadcasts to advantage, projecting his forceful personality and views into thousands of homes and cementing public support. After Lewis and the CIO enthusiastically endorsed Roosevelt's run for re-election in 1936, Green and other AFL leaders expelled the CIO and the UMWA, and maintained a neutral position during the presidential campaign.

Between 1935 and 1937, Lewis extended CIO recruitment efforts to the steel, tire, rubber, and automobile industries. He organized sit-down strikes in General Motors plants and won the corporation's recognition of noncompany unions. When confrontations between other industries and the union turned violent, Lewis appealed to President Roosevelt for help and received the reply, "A plague on both your houses." After this, Lewis, a lifelong Republican, turned against Roosevelt and tried to swing CIO support to Wendell Willkie in the 1940 election. Lewis also opposed the draft and America's participation in the war. After Roosevelt was reelected, Lewis resigned from the CIO presidency but retained leadership of the UMWA.

During the war, Lewis won concessions for miners but alienated large segments of the American public that accused him of disrupting the war effort and being a communist sympathizer. In 1946, when Lewis ordered a soft coal miners' strike, President Harry S. Truman responded by calling for government seizure of the mines. In 1947 and 1948, Lewis was convicted on contempt of court charges and his union was heavily penalized. Mounting public and legislative resentment resulted in the Taft-Hartley Act (1947), which placed restrictions on unions and precipitated a decline in power and membership that continued throughout the rest of the twentieth century.

In 1952, following a 1951 mine disaster in Illinois that took 119 men's lives, Lewis was able to persuade Congress to establish federal safety standards for mines. Lewis died in Washington, D.C., in 1969.

See also: LABOR ISSUES

For Further Information

Roberts, Ron E. *John L. Lewis: Hard Labor and Wild Justice.* Dubuque, IA: Kendall/Hunt, 1994.

Zieger, Robert H. *John L. Lewis: Labor Leader.* Old Tappan, NJ: Macmillan, 1988.

LIBERAL ACTIVISM. Liberal activism includes organizations and individuals holding progressive views, which have been under regular and heavy attack by conservatives. Liberals share a political and social philosophy that calls for freedom of the individual, nonviolent modification of political, social, and economic institutions to permit unrestricted development in all spheres of human endeavor, and governmental guarantees of individual rights and civil liberties. Unlike conservatives who insist upon a strict constructionist and literal interpretation of the U.S. Constitution, liberals prefer interpretations conditioned by current needs of the society without compromising basic principles of the Constitution and Bill of Rights. They champion political solutions that apply across a broad spectrum of issues, including economics, the environment, and social issues. They advocate open and responsive government, social justice, freedom of expression, and concern for the common good, and are committed to nonrevolutionary progress and reform.

The nation's oldest independent liberal political organization is AMERICANS FOR DEMOCRATIC ACTION (ADA), formed in 1947. Its initial leadership committee included former Vice President Hubert H. Humphrey, theologian Reinhold Niebuhr, and labor leaders DAVID DUBINSKY and WALTER P. REUTHER. ELEANOR ROOSEVELT was a charter member. From its beginnings the ADA championed antipoverty programs, higher minimum wages, consumer protection, and affirmative action.

STUDENTS FOR A DEMOCRATIC SOCIETY (SDS), organized in 1959, was a resuscitation of a 1930s leftist group. Walter P. Reuther, then president of the United Auto Workers, provided a $10,000 grant, enabling the organization to establish its headquarters in New York City. In 1962 the Port Huron Statement, drafted by TOM HAYDEN, was approved as the SDS platform. It called for an individualistic form of liberalism, condemned racism, and deplored the evils of technology and irresponsible actions of the military-industrial complex. After 1967 SDS became more militant and less liberal as U.S. involvement in the Vietnam War escalated. During its final years (1968–1972), SDS instigated bombings and other forms of terrorism.

The STUDENT NONVIOLENT COORDINATING COMMITTEE (SNCC) (1960–1970) followed a political trajectory similar to that of the SDS. For five years it committed itself to nonviolent attainment of social justice, acting in conjunction with MARTIN LUTHER KING JR.'S SOUTHERN CHRISTIAN LEADERSHIP CONFERENCE. The SNCC freedom riders displayed enormous courage in pressing compliance with desegregation despite being beaten, burnt, and murdered. In 1966 STOKELY CARMICHAEL took over SNCC, expelled its white members, and transformed it into a champion of black power to be achieved through revolutionary violence. By 1970 SNCC no longer existed.

In 1970 JOHN W. GARDNER, former secretary of health, education, and welfare under President Lyndon B. Johnson, founded COMMON CAUSE as a national citizens' lobby dedicated to "uphold the public interest against all comers—special interests, self-seeking politicians, self-perpetuating bureaucrats, industry, professional groups." Common Cause has a multiple-issue agenda, with members working on substantive problems in such areas as education, health, housing, equal rights, and campaign financing.

PUBLIC CITIZEN, founded by consumer activist RALPH NADER in 1971, is a liberal advocacy group whose members act as watchdogs and prosecutors to ensure that the common good will be respected by government and corporations. Health, safety, and preservation of the democratic process are Public Citizen's core concerns.

The most recent addition to the ranks of liberal activist organizations is PEOPLE FOR THE AMERICAN WAY, founded by television writer and producer Norman Lear in 1980 to "defend the values of pluralism, individuality, freedom of thought, expression and religion."

For Further Information

Baer, Kenneth S. *Reinventing Democrats: The Politics of Liberalism from Reagan to Clinton.* Lawrence: University Press of Kansas, 2000.

Boyle, Kevin. *The UAW and the Heyday of American Liberalism, 1945–1968.* Ithaca, NY: Cornell University Press, 1995.

Young, James P. *Reconsidering American Liberalism: The Troubled Odyssey of the Liberal Idea.* Boulder, CO: Westview Press, 1995.

LIBERTY LOBBY. Founded in 1955, the Liberty Lobby is made up of "nationalists and populists interested in political action on behalf of 110 issues which are pro-individual liberty and pro-patriotic." The group opposes federal aid to education, foreign aid, gun control, the Equal Rights Amendment, national health insurance (socialized medicine), U.S. involvement in the United Nations, hate crimes legislation, the Genocide Convention, tax-supported housing, and world government. The group supports a free gold market, lower taxes, reduced farm controls, and less government spending.

The Liberty Lobby was founded by Curtis B. Dall to promote conservatism in politics. Dall, divorced from Anna Roosevelt, President Franklin D. Roosevelt's daughter, became disenchanted with New Deal programs and believed that Roosevelt had precipitated World War II by selling out to Zionist financiers and the forces of evil. The original mission of the Liberty Lobby was to awaken the American people to internal and foreign threats, work for the realignment of the political parties, and save the nation from subjugation under a new world order. In 1960 the Liberty Lobby began rating Congress in its *Liberty Ledger* and supported Senator Barry Goldwater's candidacy for the presidency in 1964.

The architect and continuing leader of the Liberty Lobby is WILLIS ALLISON CARTO, its treasurer and chief executive officer. Francis Parker Yockey (1917–1960) provided Carto with the logical basis for the Liberty Lobby's mission in his *Imperium*, a document based on philosopher of history Oswald Spengler's *The Decline of the West*, Nazism, and anti-Semitism. The Liberty Lobby endorses racial and cultural homogeneity, and bases its political philosophy on conspiracy, cultural, and race theories. In 1969 the Liberty Lobby enlisted Dr. Henry E. Garrett, a past president of the American Psychological Association, to offer testimony before Congress that purportedly proved that Negroes were inferior to whites because they had lighter brains and less-developed frontal lobes.

In an editorial for the Liberty Lobby's publication *The Barnes Review*, titled "Why Is 'The Holocaust' Important?" Carto stated that the Holocaust is

> the ultimate in Hollywood imagery. It serves elitism by teaching that every nation may become as evil as the Germans if they try to live true to themselves (the definition of Nationalism) and oppose the international plutocratic elite. This is why the image of "The Holocaust" serves the major political movement of our day—the move away from The Constitution, national sovereignty and a structured and free society to the formlessness, chaos and tyranny of the new world order—the Global Plantation. (pp. 9–10)

The Liberty Lobby has called for abolition of the Federal Reserve and currently supports curbs on immigration, placement of armed patrols on the southern border of the United States to bar aliens' illegal entry, increased states' rights, and repeal of the Sixteenth (income tax), Seventeenth, and Twenty-fifth Amendments to the U.S. Constitution.

In 1981, Liberty Lobby membership peaked at 315,000, dropping to 90,000 by 1995. Currently it is estimated to be 121,000. Although relatively small, the Liberty Lobby is the most influential right-wing extremist organization in the United States. Headquartered in Washington, D.C., the Liberty Lobby published the *Liberty Ledger* between 1955 and 1975. *The Spotlight: Voice of the American Majority* (initially *National Spotlight*) is the group's current weekly publication, supplemented by *The Barnes Review*, a monthly. Vince Ryan is chairman of the Liberty Lobby Board of Policy.

See also: EXTREMISTS

For Further Information

Carto, Willis Allison. "Why Is the 'Holocaust' Important?" *The Barnes Review* (March/April 1998): 9–10.

Mintz, Frank P. *The Liberty Lobby and the American Right: Race, Conspiracy, and Culture.* Westport, CT: Greenwood Press, 1985.

The Spotlight, *http://www.spotlight.org*

Winston, Andrew S. "Science in the Service of the Far Right: Henry E. Garrett, the IAAEE, and the Liberty Lobby." *Journal of Social Issues* 54 (Spring 1998): 179–210.

LOVE CANAL HOMEOWNERS ASSOCIATION. *See* Center for Health, Environment and Justice.

LYND, STAUGHTON (1929–). Staughton Lynd, a radical lawyer, former professor of history, writer, and activist, was a social rebel of the 1960s and leading spokesperson of the NEW LEFT from 1960 to 1970. In 1965 he became a headline news figure when, as a Yale University history professor, he was arrested on the U.S. Capitol steps for protesting the Vietnam War. This was followed by his controversial trip to Hanoi with JANE FONDA and TOM HAYDEN to negotiate the release of American prisoners of war. Prior to that time he had been active in the civil rights movement and draft resistance. He and Hayden led the New Left, and his writings provide the most erudite and personal chronicle of this period of American radicalism.

Staughton Craig Lynd was born into a family of Quaker scholars on November 22, 1929, in Philadelphia, Pennsylvania. His parents were Robert and Helen Lynd, co-authors of *Middletown: A Study in Contemporary American Culture* (1929), a classic in the field of sociology. At Harvard College and then later at the University of Chicago, Lynd studied urban planning. During the Korean War, he lived for several years in the Macedonia Cooperative Community, a Quaker commune in Georgia. After leaving Georgia, he and his wife, Alice, moved to New York City. In 1962 he earned his doctorate in American history. From 1961 to 1964, he taught at Spelman College in Atlanta and became involved with the STUDENT NONVIOLENT COORDINATING COMMITTEE while directing the Freedom Summer Project in Mississippi. The project brought in hundreds of white students from the North for a massive voter registration drive, during which three workers were killed. This tragedy and the attendant national publicity helped to ensure passage of the Civil Rights Act of 1964 and the Voting Rights Act of 1965.

After returning from the South, Lynd joined the Yale University history faculty as a respected expert on the origins of radicalism during the American Revolutionary period. In 1965 he became troubled by the military buildup in Vietnam, helped organize a march in Washington, and was arrested along with other demonstrators for attempting to enter the U.S. House of Representatives to persuade members to adopt a declaration of peace. In a letter in the *New York Times*, Lynd urged negotiation with the National Liberation Front of Vietnam. After ascending to national prominence by traveling to North Vietnam without obtaining State Department clearance, he was recognized as leader of the New Left; he had also become unemployable as an academic. In response to pressure from angry conservative alumni and faculty, Yale University denied him tenure as a professor. Lynd resigned and applied without success to various other universities.

After being rejected by higher academe, Alice and Staughton Lynd both joined the legal profession and moved to Youngstown, Ohio, to assist working people. Staughton Lynd currently works as a labor advocacy lawyer in Niles, Ohio, where he continues to publish books and articles on the labor movement, radicalism, and civil rights.

See also: ANTIWAR/ANTI–NUCLEAR WEAPONS MOVEMENT

For Further Reading

Lynd, Staughton. *Living Inside Our Hope: A Steadfast Radical's Thoughts on Rebuilding the Movement*. Ithaca, NY: Cornell University Press, 1997.

———. *"We Are All Leaders": The Alternative Unionism of the Early 1930s*. Urbana: University of Illinois Press, 1996.

M

MALCOLM X (1925–1965). Malcolm X, the fiery spokesperson and originator of "Black Power," was born on October 25, 1925, to Earl and Louise Little, both of whom were also black activists. Earl Little was head of the Omaha, Nebraska, chapter of the Universal Negro Improvement Association (UNIA), and spoke out publicly about the desperate conditions of black people in America. Louise Little attended meetings of the UNIA and sent reports of their deliberations to the national office in Harlem, New York. The family moved to Lansing, Michigan, after being threatened by the KU KLUX KLAN in Omaha. Shortly after settling into their new home, it was burned to the ground, so the family moved again to East Lansing. Upon arrival, hostile white neighbors stoned them.

In September 1931, Earl Little died after being hit by a trolley. His wife suspected that whites who resented his speaking out about the plight of blacks and the need to unite to fight segregation had arranged his death. When Malcolm Little was thirteen, his mother was declared legally insane and sent to a mental institution. The state of Michigan separated Malcolm from his sister, placing the two siblings in separate foster homes. Malcolm Little did well in school and aspired to become a lawyer, but a teacher discouraged him by reminding him that he "needed to be realistic about being a nigger, a lawyer—that's no realistic goal for a nigger."

Malcolm Little went to live with his half-sister in Boston and worked as a shoeshine boy and red cap porter, jobs considered appropriate for blacks during the 1930s. He then moved to Harlem, where he began dealing drugs and running numbers for mobsters. After returning to Boston he was arrested for burglary in 1946 and sentenced to eight to ten years in prison. While he was in jail, his family told him about the Black Muslim movement and he began studying the world's religions, including Islam. He wrote to ELIJAH MUHAMMAD, the leader of the NATION OF ISLAM.

In 1952 Malcolm Little met Muhammad in Chicago and was accepted into the movement and renamed Malcolm X, signifying his rejection of the name given him by slave owners. After leaving prison, Malcolm X lived in Detroit with a brother, also a Muslim. By 1953 Malcolm X was asked to organize a mosque in Philadelphia, and a year later he assumed leadership of a mosque in Harlem. In 1959, as chief representative and minister of the Nation of Islam, Malcolm launched the Muslim newspaper *Muhammad Speaks*. Malcolm X drew new members to the Black Muslims through his eloquent sermons and pronouncements that whites controlled the lives of black people and that the races

Black Muslim leader Malcolm X during a visit to the Associated Press office in New York in March 1964. *AP/Wide World Photos.*

must be separated for blacks to achieve economic and spiritual independence. Recruitment was hastened by white hostility toward desegregation manifested through job dismissals, mortgage foreclosures, and an upsurge in White Citizens' Councils. Even though the Supreme Court in BROWN V. BOARD OF EDUCATION OF TOPEKA (1954) had ruled that segregation in public education was a denial of equal protection under the law and that Negroes should be admitted on a racially nondiscriminatory basis "with all deliberate speed," compliance was painfully slow.

After the assassination of President John F. Kennedy in 1963, Malcolm X publicly announced that "the chickens have come home to roost." This enigmatic statement provoked dissension between Elijah Muhammad and Malcolm X because ministers of the Nation of Islam had been ordered to refrain from commenting on the killing. In March 1964, Malcolm X resigned from the Nation of Islam and established the Muslim Mosque, Incorporated, and a sibling secular group, the Organization of Afro-American Unity. After traveling to Mecca, Malcolm X realized that not all white people were enemies and that blacks could indeed achieve their goals without resorting to violence. He also adopted a new name, el-Hajj Malik el-Shabazz.

Militant groups and some members of the Nation of Islam were enraged by Malcolm's change in attitude, and he began to receive death threats. On February 14, 1965, his home was firebombed, but no one was injured. A week later, as he began speaking at a Muslim lodge in Harlem, three Black Muslims shot him dead. All were found guilty and sentenced to life imprisonment.

Texts of Malcolm X's speeches and interviews have been compiled and published. His autobiography, written with Alex Haley, was published in 1965. In 1992 Spike Lee directed a stirring feature film based on this book that effectively depicts the dominant themes of self-determination and racial pride in Malcolm X's life.

See also: AFRICAN AMERICAN RIGHTS

For Further Information

Haley, Alex. *The Autobiography of Malcolm X.* New York: Ballantine Books, 1999.

Malcolm X. 201 min. motion picture. VHS, Beta, LV, 8mm, Letterbox. Directed by Spike Lee. Warner/Largo/Forty Acres and a Mule (Marvin Worth/Spike Lee), 1992.

Myers, Walter Dean. *Malcolm X: A Fire Burning Brightly.* New York: HarperCollins, 2000.

Rummel, Jack. *Malcolm X.* New York: Chelsea House, 1989.

MATTACHINE SOCIETY. *See* Lesbians and Gays.

MEANS, RUSSELL (1939–   ). The most controversial and radical Native American leader of the twentieth century, Russell

Means was born on November 29, 1939, on the Pine Ridge Reservation in South Dakota. When he was three years old his family moved to California, so his early exposure to reservation living was limited. When transferred to a predominantly white high school in San Leandro, Means was subjected to ethnic insults, became embittered, dropped out, and escaped into drinking, drugs, and general delinquency.

He enrolled in five different colleges, never graduated, rejected full-time employment as being incompatible with his Oglala Lakota Sioux Indian beliefs, and took temporary jobs as a cowboy, accountant, circus roustabout, and ballroom dance instructor. In 1967 Means accepted a position at the Rosebud Reservation in South Dakota but soon transferred to the government-sponsored American Indian Center in Cleveland. There he met DENNIS BANKS, co-founder of the AMERICAN INDIAN MOVEMENT (AIM), and agreed to start an AIM chapter in Cleveland.

During 1970 Means was especially active. First he filed a $9 million lawsuit against the Cleveland Indians baseball team to ban the use of their mascot, Chief Wahoo, because of its offensive and demeaning connotations. He then joined with other AIM members in climbing and occupying the Mount Rushmore monument to protest desecration of hallowed Indian ground by the U.S. government and violation of the Lakota claim to the Black Hills under an 1868 treaty. As a demonstration of how negatively most Indians regard the faces chiseled out of their holy land, Means urinated on George Washington's stone face. Later that same year, Native Americans' smoldering grievances and AIM became front-page news when Means and several other Indians took over the *Mayflower II* in Plymouth on Thanksgiving Day.

After leaving Cleveland, Means led one of AIM's three Trail of Broken Treaties caravans from Seattle to Washington, D.C. The caravans were routed to pass through all lands stolen from the Indians in alleged violation of 371 treaties and scheduled to arrive in Washington in November 1972. When the protesters reached Washington and were re-fused an audience with federal officials to discuss their claims, they took over the Bureau of Indian Affairs building. After ransacking the building and being forcibly ejected, Means returned to Pine Ridge. He reemerged into the national spotlight in 1973 by leading a seventy-one-day armed takeover of Wounded Knee, South Dakota. He and about two hundred supporters seized the site where the U.S. cavalry had massacred Chief Big Foot and 350 members of his tribe, mostly unarmed women and children, with machine-gun fire in 1890.

After a standoff with heavily armed federal marshals and FBI agents, Means negotiated a truce and a promise from federal authorities to work out a settlement, recognize Indian sovereignty, and reconsider the status of the broken treaties. The government reneged and Means escaped from custody. When he returned to Wounded Knee, he was apprehended and jailed. After a protracted trial in which he was supported by six defense attorneys, including the noted defender of dissidents William Kunstler, the charges against Means were dismissed because of illegal wiretaps, false testimony, and other improper procedures used to incriminate him.

The statuesque, ruggedly handsome, and mediagenic Means has brought hope to Indian youth living with squalor, violence, and alcoholism and has focused public attention on the problems Native Americans face in today's United States. In the 1990s Means played parts in various motion pictures: as Chingachgook in *The Last of the Mohicans*, as Chief Powhatan in *Pocahontas*, and as an evil shaman in *Natural Born Killers*. Means currently lives on a ranch in Porcupine, South Dakota.

See also: NATIVE AMERICAN RIGHTS

For Further Information

Means, Russell, with Marvin J. Wolf. *Where White Men Fear to Tread: The Autobiography of Russell Means*. New York: St. Martin's Press, 1995.

MILITIA MOVEMENTS. Militias in the twenty-first century defend their actions by citing the Second Amendment to the U.S. Constitution, framed in the context of eighteenth-century America, which mandates defense by a "well-regulated militia" and relatively small governmental military force. In *Minuteman: Restoring an Army of the People*, former Senator Gary Hart argues that a citizen militia is preferable to a standing army because its members, as stakeholders in U.S. foreign policy, would presumably be immune to the antigovernment paranoia that preoccupied and motivated members of the twentieth century's two major militia movements.

In contrast to the underground, self-appointed groups, there are legitimate militias established to protect families, communities, and the nation. The law-abiding groups are armed but not dangerous, committed to assisting with medical aid, search and rescue operations, and emergency communications in times of need. The extremist, antigovernment groups advocate military preparedness and stockpile weapons for what they predict will be an inevitable and apocalyptic conflict with federal authorities and other evil forces that threaten the nation.

The first militia movement was active between 1940 and 1945, when right-wing militias planned to dynamite Detroit, Chicago, and other U.S. cities, bomb selected buildings, terrorize Jews, assassinate congressmen, and remove Franklin Delano Roosevelt and his activist wife from the White House.

The second movement began in the 1960s as a revived KU KLUX KLAN, neo-Nazi militants, and other extremist groups surfaced to oppose the civil rights movement. In William L. Pierce's 1978 novel, *The Turner Diaries*, a popular text for militia members, a racial war occurs in which terrorists overthrow the "Zionist Occupation Government" or ZOG. The ZOG is frequently cited as being synonymous with the existing federal administration in militias' manuals and mission statements. This and other conspiracy theories are reinforced by anger directed at immigrants, affirmative action, amoral behavior in the White House, and erosion of personal income due to the widening gap between rich and poor.

Two flash points that dramatically escalated militia activity occurred in Waco, Texas (February 1993), and Ruby Ridge, Idaho (1992). The Bureau of Alcohol, Tobacco, and Firearms (BATF) attack on the Branch Davidian compound in Waco resulted in the deaths of four BATF agents and eighty residents; the Ruby Ridge attack on white supremacist Randy Weaver culminated in the shootings of his wife, son, and the family dog. Both incidents involved errors of judgment and the use of excessive force by FBI agents. However, it was the Oklahoma City bombing of a federal building in 1995 that alerted the general public to the existence of a network of militias that had been preparing for a confrontation. Investigators discovered links between terrorists and militias operating in Michigan, Montana, Idaho, and ten other states. Though small in number, recently estimated at about 170, the militias tap a deep vein of antigovernment sentiment. There may be as many as 300,000 active participants in the movement and an estimated 3 million more people who agree with its views.

Gun control legislation is a primary target of militia anger. The Brady bill, which mandates a waiting period for handgun purchasers and restrictions on sales of assault weapons, is perceived by many militia members as a treasonous and unconstitutional plot to disarm the American people in preparation for the nation's takeover by the New World Order (NWO). Many militia members are convinced that Russian and UN troops are already stationed on U.S. soil and that massive firepower will be needed to save the nation from NWO enslavement.

The militia movement is part of a long tradition steeped in the desire of people at the lower end of the economic spectrum to conjure up scapegoats and bogeymen (e.g., "big government," the UN, the Zionist Occupational Government) they can blame for their personal misfortunes. A second factor is the tendency to reduce complex and threatening trends and events to a mortal conflict between good and evil. The movement's members' firmness of purpose is further fed by the belief that they are fighting for the U.S. Constitution and the ideological legacy of the nation's founding fathers.

See also: EXTREMISTS

For Further Information

George, John, and Laird Wilcox. *The American Extremists: Militias, Supremacists, Klansmen, Communists, and Others*. Amherst, NY: Prometheus Books, 1996.

Hart, Gary. *Minuteman: Restoring an Army of the People*. New York: Simon and Schuster, 1998.

Stern, Kenneth S. *A Force upon the Plain: The American Militia Movement and the Politics of Hate*. Norman: University of Oklahoma Press, 1997.

Militia of Montana, *http://www.barefootsworld.net/mom.html*

New York Constitutional Militia, *http://www.constitution.org/mil/ny/mil_usny.htm*

MINUTEMEN. Founded in 1960 by Robert Bolivar DePugh, a chemist from Norborne, Missouri, Minutemen started as a study group and rapidly grew into a paramilitary organization, stockpiling guns and ammunition to protect the nation against communist subversion, espionage, and possible enslavement. The impetus for the group's formation was provided by DePugh, a complex, paranoid individual who believed that powerful minorities and a corrupt, inept government in Washington were losing the fight against communism. He viewed the civil rights movement and antiwar protests of the 1960s as additional symptoms of decay and endangerment. Minutemen rationalized assassination and counterterrorism as acceptable measures if needed to protect the country. It prepared and distributed manuals titled *combat intelligence, realistic combat training*, and *guerrilla warfare*.

The group was disadvantaged by its lack of a chain of command and an effective communications system. Minutemen's basic paramilitary unit was the squad, manned by members whose anonymity was strictly preserved as a precaution in the event of capture. Even if tortured, they would be unable to reveal the names of fellow members. Only the state commanders knew the identities of the squad leaders, so each unit was a miniature army, each member of which acted independently. Despite Minutemen's secrecy precautions, the FBI had little difficulty in infiltrating and monitoring the group because most of its members were affiliated with other hate groups such as the neo-Nazis, Sons of Liberty, and KU KLUX KLAN, all of which used violence as a political weapon. Further easing the task of identification was Minutemen's behavior. Its members usually had eccentric, self-glorifying personalities, imagining themselves as private eyes, soldiers of fortune, and super-patriots.

While reports of Minutemen's size ranged from 25,000 up to as many as 1 million members during the mid-1960s, the FBI estimated that there were never more than about 200 fully involved, active members supplemented by an additional 400 passive "paper tigers." Because of DePugh's threats and belligerent statements to the press, the group earned headlines and was tracked by the Internal Revenue Service and the Federal Communications Commission as well as the FBI. After Senator Barry Goldwater lost his 1964 bid for the presidency, Minutemen issued a communiqué deploring the failure of the electoral process and declaring that, in the future, it would rely upon bullets instead of ballots to achieve its agenda.

In 1966–1967, Minutemen led unsuccessful terrorist attacks on left-wing organizations' camps in New York, New Jersey, and Connecticut, and in 1967 attempted to assassinate Herbert Aptheker, director of the American Institute of Marxist Studies and a member of the U.S. Communist Party.

In 1966 DePugh formed the Patriotic Party as a political arm of Minutemen and published his *Blueprint for Victory*, containing articles excerpted from *On Target*, Minutemen's biweekly newsletter, which advised readers on how to purchase ammunition and weapons and prepare for the oncoming counterrevolution. In 1967 the Patriotic Party had about 3,000 members but soon disbanded because of DePugh's legal setbacks and imprisonment. By 1970 he had been convicted twice and indicted twelve times for violating laws controlling the transfer, manufacture, and use of automatic weapons and silencers. When he was released from prison in May 1973, Minutemen remained moribund and DePugh moved on to private publishing ventures, including development of a tabloid, the *American Patriot*, in 1982.

Minutemen publications such as *Can You Survive?* are available on the Internet, as are the addresses of kindred extremist groups that exploit xenophobia and fear of usurpation of constitutional rights and traditional American values by alien forces.

See also: EXTREMISTS; MILITIA MOVEMENTS

For Further Information

Finch, Phillip. *God, Guts and Guns: A Close Look at the Radical Right*. New York: Seaview/Putnam, 1983.

Jones, J. Harry, Jr. *The Minutemen*. Garden City, NY: Doubleday, 1968.

MOTHER BLOOR. *See* Bloor, Ella Reeve Ware Cohen Omholt

MOTHER JONES. *See* Jones, Mary Harris

MOTHERS AGAINST DRUNK DRIVING. Founded in 1980, Mothers Against Drunk Driving (MADD) works to eliminate alcohol-impaired driving by adults and teenagers, participates in reforming laws on drunk driving to require mandatory minimum punishment, and acts as the voice of victims of crashes attributable to drunk driving.

Candy Lightner, whose daughter was killed while walking along a city street by a repeat-offender drunken driver, founded MADD in 1980. MADD has been unwavering and very effective in its campaign to change laws and verdicts that have traditionally meted out minimal punishment to offenders, mostly men, who had been arrested on charges of driving while intoxicated (DWI). MADD monitors legislation and reg-

During a March 1996, vigil by Mothers Against Drunk Driving, 724 pairs of shoes, representing the 724 people killed in alcohol-related car crashes in 1995, line the rotunda of the Florida State Capitol. *AP Photo/Mark Foley.*

ulations, and promotes implementation of a nationwide legal intoxication level of 0.08 percent blood alcohol content (BAC). Its work includes campaigns to increase public awareness of the problem of drunk driving; advocacy of strict enforcement of existing drunk driving laws; operation of sobriety checkpoints; and support of victims of drunk driving offenses.

MADD's single-strand agenda, summed up in its "Don't drink *and* drive" slogan, has worked with the public and politicians. In 1984 MADD changed its name from Mothers Against Drunk Drivers to Mothers Against Drunk Driving to make clear that its mission is to save lives, minimize the problem, and educate the public, not to punish drivers. The group's avoidance of distracting alliances with prohibitionist and antidrug groups is also an important feature of its winning strategy, as is its insistence that all new MADD initiatives receive consensus support from members prior to implementation.

MADD was instrumental in raising the legal drinking age to twenty-one and continues its pressure to ensure consistent and strict enforcement. The National Highway Traffic Safety Administration's expert on drunk driving, James Fell, reported that alcohol-related highway deaths dropped by 31 percent between 1982 and 1993, from 25,165 to 17,461, and gave MADD much of the credit for this significant decline. In 1999 MADD successfully lobbied the Texas State Legislature to lower the maximum legal blood alcohol content to .08 percent, bringing to seventeen the number of states with .08 BAC laws in effect.

Nationally, MADD campaigns against advertising through the media that tends to glamorize young people's drinking. As part of this effort, it has formed Students Against Drunk Driving (SADD), an affiliate to educate and alert youth to the dangers of excessive drinking, and initiated Operation Prom/ Graduation, programs that discourage underage drinking.

MADD has 3.2 million members, making it the largest victim-advocate, anti-DWI activist organization in the world. MADD has its headquarters in Irving, Texas, and branch offices in twenty-nine states. Karolyn Nunnallee is MADD national president.

See also: ALCOHOL AND DRUG POLICIES

For Further Information

Kennedy, Joey. "Drunk Driving Makes a Comeback." *Redbook*, May 1997, pp. 89–92.

Mothers Against Drunk Driving, *http://www. madd.org*

Russell, Anne, Robert B. Voas, William Dejong, and Marla Chaloupka. "MADD Rates the States: A Media Advocacy Event to Advance the Agenda Against Alcohol-Impaired Driving." *Public Health Reports* 110 (May–June 1995): 240–245.

MUHAMMAD, ELIJAH (1897–1975).

Elijah Muhammad, leader of the black separatist movement known as the NATION OF IS-LAM, was born Elijah Poole on October 8, 1897, near Sandersville, Georgia. The son of former slaves and sharecroppers, he left home at age sixteen, married, and in 1923 moved to Detroit, where he worked on a Chevrolet assembly line. He was unemployed from 1929 until 1931 and, like his father, was for a while a Baptist minister.

In 1931 Elijah Muhammad became an assistant to Wallace D. Fard, the founder of the Nation of Islam. Fard, born in New Zealand, convinced his listeners that he had come from Mecca to save blacks from whites, the "bleached out devil race." His new sect, known as the Black Muslims, favored black separatism and rejected Christianity as a tool of oppressive whites. Abandoning his slave name in favor of the name of the Prophet, Elijah Muhammad embraced Fard's militant doctrines and committed himself to winning converts and to promoting the movement's goal of African American economic self-sufficiency.

When infighting broke out at the Detroit mosque, Muhammad moved to Chicago and established the Second Mosque of the Nation of Islam in 1934. Here he organized business enterprises and parochial schools sponsored by the Black Muslims. Fard then mysteriously disappeared, and Elijah Muhammad assumed leadership of the movement, which grew rapidly, even during his imprisonment (1942–1946) for counseling Nation of Islam members on how to evade the draft during World War II. In the late 1950s and 1960s Muhammad became critical of the integrationist agenda and nonviolent philosophy of the civil rights movement but benefited from the raised feelings of pride and personal empowerment among African Americans. By 1962 there were an estimated 250,000 Nation of Islam members.

A schism occurred in the Nation of Islam in 1965 when Muhammad's disciple MAL-COLM X opted for an "open to whites," more moderate policy closely aligned to orthodox Islam. Nation of Islam members loyal to Elijah Muhammad allegedly carried out Malcolm X's assassination in 1965.

MUHAMMAD, ELIJAH

When Elijah Muhammad died in 1975, his less radical son, Warith Deen Muhammad (1933–), took his place and persuaded a majority of Nation of Islam members to join his World Community of Islam in the West. LOUIS FARRAKHAN assumed leadership of the core of hard-liners within Nation of Islam who remained faithful to Muhammad's dogma.

See also: AFRICAN AMERICAN RIGHTS

For Further Information

Clegg, Claude Andrew, III. *An Original Man: The Life and Times of Elijah Muhammad.* New York: St. Martin's Press, 1998.

N

NADER, RALPH (1934–). Ralph Nader is America's most renowned and effective crusader for the rights of consumers and the general public, a role that has repeatedly brought him into conflict with both business and conservative politicians. He was born on February 27, 1934, in Winsted, Connecticut. Nader's parents were Lebanese immigrants who operated a restaurant in the town. The youngest of four children, Nader was influenced and encouraged by his family to develop a sense of the responsibilities of citizenship and decided he would become a "people's lawyer" while still in his teens.

He earned degrees from the Woodrow Wilson School of Public and International Affairs at Princeton University and Harvard Law School, where he was editor of the *Harvard Law Record*. He then set up a small legal practice in Hartford, Connecticut, and became a freelance journalist for the *Atlantic Monthly* and the *Christian Science Monitor*. During his travels he became aware of the indifference to social conditions in foreign nations on the part of corporate America. He began to speak out against the arrogance of big business, but this message failed to generate a wide audience.

In 1965 Nader published his most popular, shocking, and influential book, *Unsafe at Any Speed*, an indictment of the American automobile industry for manufacturing and marketing unsafe vehicles. General Motors' Corvair, a very popular car at the time, was depicted as being designed with faulty steering, enabling it to easily go out of control. General Motors Corporation retaliated by harassing Nader and prying into his private life, his family, and his sexual preferences. John Roche, president of General Motors, admitted under oath before a Senate subcommittee that his company had funded the investigation and repeated his apology in a nationally televised hearing. Nader sued General Motors and was awarded a settlement of $425,000. Meanwhile, Nader's testimony before the Senate spurred passage of the National Traffic and Motor Vehicle Safety Act of 1966. Corvair sales plummeted and the model was withdrawn from the market.

Nader's comments gained credibility, and he broadened his fight for the public interest to include safety standards in pipelines and coal mining, the release of drugs onto the market with inadequate testing, sloppy meat inspection standards in slaughterhouses, pension reform, and ethics in government. Nader was successful in his campaign for passage of the Wholesome Meat Act of 1967, legislation that mandated federal inspection standards for slaughterhouse operations and meat processing plants.

Nader then started to intensify his war

Consumer advocate Ralph Nader testifies before the National Commission on Product Safety in February 1969. *AP/Wide World Photos.*

against corporate exploitation and governmental neglect of regulatory responsibilities by building a support base for a consumers rights movement. In 1969 he founded the Washington, D.C.–based Center for the Study of Responsive Law, a think tank that works to minimize collusion between corporations and government. The Center found that regulatory agencies were susceptible to influence by the same industries they were charged to oversee. Young students who worked at the Center, conducting various investigations, became known as "Nader's Raiders."

Center staff created dozens of offshoot groups. Examples include the CENTER FOR AUTO SAFETY and CLEAN WATER ACTION. In 1971 Nader founded PUBLIC CITIZEN, a consumer lobby, which in turn spawned three other groups, the Tax Reform Research Group, the Retired Professionals Action Group, and Congress Watch. Nader and his associates scored major legislative victories in the seventies, and in 1971 a poll confirmed that he was the sixth most popular public figure in the United States. However, his influence waned in the late 1970s. He was instrumental in the creation of the Occupational Safety and Health Administration (OSHA), but his effort to have Congress approve formation of a consumer protection agency failed. While he has garnered intense antagonism from business and conservative politicians and has been criticized for his inability to compromise and his combative disposition, the American public has acknowledged his accomplishments as a powerful and effective citizen spokesperson. In 2000, Nader ran as the Green Party's candidate for U.S. president.

No spendthrift, Nader lives in a rooming house, owns a single black-and-white television for viewing the news, and purportedly wears clothing bought during his college days. Ralph Nader is a constructive force in American society and a reminder of how vitally important personal commitment is to force the U.S. Congress, state legislatures, and corporate executives to behave responsibly and in the public interest.

See also: CONSUMER RIGHTS AND SAFEGUARDS

For Further Information

Celsi, Teresa. *Ralph Nader: The Consumer Revolution*. Brookfield, CT: Millbrook Press, 1991.

Holsworth, Robert D. *Public Interest Liberalism and the Crisis of Affluence: Reflections on Nader, Environmentalism, and the Politics of a Sustainable Society*. Rochester, NY: Schenkman Books, 1981.

Nader, Ralph. *Collision Course: The Truth about Airline Safety*. New York: McGraw-Hill Professional Publishing, 1995.

———. *The Menace of Atomic Energy*. New York: W. W. Norton, 1977.

———. *No Context: How the Power Lawyers Are Perverting Justice in America*. New York: Random House, 1996.

———. *Whistle Blowing*. New York: Viking Penguin, 1974.

———. *Who Runs Congress?* New York: Viking Penguin, 1979.

———. *Winning the Insurance Game: The Complete Consumer's Guide to Saving Money*. New York: Doubleday, 1993.

NATION OF ISLAM. Nation of Islam (NOI), founded in 1930, calls for the separation of the black and white races and the return of all blacks to Islam as the only means of redemption from racial oppression. The NOI has its roots in Black Nationalist groups formed in the early twentieth century. The Moorish Science Temple of America was established in Newark, New Jersey, in 1913, by the Prophet Drew Ali, originally Timothy Drew, and one year later, MARCUS MOSIAH GARVEY JR. founded the Universal Negro Improvement Association. Both groups emphasized the Muslim origin of all blacks and predicted their return to Islam to escape white oppression.

Wallace Fard Muhammad, a New Zealand mulatto who claimed to be Moorish, emigrated to the United States in 1930 and established a mosque in Detroit in 1931. By 1934 he had recruited a large following of blacks from urban cities who believed that Fard was a reborn Muhammed destined to restore their lost dignity and primacy as a people, freeing them from whites, "the human devils." ELIJAH MUHAMMAD, born Elija Poole, succeeded Fard as leader of the Nation of Islam in 1934, revising its doctrine by blending the Bible and the Koran, pseudo-science, history, myth, and anti-Semitism. Decolonialization of African countries after World War II, widespread poverty and frustration in ghetto areas, and civil rights activism catalyzed rapid expansion of the group.

Muhammad inspired inner-city blacks to assert themselves politically and socially, to work and educate themselves, to become economically independent, and to rid themselves of drugs and crime. During the sixties, MALCOLM X, a spellbinding preacher, became NOI's chief spokesman and recruiter, and greatly increased its membership. In 1961 he launched *Muhammad Speaks*, the group's first official publication. In 1964, after a pilgrimage to Mecca, he rejected the idea of in-born white evil and attempted to change the racist thinking of leader Elijah Muhammad. After defecting from the NOI, he was gunned down in a New York hotel by three men, two of whom were NOI members.

When Elijah Muhammad died in 1975, his son, Warith Deen Muhammad, succeeded him and dramatically altered NOI policy, removing color consciousness and deification of Fard, and moving the group toward orthodox Islam. He changed the name of the group to World Community of Islam in the West, and in 1985 its members joined the American Muslim Society. In 1978 LOUIS FARRAKHAN assumed leadership of the remaining Nation of Islam adherents, keeping intact Elijah Muhammad's views.

In the 1980s NOI attracted public attention because of Farrakhan's affiliation with neo-Nazis, the KU KLUX KLAN, and other groups advocating racial separatism. Adding further to his notoriety were his receipt of a $5 million loan from Libya's Muammar Kaddafi and his extremist statements to the media. To its credit, NOI addressed extremely challenging problems like drug dealing and gang warfare in inner-city housing projects and generated great appeal among young blacks because of its ideology of discipline and order.

The 1995 Million Man March organized by Farrakhan brought 835,000 black men to Washington, and his popularity subsequently soared. In 1997–1998, he toured thirty-seven nations, with stopovers in Iraq, Libya, Nigeria, and Cuba. Recently, NOI policy and rhetoric have become more inclusive. In 1999 Sister Minister Ava Muhammad was appointed to head up the group's mosques in the southern United States, breaking with the Muslim tradition of barring women from religious leadership. More recently, the NOI Million Family March in October 2000, the second largest rally of black people to take place in Washington, D.C., was endorsed by the NATIONAL ASSOCIATION FOR THE ADVANCEMENT OF COLORED PEOPLE, the NATIONAL URBAN LEAGUE, and the SOUTHERN CHRISTIAN LEADERSHIP CONFERENCE, and included Baptists, Catholics, and followers of the Reverend Sun Myung Moon.

National headquarters for the Nation of Islam is in Chicago. Its biweekly newsletter, *The Final Call*, appears in electronic and paper versions. Louis Farrakhan is NOI chief minister.

See also: AFRICAN AMERICAN RIGHTS

For Further Information

Evanzz, Karl. *The Messenger: The Rise and Fall of Elijah Muhammad*. New York: Pantheon Books, 1999.

Lee, Martha F. *The Nation of Islam: An American Millenarian Movement*. Syracuse, NY: Syracuse University Press, 1996.

Nation of Islam, *http://www.noi.org*

NATIONAL ABORTION AND REPRODUCTIVE RIGHTS ACTION LEAGUE.

The purpose of the National Abortion and Reproductive Rights Action League (NARAL) is to "develop and sustain a pro-choice political constituency in order to maintain the right to legal abortion for all women. NARAL initiates and coordinates political action of individuals and groups concerned with maintaining the 1973 Supreme Court decision, *ROE V. WADE*, affirming the choice of abortion as a constitutional right." The group also promotes policies and programs that reduce the number of unintended pregnancies and thus the need for abortions.

Lawrence Lader, BETTY FRIEDAN, and other abortion reformers founded NARAL in 1969. Its original name was the National Association for the Repeal of Abortion Laws. In the mid-sixties, Lader, who had written a biography of MARGARET SANGER and had been referring women to physicians who would risk performing abortions, decided to start pushing for repeal of all restrictive abortion laws. After the *Roe v. Wade* ruling, NARAL changed its name to National Abortion Rights Action League and committed itself to preserving this right in the face of subsequent attempts to outlaw abortion. One of these attempts, the Hyde Amendment (1976) prohibits the use of Medicaid funds for abortions for poor women except when the mother's life is in danger or her pregnancy results from proven rape or incest. The *Webster v. Reproductive Health Services* Supreme Court decision (1989) further weakened *Roe v. Wade*, resulting in a flood of state decisions restricting abortions during the 1990s.

NARAL claimed partial responsibility for turning back the nomination of Robert Bork for the U.S. Supreme Court in 1987 but failed to stop Clarence Thomas's bid in 1991. In 1992 the March for Women's Lives, co-sponsored by NARAL and the NATIONAL ORGANIZATION FOR WOMEN, drew between 500,000 and 700,000 people to Washington in the largest pro-choice gathering ever.

NARAL was elated by the first two years of Bill Clinton's presidency because of his pro-choice policy, his nomination of Ruth Bader Ginsburg to the Supreme Court, and the appointment of Jocelyn Elders as U.S. surgeon general. In 1994 NARAL started its campaign for a Freedom of Choice Act. That same year, a triumphant Republican Party captured control of Congress; right to life supporters regained power and NARAL suffered a string of legislative defeats and a decline in membership. In 1998 alone, forty-five restrictive antiabortion measures were passed in twenty states, requiring mandatory waiting periods and parental consent or notification laws for minors. In 1997 Congress passed fifty-five similar laws, followed by an additional sixty-two in 1998.

NARAL monitors legislation, briefs lawmakers, and testifies at hearings on abortion and related issues. It also organizes grassroots affiliates, trains field representatives, and coordinates efforts with other groups that work to keep abortion legal. It alerts members to pending legislation and litigation and maintains a speakers' bureau. NARAL is currently the political arm of the pro-choice movement and the largest organization advocating women's right to reproductive choice.

Kate Michelman is executive director of NARAL. The 400,000-member group, based in Washington, D.C., publishes fact sheets, research reports, *Who Decides? A State-by-State Review of Abortion and Reproductive Rights* (annual), and the *NARAL Newsletter* (quarterly). Action Alerts inform members of the status of pending legislation affecting abortion rights.

See also: ABORTION POLICY

For Further Information

McGlen, Nancy E., and Karen O'Connor. *Women, Politics, and American Society*. 2nd ed. Upper Saddle River, NJ: Prentice-Hall, 1998.

National Abortion and Reproductive Rights Action League, *http://www.naral.org*

O'Connor, Karen. *No Neutral Ground? Abortion Politics in an Age of Absolutes*. Boulder, CO: Westview Press, 1996.

NATIONAL AMERICAN WOMAN SUFFRAGE ASSOCIATION (NAWSA).

See League of Women Voters of the United States

NATIONAL ASSOCIATION FOR THE ADVANCEMENT OF COLORED PEOPLE.

The oldest and proudest civil rights organization in the United States, the National Association for the Advancement of Colored People (NAACP) works "to insure the political, educational, social and economic equality of minority group citizens; to achieve equality of rights and eliminate race prejudice among citizens of the United States; [and] to remove all barriers of racial and other discrimination through democratic processes."

The NAACP was born in 1909 during a time when lynchings and mass violence by whites against blacks were prevalent. One such outbreak occurred in 1908 in Springfield, Illinois, and prompted Oswald Garrison Villard, grandson of the abolitionist William Lloyd Garrison, to write "The Lincoln Day Call," an exhortation to action released on the centenary of Abraham Lincoln's birth, February 12, 1909. Villard urged "all believers in democracy to join in a National Conference for the discussion of present evils, the voicing of protests, and the renewal of the struggle for civil and political liberty." The sixty people who signed this document, a multiracial group, included black historian and activist W.E.B. DU BOIS, journalist and social reformer Lincoln Steffens, social reformer JANE ADDAMS, and white civil rights activist Mary White Ovington. Du Bois chose the word "colored" because he envisioned the NAACP as a potential promoter of equity for dark-skinned people worldwide.

During its early years, the NAACP fought for antilynching legislation and worked on behalf of blacks wrongfully accused of lawbreaking. It advocated fair pay, voting rights, union representation, and improved educational opportunity. Subscriptions to *Crisis*, the NAACP magazine edited by Du Bois, reached 94,000 by 1920. In the 1940s, the group assembled a stellar legal team, including Thurgood Marshall, and in 1954 it went to the Supreme Court to challenge *Plessy v. Ferguson*, the 1896 Supreme Court decision that had upheld school segregation. Marshall argued and won the BROWN V. TOPEKA BOARD OF EDUCATION case, ensuring for the NAACP a secure place in history. Meanwhile, Du Bois, becoming frustrated by the slow pace of integration, pressed for black separatism and was forced to resign because his views clashed with the NAACP founders' policy favoring assimilation. Roy Wilkins served as executive director from 1955 until 1977.

The 1950s and 1960s ushered in the broader civil rights movement and stimulated formation of such organizations as the SOUTHERN CHRISTIAN LEADERSHIP CONFERENCE, THE STUDENT NONVIOLENT COORDINATING COMMITTEE, THE CONGRESS OF RACIAL EQUALITY, and THE BLACK PANTHER PARTY. The NAACP supplied legal and legislative advocacy skills to the new groups. By 1970 the NAACP had achieved an impressive record in winning passage of key voting rights, civil rights, and fair housing laws. The NAACP and allied organizations also succeeded in blocking President Richard Nixon's nominations of Clement Haynesworth and G. Harrold Carswell to the Supreme Court. In 1977 Benjamin L. Hooks replaced Roy Wilkins as director, and led NAACP opposition to the nominations of Robert Bork and Clarence Thomas to the Court, losing the latter battle in 1991.

When Hooks resigned in 1992, the NAACP board decided that fresh, more dynamic leadership was needed to take the organization into a new era. BENJAMIN FRANKLIN CHAVIS JR. was selected executive director in 1993 and fired only eighteen months later because of sexual and financial misconduct. Also, his overtures to NATION OF ISLAM leader LOUIS FARRAKHAN, street gang members, and hard-core rap artists had generated controversy within the organization and resulted in a loss of members and revenue.

In 1995 Myrlie Evers-Williams, widow of murdered civil rights worker Medgar Evers, was elected NAACP chair, and a year later former congressman Kweisi Mfume was installed as president and executive director. The organization's membership, morale, and finances rebounded. In 1997, in response to federal and state legislation that threatened to dismantle affirmative action initiatives, the NAACP launched a new Economic Reciprocity Program to reduce inner-city unemployment.

The NAACP remains the leading membership organization spearheading the continuing battle to secure equal justice for African Americans. It has more than 2,200 branches represented in all fifty states with a headquarters office in Baltimore, Maryland. Total membership exceeds 400,000. Kweisi Mfume is president and chief executive officer; Julian Bond is chairman of the board. *Crisis* magazine, published ten times a year, is the official NAACP journal.

See also: AFRICAN AMERICAN RIGHTS

For Further Information

Hughes, Langston. *Fight for Freedom: The Story of the NAACP.* New York: W. W. Norton, 1962.

National Association for the Advancement of Colored People, *http://www.naacp.org/*

Wedin, Carolyn. *Inheritors of the Spirit: Mary White Ovington and the Founding of the NAACP.* New York: Wiley, 1998.

NATIONAL ASSOCIATION FOR THE REPEAL OF ABORTION LAWS. *See* National Abortion and Reproductive Rights Action League

NATIONAL AUDUBON SOCIETY.

Since its formation in 1905, the purpose of the National Audubon Society has expanded to include "long-term protection and wise use of wildlife, land, water, and other natural resources; the promotion of rational strategies for energy development and use; the protection of life from pollution, radiation, and toxic substances; and the solution of global problems caused by overpopulation and the depletion of natural resources."

In the late nineteenth century, songbirds were being hunted as game, there was no bag limit on ducks, the passenger pigeon had become extinct, and the demand for ladies' feathered hats was making egrets an endangered species. George Bird Grinnell, then editor of *Forest and Stream*, was appalled by this butchery of the bird population. In 1886 he proposed an Audubon Society to protect the nation's bird population. By 1888 he had convinced 38,000 readers of his magazine to join the fledgling group, but, becoming overburdened by managerial chores, he was soon forced to disband it. In 1896 several women who were horrified by the wholesale slaughter of birds established the Massachusetts Audubon Society. By 1899 the group had expanded to include sixteen state chapters. The Lacy Act (1900), forbidding the interstate shipment of birds killed in violation of state laws, was the group's first victory.

In 1904 Albert Wilcox offered to provide a $300,000 endowment for the new organization on condition that it incorporate and expand its mission to include protection of wild animals as well as birds. In 1905 the National Association of Audubon Societies was incorporated. In 1940 the society shorted its name to the National Audubon Society, and in 1944 it started forming community-based chapters, beginning in St. Louis, Missouri. Today, there are over 500 chapters with nine regional and twelve state offices to coordinate activities.

The Society has been active in the legislative arena. It helped facilitate development of the National Wildlife Refuge system and throughout the 1960s and 1970s was heavily involved in passage of the Clean Air, Clean Water, Wild and Scenic Rivers, and Endangered Species acts. In 1969 Audubon opened a Washington, D.C., office to enhance its influence as a citizen action group. Television specials, policy reports, and programs for school-age children are produced here. International and population programs are also managed in this office.

Ongoing efforts focus on opposing efforts to open the Arctic National Wildlife Refuge to oil exploration, protecting ancient forests in the Pacific Northwest, and strengthening the Endangered Species Act. Audubon's activist network mobilizes members via the Internet. An Action Agenda identifies for each session of Congress about a dozen key actions to be taken by legislators on environmental issues (e.g., signing a letter, supporting a position, co-sponsoring a bill).

The National Audubon Society has more than a half-million members. John Flicker is current president. The national office is in New York City. *Audubon*, a bimonthly magazine, is included in membership dues. Other publications are the *Audubon Activist* (bimonthly), *Audubon Adventures*, a newspaper for children, and *Field Notes* for birders.

See also: ENVIRONMENT

For Further Information

Benneward, Patrice, ed. *From Outrage to Action: The Story of the National Audubon Society.* New York: National Audubon Society, 1982.

Graham, Frank, Jr. *The Audubon Ark: A History of the National Audubon Society.* Austin: University of Texas Press, 1992.

National Audobon Society, *http://www.audubon. org*

NATIONAL BREAST CANCER COALITION. The National Breast Cancer Coalition (NBCC), formed in 1991, seeks to eradicate breast cancer by focusing the attention of the public, health professionals, and the nation's political leadership on the disease, and by educating and converting to citizen activism women diagnosed with breast cancer and all others concerned about the issue. It operates three programs to achieve this end: (1) The Aspen Project brings together industrial, scientific, governmental, and consumer representatives to develop innovative approaches to the problem. (2) Project LEAD prepares grassroots advocates by familiarizing them with the conduct of scientific inquiry and basic terminology so they can serve as consumer representatives on peer-review panels and other scientific bodies. (3) Annual national conferences held in Washington sharpen members' lobbying skills. As part of its campaign to prick the conscience of the public, the group also sponsors *The Face of Breast Cancer*, a poignant traveling photographic exhibit depicting women devastated by the disease. The coalition's ultimate objective is development of a comprehensive national strategy to be coordinated from the White House.

Dr. Susan M. Love, a surgeon, Susan Hester, and Amy Langer planned the coalition in December 1990. In 1991 Fran Visco, a breast cancer victim, became the NBCC's president at a time when the disease had become the leading cause of death for women between the ages of thirty-two and fifty-two. The NBCC is a model of effective citizen action with a national network of 58,000 members who provide articulate, informed input for researchers and decision makers within the scientific community. More than 180 advocacy groups are united under the NBCC. In 1992 NBCC persuaded Congress to approve $400 million to support National Cancer Institute research and to improve the screening, diagnosis, and treatment of Department of Defense personnel, nearly tripling the previous allocation. By 1994 total appropriations for breast cancer had grown 450 percent, outpacing expenditures for lung cancer. Funding for breast cancer research exceeded $472 million, while research for prostate cancer totaled $36.7 million.

NBCC success was abetted in part by increased public awareness following reports that actress and ambassador Shirley Temple Black, President Gerald Ford's wife, Betty, Vice President Nelson A. Rockefeller's wife, Happy, and President Bill Clinton's mother, Virginia Kelley, had been stricken by the disease. Incidentally, veteran legislative aides observed that the Coalition provided Congress with the opportunity to demonstrate its concern about women's health despite its opposition to abortion rights and the rough treatment of Anita Hill during the confirmation hearings of Supreme Court Justice Clarence Thomas.

Legislators concur that the Coalition is informed, aggressive, and especially effective. Its current membership exceeds 58,000. Fran Visco is president. NBCC headquarters is in Washington, D.C.

See also: HUMAN HEALTH AND SAFETY

For Further Information

Erikson, Jane. "Breast Cancer Activists Seek Voice in Research Decisions." *Science* 269 (September 15, 1995): 1509–1510.

Ferraro, Susan. "The Anguished Politics of Breast Cancer," *New York Times*, August 15, 1993, late edition—final, sec. 6, p. 25.

National Breast Cancer Coalition, *http://www.natlbcc.org*

NATIONAL CIVIC LEAGUE. The mission of the National Civic League is "to strengthen citizen democracy by transforming democratic institutions." The League is an advocacy organization that accomplishes its objectives through technical assistance, training, publishing, research, and an awards program. Founded in 1894 by President Theodore Roosevelt, Supreme Court Justice Louis Brandeis, and 145 other progressive individuals representing twenty-seven different cities, the National Civic League (NCL) was created to promote better city government.

The founding group that met in Philadelphia also included President Woodrow Wilson, Chief Justice Charles Evan Hughes, Harvard College president Charles Eliot, urban landscape architect Frederick Law Olmsted, and business leader and philanthropist Marshall Field. The National Municipal League, as it was then known, was determined to make city governments more honest, efficient, and effective. Its action plan included annual conferences to alert the public to problems faced by local government; publication of the monthly *National Municipal Review* (renamed the *National Civic Review* in 1959), establishment of a Municipal Administration Service which evolved into the present Community Assistance Team; and sponsorship of research to determine optimal structures for municipal governments.

In the 1920s and 1930s, the NCL advocated the council-manager type of municipal government, developed a code of ethics that was adopted in various cities, and succeeded in decreasing corruption and bossism. In later years, it turned its attention to state government reform and helped to ensure that the "one man, one vote" ruling of the U.S. Supreme Court in *Baker v. Carr* (1962) could be realized through reapportionment.

NCL's New Politics Program promotes innovative reforms at the state and local levels. It has succeeded in negotiating campaign finance reform in eighty cities and twenty-eight states in the absence of action by the U.S. Congress and serves as a clearinghouse for information on "healthy communities."

NCL is best known for its annual All-America City and Community Awards, begun in 1949. These are presented to ten cities that have demonstrated strong grassroots citizen involvement, creative community effort, and collaborative problem solving. Besides encouraging communities to sustain high standards, the awards act as an incentive for cities with unsavory reputations to enlist the assistance of local citizen activists in upgrading the quality of their political, economic, environmental, and social health. During the 1990s, citizen participation in effecting change became more important than local government performance in determining award eligibility.

Headquarters of the National Civic League

is in Denver. The organization's membership includes over 23,000 community, business, and government leaders. Christopher T. Gates is president. NCL publishes the quarterly *National Civic Review* and two newsletters, *Civic Action* and *The Kitchen Table*.

For Further Information

National Civic League. *The Civic Index: The National Civic League Model for Improving Community Life.* Denver: National Civic League, 1998.

National Civic League, *http://www.ncl.org*

NATIONAL COALITION AGAINST DOMESTIC VIOLENCE.

Formed in 1978, the National Coalition Against Domestic Violence (NCADV) is the only grassroots organization committed to creating shelter and service programs for battered women across all social, racial, ethnic, religious, and economic groups, ages, and lifestyles. The group's mission is to eliminate personal and societal violence in the lives of women and their children. Although it is primarily a service organization, NCADV includes individual members who promote legislative measures to deter domestic violence.

The NCADV was founded by over a hundred battered women's advocates who attended the U.S. Commission on Civil Rights' hearing on battered women in Washington, D.C., in January 1978. The group's accomplishments include a significant increase in the number of shelters, from only twelve in 1975, to 700 by 1984, to over 2,000 in 1999. The first congressional appropriation of funds to develop domestic violence shelters was authorized in 1984 and followed a decade later by passage of the Vi-

At an October 2000, demonstration in front of the Statehouse in Boston, National Coalition Against Domestic Violence protestors hold signs bearing the names of women the organization says were victims of domestic violence. *AP Photo/Steven Senne.*

olence Against Women Act of 1994. The latter legislation contains provisions designed to curtail domestic violence and authorizes increased funding of domestic abuse shelters and support for state programs to prosecute rape and other crimes against women. In 1996 a generally conservative 104th Congress added interstate stalking to the list of federal crimes, and by 1998 fifteen states required police to make on-the-spot arrests when responding to domestic violence calls.

The NCADV maintains a twenty-four-hour national hotline service that refers victims of violence to local shelters. It also publishes the annually updated *National Directory of Domestic Violence Programs: A Guide to Community Shelter, Safe Homes and Service Programs*, a teen dating violence resource manual, and the *Rough Love Video and Teaching Guide* featuring discussion of verbal, emotional, physical and sexual abuse.

NCADV headquarters is in Denver, Colorado. Rita Smith is executive director. NCADV membership includes about 700 individuals and organizations. The group publishes a newsletter, *Voice*, and distributes NCADV *Legislative Updates* and *Alerts* to its membership.

See also: WOMEN'S ISSUES

For Further Information

National Coalition Against Domestic Violence. *NCADV—Organizational Background*. Denver: NCADV, 1994.
National Coalition Against Domestic Violence *http://ncadv.org/*

NATIONAL COALITION FOR THE HOMELESS. The mission of the National Coalition for the Homeless (NCH) is to end homelessness, doing this while actively involving the homeless and formerly homeless in its efforts. The organization serves as a clearinghouse for information and successful shelter models for social service and legal agencies, church groups, private charities, and individuals that want to assist the homeless. It also has a very effective lobbying arm that advocates expansion of available low-income housing and legislation to ease the plight of the homeless.

The NCH was formed in Boston in 1982 in response to the growing number of individuals and families nationwide who, because of indigence, incompetence, or crisis, had no resources for housing. Robert M. Hayes, counsel for the coalition and its first de facto executive director, was already at the forefront of the homeless battle when he founded the Coalition. In 1979 he had initiated a suit against then New York Governor Hugh Carey and New York City Mayor Edward Koch and won a consent decree requiring New York City to provide shelter to homeless men.

The NCH's first major victory was passage of the Stewart McKinney Homeless Assistance Act of 1987, providing $1 billion for emergency and transitional shelter services for the homeless. In 1992 the group introduced and spearheaded passage of the rural homelessness bill. It continues to monitor congressional reauthorization and appropriations for programs supported by the McKinney Act, along with other bills affecting housing, health, education, income, civil rights, and homeless youth and veterans. NCH is currently seeking authorization of a $50 billion Community Housing Investment Trust to create and maintain rental housing for households with annual incomes below the poverty line and establishment of a federal homeless addictive disorder treatment and recovery program.

The Coalition provides state and local technical assistance through its publications, field visits, telephone, and the Internet, striving to maximize self-empowerment of the homeless. NCH's forty-two-member board includes eleven formerly or currently homeless men and women.

The Coalition's headquarters is in Washington, D.C.; its executive director is Mary Ann Gleason. Current membership is about 12,000. NCH publishes *Safety Network*, a newsletter, six times a year.

See also: HOMELESSNESS

For Further Information

Baumohl, Jim, ed. *Homelessness in America.* Phoenix: Oryx Press, 1996.

National Coalition for the Homeless, *http://www.nationalhomeless.org/*

NATIONAL COALITION TO ABOLISH THE DEATH PENALTY.

The National Coalition to Abolish the Death Penalty (NCADP) is the only Washington-based, national organization focusing exclusively on elimination of the death penalty. The goal of the NCADP, a coalition of organizations and individuals, is unconditional rejection of the federal and state use of legalized murder as an instrument of social policy. As a grassroots organization, the NCADP concentrates its efforts at the state and local levels through consultation, publications, training, and technical support. Approximately 140 liberally oriented religious entities, civil and human rights groups, and legal advocacy organizations have joined the Coalition.

Henry Schwarzchild, director of the AMERICAN CIVIL LIBERTIES UNION's capital punishment project, founded the National Coalition Against the Death Penalty in 1976. Hugo Adam Bedau, former director of the defunct American League to Abolish Capital Punishment, chaired the new group, initially housed within the American Civil Liberties Union's offices in New York City. The impetus for formation of the NCADP was provided by the U.S. Supreme Court's *GREGG V. GEORGIA* decision in 1976, which reopened the path for executions by accepting as constitutional new laws that supposedly eliminated capriciousness, racial bias, and class discrimination in the administration of capital punishment.

Since its inception, the NCADP has grown steadily. After moving from New York City to Philadelphia in 1982, the group relocated to Washington, D.C., in 1987. In 1997 it succeeded in mobilizing public opposition to the juvenile death penalty in Mississippi, saving a minor from almost certain execution, and in Massachusetts and Michigan, NCADP affiliates held back reinstatement of the death penalty.

The Coalition's bimonthly newsletter, *Lifelines*, facilitates communication among abolitionists, death row inmates, and affected families. The *National Execution Alert*, a monthly report distributed in both paper and Internet formats, profiles inmates whose execution dates have been set and who may have been unjustly sentenced. *Stop Killing Kids*, a campaign to stem the execution of juveniles, is a recently added initiative. NCADP headquarters is in Washington, D.C. Steven W. Hawkins is executive director.

See also: DEATH PENALTY AND CHOICE IN DYING

For Further Information

Acker, James R., Robert M. Bohm, and Charles S. Lanier, eds. *America's Experiment with Capital Punishment: Reflections on the Past, Present, and Future of the Ultimate Penal Sanction.* Durham, NC: Carolina Academic Press, 1998.

National Coalition to Abolish the Death Penalty, *http://ncadp.org*

NATIONAL COALITION TO BAN HANDGUNS.

See Coalition to Stop Gun Violence

NATIONAL COMMITTEE TO PRESERVE SOCIAL SECURITY AND MEDICARE.

In 1982 James Roosevelt, the son of President Franklin D. Roosevelt, founded the National Committee to Preserve Social Security (NCPSSM) as a "people's lobby to protect the program his father had created in 1935 from being ravaged by the Reagan administration's cuts in benefits." In 1983 "Medicare" was added to the Committee's title. And in the 1990s, the NCPSSM began its campaign for universal coverage of prescription drugs to ensure coverage for the one in every three Americans over age sixty-five lacking prescription drug insurance in 1999.

Roosevelt built the NCPSSM into a major grassroots senior citizens' advocacy force, second only to the AMERICAN ASSOCIATION OF RETIRED PERSONS (AARP) in size and surpassing the AARP in its ability to mobilize constituents to apply pressure on their representatives and demonstrate its proficiency and muscle as a lobby. In 1987 Roosevelt was accused by a House Ways and Means subcommittee of terrifying the elderly with exaggerated claims that Social System and Medicare were heading toward insolvency. However, the new group's investment in purportedly alarmist letters asking seniors for $10 to protect their benefits reaped a return of $90 million within two years. In 1984 the group persuaded Congress to provide benefit increases exceeding the increase in the Consumer Price Index.

The Committee's next and more significant achievement was repeal of the 1988 Medicare Catastrophic Coverage Act, which included a surtax to cover extreme health emergencies. Its winning strategy had included use of negative ads and cleverly choreographed public confrontations with congressional leaders in which the surtax was attacked as unfair taxation for all seniors.

In 1989 Roosevelt resigned because of ill health and Martha McSteen, former acting commissioner of the Social Security Administration during President Ronald Reagan's administration, became NCPSSM president and chief executive officer. McSteen quickly won new credibility for the NCPSSM, which has become the nation's second largest senior lobbying group. In contrast to the AARP, which offers various benefits and services to its members, the NCPSSM focuses entirely on education and advocacy. Its current legislative agenda includes removal of Social Security from annual federal budget calculations, elimination of the earnings test for Social Security beneficiaries, and support of comprehensive quality health care for all Americans.

The NCPSSM has 5.5 million members. Its national headquarters is in Washington,

D.C., and Martha McSteen is president. The Committee publishes *Secure Retirement*, a bimonthly magazine, and offers its members Senior Flash, a toll-free information hotline; a legislative alert service; and monthly mailings on congressional activities affecting older adults. Because the NCPSSM's strongest asset is citizen action, it offers a program to develop local organizations' and members' political literacy. Its staff of outreach workers presents information forums to members around the country on topics such as Medigap insurance policies, raising grandchildren, and supplementary security income. The group's Minority Affairs Department focuses on concerns of low-income older adults and analyzes proposed laws affecting entitlements to ensure that they reflect the diverse needs of an aging population.

See also: SENIOR MOVEMENT

For Further Information

Dumas, K. "Budget-Buster Hot Potato: The Earnings Test." *Congressional Quarterly Weekly Report*, January 11, 1992, pp. 52–55.

McSteen, Martha A. "Medicare Prescription Drug Benefits," Testimony before the Senate Committee on Finance, 106th Cong., 1st sess. Federal Document Clearing House Congressional Testimony, Item no. 133853272032, June 23, 1999.

———. "Putting the Squeeze on the Elderly." *St. Louis Post-Dispatch*, July 21, 1989, Three Star edition, editorial section, p. 3B.

National Committee to Preserve Social Security and Medicare, *http://ncpssm.org*

NATIONAL CONGRESS OF AMERICAN INDIANS.

The oldest and largest Native American organization advocating the interests of American Indians and Alaskan natives, the National Congress of American Indians (NCAI) "protects and advances the rights of native people to continue to exercise Tribal self-government by lobbying elected federal government representatives." The NCAI was formed in 1944 by one hundred Native Americans under the leadership of Archie Phinney, a member of the Nez Percé tribe of Idaho. The NCAI's first major undertaking was to stop the U.S. government from assimilating the Indians into the dominant society and abrogating its treaty and trust obligations to Indian tribes during President Harry S. Truman's administration.

Since 1970 the NCAI has expanded its lobbying effort in response to the high unemployment rate among Indians and the extreme poverty, disease, poor education, and high suicide rates on reservations. The NCAI legislative agenda now includes protection of benefits for Indian youth and elders, education (Head Start through postsecondary), health care, environmental protection, welfare reform, nuclear waste disposal policy, and economic rights, including attraction of private capital to reservations. Other concerns include jobs creation, training, and chronic under funding of the tribal contract support provisions of the Indian Self-Determination Act of 1975; treaty and land rights; tribal gaming rights; and elimination of sports organizations and mascots bearing derogatory names such as Redskins, Redmen, and Indians.

During the 1950s NCAI succeeded in fending off compulsory assimilation and termination of Indian treaty agreements through use of the ballot and the media, mustering an 80 percent voter turnout. Other achievements include changes in sports teams' names, for example, Dartmouth College's Indians became the Big Green, and St. John's University's Redmen became the Red Storm. In 1998 the NCAI saved bison herds in Montana from being slaughtered by the cattle industry and negotiated authorization for the Makah tribe to resume its traditional whale hunts despite strong opposition from animal rights activists.

The NCAI continues its opposition to states' attempts to tax tribally owned land and businesses as well as revenue from gaming operations. Recent efforts have focused on getting money from Congress to build new schools, improve medical care, and upgrade law enforcement on tribal lands.

The National Congress of American Indians is headquartered in Washington, D.C.

JoAnn K. Chase, a Mandan-Hidatsa Indian, is executive director. Approximately 4,000 individuals and 250 tribes are members. The *NCAI Sentinel*, a quarterly bulletin, provides members with political and legislative news.

See also: NATIVE AMERICAN RIGHTS

For Further Information

Cowger, Thomas. *The National Congress of American Indians: The Founding Years.* Lincoln: University of Nebraska Press, 1999.

Gover, Kevin. "From Fear to Hope." Speech presented at the annual convention of the National Congress of American Indians, Palm Springs, California, October 6, 1999.

National Congress of American Indians, *http://www.ncai.org*

NATIONAL CONSUMERS' LEAGUE.

The National Consumers' League (NCL) "works to protect and promote the economic and social interests of America's consumers using education, research, science, investigation, publications, and the public and private sector to accomplish that mission." FLORENCE KELLEY formed the organization in New York City in 1899 to mobilize middle-class women to support improved working conditions for wage-earning females. Kelley pointed out that "not only all the foods used in private families, but a very large proportion of the furniture and books, as well as the clothing for men, women, and children, is prepared with the direct object in view of being sold to women" (p. 299).

The NCL taught women how to use their purchasing power as a weapon to effect change in their political and social status in "a campaign to be undertaken by women on behalf of women and children." The group fought labor exploitation by boycotting sweatshop products, and pioneered use of the term "advocacy" to describe their public interest lobbying. An early League motto was "To live means to buy, to buy means to have power, to have power means to have duties." A century later, this statement still remains valid for the National Consumers' League.

The NCL was a major force in winning

support and passage of minimum wage, child labor, and work hours laws in the United States. Operating out of sixty-four branches located throughout the nation, NCL members successfully applied Florence Kelley's fourfold strategy: investigate, educate, legislate, and enforce. Louis Brandeis, the League's renowned lawyer, who later served on the Supreme Court (1916–1939), won a series of pro-labor victories beginning in 1908, when the U.S. Supreme Court upheld the constitutionality of state ten-hour workday laws for women in *Muller v. Oregon*. Brandeis had developed what became known as the "Brandeis brief," in which legal points were dealt with summarily and then buttressed by a mass of sociological, economic, and historical data. This paved the way for heavy reliance on sociological data in such later cases as *BROWN V. BOARD OF EDUCATION OF TOPEKA* (1954).

NCL worked for and won passage of minimum wage laws for women in fourteen states and the District of Columbia between 1909 and 1919. In 1917 the League won extension of the laws to include men, building a base for inclusion of maximum hours and minimum wage laws in the Fair Labor Standards Act of 1938.

Four coalitions now operate under the League's umbrella: the Alliance Against Fraud in Telemarketing, the Alliance to Protect Electricity Consumers, the Child Labor Coalition, and the Ad Council. The Ad Council is a public service dedicated to teaching young children what to do in case of fire.

NCL has its headquarters in Washington, D.C. Linda Golodner is president of the 8,000-member League. It publishes four newsletters: *NCL Bulletin*, a bimonthly overview of consumer news; the *Child Labor Monitor*, a quarterly; *Community Credit Link*; and *Focus on Fraud*, produced by the Alliance Against Fraud in Telemarketing.

See also: WOMEN'S ISSUES

For Further Information

The Alliance Against Fraud in Telemarketing and Electronic Commerce, *http://www.fraud.org/*

Kelley, Florence. "Aims and Principles of the Consumers' League." *The American Journal of Sociology* 5 (November 1899): 289–304.

National Consumers League, *http://www.nclnet.org*

Storrs, Landon R. Y. *Civilizing Capitalism: The National Consumers' League, Women's Activism, and Labor Standards in the New Deal Era.* Chapel Hill: University of North Carolina Press, 2000.

NATIONAL COUNCIL OF LA RAZA.

Formed in 1968, the National Council of La Raza (NCLR), comprised of over 200 Hispanic community-based affiliated groups, is "committed to reduce poverty and discrimination, and [to] improve life opportunities for Hispanic Americans of all nationality groups in all regions of the country."

NCLR originated in a proposal written by Raul Yzaguirre for the National Organization for Mexican American Services in 1964. Influenced by the civil rights movement of the 1960s, Yzaguirre established the NCLR to reduce exploitation and discrimination against "the black man of the Southwest." NCLR's initial emphasis on bilingual education and migrant programs soon expanded to include tax cuts, the economy, health care, and Social Security. NCLR's policy analysis center is the nation's leading Hispanic think tank. Ongoing special projects focus on the Hispanic elderly, teenage pregnancy, health, AIDS, immigration, police brutality, bilingual and general education, and unemployment.

During the 1980s, Reagan era cutbacks, a severe recession, and a conservative social climate conspired to frustrate NCLR initiatives. NCLR progress was further blocked by passage of English-only laws, restrictive immigration policies, and increased anti-foreigner public sentiment. It also had to contend with factionalism within the Hispanic community, black-Hispanic friction, and low voter turnouts because of the poverty, poor education, and relative youthfulness of its Latino constituency. One of NCLR's first major achievements was a 1989 Texas Supreme Court decision mandating more equitable distribution of school funding and provision of increased appropriations to recruit students and get them into and through college.

In the 1990s affiliated community development and protest groups, following the model pioneered by SAUL DAVID ALINSKY, made major breakthroughs in East Los Angeles, San Antonio, and Phoenix. By 1998 Hispanics had achieved sufficient voting power to alter the outcomes of elections in New York, California, Texas, and Florida. Barbara Boxer and Charles Schumer won Senate races in California and New York, respectively, while Jeb and George W. Bush won gubernatorial seats in Florida and Texas. The NCLR will continue to gain electoral leverage because projections indicate that Hispanic Americans will be the largest minority population by 2010. Clinton won 61 percent of the Hispanic vote in 1992, expanded to 72 percent in 1996.

NCLR has evolved into the largest constituency-based Hispanic organization, serving over 3 million members with 200 affiliates in thirty-seven states, Puerto Rico, and the District of Columbia. NCLR's annual conventions draw over 15,000 people, including major contenders for public office. The Council's national headquarters is in Washington, D.C. Raul Yzaguirre is president. NCLR publishes a series of policy reports and training modules for its constituency. Members receive *Action Alerts, Agenda*, a quarterly newsletter, and other issue-specific newsletters on education, poverty, HIV/AIDS, and the elderly.

See also: HISPANIC AMERICAN RIGHTS

For Further Information

McKay, Emily Gantz. *The National Council of La Raza: The First Twenty-Five Years*. Washington, DC: The Council, 1993.
National Council of La Raza, *http://www.nclr.org/*

NATIONAL COUNCIL OF SENIOR CITIZENS.

The National Council of Senior Citizens (NCSC), founded in Detroit, Michigan, in 1961, led the campaign to preserve Medicare and Social Security and lobbied for enactment of a national health plan to include long-term care, reduced costs of prescription drugs, and improved housing for the elderly. The NCSC stated that it is the "only national aging organization that combines a democratic structure, political action, including candidate endorsements, annual reports on key votes by Members of Congress, and vigorous direct lobbying of Congress in support of the interests of the elderly."

The NCSC led the campaign to create the federal health benefits program for seniors, enacted as Medicare amendments to Social Security in 1965. The group opposed converting the Social Security system into "a private corporate asset" and privatizing Medicare, contending that it would deny poor citizens access to physicians of their choice.

Former Congressman Aime J. Forand (D-RI) and leaders of the United Auto Workers and United Steelworkers unions formed the NCSC in 1961. Forand served as NSCC president until 1963. In 1961 a political voice for seniors was needed in Washington because the AMERICAN ASSOCIATION OF RETIRED PERSONS had not yet developed a strong legislative lobby. Originally called the National Council of Senior Citizens for Health Care under Social Security, NCSC later adopted its current name.

NCSC's grassroots network included over 2,000 affiliated senior clubs and councils, based in more than forty states, that stimulated local and state legislative and community citizen action. Dramatic protests were often staged by NCSC. For example, in 1996, "gagged" seniors appeared on Capitol Hill to publicize their exclusion from political debate, and other senior activists placed a fourteen-foot-high Trojan Horse on the steps of the Capitol to draw attention to threatened cuts in Medicare hidden in proposed legislation.

Among senior activist groups, NCSC claimed the most achievements. In addition to Medicare, it won battles to create the Older Americans Act of 1965 and other federal programs. In 1968 NCSC was authorized to administer the U.S. Labor Department's Senior AIDES program, which has provided more than 10,500 jobs for the elderly. NCSC was also a source of low-income housing, sponsoring more than 4,000 units in thirty-seven buildings in fourteen states.

NCSC headquarters was in Silver Spring, Maryland, and its most recent executive director was Steve Protulis. The group had approximately 500,000 members. NCSC produced an annual *Congressional Voting Record* covering important votes in the House and Senate on legislation affecting older adults; its official publication was *Seniority*. *Pension Plus*, a monthly, offered advice on personal finance for seniors. Effective December 31, 2000, the National Council of Senior Citizens ceased operations. NCSC members were urged to transfer to the newly created AFL-CIO Alliance for Retired Americans at *www.retiredamericans.org*.

See also: SENIOR MOVEMENT

For Further Information

Clinton, William J. "Remarks to the National Council of Senior Citizens." *Weekly Compilation of Presidential Documents* 374 (August 3, 1998): 1523–1529 [text of speech delivered by the president of the United States on July 28, 1998].

Martin, James L., and Donald J. Senese. "The National Council of Senior Citizens: Taxpayers Fund Lobby for 'Senior-Friendly' Government Pork, Programs and Perks." *Capital Research Center: Organization Trends*, October 1997.

NATIONAL FARM WORKERS ASSOCIATION. *See* United Farm Workers of America

NATIONAL FARMERS ORGANIZATION. Founded in 1955 in Corning, Iowa, by Oren Lee Staley, the National Farmers Organization (NFO) bargains collectively to obtain profit-making contracts with buyers, processors, and exporters for the sale of farm commodities.

During the mid-1950s, the number of farms was dwindling, price support levels were eroding, hog prices had plummeted, and there was a severe drought. Oren Staley decided to induce scarcity to raise prices. Crops were stored and allowed to rot, hogs and cattle were killed and then kept off the market, and milk was dumped to lessen its availability. These coercive tactics failed because of shootings and protest demonstrations involving NFO and anti-NFO farmers. Politicians, the media, and the general public were offended by NFO's anticonsumer holding actions and seeming disregard of the needs of the hungry. The end result was backlash and less support from Washington. A second equally unsuccessful NFO strategy was to bypass distributors and retail outlets by attempting to sell beef and cheese at lower than retail prices at fairgrounds and in supermarket parking lots.

Because of its flouting of standard procedures on the commodities market, the NFO was placed on President Richard Nixon's "enemies list," and in 1973 the Securities and Exchange Commission charged the group with violating federal law by borrowing money from its members. The money was being used to pay off debts incurred as a result of President Nixon's disastrous grain deal with the Soviet Union. In 1979 Staley resigned and DeVon Woodland from Idaho took his place. After 1960 NFO endorsed all presidential nominees of the Democratic Party.

Currently the group limits its activities strictly to collective bargaining with buyers, processors, and exporters of farm commodities. NFO membership includes mostly small family owned farms that produce dairy products, grain, hogs, cattle, and specialty crops such as peanuts, sunflowers, and walnuts.

NFO pioneered in the use of telephone networks during the 1950s. Its "Minute Man" system enabled it to quickly mobilize its members to contact legislators and farm agency administrators, set up picket lines, and inform membership of unscheduled emergency meetings. The NFO's antiestablishment attitude and actions influenced the development of the populist AMERICAN AGRICULTURE MOVEMENT in the late 1970s.

Paul Olson is president of the National Farmers Organization, based in Ames, Iowa. The size of its current membership is unavailable. The group publishes the *NFO Reporter*, a monthly newsletter.

See also: FARMERS' RIGHTS

For Further Information

National Farmers Organization, *http://www.nfo.org*

Rowell, Willis. *The National Farmers Organization: A Complete History*. Ames, IA: Sigler, 1993.

NATIONAL FARMERS UNION. The National Farmers Union (NFU) was founded in Point, Texas, in 1902 by Isaac Newton Gresham to improve economic conditions for farmers and ranchers. Originally established as the Farmers' Educational and Cooperative Union of America, the group embodied progressive elements of nineteenth-century agrarian populism.

Gresham was a tenant farmer and newspaper editor. The mission of his new group was to form a federation of unions that could apply sufficient pressure in the commodities markets to drive up the prices of agricultural products and enable farmers to acquire a more equitable portion of the consumer food dollar. Until the Great Depression, NFU members were prohibited from engaging in partisan politics.

By 1905 the NFU had about 200,000 members in Southern states and in the Indian Territory. By the mid-1920s, its membership exceeded 1 million and it had become a formidable lobby with an anticapitalist bias, despite its avowedly nonpartisan beginnings. Its true politics was reflected in its exclusion of bankers, lawyers, and other individuals who speculated on the commodities market or who held anti-agriculture views. Socially responsible doctors, teachers, ministers, and journalists were welcome to join.

During the Great Depression, NFU's national president, John Simpson, advocated federal assistance and started supporting political candidates who promised to endorse NFU positions. Simpson demanded that the government guarantee farmers' recovery of production costs. In the 1940s and 1950s the NFU campaigned for high, stable price supports at more than 90 percent of parity. During President Dwight D. Eisenhower's administration, Secretary of Agriculture Ezra Taft Benson favored flexible price supports, which the NFU opposed. After 1960 the NFU switched its support to Democratic Party candidates, contributing to Jimmy Carter's margin of victory in 1976 and to the election of members of Congress in rural parts of the South. The NFU continues to advocate a national agricultural policy that would ensure survival of small, family-owned farms and opposes policies favoring the development of agribusiness conglomerates and mega-mergers. In 1999 the NFU shepherded an $8.7 billion short-term relief package through Congress and negotiated family-owned farms' representation at World Trade Organization talks.

NFU headquarters is in Aurora, Colorado. Leland H. Swenson is president. It has approximately 293,000 members. NFU publishes the *National Farmers Union News*, a monthly.

See also: FARMERS' RIGHTS

For Further Information

Crampton, John A. *The National Farmers Union: Ideology of a Pressure Group*. Lincoln: University of Nebraska Press, 1965.

Mooney, Patrick H., and Theo J. Majka. *Farmers' and Farm Workers' Movements: Social Protest in American Agriculture*. New York: Twayne, 1995.

National Farmers Union, *http://www.nfu.org*

NATIONAL FEDERATION FOR DECENCY. *See* American Family Association

NATIONAL GAY AND LESBIAN TASK FORCE. The National Gay and Lesbian Task Force (NGLTF) is the oldest national gay and lesbian civil rights advocacy organization in the United States. Founded in 1973 as the National Gay Task Force, its goal is "to eradicate prejudice, violence, and injustice against gay, lesbian, bisexual and transgendered people at the local, state and national level and to serve its members in a manner that reflects the diversity of the lesbian and gay community."

The group was founded in New York City by gay activists in response to the onslaught of the AIDS epidemic. Its original mission was to awaken the federal bureaucracy to the seriousness and extent of the AIDS crisis. Beginning in 1982, the NGLTF started campaigning against antigay violence. By 1985 it had set up its Washington, D.C., lobbying office and had won collaborative support for gay rights from the NATIONAL ORGANIZATION FOR WOMEN, AMERICAN CIVIL LIBERTIES UNION, and National Council of Churches. In 1985 "Lesbian" was added to the group's title to communicate its broadened mission, and a year later the NGLTF moved its headquarters office to Washington, D.C.

One of the group's early campaigns led to a tightening of health policies to prevent contamination of the nation's blood supply and to improve confidentiality of AIDS victims' medical records. The group also successfully pressed for revision of a Civil Service Commission ruling so that formerly disqualified homosexuals could be hired by federal agencies.

During the mid-1990s the NGLTF experienced organizational turbulence and shifted its emphasis from centralized federal lobbying focused on the AIDS issue to developing a strategy for community-based affiliates, close to the grass roots, that could deal with issues being raised by the RELIGIOUS RIGHT. These new issues included increased antigay violence, state and local initiatives restricting same-sex relationships, the repeal of sodomy laws, reform of the health care system, welfare reform, and liberalization of immigration laws. NGLTF's annual Creating Change Conference was developed as a new venue for local organizers' networking. NGLTF's new community awareness initiative, the 1999 Equality Begins at Home Campaign, included rallies, prayer breakfasts, and other activities in state capitals, in Puerto Rico, and in the District of Columbia.

NGLTF's current membership is about 40,000. Elizabeth Toledo is executive director. Offices are located in Washington, D.C., and Boston. The NGLTF Policy Institute, a nonprofit affiliate based in New York City, publishes analyses of candidates' stands on issues of concern to NGLTF people, monitors and reports on gay, lesbian, bisexual, transgender, and HIV/AIDS related legislation at the state level, maps hate crime incidents in each state, and provides many other reports for its membership.

See also: LESBIANS AND GAYS

For Further Information

Clendinen, Dudley, and Adam Nagourney. *Out for Good: The Struggle to Build a Gay Rights Movemenet in America*. New York: Simon and Schuster, 1999.

Ireland, Doug. "Rebuilding the Gay Movement." *The Nation*, July 12, 1999, pp. 11–15.

National Gay and Lesbian Task Force, *http://www.ngltf.org*

NATIONAL LEAGUE ON URBAN CONDITIONS AMONG NEGROES. *See* National Urban League

NATIONAL ORGANIZATION FOR THE REFORM OF MARIJUANA LAWS. The National Organization for the Reform of Marijuana Laws (NORML) is the oldest and largest national group dedicated solely to marijuana law reform. NORML presents its views to the public, litigates, and lobbies for what it considers to be reasonable treatment of marijuana consumers by the federal, state, and local legal systems.

R. Keith Stroup established NORML in 1970, in Washington, D.C., with the original intention of keeping college students and Vietnam War veterans out of prison for possession and use of small amounts of marijuana.

The National Organization for the Reform of Marijuana Laws (NORML) has successfully campaigned for laws enabling the medical use of marijuana in twenty-three states. *AP Photo/Panama City News Herald/ Vern Miller.*

The Playboy Foundation contributed startup money, and Ramsey Clark, attorney general under President Lyndon B. Johnson, endorsed NORML's formation. NORML argues that it is counterproductive and unjust to treat marijuana smokers as criminals.

In the 1970s, NORML led campaigns to decriminalize minor marijuana offenses in eleven states and to significantly lower penalties in all others. The decriminalization effort lost credibility and momentum in 1977 when Dr. Peter Bourne, former President Jimmy Carter's friend and adviser on health issues, was caught taking cocaine at a NORML party. In the eighties, the Reagan administration's "war on drugs" forced a temporary halt in movement on the decriminalization front.

In the late 1980s, NORML, the SIERRA CLUB, the National Coalition Against the Misuse of Pesticides, and FRIENDS OF THE EARTH joined in winning a suit requiring the Drug Enforcement Administration to file environmental impact statements when using the toxic herbicide Paraquat to eradicate marijuana on federal lands. More recently NORML has argued against mandatory urine testing for Justice Department employees and fought constitutionally dubious efforts to make some drug lawyers testify against clients.

Although NORML and Americans for Medical Rights have successfully campaigned for laws legalizing the medical use of marijuana in twenty-three states, the U.S. House of Representatives passed a resolution opposing medicinal marijuana in 1998. Most polls show strong public support for medical marijuana use, but most people do not favor legalization. Conservative groups such as the FAMILY RESEARCH COUNCIL contend that any easing of drug laws would send a dangerous signal, particularly to teens, and worsen an already serious social blight.

Headed by executive director R. Keith Stroup, a five-person staff at the NORML national office in Washington, D.C., provides an archive of literature on marijuana and free information on drug testing and urinalysis. NORML has over seventy state and local chapters and 80,000 members. It publishes a bimonthly newspaper, *Freedom at 5 NORML*.

See also: ALCOHOL AND DRUG POLICIES

For Further Information

Anderson, Patrick. *High in America: The True Story Behind NORML and the Politics of Marijuana*. New York: Viking, 1980.

Freyman, Russ. "The New Politics of Pot." *Congressional Quarterly DBA Governing Magazine*, January 1999, pp. 32–34.

Grinspoon, Lester, and James B. Bakalar. *Marihuana: The Forbidden Medicine*. New Haven: Yale University Press, 1993.

National Organization for the Reform of Marijuana Laws, *http://www.norml.org*

NATIONAL ORGANIZATION FOR WOMEN. Formed in 1966, the National Organization for Women (NOW) is the largest organization working for women's full and equal partnership with men. NOW was founded by BETTY FRIEDAN and twenty-seven other women who were attending the Third National Conference of the Commission on the Status of Women. Created in 1961 by President John F. Kennedy, the Commission, in a report issued in 1963, confirmed that women in the United States were discriminated against in virtually every aspect of life.

Betty Friedan's popular book, *The Feminine Mystique*, published in 1963, revealed to a wide readership the frustration, feelings of oppression, and ennui experienced by the average American housewife. NOW was formed to redress these problems by advocating full equality for women in government, business, the professions, churches, political parties, the judiciary, labor unions, education, science, medicine, law, and all other dimensions of American society. NOW's goals include increasing the number of women holding elected and appointed office, improving women's economic status and health coverage, ending violence against women, preserving abortion rights, and abolishing discrimination based on gender, race, age, and sexual orientation. In spite of conservatives' success in derailing states' ratification of the Equal Rights Amendment in 1982, NOW has set in motion plans for a second "Constitutional Equality Amendment."

NOW achievements include elimination of sex-segregated help wanted ads in newspapers and successful landmark lawsuits against sex discrimination in employment. The Take Back the Night marches and passage of a new federal Violence Against Women Act in 1994 are examples of other NOW achievements. In 1967 NOW spearheaded the call for the legalization of abortion and repeal of all antiabortion laws. NOW succeeded in persuading Congress to allocate $5 million to fund the International Women's Year Conference in 1977.

Lesbian rights has been a NOW priority issue since 1975. NOW supported *Belmont v. Belmont*, a 1979 case that defined lesbian partners as a nurturing family and awarded a lesbian mother custody of her two children. In 1994 NOW won a pivotal U.S. Supreme Court victory in *NOW v. Scheidler*, a decision validating the use of antiracketeering laws against extremists who employ fear, threats, or force to deny women access to abortion clinics.

NOW uses both traditional and unconventional lobbying tactics. In addition to standard advocacy and legal procedures, NOW has sponsored large-scale events such as the March for Women's Lives (1992) and the 1995 Washington Mall demonstration focusing on violence against women, which included 750,000 and 250,000 people, respectively. NOW has also resorted to picketing, work stoppages, nonviolent civil disobedience, and disruptive "zap" actions to gain media attention and public awareness.

NOW's headquarters office is in Washington, D.C. Betty Friedan served as the group's first president from 1966 to 1970. Patricia Ireland is its current president. NOW's membership—men and women—exceeds half a million contributing activists in 550 chapters in the fifty states and the District of Columbia. The *National NOW Times*, a bimonthly newspaper, is the official membership publication.

See also: WOMEN'S ISSUES

For Further Information

Carabillo, Toni. *Feminist Chronicles, 1953–1993*. Los Angeles: Women's Graphics, 1993.

Ireland, Patricia. *What Women Want*. New York: Dutton, 1997.

National Organization for Women, *http://www. now.org*

NATIONAL PARKS AND CONSERVATION ASSOCIATION.

The National Parks and Conservation Association (NPCA) is the nation's only private nonprofit citizen organization dedicated solely to "protecting, preserving, and enhancing the U.S. National Park System for present and future generations." The NPCA performs its watchdog role through publications, public outreach, advocacy, and litigation.

Robert Sterling Yard, a journalist who had lobbied for establishment of the National Park Service in 1916, founded the National Parks Association three years later, in 1919. Yard believed in the power of citizen action, declaring that "every senator and representative should receive advice from his people at home to restore the national parks to their former status and to hold them safe." In 1920 the NPCA contested legislation that would have permitted invasive federal water projects and construction within the parks. Yard's small association prevailed, killing a pending bill that had the backing of powerful special interests. Under Yard's direction the NPCA resisted pressure to open the parks to mining, logging, and hunting interests; successfully spearheaded protection of the Everglades; and convinced Congress to establish the North Cascades National Park

and Cape Cod and Assateague national seashores during the 1960s.

The NPCA saved the Chesapeake and Ohio Canal wooded corridor from being converted into a highway by enlisting the assistance of U.S. Supreme Court Justice William O. Douglas, who hiked the entire length of the canal to draw attention to its aesthetic and recreational value. The resulting media attention led Congress to redesignate the area as a new national historical park. By forming coalitions with other environmental groups, the group defeated a proposal to build dams at Echo Park and Split Mountain in Colorado that would have buried Dinosaur National Monument under billions of gallons of water. In 1970 the organization changed its name to the National Parks and Conservation Association (NPCA).

In the 1980s the NPCA resisted President Ronald Reagan's rush to reduce restrictions on commercial use of parks and preserves. In 1996 tension between the NPCA and Congress intensified when Speaker of the House Newt Gingrich's "Contract with America" called for legislation to open up the parks to motorized vehicles, petroleum and gas drilling, timber harvesting, water development, hotels, restaurants, and adjacent lands development. In response to this threat NPCA membership grew from 100,000 in 1989 to over 400,000 by 1999.

Other successes include legal action that prevented the NATIONAL RIFLE ASSOCIATION from winning its campaign to permit trapping and hunting in the parks. Another recent victory attributable to the NPCA and its allies was passage of the Underground Railroad Network to Freedom Act (1998), authorizing a comprehensive inventory of locations that provided havens for slaves en route to freedom during the Civil War. Ongoing battles are being waged by the NPCA against commercialization and overcrowding, drifting air pollution, and chronic underfunding.

The group effectively utilizes traditional lobbying techniques and information technology, sponsoring an annual March for Parks on Earth Day, working with allied organizations, alerting its Park Activist Network, and communicating pro-parks positions via phone trees, e-mail, public education, expert testimony, and litigation.

NPCA national headquarters is in Washington, D.C. Thomas C. Kiernan is president. Members receive *National Parks* magazine, published six times a year. Park Activists receive *The Park Watcher*, a bimonthly newsletter, and action alerts.

See also: ENVIRONMENT

For Further Information

Miles, John C. *Guardians of the Parks: A History of the National Parks and Conservation Association*. Washington, DC: Taylor Francis, 1995.
National Parks and Conservation Association, *http://www.npca.org*

NATIONAL RIFLE ASSOCIATION OF AMERICA.

One of the oldest associations in the United States, the NRA began life in 1871. The organization followed the British precedent of encouraging shooting, sports, and the use of firearms for hunting. Its current activities continue to include recreational and educational programs. The NRA sponsors national shooting competitions and competes worldwide in championship shooting events; it also sponsors educational programs on firearms safety and maintains a comprehensive collection of antique and contemporary firearms at its national headquarters in Fairfax, Virginia.

During the 1960s the NRA began to shift its emphasis from promotion of shooting skills to support of individual gun ownership. Its primary argument is based on the Second Amendment to the U.S. Constitution, which states that "a well regulated militia, being necessary to the security of a free state, the right of the people to keep and bear arms, shall not be infringed." Recently proposed legislation that would prevent suits against gun manufacturers is strongly supported by the NRA.

Proponents of gun control admit that a strict and literal interpretation of the Constitution may be an insurmountable legal barrier and that nullification of the Second Amendment may be a necessary precondition for enactment of effective gun control legislation.

The NRA stresses that, unlike trade and professional associations, it is a true citizens' lobby committed to preventing crime, achieving safety, protecting the home, and safeguarding the American heritage. In 1998 the NRA's almost 3 million members contributed in excess of $2 million to the political action committees of Republican (85 percent of total) and Democratic (15 percent of total) members of Congress. This figure dwarfed the approximately $150,000 given to support now defunct HANDGUN CONTROL INC. and has paid off in the thwarting of legislation that would impose restrictions on gun sales. The NRA argues that enforcement of laws already on the books is the preferred solution and that laws requiring gun registration and restrictions on gun shows would not reduce crime and would leave law-abiding American citizens more vulnerable to acts of violence by armed criminals.

The tragic shootings at Columbine High School had little effect on NRA's power on Capitol Hill. NRA lobbyists were able to kill a gun control package in Congress at the very height of public clamor for action to protect children in the nation's schools. Instead, NRA's membership rose, with an upsurge of women (now 12 percent of NRA) joining the organization in 1998 and 1999. Public opinion polls taken in 1999 showed a slim majority of women favoring stricter enforcement of existing laws over enactment of legislation restricting gun sales and use.

In 1998 actor Charlton Heston was elected NRA president. Wayne R. LaPierre Jr. is executive vice president and Tanya Metaksa, a media-savvy, articulate, pistol packing lobbyist, handles NRA's legislative affairs. Headquarters of the 3.5 million member NRA is in Fairfax, Virginia. NRA publications include three monthly magazines: *American Hunter*, *American Rifleman*, and *American Guardian*.

See also: GUN OWNERSHIP RIGHTS/GUN CONTROLS

For Further Information

Davidson, Osha Gray. *Under Fire: The NRA and the Battle for Gun Control.* New York: Henry Holt, 1993.

Dreyfuss, Robert. "The NRA Wants You." *The Nation*, May 29, 2000, pp. 11–16.

Lazare, Daniel. "Your Constitution Is Killing You." *Harper's*, October 1999, pp. 57–65.

National Rifle Association, *http://www.nra.org*

Utter, Glenn H. *Encyclopedia of Gun Control and Gun Rights.* Phoenix: Oryx Press, 1999.

NATIONAL RIGHT TO LIFE COMMITTEE.

The National Right to Life Committee (NRTLC) is the largest national grassroots organization committed to the protection of human life from abortion, euthanasia, and infanticide. The NRTLC was founded in 1973, five months after the ROE V. WADE Supreme Court decision ruled that government interference with abortion was unconstitutional during the first three months of pregnancy. During the next three months the state could regulate abortion to the extent that bears reasonable relation to protection of maternal health, and in the last three months the state could bar abortions. Pro-life activists, infuriated by the decision, came to Detroit to charter a group with a board of representatives to be chosen from every state. Physicians, constitutional lawyers, and Catholic and Protestant clergy were elected to the board, and Dr. Mildred F. Jefferson, a Harvard Medical School graduate and African American daughter of a Methodist minister, was selected as the NRTLC's first president.

Although the passage of a constitutional amendment (Human Life Amendment) banning abortion in all cases except when the mother's life is endangered has remained the primary goal of NRTLC, it also opposes physician-assisted suicide, genetic engineering (including in vitro fertilization), and infanticide. The group's symbol is a flag with a red flame within intertwining blue circles, signifying the sanctity of life ethic as an integral part of the Judeo-Christian heritage. The intensity of the abortion debate and characterization of freedom of choice proponents as "baby killers" immediately made front-page news and gave impetus to the new pro-life grassroots movement. Reinforcing the NRTLC position was PHYLLIS SCHLAFLY, who linked abortion rights to the Equal Rights Amendment and blamed *Roe v. Wade* for the decline of moral behavior and the destruction of the traditional family unit. State legislatures were soon swamped with NRTLC-endorsed proposals for laws that would require parental or spousal consent, waiting periods, and analyses of fetal development before a patient could undertake an abortion. Although efforts to win a Human Life Amendment failed, Congress passed the Hyde Amendment, named after Representative Henry J. Hyde (R-IL), prohibiting use of Medicaid for abortions in various circumstances, legislation that has been reapproved every year since 1977.

After 1980 Supreme Court decisions began to weaken the provisions of *Roe v. Wade*. By 1999 seven of nine justices rejected the idea that a woman's right to an abortion is fundamental. Although the election of Bill Clinton in 1992 led to an executive order repealing the Reagan-Bush gag rule on abortion counseling and removal of bans on fetal tissue research and testing of RU-486, an abortion pill, this countertrend was short-lived. In 1994 and 1996, national elections resulted in antiabortion majorities in Congress and reversals of the preceding changes. During 1999 Clinton signed bill riders prohibiting most federal funding of abortion and reluctantly accepted restrictions on funding of organizations that perform abortions in foreign nations.

The NRTLC wields significant influence in Congress and has been credited with being a critical factor in the 1994 and 1996 elections. In 1992 and 1996, and again in 2000, NRTLC endorsed the Republican presidential candidate. It has successfully opposed a bill that would have eliminated the ban on fetal tissue research, contending that biomedical research using fetal tissue contributes to a permissive attitude toward abortion. The NRTLC and the FAMILY RESEARCH COUN-

CIL joined forces in pressuring President George Bush to veto the legislation.

In 1999 *Fortune* magazine ranked the NRTLC as the eighth most influential lobbying group in Washington because of its enormous infrastructure, political acumen, and persuasive rhetoric. NRTLC headquarters is in Washington, D.C. David N. O'Steen is executive director and Dr. Wanda Franz is president. The organization has a political action committee and an educational trust fund. NRTLC has 3,000 local chapters in fifty states and a total membership exceeding 7 million. Its official journal is the *National Right to Life News*, a monthly.

See also: WOMEN'S ISSUES

For Further Information

McGlen, Nancy E., and Karen O'Connor. *Women, Politics, and American Society.* 2nd ed. Upper Saddle River, NJ: Prentice-Hall, 1998.

National Right to Life Committee, *http:// www.nrlc.org*

NATIONAL RIGHT TO WORK COMMITTEE.

The National Right to Work Committee (NRWC) describes itself as a nonprofit, nonpartisan citizens' coalition dedicated exclusively to the principle that all "Americans must have the right but must not be compelled to join labor unions." The affiliated National Right to Work Legal Defense Foundation, founded in 1968, is a charitable foundation providing free legal aid to employees who feel victimized by "compulsory union abuses." The Foundation litigates cases involving (1) misuse of forced union dues for political purposes; (2) union coercion violating employees' constitutional and civil rights; (3) injustices of compulsory union "hiring halls"; (4) union violations of the merit principle in public employment and academic freedom in education; (5) union violence against workers; and (6) violations of other existing legal protections against union coercion.

Former Representative Fred A. Hartley Jr. of New Jersey, co-sponsor of the Taft-Hartley Act (1947), which limited the power

of unions, founded the NRWC in 1955. In the 1930s and 1940s, the unions had made great gains until the Taft-Hartley Act reduced their power by banning the closed shop, allowing employers to sue unions for broken contracts, forbidding union contributions to political campaigns, and imposing other restrictive conditions. Impetus for NRWC formation was provided when organized labor started a campaign to repeal section 14-b, which permitted states to enact right-to-work laws. The principal goal of the NRWC is to extend and strengthen right-to-work laws nationwide. Currently such laws exist in twenty-one states.

The NRWC is a single-focus organization that directs its appeals to small businesses and others who fear Big Labor. In 1975 it targeted the common situs bill, which initially had broad bipartisan support in Congress. Under the bill, labor unions would have had the right to picket construction sites that hired nonunion labor. The NRWC and allied conservatives launched an avalanche of fundraising letters, pledging to regain control of the government from union boss–controlled radical politicians and bureaucrats. The sheer poundage of mail, exceeding 4 million letters, reinforced by full-page advertisements in fifty newspapers, each demanding President Gerald R. Ford's veto, doomed the common situs bill. Ford complied and the measure was defeated. In 1986, 1992, and 1994, the NRWC mobilized its grassroots membership to inundate legislative offices with letters, petitions, phone calls, and visitors to derail passage of a construction forced unionism bill as well as a push-button strike bill introduced by Senator Edward Kennedy of Massachusetts. Both pieces of legislation would have forced employers to fire workers who stayed on the job despite union strike orders. NRWC has also played a key role in defeating nominations of prolabor candidates to the National Labor Relations Board.

The National Right to Work Legal Defense Foundation's biggest victory was *Communications Workers of America v. Harry Beck*, a 1988 Supreme Court decision ruling that nonunion workers at "agency shops"—

where all employees must pay union dues—have the right to a refund of any portion of their dues used to pay for political advocacy with which they disagree. Foundation attorneys, working on behalf of teachers, auto workers, machinists, and airline pilots, have successfully argued six other related cases before the Supreme Court.

In 1999 Senator Jesse Helms of North Carolina was enlisted by the NRWC to lead an all-out campaign to pass the National Right to Work Act. Helms stated that any lawmakers who oppose his effort will "pay the price with the end of their political careers."

National headquarters of the 2.2 million member NRWC is in Washington, D.C. Reed E. Larson has been president since 1976. *The National Right to Work Newsletter*, a monthly, is included in membership dues.

See also: LABOR ISSUES

For Further Information

Goode, Stephen. "Larson Fights Good Fight Against Big Labor." *Insight on the News*, May 17, 1999, p. 21.

Larson, Reed. "Stop Coddling Big Labor Thugs!" *Human Events*, September 26, 1997, p. 6.

National Right to Work Committee, *http://www.nrtw.org/*

NATIONAL TAX LIMITATION COMMITTEE (NTLC).

The National Tax Limitation Committee (NTLC) is a nonprofit, grassroots activist organization that works to limit taxes and spending and strives to reduce the size of the federal government. The group advocates a balanced budget/tax limitation amendment to the U.S. Constitution.

Lewis K. Uhler and Nobel Prize–winning economist Milton Friedman formed the National Tax Limitation Committee in Roseville, California, in 1975. Initially the NTLC concentrated its efforts at the state level, working to place tax limitation proposals on ballots and pressuring state legislatures into enacting them as constitutional amendments.

In 1979 the NTLC drafted a proposed Tax Limitation/Balanced Budget Constitutional Amendment which received President Ronald Reagan's endorsement in 1982. NTLC immediately started pressuring legislators in Washington to sponsor the amendment, prompted its members to send more than a million pieces of mail to their representatives in Congress, and began to build a broad base of voter support throughout the nation. The NTLC succeeded in getting thirty-two state legislatures to pass resolutions for a constitutional convention. Mid-eighties polls indicated that over 65 percent of the public was in favor of mandating balanced budgets at the federal and state levels of government. The campaign's forward movement was temporarily stalled when the California Supreme Court invalidated an NTLC-instigated voter referendum in 1984 by ruling that only the California State Legislature could petition Congress to call a constitutional convention. Subsequently, the drive for a balanced budget amendment regained strength in 1992 and 1993 as annual federal budget deficits spiraled past the $400 billion mark and, for a brief period, bipartisan endorsement augured well for the amendment's passage. During this time NTLC membership doubled in size.

In the late 1990s, with an economic boom erasing deficits, the NTLC shifted its strategy to devising fiscal formulas for states to automatically control surpluses and limit the size of their governments, based on inflation and population variables. After this change of emphasis, the NATIONAL TAXPAYERS UNION displaced NTLC as the largest grassroots lobby concerned with capping government expenditures, cutting taxes, and fighting for taxpayer rights. Headquarters of the 200,000-member NTLC is in Roseville, California. Lewis K. Uhler is president.

See also: TAX REFORM AND GOVERNMENTAL EXPENDITURES

For Further Information

Goode, Stephen. "A Formula for Cutting Government Spending." *Insight on the News*, June 7, 1999, p. 21.

National Tax Limitation Committee, *http://www.limittaxes.org*

Uhler, Lewis K. *Setting Limits: Constitutional Control of Government*. Washington, DC: Regnery, 1989.

NATIONAL TAXPAYERS UNION.

Founded in 1969, the National Taxpayers Union (NTU) "works for constitutional limits on spending, debt and taxes, lower taxes, less wasteful spending, taxpayer rights, and accountability from elected officials at all levels of government." The NTU monitors government agencies, rates senators and members of Congress on spending and tax issues, conducts fiscal-impact studies, and has lobbied for a balanced budget amendment since 1975. The group, along with the NATIONAL TAX LIMITATION COMMITTEE and other antitax organizations, participated in the campaign to pass HOWARD JARVIS's Proposition 13, approved by California voters in 1978, which imposed tax caps on real estate. Riding the crest of the antitax rebellion, more than 100,000 people joined the NTU by 1980. Currently it is the largest and most formidable grassroots taxpayer organization in the nation, with more than 300,000 members in all fifty states. The NTU affiliate, National Taxpayers Union Foundation, a nonprofit educational research group, was created in 1977.

NTU supports privatization of Social Security and Medicare and opposes congressional pay raises, federal subsidies, foreign aid, and national health insurance. Its victories include the indexing of the federal personal income tax to prevent cost of living increases from pushing people into a higher tax bracket (1981), passage of the Internal Revenue Service Restructuring and Reform Act of 1996, and the "Taxpayers' Bill of Rights II," which shields people from abuse by IRS agents. The group also takes credit for bringing a balanced budget amendment to the Constitution to the brink of passage and saving taxpayers over $10 billion by eliminating the Superconductor Supercollider, Advanced Metal Nuclear Reactor, and Advanced Solid Rocket Motor programs. These latter programs had been requested by the American scientific community to advance knowledge of nuclear fission and improve the nation's defense capability. The NTU additionally has taken credit for defeating 90 percent of the major tax increase initiatives placed on state ballots between 1995 and 2000.

Currently the group is pushing for abolition of the Internal Revenue Service and has endorsed a national sales tax or flat tax or value-added tax to replace the income tax. In its drive to achieve deep tax cuts, NTU recommends returning one-quarter of the budget surplus to citizens and recently gathered 1.7 million signed petitions supporting enabling legislation. Presidential candidate George W. Bush used the NTU pledge to "return the money to the people" as a cornerstone policy statement in his 2000 campaign for the presidency.

In 1998 NTU launched a Web site to oppose the e-rate discount program for schools and libraries (*www.goretax.com*), arguing that action by the Federal Communications Commission had created a new stealth tax on long distance telephone service. In 1999, in response to NTU pressure, Congress introduced a bill to abolish the "Gore Tax," used to fund the wiring of classrooms and school libraries for Internet access, a project supported by the vice president. Altogether, the NTU credits itself for negotiating federal budget cuts of over $120 billion.

National Taxpayers Union headquarters is in Alexandria, Virginia. John Berthoud and David Stanley serve as president and chairman, respectively. NTU members receive the bimonthly NTU *Dollars & Sense* and the bimonthly NTU Foundation *Capital Ideas*; contributing and sustaining members additionally receive the *Tax Savings Report*.

See also: TAX REFORM AND GOVERNMENTAL EXPENDITURES

For Further Information

National Taxpayers Union. *A Call to Action*. Alexandria, VA: NTU, 1989.
National Taxpayers Union, *www.ntu.org*
Sepp, Peter J. *By Popular Demand: How Citizen-Driven Ballot Measures Have Shaped Tax Policy*

for the Better. Alexandria, VA: NTU Foundation, 1999.

NATIONAL URBAN LEAGUE. The National Urban League (NUL), founded in 1910, is an interracial social service and civil rights organization created during the Progressive era. Its formation was in reaction to the lack of jobs and the hostile social and economic environment facing African Americans who had migrated to urban areas in the North. In the years preceding World War I, the NUL established affiliates that were supported by local Community Chests, the forerunners to today's United Way organizations, and promoted vocational training to facilitate blacks' entry into the mining, steel, auto, and meat packing industries. NUL founders included George Edmund Haynes, the first black to earn a Ph.D. at Columbia University, and Ruth Standish Baldwin, a pacifist, socialist, Smith College trustee, and aunt to Roger Baldwin, founder of the AMERICAN CIVIL LIBERTIES UNION.

The current League grew out of three organizations: the Committee for Improving the Industrial Conditions Among Negroes in New York, the League for the Protection of Colored Women, and the Committee on Urban Conditions Among Negroes. The merged organization was called the National League on Urban Conditions Among Negroes until it adopted its current name in 1919.

Although not an advocacy or membership organization, the NUL is an important underwriter and promoter of black economic self-sufficiency. Its dealings with private and public sector establishment power are conciliatory rather than confrontational and it limits its agenda to employment issues. In 1941 the NUL and the NATIONAL ASSOCIATION FOR THE ADVANCEMENT OF COLORED PEOPLE planned a March on Washington to be followed by a massive rally. Reacting to this impending demonstration, President Franklin D. Roosevelt issued Executive Order 8802, banning employment discrimination in the defense industries.

Consequently the march was cancelled and the city and president saved from disruption and public embarrassment.

Under the direction of Whitney M. Young Jr. (1961–1971), NUL emerged as an important force in the civil rights movement. Young succeeded in securing large grants from corporations to support job training programs during a turbulent period when the NUL was viewed as a safer and more respectable haven than other more militant organizations, such as the STUDENT NONVIOLENT COORDINATING COMMITTEE and the BLACK PANTHER PARTY. The Department of Labor made available additional multimillion dollar grants to provide jobs for hundreds of thousands of blacks and job upgrades for an estimated 40,000 individuals. Young's plea for an "Urban Marshall Plan for America" to achieve black-white economic parity inspired President Lyndon B. Johnson's War on Poverty. After Young's accidental drowning death in 1971, successive directors Vernon Jordan Jr. (1972–1981), John Jacob (1982–1994), and Hugh B. Price (1994–   ) expanded the NUL agenda to include a voter registration program, the Campaign for African-American Achievement, and other new initiatives.

Currently, NUL has adopted a three-part strategy: (1) improvement of education and mentoring of poor children; (2) promotion of economic self-sufficiency; and (3) encouragement of racial inclusion and affirmative action. The League utilizes fully the tools of advocacy, research, program service, and systems change. Its annual conferences are major events, typically attracting some 20,000 corporate executives, local business leaders, community service workers, and, in election years, candidates for president of the United States. In 1999–2000, the NUL activated its online Opportunity Watch Grid, rating U.S. presidential candidates on their efforts to create solutions for leveling the economic, academic, and societal playing fields for blacks. The NUL has become the undisputed leader in building bridges to corporate executive suites and convincing businesses to help train and employ African Americans.

NUL headquarters is on Wall Street in New York City; Hugh Price is the executive director. NUL administers programs in thirty-four states and the District of Columbia through 115 affiliates that provide services to more than 2 million individuals each year. The League publishes *The State of Black America*, an annual that provides data on employment and wages, health disparities, and educational levels. *The Urban League News*, a quarterly, is its official journal. There are approximately 50,000 contributing members in the League.

See also: AFRICAN AMERICAN RIGHTS

For Further Information

Brooks, Lester. *Blacks in the City: A History of the National Urban League*. Boston: Little, Brown, 1971.

Dickerson, Dennis C. *Militant Mediator: Whitney M. Young, Jr.* Lexington: University Press of Kentucky, 1998.

National Urban League, *http://www.nul.org*

NATIONAL VACCINE INFORMATION CENTER.

The National Vaccine Information Center (NVIC), founded in 1982, is the oldest and largest national citizens' group advocating reform of the vaccination system, and is responsible for launching the vaccine safety movement in America in the early 1980s. Barbara Loe Fisher, Jeff Schwartz, and other parents whose children were injured or died following vaccine reactions established the NVIC. The group is also known as Dissatisfied Parents Together or DPT, the same initials used for the diphtheria/pertussis/tetanus vaccine.

At the time the NVIC was formed, of 3.5 million children receiving the DPT vaccine, 50 suffered permanent brain damage, 9,000 collapsed, and 25,000 suffered very high fevers. In Japan and the United Kingdom, the use of DPT vaccine was discontinued because of the public's fear of severe reactions. In 1984, because of vulnerability to lawsuits, major drug companies stopped distributing whooping cough vaccine in the United States. As the number of producers of polio, mumps, rubella, measles, and whooping cough vaccines shrank, costs were driven up 2,000 percent. After lawsuits against vaccine manufacturers threatened the supply of inexpensive vaccines, the NVIC, the American Academy of Pediatrics, the manufacturers, and the Communicable Disease Center worked with Congress to pass the National Childhood Vaccine Injury Act of 1986.

The act provides a vaccine injury compensation program and stipulates legal requirements for vaccine providers. Providers must give prospective recipients benefit and risk data, keep detailed records of vaccine origins, and report adverse reactions to the government. The law also preserves the right of vaccine injured persons to take their case to the court system if federal compensation is denied or proves insufficient. As of 1999, the U.S. Court of Federal Claims had awarded over $1 billion to vaccine victims. The NVIC has also spurred development of a safer, purified pertussis vaccine (DtaP) currently administered to American babies. The NVIC's most recent crusade is to win for parents the federally guaranteed right to enroll their children in a school that does not require vaccinations if they harbor doubts concerning their efficacy or fear their harmful effects.

The NVIC headquarters office is in Vienna, Virginia. Barbara Loe Fisher is president. The group has an estimated 30,000 contributing members. *The Vaccine Reaction*, a quarterly, is NVIC's official publication.

See also: HUMAN HEALTH AND SAFETY

For Further Information

Allen, Arthur. "Injection Rejection: The Dangerous Backlash Against Vaccination." *New Republic*, March 23, 1998, pp. 20–23.

Nemecek, Sasha. "Granting Immunity." *Scientific American* 282, no. 3 (March 2000): 15–16.

National Vaccine Information Center, *http://www.909shot.com*

NATIONAL WELFARE RIGHTS ORGANIZATION (NWRO). *See* Association

of Community Organizations for Reform Now.

NATIONAL WILDLIFE FEDERATION. Largest of the conservation organizations, the National Wildlife Federation (NWF) is built on a network of state affiliates that were originally sportsmen's clubs. J. N. "Ding" Darling, a popular editorial cartoonist for the *Des Moines Register*, founded what was initially named the General Wildlife Federation (GWF) in 1936. Darling had been administrator of the U.S. Biological Survey in 1934 and organizer of the Migratory Waterfowl Division. It was Darling who obtained funding for wildlife refuges for duck breeding and convinced Congress to enact the Duck Stamp Act. By the time he left government service in 1935, he was convinced that commercial and business interests would endanger natural resources unless prevented from doing so by a strong national counterforce.

Darling founded the GWF to ensure "the wise use, conservation, aesthetic appreciation, and restoration of wildlife and other natural resources." To distinguish his group from the Audubon Societies and the IZAAK WALTON LEAGUE, he structured it as a federation of local and state sports and conservation clubs. Today, the organization includes affiliates and autonomous groups in each of the fifty states and territories. The affiliates send representatives to the annual meetings to set national policies and state priorities.

The General Wildlife Federation's first lobbying success was passage of the Pittman-Robertson Wildlife Restoration Act of 1937, creating a federal excise tax on guns and ammunition. In 1938 the group was renamed the National Wildlife Federation (NWF). In 1949, the NWF appointed its first executive director and by 1956 had attracted over a million members. Fear of losing tax-exempt status inhibited NWF lobbying until 1976. After that, attorneys were added to the staff and litigation victories stiffened states' enforcement of surface mining reclamation laws

and limited mining on federal lands. In the 1980s the NWF advocated removal of Secretary of the Interior James Watt and fought against the Reagan administration's policies that favored business over environmental interests.

Currently the NWF focuses its efforts on five issues: endangered habitats, land stewardship, wetlands preservation, pollution reduction, and maintenance of pollution-free and uncrowded human habitats. The NWF's informative and easily navigable Web site, e-mail action alerts, grassroots connections, occasional involvement in lobbying coalitions, educational programs and publications, litigation, and sheer size make it the most influential mainstream citizen action organization in the environmental policy arena.

The NWF has its headquarters in Washington, D.C. and claims a membership of over 4.4 million members and individual conservationist-contributors. Mark Van Putten is the organization's president and chief executive officer. *National Wildlife*, a bi-monthly, is included in membership dues. NWF produces *Ranger Rick's Nature Magazine* for young children and *Your Big Backyard* for preschoolers. Its *EnviroAction*, a monthly, informs activists of pending legislation and critical environmental issues. NWF also produces television specials and series, and popular movies, including the IMAX films.

SEE ALSO: ENVIRONMENT

For Further Information

Allen, Thomas B. *Guardian of the Wild: The Story of the National Wildlife Federation*. Bloomington: Indiana University Press, 1987.

National Wildlife Federation. *Your Choices Count: National Wildlife Federation Citizen Action Guide*. Washington, DC: The Federation, 1990.

National Wildlife Federation, *http://www.nwf.org*

NATIONAL WOMEN'S HEALTH NETWORK. The National Women's Health Network (NWHN) is an independent, science-based advocacy organization committed to giving women a voice in decisions affecting U.S. health care policies and practices. In 1974 two feminists, Barbara Seaman and Belita Cowan, decided that a Washington, D.C.–based lobby was needed to influence federal health policy and serve as a counterforce to organized medicine and the pharmaceutical industry. The group was formally established under its current name in 1976.

ABC Television ran coverage of the NWHN's first demonstration staged at the U.S. Food and Drug Administration (FDA) headquarters to protest the hazards of estrogen drugs. Marlene Sanders's 1976 ABC *Close-Up* special, "Women's Health: A Question of Survival," aired the group's concerns to a nationwide audience.

NWHN founder Barbara Seaman had cited the dangers of oral contraceptives, especially DES (diethylstilbestrol) and estrogen replacement therapy, in her 1969 book, *The Doctors' Case Against the Pill*. Problems she cited included blood clots, heart attacks, strokes, depression, suicide, obesity, and lessened sex drive. NWHN actions eventually resulted in the mandated inclusion of patient package inserts (PPIs) with each prescription of birth control pills in 1995. The group's grassroots advocacy also resulted in FDA support for the approval of the cervical cap as a birth control device in 1988. Currently the NWHN serves as an information clearinghouse and monitors federal health policies and legislation as they pertain to older women's health, contraception, breast cancer, abortion, unsafe drugs, and AIDS.

Cynthia Pearson is executive director, and NWHN headquarters is in Washington, D.C. *Network News*, a bimonthly newsletter, and the group's Women's Health Information Service are available to members. Contributors at the $45 level receive free copies of *Our Bodies, Ourselves*, the best-selling women's health and wellness guide. The group has about 12,000 members.

See also: HUMAN HEALTH AND SAFETY; WOMEN'S ISSUES

For Further Information

Davis, Flora. *Moving the Mountain: The Woman's Movement in America since 1960.* Champaign: University of Illinois Press, 1999.

National Women's Health Network, *http://www.womenshealthnetwork.org*

Null, Gary. *For Women Only! Your Guide to Health Empowerment.* New York: Seven Stories Press, 2000.

Pearson, Cynthia. "National Women's Health Network and the US FDA: Two Decades of Activism." *Reproductive Health Matters*, no 6, (1995): 132–141.

NATIONAL WOMEN'S POLITICAL CAUCUS. Founded in 1971, the National Women's Political Caucus (NWPC) is the only national grassroots organization committed to increasing the number of pro-choice feminist women in elected and appointed positions at all levels of government, regardless of party affiliation. Congresswoman BELLA ABZUG, who had been an organizer of the Women's Strike for Peace (1961) and a co-founder of the New Democratic Coalition, Representative Shirley Chisholm, a contender for the vice presidential nomination at the 1972 Democratic National Convention; BETTY FRIEDAN, and GLORIA STEINEM were the four founders of the NWPC.

Initially, NWPC's objectives were very broad, encompassing civil and economic rights, ratification of the Equal Rights Amendment to the U.S. Constitution, passage of comprehensive legislation legalizing abortion, establishment of child care centers, and elimination of sexism within the criminal justice system.

Since its inception, the NWPC has urged appointments of more women to top governmental positions, enactment of the Women's Education Act, and federal support of state commissions on the status of women. NWPC took credit for convincing more women to run for local, state, and national offices in 1974. At the 1976 Democratic National Convention, NWPC successfully negotiated revision of rules to mandate that

Members of the National Women's Political Caucus appear at a July 1971 news conference to announce their goal of having half the delegates at the 1972 political conventions be women. Seated (from left to right) are Gloria Steinem, Rep. Shirley Chisholm (D-NY), and Betty Friedan; standing is Rep. Bella Abzug (D-NY). *AP/Wide World Photos.*

women would make up 50 percent of the 1980 delegates. Although NWPC is nonpartisan, it has had only marginal success in pursuing reform within the Republican Party, perhaps because of Democrats' sizable majority within NWPC and the conservative nature of recent Republic leadership. NWPC attributed increased representation of women in the federal courts, up from five in 1977 to forty-two by 1980, to its persistent lobbying.

Each year, NWPC convenes its Coalition for Women's Appointments, comprising representatives from more than seventy women's and public interest groups, to identify strong female candidates for high-ranking governmental positions. Their names and resumés are forwarded to the White House, after which lobbying for the appointment commences. Nominees have been submitted to the administrations of Jimmy Carter, George

Bush, Bill Clinton, and George W. Bush. Women recommended by NWPC include U.S. Secretary of State Madeleine Albright, U.S. Secretary of Labor Alexis Herman, U.S. Trade Representative Charlene Barshefsky, and U.S. Small Business Administrator Aida Alvarez. They also recommended the following women who have since been nominated by President George W. Bush for cabinet or appointed to senior-level posts: Elaine Chao, Labor Secretary; Condoleezza Rice, National Security Advisor; Ann M. Veneman, Secretary of Agriculture; and Christine Todd Whitman, Environmental Protection Agency. More than 50,000 women participate in NWPC activities each year. In 1996 the Caucus endorsed one hundred women running for federal and statewide offices and hundreds of pro-choice women competing for other state and local offices.

NWPC sponsors leadership and campaign skills training programs for girls, young women, and corporate women executives. It also honors woman-championing men with Good Guys Awards and pro-woman media representatives with Exceptional Merit Media Awards, presented annually.

NWPC headquarters is in Washington, D.C., and its current president is Roselyn O'Connell, the first Republican to take the helm in over fourteen years. NWPC has about 75,000 members. Its publications include *Campaigning to Win, Fact Sheet on Women's Political Progress*, and *National Directory of Women Elected Officials*. The group's official publication is *Women's Political Times*, a quarterly newsletter with legislative updates.

See also: WOMEN'S ISSUES; ABORTION POLICY

For Further Information

Friedan, Betty. "Battling for Women While Being Beaten at Home." *George* 5 (May 2000): 82–89.

McGlen, Nancy E., and Karen O'Connor. *Women, Politics, and American Society.* 2nd ed. Upper Saddle River, NJ: Prentice-Hall, 1998.

Mills, Kay. "Interview: Anita Perez Ferguson; On Bringing Women—and the Personal—into Public Office." *Los Angeles Times*, July 14, 1996, home edition, part M, opinion desk, p. 3.

National Women's Political Caucus, *http://www.nwpc.org/*

The Women's Appointments Project convened by the NWPC and the National Council of Women's Organizations (NCWO), *http://www.appointwomen.com*

NATIVE AMERICAN RIGHTS. About 2.3 million Native Americans (Indians) live in the United States, about half of them on reservations. The Bureau of Indian Affairs, an agency of the Department of the Interior, manages the federal reservations. In 1924 Congress passed the Indian Citizenship Act, granting citizenship status to all Indians born within the United States. Only in the mid-1930s did the U.S. Congress pass legislation enabling cooperation between federal and state governments in improving education, health care, and welfare for Native Americans. In sharp contrast to the prosperity of most other Americans, Native Americans have an unemployment rate exceeding 50 percent and are plagued by poverty, disease, high infant mortality rates, inferior education, and alcoholism.

In 1944 Indian leaders founded the NATIONAL CONGRESS OF AMERICAN INDIANS, the first activist group to represent Native American political interests. In 1953 Congress passed a resolution that denied federal support and protection to Indians on many of the reservations in violation of earlier treaty agreements and called for rapid assimilation into the dominant white culture. Opposition by the Indian lobby pressured the government to retract the resolution.

During the 1960s, because of the many injustices suffered by Indians since 1492 and because of Washington bureaucrats' continuing inaction, some of the tribal leaders became convinced that militant activism was necessary to effect change. DENNIS BANKS, a Chippewa, and RUSSELL MEANS, an Oglala Sioux, founded the AMERICAN INDIAN MOVEMENT (AIM) in 1968. AIM accused the Bureau of Indian Affairs (BIA) of being inefficient, paternalistic, and unfair in carrying out governmental policies. In 1972 AIM forcibly took over the BIA office in Washington for several days. A year later, in February 1973, AIM seized the village of Wounded Knee, South Dakota, to attract public attention to the U.S. government's violation of treaty agreements.

In the 1980s, the U.S. Supreme Court ordered the federal government to pay $122.5 million to Sioux Indian tribes to compensate for illegal government seizure of South Dakotan Indian land in 1877. A later Court decision further extended Indian power by ruling that tribes could tax corporate extraction of oil, natural gas, and minerals on reservations.

By the end of the twentieth century, Indian tribes were gaining new wealth that enabled them to become more effective in their lobbying to protect their sovereignty as sep-

In March 1973, American Indian Movement leaders Russell Means (left) and Dennis Banks meet with reporters about the group's ongoing occupation of the village of Wounded Knee, South Dakota. *AP/Wide World Photos.*

arate nations. The proliferation of casino gambling on reservations and the flow of income from gas and oil receipts provided the necessary revenue to contribute large sums of money to political races of candidates supporting their causes. In 1998 tribes gave over $100,000 to Republican and Democratic campaign coffers. In addition, the Saginaw Chippewa, Mashantucket Pequot, and other tribes were able to move into legislative offices on prestigious Embassy Row in Washington, D.C. Native American political power had come of age.

For Further Information

Grossman, Mark. *The ABC-CLIO Companion to the Native American Rights Movement.* Santa Barbara: ABC-CLIO, 1996.

Josephy, Alvin, Jr., and others. *Red Power: The American Indians' Fight for Freedom.* Lincoln: University of Nebraska Press, 1999.

NATURAL RESOURCES DEFENSE COUNCIL. The Natural Resources Defense Council (NRDC) is dedicated to protecting wildlife and wild places. It uses law and science "to ensure a safe and healthy environment for all living things," working to "foster the fundamental right of all people to have a voice in decisions that affect their environment. It seeks to break down the pattern of disproportionate environmental burdens borne by people of color and others who face social or economic inequities."

The NRDC was formed in 1970, with seed money from a Ford Foundation grant, by a group of young lawyers, including James Gustave Speth, Richard Ayres, David Sive, and Stephen P. Duggan. Duggan had already played a major role in the Storm King case, blocking activation of a nuclear power plant on the Hudson River. Although initially made up mostly of lawyers and scientists, the

NRDC soon attracted an increasing number of laypersons. It has won a reputation for shrewdness and aggressiveness, becoming an organization that can provide exemplary legal representation and policy analysis on demand, and has been at the center of every major environmental debate for three decades.

NRDC lawsuits have resulted in landmark decisions influencing the laws governing air and water pollution, toxic wastes, drinking water, pesticides, nuclear energy, conservation, and land use. Due to its efforts, government regulators must take into account environmental concerns when issuing licenses for construction of nuclear power plants. It has widely publicized problems imposed by unclean air, polluted water, and sulfur dioxide emissions. Successes include reduction of lead in gasoline and improved control of chlorofluorocarbons and other chemicals that deplete the ozone layer. The NRDC compelled the Environmental Protection Agency (EPA) to enforce the Clean Water Act and control industrial pollutants.

In 1989, when the EPA revealed that Alar, an apple ripening agent, contained daminozide but nonetheless would permit the product to remain on the market for another eighteen months, the NRDC took action. It issued a report, "Intolerable Risks: Pesticides in Our Children's Food," followed by a coast-to-coast telecast of the topic on CBS's *60 Minutes*. This was reinforced by a *Consumer Reports* article and topped off by actress Meryl Streep's anti-Alar public education campaign. Apple growers' and pesticide producers' abandonment of Alar followed.

Recently, NRDC has focused on Detroit auto manufacturers' disregard of "earth-smart," hybrid gasoline-electric cars in favor of polluting, internal combustion engine vehicles and on proposed changes to the Clean Water Act that would permit mining companies to dump waste in mountain streams. These concerns are high priority targets for citizen action.

John H. Adams has been executive director of NRDC since its founding. Head-quartered in New York City, NRDC has over 350,000 members. Organization publications include *The Amicus Journal*, a quarterly, and *Earth Action: The Bulletin for Environmental Activists*, a bimonthly, which identifies urgent issues requiring grassroots action.

See also: ENVIRONMENT

For Further Information

The Amicus Journal, 1980– .

Mott, Laurie. *Our Children at Risk: The Five Worst Environmental Threats to Their Health*. New York: Natural Resources Defense Council, 1997.

National Resources Defense Council, *http://www.nrdc.org*

Natural Resources Defense Council. *Twenty-Five Years Defending the Environment: Natural Resources Defense Council, 1970–1995*. New York: NRDC, 1995.

NEW LEFT. The New Left was a radical leftist political movement that was particularly active in the 1960s and 1970s, comprising mostly college students and young intellectuals whose goals included racial equality, deescalation of the arms race, nonintervention in foreign affairs, and other major changes in the political, economic, social, and educational systems of the United States. In a "Letter to the New Left," written in 1960, C. Wright Mills derided the outdated legacy bequeathed by a "Victorian Marxism." Echoing Mills, TOM HAYDEN told the STUDENTS FOR A DEMOCRATIC SOCIETY (SDS) executive council in 1962 that the working class "is just not the missionary force we can count on." Coming of age after 1956, the young leftists could not identify with the anti-Stalinism of Old Left spokesmen like Irving Howe or with labor leaders like Michael Harrington and Bayard Rustin. The Old Left had wanted to build a reformist coalition of labor, civil rights groups, churches, liberals, and intellectuals within the Democratic Party. They believed that an effective peace movement had to reach out and build bridges with other groups. The Old Left wanted to exclude communists.

The New Left wanted to create independent constituencies to oppose the establishment and argued that any movement's fight for the freedom of one group could not exclude another, including the communists. Carl Oglesby, the leader of SDS, rejected any compromise with the establishment and blamed liberals for the embourgeoisement of blacks, the decay of the cities, the bureaucratization of the universities, and the distortion of national priorities. The New Left believed in the collective expression of a moral society. During its beginnings it was committed to participatory democracy, but by the close of the 1960s its adherents were rationalizing, romanticizing, and sometimes even glorifying the societal advances of repressive political regimes in Vietnam and Cuba. However, with the election of President Richard Nixon in 1968, members of the New Left felt that they had failed. SDS, the STUDENT NONVIOLENT COORDINATING COMMITTEE, and other allied organizations buckled and broke apart, with some members becoming anarchists and others joining the hippies or retreating to normalcy.

Although the New Left failed in its grandly ambitious attempt to make over American society, it altered the public view of military interventions in foreign countries, led to a liberalization of teaching and curriculums in academic institutions and, because of the extreme male chauvinism of its later stages, hastened development of the women's movement.

See also: LIBERAL ACTIVISM

For Further Information

Gitlin, Todd. *The Sixties: Years of Hope, Days of Rage*. New York: Bantam, 1987.

Isserman, Maurice. *If I Had a Hammer . . . : The Death of the Old Left and the Birth of the New Left*. New York: Basic Books, 1987.

NEWTON, HUEY P. (1942–1989).

A controversial, militant political activist, Huey P. Newton co-founded the BLACK PANTHER PARTY in 1966. He articulated African Americans' anger and eagerness to escape from oppressive inner-city poverty and took up arms against the racist brutality of the Oakland, California, police. Newton captured the hearts and minds of the many who believed that only violent, in-your-face measures could bring "Power to the People." A widely distributed photo shows him posed on a thronelike rattan chair, a spear in one hand and a rifle in the other. Newton was viewed as a hero of the radical left during the sixties, and JANE FONDA lauded him as the only man she had ever met who approached sainthood.

Born on February 17, 1942, in Monroe, Louisiana, Huey Percy Newton was named after Huey Long, Louisiana's publicly venerated, benevolent, but corrupt governor (1928–1931). When he was one year old, his family moved to Oakland, California, so that his father could work in a shipyard. After the war, his father had to take two or three jobs at a time just to survive, and Oakland became a divided city, with blacks living in the depressed inner city and wealthy whites living in the surrounding hilly suburbs. Although he was a very bright student in the elementary grades, Newton soon became labeled by teachers as a below-average student, was repeatedly suspended, and graduated as an illiterate with a D average. After teaching himself to read, he went on to college, attending San Francisco Law School, where he met BOBBY SEALE.

After 1962 he began a long sequence of illegal activities and crimes, including book pilferage, battery, assault with a deadly weapon, pistol whipping his tailor, and the murder of a seventeen-year-old prostitute.

In 1966 the Black Panther Party was formed with Huey Newton as minister of defense, and Bobby Seale as chairman; in 1967 ELDRIDGE CLEAVER joined as minister of information. Later that same year Newton was arrested and charged with killing an Oakland police officer during a dispute, precipitating a much-publicized "Free Huey" campaign organized by the Panthers. Although his 1968 conviction was overturned due to procedural errors, he later expressed pride in the killing, arguing that his act had reduced police brutality in the black community.

Newton escaped other criminal charges by fleeing to Cuba in 1973. He returned in 1977 and in 1980 earned a doctorate in philosophy from the University of California, Santa Cruz. Despite his book smarts he never broke free from his "mean streets" past, fell prey to alcohol and drug abuse, and was shot to death in 1989 for strong-arming crack cocaine from a dealer.

See also: AFRICAN AMERICAN RIGHTS; EXTREMISTS

For Further Information

Haskins, James. *Power to the People: The Rise and Fall of the Black Panther Party.* New York: Simon and Schuster Books for Young Readers, 1997.

Pearson, Hugh. *The Shadow of the Panther: Huey Newton and the Price of Black Power in America.* New York: Addison-Wesley, 1994.

NORMA RAE. *See* Jordan, Crystal Lee

O

OLDER WOMEN'S LEAGUE. The Older Women's League (OWL) is a national network of grassroots organizations of women "dedicated to winning economic, political and social equity for midlife and older women." OWL's voice has been heard in legislative chambers from community to state and national levels on such issues as defense and reform of Social Security and Medicare, pension equity and access to quality health care, and support of family caregivers.

Laurie Shields, founder of the Displaced Homemakers Network, and Tish Sommers, former chair of the NATIONAL ORGANIZATION FOR WOMEN's Task Force on Older Women, founded OWL in Des Moines, Iowa, in 1980. During its early years, OWL was guided by the slogan "Don't Agonize, Organize," and concentrated on assisting women who become destitute after divorce or their husbands' deaths. OWL is particularly disturbed by the "feminization of poverty" that denies security, dignity, and independence to women in their later years and warehouses the infirm elderly in nursing homes.

OWL has been effective in advocating tax credits for caregivers and purchasers of long-term care insurance. In 1999 it campaigned against "Flo," the grandmotherly star of a multimillion-dollar ad campaign underwritten by the Pharmaceutical Research and Manufacturers of America (PhRMA). The ads featured Flo worrying about "big government getting into her medicine cabinet." OWL distributed "Flo is a fake" leaflets to its chapters nationwide, picketed PhRMA headquarters, and explained that seniors could opt in or out of the proposed federal prescription payment program, which would cover every drug category. The pharmaceutical industry opposed the Clinton plan because it could impose price controls on drugs.

OWL headquarters is in Washington, D.C., and Deborah Briceland-Betts is executive director of the 21,000-member organization. OWL operates a speakers' bureau, compiles statistical reports, and distributes educational materials to members. Its official newsletter is the *OWL Observer*, a bimonthly. OWL also publishes reports, issue papers, and fact sheets, available at no charge, on such topics as health care, displaced homemakers, divorce, pension plans, and employment problems.

See also: SENIOR MOVEMENT; WOMEN'S ISSUES

For Further Information

Huckle, Patricia. *Tish Sommers, Activist, and the Founding of the Older Women's League.* Knoxville: University of Tennessee Press, 1991.

Older Women's League, *http://www.owl-national.org/*

Toner, Robin. "The Debate on Aid for the Elderly Focuses on Women." *New York Times*, September 13, 1999, late edition, p. A1.

OMB WATCH. OMB Watch is a research and advocacy organization that monitors and interprets the policies and activities of the Office of Management and Budget in an effort to make the governmental decision-making process publicly accountable. The organization was formed in 1983 to "lift the veil of secrecy shrouding the White House Office of Management and Budget" during President Ronald Reagan's administration. Although the OMB oversees regulations, the budget, information collection and dissemination, proposed legislation, and testimony by agencies, many of its decisions and operations remained hidden and unaccountable to Congress and the general public.

Gary D. Bass, the founder of OMB Watch, holds doctorates in education and psychology and had worked with juveniles in prison systems and child abuse victims before coming to Washington in 1980. He was aware of federal budget cuts' devastating impact on community nonprofit human services organizations and the general public's unawareness of OMB's secret operation and its ability to affect their lives. Energized by his desire to make government more accountable, Bass toured forty cities to alert local organizations and to recruit members to his group.

In 1983 OMB Watch organized opposition to OMB Circular A-122, containing regulations designed to throttle nonprofit lobbying. And in 1995 and 1996, OMB Watch joined with Independent Sector, Let America Speak, the American Library Association, and other groups in opposing the Istook Amendment, which would have cut off federal funding to nonprofit organizations that spend more than 5 percent of their budgets on advocacy. Other OMB Watch victories included defeat of a Reagan era policy initiative that would have required federal agencies to prepare detailed impact analysis statements for all proposed regulations and the public disclosure of OMB's attempt to delay and thwart Center for Disease Control research on dioxin's toxicity. Currently the group is monitoring federal agencies' compliance with the Electronic Freedom of Information Act's public access requirements.

OMB Watch also administers an online service providing environmental, census, housing, and bank loan data and teaches public service organizations how to use the Internet and other information technologies. The group continually seeks opportunities to work on emerging issues for which there is little financial and political support, but where neglect may have widespread and serious social consequences. The Right-to-Know Network (RTK NET, *http://www.rtk.net*) is one such venture, providing free access to numerous databases and enabling its users to identify amounts of toxic pollutants produced by specific factories in communities throughout the nation.

Headquarters of the 1,000-member OMB Watch is in Washington, D.C. Gary D. Bass is executive director. OMB Watch publishes two bimonthlies, *The OMB Watcher* and *The Government Information Insider*.

See also: CONSUMER RIGHTS AND SAFEGUARDS; LIBERAL ACTIVISM

For Further Information

Cochran, Steve, and Gary D. Bass. "Beltway Web Wrangling Puts Public in the Dark." *Journal of Commerce*, March 8, 2000, p. 7.

Kriz, Margaret E. "Gary D. Bass: Lobbing Hardballs at the Budget Office." *National Journal*, June 20, 1987, p. 1604.

OMB Watch, *http://www.ombwatch.org/ombwatch.html*

OPERATION RESCUE. *See* Operation Save America

OPERATION SAVE AMERICA. Operation Rescue National, renamed Operation Save America (OSA) in 1999, is a Christian pro-life group that has declined in influence but remains committed to stopping abortions. Its statement of purpose declares that it "unashamedly takes up the cause of pre-born children in the name of Jesus Christ. . . . There are no cheap political solutions to the holocaust presently ravaging our nation. Like slavery before it, abortion is preeminently a Gospel Issue. The Cross of Christ is the only solution."

RANDALL TERRY founded the group in 1987 to protect America from "moral pollution" and to "save the lives of innocent children." OSA debuted as an activist force during the 1988 Democratic National Convention in Atlanta, Georgia, where it blockaded entry to several local clinics and a feminist health center. By 1999 the group had recruited an estimated 35,000 members.

In the 1990s, the OSA conducted weeks-long "rescues" at family planning clinics that included the obstructing of client access, protesters chaining themselves to clinic doors, and verbal and physical abuse of staff and patients. OSA also established programs to prepare activists to lead protests in their local communities. Suggested actions included picketing homes of abortion clinic staff, using vehicle license plate numbers to trace physicians' and patients' home addresses, and overloading clinic telephone lines to bar patients from making appointments.

In response to escalating threats and violence, the Freedom of Access to Clinic Entrances Act (FACE) was passed by Congress in 1994. The U.S. Supreme Court ruled in 1999 that pro-life activists had to pay $600,000 in fines and attorneys' fees for blockading New York City abortion clinics in 1989. Shootings of doctors and clinic personnel in Florida, Buffalo, New York, and elsewhere between 1994 and 1998 were attributed to OSA-incited extremists, and the group has since distanced itself from activists who condone violence. In 1998 and 1999 its protests drew fewer participants and less coverage by the press than in prior years. In 1999, Operation Save America expanded its policy agenda to include opposition to homosexual activity and child pornography, with its director, the Reverend Philip (Flip) Benham, vowing to "take the gospel of Jesus Christ to every gate of hell."

Headquarters of the 2,000-member organization is in Dallas, Texas. Philip L. Benham is director.

See also: ABORTION POLICY; RELIGIOUS RIGHT

For Further Information

Diamond, Sara. "No Place to Hide." *Humanist*, September/October 1993, pp. 39–41.

Operation Save America, *http://www.operation saveamerica.org*

P

PARKS, ROSA (1913–). Rosa Parks, by refusing to yield her seat to a white man on a segregated bus on December 1, 1955, sparked the Montgomery, Alabama, bus boycott, and in making her quietly courageous protest marked the beginning of the modern civil rights movement.

Parks was born Rosa Louise McCauley, on February 4, 1913, in Tuskegee, Alabama. Her mother was an elementary school teacher; her father was a carpenter and member of the NATIONAL ASSOCIATION FOR THE ADVANCEMENT OF COLORED PEOPLE (NAACP). She worked as a seamstress and housekeeper after leaving high school. In 1943, as the only woman attending a Montgomery, Alabama, NAACP chapter meeting, she was elected secretary and remained in that post until 1953. One of her tasks was to prepare records of cases of racial discrimination. She also assisted the NAACP Youth Council in recruiting new members.

At the time Parks was arrested for refusing to give up her seat, civil rights activists had been planning to test the authority of the U.S. Supreme Court decision *BROWN V. BOARD OF EDUCATION OF TOPEKA* (1954), ruling that segregation in the public schools was unconstitutional. They wanted to make it clear that the ruling applied to busing and public accommodations as well as the public schools. Rosa Parks's decision to disobey the segregated seating policy was made without knowledge of the planned test. Her refusal provided the pretext for MARTIN LUTHER KING JR. and the Montgomery Improvement Association to organize a citywide boycott of the bus company and to file a federal suit seeking to outlaw segregation of public transportation in Montgomery. King was found guilty of instigating the boycott and given the alternative of paying $1,000 or spending 386 days in jail at hard labor, the same number of days as the boycott. Parks and her husband lost their jobs and were forced to move to Detroit, where they remained active in civil rights. From 1965 until 1988, Parks worked for Democratic senator John Conyers of Michigan.

During her retirement, Parks has committed herself to work with the Rosa and Raymond Parks Institute for Self-Development, an agency she cofounded to help typical inner-city teenagers pursue education and productive lives. Rosa Parks's extensive array of awards and honors reflects Americans' appreciation of her contribution to personal freedom, dignity, and eradication of the blight of racial discrimination.

See also: AFRICAN AMERICAN RIGHTS

For Further Information

Hull, Mary. *Rosa Parks: Civil Rights Leader.* Broomall, PA: Chelsea House, 1994.

Rosa Parks, whose refusal to move to the back of a bus touched off the Montgomery, Alabama, bus boycott, is fingerprinted in February 1956. *AP Photo/Gene Herrick.*

Parks, Rosa, with Jim Haskins. *Rosa Parks: My Story.* New York: Penguin Putnam Books for Young Readers, 1992.

PARTNERSHIP FOR CARING: AMERICA'S VOICES FOR THE DYING. *See* Choice in Dying

PATRIOTIC PARTY. *See* Minutemen

PAUL, ALICE (1885–1977). Alice Paul was one of the leading figures responsible for passage of the Nineteenth Amendment to the U.S. Constitution and the original framer of the Equal Rights Amendment (ERA). She was certain that most of the world's man-made woes could be blamed on the absence and repudiation of the power of women and committed her life to seeing that women gained more control in all matters that affected them.

Paul was born on January 11, 1885, into a wealthy Quaker family in Moorestown, New Jersey, and earned an A.B. degree at Swarthmore College in 1905. Her first encounter with social activism was as a settlement worker in New York City. In 1906, while doing settlement work in England, she became involved with the suffrage movement there and was jailed three times as an agitator. By 1912 she had earned master's and doctoral degrees from the University of Pennsylvania to add to the knowledge she had acquired at the universities of Birmingham and London. Upon her return to the United States, Paul became a central figure in the American suffrage movement. As newly elected chair of the National American Woman Suffrage Association's congressional committee, she organized a protest march of 5,000 women in 1913 in Washington to co-

Alice Paul in 1920. *Library of Congress, Prints and Photographs Division, LC-USZ62–20176 DLC.*

incide with President Woodrow Wilson's inauguration. The women were attacked by the crowd and had to be protected by the police. The publicity benefited the cause, but the march was considered unnecessarily militant by the National American Woman Suffrage Association. Frustrated by the Association's faint-heartedness, Paul founded a new organization, which evolved into the National Woman's Party (1917), in which she played a prominent role for thirty years.

Paul and her followers adopted British suffragists' tactics, engaging in acts of civil disobedience, hunger strikes, and the picketing of governmental buildings, including the White House, until their goal was realized with ratification of the Nineteenth Amendment on August 18, 1920. Although she is perhaps best known today for originating the Equal Rights Amendment in 1923, Paul's accomplishments as a feminist and internation-

alist were myriad. For example, it was due to her initiative that an affirmation of the equality of women and men was included in the preamble to the charter of the United Nations.

In 1942 Paul was elected head of the National Woman's Party and resumed her battle for the Equal Rights Amendment until 1974, when she suffered a stroke and was placed in a nursing home. Although the ERA was defeated in 1982, the battle for its passage continues.

See also: WOMEN'S ISSUES

For Further Information

Lunardini, Christine A. *From Equal Suffrage to Equal Rights: Alice Paul and the National Woman's Party, 1910–1928*. New York: New York University Press, 1988.

PEOPLE FOR THE AMERICAN WAY. People for the American Way (PFAW), a liberal organization founded by Norman Lear in 1980, "defends the values of pluralism, individuality, freedom of thought, expression and religion, a sense of community, and tolerance and compassion for others." Its membership includes leaders of the religious, business, media, and labor communities who are dedicated to work for "a climate in which every citizen has the right to believe, worship, think, and speak freely."

Norman Lear, the writer-producer of the television sitcoms *All in the Family, Maude,* and *Mary Hartman, Mary Hartman,* decided to form PFAW while gathering material for a movie on radio and television evangelicals. Videos of JERRY FALWELL's *Old Time Gospel Hour* and PAT ROBERTSON's *700 Club* awakened him to the need to oppose the 6.5 million member Moral Majority's full-scale attack on the Equal Rights Amendment, abortion, gays and lesbians, the Department of Education, the Strategic Arms Limitation Treaty II, and the separation of church and state clause in the First Amendment to the U.S. Constitution. Lear counterattacked the RELIGIOUS RIGHT with a spot featuring a steelworker on a forklift who

At a March 1979, party for the Equal Rights Amendment, People for the American Way founder Norman Lear and his wife Frances (far left) join NOW president Eleanor Smeal, actress Joan Hackett, and Maureen Reagan, daughter of Ronald Reagan (left to right), in giving a thumbs up. *AP/Wide World Photos.*

spoke of preachers on television telling folks who's a good Christian and who's not, depending on their political beliefs. The tag line was "That's *not* the American way"—a statement that inspired the group's name.

PFAW's founding board included Father Theodore Hesburgh, then president of Notre Dame University, former Senator Harold Hughes of Iowa and former Congresswoman Barbara Jordan of Texas. PFAW mobilized the media, producing op-ed page articles, radio commentaries, and television spots that enabled it to grow quickly and build a substantial financial base. By 1984 the group was able to turn back a constitutional amendment permitting prayer to be part of public school curricula and convinced the Texas Board of Education to repeal a ten-year ruling that evolution be taught as "only one of several explanations of the origins of man-

kind." PFAW defended school boards in censorship cases in Alabama and Tennessee, persuaded publishers to reinstate coverage of evolution in high school biology texts, and helped defeat an amendment by Senator Orrin Hatch that would have prohibited funding of school districts that taught "secular humanism." PFAW was prominently involved in opposing the Supreme Court nominations of Robert Bork and Clarence Thomas.

PFAW and its affiliated PFAW Foundation assumed leadership in the battle to overturn the Communications Decency Act and attempts to mandate library filtering software in Loudon County, Virginia. The group has published an annual report, *Attacks on the Freedom to Learn*, that chronicles attempts at public school library and classroom censorship occurring since 1983. This publication is now online, as are *Right Wing Watch* and *Education Activist*, which monitor the Religious Right's statements in the media and alert members to political activity affecting public schools.

People for the American Way is based in Washington, D.C., and has a current membership of about 300,000. Ralph G. Neas is president.

See also: CONSTITUTIONAL RIGHTS AND CIVIL LIBERTIES PROTECTION; LIBERAL ACTIVISM

For Further Information

People for the American Way, *http://www.pfaw.org*

Sweeney, Louise. "Norman Lear's PAW Takes a Swipe at the New Right." *Christian Science Monitor*, July 23, 1981, p. 14.

Zeller, Shawn. "Ready to Rumble with the Right." *National Journal* 32, no. 8 (February 19, 2000): 564.

PEOPLE FOR THE ETHICAL TREATMENT OF ANIMALS. People for the Ethical Treatment of Animals (PETA), founded in 1980 by Ingrid Newkirk and Alex Pacheco, is the largest animal rights organization in the world. PETA is dedicated to establishing and protecting the rights of all animals, operating under the principle that animals do not exist for people to eat, wear, experiment on, or use for entertainment. According to Newkirk, animals are not inferior to humans, just different.

In 1981, while working as a volunteer at the Institute for Behavioral Research (IBR) in Silver Spring, Maryland, Pacheco videotaped experiments being conducted on monkeys. Supported by veterinarians and primatologists, he disclosed his findings to the Montgomery County police. As a result of the investigation, Dr. Edward Taub, the laboratory's lead scientist, became the first animal experimenter to be charged and convicted of cruelty to animals, although four scientific societies exonerated him and his conviction was overturned.

Use of animals in research labs continues to be one of PETA's four areas of concern. Stating that such research is needless and redundant, the group aims to curtail animal experimentation in medicine. PETA has widely publicized its evidence of alleged maltreatment. Cases it has cited include an investigation of the effects of an osteoporosis drug on beagles in 1997 and a study of pain inflicted by fire ants on fawns in a Texas A&M University experiment conducted in 1999. When eighty-seven razorblade-laced letters were mailed to primate researchers in 1999 by the extremist animal rights group Justice Department, Newkirk commented that "perhaps the mere idea of receiving a nasty missive will allow animal researchers to empathize with their victims for the first time in their lousy careers."

PETA's second area of concern is the procedures used in raising and slaughtering animals for human consumption. The organization disapproves of "factory farms" that purportedly minimize costs while maximizing animals' discomfort and pain. *The Compassionate Cook: A Vegetarian Cookbook* has been produced by PETA to assist people who are trying to kick the meat-eating habit.

Animal furs are the third focus for PETA. Since 1988 the group has staged protests at fashion shows, collected donated fur coats for educational purposes, and recruited celebrities for antifur advertisements. Sales of fur products declined by 50 percent during the 1990s, partially because of the efforts of PETA and other animal rights organizations.

PETA's fourth target is the use of animals for entertainment in circuses, zoos, rodeos, and aquariums, and in hunting and sports events. In 1996 PETA members began protesting at fishing events. Because fish are the most frequently killed fauna for sport or food, PETA is advocating a ban on fishing activities, including catch and release tournaments.

Headquartered in Norfolk, Virginia, the 700,000-member PETA maintains offices in London, Amsterdam, and Stuttgart. As a nonprofit organization, it remains dependent on contributions from its members. PETA operates on a $17 million annual budget and has 120 salaried employees on its staff. Its publications include *The Compassionate Cook, 2001 Shopping Guide for Caring Consumers, PETA News,* a quarterly, and *GRRR!,* PETA's magazine just for kids. The PETA Web site summarizes current news, ongoing investigations, and pending legislation. A directory of addresses and instructions for reporting improper treatment of animals is also provided. Ingrid Newkirk is PETA president.

See also: ANIMAL WELFARE AND RIGHTS

For Further Information

Guither, Harold D. *Animal Rights: History and Scope of a Radical Movement.* Carbondale: Southern Illinois University Press, 1998.

Newkirk, Ingrid. *Free the Animals! The Inside Story of the U.S. Animal Liberation Front and Its Founder, "Valerie."* Chicago: Noble Press, 1992.

People for the Ethical Treatment of Animals, *www.peta-online.org*

Welch, Aimee. "Fur Flies in PETA's Fight for Animals." *Insight on the News*, July 17, 2000, p. 15.

PLANNED PARENTHOOD FEDERATION OF AMERICA.

The Planned Parenthood Federation of America (PPFA) is the world's largest and oldest voluntary family planning organization. Its 129 affiliates operate 875 local health centers across the country, which provide professional medical, education, and counseling services to women, men, and their families. Planned Parenthood "believes in the fundamental right of each individual to manage his or her fertility, regardless of the individual's income, marital status, race, ethnicity, sexual orientation, age, national origin, or residence."

The PPFA had its origins in MARGARET SANGER's birth control clinic, opened in 1916 in Brooklyn, New York. The clinic was immediately shut down for violating New York State's 1873 Comstock Law forbidding discussion and dissemination of birth control. In 1923 Sanger founded the Birth Control Clinical Research Board, and in 1937 the American Medical Association approved birth control as a legitimate medical practice.

Rival factions of the American birth control movement merged in 1939 to form the American Birth Control Federation. The name was changed in 1942 to Planned Parenthood Federation to reflect the group's neutral position on fertility and its importance for men as well as for women. When Alan Guttmacher became PPFA president in 1959, social acceptance of birth control enabled the group to place greater emphasis on service and less on activism. Currently PPFA's promise is being realized nationwide in 875 centers that offer medically supervised reproductive health services and educational programs.

The PPFA's second wave of activism was provoked by Massachusetts and Connecticut laws, still in effect in 1960, that banned the use of contraceptives and the giving of medical advice as to their use. PPFA opened a clinic in New Haven to challenge Connecticut's law, resulting in the conviction of its director and a cooperating physician. The challenge was referred to the U.S. Supreme Court, which ruled the statute unconstitutional in GRISWOLD V. CONNECTICUT (1965) because it violated the First, Third, Fifth, Ninth, and Fourteenth Amendments to the U.S. Constitution. The landmark 1973 ROE V. WADE decision relied heavily on the right to privacy as upheld in *Griswold v. Connecticut.*

In 1976 congressional passage of the Hyde Amendment, legislation limiting the use of Medicaid for abortions for poor women, signaled the resurgence of the RELIGIOUS RIGHT and right-to-life factions. During the administrations of Ronald Reagan and George Bush and the later years of Bill Clinton's presidency, a more conservative Supreme Court also came very close to overruling *Roe v. Wade.* After the 1992 Supreme Court decision in *Planned Parenthood of Southeastern Pennsylvania v. Case* sanctioning restrictions on access to abortion, the PPFA ran full-page ads in the *New York Times* and the *Washington Post* urging Americans to "counter the court's evisceration of *Roe v. Wade* by supporting the Freedom of Choice Act." The Planned Parenthood Ac-

Daniel (left) and Philip Berrigan, leaders of the Plowshares Movement, talk to supporters outside the courthouse in Norristown, Pennsylvania, during the 1981 Plowshare 8 trial of the Berrigans and six other anti-nuclear activists. *AP/Wide World Photos.*

tion Fund was created in 1996 to strengthen the campaign for freedom of choice and to offset right-to-life groups and a conservative Congress from further encroachment on women's right of reproductive choice.

The PPFA has its national headquarters in New York City, a legislative office in Washington, D.C., and regional branches in Atlanta, San Francisco, and Chicago. Gloria Feldt is PPFA president. An estimated 400,000 contributing members serve as activists in behalf of individual reproductive freedom.

See also: ABORTION POLICY; WOMEN'S ISSUES

For Further Information

Planned Parenthood Federation of America, *http://www.plannedparenthood.org/*

Wattleton, Faye. *Life on the Line.* New York: Ballantine Publishing Group, 1996.

PLOWSHARES MOVEMENT. The Plowshares Movement uses civil disobedience to expose and condemn what its members view as "the criminality of nuclear weaponry and corporate piracy" by breaking into defense installations, damaging nuclear components with hammers, tearing up blueprints, and pouring vials of their own blood over military hardware. Begun in the 1980s, Plowshares is an outgrowth of the 1930s CATHOLIC WORKER MOVEMENT. Plowshares is committed to beating swords (nuclear weapons) into plowshares as described in the biblical prophecies of Isaiah 2:4 and Micah 4:3.

The movement started when Catholic priests DANIEL and PHILIP BERRIGAN, along with a divinity student, another priest, a nun, a history professor, a lawyer, and a homemaker, distracted a guard and entered the

General Electric complex in King of Prussia, a Philadelphia suburb, on September 9, 1980. The group, later named the Plowshares 8, found two metal nose cones that protect and guide nuclear warheads to their targets and beat them with hammers, inflicting damage later estimated at $28,000. They also poured blood on the nose cones, desks, work orders, and blueprints. The King of Prussia protest became one of most publicized antiwar incidents in the United States since the Vietnam War.

Even though concern about the nuclear arms race faded during the 1980s, Plowshares clung to its antiwar mission, invading a Martin Marietta weapons plant in 1984 and damaging Pershing 2 missile components. Subsequent Plowshares actions included the illegal boarding of the U.S.S. *Iowa* (1988) and dumping of blood on the *Tucson*, a nuclear-powered submarine (1993). In 1994, Philip Berrigan and three other antiwar activists vandalized a U.S. Air Force fighter-bomber at a North Carolina military base, and again caused damage with blood and hammers. And in May 1997, six Plowshares members, headed by Philip Berrigan, "symbolically destroyed and converted" the U.S.S. *The Sullivans*, a billion-dollar missile-launching destroyer. Between 1980 and 2000, Plowshares conducted more than sixty such actions, some directed by Philip Berrigan from his jail cell.

Inspired by radical theology, Plowshares replaced abhorrence of the Vietnam War with a new fervor directed against nuclear war. Plowshares' status and influence remains minimal, and its members are generally regarded as quixotic extremists. However, with nuclear weaponry coming into the hands of rogue nations, the group could again attract a larger following in the years ahead. Plowshares has an estimated two to three hundred active members with several thousand others assisting the group with housing, food, and transportation.

See also: ANTIWAR/ANTI-NUCLEAR WEAPONS MOVEMENT

For Further Information

Wilcox, Fred A. *Uncommon Martyrs: The Berrigans, the Catholic Left, and the Plowshares Movement.* Reading, MA: Addison-Wesley, 1991.

POOLE, ELIJAH. *See* Muhammad, Elijah

PORT HURON STATEMENT. *See* Hayden, Tom; Students for a Democratic Society

POSSE COMITATUS. Posse Comitatus believes that the sole legitimate governing authority in the United States is vested in self-declared "sheriffs" at the county level who cannot be constrained by state or federal government. Posse members wear badges, claim the right to perform citizen arrests, and refuse to pay state and federal taxes. The group maintains that the U.S. Constitution forbids collection of federal taxes and that the Federal Reserve is part of an evil international Zionist conspiracy.

Henry Beach and William Potter Gale founded Posse Comitatus in 1969. Gale was a retired colonel who had led guerrilla units in the Philippines for General Douglas MacArthur during World War II. Posse is a product of the prolonged depression that has plagued American agriculture and resulted in mortgage foreclosures and farmers being evicted from land they consider their birthright. In keeping with populist history in the Midwest, many farmers have been refusing to pay taxes in a desperate effort to maintain their agrarian lives and to separate themselves from an economy and society that no longer seem to value or support what they do for a living.

Posse gained headline attention in 1983 when one of its leaders, Gordon Kahl, was shot and killed by a federal marshal. Kahl, the Texas coordinator of Posse, and five other members had urged people to stop paying income taxes on a television show aired in 1976. When the authorities caught up with

Kahl in February 1983, his son and dog were shot and a marshal and deputy marshal killed in a gun battle. Four months later Kahl was killed and became a martyr for extremist groups.

Posse Comitatus, in common with the neo-Nazis, the KU KLUX KLAN, skinheads, and Christian Identity, is antigovernment, isolationist, and racist, espouses conspiracy theories, and is prone to violence. Its current director, James P. Wickstrom, proclaims on his group's Web site: "His Kingdom will not be brought into this multicultural cesspool where the Satanic son's and daughter's [*sic*] of Cain are allowed to rule over His True son's and daughter's [*sic*], where homosexuals and perverts have more rights than His TRUE chosen people—the WHITE RACE."

Pastor James P. Wickstrom is director and Pastor August B. Kreiss is information director of Posse Comitatus. The group has about a thousand members.

See also: EXTREMISTS

For Further Information

Dobratz, Betty A., and Stephanie L. Shanks-Meile. *"White Power, White Pride!": The White Separatist Movement in the United States.* New York: Twayne, 1997.

Posse Comitatus, *http://www.posse-comitatus.org*

PRINTZ V. UNITED STATES (521 U.S. 98) (1997). In *Printz v. United States*, the Supreme Court invalidated a key portion of the Brady gun control law, ruling by a 5–4 margin that Congress had overstepped its powers by giving the federal government the authority to require local and state government officials to check the backgrounds of gun buyers. This provision was part of a broader law inspired by James S. Brady, who was disabled in the 1981 assassination attempt on President Ronald Reagan. The law marked the first major effort by Congress to regulate firearms in two decades, and passed in 1993 after seven years of fractious debate and despite the strong opposition of the NATIONAL RIFLE ASSOCIATION. The petitioners, Montana sheriff Jay Printz and Arizona sher-

iff Richard Macke, had challenged the constitutionality of background checks, claiming the procedure was too time-consuming and distracted their deputies from enforcing local laws.

The Printz decision was one of a series handed down by the conservative Court majority comprising Chief Justice William H. Rehnquist and Justices, Sandra Day O'Connor, Antonin Scalia, Anthony M. Kennedy, and Clarence Thomas. The dissenters were Justices John Paul Stevens, David H. Souter, Ruth Bader Ginsburg, and Stephen G. Breyer. Justice Stevens reminded the Court that the Brady Act's legislative history included the statement that

> 15,377 Americans were murdered with firearms in 1992 and that 12,489 of these deaths were caused by handguns. Congress expressed special concern that the level of firearm violence in this country is, by far, the highest among developed nations. The partial solution contained in the Brady Act, a mandatory background check before a handgun may be purchased, has met with remarkable success. Between 1994 and 1996, of approximately 6,600 firearm sales each month to potentially dangerous persons prevented by Brady Act checks, over 70% of the rejected purchasers were convicted or indicted felons. . . . If Congress believes the Brady Act will benefit the people of the nation . . . we should respect both its policy judgment and its appraisal of its constitutional power.

In his majority opinion Justice Scalia wrote, "Congress cannot compel the states to enact or enforce a federal regulatory program."

The case held great significance because of the limits it placed on future laws affecting national social policies. Scores of federal laws, including those affecting the environment, equal employment, public safety, the reporting of missing children, and storage of hazardous waste, would be impacted. The Court narrowly construed federal authority and gave sovereignty to the states. Scalia said, "[I]t is no more compatible with states' independence and autonomy that their police officers be dragooned into administering federal law than it would be compatible with the independence and autonomy of the United States that its officers be impressed into service for the execution of state laws."

In a lengthy and angry dissent, Justice Stevens wrote, "[T]here is not a clause, sentence, or paragraph in the entire text of the Constitution of the United States that supports the proposition that a local police officer can ignore a command contained in a statute enacted by Congress pursuant to an express delegation of power enumerated in Article I."

See also: GUN OWNERSHIP RIGHTS/GUN CONTROLS

For Further Information

Gibeaut, John. "Keeping Federalism Alive." *ABA Journal* 84 (January 1998): 38–39.

PROMISE KEEPERS. Promise Keepers (PK) is an Evangelical Christian organization whose membership is restricted to men and made up almost entirely of conservative Christians. PK had a small beginning in 1990 when seventy-two men gathered in prayer in Boulder, Colorado. In 1991, 4,200 men attended meetings. As of 1997, a total of 2.6 million men (and at least one woman) attended mass rallies across the United States and Canada.

PK's aim is "to unite men through vital relationships to become godly influences in their world." They are enjoined to accomplish this by making seven lifelong promises to Jesus Christ and to one another, fulfilling them in the areas of their personal finances, sex life, and relationship to God. A manifestation of religious revivalism, Promise Keepers was founded in 1990 by Bill McCartney, former head coach of the University of Colorado football team, with the support of FOCUS ON THE FAMILY and other Christian Right groups.

The stated goal of this Christian outreach movement is "to celebrate Biblical manhood and motivate men towards a Christ-like integrity." PK programs include regional stadium rallies, pastors' conferences, one-day leadership training seminars, books and videos, a newsletter, and an Internet Web site. PK appeals as well to conservative women because it encourages their husbands to be responsible and faithful in exchange for "submitting themselves unto their own husbands, as under the Lord" (Ephesians 5:22). The official PK view of homosexuality is that it "violates God's creative design for a husband and wife and that it is a sin," a view based on the biblical texts Leviticus 18:22, Romans 1:24–27, and 1 Corinthians 6:9–10.

At its peak of popularity in 1997, PK held men's rallies in twenty-two major U.S. cities that were attended by more than 1.1 million men, each paying a $60 registration fee. During such rallies the men shout, sing, weep, hug one another, and pray in response to a preacher on stage. The men are then instructed to return home and spread the fundamentalist message to family, friends, and fellow workers. PK's much publicized and spectacularly successful 1997 "Stand in the Gap" rally on the Mall in Washington, D.C., rivaled LOUIS FARRAKHAN's 1995 Million Man March. Ten million dollars was budgeted for this free event, which drew between 500,000 and 700,000 attendees. PK thenceforth stopped charging registration fees for its conferences "in response to a directive from God," and plummeting income soon forced cuts in its staffing and programs. In 1999, 306,700 people attended fifteen events, and fifteen cities were scheduled for rallies in 2000.

Promise Keepers offers a sense of security and personal worth to men who are confused by changing gender roles. It does this by using a mix of New Age marketing and evangelical ideology, and by providing settings where mass hysteria can act as a psychic purgative. Many of the participants report significant improvement in the quality of their family lives, where they rule supreme but are kinder, gentler, and more spiritual "dads" than the distant patriarchs of the 1950s.

Bill McCartney is Promise Keepers president, and ministry headquarters is in Denver, Colorado. Field offices are located in Dallas,

At a September 1998, conference in Colorado Springs, Colorado, Promise Keepers founder Bill McCartney (appearing on the monitor) leads conference attendees in prayer. *AP Photo/Chuck Bigger.*

Indianapolis, Nashville, New York City, Charlotte, Washington, D.C., and Ontario, California. Current size of the organization is unknown.

See also: RELIGIOUS RIGHT

For Further Information

Abraham, Ken. *Who Are the Promise Keepers?* New York: Doubleday, 1997.

McCartney, Bill. *Sold Out: Becoming Man Enough to Make a Difference.* Nashville: Word Publishing, 1997.

Morley, Patrick. "The Next Christian Men's Movement." *Christianity Today*, September 4, 2000, pp. 84–86.

Promise Keepers, *http://www.promisekeepers.org/*

PUBLIC CITIZEN. Public Citizen (PC) is a national nonprofit organization that "fights for corporate and government accountability in order to guarantee the individual's right to safe products, a healthy environment and workplace, fair trade, and clean and safe energy sources." It is also an advocate for campaign finance reform and citizens' civil rights, making its points in every public forum, Congress, the courts, government agencies, and the news media.

PC was founded by RALPH NADER, inspired by his belief that citizens should become watchdogs and prosecutors for the public interest—that they must do what the government may or will not do, enforce laws and regulations. In 1971 Nader sent out a mass mailing that brought in 62,000 contributions and built a solid financial base for the organization. Public Citizen continues to derive its funding from individual supporters and does not accept government or corporate grants.

There are six divisions within Public Citizen. Congress Watch monitors consumer-related legislation on Capitol Hill, exposes campaign financing abuses, and seeks to counter the influence of big money and to return the democratic process to the people. The Health Research Group fights for protection against unsafe foods, drugs, and medical devices, and for universal health insurance. The Litigation Group brings class action suits against government agencies and corporations on behalf of citizens. A fourth group, the Critical Mass Energy Project, lobbies for nuclear safety, affordable energy, and decreased reliance on fossil fuels. Global Trade Watch monitors the North American Free Trade Agreement (NAFTA) and the General Agreement on Tariffs and Trade (GATT). Finally, Buyers Up is a home heating oil cooperative that also produces data on quality and pricing of gasoline sold to consumers.

In December 1999 the protests that upstaged the World Trade Organization (WTO) meetings in Seattle were in large part organized by Public Citizen, which contends that the WTO is "a secretive, undemocratic institution whose rulings undermine critical health, labor, safety and environmental standards throughout the world."

Joan Claybrook, president since 1982, was director of the National Highway Traffic Safety Administration from 1977 to 1981. She implemented the first passive-restraint regulations for automobiles and lobbied for mandatory airbag installation.

Public Citizen has achieved many successes, a sampling of which follows. Its Health Research Group campaigned against silicone gel breast implants and sought criminal prosecution of Dow Corning Corporation. The Critical Mass Energy Project published *Nuclear Lemons*, which drew lawmakers' attention to the nation's fifty unsafest plants and alerted the Nuclear Regulatory Commission to the need for minimum standards for reactors. PC blocked the Nuclear Waste Policy Act, which would have mandated transportation of 100,000 shipments of radioactive waste through forty-three states over a period of thirty years. The group also played a crucial role in the Supreme Court decision to invalidate the line item veto, which would have allowed the president to usurp the role of Congress and violate the separation of powers. PC ordered the U.S. archivist to formulate standards for evaluating and preserving electronic records and compelled agencies to comply with the Electronic Freedom of Information Act.

Public Citizen headquarters is in Washington, D.C. Joan Claybrook is president. Current membership is approximately 120,000. *Public Citizen News*, a bimonthly magazine, is mailed to all members; *Health Letter*, a monthly, is mailed to those with "combination memberships." Popular PC publications include *Worst Pills Best Pills News, The Perils of Nuclear Energy*, and *Corporate Greed*.

See also: LIBERAL ACTIVISM

For Further Information

Congressional Quarterly. *Public Interest Profiles, 1998–1999*. Washington, DC: CQ, 1998.

Conniff, Ruth. "Joan Claybrook." *Progressive*, March 1999, pp. 33–37.

Public Citizen, *http://www.citizen.org*

PUBLIC VOICE FOR FOOD AND HEALTH POLICY.

Established in 1982, Public Voice for Food and Health Policy promoted "a safer, healthier and more affordable food supply," protecting the interests of consumers by encouraging food and agriculture policies designed to improve public health and protect the environment.

Ellen Haas, five-time president of the CONSUMER FEDERATION OF AMERICA, founded Public Voice in response to President Ronald Reagan's policies on food safety, nutrition assistance, and agricultural subsidies. Haas began her activist career while a student at the University of Michigan, protesting the Vietnam War with TOM HAYDEN. In 1973 she founded the Maryland Citizens' Consumer Council, gained national attention by picketing and demonstrating against then Secretary of Agriculture Earl L. Butz's policies, and succeeded in pushing four important consumer protection measures through the Maryland legislature. She was then elected Consumer Federation of America president.

With Haas at its helm, Public Voice became a potent force in reversing federal policies that had relaxed meat and poultry inspection standards and drastically cut food assistance programs during a period of high unemployment. In 1985 and 1986, Public Voice issued reports confirming the severity of America's nutritional problems, the decline in women's health, and the high infant mortality among the rural poor, all made worse by cuts in federal assistance.

Although the group's efforts to curb dairy, sugar, wheat, and peanut price support programs failed, Public Voice was able to take credit for initiating the first mandatory regulation of seafood sold in the United States. The group's forty-four-page report, *The Great American Fish Scandal* (1986), had shown that 24 percent of food poisoning episodes in the United States were caused by chemical contamination and harmful bacteria in seafood. At the time, Commerce Department inspections had become voluntary and Food and Drug Administration checks for problems were limited by severe staff and funding shortfalls. Public Voice, backed by consumers and industry, also succeeded in negotiating a change in federal beef grades that gave more prominence to lean beef and prodded the United States Department of Agriculture (USDA) into increasing the thoroughness of its inspection of all red meats and poultry.

With a staff of fourteen and an impressive track record, Public Voice reached its peak membership of 2,000 in 1992. In May 1993, Haas left Public Voice to serve in President Bill Clinton's administration as assistant secretary of food, nutrition, and consumer services in the USDA, and Mark Epstein took her place as director at Public Voice. That same year, the group conducted a nationwide survey of forty-one school districts and found that a majority served lunches loaded with fat and deficient in fruit and vegetables. Another report showed that grocery stores in inner cities had more expensive, fewer, and inferior food products than their counterparts in high-income neighborhoods.

Public Voice closed down in 1999 after waging a losing battle to block legislation allowing New England and New York State dairy farmers to increase prices as much as 25 percent above federal guidelines, pitting dairy interests against those of the poor. In May 1999, the group announced its absorption within the Consumer Federation of America with CFA to play a bigger role in monitoring food and agricultural policy legislation and regulations, and promoting consumer interests.

Public Voice for Food and Health Policy was headquartered in Washington, D.C., and Art Jaeger was its executive director until appointed assistant director of the Consumer Federation in 1999.

See also: CONSUMER RIGHTS AND SAFEGUARDS; HUMAN HEALTH AND SAFETY

For Further Information

Sinclair, Ward. "Ellen Haas: Bringing a New Approach to the Consumer Movement," *Washington Post*, August 18, 1986, 15.

Weinstein, Michael M. "Bringing Markets to Milk," *New York Times*, Sunday, April 11, 1999, sec. 3, p. 9.

Yablonski, C. R. Hegblom, and A. Fulk. *Guide to Nonprofit Advocacy and Policy Groups.* Washington, DC: Capital Research Center, 1997.

R

RAINBOW/PUSH COALITION. The Rainbow/PUSH Coalition (RPC), "a multiracial, multi-issue, international membership organization," was founded by JESSE JACKSON. Its mission is "to move the nation and the world toward social, racial and economic justice."

In 1996 Jesse Jackson merged Operation PUSH and the National Rainbow Coalition into a single action network, the Rainbow/PUSH Coalition. The roots of RPC extend back to 1966, at which time Jackson launched Operation Breadbasket, the SOUTHERN CHRISTIAN LEADERSHIP CONFERENCE's economic and social justice project. PUSH, established by Jackson in 1971, was organized to upgrade black education, jumpstart black business enterprises, and increase black voter registration. Jackson stressed the value of education as a means for young blacks to attain social status and wealth. On a larger dimension, Jackson envisioned PUSH as a powerful nationwide lobby that would persuade government and industry to grant black Americans economic development protective and rehabilitative assistance equivalent to that given to Germany and Japan at the conclusion of World War II.

PUSH has effectively employed boycotts and hard bargaining, education, and research to open up opportunities for blacks in corporate America. It has successfully challenged broadcast station licenses to ensure equal employment opportunities in the media. Additionally, PUSH has negotiated covenants with major corporations, resulting in a significant increase in minority-owned franchises and car dealerships. PUSH and the Rainbow Coalition were both instrumental in registering millions of voters, and consequently influenced the outcomes of presidential, congressional, Senate, and mayoral elections. Although the Rainbow Coalition failed to generate a sufficiently massive turnout of women, blacks, and other minorities to unseat President Ronald Reagan, Senator Jesse Helms, and other conservative Republicans, it proved effective in the larger cities. Since 1965 New York, Los Angeles, Chicago, Philadelphia, Detroit, and at least six other major cities have elected a black mayor by combining black, Hispanic, and liberal white votes. Statewide elections have exhibited a similar trend.

The new Rainbow/PUSH Coalition is committed to improving the electoral and economic power of African Americans. Jesse Jackson is RPC's president and chief executive officer. Current information on the numbers of its members worldwide is unavailable. RPC has its headquarters in Chicago and a legislative bureau in Washington, D.C. In addition to establishing chapters across the United States, there are plans establish a chapter in Japan to create opportunities for black enterprises in Pacific Rim countries.

See also: AFRICAN AMERICAN RIGHTS

For Further Information

Crockett, Roger O., and others. "Jesse's New Target: Silicon Valley." *Business Week*, July 12, 1999, pp. 111–112.

"National Report." *Jet*, August 30, 1999, p. 4.

Rainbow/PUSH Coalition, *http://www.rainbow push.org*

Reddy, Patrick. "Ten Years Later: How's Jesse's Rainbow Coalition?" *Public Perspective* 6 (November–December 1994): 28–29.

RANDOLPH, A(SA) PHILIP (1889–1979).

Asa Philip Randolph, labor leader and activist, often referred to as the father of the civil rights movement, played a key role in the struggle for black rights from the 1920s until the 1960s. Born on April 15, 1889, in Crescent City, Florida, he attended the local black high school. As a teenager he was humiliated by being denied access to the "whites only" public library. In 1907 he moved north to study economics, philosophy, and science at the City College of New York (CUNY). While at CUNY, Randolph became intrigued by Karl Marx's socialist theories. He concluded that socialism would eliminate the disparities between blacks and whites, and ultimately end racism.

After leaving CUNY, Randolph took various menial jobs and made a first attempt to unionize black workers. He encountered ignorance and apathy among laborers and was repeatedly fired by managers who feared that he would be a troublemaker and incite rebellion against the status quo in the workplace.

In 1916 Randolph and a fellow student, Owen Chandler, joined the Socialist Party and started a journal, *The Messenger*. Initially a supporter of Black Nationalists MARCUS MOSIAH GARVEY JR. and W.E.B. DU BOIS, Randolph aired his opposition to the idea of economic separatism in his new journal. *The Messenger* also included Randolph's controversial statements favoring atheism and so-cialism, and encouraging readers to revolt and take over the government. These insurrectionist views led to the arrest of Randolph and Chandler for espionage, charges subsequently dropped by the judge. The court proceedings generated national publicity for the magazine and its founders. Soon after, both men resigned from the Socialist Party because of its indifference to the plight of black workers.

In 1925 Randolph organized the Brotherhood of Sleeping Car Porters, the first black union to win major successes, including its recognition by the Pullman Company as a legitimate bargaining unit. In 1941, at the beginning of World War II, blacks were excluded from jobs in the defense industry. Randolph threatened to lead a march on Washington to demand equal employment opportunities for blacks and the banning of racial segregation in housing and in the armed forces. President Franklin D. Roosevelt reluctantly decided to negotiate with Randolph rather than deal with the negative publicity that would be generated by the march. He acceded to Randolph's demands by establishing the Fair Employment Practices Committee, issuing orders mandating fair housing practices, and making it illegal for defense contractors to refuse to hire blacks. Later, in 1948, Randolph met with President Harry S. Truman to request an end to segregation in the military. Truman responded by issuing Executive Order 9981, enforcing integration in the armed forces.

During the civil rights movement of the 1960s, Randolph helped organize the March on Washington for Jobs and Freedom (August 28, 1963), the biggest demonstration in the history of Washington, D.C. Although President John F. Kennedy requested that the march be postponed or cancelled, over a quarter of a million people came to the Capitol to show their support for a new civil rights bill. It was during this event that MARTIN LUTHER KING JR. gave his memorable "I have a dream" speech.

Randolph was awarded the Medal of Freedom by President Lyndon B. Johnson in 1964, and later that same year Randolph es-

Asa Philip Randolph (center), president of the Brotherhood of Sleeping Car Porters, meets with President Lyndon Johnson and National Urban League Executive Secretary Whitney Young at the White House in August 1965. *AP/Wide World Photos.*

tablished an institute to train blacks for skilled jobs. A. Philip Randolph died in 1979 in New York City at the age of ninety.

See also: AFRICAN AMERICAN RIGHTS; LA-BOR ISSUES

For Further Information

Patterson, Lillie. *A. Philip Randolph: Messenger for the Masses.* New York: Facts on File, 1996.

Pfeffer, Paula F. *A. Philip Randolph, Pioneer of the Civil Rights Movement.* Baton Rouge: Louisiana State University Press, 1990.

REED, RALPH (1961–). Ralph Reed transformed the CHRISTIAN COALITION from a minor footnote in the news into a major, 1.9 million strong force in Republican politics, backed up by a $25 million operating budget. Over a seven-year period (1991–1997), Reed's Christian Coalition was gen-

erally acknowledged to be the most powerful force in Republican politics.

Born June 24, 1961, in Portsmouth, Virginia, Reed entered the University of Georgia at Athens in 1979 and immediately became active in campus Republican politics. After earning a B.A. in history in 1983, he moved to Washington, D.C., and joined the National College Republicans, eventually becoming the organization's executive director. In September 1983 Reed joined the Evangelical Assembly of God in Camp Springs, Maryland, and became a born-again Christian.

In 1984 Reed enrolled in Students for America (SFA) and campaigned to reelect Senator Jesse Helms of North Carolina. SFA is a conservative group with an evangelical tint, according to Reed. Over the next four years, Reed advised over twenty congressional and gubernatorial candidates on campaign strategy. He completed his formal education at Emory University in 1991. In his doctoral dissertation, he criticized church-related colleges that had deserted their chartered commitments to Christian values in order to attract increased endowments.

In 1989 he met televangelist PAT ROBERTSON at a dinner honoring the inauguration of President George Bush. Robertson was impressed by Reed's organizational and political skills and immediately hired him as executive director of the Christian Coalition. Reed sees his mission as promoting the "family" agenda at every level of government from local school board to Congress and the presidency, working for the election of conservative Republicans nationwide who will enact legislation that favors traditional Christian values. He lobbied aggressively for former Speaker of the House Newt Gingrich and the "Contract with America" while promoting his own parallel "Contract with the American Family."

Reed is pro-life, pro-family, and pro–free enterprise, and he favors erasure of constitutional barriers to prayer in the public schools, tax relief for families with children attending parochial schools, displacement of welfare by workfare, and drastic reductions in federal spending. Reed has assisted in the successful campaigns of conservative candidates, including Senator Richard C. Shelby (Alabama) and former Representative Frank Cremeans (Ohio), along with several dozen other Republican incumbents and challengers. His role for conservative Republicans is analogous to that of political consultant and campaign manager James Carville for the Democrats. Under Reed's direction, the Christian Coalition claimed considerable credit for the Republican sweep of the 1994 midterm congressional election and Robert Dole's presidential nomination in 1996.

In 1997 Reed left the leadership of the Christian Coalition to work directly in electoral politics. Returning to Alabama, he established Century Strategies, a Republican consulting firm. His intention is to create a team of hundreds of candidates who will run

for positions at every level of government. It is expected that his influence on political outcomes as an independent citizen activist will be significant.

See also: RELIGIOUS RIGHT

For Further Information

Gerson, Michael J. "Christian Coalition in Unprecedented Crisis." *U.S. News & World Report*, February 16, 1998, pp. 33–34.

Reed, Ralph. *Active Faith: How Christians Are Changing the Soul of American Politics.* New York: The Free Press, 1996.

Watson, Justin. *The Christian Coalition: Dreams of Restoration, Demands for Recognition.* New York: St. Martin's Press, 1997.

RELIGIOUS RIGHT. The Religious Right takes a political position that seeks to minimize the role of the federal government in the economy and to reestablish moral order in a culture that it believes has become overly secular and permissive. In the United States, the Religious or New Christian Right is rooted primarily in theologically conservative white Protestant religious groups. The New Christian Right emerged in the late 1970s and by the mid-1990s had become a central part of the American conservative establishment and a potent force in American politics.

In the nineteenth century Alexis de Tocqueville noted the large number of American churchgoers and predicted that churches were much more likely to be the focus of civic life than in other countries. For example, in Europe, the political parties and unions, not the churches, take the lead in mobilizing citizens' civic action.

American evangelical churches are energized by a distinctive kind of Protestant moralism. Evangelicalism stresses the importance of individual salvation, to be gained through a born-again experience and a personal relationship with God, and of Christianizing and reforming a sinful world. Evangelicals cherish the idea of America as a "New Israel," destined to play a special role in the divine design for humankind.

During the early twentieth century, fundamentalism arose as a foil against liberal Protestants who had decided that the Bible had to be interpreted in the light of modern science and contemporary societal contexts. The fundamentalists defended a literal reading of the Bible and fought to block the teaching of Darwin's theory of evolution in the public schools. The AMERICAN COUNCIL OF CHRISTIAN CHURCHES (ACCC), formed in 1941, promoted strict fundamentalism. Communism and liberalism were viewed by the ACCC as the new archenemies, so grassroots members urged the use of nuclear weapons to ensure total victory in Vietnam and opposed diplomatic recognition of the People's Republic of China. In 1948 Billy James Hargis founded the Christian Crusade, which by 1973 was operating a network of religious and educational institutions preaching against communism.

The Religious Right that emerged after the mid-1970s believed that America's problems stemmed from secular humanism in government, the media, the schools, and other cultural institutions. Its adherents believed that the nation had become awash in social problems because denial of God had snapped its moral moorings and it was foundering on the shoals of sin. These shoals included the loss of family cohesion, feminism, ROE V. WADE (1973), homosexuality, affirmative action, crime, drug use, promiscuity, and generally decadent behavior. As antidotes, the Religious Right advocated overturning *Roe v. Wade*, outlawing abortion, limiting gay rights, and legalizing and encouraging of religious activities in the schools and other public places. Capitalism and a virtuous America should be extolled in school curricula and male-centered families with one primary wage earner, the father, promoted.

The following Religious Right leaders and organizations endorse the preceding views: PHYLLIS SCHLAFLY, founder of the EAGLE FORUM, best known for her role in the defeat of the Equal Rights Amendment; ANITA BRYANT, leader of the first campaign against gay rights, launched in Dade County, Florida in 1976; the AMERICAN FAMILY ASSOCIA-

TION, which focuses mostly on combating profanity, adultery, homosexuality, other amoral behavior, and foul language used on television; and JAMES DOBSON, founder of FOCUS ON THE FAMILY, a national organization that deploys magazines, radio, and television to inspire evangelical Christians to assume an active pro-family role in the political process.

In the late 1970s, the Religious Right extended its reach via electronic ministries by using cable and satellite television and direct mail technology. Evangelicals became very active politically, voting in large numbers and lobbying vigorously for their causes. JERRY FALWELL established the Moral Majority, Inc., in 1979 and used media to influence the votes of more than 14 million people in the 1980 election. That same year Beverly LaHaye started CONCERNED WOMEN FOR AMERICA as a conservative alternative to the NATIONAL ORGANIZATION FOR WOMEN.

Founded in 1981, the FAMILY RESEARCH COUNCIL has been directed by Gary Bauer since 1994. CITIZENS FOR EXCELLENCE IN EDUCATION, established in 1983, aims to save Christian children in the public schools from "atheism, homosexuality, brainwashing, and humanistic literature." PAT ROBERTSON founded the CHRISTIAN COALITION in 1989 as a grassroots organization that would stem moral decay in government. The Christian Coalition distributed a total of 78 million voter guides in the 1994 and 1996 elections and influenced the political balance of power within the U.S. Congress. In 1989 RALPH REED was hired as executive director of the Christian Coalition and quickly transformed it into a 1.9 million strong force of conservative Republicans.

The PROMISE KEEPERS, a manifestation of male religious revivalism that celebrates biblical manhood, was started in 1990 with financial support from Focus on the Family. Family Friendly Libraries, founded in 1995 by Karen Jo Gounaud, combats the allegedly anti-family policies of the American Library Association (ALA). Family Friendly Libraries claims that "the ALA not only seeks to influence the field of librarianship, but their official *Manual of Public Policy Positions* states that their membership is expected to support the ERA, the concept of a nuclear freeze, gay rights, opposition to mandatory AIDS testing, national health insurance, and minors' access to sexual resources both in and out of the library." Further, they claim that any master's of library science program "is in violation of [ALA] standards if school policy includes any discrimination against homosexuality or other 'lifestyles' or orientations.'"

As the twentieth century concluded, the Religious Right had formed a solid conservative bloc and the number of coalitions and groups dedicated to cleansing the secular culture was growing. Abortion, the public schools, gay marriage, gun control, humanism, and open access to information in libraries and on the Internet were all being subjected to increasing scrutiny and attack.

For Further Information

Family Friendly Libraries, *http://www.fflibraries. org/*

Heineman, Kenneth J. *God Is a Conservative: Religions, Politics, and Morality in Contemporary America*. New York: New York University Press, 1998.

Martin, William C. *With God on Our Side: The Rise of the Religious Right in America*. New York: Bantam Books, 1996.

Wilcox, Clyde. *Onward Christian Soldiers? The Religious Right in American Politics*. Boulder, CO: Westview Press, 1996.

REUTHER, WALTER PHILIP (1907–1970). Liberal social reformer and leader of the United Auto Workers (AUW) for twenty-four years, Walter Philip Reuther was born on September 1, 1907, in Wheeling, West Virginia. He left school at age sixteen to work as an apprentice at the Wheeling Steel Company, but was fired for mobilizing a protest against Sunday and holiday work. Moving to Detroit in 1926, he was hired by the Briggs Manufacturing Company, then General Motors, and finally Ford. During this time he completed high school and took night classes at Wayne State University. In 1931 Ford dismissed him because of his un-

ion activism. Reuther then traveled to Europe, the Far East, and the Soviet Union, working for a brief time in a Ford-built plant in Gorki, an industrial center in Soviet Russia.

Upon his return to Detroit, Reuther was determined to increase labor's ability to deal with antiunion automobile plant management and to act as a responsible force for social change. He helped organize AUW Local 174, pumping up its membership from 78 to 30,000 within a single year, and establishing himself as the lead figure in the UAW, serving as president from 1946 until 1970. In 1936 he organized the first of several UAW sit-down strikes that, in spite of considerable violence and threats to his life, resulted in recognition of the union by GM and Chrysler in 1937, with Ford following suit in 1941.

In November 1945 Reuther ordered the 200,000 UAW members to strike against GM, and by March 1946 the union had won major wage concessions and improvements in working conditions. In 1948 Reuther was shot in a bungled assassination attempt and never recovered the full use of his left arm.

After being elected president of the Congress of Industrial Organizations (CIO) in 1952, Reuther negotiated a merger between the CIO and the American Federation of Labor. Sixteen years later, because of harsh disagreements with more conservative AFL-CIO head George Meany, Reuther took the UAW out of the AFL-CIO, and formed the Alliance for Labor Action with the Teamsters Union in 1969.

Reuther was an active civil rights promoter in Detroit, writing numerous articles and a book, with Edith Green, titled *Education and the Public Good*. A pragmatic, incorruptible radical and idealist, he created a strong alliance of union members, middle class liberals, and African Americans, and in 1947 received a CIO award for furthering the fight against racial discrimination. A skillful negotiator, he led the way in winning pensions, pay increases tied to the cost of living and productivity, profit sharing, and early retirement benefits for his union. He died in an airplane crash near Pellston, Michigan, on May 10, 1970.

See also: LABOR ISSUES

For Further Information

Carew, Anthony. *Walter Reuther*. New York: St. Martin's Press, 1993.

Lichtenstein, Nelson. *The Most Dangerous Man in Detroit: Walter Reuther and the Fate of American Labor*. New York: Basic Books, 1995.

ROBERTSON, MARION GORDON (PAT) (1930–).

Marion Gordon "Pat" Robertson, American televangelist, businessman, and politician was born on March 22, 1930, in Lexington, Virginia. His father, Absalom Willis Robertson, a conservative Democrat, served in Congress for thirty-four years, first in the House and later in the Senate, where he chaired the Banking and Commerce Committee. His mother was a devout born-again Christian who urged her son to stay out of politics and give himself to Jesus Christ. The young Robertson initially followed in his father's tracks, attending Washington and Lee College and graduating from Yale Law School. In 1956 he headed up the Richmond County Staten Island Adlai Stevenson for President Committee.

After he met Cornelius Vanderbreggen, a mystical Dutch evangelist, Robertson's life changed. He found God and enrolled in the New York Theological Seminary. In 1961 he was ordained a Southern Baptist clergyman. Returning to his roots in Tidewater, Virginia, he bought a deserted, bankrupt UHF television station and started up his Christian Broadcasting Network (CBN). Monthly operating costs for the new station were approximately $7,000, which he raised by asking 700 members of his audience to each contribute $10 per month. Thus was born the 700 Club, a venture that pioneered interactive television. By 1977 CBN was transmitting its programs by satellite to the sixty top markets in the United States. Soon CBN was beaming nationwide programs that featured religious conversions, miraculous healing, and discussions of the evils of abortion, secular humanism, sexual deviation, and women's liberation.

In 1977 Robertson founded Regent University, a fully accredited institution offering graduate degrees in law, journalism, government, religion, and other subjects. He serves as chancellor of the school, which has an enrollment of nearly 1,800 students. He also owns profitable businesses in Asia, the Middle East, and Africa, a four-star hotel, and a jet chartering service.

Between 1977 and 1982, members of the 700 Club received Pat Robertson's *Perspective*, a newsletter that provided information on U.S. fiscal policy, foreign trade, and investment trends. In 1981 Robertson cofounded the Freedom Council, a nonprofit grassroots foundation established to support and groom evangelical Christians for political action. Later the Internal Revenue Service determined that Robertson's Christian Broadcasting Company had contributed a total of $8.5 million in 1985 and 1986 to the Freedom Council to support the Robertson 1988 Republican presidential campaign.

In 1986 Robertson disbanded the group and started up two other related groups, the Committee for Freedom and the National Perspectives Institute, along with the American Center for Law and Justice, a Christian civil rights group that opposes positions taken by liberal legal centers. Robertson resigned as a Southern Baptist minister in 1987, prior to announcing his candidacy for the U.S. presidency. Although he failed in his attempt to win the Republican Party nomination for president, he continues to mold policy making through his leadership of the CHRISTIAN COALITION. It is generally conceded that Robertson and his followers were key players in the so-called Republican Revolution of 1994, taking Christian evangelicalism from a remote and nonpartisan, stagnant backwater and placing it in the mainstream of public political engagement. An estimated 70 million guides educating voters about candidates' positions on issues of interest to religious conservatives were distributed through houses of worship, over the

700 Club co-host Pat Robertson speaks at a press conference at the CBN studio in Virginia Beach, Virginia, in February 1998. *AP Photo/The Virginian-Pilot/Bill Tiernan.*

Internet, and elsewhere during the 2000 national election.

In 1997 Rupert Murdoch bought Robertson's International Family Entertainment (IFE), a TV channel he had formed in 1990, for $1.9 billion. IFE's principal business had been the Family Channel, a satellite-delivered cable television network with 63 million U.S. subscribers.

Robertson is the author of ten books, including *The Secret Kingdom, Answers to 1,000 of Life's Most Probing Questions*, and *The New World Order*, each of which became the number one religious book in America during its year of publication. His most recent book, *The End of the Age*, is an apocalyptic novel.

See also: RELIGIOUS RIGHT

For Further Information

Boston, Robert. *The Most Dangerous Man in America? Pat Robertson and the Rise of the Christian Coalition.* Amherst, MA: Prometheus, 1996.

The Christian Broadcasting Network, *http://www.cbn.org*

Harrell, David Edwin, Jr. *Pat Robertson: A Personal, Religious, and Political Portrait.* San Francisco: Harper and Row, 1987.

Robertson, Pat. *The End of the Age.* Nashville, TN: Word, 1995.

ROE V. WADE (410 U.S. 113) (1973). The 1973 U.S. Supreme Court decision that legalized abortion was one of the most stunning, far-reaching, and controversial decisions the high court ever made. *Roe v. Wade* involved a pregnant woman's challenge to a Texas law that prohibited abortions except to save a mother's life. Because "Jane Roe's" (pseudonym for Norma McCorvey) pregnancy was not life-threatening, she could not get a legal abortion in Texas and was advised to seek one out of state. Lacking the money to do this, and on advice of legal counsel, she went to court to challenge the constitutionality of the Texas law.

The court ruled in its 7–2 decision that state abortion laws were a violation of a woman's right to privacy and struck down the existing state abortion laws. Justice Harry Blackmun recognized the gravity of the decision, stating that the Court acknowledged its "awareness of the sensitive and emotional nature of the abortion controversy, of the vigorous opposing views, even among physicians, and of the deep and seemingly absolute convictions that the subject inspires. One's philosophy, one's experiences, one's exposure to the raw edges of human experience, one's religious training, one's attitudes toward life and family, and their values, and the moral standards one establishes and seeks to observe are all likely to influence and to color one's thinking and conclusions about abortion." He then said that the right of privacy "is broad enough to encompass a woman's decision whether or not to terminate her pregnancy." He grounded the decision on the U.S. Constitution's Fourteenth Amendment concept of personal liberty and on the Ninth Amendment's reservation of rights to the people. In summary, the Court ruled that a woman's right to abortion was constitutionally protected.

The Court further ruled that recognition be given to the claim that as long as at least potential life is involved, the state may assert interests beyond the protection of the pregnant woman alone. In the first trimester, the state could not intervene in any way to regulate abortion. In the second trimester, it could intervene to protect the woman's health; and in the third trimester, or at the approximate point of viability, when the fetus presumably has the capability of meaningful life outside the mother's womb, the state could intervene to protect it.

Roe v. Wade galvanized the right to life movement and the RELIGIOUS RIGHT because they found the decision abhorrent on moral and religious grounds. Abortion con-

cerns nothing less than the value society places on human life, and those who oppose abortion contend that the sanctity of human life from conception must be held collectively, that one standard must apply to everyone and to all circumstances. In contrast, freedom of choice proponents believe that the choice should only be made by the individual woman.

See also: ABORTION POLICY; EXTREMISTS; WOMEN'S ISSUES

For Further Information

Faux, Marian. *Roe v. Wade: Marking the Twentieth Anniversary of the Landmark Supreme Court Decision that Made Abortion Legal*. New York: Penguin Group, 1989.

Romaine, Deborah S. *Roe v. Wade: Abortion and the Supreme Court*. San Diego: Lucent Books, 1998.

Solinger, Rickie, ed. *Abortion Wars: A Half Century of Struggle, 1950–2000*. Berkeley: University of California Press, 1998.

ROOSEVELT, ELEANOR (1884–1962).

Diplomat, civil rights activist, teacher, and precedent-shattering first lady, Eleanor Roosevelt was already well known at the time her husband, Franklin Delano Roosevelt, was elected governor of New York in 1928. She ultimately became one of the twentieth century's most civic-minded and universally admired American women.

Eleanor Roosevelt was born on October 11, 1884, in New York City to a life of genteel privilege. Her parents died during her childhood, and she was sent to England for schooling. In 1905 she married a distant cousin, Franklin Delano Roosevelt, the future thirty-second president of the United States. Over the next decade she gave birth to six children, one of whom died in infancy.

Active since World War I in advocating equal rights for women, and better working conditions in factories, and in improving facilities for the mentally ill, Eleanor Roosevelt served as her husband's "legs" after he suffered a crippling attack of polio in 1921.

Eleanor Roosevelt c. 1933. *Library of Congress, Prints and Photographs Division, LC-USZ62–25812 DLC.*

She spoke in his place, campaigned for Democratic candidates during his run for governor of New York, and, serving as his eyes and ears, kept him linked to his constituency and to political happenings in the field. She also visited and reported on conditions in state hospitals, prisons, and nursing homes.

Roosevelt was a pioneer in expanding her sphere of action as an independent political first lady, holding weekly press conferences and launching a nationally syndicated newspaper column, "My Day," that by 1939 was dealing with public affairs as well as women's issues. At a time when such advocacy was rare and required immense courage, she championed minority rights. When she resigned from the Daughters of the American Revolution (DAR) because of its refusal to permit the world-renowned African American singer Marian Anderson to use Constitution Hall in Washington for a concert, she publicly condemned the DAR's racist policy in "My Day." This was followed by a White House invitation to Anderson to sing on the steps of the Lincoln Memorial in a concert attended by 75,000 people. Roosevelt's assertive espousal of liberal causes earned her personal insults, accusations of being a communist sympathizer, and taunts from Republicans who called her a Bolshevik.

Although she was a pacifist, Roosevelt supported the war effort when America entered World War II. She traveled to the war fronts, logging 23,000 miles in the summer of 1943 while visiting field hospitals in Australia and the South Pacific. After Franklin Roosevelt's death in 1945, President Harry S. Truman appointed her as a U.S. delegate to the United Nations. As chair of the UN Commission on Human Rights she assisted in the drafting and adoption of the UN Universal Declaration of Human Rights in 1948. When Republican Dwight D. Eisenhower became president in 1952, Roosevelt resigned from her UN post and for the next decade traveled throughout the world as a leading spokesperson for civil rights and nuclear disarmament. Eleanor Roosevelt died in New York City on November 7, 1962.

As a public figure Eleanor Roosevelt still remains controversial, her strong stands on civil rights and other social issues making her many enemies—even as millions vote her "most admired American woman" year after year.

See also: AFRICAN AMERICAN RIGHTS; WOMEN'S ISSUES

For Further Information

Black, Allida M. *Casting Her Own Shadow: Eleanor Roosevelt and the Shaping of Postwar Liberalism.* New York: Columbia University Press, 1996.

Cook, Blanche Wiesen. *Eleanor Roosevelt.* New York: Viking, 1992.

Freedman, Russell. *Eleanor Roosevelt: A Life of Discovery*. New York: Clarion Books, 1993.

Roosevelt, Eleanor. *Courage in a Dangerous World: The Political Writings of Eleanor Roosevelt*. Edited by Allida M. Black. New York: Columbia University Press, 1999.

RUDD, MARK (1947–). The campus radical responsible for the 1968 student activist takeover of Columbia University, Mark Rudd was born June 2, 1947, in Newark, New Jersey. His family moved to Maplewood, where his father built up a flourishing real estate business. In high school, Mark read Allen Ginsberg, Lawrence Ferlinghetti, and the *Village Voice*, and upon entering Columbia University, linked up with campus radicals, including John Jacobs, a fellow student who was a member of the Progressive Labor Party, a splinter faction of the American Communist Party.

In 1964 Rudd joined members of the Columbia Independent Committee on Vietnam in an antiwar march down New York City's Fifth Avenue. During his sophomore year, radicals started confronting Columbia over its secret affiliation with the Institute for Defense Analysis (IDA) and on-campus recruiting by the CIA and the U.S. Marine Corps. In February 1968 Rudd led a demonstration against campus recruiters from Dow, the napalm manufacturer, and was elected chair of the Columbia chapter of the STUDENTS FOR A DEMOCRATIC SOCIETY (SDS). He read Regis Debray's book on the Cuban revolution extolling the theory of *foco*, the ability of small vanguard groups to win people over to radicalization, and began envisioning SDS as a guerrilla organization. During the previous summer, Rudd had visited Cuba, toured a collective farm, and chatted with intellectuals. He adopted Che Guevara as a hero and rhapsodized over Castro's "extremely humanist government" in the campus paper.

In spring 1968 Rudd led SDS in a rally protesting construction of a new gymnasium on the site of a public park that separated the elite school from the black neighborhood it abutted. Planned low-income housing would be displaced by a facility for faculty, staff, and student athletes. Rudd exploited Columbia's public relations blunder and quickly made a name for himself. On April 23, 1968, the Battle of Morningside Heights was joined. Students tore down the fence at the gymnasium site and then took over Hamilton Hall, barricaded it, and held a dean hostage in his office. The next day the dean was freed, but by then other student platoons had seized the Low Library, which housed administrative offices, the mathematics building, and three other halls. President Grayson Kirk's office was trashed and classes were canceled as mobs of student rebels took control of the campus.

The Columbia takeover made national news, with a photo of a student at Kirk's mahogany desk puffing one of his cigars outraging many Americans but delighting radicals. On April 30 police cleared the buildings, removed 524 students, and arrested 692 people. Over 100 were injured. Rudd was charged with inciting a riot and trespassing, and was expelled from the university, but the SDS had won several concessions and set a precedent. The gymnasium was not built, the blanket ban on demonstrations was rescinded, Columbia dissolved its relationship with the IDA, new disciplinary procedures were adopted, and President Kirk resigned. Thousands of other students were stirred up by seeing their counterparts being beaten up on television. Within a year, Berkeley, Brown, Chicago, Harvard, and other universities were experiencing student rebellions. By 1969 the student movement had split into factions. These included the Revolutionary Youth Movement, the BLACK PANTHER PARTY, SDS, the Progressive Labor Party, and others. Rudd, along with Bernadine Dohrn, split off from SDS and formed the WEATHERMAN, a group committed to violent militancy.

In 1970 Rudd left the Weatherman and went underground until 1977, at which time he resurfaced in the district attorney's office in New York City. All federal felonies against him were dropped. He married, and moved to New Mexico in 1978. After earning an education degree he took a job teaching remedial mathematics to junior college students. Currently Rudd lives with his second wife in Albuquerque.

See also: EXTREMISTS

For Further Information

Gross, Michael. *My Generation: Fifty Years of Sex, Drugs, Rock, Revolution, Glamour, Greed, Valor, Faith, and Silicon Chips*. New York: Cliff Street/HarperCollins, 2000.

Jacobs, Ron. *The Way the Wind Blew: A History of the Weather Underground*. New York: Verso, 1997.

S

SANE, THE NATIONAL COMMITTEE FOR A SANE NUCLEAR POLICY. The National Committee for a Sane Nuclear Policy (SANE) was conceived in 1957 to promote the international control of nuclear weapons and to eliminate testing worldwide. Veteran peace activists persuaded Norman Cousins, then editor of the *Saturday Review*, and Clarence Picket of the American Friends Service Committee, to serve as co-chairmen. At the time of SANE's formation, the U.S.-Soviet arms race was raising the specter of instant annihilation. This anxiety was reinforced by governmental plans for civil defense, discussions regarding bomb shelters, reports of radioactive fallout from bomb tests, and public viewing of such films as *On the Beach* and *Dr. Strangelove*.

SANE kicked off its public relations with a full-page advertisement in the *New York Times* featuring Dr. Benjamin Spock and warning that "we are facing a danger unlike any danger that has ever existed." Linus Pauling, MARTIN LUTHER KING JR., ELEANOR ROOSEVELT, Albert Schweitzer, and Hollywood actors Marlon Brando, Henry Fonda, Kirk Douglas, and Gregory Peck were early SANE sponsors.

By 1958 SANE had 25,000 members, and in 1960 it mounted a rally in Madison Square Garden that drew over 20,000 people. John F. Kennedy's election in 1960 led to reduced emphasis on nuclear weaponry despite the Berlin Wall and the Cuban missile crisis. SANE became a major force stimulating creation of the U.S. Arms Control and Disarmament Agency in 1961, and a year later the Limited Test Ban Treaty was signed, prohibiting atmospheric testing of nuclear weapons.

With the onset of the Vietnam War, the drive for disarmament was deferred and arguments between liberal and radical factions concerning tactics flared up within SANE. Throughout the 1970s, the group lobbied for arms control and opposed the B-1 bomber, Trident submarine, and Cruise missile programs. After the Vietnam War, SANE membership dwindled to 6,000. In 1976 David Cortright came in and intensified SANE's efforts, urging ratification of the SALT II treaty, working to block funds for the B-1 bomber and the MX missile system, attempting to shift the focus of nuclear energy research and development from military to nonmilitary applications, and opposing President Ronald Reagan's interventions in Central America.

Meanwhile, Randall Forsberg launched the Nuclear Freeze campaign, advocating a bilateral verifiable freeze in the production, testing, and deployment of nuclear weaponry. In 1982 anti-nuclear sentiment peaked, with over half of the nation's religious leaders endorsing a freeze, and supportive resolutions being passed by eleven state legislatures and in communities coast to coast. The campaign climaxed in New York City on June 12, 1982, as the UN General Assembly was convening a special session on disarmament. An estimated 1 million people marched outside the UN in the largest demonstration in American history. Forsberg's group then merged with SANE to form SANE/ FREEZE, which briefly attracted a membership of 150,000. The organization's purpose was undercut when, in his second term, President Reagan co-opted its mission by calling for deep reductions in nuclear weapons stockpiles in summit meetings with Soviet leader Mikhail Gorbachev in 1985 and 1986. Media coverage ceased, and by 1988 the newly combined organization had expired.

See also: ANTIWAR/ANTI–NUCLEAR WEAPONS MOVEMENT

For Further Information

Boyer, Paul. "From Activism to Apathy: The American People and Nuclear Weapons, 1963–1980." *Journal of American History* 70 (March 1984): 821–844.

Cortright, David. *Peace Works: The Citizen's Role in Ending the Cold War*. Boulder, CO: Westview Press, 1993.

SANGER, MARGARET (1879–1966).
Margaret Sanger was the twentieth century's first and most important activist in the area of birth control and reproductive health. Born Margaret Louise Higgins on September 14, 1879, in Corning, New York, Sanger was the sixth of eleven children. Her father, an unsuccessful stonecutter, militant freethinker, and labor rights advocate, constantly debated social issues and philosophy; her mother remained faithful to her Irish Catholic upbringing and struggled to raise her large family. From the onset, Sanger was molded by her parents' conflicting attitudes of defiance and compliance with societal norms.

Sanger attended Claverack College and subsequently took a teaching position in New Jersey until forced to return home to care for her ailing mother. She then entered a nurse-training program at the White Plains, Hospital in New York, but this was interrupted by bouts of tuberculosis. In 1902 she married William Sanger, a young architect. The couple had three children within the first six years of their marriage.

In 1910 the Sangers moved to Manhattan, joined the Socialist Party, and became active in the labor movement. Margaret Sanger then met anarchist and feminist Emma Goldman, who was advocating sexual freedom and urging women to break loose from the bonds of marriage and motherhood. Sanger contributed two series of articles on health to the woman's page of the socialist newspaper *Call*, "What Every Mother Should Know" and "What Every Girl Should Know." Because her articles mentioned venereal disease, they were banned as obscene by postal authorities.

As a midwife, Sanger dealt daily with the misery, helplessness, and frequent deaths suffered by poverty-stricken pregnant women. On maternity assignments, labor would often terminate before the doctor arrived and she would perform the delivery herself. She witnessed many young mothers prematurely burnt out, depressed, and distraught by seeing their children undernourished and poorly clad. While Sanger was nursing one mother back to health after a self-induced abortion, the doctor came in to examine the patient. When the young mother asked the doctor to provide something to prevent further pregnancies, the doctor advised her to tell her husband to sleep on the roof. Sanger glanced quickly at the woman and through her sudden tears could see stamped on her face an expression of total despair. When, three months later, the woman died after another self-induced abortion, Sanger realized that her work was only palliative and would not erase the misery she witnessed. Her search for current medical data took her to France, where she gathered information from doctors, midwives, pharmacists, and mothers. She incorporated these findings in her book, *Family Limitation*. After returning to New

York, she was arrested repeatedly for publishing materials on contraception.

In 1914 Sanger founded the National Birth Control League, precursor to the PLANNED PARENTHOOD FEDERATION OF AMERICA, and launched a magazine, *Woman Rebel*, bearing the slogan "No gods; no masters!" Included in the premier issue was the following list of seven conditions that would justify birth control: (1) either spouse has a transmittable disease; (2) the wife suffers a temporary infection of the lungs, heart, or kidneys, the cure for which might be retarded in pregnancy; (3) the mother is physically unfit; (4) the mother already has subnormal children; (5) the parents are adolescents; (6) their income is inadequate; or (7) conception occurs during the first year of marriage.

Sanger was persecuted and imprisoned because of her crusade for contraception. In 1915 she was indicted for sending pleas for birth control through the mail, and a year later she was arrested for operating a birth control clinic in the Brownsville section of Brooklyn, New York. Nevertheless, she won financial support from influential wealthy society women that enabled her to further her clinical research and professional training. She launched and edited the *Birth Control Review* (1917–1940) while still in prison. This activity, combined with extra-marital affairs, placed an intolerable strain on her marriage, and she divorced her husband in 1920. After her daughter died, she married millionaire J. Noah Slee, seventeen years her senior, who contributed generously to her cause until his death in 1943.

Sanger's political instincts led her to convert birth control from an exclusively female concern into a general human health issue that legislators could support without alienating their mostly male constituents. After organizing national and international conferences, founding the Birth Control Clinical Research Bureau, and writing and testifying on behalf of her cause, Sanger won a ruling by a federal court in 1936 that permitted doctors to prescribe contraceptives and educate the public. Margaret Sanger's lobbying and organizational efforts resulted in significant policy changes within the medical establishment and landmark court decisions, culminating in *ROE V. WADE* (1965). Because abortion rights and family values occupy center stage in current political debates, her courageous contribution has especial value today.

See also: WOMEN'S ISSUES

For Further Information

Chesler, Ellen. *Woman of Valor: Margaret Sanger and the Birth Control Movement in America.* New York: Simon and Schuster, 1992.

Sanger, Margaret. *Margaret Sanger: An Autobiograhy.* New York: W. W Norton, 1938.

Sanger, Margaret. *The Margaret Sanger Papers.* Collected Documents Series. Bethesda, MD: University Publications of America, 1997.

———. *My Fight for Birth Control. Volume 4.* Elkins Park, IL: Franklin Book Co., 1959.

SAVIO, MARIO (1942–1996). Mario Savio was one of the finest, most fiercely honest, and most democratic thinkers of the 1960s generation, using his oratorical talent to voice the moral outrage felt by many young people at that time. He led the fall 1964 student uprising that immobilized the University of California at Berkeley campus and secured for students and faculty the freedom to discuss political ideas.

Born on December 8, 1942, in New York, the son of a machinist in a working-class Italian Catholic family, Savio was a superior student—serious, responsible, cerebral, and polite. He began his college education in New York but eventually ended up at the University of California at Berkeley as a philosophy student searching for a rigorous education. During the summer of 1964, he had worked with the STUDENT NONVIOLENT COORDINATING COMMITTEE (SNCC) in Mississippi to hasten integration. Upon returning to Berkeley in the fall, he found that unreasonable limits were being placed on students' First Amendment rights.

In the previous spring, Berkeley students had organized protests against racist hiring

Mario Savio (left), the leader of the Free Speech Movement, stands with folk singer Joan Baez at a free speech rally before Sproul Hall on the University of California, Berkeley campus in 1964. © *Ted Streshinsky/ CORBIS.*

practices in the San Francisco area. Buckling under pressure from local businesses, the university had decided to ban all political activity on the Berkeley campus, including distribution of leaflets and petitions and solicitation of donations.

Clark Kerr, then president, defined the university as a "knowledge factory" designed to serve American industry. All the student groups on campus united to challenge the ban. When they surrounded a police car containing an arrested student, the protesters began to give speeches. Mario Savio was one of many who spoke, but his statement was the most rousing. He had stuttered all of his life, but passion and conviction liberated his tongue during his speeches. He confided in an interview that the term "free speech" had for him an added private meaning.

Although he was "appalled" by his selection as leader, he was indeed instrumental in rallying the full spectrum of students for a sit-in at Sproul Hall and in negotiating an agreement with the university administration. Savio had the ability to relate to students across the entire political spectrum because of his honesty and choice of simple, nonideological terms that highlighted basic human rights. He said, "[T]here is a time when the operation of the machine becomes so odious, makes you so sick at heart, that you can't take part; you can't even passively take part, and you've got to put your bodies upon the gears and upon the wheels, upon the levers, upon all the apparatus, and you've got to make it stop. And you've got to indicate to the people who run it, to the people who own it, that unless you're free, the machine will be prevented from working at all!" (Goines, p. 361).

Berkeley's Free Speech Movement heated latent frustrations past the auto-ignition point, setting off a nationwide conflagration of activism in the form of marches, protests, sit-ins, and acts of civil disobedience in the 1960s. Ironically, it was Clark Kerr, president of the University of California system, who predicted in 1959 that "employers are going to love this generation—they are going to be easy to handle. There aren't going to be any riots" (*Reader's Digest*, p. 346).

Savio was eventually arrested, served four months in jail, and was expelled from Berkeley. Before earning an M.A. summa cum laude in physics from San Francisco State University, he took temporary jobs as bartender, bookstore clerk, and math tutor. He went on to teach logic and physics at Sonoma State University, married, and tried to lead a low-profile existence. In the 1990s he briefly emerged from obscurity to protest conservative propositions aimed at curtailing affirmative action and illegal immigration, and increased student fees at Sonoma State. He died of a heart attack following a debate with the Sonoma State University president.

Savio became disenchanted with the Free Speech Movement after it shifted its attention from free speech and educational reform to "filthy speech," sexual freedom, and other issues of concern to the emerging hippie culture. Although the Free Speech Movement was soon disbanded after winning revocation of the university's restrictions, Mario Savio's name remains permanently linked to this 1960s activism landmark. In 1998 Berkeley history professor Leon Litwack said, "Mario Savio gave as much to the life of our campus as any financial contributor, athletic coaches or even Nobel Laureates."

See also: CONSTITUTIONAL RIGHTS AND CIVIL LIBERTIES PROTECTION

For Further Information

Garson, Barbara. "Obituary: Mario Savio: Stirring Up the Students." *The Guardian* (London), November 9, 1996, Guardian Features section, p. 19.

Goines, David L. *The Free Speech Movement: Coming of Age in the 1960s*. Berkeley, CA: Ten Speed Press, 1993.

Orlans, Harold. "Thirty-Three Years Later." *Change* 30 (July/August 1998): 10.

Reader's Digest. Our Glorious Century. Pleasantville, NY: Readers Digest, 1994.

The Free Speech Movement Archives at University of California, Berkeley, *http://www.fsm-a.org/stacks/covers/savio-cvr.html*

SAVITZKY, BELLA. *See* Abzug, Bella

SCHLAFLY, PHYLLIS (1924–   ). Phyllis Schlafly has been a national leader of the conservative movement since the publication of her best-selling 1964 book, *A Choice, Not an Echo*, which helped Senator Barry Goldwater win the Republican presidential nomination. A crusader for the pro-family movement since 1972, she led pro-family allies to victory over the principal legislative goal of liberal feminists, the Equal Rights Amendment, which failed to achieve ratification in 1982.

As editor of the *Phyllis Schlafly Report* and the *Eagle Forum Newsletter*, Schlafly has penned hundreds of articles and delivered

Phyllis Schlafly talks with reporters during a "Stop the Equal Rights Amendment" rally at the Illinois State Capitol in March 1975. © *Bettmann/ CORBIS.*

speeches in every state condemning contemporary feminism as a destroyer of families. Her sixteen books include *The Power of the Positive Woman, Who Will Rock the Cradle? Pornography's Victims*, and *First Reader*, which promotes phonics. She has been a delegate to the Republican National Convention eight times, starting in 1956, and is a former president of the National Federation of Republican Women. Schlafly ran unsuccessfully for Congress in 1952 and again in 1972.

Born Phyllis Stewart in St. Louis, Missouri, on August 15, 1924, Schlafly graduated Phi Beta Kappa from Washington University in 1944, while working full-time at the St. Louis Ordnance Plant, testing the accuracy of rifles and machine-guns. Awarded a scholarship, she received an M.A. in political science from Radcliffe College in 1945. In

1978 Washington University awarded her a J.D. degree.

Schlafly was Senator Joseph R. McCarthy's research assistant during the early 1950s and, with her husband, established the Cardinal Mindszenty Foundation in 1958 to warn the world about the perils of communism. The mother of four boys and two girls, Schlafly believes that raising a family is the most important career for a woman, that caring for a baby provides the greatest joy, and that women would rather be loved than liberated. Even her worst enemies concede that she is a paragon of maternal virtue.

In 1972 Schlafly founded the EAGLE FORUM as "an answer to women's lib" and led it to a victory over feminists' principal legislative goal, ratification of the Equal Rights Amendment. For over thirty years, she has campaigned against abortion, sex education in the public schools, violence and sex on television, and same-sex marriages. A devout Catholic and a member of the Daughters of the American Revolution, Schlafly continues her promotion of conservative policies as they pertain to child care, education, national defense, women's rights, and government intrusion into citizens' lives. Working from the Eagle Forum's national headquarters in St. Louis, Missouri, she airs her positions in a column syndicated in more than one hundred newspapers and in the *Phyllis Schlafly Report* broadcast by sixty-five radio stations.

See also: ABORTION POLICY; CONSERVATIVES (FAR RIGHT); RELIGIOUS RIGHT; WOMEN'S ISSUES

For Further Information

Eagle Forum, *http://www.eagleforum.org*
Felsenthal, Carol. *The Sweetheart of the Silent Majority: The Biography of Phyllis Schlafly*. Garden City, NY: Doubleday, 1981.
Schlafly, Phyllis. *A Choice, Not an Echo*. Alton, IL: Pere Marquette Press, 1964.
———. *First Reader*. Alton, IL: Pere Marquette Press, 1994.

SCHLESSINGER, LAURA (1947–).

One of America's favorite radio talk show hosts, Laura Schlessinger preaches and chats to over 20 million fans who are addicted to her daily dosages of nagging and nuggets of advice on how to redress their violations of traditional moral codes and good judgment. Born on January 16, 1947, Laura Schlessinger grew up on Avenue U in Brooklyn, New York, one of two daughters born to Monroe Schlessinger, a civil engineer, and Yolanda Ceccovi, an Italian he met and married during World War II. The marriage was strained because Schlessinger's Jewish family could not accept his Catholic wife, and Schlessinger's childhood was not a happy one. When her family moved to Long Island, New York, Schlessinger, who had an aptitude for science, converted the basement into a laboratory.

Schlessinger earned a B.S. in biology at the State University of New York at Stonybrook and a doctorate in physiology at Columbia University (1974), writing her dissertation on the effect of insulin on fat cells. She married a classmate whom she divorced in 1978. She then joined the faculty of the University of Southern California, became the host of a local radio show, and earned a certificate in marriage and family counseling. By 1980 she had established a private practice. In 1984 she married Lew Bishop who currently serves as her business manager. The couple had a son, Deryk, in 1986.

In 1990 KFI in Los Angeles launched the *Dr. Laura* show, and the program became nationally syndicated in 1994. Her career as the nation's favorite radiotherapist skyrocketed, with her show becoming second in popularity only to Rush Limbaugh's in 1999. Schlessinger labels her program a morality show and only addresses listeners' personal or interpersonal problems. A convert to Orthodox Judaism, she denounces premarital sex, extramarital affairs, divorce, and mixed religion marriages. She has labeled homosexuality a biological error and recommends reparative therapy to modify gay-lesbian behavior. With brash and pithy responses and a brisk staccato style, "Dr. Laura" urges her callers to stop blaming others, accept personal responsibility, and stop their whining and self-pity.

When asked if she is part of a movement to reinstate conservative values, she responds, "I'm not part of a movement; I am a movement."

In 1999 Schlessinger denounced the American Library Association (ALA) for its recommendation of the *Go Ask Alice* site on the ALA Teen Hoopla Web page and for supporting minors' unrestricted access to the Internet. Her crusade against the ALA gained momentum when she asked her millions of listeners to eliminate library budgets and to participate in ALA annual conferences and chapter meetings as a "polite conservative voice." In response to the negative fallout from the Schlessinger broadcasts, Toys R Us cancelled its plans to fund children's reading rooms in public libraries throughout the United States.

Schlessinger is author of four best sellers: *Ten Stupid Things Women Do to Mess Up Their Lives; How Could You Do That?; Ten Stupid Things Men Do to Mess Up Their Lives;* and *The Ten Commandments: The Significance of God's Law in Everyday Life.* Her latest book for children is *Why Do You Love Me?*

In 1993 Schlessinger discontinued her private practice to devote more time to her family, and in 1997 her weekly syndicated column was appearing in fifty-five newspapers. Her numerous awards include the 1997 Marconi Radio Award and Israel's Fiftieth Anniversary Tribute Award for her contributions to humanity. She holds a black belt in karate and owns residences in the San Fernando Valley and in Lake Arrowhead, California.

See also: RELIGIOUS RIGHT

For Further Information

Bane, Vickie. *Dr. Laura Schlessinger.* 2nd ed. New York: St. Martin's Press, 1999.

Dr. Laura.com, *http://www.drlaura.com*

SEA SHEPHERD CONSERVATION SOCIETY. The Sea Shepherd Conservation Society (SSCS) is an activist group that investigates and documents "violations of international laws, regulations and treaties protecting marine wildlife species." Whenever national governments or international regulatory organizations fail to comply with or enforce existing laws because of "absence of jurisdiction or lack of political will," the SSCS takes aggressive action.

The SSCS was founded by Paul Watson, a co-founder of GREENPEACE who was expelled in 1977 for advocating the use of force against whalers and seal hunters. He had snatched a club from the hand of a Newfoundland baby seal hunter during a 1977 Greenpeace expedition and tossed it into the sea. Watson contends that Greenpeace has become passive, bureaucratic, wealthy, and too willing to accommodate industrial and governmental interests.

The SSCS advocates strict compliance with International Whaling Commission rulings. Watson, a Canadian by birth, participated in the 1970s Earth Day demonstrations, protested against Atomic Energy Commission H-bomb tests in Amchitka, and served as a medic during the AMERICAN INDIAN MOVEMENT occupation of Wounded Knee before starting up Greenpeace. Money donated from animal welfare groups, including the Cleveland Amory Fund for Animals and the British Royal Society for the Prevention of Cruelty to Animals, enabled the SSCS to purchase two ships to wage war against allegedly illegal whalers, seal hunters, and dolphin killers. Ed Asner, Bo Derek, Mike Farrell, Ida Lupino, Loretta Swit, Jon Voigt, and other Hollywood stars have also made pledges to Sea Shepherd. Rather than being salaried employees, crew members aboard SSCS vessels pay between $500 and $1,500 for the privilege of serving the Society.

In 1986 the SSCS became front-page news because of its attempt to subvert Iceland's plans to resume whaling despite a moratorium decreed by the International Whaling Commission. The SSCS scuttled two of Iceland's four whaling ships and sabotaged equipment in a whale processing plant. The ensuing negative publicity and the threat of international boycotts forced Iceland to abandon its commercial whaling operation.

Earlier, in 1980, the group had used hull-attached mines to sink a Cypriot whaling ship in Lisbon and two Spanish whalers. Other SSCS actions have included attacks on trawlers in the Faeroe Islands to prevent residents from killing an estimated 2,000 pilot whales per year and destruction of five-mile-long Japanese drift nets in the North Pacific responsible for killing sea life and birds. By 1994 the group had acquired two vessels and a British two-man submarine and had sunk ten ships involved in anti–marine life operations.

More recently, in 1999, the group attempted to stop the Makah Nation, a tribe based in Neah Bay, Washington, from canoeing into the Pacific Ocean to harpoon a whale. The Makah had received permission from the International Whaling Commission to hunt up to five California gray whales a year for five years to revive a tribal tradition. SSCS insisted that commercial whalers would use the hunt as a pretext to break the moratorium.

The SSCS has its headquarters in Venice, California, and branch offices in Germany, the United Kingdom, and the Netherlands. The group publishes the *Sea Shepherd Log*, a quarterly newsletter. SSCS has 35,000 members, over half of them living in the United States. Captain Paul Watson is president.

See also: ANIMAL WELFARE AND RIGHTS

For Further Information

Morris, David B. *Earth Warrior: Overboard with Paul Watson and the Sea Shepherd Conservation Society.* Golden, CO: Fulcrum Publishing, 1995.

Sea Shepard Conservation Society, *http://www.seashepherd.org*

SEALE, ROBERT G. ("BOBBY")

(1936–). Radical civil rights activist and co-founder of the BLACK PANTHER PARTY with HUEY NEWTON, Robert G. Seale, better known as Bobby Seale, was born in Dallas, Texas, on October 22, 1936. When he was seven, his family moved to Oakland, California, where he taught himself the basics of carpentry while working in his father's building and furniture store. Following a three-year stint in the U.S. Air Force, he entered Merritt College, in Oakland. There, in 1962, he heard MALCOLM X speak and met Huey Newton. Although aware of the nonviolent resistance philosophy of MARTIN LUTHER KING JR., Seale and Newton were most influenced by Mao Zedong, Frantz Fanon, and Marxist-Leninist rhetoric, and adopted paramilitary tactics to win black empowerment.

Seale and Newton founded the Black Panther Party for Self-Defense in 1966 to protect the black community from the bias-driven brutality of the Oakland police. In 1969 Seale was indicted in Chicago with seven others for having conspired to incite riots during the 1968 Democratic National Convention. During the trial, Judge Julius Hoffman had Seale bound and gagged because of his repeated insistence that he was being denied his constitutional rights, his foul language, and disorderly behavior. The judge ordered his case to be severed from those of the other seven defendants and had him removed from the court. Seale was convicted of contempt of court and received a four-year sentence. In 1971 he was accused of the 1969 murder of a suspected Black Panther police informant but later acquitted.

Seale ran for mayor of Oakland in 1973 and lost, getting 42 percent of the vote. During his later years as Black Panther Party chair, Seale renounced violence and initiated community-based service programs, including breakfasts for school children, free busing for seniors, Seniors Against a Fearful Environment (SAFE), a preventative health care program, cooperative housing, and mass voter registration drives. In 1979 he went to Washington, D.C., and established a nonprofit group, Advocates Scene, Inc., to assist community activists, and is currently working to improve social services for blacks in Pennsylvania.

Seale's writings include *Seize the Time: The Story of the Black Panther Party and Huey P.*

Newton (1970) and a cookbook, *Barbeque'n with Bobby.*

See also: AFRICAN AMERICAN RIGHTS

For Further Information

Bobby Seale, *http://www.bobbyseale.com/*

Haskins, James. *Power to the People: The Rise and Fall of the Black Panther Party.* New York: Simon and Schuster Books for Young Readers, 1997.

Seale, Bobby. *Barbeque'n with Bobby.* Berkeley, CA: Ten Speed Press, 1988.

SENIOR MOVEMENT. The senior movement, as defined by the development of organizations and leaders able to exert political influence and shape social policy to benefit older Americans, did not come into existence until the 1930s. Although various veterans' groups had been agitating for increased pension benefits, it was the Depression that made clear to Congress the plight of the aged, so many of whom had lost their savings, jobs, health, and homes, and the need for publicly supported pensions and economic security insurance.

The first citizens' campaign for federal assistance programs for the elderly was launched in 1933. Francis Everett Townsend (1867–1960), a retired physician in Long Beach, California, advocated a $200-a-month pension for every retired citizen over sixty. It was to be funded by a national sales tax, paid in scrip, and spent by the recipients within a month. Townsend promoted his proposal with messianic zeal and within three years had built a formidable lobby of 30 million Townsendites. He won support in Congress despite the plan's condemnation by respected economists. Though repeatedly defeated in Congress, the Townsend Plan helped ease passage of the Social Security Act of 1935. Most of the elderly continued to be destitute, dependent on others, and medically neglected because Social Security provided only a bare subsistence income.

Seniors' next big breakthrough was the founding of the National Retired Teachers Association (NRTA), established in 1947 by Dr. Ethel Percy Andrus, a high school principal in California. In 1958 the NRTA spun off a parallel organization, the AMERICAN ASSOCIATION OF RETIRED PERSONS (AARP), to extend retirement benefits to all elderly persons. Three years later the NATIONAL COUNCIL OF SENIOR CITIZENS (NCSC) was founded by liberal Democrats, the United Auto Workers, and the United Steelworkers. The AARP had not yet developed its lobbying operation, and the NCSC would provide a strong voice in Washington.

Led by MAGGIE KUHN, a persistent pioneer leader in the fight to repeal mandatory retirement laws, the GRAY PANTHERS was formed in 1970. The OLDER WOMEN'S LEAGUE (OWL) was created in 1980 so that widows and divorcees could advocate a legislative agenda to improve the status of elderly destitute women.

In 1982 James Roosevelt formed the NATIONAL COMMITTEE TO PRESERVE SOCIAL SECURITY, fearing that President Ronald Reagan's administration would cut senior benefits provided through existing federal entitlement programs created by his father, President Franklin D. Roosevelt.

In 1988 elderly citizen activists inadvertently created an irresistible opportunity for conservative groups to move into a lobbying domain that was being monopolized by middle-of-the-road and liberal organizations. The AARP had supported the Medicare Catastrophic Coverage Act of 1989, a health plan to protect the elderly poor from being financially ruined by expenses incurred by disastrous illness. The act would have levied a small surtax on well-to-do Medicare recipients. Within months the AARP lost an estimated 60,000 middle-class and wealthy members who favored broadened social health insurance only if it had no adverse impact on their own pocketbooks. RICHARD VIGUERIE, a master of the art of using direct mail to establish right-wing groups, created SENIORS COALITION to demonstrate to Congress that the behemoth AARP did not reflect the views of the majority of the nation's elderly. Viguerie's multiple mailings proved to be so expensive that the group's director complained that "after a year or two, we had an enormous amount of debt because we mailed so much and the cost was unbelievable. It wasn't Viguerie's debt, it was ours." Viguerie then established a second conservative seniors group, the UNITED SENIORS ASSOCIATION, which prospected for new members using the Seniors Coalition mailing list (in which Viguerie had a proprietary interest). Viguerie went on to develop a third seniors group, 60 PLUS, drawing upon the same constituency as the two earlier groups.

The new renegade groups, which differed from AARP on catastrophic health care policy, succeeded in getting 240 members of Congress to switch their votes from support of the act in June 1988 to support of its repeal only sixteen months later. This was the first time the U.S. Congress had ever voted to repeal a major social benefit it had created. In 1999, 60 Plus was conducting a second full press campaign to eliminate the inheritance tax, a change that would disproportionately favor very wealthy seniors.

Seniors remain the nation's most powerful citizen activists because they read, analyze issues, communicate views to legislators, and vote more often than younger people. They are an enormous and expanding bloc that votes primarily for candidates, regardless of party affiliation, who speak to their concerns. Candidates who win senior support on such issues as income, health care, neighborhood crime, energy costs, and taxes become almost invulnerable to defeat.

For Further Information

Serafini, Marilyn Werber. "Senior Schism," *The National Journal*, May 6, 1995, p. 1089.

Powell, Lawrence A. *The Senior Rights Movement: Framing the Policy Debate in America*. New York: Twayne, 1996.

Wallace, Steven P. *The Senior Movement: References and Resources*. New York: Macmillan, 1992.

SENIORS COALITION. The mission of the 3 million member Seniors Coalition is "to protect the quality of life and economic well-being that older Americans have earned while supporting common sense solutions to the challenges of the future." In addition to Medicare and Social Security, Seniors Coalition issues include balancing the federal budget, protecting the free market and traditional family values, and streamlining FDA approval of new drugs.

Founded in 1989, the Coalition grew out of the Taxpayers Education Lobby, a conservative direct mail group started by Dan Alexander and his wife, Fay. In the mid-1980s, Dan Alexander, a former school board president from Mobile, Alabama, had been convicted of receiving kickbacks on school construction projects and was in jail, so Fay Alexander served in his place as the Coalition's first leader. The Coalition exploited the window of opportunity created by the Medicare Catastrophic Coverage Act of 1989, a health plan designed to protect less well-to-do elderly from being devastated by a catastrophic illness by charging a surtax on more affluent Medicare recipients. The AMERICAN ASSOCIATION OF RETIRED PERSONS (AARP) had supported the health plan, but when news of the surtax spread among the elderly, there was an explosion of protest and mass defection of AARP members. At this point, RICHARD VIGUERIE, an expert on direct mail fundraising for conservative causes, stepped in to organize a write-in campaign for the Coalition that succeeded in pressuring Congress to repeal the act. Viguerie also recruited members by allegedly scaring seniors into contributing money to "the responsible alternative to the AARP," most of which was used to help his private business. In 1992 the group severed its connection to Viguerie and the Taxpayers Education Lobby and hired a new chief executive, Paul Bramell, who transformed the group into an effective supporter of the Republican health care agenda. The organization dropped its original name, the Seniors Coalition Against the Tax, and was chartered in 1992 under its current name and soon became one of the more powerful citizens' lobbies on Capitol Hill.

Opposition to the Kyoto Treaty and support of a constitutional amendment to protect the flag are on the Coalition's current agenda. In 1999 it presented its annual Friend of Seniors Award to the American Petroleum Institute for providing information to seniors on the true cost of the Kyoto Global Climate Protocol.

Senior Coalition headquarters is in Springfield, Virginia. Thair Phillips is chief executive officer and Mary Martin serves as executive director and chairman of the board. *The Advocate*, a quarterly magazine, is the group's membership publication. SCAT, the Seniors Coalition Action Team, "serves as the eyes, ears, and voice of conservative seniors in each congressional district." SCAT members additionally receive *The Activist*, a quarterly newsletter.

See also: FALSE FRONT ORGANIZATIONS; SENIOR MOVEMENT

For Further Information

Seniors Coalition, *http://www.seniors.org*
Serafini, Marilyn Werber. "A Ruckus at the Seniors Coalition." *National Journal*, January 26, 1996, p. 203.

SHANKER, ALBERT (1928–1997). Outspoken, combative, and expert in the philosophy and practice of education, Albert Shanker became the most prominent voice affecting the status of the American teaching profession during the second half of the twentieth century. As president of the American Federation of Teachers (1974–1986) he represented over a fourth of the nation's public school teachers.

Shanker was born September 14, 1928, in lower Manhattan, son of a Polish immigrant and former rabbinical student who earned his living as a newspaper deliveryman. His mother was a sewing machine operator in a sweatshop. After the family moved to a section in Queens made up primarily of Irish and Italian working-class families, Shanker was subjected to racist taunts, called a "Christkiller," and threatened with crucifixion and garroting by neighborhood

toughs. He graduated from prestigious Stuyvesant High School near the top of his class, studied philosophy at the University of Illinois (Urbana), where he joined the Young People's Socialist League, and went on to Columbia University for graduate studies in philosophy and mathematics. In 1952, after being awarded an M.A. degree, he abandoned his pursuit of a doctorate, choosing instead to teach mathematics in a junior high school in East Harlem.

Shanker was appalled by the tensions, low pay, squalid conditions, and inability of the existing New York Teachers' Guild to organize and achieve tangible results. He joined the Guild and became an organizer of the American Federation of Teachers. From 1974 until his death, he was president of the AFT, which under his direction grew from about 400,000 to over 900,000 members. He revolutionized the profession by injecting it with trailblazing ideas about teachers' rights and education reform, converting teachers from underpaid public servants into self-respecting professionals.

However, despite Shanker's unimpeachable record as a civil rights activist and veteran of sit-ins and freedom marches, he became ensnared in a vicious racial and religious crossfire during the United Federation of Teachers' fifty-five-day strike against the New York City Schools in 1968–1969. He led the strike to halt a plan to permit local community boards to control educational policy. City authorities and the black residents favored local control as a strategy to help minority neighborhoods to improve their schools' accountability and quality. In April 1968, in the initial stage of the decentralization experiment, thirteen white teachers and administrators were summarily transferred out of a poor minority-dominated district in violation of civil service laws and union contracts. Shanker, fearing that the involuntary transfers would spread to other schools, won the support of the courts, but city leaders refused to fan community resentment by enforcing reinstatement of the transferred staff. Shanker was vilified and jailed for fifteen days for calling the strike but later proven right when corruption, violations of teachers' rights, and anti-Semitic incidents increased significantly following decentralization.

In his weekly AFT-subsidized column in the Sunday *New York Times*, Shanker fulminated against such educational fads as Ebonics, self-concept change, and discipline by the numbers, insisting that there was no easy shortcut to learning. An old-fashioned, pragmatic liberal, Shanker championed rigorous national educational standards, centralization, graduation based on academic readiness, and national competency tests and merit raises for teachers. He built the AFT into a major presence in education and fought to improve public schools' capacity to create a better life for all Americans. Albert Shanker died of bladder cancer in 1997.

See also: LABOR ISSUES

For Further Information

Mungazi, Dickson A. *Where He Stands: Albert Shanker of the American Federation of Teachers.* Westport, CT: Greenwood Publishing Group, 1995.

Weiner, Lois. "Albert Shanker's Legacy." *Contemporary Education* 69 (Summer 1998): 196–201.

SHUTTLESWORTH, REVEREND FRED (1922–).

Co-founder of the SOUTHERN CHRISTIAN LEADERSHIP CONFERENCE (SCLC) and a legendarily fearless advocate of racial justice, the Reverend Fred Shuttlesworth was born on March 18, 1922, in Montgomery County, Alabama, as Freddie Lee Robinson. It was he who brought the Birmingham protests to a boil by inviting MARTIN LUTHER KING JR. to lead boycotts and demonstrations in Birmingham, Alabama, thereby hastening passage of the Civil Rights Act of 1964 and integration of public accommodations.

Shuttlesworth was the son of unmarried parents. His father lived in a shack and earned a meager living keeping dogs and repairing watches and guns. After his mother had a second child by the same man, she moved to Birmingham. In 1926 she married William Nathan Shuttlesworth, a bootlegger and farmer. Young Fred and his sibling were given his stepfather's surname, Shuttlesworth. His mother worked as a domestic and in the fields, and the family lived according to the slogan "Let Roosevelt feed you and the good Lord lead you."

As a teenager, Shuttlesworth became a Sunday school superintendent, also taking odd jobs as a physician's orderly, quarry worker, and truck driver. When he was twenty-six, he became an ordained Baptist minister and pastor of Selma, Alabama's, First Baptist Church. Because of his growing involvement in civil rights activism, the time he committed to church functions such as counseling, weddings, and funerals became minimal. In 1952 he left Selma to become pastor at Birmingham's Bethel Baptist Church, where he rapidly built up a large and socially conscious following. The group he founded in 1956, the Alabama Christian Movement for Human Rights (ACMHR), soon became the SCLC's strongest local affiliate.

By 1956 Shuttlesworth had become a prominent black leader, aggressively pushing authorities to hire black police officers and end segregation on buses, at stores, and in public facilities. Because of the size, loyalty, and fervor of his followers, Martin Luther King Jr. decided to honor Shuttlesworth's request for assistance in the battle for integration by spotlighting Birmingham with a massive direct action campaign in April 1963.

Meanwhile, racial bigots and the KU KLUX KLAN repeatedly tried to intimidate or eliminate Shuttlesworth, hurling bricks through his windows, beating him with baseball bats, brass knuckles, and chains, and dynamiting his parsonage on Christmas Eve, 1956. Altogether he survived eight different attempts on his life and his church was bombed three times.

Theophilus Eugene "Bull" Connor, Birmingham's segregationist commissioner of public safety, became Shuttlesworth's principal antagonist. Because of the two men's highly combustible, hard-edged personalities, Shuttlesworth was able to goad Connor into taking extreme and illegal actions in 1963, for example, brutally attacking protesters with police dogs, clubs, and high-pressure spray from fire hoses. Television footage of these actions shamed local whites, shocked the entire nation, and convinced President John F. Kennedy that at long last there was sufficient public support to justify enactment of federal civil rights legislation. Shuttlesworth also assisted King with his Montgomery bus boycott and JAMES FARMER with his Freedom Rides, and supported sit-ins conducted by students on various southern college campuses in the 1960s. In 1961 Shuttlesworth moved to Cincinnati, Ohio, where he is currently pastor of the Greater New Light Baptist Church.

For Further Information

Manis, Andrew M. *A Fire You Can't Put Out: The Civil Rights Life of Birmingham's Reverend Fred Shuttlesworth.* Tuscaloosa: University of Alabama Press, 1999.

SIERRA CLUB. Founded in 1892, the Sierra Club is dedicated to conserving the environment by influencing public policy at the legislative, administrative, legal, and electoral levels. It is the nation's oldest, largest, and most influential nonprofit environmental organization. The Club's purpose is "to explore, enjoy, and protect the wild places of the earth; to practice and promote the responsible use of the earth's ecosystems and resources; to educate and enlist humanity to protect and restore the quality of the natural and human environment; and to use all lawful means to carry out these objectives."

The Sierra Club was established by the renowned naturalist John Muir "to enlist the support and cooperation of the people and the government in preserving the forests and other natural features of the Sierra Nevada Mountains." Muir's books, among them *The Mountains of California* (1894), *Our National Parks* (1901), and *The Yosemite* (1912), popularized the concept of preservation. Theodore Roosevelt, the first conservation-minded president, camped with

President Theodore Roosevelt (left) and Sierra Club founder John Muir on Glacier Point, Yosemite Valley, California c. 1906. *Library of Congress, Prints and Photographs Division, LC-USZ62–8672 DLC.*

Muir in the Sierras and became an ally. However, after achieving initial success in preserving Yosemite and Sequoia Parks, the Club suffered its first and worst defeat. In the wake of the great earthquake of 1906 and six previous disastrous fires, San Francisco's civic leaders insisted on development of an adequate and reliable city water supply. Hetch Hetchy Valley, a nearly exact counterpart of Yosemite, was chosen as the preferred site for a water reservoir. In response, the Sierra Club formed coalitions and lobbied vigorously to oppose the plan, but in 1913 the Raker Act authorized construction of the O'Shaugnessy Dam, an event that temporarily traumatized the nation's young conservation movement. Some eighty-five years after its completion, the Sierra Club continues to fight for restoration of the flooded valley.

In 1916 the Club was instrumental in establishing the National Park Service and the National Forest Service and negotiated legislation creating Kings Canyon and Olympic National Parks. In the 1940s and 1950s, the Club protected Dinosaur National Monument from dams but failed to stop construction of the Glen Canyon Dam on the Colorado River. At this time the Club remained small, and it was not until DAVID BROWER was appointed its first executive director in 1952 that it started to make its mark as a lobby. The Echo Park Dam in Dinosaur Park was halted, and this success stimulated a rise in membership from 7,000 in 1950 to 15,000 in 1960, the year the Sierra Club Foundation launched its Exhibit Format book series, graced by spectacular color photographs. In 1966 the Sierra Club's full-page newspaper ads urging protection of the Grand Canyon from damming prompted the Internal Revenue Service to rescind the group's tax-deductible status. The resulting publicity generated contributions and a surge in membership, and led to creation of a separate Sierra PAC. Subsequent legislative victories included passage of the Toxic Substances Control Act (1976) and the Alaskan National Interest Lands Conservation Act (1980).

In 1982 Sierra Club members competed in more than 170 congressional races and various state and local contests, and won a majority of races. The successful campaign to remove President Ronald Reagan's secretary of the interior, James Watt, an extreme conservative and enviro-enemy, spurred further growth of Club membership, which peaked at 600,000 in 1990. The California Desert Protection Act (1994), creation of the Escalante National Monument in Utah (1996), protection of polar regions from commercial exploitation, and election of pro-environment candidates in thirty-eight congressional races (1998) were additional victories.

Today the Sierra Club, with its dedicated action network of 85,000 members, is one of the nation's most effective grassroots lobbies. Club campaigns include a call for more stringent automobile fuel efficiency standards, reduction of contamination of human drinking water by animal waste, protection of the Arctic National Wildlife Refuge in Alaska from oil drilling, and initiatives to counter global warming.

The 550,000 member Sierra Club has 65 state and 398 local chapters; its headquarters is in San Francisco. Carl Pope is executive director. The Club publishes *Sierra*, a bimonthly magazine.

See also: ENVIRONMENT

For Further Information

Mesnikoff, Ann R. "Efforts to End Global Warming." Testimony Before the U.S. Senate Committee on Commerce, Science, and Transportation, 107th Cong., 2nd sess. Federal Document Clearing House Congressional Testimony, Item no. 32Y20009200005102, September 21, 2000.

Sierra Club, *http://www.sierraclub.org*

Turner, Tom. *Sierra Club: One Hundred Years of Protecting Nature*. New York: Harry N. Abrams, 1993.

SILKWOOD, KAREN GAY (1946–1974). Born February 19, 1946, in Longview, Texas, Karen Silkwood has been memorialized as a martyr of the anti–nuclear power movement in the motion picture *Silkwood* (1983), directed by Mike Nichols and starring Meryl Streep. As a legendary whistle-blower she shook the nation's confidence in the nuclear power industry and precipitated a significant slowdown in plant construction.

Silkwood studied medical technology and chemistry at Lamar State College in Beaumont, Texas, on a scholarship. In 1965 she married William Meadows, whom she divorced in 1972. Leaving her three children behind, she moved to Oklahoma and was hired as a laboratory analyst at the Cimarron River plutonium plant of the Kerr-McGee Nuclear Corporation. By 1974 she had become the first female member of the Oil, Chemical and Atomic Workers Union, with the task of reviewing health and safety issues

An undated photo of Karen Silkwood. *AP/Wide World Photos.*

at Kerr-McGee. She suspected that workers at the plant were being poisoned by radiation because of negligence and disregard of safety regulations and led a union campaign to improve conditions. At that time Kerr-McGee was already dealing with litigation involving worker safety and environmental contamination, and Silkwood had been asked to testify to charges before the Atomic Energy Commission.

During September 1974, Silkwood flew to Washington, D.C., to inform union headquarters officials about the life-endangering conditions at the plant. Steve Wodka, a union official at the time, noted that her clear and consistent recollection of places, times, and people's names leant credibility to her statement. A month later, Silkwood became convinced that she was being deliberately contaminated as part of a cover-up conspiracy. She gathered additional documentation, and Wodka set up a meeting with an

Atomic Energy Commission official and David Burnham, a *New York Times* reporter, in Oklahoma City. Silkwood was to bring with her falsified fuel-rod quality control assurance records and evidence revealing that forty pellets of deadly plutonium had gone unaccountably missing from the plant's inventory. On November 13, 1974, while en route to the meeting, she was killed in a car crash that occurred under suspicious circumstances, and the potentially incriminating materials disappeared. A Dallas, Texas, accident reconstruction firm investigated the crash and concluded that her car had been bumped from behind and forced off the road.

Silkwood's household goods purportedly were buried in a nuclear waste site because of the high levels of plutonium radiation found in her apartment, which took three months to decontaminate. Her estate filed a civil suit against Kerr-McGee that was settled out of court for $1.3 million in 1986. Eventually Kerr-McGee closed the nuclear plant.

See also: ANTI–NUCLEAR POWER MOVEMENT

For Further Reading

Gay, Kathlyn, and Martin Gay. *Heroes of Conscience*. Santa Barbara: ABC-CLIO, 1996.

Rashke, Richard L. *The Killing of Karen Silkwood: The Story Behind the Kerr-McGee Plutonium Case*. Boston: Houghton Mifflin, 1981.

60 PLUS ASSOCIATION. Founded in 1992, the 60 Plus Association is an influential lobby for the elderly, positioning itself as the conservative alternative to the AMERICAN ASSOCIATION OF RETIRED PERSONS (AARP). It describes itself as "a non-partisan seniors advocacy group with a free enterprise, less government, less taxes approach to seniors issues." Jim Martin, president of 60 Plus, has referred to the AARP as the "American Association *Against* Retired Persons."

60 Plus has built up a membership base that succeeded in raising $2.9 million in campaign contributions during 1997, when Medicare revisions were being considered by

Congress. The group has accused liberal politicians of "shamelessly rid[ing] the twin horses of hypocrisy—Social Security and Medicare." 60 Plus advocates privatization of Social Security, claiming that "[j]ust as Generation Xer's believe more in UFOs than that Social Security will be solvent when they retire, seniors believe more in the second coming of Elvis than in the system's remaining solvent."

60 Plus, SENIORS COALITION, and UNITED SENIORS ASSOCIATION were all established with the assistance of the politically conservative direct mail fundraiser RICHARD A. VIGUERIE. The three groups got their start by exploiting a tactical error committed by the AARP, which in 1988 endorsed federal governmental coverage of excessive medical expenses through the Catastrophic Coverage Act. The act was designed to protect poor and lower middle income elderly from being bankrupted by costs incurred for treatment of severe illnesses. Benefits would be slightly reduced for the wealthy in order to support the needy elderly. Upper-income seniors revolted against the plan because they would have been charged a surtax, and for the first time ever, Congress was forced to repeal health benefits legislation within a year of its enactment. During this period, many of the outraged elderly switched their allegiance to one of the three newly formed organizations.

60 Plus issues an annual Congressional Scorecard. In its rating of the 1997–98 (105th Congress), 60 Plus awarded scores of 0 percent to liberal Democrats Senator Ted Kennedy, Senator Barbara Boxer, and then Representative Charles Schumer, and scores of 100 percent to conservative Republicans Senator Strom Thurmond and Representatives Dick Armey and Henry Hyde.

The group endorses elimination of the inheritance tax, which it refers to as the "death tax," and has backed bills that would ensure a balanced federal budget. The group also supported a ban on partial birth abortion and elimination of funding of the National Endowment for the Arts because it assists "projects that coarsen our society to the detriment and distress of senior citizens." 60 Plus opposed statistical sampling for the U.S. Census because of its concern that currently undercounted minorities would be counted and their inclusion would weaken seniors' electoral representation. In 1999, 60 Plus opposed U.S. ratification of the Kyoto Treaty, contending that the scientific findings about global warming are unreliable and that treaty implementation would impose unnecessary hardships on senior citizens.

The group presents annual Guardian of Seniors' Rights Awards. Recipients have included former Senator Robert Dole, Senator Trent Lott, and former House Speaker Newt Gingrich. The 475,000 members of 60 Plus receive subscriptions to the monthly newsletter *Senior Voice*. Former U.S. Representative Roger Zion (R-IN) serves as honorary chairman of 60 Plus. Organization headquarters is in Arlington, Virginia.

See also: FALSE FRONT ORGANIZATIONS; SENIOR MOVEMENT

For Further Information

Goode, Stephen. "Martin Sounds Death Knell for 'Death Tax' " (Interview with 60 Plus Association head Jim Martin). *Insight on the News* 14, no. 46 (December 14, 1998): 21.

Martin, James L. "Seniors and Global Warming: The Kyoto Treaty." Speech delivered at the Global Warming, Science and Public Policy Conference, Frontiers of Freedom Institute, Washington, D.C., April 3, 2000, *Vital Speeches of the Day*, 66, no. 14 (May 1, 2000): 445–447.

60 Plus Association, *http://www.60plus.org*

SLIWA, CURTIS (1954–). Curtis Sliwa is best known for having founded the Guardian Angels, a citizens' patrol group formed in 1979 to protect New York City subway riders from muggers and molesters. Born in the Canarsie section of Brooklyn on March 26, 1954, Sliwa was a bright but rebellious student who dropped out of high school. As a fourteen-year-old, he already displayed a strong sense of civic responsibility by creating a five-ton tower of recyclable paper in the family front yard, an unsightly proof of his commitment to conservation. Two years later, he rescued several people from a burning building while on his paper route, and for this heroic feat and his community spirit, the *New York Daily News* named him Newsboy of the Year and arranged a personal meeting with President Richard Nixon in Washington.

After leaving school and taking jobs as a gas station attendant, supermarket clerk, and assistant manager of a McDonald's, Sliwa organized the Rock Brigade, a neighborhood litter cleanup squad. Early in 1979, he formed the Magnificent 13, a volunteer citizen patrol to guard passengers on the notoriously crime-ridden subway train known as the "Muggers' Express." Within a year, Sliwa had drawn scores of mostly minority teenagers to his group and renamed it Guardian Angels. Although the police and New York City mayor Edward Koch viewed the Angels as a disreputable, untrained, and potentially dangerous paramilitary presence, the then lieutenant governor, Mario Cuomo, praised them as being "a better expression of morality than the city deserves."

By 1981 over 700 Guardian Angels were working the subways and making dozens of citizen's arrests. They carried officially authorized identification cards, wore badges, and were granted a modicum of respect and cooperation from law enforcement agencies.

Most Guardians are between seventeen and twenty-four years old and have profited from choosing membership as an alternative to drugs, crime, and gang activity. Currently, Sliwa's group claims some 7,000 members in unarmed volunteer groups combating crime in about thirty cities, including Denver, Atlanta, San Juan, Los Angeles, Boston, Phoenix, and Washington, D.C. Overseas, groups have been formed in London, Nottingham, Bristol, Milan, and Tokyo. Members wear red berets and are admitted to the group only if recommended by other Angels.

In 1995 Sliwa launched Cyberangels, a child/teenage safety organization that addresses pornography, hate sites, cyberpredators, and violence on the Internet. Sliwa continues to lead the New York Angels and hosts a talk show on WABC radio.

For Further Information

Haskins, James. *Guardian Angels*. Berkeley Heights, NJ: Enslow, 1983.
Guardian Angels, *http://www.guardianangels.org/; http://www.cyberangels.org/guardianangels/*

SMITH, GERALD L.K. (1898–1976). The Reverend Gerald Lyman Kenneth Smith was a fundamentalist clergyman, famous between 1940 and 1976 for his anti-Semitic and anticommunist oratory, his monthly magazine *The Cross and the Flag* promoting "a White, Christian America," his hate radio programs broadcast from WJR in Detroit, and his spellbinding oratory. Born February 27, 1898, in Pardeeville, Wisconsin, Smith was the descendent of four generations of Bible-pounding, fire and brimstone circuit-riding preachers. He became a minister in an evangelical denomination after earning a degree in oratory from Valparaiso University. A precocious student, he graduated in 1917 and took various fill-in posts in churches when regularly assigned ministers were unavailable. In 1922 he married and became pastor of the Seventh Christian Church of Indianapolis and subsequently of the Butler University Church in the same city.

His next congregation was the King's Highway Christian Church in Shreveport, Louisiana. In 1931, during the Great Depression, he ran afoul of conservatives after convincing Senator Huey P. Long to intercede on behalf of poor church members who were facing foreclosures on their mortgages. Smith then became director of Long's Share Our Wealth Society, a social services and public works program which to many was perilously akin to socialism. After leaving this position and adopting more conservative views, Smith started capitalizing on his public speaking skills. H. L. Mencken dubbed him "the gutsiest and goriest, the loudest and lustiest, the deadliest and damnedest orator" he had ever heard.

After Huey Long was assassinated in 1935, Smith assisted Dr. Francis Everett Townsend in promoting his Old Age Revolving Pension

Plan. He then joined FATHER CHARLES COUGHLIN and Townsend in forming the ill-fated Union Party. William Lemke, an obscure member of Congress from North Dakota, ran as its presidential candidate against President Franklin D. Roosevelt in 1936. At the party convention in Cleveland, Ohio, Smith predicted that "[t]hese great phenomenal assemblies, whether they be headed by Dr. Francis E. Townsend, Gerald Smith, or Father Charles E. Coughlin, represent the unmistakable edict that is being issued to the corrupt, seething politicians of America that the baby-having, stump-grumping, sod-busting, go-to-meeting, God-fearing American people are about to take over the United States Government of America." Lemke garnered 2 percent of the popular vote and no electoral votes.

In 1937 Smith formed the Committee of One Million, which had as its mission the destruction of communism and promotion of an all-white, Christian America. The Committee floundered and failed within a year. Smith then moved to Detroit and set up his Federation of Americanization, which met a similar fate. In 1942 Smith began publishing his monthly magazine, *The Cross and the Flag*, a venture that thrived for over thirty-five years. He also ran as an independent for U.S. senator in Michigan, drawing over 32,000 votes.

In 1947 he established what would be his most influential organization, the Christian Nationalist Crusade, and transferred its operation to Los Angeles in 1953. *The Cross and the Flag* readership expanded to over 25,000 subscribers in the 1960s and 1970s. Its circulation, the largest of any extreme right periodical, exceeded that of *The Nation* and *The New Republic*. Smith's other publications included pamphlets with titles proclaiming his bigotry, examples being *The Jew Created Communism* and *Jews Strive for World Control*.

The Christian Nationalist Crusade was largely responsible for fanning public protests against the activist, pro–civil rights Supreme Court, which Smith said was "packed with judges who were soft on Communism."

Hundreds of billboards appearing along highways throughout the Midwest, urging impeachment of Chief Justice Earl Warren, were funded by the Crusade. In 1967 Robert F. Kennedy became one of Smith's prime targets. In the March 21, 1968 issue of *The Cross and the Flag*, Smith warned that electing Bobby Kennedy to the presidency "would be the most catastrophic misfortune that could befall the U.S.A." and that under Kennedy "anti-Semitism would become a crime, punishable by prison or death."

In the late 1960s Smith won national media attention with his plan to build a theme park, featuring a huge statue of Jesus, near Eureka Springs, Arkansas. Despite controversy over the use of federal funds to construct roads to the park, the project proceeded. A seven-story "Christ of the Ozarks" mortar statue was completed that constitutes Smith's most enduring legacy. In 1976 Gerald L.K. Smith died and was laid to rest at the foot of the ivory-white statue.

A spellbinding speaker, Smith had dedicated himself to vilification of Jews and communists as omnipresent evil agents, with blacks as their dupes and fellow travelers. He once wrote, "I expect to live and die a misunderstood man by millions of my compatriots." And thankfully he did, for the good of the nation.

See also: EXTREMISTS

For Further Reading

George, John, and Laird Wilcox. *Nazis, Communists, Klansmen, and Others on the Fringe: Political Extremism in America*. Buffalo, NY: Prometheus Books, 1992.

Jeansonne, Glen. *Gerald L.K. Smith: Minister of Hate*. New Haven: Yale University Press, 1988.

SNYDER, MITCHELL DARRYL (1943–1990).

The leader of the nation's homeless from 1978 until 1990, Mitchell Darryl Snyder was born August 14, 1943, in Brooklyn, New York. His father left Mitch's mother for another woman when Mitch was nine years old, severing all ties to his family and leaving them destitute. As a teenager, Snyder was re-

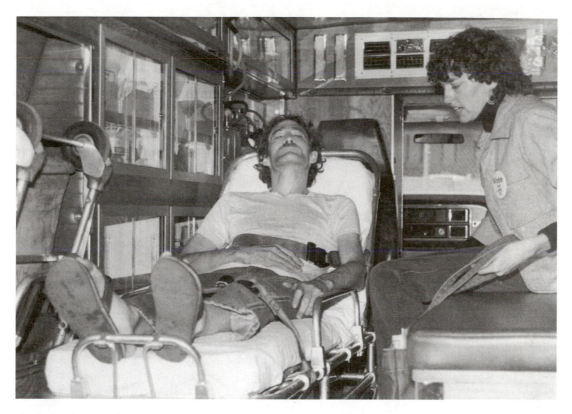

Mitch Snyder, an advocate for the homeless, ends a fifty-one-day fast in November 1984 after President Ronald Reagan accedes to his demand that a Washington homeless shelter be refurbished. *AP Photo/Lana Harris.*

peatedly arrested for breaking open parking meters for spare change to supplement his household's meager income. When he was sixteen, he was sent to a reform school in upstate New York for bright but antisocial youngsters.

In 1963 he married Ellen Kleiman and fathered two sons. His various jobs—selling vacuum cleaners and dishwashers, doing road construction, working as a job counselor—earned insufficient income to pay the rent. Frequently he left his family without forewarning, and during one of these disappearances (1970) was arrested for auto theft in Las Vegas and transferred to a federal prison in Danbury, Connecticut. His cellmates included DANIEL and PHILIP BERRIGAN, famed radical, antiwar Catholic priests who had been jailed for destroying draft records. He joined them in a thirty-three-day hunger strike protesting the treatment of prisoners in Vietnam.

After leaving prison in 1973, Snyder resettled in Washington, D.C., and joined the Community for Creative Non-Violence, an antiwar group. He lost contact with his family until 1985, when he was featured on the CBS News program *60 Minutes* and spotted by his sons and former wife. After a brief family reunion, they again went their separate ways.

In 1978 Snyder started campaigning on behalf of the homeless by parading a coffin around a Washington, D.C. building and dousing its walls with blood to protest city government's inattention to the needs of the homeless. He broke into national prominence during the 1984 presidential campaign when he began a long fast to pressure President Ronald Reagan to approve use of an abandoned federal building in Washington as a shelter for 1,200 homeless men and women. On the fifty-first day of the fast, forty-eight hours before the election, the government acceded to Snyder's demands.

Snyder's life and advocacy of the homeless became the subject of a 1986 CBS documentary, *Samaritan: The Mitch Snyder Story*, starring Martin Sheen. A year later, Sheen, Dennis Quaid, Cicely Tyson, and other celebrities and politicians joined Snyder in sleeping overnight on grates to dramatize federal neglect of the homeless. Snyder held public funerals for unknown homeless victims of the cold, served Thanksgiving and Christmas dinners to thousands of the poor on the Capitol lawn, and deployed other tactics to keep the public continuously aware of the plight of the homeless.

Snyder hanged himself in July 1990, despondent because of a sequence of failed initiatives to ease the plight of the homeless and the rejection of his matrimonial proposal to his longtime companion, Carol Fennelly. JESSE JACKSON, Cher, Martin Sheen, and Dick Gregory were among the many notables who attended his funeral in Washington and delivered eulogies.

A charismatic individual, Snyder had raised more than $100,000 each year in speaking fees that helped fund the Community for Creative Non-Violence shelter that he helped to develop. He possessed a unique ability to goad the establishment into action and to command compassion for the jobless, mentally ill, addicted, and all others who are shut out in the cold.

See also: HOMELESSNESS

For Further Information

DeParle, Jason. "Mitch Snyder, 46, Advocate of Homeless." *New York Times*, July 6, 1990, late edition—final, p. 16.
Samaritan: The Mitch Snyder Story. Television drama featuring Martin Sheen; Richard T. Heffron, director [90 min. Color, VHS, Beta]. New York: CBS, 1986.

SOCIETY FOR THE RIGHT TO DIE.
See Choice in Dying

SOUTHERN CHRISTIAN LEADERSHIP CONFERENCE.
The Southern Christian Leadership Conference (SCLC) was established by the Reverend MARTIN LUTHER KING JR. and his followers in 1957 and was the mainspring of the civil rights movement during the 1950s and 1960s. The SCLC coordinated and served local organizations in their struggle to win for African Americans full citizenship rights, equality, and integration into American society. SCLC worked primarily in the South, adhering to Gandhian principles of nonviolent resistance while conducting leadership training programs on registration and voting, social protest, use of the boycott and picketing, the causes of prejudice, and politics. In 1963 SCLC played a major role in the civil rights march on Washington, D.C., where King delivered his memorable and stirring "I have a dream" speech to over 200,000 people.

SCLC's major victories included passage of the Civil Rights Act of 1964 and the Voting Rights Act of 1965, which suspended the practice of using literacy tests to prevent blacks from voting. In 1965 SCLC purposely provoked authorities to create tension that resulted in the nation's exposure to the shocking sight of defenseless blacks being beaten with clubs and chased by mounted policemen. SCLC's influence declined after its campaign to organize open-housing marches in Chicago floundered in 1966. STUDENT NONVIOLENT COORDINATING COMMITTEE chairman STOKELY CARMICHAEL's popularization of "Black Power" and the more militant actions of other groups such as the CONGRESS OF RACIAL EQUALITY (CORE) diverted public attention from SCLC. Also, King's denunciation of American involvement in Vietnam, his shift toward leftist radicalism and agitation for a guaranteed minimum income, and announced intention to sever SCLC's affiliation with the Democratic Party estranged him from the Lyndon B. Johnson White House and the political establishment.

After King's assassination in April 1968, Reverend RALPH ABERNATHY took his place as SCLC president and resolved to carry out the previously planned Poor People's Campaign. Thousands of blacks and members of other minority groups came to Washington, where they erected "Resurrection City," made up of unsightly temporary structures and tents on federal property between the Capitol and the White House. The occupants were forcibly removed and arrested. After this, the SCLC joined other groups in protesting against the Vietnam War, and in 1972 supported Senator George McGovern's nomination for the presidency. Thenceforth the organization ceased its large-scale demonstrations and focused its attention mostly in the South. In 1977 Abernathy resigned to seek the congressional seat vacated by Andrew Young, and Reverend Joseph E. Lowery, a co-founder of SCLC, succeeded him as president.

Currently the SCLC works primarily in sixteen southern and border states to improve civic, economic, and cultural conditions. It also administers Crusade for the Ballot, a program that aims to increase black electoral participation and voter registration.

Martin Luther King III, the son of Martin Luther King Jr., was elected fourth SCLC president in 1998. The organization's headquarters is in Atlanta, Georgia. The size of SCLC's membership is unavailable.

See also: AFRICAN AMERICAN RIGHTS

For Further Information

Fairclough, Adam. *To Redeem the Soul of America: The Southern Christian Leadership Conference and Martin Luther King, Jr.* Athens: University of Georgia Press, 1987.

Garrow, David J. *Bearing the Cross: Martin Luther King, Jr. and the Southern Christian Leadership Conference.* New York: Morrow, 1986.

STEINEM, GLORIA (1934–). As a writer and activist, Gloria Steinem has been a leader in the late twentieth century women's rights movement and founder of *Ms.* magazine, published for and by women. Born on March 25, 1934, in Toledo, Ohio, she is the daughter of Leo and Ruth Nuneviller Steinem. She was very close to her fa-

ther and his mother, who had served as president of the Ohio Women's Suffrage Association and been a delegate to the 1908 meeting of the International Council of Women. Gloria spent her childhood years traveling from point to point in a trailer while her father, who dealt in antiques, tried to find work. In 1944 her parents were divorced and Steinem went to live with her mother in Toledo. Her mother had a degree in journalism yet was unable to continue her work as Sunday editor for a local paper because of bouts of anxiety neurosis, depression, and agoraphobia. Consequently Steinem became her primary caregiver. In her senior year of high school, she moved to Washington, D.C., and applied to Smith College. She graduated in 1956 with high honors and was offered a fellowship to study in India for two years with a radical humanist group.

Upon returning to the United States, Steinem aspired to a career in journalism in New York City, working with *Help!*, a humor magazine, and publishing her first major article, "The Moral Disarmament of Betty Coed," in *Esquire*. In 1963 she attained high visibility with "I Was a Playboy Bunny," an article exposing her undercover experiences in Hugh Hefner's mansion. In 1968 she was assigned a weekly column in *New York* magazine, "The City Politic" completing the transition from the frivolous to the gritty by handling such subjects as the Poor People's March, Democratic politics, and the Committee for Legal Defense. However, at this point, Steinem was still viewed as marginal and superficial by the media.

She became an active feminist in 1968. The initial issue that drew her attention was abortion, drawing upon her feelings about her own abortion, for which she had to travel to England soon after leaving college. Overnight, she became a popular presenter on the lecture circuit and on talk shows. A co-founder of Women's Action Alliance (1970) and the NATIONAL WOMEN'S POLITICAL CAUCUS (1971), she was instrumental in developing and editing *Ms.* magazine (1973), which was owned and staffed by women and brought their issues to the fore. By the mid-

1970s, the magazine had attracted a readership of over 500,000. Steinem and *Ms.* magazine were attacked by Marxist and lesbian factions of the women's movement for being behind the times, and she was accused of having worked for the Central Intelligence Agency. She survived these attacks and was invited by President Jimmy Carter to take part in the National Committee on the Observance of the International Women's Year. Other organizations she has helped establish include the Coalition of Labor Union Women, Voters for Choice, Women Against Pornography, and Women USA.

As a political activist Steinem assisted in the rise of such leaders as Senators Dianne Feinstein, Barbara Boxer, and Kay Bailey Hutchinson, and former Representative Pat Schroeder, Governor Anne Richards of Texas, Secretary of Transportation Elizabeth Dole, and Attorney General Janet Reno. During recent years, Steinem has continued to write and speak out on the roles of men and women in contemporary society and has fought to empower women in business, politics, the arts, and every walk of life.

See also: WOMEN'S ISSUES

For Further Information

Steinem, Gloria. *Outrageous Acts and Everyday Rebellions.* New York: Henry Holt, 1995.
———. *Revolution from Within: A Book of Self Esteem.* New York: Little, Brown, 1992.
———. *Road to the Heart.* New York: Random House, 1998.

STONEWALL INN RAID. *See* Lesbians and Gays

STUDENT ACTIVISM. Student activism, most often originating on college and university campuses, is rebellion against existing social conditions such as the nation's participation in a war, widespread poverty, segregation and denial of civil rights, and exploitation and manipulation of fellow human beings; it is an organized expression of dissatisfaction with the present state of affairs and the desire for a better and more just society. Activism can follow whenever youth develop values that conflict with those of their parents and wielders of power in society. Students tend to be idealistic, more open to new ideas than their elders, politically naïve, and accepting of deviant views of social reality. Student activists usually begin by seeking reforms in the existing system; if frustrated in their efforts, they either resign themselves to the status quo or advocate the replacement and overthrow of the current system through revolution. STUDENTS FOR A DEMOCRATIC SOCIETY (SDS) is an example of an organization that made the transition from promoting reform to fomenting revolution. Student activism became sufficiently organized, strong, and prolonged to assume the form of student movements at three different times during the twentieth century: 1929–1941, 1960–1972, and 1998–2000.

In 1914, during the early months of World War I, classes, parties, and sports events on college campuses were unruffled by the unfolding conflict in Europe. At Columbia University, the student newspaper focused on a song contest and a recent regatta crew victory. However, the campuses' cocoon of unconcern was punctured when the Germans destroyed the University of Louvain in Belgium and began unrestricted submarine warfare against allied shipping. These events shocked students and faculty, consolidating their support of Britain and France. After the 1915 sinking of the *Lusitania*, Charles W. Eliot, president emeritus of Harvard, spoke out on the Germans' lack of chivalry, mercy, and humanity.

By mid-October 1916, the heads of colleges and universities had drawn up a list of schools that would offer compulsory military training and establish Reserve Officer Training Corps (ROTC) units on their campuses. Most institutions agreed to award credit toward academic degrees for ROTC and military science courses. During the first two years of the war, student activism was on the rise. Many students and faculty believed that preparedness measures were a smokescreen to maneuver the United States into a dangerous foreign conflict irrelevant to American interests. Highly respected peace advocates, including civic reformers Rabbi Stephen Wise and JANE ADDAMS, advised against American entanglement, and in 1915 students formed the Collegiate Anti-Militarism League. Letters were sent to 80,000 students questioning the value of summer military camps that had been started by General Leonard Wood. A majority of respondents, 63,000, disapproved of the military drills and preparedness measures.

In 1916, an election year, the pace of debate picked up on and off campus. Antiwar rallies were held at Columbia University, and in April 1916 the head of the Anti-Militarism League told his audience that the real purpose of the summer military camps was to provide profits for shareholders backing the Army and Navy Co-operating Company. By November 1916, League influence had faded as the bloody tide of war rose in Europe. Still, in mid-January 1917, Columbia University retained a small nucleus of pro-peace student activists. A meeting to mobilize campus sentiment against a proposed universal military training bill attracted 200 students, but the vast majority stayed away. On February 3, 1917, the United States severed all diplomatic relations with Germany and academic freedom became the victim of a national wave of xenophobic hysteria. As early as 1915, there had been attacks on pro-German and German-born faculty, and these became more vitriolic as the war continued. Student editors were censored and atavistic emotion abrogated democratic principles. Critical insights were disallowed and scholars were denied their basic civil rights.

After the war, student hostility to ROTC strengthened, and by the end of the 1920s only 197 of the 382 colleges that had offered military science courses in 1919 continued to list such courses as prerequisites for graduation.

Beginning in 1929, student antimilitarism campaigns resumed. The economic ravages of the Great Depression and the vulnerability of youth to radicalism as a panacea became the yeast of student rebellion. In spring 1934, the first student Strike Against War drew 25,000 demonstrators. A year later, the Strike for Peace was supported by over 175,000 antiwar demonstrators in large and small, private and public colleges and universities. Placards reading "Abolish ROTC," "Scholarship Not Battleships," and "Jesus Not Mars" were posted on campuses, especially those located in the northeastern United States. On April 22, 1936, half a million college students took part in the largest Strike for Peace of the decade. Organizers included members of left-wing groups such as the American Student Union along with newly formed student organizations such as the Veterans of Future Wars (VFW) and Gold Star Mothers of the Future. The students' VFW established 415 collegiate chapters and attracted as many as 5,000 members. The apogee of student antiwar activity was reached in 1936–1937.

In 1936 the Spanish Civil War muddied student antiwar sentiment because Benito Mussolini and Adolf Hitler were delivering military hardware to the fascist rebels so that they could eliminate the Spanish Loyalists. The U.S. Congress passed a joint resolution forbidding the import of munitions to either side, and this worked to the disadvantage of the Loyalists because the rebels had weapons donated by Italy and Germany. Although the majority of students continued to push for noninvolvement unless the United States was invaded, some became uneasy with this position as the conflict spread across Europe and started to envelop China and Japan. In 1939 students formed the American Independence League as a successor to the Collegiate League Against Militarism, but dissolved it by 1941.

The Selective Service Act, passed in 1940, authorized the first peacetime draft in American history, creating a wave of uncertainty, fear, and resentment among students. Some student groups, for example, the Student Defenders of Democracy and the American Student Defense League, backed U.S. efforts to help the beleaguered British, while pro-communist groups, for example, the American Youth Congress, paraded with signs reading "The Yanks Are *Not* Coming." After Hitler's surprise attack in June 1941 on his former ally, the Soviet Union, the leftist groups promptly reversed field and called for "All Out Aid for the Allies."

With America's entry into the war on December 7, 1941, this first student movement came to an end. It had produced a less naïve and better informed student body and laid a foundation for the second student movement, the explosive campus uprisings against the Vietnam War in the 1960s.

Most important as a catalyst was the civil rights movement, which inspired a new generation of young activists. The tone of the time was best conveyed by the Port Huron Statement, TOM HAYDEN's founding document for the SDS in 1962. Its authors identified themselves as "people of this generation, bred in at least modest comfort, housed now in universities, looking uncomfortably to the world we inherit." This complacency was being shattered by events "too troubling to dismiss," the first of which was "the permeating and victimizing fact of human degradation, symbolized by the Southern struggle against racial bigotry." It was in the South that the student leaders gained formative political expertise, by taking part in mass demonstrations and civil disobedience at Montgomery and Selma, joining the Freedom Riders, and learning from mentors at the HIGHLANDER FOLK SCHOOL.

In what would be the event that ignited a nationwide series of campus rebellions, the students at the University of California, Berkeley, decided to test the rules limiting political speakers on campus. In the 1940s and 1950s, the university administration had the authority to rule on the acceptability of speakers that student organizations wished to invite to the campus. At Berkeley, by 1952, the policy enforcing political neutrality was so stringent that it barred presidential candidate Adlai Stevenson from appearing on campus. Subsequently the barriers were removed and the number of political speakers admitted increased from only 7 in 1954–1955, to 68 in 1962–1963, to 188 in 1964–1965, when MARIO SAVIO and the Free

Speech Movement lifted the university's quarantine from exposure to the discontents of society beyond its borders. The Berkeley faculty voted to end all regulation on the content of speech on campus and to uphold due process in the enforcement of university regulations.

At the time of the Berkeley crisis anti–Vietnam War sentiment was still minimal and limited to students at premier colleges and universities. The peak of student involvement was to come between 1968 and 1970. By then, other causes—feminism, environmentalism, consumer activism, civil rights, homelessness, Native American rights, migrant workers' rights, aid to the poor—were to further energize the student movement.

In the late 1960s, the military draft became the biggest issue for students. More than any other single factor, the draft forced college men to oppose the Vietnam War. Fighting was not a source of pride; it was a misfortune and a penalty reserved for young men lacking the wealth, powerful connections, or intelligence to avoid it. A 1971 Harris Poll confirmed that most Americans believed that those who went to Vietnam were fools, risking their lives in the wrong war, in the wrong place, at the wrong time. Students risked and sometimes suffered prison sentences for refusing to register for the draft, picketed military recruiters on campuses, organized mass demonstrations to shut down or burn down college ROTC units, and gathered by the hundreds of thousands with other antiwar activists in major cities across the country. The civil rights movement had taught them that democracy must be fought for in the streets. Draft evaders and resisters became numerous, with over 150,000 emigrating to Canada and other countries. Many avoided conscription by studying abroad. Enrollments in defense-related fields expanded, and graduate schools and the National Guard became popular options. On April 15, 1967, several hundred thousand people demonstrated outside the United Nations headquarters in New York City. On Vietnam Moratorium Day (October 15, 1969), over 2 million Americans participated in antiwar rallies, joined by fifty members of Congress.

Meanwhile formerly nonviolent student groups, particularly the Students for a Democratic Society, were resorting to force. MARK RUDD led a takeover of Columbia University, and riots erupted at the University of Wisconsin, Harvard, San Jose State College, and elsewhere. During the 1969–70 academic year, there were 9,400 such outbreaks. Bombings occurred at Berkeley, Stanford, and Cornell. And in 1970, when President Richard Nixon disclosed that troops had been sent into Cambodia, his "get tough" action triggered a nationwide shutdown of more than 130 colleges and universities in which more than 4 million students took part. At Kent State University, in northern Ohio, students rampaged in protest to Nixon's decision. On May 2 they burned down an ROTC building, and Governor James A. Rhodes dispatched units of the Ohio National Guard to restore law and order. A curfew was imposed, but angry students continued to riot. For three successive nights they tore through the town of Kent, smashing windows and setting fires. On May 4, when a large band of students converged on the university commons to attend a protest rally, National Guardsmen repelled them with tear gas. Students responded by hurling rocks, chunks of pavement, and smoking canisters. One platoon of soldiers started to move away, then suddenly wheeled about, aimed at the demonstrators, and fired. Four students were killed; eight others were wounded. At Jackson State College in Mississippi, a similar incident on May 14 culminated in the death of two students and the wounding of fourteen others. After these events, President Nixon began winding down Americans' involvement in Southeast Asia.

By 1971 students' antiwar protests had ceased and withdrawal to academic pursuits was displacing activism. The economic downturn, beginning in 1970, created a scarcity of new job openings for graduates, and in this buyers' market, fewer students were willing to jeopardize careers by defending their principles. The SDS became fragmented, with the WEATHERMAN, Motherfuckers, and Crazies splitting off from the core organization.

During the 1980s, student organizing became associated with matters of personal identity and rights, focusing on such issues as abortion policy, ethnic group empowerment, animal rights, affirmative action, and lesbian and gay initiatives. Feminist and mainstream gay issues became less prominent, with gays shifting their attention to such concerns as inclusion in the military, gay marriage, and hate-crimes legislation, not the kinds of global issues that inspire large-scale student activism. Most students preferred to focus on getting good grades and jobs, while distancing themselves from politics and citizen action.

Gradual resurgence of student involvement started in the 1990s. In 1995 a new campaign to close sweatshops got under way as students discovered that the sneakers, clothing, toys, and electronic products acquired by Americans are often manufactured under appalling conditions. American labor groups' drive to eliminate such practices took off in the United States and became linked to similar efforts in Europe and Asia. Impetus was given to a third student movement when Nike had to defend itself against well-documented charges that it was locating factories in countries with regimes that suppress organized labor and that its contractors were paying sub-minimum wages, demanding overly long work weeks, and even physically abusing employees. Students, under the aegis of UNITED STUDENTS AGAINST SWEATSHOPS, joined this campaign by pressuring the sweatshop manufacturers of clothing bearing the names and symbols of some of the top universities to improve their labor standards. The new surge of student activism soon became the biggest since the early 1980s, when students had pressured colleges to sell their shares of stocks in companies that were doing business in South Africa during the waning days of apartheid.

The new student groups are anticorporatist and linked to organized labor. Examples include the 180 Movement for Democracy and Education (MDE), the Student Alliance to Reform Corporations (STARC), and Students for Socially Responsible Investing. The 180 MDE mission statement says, "We [are] dedicated to helping build a campus-based movement for political empowerment and participatory democracy. Through education and organizing we hope to encourage a radical political presence in our schools to transform them and our communities into truly democratic spaces. We oppose corporate control of the university and society, inequitable and disempowering elementary education, shrinking access to higher education, and the racism, sexism, homophobia, and other forms of systematic oppression in our world." One of the group's catchphrases is "Corporate Scum, Here We Come!" The group has links to the ASSOCIATION OF COMMUNITY ORGANIZATIONS FOR REFORM NOW, EARTH FIRST!, and other extreme liberal groups. Formed in 1998, 180 MDE is headquartered at the University of Wisconsin (Madison) with chapters at the University of Chicago, Brown University, and other campuses.

STARC, founded in 1999 at Yale University, declared in its mission statement that it was "linked by a common concern, the lack of democratic accountability by corporations. Corporate influence within our government, our media, and our universities has shifted power away from the people, the relentless pursuit of profit without conscience or regard to consequences has inflicted countless wounds on our people and our environment. We must take action. The era in which corporate interests take precedence over justice will end." STARC became part of 180 MDE in 2000.

In the year 2000, students were on the verge of creating a new anticorporatist movement that could generate public outrage. It appeared that the labor movement, church groups, and women's organizations, all historically opposed to sweatshops, would join with the students, widen the campaign, and spread the word to mainstream America.

For Further Information

Cooper, Marc. "No Sweat: Uniting Workers and Students, a New Movement Is Born." *The Nation* 268, no. 21 (June 7, 1999): 11–12+.

Featherstone, Liza. "The New Student Movement." *The Nation* 270, no. 19 (May 15, 2000): 11–16.

Loeb, Paul Rogat. *Generation at the Crossroads: Apathy and Action on the American Campus.* New Brunswick, NJ: Rutgers University Press, 1994.

180-Movement for Democracy and Education, *http://www.corporations.org/democracy/*

Rudy, Willis. *The Campus and a Nation in Crisis: From the American Revolution to Vietnam.* Madison, NJ: Fairleigh Dickinson University Press, 1996.

Student Alliance to Reform Corporations, *http://www.corpreform.org*

Sweatshop Watch, *http://sweatshopwatch.org/*

STUDENT NONVIOLENT COORDINATING COMMITTEE.

Organized in 1960 by sixteen black and white college students, the Student Nonviolent Coordinating Committee (SNCC) affirmed in its founding statement the "ideal of nonviolence and integration as a first step towards a social order of justice." SNCC's aim was to desegregate the South, acting as an adjunct to MARTIN LUTHER KING JR.'s SOUTHERN CHRISTIAN LEADERSHIP CONFERENCE (SCLC).

The motivation for SNCC's formation was the successful sit-in at Greensboro, North Carolina, in 1960. The group peacefully forced desegregation by occupying "whites only" spaces at lunch counters, swimming pools, beaches, and hotels, and in other public accommodations. Unlike SCLC, with its charismatic spokesmen Martin Luther King Jr. and RALPH DAVID ABERNATHY, its big budget, big crowds, and media, SNCC adopted a group-centered leadership. It concentrated on encouraging grassroots lobbying and teaching black people to develop self-reliance. The SNCC freedom riders exhibited unparalleled bravery, prevailing in their four-year suffrage campaign despite beatings, threats, arrests, and murders. Their protest resulted in many blacks winning political offices throughout the South, built a foundation for the Selma campaign, and helped to ensure passage of the Voting Rights Act of 1965.

Initially interracial in its composition, SNCC grew rapidly in the early sixties as members were recruited from college campuses and field offices established in key southern cities. Gradually, as conflicts with white supremacists and local authorities became increasingly violent, SNCC began to adopt more militant tactics and to distance itself from the older, more cautious religious leaders of the civil rights movement. In 1966 STOKELY CARMICHAEL assumed command of SNCC, bringing with him a new and more combative style of leadership. He questioned the validity of the democratic system, advocated revolutionary violence, voiced his antipathy toward the Vietnam War as an act of American imperialism, and called upon blacks to take pride in their heritage and to define their separate goals. After King's assassination, he required white students to return to their campuses and initiated a "Black Power" policy. These changes attracted radical activists to SNCC but alienated others who believed in the validity of integration and American democracy.

As public opinion soured on black radicalism and the Vietnam War came to an end, former supporters defected and SNCC's financial base evaporated. Internal dissension further weakened the organization, resulting in its demise by 1970.

See also: AFRICAN AMERICAN RIGHTS; STUDENT ACTIVISM

For Further Information

Lewis, John. *Walking with the Wind*. New York: Simon and Schuster, 1998.

Lyon, Danny. *Memories of the Southern Civil Rights Movement*. Chapel Hill: University of North Carolina Press, 1992.

STUDENTS FOR A DEMOCRATIC SOCIETY.

Students for a Democratic Society (SDS) began life as the student wing of the League for Industrial Democracy, a moribund social democratic group formed in the 1930s. In 1959 the League detected new signs of leftist activism and reorganized the group as the Students for a Democratic Society.

SDS was a unique organization, employing antiestablishment tactics that have left a lasting imprint on youth culture, educational curricula, and teaching methodology. "Political correctness," the insistence upon inclusive, liberal pedagogy and principles that dominated academic life on many American campuses in the 1990s, is one of SDS's legacies.

In 1960 Robert Allen Haber was elected president at the first SDS national convention, held in New York City. During the next several years, the SDS recruited heavily on university campuses, and its social action program broadened considerably when delegates from eleven colleges convened at Port Huron, Michigan, in 1962. Here the SDS adopted a sixty-page declaration of principles drafted by TOM HAYDEN. SDS would "seek the establishment of a democracy of individual participation governed by two central aims: that the individual share in those social decisions determining the quality and direction of his life; that society be organized to encourage independence in men and provide the media for their common participation." Tom Hayden had worked with the STUDENT NONVIOLENT COORDINATING COMMITTEE on voter registration drives in Georgia and Mississippi and sent back vivid reports to SDS members. He and Haber envisioned the emergence of a white student movement parallel to the pioneering black student movement, with which it might coalesce. Hayden's Port Huron Statement derived its content from the writings of C. Wright Mills, John Stuart Mill, Albert Camus, and John Dewey, criticized the racism, militarism, and apathy of American society, and looked ahead to a regenerated society. The universities would catalyze positive change and students would be the change agents. Alliances would be formed with black activists, the peace movement, the labor unions, and liberal Democrats.

In 1964, as President Lyndon B. Johnson increased America's involvement in Vietnam, SDS began organizing antiwar protests. A year later, SDS leadership cut its ties to the League for Industrial Democracy, decentralized its operation, and urged its chapters to develop projects independently. The SDS Free University Committee launched a campaign for open admissions and course offerings on "relevant" topics such as Zen Buddhism, Marxism, and anarchism.

Resistance to the Vietnam War escalated after 25,000 SDS members participated in a Washington demonstration in April 1965 that linked antiwar and civil rights activists. Journalist I. F. Stone, singers Joan Baez and Judy Collins, Dr. Benjamin Spock, and many other prominent speakers attracted publicity, generating increases in SDS membership.

When draft deferments for students with low grades were revoked in 1966, SDS reacted by conducting sit-ins and takeovers of buildings on college campuses, became militantly anti-ROTC, and threatened Dow Chemical and Monsanto, the producers of napalm. In 1967 and 1968, as SDS became more belligerent, bombs started exploding on campuses, draft records were destroyed, and a Vietcong National Liberation Front flag was placed in front of the Pentagon.

The critical transition year for SDS was 1968. Bernadine Dohrn and Mike Klonsky, revolutionary communists, were elected to national offices; Robert Kennedy and MARTIN LUTHER KING JR. were assassinated; and Columbia University became the site for a headline-grabbing demonstration. SDS organized a takeover of the Columbia campus to protest the university's relationship with the Institute for Defense Analysis. The student uprising shut down the campus and forced cancellation of classes for several weeks. Following the Columbia occupancy, over 3,000 other campus protests occurred and SDS membership peaked at over 100,000 members in 500 chapters.

Following the Columbia University seizure, radical groups within SDS moved the organization further to the left, endorsing terrorist and guerrilla tactics. The group broke into contending factions and never recovered the resources and power it had held in 1968. Some of the splinter groups, notably the Weather Underground (see WEATHERMAN), were responsible for bombings and robberies. Other groups, for example, the BLACK PANTHER PARTY, cut their ties to SDS and worked under entirely separate leadership. The newly invigorated women's movement, formation of the NATIONAL ORGANIZATION FOR WOMEN in 1966, and the inability of the SDS to involve women in key positions led to the defection of many more members. The remaining factions within SDS, such as Puerto Rican rights advocates, Native Americans, and gays and lesbians, squabbled among themselves. Other members resigned in order to support Eugene McCarthy's and Robert Kennedy's bids for the Democratic presidential nomination. These problems exhausted SDS resources, and the end of the Vietnam War eliminated an important justification for its existence. By that time SDS had disappeared.

See also: EXTREMISTS; STUDENT ACTIVISM

For Further Information

Breines, Wini. *Community and Organization in the New Left: 1962–1968. The Great Refusal.* New York: Praeger, 1982.

Unger, Irwin. *The Movement: A History of the American New Left, 1959–1972.* New York: Dodd, Mead, 1974.

SWEENEY, JOHN J. (1934–). The son of Irish immigrants, John Joseph Sweeney has revitalized the U.S. labor movement after a fifty-year decline in its membership, influence, and relevance. Sweeney was born May 5, 1934, in the Bronx, New York, and raised in Yonkers. He grew up in a strongly pro-union home; his father was a city bus driver and an active member of the Transportation Workers Union (TWU), and his mother was a domestic worker. John's father took him to union meetings, and he read the TWU newspaper and joined his father during strike actions.

After graduating from Iona College in

AFL-CIO President John Sweeney leads a labor march and rally in New York's garment district in October 1995. *AP Photo/Ed Bailey.*

1956 with an economics degree, Sweeney was initially employed by IBM but soon moved to a job as researcher for the International Ladies Garment Workers Union. In 1960 Sweeney was asked by Thomas R. Donahue to join the staff of the Service Employees International Union (SEIU) as a contract director. By 1981 Sweeney had risen to the presidency of the international SEIU after leading a series of successful strikes that won workers better job security and higher pay.

Under his leadership, the SEIU initiated research on the impact of repetitive stress syndrome among keyboarders and the effects of video display terminal radiation, launched a "Dignity, Rights, and Respect" campaign for nursing home attendants, and organized a "Justice for Janitors" campaign. Sweeney converted the union into a uniquely upbeat, integrated, and winning operation. The SEIU was an active campaigner for passage of the federal Family and Medical Leave Act, Occupational Safety and Health Administration regulations, and federal regulations banning sexual harassment and discrimination in the workplace. The SEIU experienced remarkable expansion, moving past the million mark by 1995, during a time when other unions were losing members. Unusual because of its pacesetting inclusiveness was the SEIU's Lavender Caucus, representing gay and lesbian interests.

Sweeney has pinpointed problems of "stagnant wages, corporate greed, and a fractured society" and deplores blue-collar workers' willingness to "blame scapegoats put forth by the Rush Limbaughs and Patrick Buchanans of the world instead of attacking the true sources of their economic woes."

In October 1995, Sweeney was elected president of the AFL-CIO and since that time has injected enthusiasm and ardor, sharpened the union's political teeth, and aggressively built up its membership. In 1999 union membership nationwide rose faster than at any time in the previous two decades. The union is reemerging as an assertive, confrontational, politically potent force for labor and social justice. Sweeney has kept his promise that, if elected union head, he would stop labor from being treated "like so much road kill on the highway of American life."

See also: LABOR ISSUES

For Further Information

Sweeney, John J. *America Needs a Raise: Fighting for Economic Security and Social Justice.* New York: Houghton Mifflin, 1996.

SYMBIONESE LIBERATION ARMY.
The Symbionese Liberation Army (SLA) was a ragged band of leftists who terrorized California in the early 1970s, murdering alleged enemies of the people, planting bombs, robbing banks, and kidnapping newspaper heiress Patricia Hearst.

Young Maoist radicals and black convicts formed the SLA in 1972 at Vacaville Prison, near Sacramento, California. Donald De-

Freeze, who had escaped from Soledad Prison in March 1973, assumed command of the fledgling group as Field Marshal Cinque Mtume (fifth prophet in Swahili). His small band of mostly upper-middle-class white young people stated in their founding document that it represented "Asian, Black Brown, Indian, White, Women, Grey and Gay Liberation Movements in a war against the Fascist Capitalist Class, and all their agents of murder, oppression and exploitation." The name "Symbionese" was based on the noun "symbiosis" to define the group as "a body of dissimilar organisms living in deep and loving harmony and partnership in the best interest of all within the body" that would aim to "liquidate the common enemy and overthrow the fascist American government."

In November 1973, two SLA members murdered Marcus Foster, an Oakland, California, school superintendent, with cyanide-coated bullets, after notifying a local radio station that the "court of the people" had ordered the execution. SLA had called Foster, a black administrator, "a fascist insect who preys upon the masses" because he ruled that students must carry school photo-identification cards.

The SLA became national headline news in February 1974 when nineteen-year-old Patricia Hearst, granddaughter of newspaper tycoon William Randolph Hearst, was abducted from her Berkeley, California, apartment. Her captors demanded hundreds of millions of dollars worth of free food to be distributed to the needy in California in exchange for her release. Meanwhile Patty was kept in a closet, bound and blindfolded for fifty-seven days, allegedly raped, mentally tortured, and, under duress, converted from victim to villain. A photo of her, wearing a beret and carrying a rifle while helping to rob a bank, and tapes of her antifascist ravings were made public on national media. After

being recaptured by FBI agents, she was arrested and convicted of robbery, but served only twenty-two months of a seven-year term before having her sentence commuted by President Jimmy Carter in 1979.

FBI agents had earlier traced DeFreeze and five other SLA members to a bungalow in Compton, California, where, in a cataclysmic gunfight and fire, they killed the entire group. The SLA, a close-knit group of not more than a dozen, faded from view and presumably disbanded by 1977.

In 1999 interest in the group was rekindled when Sara Jane Olson, respectable mother of three and a doctor's wife, was arrested in St. Paul, Minnesota, and identified as Kathleen Soliah, a former SLA activist. Soliah had hidden SLA members after the Hearst kidnapping and allegedly placed pipe bombs, which failed to detonate, under two Los Angeles police cars in retaliation for the Compton shoot-out. Olson was first scheduled to go on trial for attempted murder in spring 2001, then postponed until fall 2001. On October 31, 2001, Olson pleaded guilty to planting two bombs, reversing her earlier denial only because of the change in the nation's mood after the terrorist attacks of September 11, 2001.

See also: EXTREMISTS

For Further Information

U.S. House Committee on Internal Security. *The Symbionese Liberation Army: A Study for the Use of the Committee on Internal Security, House of Representatives.* Washington, DC: FBI, February 18, 1974.

Hearst, Patricia. *Every Secret Thing.* Garden City, NY: Doubleday, 1982.

Miller, Mark. "A Bloody 'Army' on Trial: A Court Plans to Relive the '70s Revolution—and Bring Back Patty Hearst." *Newsweek*, February 7, 2000, p. 38.

Sterngold, James. "70's Radical Pleads Guilty in Bomb Plot." *New York Times*, November 1, 2001, p. A 18.

T

TAX REFORM AND GOVERN-MENTAL EXPENDITURES. Tax reform and governmental expenditures are issues that have concerned Americans since the Boston Tea Party (Taxation without Representation) and formation of the nation. What is the proper division between the people's and the government's money? For what purposes should tax dollars be committed? What are the most fair, progressive, and effective ways to distribute tax dollars among local, state, and federal jurisdictions? These questions plague politicians, taxpayers, and economists because the solutions preferred by conservatives and liberals are incompatible. One camp contends that what is good for business is good for the country: minimize taxes on corporations and eliminate capital gains and inheritance taxes, and the ensuing prosperity will raise the standard of living for all people. The opposing faction argues that federal support of social programs and closing the gap between rich and poor is preferable to providing "corporate welfare" through tax reduction and loopholes.

One of the more important reforms of the twentieth century was passage of the Revenue Act of 1935 (known as the Wealth Tax Act), which implemented a graduated income tax to reduce the unjust concentration of wealth and economic power in the hands of a small number of corporations and indi-viduals. It was designed to narrow the gap between rich and poor to a distance acceptable in a democracy. This utilitarian concept of the greatest good to the greatest number was praised by Justice Oliver Wendell Holmes, who said that "taxes are the price we pay for civilization." Other types of taxes, for example, sales, property, and value-added taxes, have not been as readily accepted and are considered by many economists to be regressive.

The NATIONAL TAXPAYERS UNION (NTU) was founded in 1969 to reduce taxes and lobby for taxpayers' rights. Its formation signaled the beginning of a "taxpayer revolt" that lasted through the succeeding thirty years. The NTU is the nation's largest and oldest taxpayers' rights group, representing 300,000 members in all fifty states. It analyzes votes taken in Congress and assigns ratings to legislators. The NTU encouraged HOWARD JARVIS in his successful campaign to pass Proposition 13 in California, a measure that placed a cap on property taxes and set a precedent followed elsewhere.

The NATIONAL TAX LIMITATION COMMITTEE was co-founded by conservative economist Milton Friedman in 1975. It seeks constitutional and other limits on taxes, spending, and deficits at the state and federal levels. It also monitors and rates legislators in Congress.

On June 7, 1978, Howard Jarvis (right) and Paul Gann raise their hands in triumph after passage of Proposition 13, the California property tax relief initiative the two coauthored. *AP Photo/Staff.*

In 1979 CITIZENS FOR TAX JUSTICE was established as a liberal group to correct inequities in the tax code and to redress damage done to underfunded public services and institutions hurt by passage of California's Proposition 13. During President Ronald Reagan's administration, OMB WATCH was founded to open up to public scrutiny the operation of the White House's Office of Management and Budget.

CITIZENS AGAINST GOVERNMENT WASTE, created in 1984, has over 600,000 members and a separate lobbying unit, the Council of Citizens Against Government Waste, that monitors and opposes allegedly excessive federal expenditures. AMERICANS FOR TAX REFORM, a conservative group organized by Grover Norquist in 1985, has 60,000 members who advocate a flat income tax and seek antitax pledges from state and federal candidates for public office. The CONCORD COALITION, a nonpartisan grassroots organization established in 1992, advocates retirement of the U.S. national debt and reduction of government expenditures.

For Further Information

Smith, Daniel A. *Tax Crusaders and the Politics of Direct Democracy.* New York: Routledge, 1998.

TERM LIMITS. Term limits, popular during the 1990s, reflected the public's deep distrust of elected legislators and governors. In 1990 polls indicated that 70 percent of Americans favored an automatic "kick the rascals out" policy. George K. Will argued that "the tireless quest to hang on to office has left individual members of both parties dependent on pleasing special interests, which has all but robbed Congress of any larger notion of the public good." It was expected that the mandatory expulsion of legislators from office after two terms would help restore public faith, deliberative democracy, and congressional supremacy.

Opponents of term limits deplore the bypassing of the electoral process and preplanned expulsion of experienced, competent, engaged, and popular political leaders. They point out that lobbyists for special interests will transfer their pleading and pressure for special treatment to appointed legislative aides who are immune to the automatic dismissal process. Others predict that talented and dedicated individuals will no longer be motivated to run for public office. Additionally, it has been noted that the eighteenth-century model recommending rotation in office often cited by term limits proponents was designed during a time when the conduct of public affairs was dominated by property owners and voting rights were exercised almost exclusively by wealthy white males. Finally, until the mid-1990s, opponents of term limits argued that the drive for their enactment was basically a partisan, conservative-financed plot to dislodge Democrats from longstanding majorities in Congress and state legislatures. And indeed, many citizen groups that had appeared in the early 1990s faded from view after 1995, the year the Republicans recaptured the House of Representatives for the first time in forty years. Temporary, now-defunct citizen groups include Americans Back in Charge, Americans to Limit Congressional Terms, Citizens for Congressional Reform, Citizens for Terms Limits, and Term Limits Legal Institute.

In 1991 Citizens for Congressional Reform claimed over 200,000 members but disbanded within months amid controversy surrounding its funding sources. Its assets were transferred to U.S. TERM LIMITS. U.S. Term Limits, founded in 1990 by libertarian Paul Jacob, is based in Washington and has 151,000 contributors and 175,000 members.

Americans to Limit Congressional Terms, founded in 1989 by former congressman James K. Coyne, filed for bankruptcy in April 1993, following a dispute with RICHARD A. VIGUERIE's direct mailing firm involving a debt of $1.2 million.

For Further Information

Kamber, Victor, and others. *Giving Up on Democracy: Why Term Limits Are Bad for America.* Washington, DC: Regnery Publishing, 1995.

Will, George F. *Restoration: Congress, Term Limits and the Recovery of Deliberative Democracy.* New York: The Free Press, 1993.

TERRY, RANDALL A. (1959–).

Randall Terry was the most prominent figure on the "right to life" side of the fiercely confrontational battle over the abortion issue while in his role as director of Operation Rescue in the late 1980s and early 1990s. A Christian Evangelical lay missionary, with fervor fed by his belief that he was doing what God told him to do, and convinced that the final judgment must punish a society that condones abortion, Terry became the symbol of antiabortion protest between 1984 and 1990.

Born on April 25, 1959, in Rochester, New York, Terry was the son of public school teachers. A rebellious adolescent, he dropped out of school and then attended Elim Bible Institute in Lima, New York. In 1976 he became a born-again Christian, joining a charismatic congregation and developing a lifelong loathing of secular humanism and situational ethics. Terry's anger was reinforced by the Supreme Court's continued adherence to ROE V. WADE (1973) and further fueled by the failure of a conservative Congress, during Ronald Reagan's presidency, to pass a constitutional amendment banning abortion.

In 1984 Terry and his wife opened the House of Life, a crisis pregnancy center, in Binghamton, New York. It was a prototype of other centers where expectant mothers could receive free pregnancy tests, counseling, baby clothes, referral services, and offers of free lodging. That same year he founded Operation Rescue, a citizen action antiabortion organization that in its early stages used nonviolent, civil disobedience tactics.

In 1986 Terry began his pro-life crusade by picketing a Binghamton abortion clinic and doing sidewalk counseling to persuade pregnant women to "choose life" for their unborn offspring. A year later, Operation Rescue started blockading access to abortion clinics, first in Cherry Hill, New Jersey, and in May 1988, in New York City and Long Island. Catholic and Protestant clergy and rabbis joined the more than 1,500 demonstrators who were arrested.

The "Siege of Atlanta," during and after the Democratic National Convention in 1988, resulted in 1,235 people being arrested in twenty-four different "rescues" and drew increased publicity and funding, including a $10,000 check from REVEREND JERRY FALWELL. In Atlanta, Terry was convicted on felony charges of inciting police assault and criminal trespass. During its peak years, 1988–1990, Operation Rescue (which later became OPERATION SAVE AMERICA) claimed more than 100,000 members and mounted blockades at 683 sites in thirty-five states, during which 41,000 demonstrators were jailed. Operation Rescue is credited with laying the groundwork for the subsequent wave of terrorism that included the murders of Dr. David Gunn and Dr. James Barrett, and clinic staff during the 1990s.

After 1988 Operation Rescue's bank accounts were seized and its national headquarters closed, and in 1990 only thirty-four clinics were blockaded and 1,363 persons arrested. Terry then left Operation Rescue to focus his attention on the "Godless, pro-abort judges who serve as lapdogs and lackeys to the NATIONAL ORGANIZATION FOR WOMEN."

In 1998 Terry, who had taken a job as a Binghamton talk radio host, ran as a Right to Life Party candidate against Democrat Maurice Hinchey in New York State's Twenty-Sixth Congressional District. His platform called for a constitutional amendment to ban all property taxes, the elimination of Social Security, and repeal of the federal income tax. Fearing a possible upset victory, centrist Republicans ran a clip from a 1993 speech in which Terry had said to his audience, "Let a wave of intolerance wash over you. I want to let a wave of hatred wash over you. Yes, hate is good." Terry won only 7 percent of the total vote, 12 percent in his home county. The Terrys currently reside near Harpursville, New York.

See also: ABORTION POLICY; EXTREMISTS

For Further Information

Risen, James, and Judy L. Thomas. *Wrath of Angels: The American Abortion War*. New York: Basic Books, 1998.
"Terry, Randall A., Apr. 25, 1959– Antiabortion Activist." *Current Biography*, New York: H. W. Wilson, 1994, pp. 589–593.

20/20 VISION. 20/20 Vision was started in Amherst, Massachusetts, in 1986 by Lois Barber to accommodate busy people who have little time but want to lobby on behalf of issues they care about. Barber, a former grassroots organizer of antiwar and nuclear freeze activists, established 20/20 Vision for people who promise to commit $20 a year and at least twenty minutes each month to convenient, simple, but effective lobbying activity.

Initially the group focused exclusively on efforts to end the nuclear arms race and increase world security. In 1999 the group broadened its agenda to include environmental conservation, handgun control, campaign financing, and other progressive issues, collaborating with other citizen action groups to achieve maximum effectiveness.

The operation of 20/20 Vision is ingenious and effective. A small staff of researchers collects information from newspaper clippings, congressional briefings, individual experts, lobbyists, and libraries, distilling it into issue summaries with recommended twenty-minute actions to be undertaken by 20/20 Vision members. This information is posted on the Internet and sent in the form of a "national postcard" each month. Core group leaders at the congressional district level then produce and distribute locally relevant postcards containing succinct recommendations for action.

Strip mining, wasteful government projects that harm the environment, and genetically altered foods are among current concerns of the group. 20/20 Vision does not expect its members to take part in demonstrations, appear at hearings, deliver testimony, recruit, raise money, or spend time in organizational meetings. Results of group actions are evaluated at six-month intervals and reported to members.

The group has been able to influence legislative decisions because, during action alerts, some 65 percent of 20/20 Vision subscribers write letters or make phone calls to their representatives' offices. This is in contrast to the less than 10 percent response rate achieved by other public interest groups. 20/20 Vision helped to get Congress to approve the Chemical Weapons Convention, an international treaty condemning the manufacture and use of poison gas; pushed EPA development of new clean air standards for pesticide and soot; and urged implementation of tighter idle emission standards for sports utility vehicles, light trucks, and automobiles. The group also helped to get Congress to approve payment of U.S. dues to the United Nations and publicized the need for the United States to ratify the Comprehensive Test Ban Treaty.

20/20 Vision headquarters is in Washington, D.C. James K. Wyerman is executive director, Natalie Hildt is outreach coordinator, and Laura Kriv serves as legislative director. The organization has an estimated 10,000 members comprising thirty core groups in 102 congressional districts. New members receive packets of information tailored to their particular political address.

See also: ANTIWAR/ANTI–NUCLEAR WEAPONS MOVEMENT; CONSUMER RIGHTS AND SAFEGUARDS; ENVIRONMENT; HUMAN HEALTH AND SAFETY; TAX REFORM AND GOVERNMENTAL EXPENDITURES

For Further Information

Motavalli, Jim. "The 20/20 Vision Thing." *E Magazine: The Environmental Magazine*, March/April 1999, pp. 26–27.
20/20 Vision, *http://www.2020vision.org*

U

UNITED FARM WORKERS OF AMER-ICA. The United Farm Workers of America (UFW) helps its members negotiate wages, benefits, and better working conditions, and conducts training programs and workshops. It focuses on immigration and migrant workers, monitoring legislation and regulations that affect farm workers concentrated in the southwestern states.

Hispanic farm workers were organized for the first time by CESAR CHAVEZ in 1962 to combat exploitation by agribusiness. Under Chavez's direction, farm workers mustered allies in other unions, in churches, and in groups affiliated with the growing civil rights movement to fight for improved wages, working standards, and living conditions. The UFW began as the National Farm Workers Association in 1962, and in 1966 merged with another union to form the United Farm Workers Organizing Committee. In 1973 the group adopted its current name.

In achieving UFW objectives, Chavez employed Gandhi's nonviolent tactics of passive resistance and fasting, economic warfare, and group action backed by a firm commitment to egalitarianism and diversity. By 1966 the UFW Organizing Committee had negotiated the first collective bargaining agreement between farm workers and growers in the continental United States. Soon union contracts broke new ground by requiring rest periods, clean drinking water, hand-washing facilities, protective clothing against pesticide exposure, and union hiring halls to guarantee farm workers' seniority rights and job security. Chavez inspired workers to take part in hunger strikes and convinced consumers to boycott lettuce and grapes during the 1970s. He moved the plight of migrant farm workers into the national spotlight and won major concessions such as pensions and increased independence for the union. Membership peaked at 80,000 in 1970.

After Chavez's death in 1993, his son-in-law, Arturo Rodriguez, became union head. He won additional contracts for rose and mushroom laborers and in 1999 conducted federal class action lawsuits against strawberry distributors on workers' behalf. Although UFW had dwindled to only 21,000 at the time of Chavez's death it has rebounded to about 30,000. The UFW is active in many parts of the United States, especially in California, Washington, Florida, and the Northeast. It is associated with the American Federation of Labor and Congress of Industrial Organizations (AFL-CIO). UFW's headquarters office is in Keene, California, near Bakersfield. Arturo S. Rodriguez is president.

See also: HISPANIC AMERICAN RIGHTS; LABOR ISSUES

For Further Information

Ferriss, Susan. *The Fight in the Fields: Cesar Chavez and the Farmworkers Movement.* San Diego: Harcourt, 1998.

United Farm Workers of America, *http://www.ufw.org*

UNITED MINE WORKERS OF AMERICA.

The United Mine Workers of America (UMWA) represents coal miners and other workers in the metals extraction business, acting on their behalf in collective bargaining with industry. UMWA conducts education, housing, and health and safety training programs and monitors federal regulations governing mine safety.

Organized by pit miners in Columbus, Ohio, in 1890, the UMWA became the largest, most powerful, and most progressive labor organization within the American Federation of Labor. In its early days, bitter, often violent disputes broke out against coal mine operators as miners fought to obtain subsistence wages and safe working conditions. Miners were killed during the Lattimer strike in Pennsylvania in 1897 and the Ludlow strike in Colorado in 1913. At Ludlow, a detective agency used a machine-gun mounted on an armored car, the "Death Special," and ignited kerosene to massacre miners along with their wives and children.

Over the years the UMWA has been a pioneer in interracial and interethnic integration. In 1985, during a fifteen-month battle with a coal company, the union employed tactics reminiscent of civil rights demonstrations, including a march of 800 union members chanting "We shall not be moved." This was in response to mine owners who had been using helicopters and an armored personnel carrier to break the strike. In 1988 the union struck the Pittston Coal Company when it attempted to evade an industrywide contract obligation to provide health benefits for retired coal miners. Cecil Roberts, the current UMWA president, received a Rainbow Coalition medal for his role in the strike and an award from CITIZEN ACTION.

Although the union grew rapidly from 1898 until 1908 under John Mitchell, it was the legendary leadership of JOHN L. LEWIS that took it to its zenith of influence in the 1940s. The eloquent and fiery Lewis remained president from 1919 until his retirement in 1960. He took maximum advantage of the pro-labor policy of the New Deal and organized Appalachian miners. Because the UMWA had provided solid support for President Franklin D. Roosevelt in the 1936 election, his Democratic administration could be counted upon as an ally. Lewis and the UMWA became the nucleus of the Committee for Industrial Organization, founded in 1935 and renamed the Congress of Industrial Organizations (CIO) in 1938. In 1942 Lewis broke away from the CIO, and except for a brief reaffiliation (1946–1947), the UMWA remained independent until it joined the AFL-CIO in 1989. At the pinnacle of UMWA power, Lewis proclaimed that "when we control the production of coal, we hold the vitals of our society right in our hands. I can squeeze, twist and pull until we get the inevitable victory." This was at a time when the UMWA had 595,000 members.

After Lewis's retirement, leadership of the union became erratic and corrupt until the early 1980s. One president, W. A. ("Tony") Boyle (1963–1972), was convicted of conspiracy in the murder of insurgent union leader Joseph Yablonski and his wife and daughter in 1969.

In 1968 Consolidated Coal's No. 9 mine in West Virginia collapsed, and seventy-eight minors were trapped and killed in the cave-in. This tragedy, a series of wildcat strikes, and a march on the state capitol shocked the public, creating an opportunity for the UMWA to lobby for mine safety legislation in Congress. Even though President Richard Nixon opposed such legislation, he felt compelled to sign the bill that Congress sent him.

In the 1990s the UMWA no longer represented workers in most of the coal mines and coal-processing industries in the United States. Automation, the closing of unproductive mines, a shift to less labor-intensive surface mining, antipollution requirements set by the 1990 Clean Air Act, the rising use of alternative sources of energy, a general decline in unionism, and the shift from a smokestack to an information economy were clouding the UMWA's future. Added to these problems was the movement of mining to western states where the union has had little success in organizing workers. By 1998 UMWA mines produced less than 30 percent of the nation's coal.

UMWA headquarters is in Washington, D.C. Cecil E. Roberts is currently president of the 187,000-member union.

See also: LABOR ISSUES

For Further Reading

Laslett, John M., ed. *The United Mine Workers of America: A Model of Industrial Solidarity*. University Park: Pennsylvania State University Press, 1996.
United Mine Workers of America, *http://www. umwa.org*

UNITED SENIORS ASSOCIATION.

Formed in 1991, United Seniors Association (USA) describes itself as "a nonpartisan, nonprofit, public interest organization dedicated to educating and informing senior citizens about Social Security, Medicare, taxes, and other issues related to traditional values, national security, and economic prosperity." The group warns its members about governmental reductions of their health care options and endorses a free market approach to Medicare.

Based in Fairfax, Virginia, USA is the second of three different conservative seniors lobbying groups established by RICHARD A. VIGUERIE, a master builder of far right organizations through direct mail. The first group seeded by Viguerie was the SENIORS COALITION, formed to counteract the impact of the allegedly liberal AMERICAN ASSOCIATION OF RETIRED PERSONS. The third Viguerie-inspired group is the 60 PLUS ASSOCIATION, set up in 1992.

Over a million letters mailed by USA used the acronym ALARM (Americans Lobbying Against Rationing of Medical Care) to scare seniors into joining and contributing to the organization. In line with its conservative position, USA has opposed a provision in the Balanced Budget Act that would forbid doctors who contract privately from participating in Medicare for at least two years. The provision would discourage double billing and other possible abuses. Because USA promotes private contracting and a free market approach to health care, it has filed a lawsuit to overturn this restriction. USA argues that the existing law is "anti-senior" when, in fact, it permits doctors and seniors to avoid Medicare if they so choose. If the USA campaign should succeed, doctors would be free to avoid Medicare cost controls and increase seniors' fees.

USA lobbied vigorously against the Clinton proposal for government-administered health care in 1992 and 1993 and claims that its education efforts were in part responsible for the American public's paltry 6 percent support for the bill and its defeat. USA, Inc. Grassroots Leaders groups are now being mobilized to ensure that the group's voice is heard in each congressional district.

Current USA membership exceeds 685,000. The organization's headquarters is in Fairfax, Virginia. Its president is Sandra Butler and its membership chairman is Pat Boone.

See also: FALSE FRONT ORGANIZATIONS; SENIOR MOVEMENT

For Further Information

Quinn, Jane Bryant. "Senior Citizen Groups Mislead Constituency." *Washington Post*, March 8, 1998, Financial section, p. 2.
United Seniors Association, *http://www. unitedseniors.org*

U.S. PUBLIC INTEREST RESEARCH GROUP.

The U.S. Public Interest Research Group (USPIRG) "researches consumer and environmental issues, monitors corporate and governmental actions, and lobbies for reforms at the national level." USPIRG serves as "the national lobbying office for state Public Interest Research Groups (PIRGS), which are nonprofit . . . statewide research and advocacy organizations."

USPIRG was established in 1983 to lobby on behalf of state public interest research groups for passage of national versions of progressive legislation proven effective at the state level. The original PIRGs were founded in 1971 by RALPH NADER to promote consumer protectionism at the state level. Nader critics have noted that the PIRGs were conceived as a means of getting idealistic liberal college students to help subsidize the "public interest" movement. Students would volunteer to work on such issues as pollution, consumer fraud, antibusiness initiatives, opposition to nuclear power, women's rights, and education funding programs. Teams of legal investigators, known as "Nader's Raiders," were formed that produced a series of reports alerting the public to dangerous products and environmental threats. Unsafe vehicles, water pollution, chemical hazards, and other problems attributable to alleged corporate cost-cutting procedures and negligence were widely publicized.

Organizations such as PUBLIC CITIZEN, CENTER FOR AUTO SAFETY, and CLEAN WATER ACTION are among the many watchdog groups Nader founded. He, along with MARTIN LUTHER KING JR. and SAUL DAVID ALINSKY, is considered by many to be one of the most influential citizen activists of the twentieth century. All three fought to make democracy work and inspired their followers to advocate remedial measures that have advanced equity and the quality of life.

In over seventy lawsuits brought by the PIRGs against polluting companies, the groups have won at least $34 million in penalties, forced violators to install new equipment, and shut down illegal sources of pollution. In 1997 Congress eliminated all subsidies for commercial nuclear research and development, a victory for USPIRG staff and coalition partners. The group has also defeated a U.S. Senate bill that would have increased limits on campaign contributions and has beaten back congressional attempts to weaken provisions in the Endangered Species Act.

Other areas monitored by USPIRG include banking practices, product safety, consumer fraud and illegal business practices, global warming, and privacy rights, particularly in the area of credit reporting.

There are an estimated 500,000 PIRG members, more than half of whom are college students, based in twenty-four states. The group sponsors internships and provides opportunities for students to receive academic credit for activities such as legislative research, lobbying, public education, and organizing advocacy.

USPIRG headquarters is in Washington, D.C. Gene Karpinski is executive director. Members receive *U.S. PIRG Citizen Agenda*, an annual report.

See also: CONSUMER RIGHTS AND SAFEGUARDS; ENVIRONMENT

For Further Information

Congressional Quarterly Foundation for Public Affairs. *Public Interest Profiles, 1998–1999.* Washington: CQ, 1998.

Friedly, Jock. "Charges Fly over Advocacy Research." *Science*, March 7, 1997, pp. 1411–1412.

Oldenburg, Don. "Consummate Consumer: Reporting 'Trouble in Toyland.'" *Washington Post*, November 24, 1999, final edition, Style section, p .4.

State PIRGs, *http://www.pirg.org*

U.S. TERM LIMITS. U.S. Term Limits (USTL) was founded in 1990 by businessman and Libertarian Howard Rich in Washington, D.C., to "restore citizen control of government by rallying Americans to limit congressional, state, and local terms." The group was motivated by reelection rates averaging over 90 percent that had created a class of career incumbent politicians "insulated from the public and not representative of the people."

USTL has stated that it is leading the most successful grassroots movement since women's suffrage. During the 1990s, the "kick the rascals out" movement resulted in eighteen state legislatures setting term limits for their members. Cincinnati, Dallas, Denver, New York, Los Angeles, San Francisco, Washington, D.C., and 3,000 other cities and counties had set term limits by 1999.

In 1994 a term-limit pledge was a key part of former House Speaker Newt Gingrich's action agenda for incoming Republicans, known as the "Contract with America." Beginning during the congressional elections in 1994, more than 200 candidates for office signed a voters' contract, pledging their support for legislation that would limit legislators to three terms in the House and two in the Senate. Although the "grassroots" campaign spearheaded by USTL has been funded primarily by corporate and wealthy donors, over 70 percent of the general public favored term limits at the time the Republicans took over Congress in 1994. By 1999 several supporters had recanted their vows and refused to give up their legislative seats, protesting that their work was not yet accomplished, while others were concerned about forced Republican exits resulting in Democratic control of the House in the 107th Congress.

Critics of term limits point out that forced expulsion of seasoned legislators results in the loss of conscientious politicians, those who know about the intricacies of governmental decision making and possess the skills and incentive to work on problems not amenable to quick and easy solutions. The arbitrary dumping of the good along with the bad is a declaration of distrust between voters and their representatives, moving power from elected officials into the hands of lobbyists and appointed legislative staff, while weakening voter suffrage and making government less responsive. Efforts in Congress to produce a constitutional amendment mandating congressional term limits failed to muster the two-thirds majorities required in both the House and Senate in 1995 and again in 1997.

U.S. Term Limits and its affiliated foundation are located in Washington, D.C. Howard Rich is president; Paul Jacob administers the foundation and is national director of the 174,000-member USTL.

See also: TERM LIMITS

For Further Information

Carey, John M. *Term Limits and Legislative Representation*. New York: Cambridge University Press, 1998.
U.S. Term Limits, *http://www.termlimits.org/*

UNITED STUDENTS AGAINST SWEATSHOPS. United Students Against Sweatshops (USAS) is an international student coalition comprising campuses and individual students fighting for sweatshop-free labor conditions and workers' rights. USAS is part of a campaign that began in 1995 against global sweatshops.

Since its formation in late 1998, USAS has grown rapidly into a loose alliance of over 200 student groups (chapters) located on campuses throughout the United States and Canada. USAS has organized sit-ins on major university campuses (e.g., Princeton, University of North Carolina, Purdue, Duke, Tulane, SUNY-Albany, Georgetown, Michigan, Wisconisn, Oregon), picketed, held rallies, and in other ways pressured clothing manufacturers to improve pay and working conditions in factories worldwide. Their prime target has been the College Licensing Company (CLC), the agency that handles athletic goods produced by Nike, Gap, Wal-Mart, Starbucks, Disney, Reebok, Phillips–Van Heusen, and other corporations that are for sale at more than 2,000 retail outlets located on nearly 200 university campuses.

Until 1998 the leading garment makers had attempted to placate anti-sweatshop activists by hiring auditors to inspect overseas factory working conditions without divulging their findings to the public. Therefore USAS activists had good reason to celebrate when, in April 2000, Nike, after three years of prodding, agreed to make public complete audits of its 600 plants that manufacture shoes and apparel. Jansport and Reebok International immediately followed suit by releasing locations of their factories. Leading up to this point, USAS had succeeded in persuading over fifty colleges and universities (including Brown, Bard, Smith, Georgetown, Cornell,

In April 2000, members of United Students Against Sweatshops unfurl a banner at a Niketown store in New York accusing Nike of using sweatshop labor to produce its athletic apparel. *AP Photo/Tina Fineberg.*

Columbia, and the University of California system) to join the Worker Rights Consortium (WRC) and quit the Fair Labor Association (FLA), an industry-backed monitoring system that evolved from a White House task force and various human rights groups. The students contended that the FLA would permit corporate cover-ups and the continuation of intolerable factory conditions.

The WRC is a nonprofit organization that supports and verifies licensee compliance with production codes of conduct. Colleges and universities have developed the codes to ensure that goods are produced under conditions that respect the basic rights of workers. The WRC governing board includes USAS members, university faculty, representatives of labor and religious organizations, and members of Congress. The WRC demands that all collegiate licensees monitor their suppliers and provide full disclosures of their findings. If they fail to do so, they forfeit their university contracts. After USAS succeeded in pressuring the University of Oregon to drop FLA and join the WRC, Nike chief executive officer Phil Knight retaliated by retracting the $30 million he had donated to his alma mater to build a sports stadium.

USAS has strong ties to unions that share its anticorporatist objectives. JOHN J. SWEENEY and the AFL-CIO are allies, as is George Becker, president of the United Steelworkers. In 1999 Becker denounced the University of Wisconsin administration's use of police to expel fifty-four anti-sweatshop protesters. USAS was one of the many liberal and extremist groups that participated in the demonstrations against the World Trade Organization in Seattle in December 1999.

United Students Against Sweatshops is headquartered in Washington, D.C., and has a contact office at the University of Michigan. Information on leadership and the size of the group is unavailable.

See also: STUDENT ACTIVISM

For Further Information

Featherstone, Liza. "The Student Movement Comes of Age." *The Nation*, October 16, 2000, pp. 23–26.
United Students Against Sweatshops, *http://www.usasnet.org*

URBAN COALITION ACTION COUNCIL. *See* Common Cause

V

VETERANS' ISSUES. Veterans' issues include pensions, service-connected disability payments, burial benefits, education, training, vocational rehabilitation, employment, housing loans, special housing for paraplegics, provisions for readjustment to civilian life for disabled veterans, assistance for survivors of deceased veterans, and construction of medical facilities.

Veterans' concerns have elicited scant attention from nonveteran citizen activists. In contrast, Supreme Court decisions and legislation that affect such areas as the environment, freedom of expression, civil rights, minority and women's rights, occupational safety and health, and the separation of church and state have inspired massive lobbying efforts to influence politicians in state capitols and in Washington. When a veterans' compensation bill came before Congress in 1991, no citizen action group appeared to argue for or against a standard of living adjustment for disabled veterans or entered into the controversy over illnesses caused by exposure to Agent Orange, a defoliant used during the Vietnam War. This is because veterans have never been a weak or underrepresented constituency. Their status as patriotic defenders and heroes/heroines is unassailable, and they have developed strong, effective support groups and so require little outside help in capturing the attention of Congress.

The AMERICAN LEGION, founded in 1919, is the largest veterans' organization, numbering about 3 million men and women who have served in one or more of the eight U.S. military engagements that took place during the twentieth century, from World War I through the Kosovo intervention. The Legion has advocated key legislation, beginning with the National Defense Act of 1920 and the Soldiers' Bonus Act of 1924. The bonus was originally in the form of twenty-year endowment policies on which ex-servicemen might borrow from the government up to about 25 percent of full value. Because cash payments were disallowed, World War I veterans formed the BONUS ARMY, set up encampments near the Capitol in Washington, and had to be forcibly removed. By 1936 a bill calling for full cash payment of adjusted service certificates (the bonus) was enacted over President Franklin D. Roosevelt's veto.

The AMERICAN VETERANS COMMITTEE (AVC) was established in 1943 as a more liberal and less narrowly focused alternative to the American Legion and Veterans of Foreign Wars. The AVC motto is "Citizens first, veterans second," and its members have fought racial discrimination in the armed forces, advocated women veterans' issues, and worked for international cooperation and peace.

The most recently established group is

AMERICAN VETERANS OF WORLD WAR II, KOREA AND VIETNAM (AMVETS). AMVETS promotes benefits for veterans who served in the military after September 15, 1940. It helps its members obtain benefits, participates in community programs, and operates a volunteer service that donates time to hospitalized veterans.

For Further Information

Bolté, Charles G. *The New Veteran: Hero or Problem?* New York: Reynal and Hitchcock, 1945.

Daniels, Roger. *The Bonus March: An Episode of the Great Depression.* Westport, CT: Greenwood Press, 1971.

Flanagan, Richard W. *AMVETS: Fifty Years of Proud Service to America's Veterans.* Lanham, MD: AMVETS (American Veterans of World War II, Korea and Vietnam), 1994.

Rumer, Thomas A. *The American Legion: An Official History, 1919–1989.* New York: M. Evans and Co., 1990.

VIGUERIE, RICHARD A. (1933–).

Born September 23, 1933, in Golden Acres, Texas, in the midst of the Great Depression, Richard Viguerie takes credit for revolutionizing American politics in the 1960s and 1970s when he combined computers, direct mail, and politics to create the first political campaigns and political movements financed by a broad base of grass roots supporters, rather than a small coterie of "fat cats." A significant number of members of the U.S. House and Senate, state legislators, and city public officials have gained public office because of media blitzes organized by Viguerie. By generating over 1.5 billion letters, his direct mail operations have made him a millionaire and a major factor in the conservative successes that led to the "Reagan Revolution."

While enrolled as an engineering student at Texas A&M University at Kingsville, Viguerie assisted in Dwight D. Eisenhower's presidential campaign and in John Tower's successful bid to become the first Republican senator from Texas. Viguerie transferred to the University of Houston and earned a B.S. in political science in 1956 but failed to obtain his law degree.

In 1961 the newly formed conservative group Young Americans for Freedom (YAF) hired Viguerie as its executive secretary, and he took on the responsibility of raising funds to eliminate YAF's $20,000 debt. It was then that he discovered his talent as a direct mail fundraiser.

He left YAF and started his own direct mail business, using a list of 12,500 contributors to Senator Barry Goldwater's 1964 presidential campaign. By 1975 he had set up a corporation and was publishing the *New Right Report* and *Conservative Digest*. He absorbed arch-segregationist Governor George Wallace's direct mail operation in 1973 and raised over a million dollars by 1976. In 1980 he published *The New Right: We're Ready to Lead*, a self-defining political manifesto, in which he stated his intention to roll back the Great Society legislation of the 1960s. Democrats George McGovern, Frank Church, and Birch Bayh were among the many liberals who lost their seats in 1980 because of Viguerie's mailed pleas to "topple the establishment and return the power to the people."

Viguerie, more than another other political professional, has popularized direct mail, creating a breakthrough message-delivery system that unites information technology with political strategy. By computerizing and merging lists of donors to conservative candidates including Jesse Helms, Oliver North, and Patrick Buchanan, Viguerie developed the consummate right-wing mailing list. Additionally, his mailings have served as recruitment, public education, and movement-building tools. Typically the letters are in three parts: they raise an alarm (e.g., the government will confiscate your privately owned guns), identify the perpetrator (e.g., liberal gun control legislation will deprive you of your constitutional right to defend your home and engage in recreational shooting), and suggest corrective action (e.g., lobby against gun control).

In the 1970s and 1980s Viguerie's mass mailings were new and extremely effective because the public was not yet aware of their manipulative nature. During the 1990s many new right-wing organizations sprang up, seemingly out of nowhere, inspired by the emotion-laden, anger-inducing appeals that Viguerie mailed to hundreds of thousands at a time. For example, his direct mail operation facilitated the funding and development of three different conservative senior groups, the SENIORS COALITION, UNITED SENIORS ASSOCIATION, and 60 PLUS.

In 1999 Viguerie had been crafting letters for Mayor Rudolph Giuliani's New York senatorial campaign against Hillary Rodham Clinton until the mayor vacated the race because of personal and health problems. Viguerie then stepped down from his position as president of American Target Advertising to launch a new activist venture, ConservativeHQ.com, in January 2000, ex-pected to reach "the more than 40 million conservatives who will be online by the year 2002." Viguerie's vision is to create a site that will "address the social, cultural and political needs of American conservatives and provide a new forum for leadership and unity using what is potentially the most potent grassroots medium we have ever seen."

See also: CONSERVATIVES (FAR RIGHT)

For Further Information

Site of the Month Supplement. *Campaigns and Elections*, June 2000, p. 51.

Viguerie, Richard A. *The Establishment vs. the People: Is a New Populist Revolt on the Way?* Washington, DC: Regnery, 1984.

———. *The New Right: We're Ready to Lead*. Falls Church, VA: Caroline House, 1980.

Richard Viguerie's Conservative Headquarters.com, *http://www.conservativehq.com*

W

WALSH, JOHN (1945–). Born in Auburn, New York, December 26, 1945, John Walsh, the father of abduction and murder victim Adam Walsh, converted his rage into an obsessive and successful campaign for passage of the Missing Children's Assistance Act of 1982. In 1983 Daniel J. Travanti played Walsh in an NBC made-for-TV movie about the case, *Adam*, which became one of the most widely watched TV movies. Because of Walsh's unremitting effort, the National Center for Missing and Exploited Children was established in 1984 as a public-private partnership, operating as the national clearinghouse for information on missing children and the prevention of child victimization.

Walsh spent his early years in Auburn, New York, attended the University of Buffalo, and built a career in hotel management. In 1981 he was planning a $26 million hotel complex in the Bahamas and living in Hollywood, Florida. On July 27, 1981, his wife Reve needed a new lamp, and she and Adam went to Sears. Adam was permitted to play video games while she shopped only three aisles away. Adam vanished, and after a two-week search, several fishermen in Vero Beach, Florida, found his severed head floating in a canal. When the Walshes contacted the police, they were horrified to discover that no mechanism existed to search for a missing child on a statewide or nationwide level. During the months immediately following the grisly killing, Walsh launched a crusade to develop an improved search and rescue system, testifying and lobbying in forty-seven states for tougher and more uniform laws for crimes involving children.

In 1987 the Fox television network was developing a true-crime show, a series that would profile some of the nation's most dangerous fugitives from justice and reenact their crimes. The executive producer of *America's Most Wanted* selected John Walsh as host of the show, which premiered in 1988. As of 1997, it had been instrumental in apprehending 433 fugitives, 11 of them on FBI "ten most wanted" lists.

In 1999 the National Center for Missing and Exploited Children moved into a new state-of-the-art headquarters building in Alexandria, Virginia. The Center has helped locate over 47,000 children and has achieved a recovery rate of over 90 percent. Its online, multilingual database of images and age-progression technology makes possible identification from photographs, even years after a child's disappearance. The Center's Web site, *www.missingkids.com*, receives more than 2 million hits per day.

See also: CHILD AND YOUTH-RELATED ISSUES

John Walsh (left) and Fred Goldman, whose son Ron was killed with Nicole Brown Simpson in 1994, prepare to discuss the proposed Victim's Rights Amendment at a Washington press conference in April 1997. *AP Photo/Joe Marquette.*

For Further Information

Szegedy-Maszak, Marianne. "Avenging Adam." *Biography* 1, no. 5 (May 1997): 4–7.

WEATHERMAN. Weatherman was founded in 1969 in Chicago by the Revolutionary Youth Movement, a group that split off from the STUDENTS FOR A DEMOCRATIC SOCIETY (SDS) and declared that the "main struggle going on in the world today is between U.S. Imperialism and the national liberation struggle against it." The splinter group, led by Bernadine Dohrn, included Bill Ayers, John Jacobs, Karen Ashley, Jim Mellen, and MARK RUDD. Although their declaration concluded with the revolutionary cry "Long live the victory of the people's war of the People's Republic of China," the group was more anarchistic than Maoist in its struc-ture. At an early organizational meeting, surrounded by photos of Fidel Castro, Che Guevara, Ho Chi Minh, Mao Zedong, and Lenin, Rudd rhapsodized over "the wonderful feeling aroused by hitting a pig [slaying a police officer]."

The name "Weatherman" was inspired by the line "You don't need a weatherman to know which way the wind blows" from the Bob Dylan song "Subterranean Homesick Blues." After becoming "Weatherpeople" to placate feminists, the group renamed itself "Weather Underground" and expelled three-quarters of its members, who questioned the value of terrorism.

During October 1969, the group hoped to recruit 15,000 activists to take part in an antiestablishment rampage, dubbed "Days of Rage." The much smaller force of about 200 that materialized began its action by blowing up a monument to policemen in Chicago's

Haymarket Square and followed this by demolishing cars and business property. By February 1970, the group had dispersed into small communes or cells. Thereafter, they started using high explosives, collaborating with Revolutionary Force 9 in a series of New York City bombings. Although the resulting property damage was extensive, loss of life was minimal, with most of the fatalities being caused by bumbling Weathermen who had accidentally blown themselves up. On March 6, 1970, a bomb factory in a house in Greenwich Village exploded and three more Weathermen perished. Subsequent bombings occurred at the Capitol and the State Department in Washington, D.C., and Bernardine Dohrn displaced ANGELA DAVIS on the FBI's most wanted list. Dohrn and Bill Ayers reappeared in 1980, were indicted, served time in prison, and were married in 1982.

In 1981 Kathy Boudin and several other Weathermen robbed a Brink's armored truck near Nyack, New York, and killed two police officers and a guard. Boudin was captured and found guilty of the crime, thereby concluding the final episode of the New Left movement.

Terrorist tactics, self-destructive behavior, and rabid allegiance to unconstitutional principles resulted in the demise of the Weatherman Underground. Their activities had discredited the antiwar movement and given President Richard Nixon's administration the justification it needed to launch a full-scale assault against dissent.

See also: EXTREMISTS

For Further Information

Castellucci, John. *The Big Dance: The Untold Story of Kathy Boudin and the Terrorist Family that Committed the Brink's Robbery Murders*. New York: Dodd, Mead, 1986.

George, John, and Laird Wilcox. *American Extremists: Militias, Supremacists, Klansmen, Communists, and Others*. Amherst, NY: Prometheus Books, 1996.

WEBSTER V. REPRODUCTIVE HEALTH SERVICES (492 U.S. 490)

(1989). In its *Webster v. Reproductive Health Services* decision the Supreme Court ruled that states may sharply limit abortion practices. The 5–4 decision upheld a controversial Missouri abortion law but stopped short of overturning the landmark *ROE V. WADE* (1973) case, which had legalized abortion on demand. However, *Webster* made abortions more difficult and expensive to obtain.

Webster upheld three states' restrictions on abortion. The Court ruled that states may forbid abortions in public hospitals or other taxpayer-supported facilities, may forbid public employees to perform elective abortions, and may require viability tests for fetuses estimated to be at least twenty weeks old. Chief Justice William Rehnquist recommended a further "narrowing of *Roe v. Wade* in succeeding cases" if given the opportunity. Justice Antonin Scalia stated that there were "valid and compelling reasons to overturn *Roe v. Wade*," and Justice Sandra Day O'Connor found the decision "problematic."

The author of the *Roe v. Wade* decision, Justice Harry Blackmun, attacked the majority in *Webster* and wrote, "I have fear for the future. While for today, at least, the law of abortion stands undisturbed, the signs are very evident and very ominous, and a chill wind blows." In the year 2000, *Roe v. Wade*, permitting elective, though restricted, abortion, was still intact, but its eventual nullification seemed likely. In the late 1990s, a Republican Congress was seeking ways to further confine abortion rights. Some states had no restrictions, others had imposed bans on abortions in public facilities, added parental consent requirements and waiting periods, and prescribed detailed informed consent procedures designed to deter women from exercising what was still their constitutional, albeit limited, right.

See also: WOMEN'S ISSUES

For Further Information

Tribe, Laurence H. *Abortion: The Clash of Absolutes*. New York: W. W. Norton, 1992.

WILDERNESS SOCIETY. The Wilderness Society (WS) was founded in 1935 by the militant conservationist Robert Marshall "to preserve wilderness and wildlife, protect America's forests, parks, rivers, shorelands, deserts, and all other public lands and foster the development of an American land ethic." WS defines itself as being the only conservation organization devoted exclusively to issues relating to all federal public lands.

Robert Sterling Yard, a former director of the NATIONAL PARKS AND CONSERVATION ASSOCIATION, Benton MacKaye, "Father of the Appalachian Trail," and naturalist Aldo Leopold were the Society's co-founders. Their intent was to create a broad, committed, and influential constituency that would insist that political leaders support wilderness preservation and land protection.

WS relies on a combination of grassroots organizing, public education, advocacy, and economic and ecological analysis. The Society monitors and takes positions on federal, legislative, and administrative actions affecting national forests, parks, and wildlife refuges, and Bureau of Land Management lands. It encourages Congress to designate appropriate public lands as wilderness areas.

The group was instrumental in the drafting and passage of the Wilderness Act of 1964. Although membership quadrupled between 1960 and 1970, in later years the Society was beleaguered by the cost of legislative campaigns, increased staff, and an expensive, futile lawsuit against Alaskan oil pipeline proponents. In 1978 William A. Turnage became executive director and brought in new grants, new administrators, and new members. WS reemerged as a leader in engineering passage of important pieces of legislation including the Omnibus Parks Act (1978), Alaska Lands Act (1980), Tongass Timber Reform Act (1990), and California Desert Protection Act (1994). In the late 1990s, WS, along with its allies, was fighting congressional efforts to reduce protection for scenic lands and wildlife. Pending bills and riders to appropriations would permit overlogging, oil and gas development, off-road vehicles on public lands, increased noise pollution from motors, grazing, and elimination of many existing environmental protections.

The Wilderness Society is headquartered in Washington, D.C., with field offices in Anchorage, Seattle, San Francisco, Boise, Bozeman, Denver, Atlanta, and Boston. William H. Meadows III is current president of the 200,000-member organization. Publications include *Wilderness America*, a biannual newsletter, *Wilderness* (annual), and numerous reports on environmental issues. An e-mail publication, *WildAlert*, provides weekly news about threats to wildlands, in the field and in Washington, and advises readers regarding appropriate action they should take.

See also: ENVIRONMENT

For Further Information

Glover, James M. *A Wilderness Original: The Life of Bob Marshall*. Seattle: Mountaineers, 1986.
Wilderness Society, *http://www.wilderness.org/*
The Wilderness Society 1, 1 (Winter 1998–1999).
Zakin, Susan. *Coyotes and Town Dogs*. New York: Viking, 1993.
Zaslowsky, Dyan. *These American Lands*. New York: Holt, 1986.

WOMEN'S ACTION FOR NEW DIRECTIONS. Women's Action for New Directions (WAND) is a grassroots organization that works to "(1) empower women to act politically, (2) reduce militarism and violence, and (3) redirect excessive military resources toward human and environmental needs." Dr. Helen Caldicott started WAND in 1980 with the aim of ending the threat of nuclear annihilation. An Australian mother and physician, Caldicott had been an effective spokesperson for the nuclear disarmament movement in the South Pacific. She coined the slogan "Nuclear disarmament is the ultimate form of preventative medicine."

After moving to the United States, Caldicott founded the Women's Party for Survival, which in 1980 was renamed Women's Action for Nuclear Disarmament. In 1991 the organization adopted its current, more inclusive title, Women's Action for New

Directions. In 1981 a tax exempt 501©(3) sister organization, the WAND Education Fund (WAND EF), was established to develop educational materials for training and briefing grassroots activists, legislators, and the media. WAND EF sponsors lectures and holds annual media celebrations on Mother's Day, seeking to restore the day to its original purpose (suffragist and reformer Julia Ward Howe's concept) as a call for women to speak out on issues of war and peace. WAND has a separate related political action committee, set up to endorse and contribute financial support to WAND-friendly candidates for public office.

In 1997 the Code of Conduct on Arms Transfers, a bill drafted and spearheaded by WAND, was passed by Congress. This measure prohibited sales of arms to countries with human rights abuses.

WAND has its national office in Arlington, Massachusetts, a legislative office in Washington, D.C., and a national field office in Atlanta, Georgia. Susan Shaer serves as executive director of the 10,000-member organization.

See also: WOMEN'S ISSUES

For Further Information

Laidler, John. "Hildt, Shaer Give Group Strong Base in This Area." *Boston Globe*, October 19, 1997, Northwest Weekly section, p. 1.

Women's Action for New Directions, *http://www.wand.org*

WOMEN'S ISSUES. Suffrage, the right to vote, was one of the two dominant women's issues during the first twenty years of the twentieth century. The National American Woman Suffrage Association, formed from two previous groups in 1890, held conferences, campaigned widely, and distributed literature. British women suffragists set the pace for progress with their nonviolent parades and outdoor speeches, inspiring American women to employ similar lobbying tactics. The early equal rights feminists directed their appeals for suffrage to women laborers, professionals, and college educated individuals, all of whom had an incentive to gain access to more responsible and better paying jobs.

In 1920 the United States adopted the Nineteenth Amendment to the Constitution, granting American women their voting rights. At this point, most of the women who had been fighting for suffrage were also caught up in the temperance and progressive movements. These middle- and upper-class women favored prohibition and campaigned for improvement of the cruel and dangerous working conditions forced upon less fortunate women and children. They also took pride in their traditional roles as mothers and wives. Although Elizabeth Cady Stanton, a militant feminist, believed that motherhood and marriage were only incidental responsibilities, most of her peers continued to consider motherhood and marriage not only sacred, but the best justification for their right to vote.

Birth control became the second big issue of the time. MARGARET SANGER took the lead in the fight to legalize contraception and in promoting planned parenthood. She advocated birth control, not as a woman's issue, but as a social reform, while publicly denouncing abortion.

The next burst of activity for the women's movement came in the 1960s, with the publication of BETTY FRIEDAN's *The Feminine Mystique* (1963). The concurrent civil rights movement provided support from college students and other activists involved with such organizations as the SOUTHERN CHRISTIAN LEADERSHIP CONFERENCE, CONGRESS OF RACIAL EQUALITY, and STUDENT NONVIOLENT COORDINATING COMMITTEE. However, as these groups reached a more militant stage during the mid- and late 1960s, they became sexist and antifeminist.

The 1970s women's groups shifted their attention to other concerns such as health care, domestic violence, and the 'glass ceiling' in corporate and public sector America that imposed an arbitrary limit on women's upward professional mobility. After 1973 and the *ROE V. WADE* Supreme Court decision, a countermovement got under way.

A group of men look into the windows of the National Anti-Suffrage Association headquarters c. 1911. *Library of Congress, Prints and Photographs Division, LC-USZ62–25338 DLC.*

The RELIGIOUS RIGHT, political conservatives, and traditional family values proponents, led by PHYLLIS SCHLAFLY and others, established the EAGLE FORUM and CONCERNED WOMEN FOR AMERICA to stem the tide of feminism. Additional conservative groups mobilized to block further expansion of women's rights.

Although the Republicans emphasized the theme of family values at their 1992 nominating convention, Democrat Bill Clinton won the presidency and there followed a brief respite from attack. However, in 1994, with Republicans winning control of both houses of Congress, the feminists' gains were subjected to renewed assault. By 1999 a conservative trend was apparent with the likelihood of reversal of earlier advances and nullification of *Roe v. Wade* increasing.

A chronology identifying key people and groups associated with women's issues follows.

Chronology of Developments

1900–1904   CARRIE CHAPMAN CATT serves as president of the North American Woman Suffrage Association. Catt campaigns for passage of the Nineteenth Amendment (1920).

1908   In *Muller v. Oregon*, the U.S. Supreme Court rules that protective legislation for women in the workplace is unconstitutional.

1908   Jovita and Soledad Pena organize La Liga Feminil Mexicanista (League of Mexican Feminists) in Laredo, Texas. Its motto is "Educate a woman and you educate a family."

1913   ALICE PAUL and Lucy Burns organize the Congressional Union, later to become the National Woman's Party. Paul pickets the White House and pioneers other forms of nonviolent civil disobedience. Eight thou-

Calling upon President Woodrow Wilson to support voting rights for women, a group of women suffragists form a picket line in front of the White House in February 1917. *Library of Congress, Prints and Photographs Division, LC-USZ62–31799 DLC.*

sand women march up Pennsylvania Avenue to dramatize women's desire for an amendment to the Constitution giving them the right to vote.

1914 Margaret Sanger publishes the radical feminist magazine *The Woman Rebel*, offering advice on contraception.

1915 Margaret Sanger opens the first American birth control clinic, in Brooklyn, New York.

1915–1947 Carrie Chapman Catt again serves as president of the North American Woman Suffrage Association. She continued as honorary president of LWV until her death.

1916 The PLANNED PARENTHOOD FEDERATION OF AMERICA is founded by Margaret Sanger. The Federation is "dedicated to the principle that every woman has the fundamental right to choose when or whether to have children." Sanger is arrested and imprisoned for operating her birth control clinic.

1920 Tennessee, by a margin of one vote, becomes the thirty-fifth and final state to ratify the Nineteenth Amendment to the Constitution, granting women the right to vote.

1920 The LEAGUE OF WOMEN VOTERS is established by Carrie Chapman Catt as the successor to the National American Woman Suffrage Association to educate newly enfranchised voters about political issues.

1921 FLORENCE KELLEY becomes president of the NATIONAL CONSUMERS' LEAGUE and promotes women's influence in the marketplace as buyers of household goods and boycotters of sweatshop-produced clothing.

1921   The AMERICAN ASSOCIATION OF UNIVERSITY WOMEN is founded.

1923   Alice Paul and the National Woman's Party succeed in getting an Equal Rights Amendment introduced in Congress stating that "men and women shall have equal rights throughout the United States and every place subject to its jurisdiction." In 1943 a revision was reintroduced as the Equal Rights Amendment.

1936–1962   ELEANOR ROOSEVELT plays a major role in championing civil rights and sets a precedent as an independent and activist first lady. She works with Florence Kelley, coordinates the League of Women Voters legislative program, and lobbies for the appointment of women to high-level political positions.

1945–1952   After President Franklin D. Roosevelt's death, President Harry S. Truman appoints Eleanor Roosevelt U.S. delegate to the United Nations.

1961   President John F. Kennedy establishes the President's Commission on the Status of Women and designates Eleanor Roosevelt as its chair. Fifty parallel state commissions are eventually set up.

1963   Betty Friedan's best seller, *The Feminine Mystique*, details women's role in American society and their frustrations, laying the foundation for the modern feminist movement

1964   In *GRISWOLD V. CONNECTICUT* (381 U.S. 479) the U.S. Supreme Court holds unconstitutional a Connecticut birth control statute that banned the use of contraceptives and giving medical advice as to their use as a violation of marital privacy, emanating from the First, Third,

Fifth, Ninth, and Fourteenth Amendments.

1966   The NATIONAL ORGANIZATION FOR WOMEN (NOW) is founded by twenty-eight women angered by the Equal Employment Opportunity Commission's disregard of gender discrimination complaints.

1969   The NATIONAL ABORTION RIGHTS ACTION LEAGUE is founded.

1970   The Equal Rights Amendment is reintroduced in Congress.

1971–1972   *Ms.* magazine premieres as an insert in *New York* magazine. GLORIA STEINEM, *Ms.* co-founder and editor, becomes prominent in the media and a strong spokesperson for the women's movement.

1971   The NATIONAL WOMEN'S POLITICAL CAUCUS, a nonpartisan grassroots group, is formed to increase the number of women running for public office.

1973   In *Roe v. Wade* (410 U.S. 113), the U.S. Supreme Court establishes a woman's right to abortion, effectively canceling the antiabortion laws of forty-six states.

1973   The NATIONAL RIGHT TO LIFE COMMITTEE is founded by pro-life activists in response to the *Roe v. Wade* Supreme Court decision.

1975   Phyllis Schlafly, crusader for traditional family values, establishes the Eagle Forum and launches her campaign against states' ratification of the Equal Rights Amendment.

1976   The NATIONAL WOMEN'S HEALTH NETWORK is established to give women a voice in legislative decisions affecting U.S. health care policies and practices.

1976   The Alliance for Displaced Homemakers is founded to advocate the rights of divorced and widowed homemakers seeking employment.

1977   The NATIONAL COALITION AGAINST

DOMESTIC VIOLENCE is established by battered women's advocates in Washington, D.C.

1977   Congress passes the Hyde Amendment, eliminating federal funding for most poor women's abortions.

1978   The OLDER WOMEN'S LEAGUE is founded to address age and gender discrimination issues including health insurance and retirement benefits.

1979   Beverly LaHaye founds CONCERNED WOMEN FOR AMERICA as an antichoice, antigay, anti–sex education activist group.

1980   Dr. Helen Caldicott founds WOMEN'S ACTION FOR NEW DIRECTIONS to empower women to act politically to reduce militarism and violence and support human and environmental needs.

1982   Phyllis Schlafly's STOP-ERA group succeeds in blocking ratification of the Equal Rights Amendment.

1984   EMILY'S LIST (Early Money Is Like Yeast: It Makes the Dough Rise) is founded to raise money for Democratic feminist candidates for public office.

1987   Operation Rescue, later renamed OPERATION SAVE AMERICA, is founded by RANDALL TERRY to protect America from "moral pollution" and "save the lives of innocent children." In the 1990s "rescues" at abortion clinics turn violent and shootings of doctors and clinic personnel follow.

1987   The FEMINIST MAJORITY Foundation is established by Eleanor Smeal to help women candidates win public offices.

1989   The U.S. Supreme Court, in WEBSTER V. REPRODUCTIVE HEALTH SERVICES, rules that states can deny public funding for abortions and prohibit public hospitals from performing abortions. The Court declares that life begins at conception and mandates viability tests after twenty weeks gestation. The decision marks the first time that five justices, the majority, do not explicitly reaffirm *Roe v. Wade*.

1991   The NATIONAL BREAST CANCER COALITION is formed to focus political leadership on the disease and to educate cancer victims.

1993   The Family Medical Leave Act is authorized. Vetoed by President George Bush, it is the first bill to be signed by President Bill Clinton.

1993   The Susan B. Anthony List is founded to help elect pro-life women to high public office and to counterbalance the allegedly pro-abortion EMILY's List. It is named after the nineteenth-century suffragist who wrote of abortion in 1869 that "we want prevention, not merely punishment. We must reach the root of evil."

1994   In the U.S. Supreme Court case *National Organization for Women v. Scheidler* (510 U.S. 249) the Court unanimously affirms NOW's right to use the Racketeer Influenced and Corrupt Organizations (RICO) chapter of the Organized Crime Control Act of 1970 to prosecute antiabortion extremists who organize others to block and bomb abortion clinics or intimidate patients and health care providers.

2000   The U.S. Supreme Court, by a 5–4 margin, declares unconstitutional the civil remedy provision of the Violence Against Women Act of 1994 in *United States v. Morrison*. This closes the door to rape victims seeking compensatory and punitive damages through the federal courts. Conservatives hail the decision as an appropriate elimination of federal intrusion and an affirmation of states' and localities' exclusive right to adjudicate cases involving gender-based violence. Chief Justice William H. Rehnquist writes the majority opinion; Justice David H. Souter writes the dissent.

For Further Information

Berg, Barbara J. *The Women's Movement and Young Women Today: A Hot Issue.* Berkeley Heights, NJ: Enslow, 2000.

Ireland, Patricia. *What Women Want.* New York: Dutton, 1996.

Rosen, Ruth. *The World Split Open: How the Modern Women's Movement Changed America.* New York: Viking, 2000.

Tobias, Sheila. *Faces of Feminism: An Activist's Reflections on the Women's Movement.* Boulder, CO: Westview Press, 1997.

WOUNDED KNEE (FEBRUARY 28–MAY 8, 1973). *See* American Indian Movement; Banks, Dennis; Means, Russell

Directory of Organizations

ACT UP New York
332 Bleecker Street
Suite 5G
New York, NY 10014–2980
Phone/Fax: (212) 966–4873
E-Mail: *actupny@panix.com*
URL: *http://www.actupny.org*

ACT UP Philadelphia
Post Office Box 22439
Land Title Station
Philadelphia, PA 19110–2439
Phone: (215) 731–1844
Fax: (215) 731–1845
E-Mail: *jdavids@critpath.org*
URL: *http://www.critpath.org/actup/*

AIDS Action
1906 Sunderland Place, NW
Washington, DC 20036
Phone: (202) 530–8030
Fax: (202) 530–8031
E-Mail: *aidsaction@aidsaction.org*
URL: *http://www.aidsaction.org*

American Agriculture Movement
P.O. Box 399
Sunray, TX 79086
Phone: (806) 733–2203
Fax: (806) 733–2965
E-Mail: *parity79@hotmail.com*
URL: *http://www.aaminc.org*

American Anti-Vivisection Society
801 Old York Road #204
Jenkintown, PA 19046–1685
Phone: (215) 887–0816; (800) 729–2287
Fax: (215) 887–2088
E-Mail: *aavsonline@aol.com*
URL: *http://ww.aavs.org*

American-Arab Anti-Discrimination Committee
4201 Connecticut Ave., NW
Suite 300
Washington, DC 20008
Phone: (202) 244–2990
Fax: (202) 244–3196
E-Mail: *adc@adc.org*
URL: *http://www.adc.org*

American Association of Retired Persons
601 E Street, NW
Washington, DC 20049
Phone: (202) 434–2560; (800) 424–3410
Fax: (202) 434–2588
E-Mail: *member@aarp.org*
URL: *http://www.aarp.org*

American Association of University Women
1111 16th Street, NW
Washington, DC 20036–4873
Phone: (202) 785–7700; (800) 326–2289
Fax: (202) 872–1425
E-Mail: *info@aauw.org*
URL: *http://www.aauw.org*

DIRECTORY OF ORGANIZATIONS

American Civil Liberties Union
125 Broad Street
New York, NY 10004–2400
Phone: (212) 549–2500
Fax: (212) 549–2646
E-Mail: *aclu@aclu.org*
URL: *http://www.aclu.org*

American Conservative Union
1007 Cameron Street
Alexandria, VA 22314–2426
Phone: (703) 836–8602; (800) 228–7345
Fax: (703) 836–8606
E-Mail: *acu@conservative.org*
URL: *http://www.conservative.org*

American Council of Christian Churches
P.O. Box 5455
Bethlehem, PA 18015
Phone: (610) 865–3009
Fax: (610) 865–3033
E-Mail: *acc@juno.com*
URL: *http://www.amcouncilcc.org/*

American Council on Alcohol Problems
2376 Lakeside Drive
Birmingham, AL 35244
Phone: (205) 985–9062
Fax: (205) 985–9015

American Disabled for Attendant Programs To-
    day—ADAPT
201 S. Cherokee
Denver, CO 80223
Phone: (303) 733–9324; (303) 333–6698;
    (303) 744–0717
Fax: (303) 733–6211
E-Mail: *national@adapt.org*
URL: *http://www.adapt.org*

American Enterprise Institute for Public Policy
    Research
1150 17th Street, NW
Washington, DC 20036–4603
Phone: (202) 862–5800
Fax: (202) 862–7177
E-Mail: *info@aei.org*
URL: *http://www.aei.org*

American Family Association
P.O. Drawer 2440
Tupelo, MS 38803
Phone: (601) 844–5036
Fax: (601) 842–7798

E-Mail: *afa@afa.net*
URL: *http://www.afa@afa.net*

American Farm Bureau Federation
225 Touhy Ave.
Park Ridge, IL 60068
Phone: (847) 685–8600
Fax: (847) 685–8969
E-Mail: *webmaster@fb.org*
URL: *http://www.fb.org/*

American Indian Movement
P.O. Box 13521
Minneapolis, MN 55414
Phone: (612) 721–3914
Fax: (612) 721–7826
E-Mail: *aimggc@worldnet.att.net*
URL: *http://www.aimovement.org*

American Jewish Committee
c/o Institute of Human Relations
165 E. 56th Street
New York, NY 10022
Phone: (212) 751–4000
Fax: (212) 838–2120
E-Mail: *info@ajc.org*
URL: *http://www.ajc.org*

American Jewish Congress
15 East 84th Street
New York, NY 10028
Phone: (212) 879–4500
Fax: (212) 249–3672
E-Mail: *webmaster@ajc.org*
URL: *http://www.ajcongress.org*

American Legion
c/o Public Relations Division
700 N. Pennsylvania Street
Indianapolis, IN 46206
Phone: (317) 630–1200
Fax: (317) 630–1223; (800) 433–3318
E-Mail: *natlcmdr@legion.org*
URL: *http://www.legion.org/*

American Society for the Prevention of Cruelty
    to Animals
424 E. 92nd Street
New York, NY 10128–6804
Phone: (212) 876–7700
Fax: (212) 876–9571
E-Mail: *webmaster@aspca.org*
URL: *http://www.aspca.org*

American Veterans Committee
6309 Bannockburn Drive
Bethesda, MD 20817
Phone/Fax: (301) 320–6490

Americans for Democratic Action
1625 K Street, NW
Suite 210
Washington, DC 20006
Phone: (202) 785–5980; (800) 787–2734
Fax: (202) 785–5969
E-Mail: *adaction@ix.netcom.com*
URL: *http://www.adaction.org*

Americans for Tax Reform
1320 18th Street, NW
Suite 200
Washington, DC 20008
Phone: (202) 785–0266
Fax: (202) 785–0261
E-Mail: *info@atr.org*
URL: *http://www.atr.org*

Americans United for Separation of Church and
State
1816 Jefferson Place, NW
Washington, DC 20036
Phone: (202) 466–3234
Fax: (202) 466–2587
E-Mail: *americansunited@au.org*
URL: *http://www.au.org*

AMVETS (American Veterans of World War II,
Korea and Vietnam)
4647 Forbes Blvd.
Lanham, MD 20706–4380
Phone: (301) 459–9600
Fax: (301) 459–7924
E-Mail: *amvets@amvets.org*
URL: *http://www.amvets.org*

Anti-Defamation League
823 United Nations Plaza
New York, NY 10017
Phone: (212) 885–7700
Fax: (212) 867–0779
E-Mail: *webmaster@adl.org*
URL: *http://www.adl.org*

Association of Community Organizations for Reform Now (ACORN)
1024 Elysian Fields Ave.
New Orleans, LA 70117
Phone: (504) 943–0044

Fax: (504) 944–7078
E-Mail: *acorn@acorn.org*
URL: *http://www.acorn.org*

Cambio Cubano
9600 Southwest 8th Street
Miami, FL 33174
Phone: (305) 220–0909
URL: *http://www.cambiocubano.com/*

Campus Outreach Opportunity League (COOL)
1531 P Street, NW
Suite LL
Washington, DC 20005
Phone: (202) 265–1200
Fax: (202) 265–3241
E-Mail: *homeoffice@cool2serve.org*
URL: *http://www.cool2serve.org*

Catholic Worker
36 East 1st Street
New York, NY 10003
Phone: (212) 254–1640; (212) 473–8973
E-Mail: *jallaire@home.com*
URL: *http://www.catholicworker.org/*

Cato Institute
1000 Massachusetts Avenue, NW
Washington, DC 20001–5403
Phone: (202) 842–0200
Fax: (202) 842–3490
E-Mail: *cato@cato.org*
URL: *http://www.cato.org*

Center for Auto Safety
1825 Connecticut Avenue
Suite 330
Washington, DC 20009–5708
Phone: (202) 328–7700
URL: *http://www.autosafety.org*

Center for Health, Environment and Justice
P.O. Box 6806
Falls Church, VA 22040
Phone: (703) 237–2249
Fax: (703) 237–8389
E-Mail: *chej@chej.org*
URL: *http://www.chej.org*

Center for Science in the Public Interest
1875 Connecticut Avenue, NW
Suite 300
Washington, DC 20009–3728
Phone: (202) 332–9110

Fax: (202) 265–4954
E-Mail: *cspi@cspinet.org*
URL: *http://www.cspinet.org*

CFIDS (Chronic Fatigue and Immune Dysfunc-
tion Syndrome) Association of America
P.O. Box 220398
Charlotte, NC 28222–0398
Phone: (704) 364–0016; (800) 442–3437
Fax: (704) 365–9755
E-Mail: *info@cfids.org*
URL: *http://www.cfids.org*

Children's Defense Fund
25 E Street, NW
Washington, DC 20001
Phone: (202) 628–8787
Fax: (202) 662–3510
E-Mail: *cdinfo@childrensdefense.org*
URL: *http://www.childrensdefense.org*

Choice in Dying
1035 30th Street, NW
Washington, DC 20007
Phone: (202) 338–9790; (800) 989–9455
Fax: (202) 338–0242
E-Mail: *cid@choices.org*
URL: *http://www.choices.org*

Christian Coalition of America
1801 Sara Drive
Suite L
Chesapeake, VA 23320
Phone: (757) 424–2630
Fax: (757) 424–9068
URL: *http://www.cc.org*

Citizens Against Government Waste
1301 Connecticut Avenue, NW
Suite 400
Washington, DC 20036
Phone: (202) 467–5300;(800) 232–6479
Fax: (202) 467–4253
URL: *http://www.cagw.org*

Citizens for a Better Environment
CBE Illinois
407 South Dearborn Street
Suite 1775
Chicago, IL 60605
Phone: (312) 939–1530
Fax: (312) 939–2536
E-Mail: *ilcbe@chemw.org*
URL: *http://www.cbemw.org*

Citizens for Excellence in Education
A Division of the National Association of Chris-
tian Educators
Box 3200
Costa Mesa, CA 92628
Phone: (949) 251–9333
E-Mail: *info@nace-cee.org*
URL: *http://www.nace-cee.org*

Citizens for Tax Justice
1311 L Street, NW
Suite 400
Washington, DC 20005
Phone: (202) 626–3780
Fax: (202) 638–3486
E-Mail: *ctj@ctj.org*
URL: *http://www.ctj.org*

Clean Water Action
4455 Connecticut Avenue, NW
Suite A300
Washington, DC 20008–2328
Phone: (202) 895–0420
Fax: (202) 895–0438
E-Mail: *cwa@cleanwater.org*
URL: *http://www.cleanwateraction.org*

Coalition to Stop Gun Violence
1000 16th Street, NW
Suite 603
Washington, DC 20036
Phone: (202) 530–0340
E-Mail: *webmaster@csgv.org*
URL: *http://www.gunfree.org*

Common Cause
1250 Connecticut Avenue, NW
6th Floor
Washington, DC 20036
Phone: (202) 833–1200
Fax: (202) 659–3716
E-Mail: *grassroots@commoncause.org*
URL: *http://www.commoncause.org*

Concerned Women for America
1015 15th Street, NW
Suite 1100
Washington, DC 20005
Phone: (202) 488–7000; (800) 458–8797
Fax: (202) 488–0806
E-Mail: *mail@cwfa.org*
URL: *http://www.cwfa.org*

Concord Coalition
1019 19th Street, NW
Suite 810
Washington, DC 20036
Phone: (202) 467–6222
Fax: (202) 467–6333
E-Mail: *concord@concordcoalition.org*
URL: *http://www.concordcoalition.org*

Congress of Racial Equality
817 Broadway
3rd Floor
New York, NY 10003
Phone: (212) 598–4000
Fax: (212) 598–4141
E-Mail: *coreny@msn.com*
URL: *http://www.core-online.org/*

Consumer Alert
1001 Connecticut Avenue, NW
Suite 1128
Washington, DC 20036
Phone: (202) 467–5809
Fax: (202) 467–5814
E-Mail: *info@consumeralert.org*
URL: *http://www.consumeralert.org*

Consumers Union of the United States
101 Truman Avenue
Yonkers, NY 10703–1057
Phone: (914) 378–2000
Fax: (914) 378–2900
URL: *http://www.consumersunion.org*

Council for a Livable World
110 Maryland Avenue, NW
Suite 409
Washington, DC 20002
Phone: (202) 543–4100
Fax: (202) 543–6297
E-Mail: *clw@clw.org*
URL: *http://www.clw.org*

Council on American-Islamic Relations
453 New Jersey Avenue, SE
Washington, DC 20003–2604
Phone: (202) 659–2247
Fax: (202) 659–2254
E-Mail: *cair@cair-net.org*
URL: *http://www.cair-net.org*

Cuban American National Foundation
1312 SW 27th Avenue
Miami, FL 33145

Phone: (305) 592–7768
Fax: (305) 592–7889
E-Mail: *canfnet@icanect.net*
URL: *http://www.canfnet.org*

Defenders of Wildlife
1101 14th Street, NW
Suite 1400
Washington, DC 20005–5601
Phone: (202) 682–9400
Fax: (202) 682–1331
E-Mail: *information@defenders.org*
URL: *http://www.defenders.org*

Ducks Unlimited
One Waterfowl Way
Memphis, TN 38120–2351
Phone: (901) 758–3825; (800) 753–8257
Fax: (901) 758–3850
E-Mail: *webmaster@ducks.org*
URL: *http://www.ducks.org*

Eagle Forum
P.O. Box 618
Alton, IL 62002
Phone: (618) 462–5415
Fax: (618) 462–8909
E-Mail: *eagle@eagleforum.org*
URL: *http://www.eagleforum.org*

Earth First!
P.O. Box 1415
Eugene, OR 97440
Phone: (541) 344–8004
Fax: (541) 344–7688
E-Mail: *earthfirst@igc.org*
URL: *http://www.earthfirst.org*

EMILY's List
805 15th Street, NW
Suite 400
Washington, DC 20005
Phone: (202) 326–1400
Fax: (202) 326–1415
URL: *http://www.emilyslist.org*

Environmental Defense National Headquarters
257 Park Avenue South
New York, NY 10010
Phone: (212) 505–2100; (800) 684–3322
Fax: (212) 505–2375
E-Mail: *Contact@environmentaldefense.org*
URL: *http://www.edf.org*

Families USA
1334 G Street, NW
Suite 300
Washington, DC 20005–3169
Phone: (202) 628–3030
Fax: (202) 347–2417
E-Mail: *info@familiesusa.org*
URL: *http://www.familiesusa.org*

Family Research Council
801 G Street, NW
Washington, DC 20001
Phone: (202) 393–2100; (800) 225–4008
Fax: (202) 393–2134
E-Mail: *corrdept@frc.org*
URL: *http://www.frc.org*

Fellowship of Reconciliation
P.O. Box 271
Nyack, NY 10960
Phone: (914) 358–4601
Fax: (914) 358–4924
E-Mail: *fornatl@igcapc.org*
URL: *http://www.nonviolence.org/for*

Feminist Majority
1600 Wilson Blvd.
Suite 801
Arlington, VA 22209
Phone: (703) 522–2214
Fax: (703) 522–2219
E-Mail: *femmaj@feminist.org*
URL: *http://www.feminist.org*

Feminists for Life of America
733 15th Street, NW
Washington, DC 20005
Phone: (202) 737–3352
Fax: (202) 737–0414
E-Mail: *fems4life@aol.com*
URL: *http://www.feministsforlife.org*

Focus on the Family
8605 Explorer Drive
Colorado Springs, CO 80920
Phone: (719) 531–3400; (800) 232–6459
Fax: (719) 548–4525
E-Mail: *mail@fotf.org*
URL: *http://www.fotf.org*

FORMULA
1815 North Hartford Street
Arlington, VA 22201

Phone: (702) 527–7171
E-Mail: *Laskin1@aol.com*

Free Congress Research and Education Foundation
717 Second Street, NE
Washington, DC 20002
Phone: (202) 546–3000
Fax: (202) 543–5605
E-Mail: *gblake@fcref.org*
URL: *http://www.freecongress.org*

Friends of the Earth
1025 Vermont Avenue, NW
Suite 300
Washington, DC 20005–6303
Phone: (202) 783–7400
Fax: (202) 783–0444
E-Mail: *foe@foe.org*
URL: *http://www.foe.org*

Gay and Lesbian Alliance Against Defamation
(GLAAD)
8455 Beverly Blvd.
Suite 305
Los Angeles, CA 90048
Phone: (323) 658–6775
Fax: (323) 658–6776
E-Mail: *glaad@glaad.org*
URL: *http://www.glaad.org*

Gay Men's Health Crisis
The Tisch Building
119 W. 24th Street
New York, NY 10011–1913
Phone: (212) 367–1000; (800) 243–7692
Fax: (212) 367–7386
E-Mail: *hotline@gmhc.org*
URL: *http://www.gmhc.org*

Gray Panthers
733 15th Street, NW
Suite 437
Washington, DC 20005
Phone: (202) 737–6637; (800) 280–5362
Fax: (202) 737–1160
E-Mail: *info@graypanthers.org*
URL: *http://www.graypanthers.com*

Greenpeace USA
1436 U Street, NW
Washington, DC 20009
Phone: (202) 462–1177; (800) 326–0959
Fax: (202) 462–4507

E-Mail: *info@wdc.greenpeace.org*
URL: *http://www.greenpeaceusa.org*

Gun Owners of America
8001 Forbes Place
Suite 102
Springfield, VA 22151
Phone: (703) 321–8585
Fax: (703) 321–8408
URL: *http://www.gunowners.org*

Handgun Control, Inc.
1225 Eye Street, NW
Suite 1100
Washington, DC 20005
Phone: (202) 898–0792
Fax: (202) 371–9615
URL: *http://www.handguncontrol.org*

Hemlock Society USA
P.O. Box 101810
Denver, CO 80250–1810
Phone: (303) 639–1202; (800) 247–7421
Fax: (303) 639–1224
E-Mail: *hemlock@privatei.com*
URL: *http://www.hemlock.org*

Heritage Foundation
214 Massachusetts Avenue, NE
Washington, DC 20002–4999
Phone: (202) 546–4400; (800) 546–2843
Fax: (202) 546–8328
E-Mail: *info@heritage.org*
URL: *http://www.heritage.org*;
http://www.townhall.com

Highlander Research and Education Center
1959 Highlander Way
New Market, TN 37820
Phone: (865) 933–3443
URL: *http://www.hrec.org*

Home School Legal Defense Association
P.O. Box 3000
Purcellville, VA 20134–9000
Phone: (540) 338–5600
Fax: (540) 338–2733
E-Mail: *mailroom@hslda.org*
URL: *http://www.hslda.org*
http://www.nheri.org

Human Rights Campaign
919 18th Street, NW
Suite 800

Washington, DC 20006
Phone: (202) 628–4160
Fax: (202) 347–5323
E-Mail: *hrc@hrc.org*
URL: *http://www.hrc.org*

Humane Society of the United States
2100 L Street, NW
Washington, DC 20037
Phone: (202) 452–1100
Fax: (202) 778–6132
E-Mail: *hsuceo@ix.netcom.com*
URL: *http://www.hsus.org*

Industrial Areas Foundation
220 W. Kinzie Street
5th Floor
Chicago, IL 60610–4412
Phone: (312) 245–9211
Fax: (312) 245–9744

INFACT
46 Plympton Street
Boston, MA 02118
Phone: (617) 695–2525
Fax: (617) 695–2626
E-Mail: *infact@igc.org*
URL: *http://www.infact.org*

Izaak Walton League of America
707 Conservation Lane
Gaithersburg, MD 20878
Phone: (301) 548–0150; (800) 453–5463
Fax: (301) 548–0146
E-Mail: *general@iwla.org*
URL: *http://www.ila.org*

Jewish Defense League
P.O. Box 480370
North Hollywood, CA 91601
Phone: (818) 980–8535
E-Mail: *jdljdl@aol.com*
URL: *http://www.jdl.org*

John Birch Society
P.O. Box 8040
Appleton, WI 54913
Phone: (920) 749–3780
Toll-Free Phone: 1–800–527–8721
Fax: (920) 749–5062
E-Mail: *jbs@jbs.org*
URL: *http://www.jbs.org/*

Knights of the Ku Klux Klan
P.O. Box 2222
Harrison, AR 72601
Phone: (870) 427–3414
E-Mail: *the6thera@hotmail.com*
URL: *http://www.kukluxklan.org*

Ku Klux Klan
Church of American Knights of the Ku Klux
  Klan
7238 SR 8
Butler, IN 46721
Phone: (219) 337–5555
E-Mail: *info@americanknights.com*
URL: *http://www.americanknights.com*

League of Conservation Voters
1920 L Street, NW
Suite 800
Washington, DC 20036
Phone: (202) 785–8683
Fax: (202) 835–0491
E-Mail: *lcv@lcv.org*
URL: *http://www.lcv.org*

League of United Latin American Citizens
221 N. Kansas
Suite 1200
El Paso, TX 79901
Phone: (915) 577–0726
Fax: (915) 577–0914
E-Mail: *lulac@aol.com*
URL: *http://www.lulac.org*

League of Women Voters of the United States
1730 M Street, NW
Suite 1000
Washington, DC 20036–4508
Phone: (202) 429–1965
Fax: (202) 429–0854
E-Mail: *lwv@lwv.org*
URL: *http://www.lwv.org*

Liberty Lobby
300 Independence Avenue, SE
Washington, DC 20003
Phone: (202) 546–5611
E-Mail: *libertylobby@earthlink.net*
URL: *http://www.spotlight.org*

Mothers Against Drunk Driving (MADD)
511 John Carpenter Freeway
Suite 700
Irving, TX 75062–8187

Phone: (972) 744–6233; (800) 438–6233
Fax: (972) 869–2206
URL: *http://www.madd.org*

Nation of Islam
Mosque Maryam
7351 South Stoney Island Avenue
Chicago, IL 60649
Phone: (773) 324–6000
E-Mail: *email@noi.org*
URL: *http://www.noi.org*

National Abortion and Reproductive Action
  League (NARAL)
1156 15th Street, NW
Suite 700
Washington, DC 20005
Phone: (202) 973–3000
Fax: (202) 973–3096
E-Mail: *naral@newmedium.com*
URL: *http://www.naral.org*

National Association for the Advancement of
  Colored People (NAACP)
4805 Mount Hope Drive
Baltimore, MD 21215
Phone: (410) 358–8900
Fax: (410) 486–3818
URL: *http://www.naacp.org*

National Audubon Society
700 Broadway
New York, NY 10003
Phone: (212) 979–3000
Fax: (212) 353–0377
E-Mail: *webmaster@list.audubon.org*
URL: *http://www.audubon.org*

National Breast Cancer Coalition
1707 L Street, NW
Suite 1060
Washington, DC 20036
Phone: (202) 296–7477; (800) 622–2838
Fax: (202) 265–6854
URL: *http://www.natlbcc.org*

National Civic League
1445 Market Street
Suite 300
Denver, CO 80202–1717
Phone: (303) 571–4343; (800) 223–6004
Fax: (303) 571–4404
E-Mail: *ncl@ncl.org*
URL: *http://www.ncl.org/ncl*

National Coalition Against Domestic Violence
P.O. Box 18749
Denver, CO 80218–0749
Phone: (303) 839–1852; (800) 799–7233
Fax: (303) 831–9251
URL: *http://www.ncadv.org*

National Coalition for the Homeless
1012 14th Street, NW
Suite 600
Washington, DC 20005–3406
Phone: (202) 737–6444
Fax: (202) 737–6445
E-Mail: *nch@ari.net*
URL: *http://www.nationalhomeless.org/*

National Coalition to Abolish the Death Penalty
1436 U Street, NW
Suite 104
Washington, DC 20009
Phone: (202) 387–5590; (888) 286–2237
Fax: (202) 387–5590
URL: *http://www.ncadp.org*

National Committee to Preserve Social Security
  and Medicare
10 G Street, NE
Suite 600
Washington, DC 20002–4215
Phone: (202) 216–0420; (800) 966–1935
Fax: (202) 216–0451
E-Mail: *webmaster@ncpssm.org*
URL: *http://ncpssm.org*

National Congress of American Indians
1301 Connecticut Avenue, NW
Suite 200
Washington, DC 20036
Phone: (202) 466–7767
Fax: (202) 466–7797
URL: *http://www.ncai.org*

National Consumers' League
1701 K Street, NW
Suite 1201
Washington, DC 20006
Phone: (202) 835–3323
Fax: (202) 835–0747
E-Mail: *nclncl@aol.com*
URL: *http://www.nclnet.org; http://www.fraud.org*

National Council of La Raza
1111 19th Street, NW

Suite 1000
Washington, DC 20036
Phone: (202) 785–1670
Fax: (202) 776–1792
URL: *http://www.nclr.org*

National Council of Senior Citizens
8403 Colesville Road
Suite 1200
Silver Spring, MD 20910–3314
Phone: (301) 578–8800
Fax: (301) 578–8999
E-Mail: *comments@ncscinc.org*
URL: *http://www.nscinc.org*

National Farmers Organization
2505 Elwood Avenue
Ames, IA 50010–2000
Phone: (515) 292–2000
Fax: (515) 292–7106
E-Mail: *info@netins.net*
URL: *http://www.nfo.org*

National Farmers Union
11900 E. Cornell Avenue
Aurora, CO 80014–3194
Phone: (303) 337–5500; (800) 347–1961
Fax: (303) 368–1390
E-Mail: *NFU@NFU.org*
URL: *http://www.nfu.org*

National Gay and Lesbian Task Force
1700 Kalorama Road, NW
Washington, DC 20009–2624
Phone: (202) 332–6483
Fax: (202) 332–0207
E-Mail: *nglt@nglt.org*
URL: *http://www.ngltf.org*

National Organization for the Reform of Mari-
  juana Laws (NORML)
1001 Connecticut Avenue, NW
Suite 710
Washington, DC 20036
Phone: (202) 483–5500
Fax: (202) 483–0057
E-Mail: *natlnorml@aol.com*
URL: *http://www.norml.org*

National Organization for Women (NOW)
1000 16th Street, NW
Suite 700
Washington, DC 20036
Phone: (202) 331–0066

Fax: (202) 785–8576
E-Mail: *now@now.org*
URL: *http://www.now.org*

National Parks and Conservation Association
1776 Massachusetts Avenue, NW
Suite 200
Washington, DC 20036–6404
Phone: (202) 223–6722; (800) 628–7275
Fax: (202) 659–0650
E-Mail: *npca@npca.org*
URL: *http://www.npca.org*

National Rifle Association (NRA)
11250 Waples Mill Road
Fairfax, VA 22030
Phone: (703) 267–1000; (800) 672–3888
Fax: (703) 267–3989
E-Mail: *comm@nrahq.org*
URL: *http://www.nra.org*

National Right to Life Committee
419 7th Street, NW
Suite 500
Washington, DC 20004–2293
Phone: (202) 626–8800
Fax: (202) 737–9189
E-Mail: *nrlc@nrlc.org*
URL: *http://www.nrlc.org*

National Right to Work Committee
8001 Braddock Road
Suite 500
Springfield, VA 22160
Phone: (703) 321–9820; (800) 325–7892
Fax: (703) 321–7342
E-Mail: *info@nrtw.org*
URL: *http://www.nrtw.org/*

National Tax-Limitation Committee
151 N. Sunrise Avenue
Suite 901
Roseville, CA 95661
Phone: (916) 786–9400

National Taxpayers Union
108 North Alfred Street
Alexandria, VA 22314
Phone: (703) 683–5700; (800) 829–4258
Fax: (703) 683–5722
E-Mail: *ntu@townhall.com*
URL: *http://www.ntu.org*

National Urban League
120 Wall Street
New York, NY 10005
Phone: (212) 558–5300
Fax: (212) 344–5332
E-Mail: *info@nul.org*
URL: *http://www.nul.org*

National Vaccine Information Center
512 W. Maple Avenue
Suite 206
Vienna, VA 22180
Phone: (703) 938–3783; (800) 909–7468
Fax: (703) 938–5768
E-Mail: *kwnvic@aol.com*
URL: *http://www.909shot.com*

National Wildlife Federation
8925 Leesburg Pike
Vienna, VA 22184
Phone: (703) 790–4000
Fax: (703) 442–7332
E-Mail: *info@nwf.org*
URL: *http://www.nwf.org/*

National Women's Health Network
514 10th Street, NW
Suite 400
Washington, DC 20004
Phone: (202) 347–1140
Fax: (202) 347–1168
URL: *http://www.womenshealthnetwork.org*

National Women's Political Caucus
1630 Connecticut Avenue, NW
Suite 201
Washington, DC 20009
Phone: (202) 785–1100; (800) 729–6972
Fax: (202) 785–3605
E-Mail: *nwpc@aol.com*
URL: *http://www.nwpc.org*

Natural Resources Defense Council
40 West 20th Street
New York, NY 10011
Phone: (212) 727–2700
Fax: (212) 727–1773
E-Mail: *nrdcinf@nrdc.org*
URL: *http://www.nrdc.org*

Older Women's League (OWL)
666 11th Street, NW
Suite 700
Washington, DC 20001

Phone: (202) 783–6686; (800) 825–3695
Fax: (202) 638–2356
E-Mail: *owlinfo@owl-national.org*
URL: *http://www.owl-national.org*

OMB Watch
1742 Connecticut Avenue, NW
Washington, DC 20009
Phone: (202) 234–8494
Fax: (202) 234–8584
E-Mail: *ombwatch@ombwatch.org*
URL: *http://www.ombwatch.org/ombwatch.html*

Operation Save America
P.O. Box 740066
Dallas, TX 75374
Phone: (972) 494–5316
Fax: (972) 276–9361
E-Mail: *osa@operationsaveamerica.org*
URL: *http://www.operationsaveamerica.org*

People for the American Way
2000 M Street, NW
Suite 400
Washington, DC 20036
Phone: (202) 467–4999; (800) 326–7329
Fax: (202) 293–2672
E-Mail: *pfaw@pfaw.org*
URL: *http://www.pfaw.org*

People for the Ethical Treatment of Animals
  (PETA)
501 Front Street
Norfolk, VA 23510
Phone: (757) 622–7382
Fax: (757) 622–0457
E-Mail: *peta@peta-online.org*
URL: *http://www.peta-online.org*

Planned Parenthood Federation of America
810 Seventh Avenue
New York, NY 10019
Phone: (212) 541–7800
Fax: (212) 245–1845
E-Mail: *communications@ppfa.org*
URL: *http://www.plannedparenthood.org*

Posse Comitatus
P.O. Box 103
Ulysses, PA 16948
E-Mail: *posse@penn.com*
URL: *http://www.posse-comitatus.org/*

Promise Keepers
4045 Pecos Street
Denver, CO 80211
Phone: (303) 964–7600; (800) 888–7595
Fax: (303) 433–1036
URL: *http://www.promisekeepers.org*

Public Citizen
1600 20th Street, NW
Washington, DC 20009
Phone: (202) 588–1000
Fax: (202) 588–7798
E-Mail: *public_citizen@citizen.org*
URL: *http://www.citizen.org*

Rainbow/PUSH Coalition
950 East 50th Street
Chicago, IL 60615–2702
Phone: (773) 373–3366
Fax: (773) 373–3571
E-Mail: *info@rainbowpush.org*
URL: *http://www.rainbowpush.org*

Sea Shepherd Conservation Society
P.O. Box 2616
Friday Harbor, WA 98250–2616
Phone: (360) 370–5500; (888) 942–5322
Fax: (360) 370–5501
E-Mail: *ft@elfweb.com*
URL: *http://www.seashepherd.org*

Seniors Coalition
9001 Braddock Road
Suite 200
Springfield, VA 22151
Phone: (703) 239–1960
Fax: (703) 239–1985
E-Mail: *tsc@senior.org*
URL: *http://www.senior.org*

Sierra Club
85 Second Street
Second Floor
San Francisco, CA 94105–3441
Phone: (415) 977–5500
Fax: (415) 977–5799
E-Mail: *information@sierraclub.org*
URL: *http://www.sierraclub.org*

60 Plus Association
1655 N. Ft. Myers Drive
Suite 355
Arlington, VA 22209
Phone: (703) 807–2070

Fax: (703) 807–2073
E-Mail: *60plus@60plus.org*
URL: *http://www.60plus.org*

Southern Christian Leadership Conference
  (SCLC)
334 Auburn Avenue, NE
Atlanta, GA 30303
Phone: (404) 522–1420
Fax: (404) 659–7390

Stand for Children
1834 Connecticut Avenue, NW
Washington, DC 20009
Phone: (202) 234–0095; (800) 663–4032
Fax: (202) 234–0217
E-Mail: *tellstand@stand.org*
URL: *http://www.stand.org*

20/20 Vision
1828 Jefferson Place, NW
Washington, DC 20036
Phone: (202) 833–2020
Fax: (202) 833–5037
E-Mail: *vision@2020vision.org*
URL: *http://www.2020vision.org*

United Farm Workers of America, AFL-CIO
P.O. Box 62
19700 Woodford-Tehachapi Road
Keene, CA 93531
Phone: (661) 822–5571
Fax: (661) 822–6103
E-Mail: *UFWofamer@aol.com*
URL: *http://www.ufw.org*

United Mine Workers of America
8315 Lee Highway
Fairfax, VA 22031
Phone: (703) 208–7200
E-Mail: *tblount@umwa.org*
URL: *http://www.umwa.org*

United Seniors Association
3900 Jermantown Road
Suite 450
Fairfax, VA 22030

Phone: (703) 359–6500; (800) 887–2872
Fax: (703) 359–6510
E-Mail: *usa@unitedseniors.org*
URL: *http://www.unitedseniors.org*

U.S. Public Interest Research Group
218 D Street, SE
Washington, DC 20003
Phone: (202) 546–9707
Fax: (202) 546–2461
E-Mail: *uspirg@pirg.org*
URL: *http://www.pirg.org*

U.S. Term Limits Foundation
10 G Street, NE
Suite 410
Washington, DC 20002
Phone: (202) 379–3000; (800) 733–6440
Fax: (202) 379–3010
E-Mail: *admin@ustermlimits.org*
URL: *http://www.termlimits.org*

United Students Against Sweatshops
1413 K Street, NW
9th Floor
Washington, DC 20005
Phone: (202) 667–9329
Fax: (202) 393–5886
URL: *http://www.usasnet.org*

Wilderness Society
1615 M Street, NW
Washington, DC 20036
Phone: (202) 833–2300; (800) 843–9453
Fax: (202) 429–3958 or (202) 429–8443
E-Mail: *tws@wilderness.org*
URL: *http://www.wilderness.org*

Women's Action for New Directions (WAND)
WAND/WiLL
691 Massachusetts Avenue
Arlington, MA 02476
Phone: (781) 643–6740
Fax: (781) 643–6744
E-Mail: *info@wand.org*
URL: *http://www.wand.org*

Bibliography

Abbey, Edward. *Confessions of a Barbarian.* New York: Little, Brown, 1994.

———. *The Monkey Wrench Gang.* New York: Lippincott, 1975.

Abbott, Cathryn. *Cesar Chavez: Labor Leader.* New York: Vantage Press, 1997.

Abernathy, Ralph David. *And the Walls Came Tumbling Down.* New York: Harper, 1989.

Abraham, Ken. *Who Are the Promise Keepers?* New York: Doubleday, 1997.

Abzug, Bella, with Mim Kelber. *Gender Gap: Bella Abzug's Guide to Political Power for American Women.* New York: Houghton Mifflin, 1984.

Acker, James R., Robert M. Bohm, and Charles S. Lanier, eds. *America's Experiment with Capital Punishment: Reflections on the Past, Present, and Future of the Ultimate Penal Sanction.* Durham, NC: Carolina Academic Press, 1998.

Adam, Barry D. *The Rise of a Gay and Lesbian Movement.* Boston: Twayne, 1987.

Alexander-Moegerle, Gil. *James Dobson's War on America.* Amherst, MA: Prometheus Books, 1997.

Alinsky, Saul David. *Reveille for Radicals.* Chicago: University of Chicago Press, 1945.

———. *Rules for Radicals: A Practical Primer for Realistic Radicals.* New York: Vintage Books, 1971.

Allen, Thomas B. *Guardian of the Wild: The Story of the National Wildlife Federation.* Bloomington: Indiana University Press, 1987.

Andersen, Christopher P. *Citizen Jane: The Turbulent Life of Jane Fonda.* New York: Henry Holt, 1990.

Anderson, Patrick. *High in America: The True Story Behind NORML and the Politics of Marijuana.* New York: Viking, 1980.

Andryszewski, Tricia. *School Prayer: A History of the Debate.* Berkeley Heights, NJ: Enslow, 1997.

Aronowitz, Stanley. *From the Ashes of the Old: American Labor and America's Future.* Boston: Houghton Mifflin, 1998.

Back, Kurt W. *Family Planning and Population Control: The Challenges of a Successful Movement.* Boston: Twayne, 1989.

Baer, Kenneth S. *Reinventing Democrats: The Politics of Liberalism from Reagan to Clinton.* Lawrence: University Press of Kansas, 2000.

Bane, Vickie. *Dr. Laura Schlessinger.* 2nd ed. New York: St. Martin's Press, 1999.

Bauer, Gary. *Our Hopes—Our Dreams: A Vision for America.* Colorado Springs: Focus on the Family Publishing, 1996.

Baum, Dan. *Citizen Coors: An American Dynasty.* New York: HarperCollins, 2000.

Baumohl, Jim, ed. *Homelessness in America.* Phoenix: Oryx Press, 1996.

Bedau, Hugo Adam. *Death Is Different: Studies in the Morality, Law, and Politics of Capital Punishment.* Boston: Northeastern University Press, 1987.

Bekoff, Marc, ed. *Encyclopedia of Animal Rights.* Westport, CT: Greenwood Press, 1988.

Bellah, Robert. *Habits of the Heart: Individualism and Commitment in American Life.* Berkeley: University of California Press, 1985.

Belth, Nathan C. *A Promise to Keep: A Narrative*

of American Encounters with Anti-Semitism. New York: Times Books, 1979.

Benneward, Patrice, ed. From Outrage to Action: The Story of the National Audubon Society. New York: National Audubon Society, 1982.

Berg, Barbara J. The Women's Movement and Young Women Today: A Hot Issue. Berkeley Heights, NJ: Enslow, 2000.

Berrigan, Daniel J. Daniel: Under the Siege of the Divine. Farmington, PA: Plough Publishing House, 1998.

———. To Dwell in Peace: An Autobiography. San Francisco: Harper, 1987.

Berrigan, Philip F. Fighting the Lamb's War. Monroe, ME: Common Courage Press, 1997.

Betzold, Michael. Appointment with Doctor Death. Troy, MI: Momentum Books, 1996.

Black, Allida M. Casting Her Own Shadow: Eleanor Roosevelt and the Shaping of Postwar Liberalism. New York: Columbia University Press, 1996.

Bloor, Ella Reeve. We Are Many: An Autobiography. New York: International Publishers, 1940.

Blumberg, Rhoda Lois. Civil Rights: The 1960s Freedom Struggle. Rev. ed. Boston: Twayne, 1991.

Bolté, Charles G. The New Veteran: Hero or Problem? New York: Reynal and Hitchcock, 1945.

Boston, Robert. The Most Dangerous Man in America? Pat Robertson and the Rise of the Christian Coalition. Amherst, MA: Prometheus, 1996.

Boyle, Kevin. The UAW and the Heyday of American Liberalism, 1945–1968. Ithaca, NY: Cornell University Press, 1995.

Boyte, Harry C. The Backyard Revolution: Understanding the New Citizen Movement. Philadelphia: Temple University Press, 1980.

Boyte, Harry C., Heather Booth, and Steve Max. Citizen Action and the New American Populism. Philadelphia: Temple University Press, 1986.

Breines, Wini. Community and Organization in the New Left: 1962–1968. The Great Refusal. New York: Praeger, 1982.

Brobeck, Stephen, Robert N. Mayer, and Robert O. Herrmann, eds. Encyclopedia of the Consumer Movement. Santa Barbara: ABC-CLIO, 1997.

Brooks, Lester. Blacks in the City: A History of the National Urban League. Boston: Little, Brown, 1971.

Brower, David Ross. Let the Mountains Talk, Let

the Rivers Run: A Call to Those Who Would Save the Earth. San Francisco: HarperCollins, 1995.

Bruce, Rich. Mortgaging the Earth: The World Bank, Environmental Impoverishment, and the Crisis of Development. Boston: Beacon Press, 1995.

Bryant, Anita. A New Day. Nashville: Broadman and Holman, 1992.

Burns, James MacGregor. The People's Charter: The Pursuit of Rights in America. New York: Alfred A. Knopf, 1991.

Burns, Steward. Social Movements of the 1960s: Searching for Democracy. Boston: Twayne, 1990.

Button, John, comp. The Radicalism Handbook: Radical Activists, Groups and Movements of the Twentieth Century. Santa Barbara: ABC-CLIO, 1995.

Byrnes, Patricia. Environmental Pioneers. Minneapolis: Oliver Press, 1998.

Camp, Helen C. Iron in Her Soul: Elizabeth Gurley Flynn and the American Left. Pullman: Washington State University Press, 1995.

Capital Research Center. Gun Control: Is the Tide Turning? Battleground Shifts to the States. Washington, DC: Capital Research Center, 1996.

Carabillo, Toni. Feminist Chronicles, 1953–1993. Los Angeles: Women's Graphics, 1993.

Carew, Anthony. Walter Reuther. New York: St. Martin's Press, 1993.

Carey, John M. Term Limits and Legislative Representation. New York: Cambridge University Press, 1998.

Carlson, Peter. Roughneck: The Life and Times of Big Bill Haywood. New York: W. W. Norton, 1983.

Carson, Rachel. The Edge of the Sea. Boston: Houghton Mifflin, 1955.

———. The Sea Around Us. New York: Oxford University Press, 1951.

———. Silent Spring. Boston: Houghton Mifflin, 1962.

Carter, Gregg Lee. The Gun Control Movement. New York: Twayne, 1997.

Castellucci, John. The Big Dance: The Untold Story of Kathy Boudin and the Terrorist Family that Committed the Brink's Robbery Murders. New York: Dodd, Mead, 1986.

Celsi, Teresa. Ralph Nader: The Consumer Revolution. Brookfield, CT: Millbrook Press, 1991.

Chatfield, Charles. The American Peace Movement: Ideals and Activism. New York: Twayne, 1992.

Cheatham, Karyn. Dennis Banks: Native American Activist. Berkeley Heights, NJ: Enslow Publications, 1997.

Chesler, Ellen. *Woman of Valor: Margaret Sanger and the Birth Control Movement in America.* New York: Simon and Schuster, 1992.

Children's Defense Fund. *The State of America's Children Yearbook, 2000.* Boston: Beacon Press, 2000.

Chrislip, David, and Carl Larson. *Collaborative Leadership: How Citizens and Civic Leaders Can Make a Difference.* San Francisco: Jossey-Bass, 1994.

Clark, Septima. *Echo in My Soul.* New York: Dutton, 1962.

———. *Ready from Within.* Navarro, CA: Wild Tree Press, 1986.

Claybrook, Joan. *Retreat from Safety: Reagan's Attack on America's Health.* New York: Pantheon Books, 1984.

Cleaver, Eldridge. *Soul on Ice.* New York: Dell, 1999.

Clegg, Claude Andrew, III. *An Original Man: The Life and Times of Elijah Muhammad.* New York: St. Martin's Press, 1998.

Clendinen, Dudley, and Adam Nagourney. *Out for Good.* New York: Simon and Schuster, 1999.

Cohen, Peter F. *Love and Anger: Essays on AIDS, Activism, and Politics.* New York: Haworth Press, 1998.

Coles, Robert. *Dorothy Day: A Radical Devotion.* Reading, MA: Addison-Wesley, 1987.

Coles, Robert, and John Erickson. *A Spectacle unto the World: The Catholic Worker Movement.* New York: Viking Penguin, 1974.

Congressional Quarterly. *Public Interest Profiles, 2000–2001.* Washington, DC: CQ Press, 2000.

Cook, Blanche Wiesen. *Eleanor Roosevelt.* New York: Viking, 1992.

Cortright, David. *Peace Works: The Citizen's Role in Ending the Cold War.* Boulder, CO: Westview Press, 1993.

Costanzo, Mark. *Just Revenge: Costs and Consequences of the Death Penalty.* New York: St. Martin's Press, 1997.

Cowger, Thomas. *The National Congress of American Indians: The Founding Years.* Lincoln: University of Nebraska Press, 1999.

Crampton, John A. *The National Farmers Union: Ideology of a Pressure Group.* Lincoln: University of Nebraska Press, 1965.

Crane, Edward H., and David Boaz, eds. *Cato Handbook for Congress: Policy Recommendations for the 106th Congress.* Washington, DC: Cato Institute, 2000.

Crawford, Alan. *Thunder on the Right: The "New Right" and the Politics of Resentment.* New York: Pantheon Books, 1980.

Daniels, Roger. *The Bonus March: An Episode of the Great Depression.* Westport, CT: Greenwood Press, 1971.

Davidson, Osha Gray. *Under Fire: The NRA and the Battle for Gun Control.* New York: Henry Holt, 1993.

Davis, Allen F. *American Heroine: The Life and Legend of Jane Addams.* New York: Oxford University Press, 1973.

Davis, Angela Y. *Angela Davis: An Autobiography.* New York: International Publishers, 1988.

Davis, Flora. *Moving the Mountain: The Woman's Movement in America since 1960.* Champaign: University of Illinois Press, 1999.

Day, Dorothy. *The Long Loneliness.* New York: Harper, 1952. Reprint, San Francisco: Harper, 1982.

DeCew, Judith Wagner. *In Pursuit of Privacy: Law, Ethics, and the Rise of Technology.* Ithaca, NY: Cornell University Press, 1997.

Delgado, Gary. *Organizing the Movement: The Roots and Growth of ACORN.* Philadelphia: Temple University Press, 1986.

Dell Orto, Arthur E., and Robert P. Marinelli, eds. *Encyclopedia of Disability and Rehabilitation.* New York: Macmillan Library Reference USA, 1995.

Dickerson, Dennis C. *Militant Mediator: Whitney M. Young, Jr.* Lexington: University Press of Kentucky, 1998.

Didion, Joan. *Miami.* New York: Vintage Books, 1999.

Dilling, Elizabeth Kirkpatrick. *The Red Network: A "Who's Who" and Handbook of Radicalism for Patriots.* Kenilworth, IL: Privately printed, 1934.

———. *The Roosevelt Red Record and Its Background.* Kenilworth, IL: Privately printed, 1936.

Dinnerstein, Leonard. *Antisemitism in America.* New York: Oxford University Press, 1994.

Dizard, Jan E., Robert Merrill Muth, and Stephen P. Andrews, eds. *Guns in America: A Reader.* New York: New York University Press, 1999.

Dobratz, Betty A., and Stephanie L. Shanks-Meile. *"White Power, White Pride!": The White Separatist Movement in the United States.* New York: Twayne, 1997.

Dobson, James C. *The New Dare to Discipline.* Wheaton, IL: Tyndale House, 1992.

———. *Parenting Isn't for Cowards.* Nashville, TN: Word Publishing, 1997.

————. *What Wives Wish Their Husbands Knew about Women*. Wheaton, IL: Tyndale House, 1979.

Dolan, Edward F., Jr. *Protect Your Legal Rights: A Handbook for Teenagers*. Parsippany, NJ: Silver Burdett Press, 1983.

Donohue, William A. *The Politics of the American Civil Liberties Union*. Princeton, NJ: Transaction Books, 1985.

Du Bois, W.E.B. *The Souls of Black Folk*. New York: Signet Classic, 1995.

Dubinsky, David. *David Dubinsky: My Life with Labor*. New York: Simon and Schuster, 1977.

Dunn, John M. *The Civil Rights Movement*. San Diego: Lucent Books, 1998.

Edelman, Marian Wright. *The Measure of Our Success: A Letter to My Children and Yours*. Boston: Beacon Press, 1994.

————. *The State of America's Children Yearbook, 1999: A Report from the Children's Defense Fund*. Boston: Beacon Press, 1999.

Edwards, Lee. *The Conservative Revolution: The Movement that Remade America*. New York: The Free Press, 1999.

————. *The Power of Ideas: The Heritage Foundation at Twenty-five Years*. Ottawa: Jameson Books, 1998.

Epstein, Barbara. *Political Protest and Cultural Revolution: Nonviolent Direct Action in the 1970s and 1980s*. Berkeley: University of California Press, 1991.

Epstein, Steven. *Impure Science: AIDS, Activism, and the Politics of Knowledge*. Berkeley: University of California Press, 1996.

Euchner, Charles C. *Extraordinary Politics: How Protest and Dissent Are Changing American Democracy*. Boulder, CO: Westview Press, 1996.

Evanzz, Karl. *The Messenger: The Rise and Fall of Elijah Muhammad*. New York: Pantheon Books, 1999.

Evers, Charles. *Have No Fear*. New York: Wiley, 1997.

Fairclough, Adam. *To Redeem the Soul of America: The Southern Christian Leadership Conference and Martin Luther King, Jr*. Athens: University of Georgia Press, 1987.

Falwell, Jerry. *Falwell: An Autobiography*. Lynchburg, VA: Liberty House, 1997.

Farmer, James. *Lay Bare the Heart: An Autobiography of the Civil Rights Movement*. New York: Arbor House, 1985.

Farrington, Selwyn Kip. *The Ducks Came Back: The Story of Ducks Unlimited*. New York: Coward-McCann, 1945.

Faux, Marian. *Roe v. Wade: Marking the Twentieth Anniversary of the Landmark Supreme Court Decision that Made Abortion Legal*. New York: Penguin Group, 1989.

Feldman, Douglas A., and Julia Wanger Miller. *The AIDS Crisis: A Documentary History*. Westport, CT: Greenwood Press, 1998.

Felsenthal, Carol. *The Sweetheart of the Silent Majority: The Biography of Phyllis Schlafly*. Garden City, NY: Doubleday, 1981.

Ferrara, Peter J., and Michael Tanner. *A New Deal for Social Security*. Washington, DC: Cato Institute, 1998.

Ferriss, Susan. *The Fight in the Fields: Cesar Chavez and the Farmworkers Movement*. San Diego: Harcourt, 1998.

Fetherling, Dale. *Mother Jones, the Miners' Angel: A Portrait*. Carbondale: Southern Illinois University Press, 1974.

Finch, Phillip. *God, Guts and Guns: A Close Look at the Radical Right*. New York: Seaview/Putnam, 1983.

Finks, P. David. *The Radical Vision of Saul Alinsky*. New York: Paulist Press, 1984.

Flanagan, Richard W. *AMVETS: Fifty Years of Proud Service to America's Veterans*. Lanham, MD: AMVETS (American Veterans of World War II, Korea and Vietnam), 1994.

Foner, Eric. *The Story of American Freedom*. New York: W. W. Norton, 1998.

Foner, Philip S. *The Case of Joe Hill*. New York: International Publishers, 1965.

Foster, William Z. *The Great Steel Strike and Its Lessons*. New York: B. W. Huebsch, 1920. Reprint, New York: Da Capo Press, 1971.

Fowler, Robert Booth. *Carrie Catt: Feminist Politician*. Boston: Northeastern University Press, 1986.

Fox, Elaine. *Come Lovely and Soothing Death: The Right to Die Movement in the United States*. New York: Twayne, 1999.

Frady, Marshall. *Jesse: The Life and Pilgrimage of Jesse Jackson*. New York: Random House, 1996.

Fraser, Steven. *Labor Will Rule: Sidney Hillman and the Rise of American Labor*. New York: The Free Press, 1991.

Free Congress Research and Education Foundation. *Cultural Conservatism: Toward a New National Agenda*. Washington, DC: The Foundation, 1988.

Freedman, Russell. *Eleanor Roosevelt: A Life of Discovery*. New York: Clarion Books, 1993.

Freeman, Jo, ed. *Social Movements of the Sixties and Seventies*. New York: Longman, 1983.

Freeman, Martha, ed. *Always Rachel: The Letters of Rachel Carson and Dorothy Freeman, 1952–1964.* Boston: Beacon Press, 1995.

Friedan, Betty. *Beyond Gender: The New Politics of Work and Family.* Baltimore: Johns Hopkins University Press, 1997.

———. *The Feminine Mystique.* 3rd ed. New York: W. W. Norton, 1997.

———. *The Second Stage: With a New Introduction.* Cambridge, MA: Harvard University Press, 1999.

Gagné, Patricia. *Battered Women's Justice: The Movement of Clemency and the Politics of Self-Defense.* New York: Twayne, 1998.

Garcia, Mario T. *Mexican Americans: Leadership, Ideology, and Identity, 1930–1960.* New Haven: Yale University Press, 1989.

Garcia, Raymond. "The Citizen Groups in the Nuclear Power Protest Movement: A Reassessment." Master's thesis, Michigan State University, Department of Sociology, 1993.

Gardner, John W. *In Common Cause.* New York: W. W. Norton, 1972.

Garey, Diane. *Defending Everybody: A History of the American Civil Liberties Union.* New York: TV Books, 1998. [Accompanies 1998 PBS special on the history of the ACLU.]

Garrow, David J. *Bearing the Cross: Martin Luther King, Jr. and the Southern Christian Leadership Conference.* New York: Morrow/Avon, 1999.

———. *Liberty and Sexuality: The Right to Privacy and the Making of Roe vs. Wade.* Berkeley: University of California Press, 1998.

Garvey, Amy. *Philosophy and Opinions of Marcus Garvey.* New York: Atheneum, 1992.

Gay, Kathlyn, and Martin Gay. *Heroes of Conscience.* Santa Barbara: ABC-CLIO, 1996.

George, John, and Laird Wilcox. *American Extremists: Militias, Supremacists, Klansmen, Communists, and Others.* Amherst, NY: Prometheus Books, 1996.

Gibbs, Lois Marie. *Dying from Dioxin: A Citizen's Guide to Reclaiming Our Health and Rebuilding Democracy.* Cambridge, MA: South End Press, 1995.

———. *Love Canal: The Story Continues.* North Kingstown, CT: New Society, 1998.

Gillon, Steven M. *Politics and Vision: The ADA and American Liberalism, 1947–1985.* New York: Oxford University Press, 1987.

Gitlin, Todd. *The Sixties: Years of Hope, Days of Rage.* Toronto: Bantam Books, 1987.

Glen, John. *Highlander: No Ordinary School, 1932–1962.* Lexington: University of Kentucky Press, 1988.

Glover, James M. *A Wilderness Original: The Life of Bob Marshall.* Seattle: Mountaineers, 1986.

Goines, David I. *Free Speech Movement.* Berkeley: Ten Speed Press, 1993.

Goldmark, Josephine. *Impatient Crusader: Florence Kelley's Life Story.* Urbana: University of Illinois Press, 1953.

Goldstein, Leslie Friedman. *Contemporary Cases in Women's Rights.* Madison: University of Wisconsin Press, 1994.

Goldwin, Robert A., and William A. Schambra. *The Constitution, the Courts, and the Quest for Justice.* Washington, DC: American Enterprise Institute for Public Policy Research, 1989.

Goodwyn, Lawrence. *Democratic Promise: The Populist Moment in America.* New York: Oxford University Press, 1976.

Grabowski, John F. *The Death Penalty.* San Diego: Lucent Books, 1999.

Graham, Frank, Jr. *The Audubon Ark: A History of the National Audubon Society.* Austin: University of Texas Press, 1992.

Graves, Charles Parlin. *Father Flanagan: Founder of Boys Town.* Dallas: Garrard Publishing, 1972.

Greider, William. *Who Will Tell the People: The Betrayal of American Democracy.* New York: Simon and Schuster, 1992.

Greile, Janet Zollinger. *Two Paths to Women's Equality: Temperance, Suffrage, and the Origins of Modern Feminism.* New York: Twayne, 1995.

Grinspoon, Lester, and James B. Bakalar. *Marihuana: The Forbidden Medicine.* New Haven: Yale University Press, 1993.

Griswold del Castillo, Richard. *Cesar Chavez: A Triumph of Spirit.* Norman: University of Oklahoma Press, 1995.

Gross, Michael. *My Generation: Fifty Years of Sex, Drugs, Rock, Revolution, Glamour, Greed, Valor, Faith, and Silicon Chips.* New York: Cliff Street/HarperCollins, 2000.

Grossman, Mark. *The Native American Rights Movement.* Santa Barbara: ABC-CLIO, 1996.

Guither, Harold D. *Animal Rights: History and Scope of a Radical Social Movement.* Carbondale: Southern Illinois University Press, 1998.

Gwyn, Douglas. *A Declaration of Peace: In God's People the World's Renewal Has Begun. A Contribution to Ecumenical Dialogue.* Scottdale, PA: Herald Press, 1991.

Haas, Carol. *Engel v. Vitale: Separation of Church and State.* Hillside, NJ: Enslow, 1994.

BIBLIOGRAPHY

Haiek, Joseph R., ed. *Arab-American Almanac.* 5th ed., rev. Glendale, CA: News Circle, 1998.

Haines, Herbert H. *Against Capital Punishment: The Anti–Death Penalty Movement in America, 1972–1994.* New York: Oxford University Press, 1996.

Halevi, Jossi Klein. *Memoirs of a Jewish Extremist: An American Story.* Boston: Little, Brown, 1995.

Haley, Alex. *The Autobiography of Malcolm X.* New York: Ballantine Books, 1999.

Hardisty, Jean. *Mobilizing Resentment: Conservative Resurgence from the John Birch Society to the Promise Keepers.* Boston: Beacon Press, 1999.

Harrell, David Edwin, Jr. *Pat Robertson: A Personal, Religious, and Political Portrait.* San Francisco: Harper and Row, 1987.

Harris, LaDonna. *LaDonna Harris: A Comanche Life.* Lincoln: University of Nebraska Press, 2000.

Hart, Gary. *Minuteman: Restoring an Army of the People.* New York: Simon and Schuster, 1998.

Haskins, James. *Guardian Angels.* Berkeley Heights, NJ: Enslow, 1983.

———. *Jesse Jackson: Civil Rights Activist.* Berkeley Heights, NJ: Enslow, 2000.

———. *Power to the People: The Rise and Fall of the Black Panther Party.* New York: Simon and Schuster Books for Young Readers, 1997.

Hayden, Tom. *The Port Huron Statement: The Founding Manifesto of Students for a Democratic Society.* Reprint, Chicago: Charles H. Kerr, 1990.

———. *Reunion: A Memoir.* New York: Random House, 1988.

———. *Tom Hayden: An Activist Life.* Niwot, CO: Roberts Rinehart, 1997.

Hearst, Patricia. *Every Secret Thing.* Garden City, NY: Doubleday, 1982.

Heineman, Kenneth J. *God Is a Conservative: Religion, Politics, and Morality in Contemporary America.* New York: New York University Press, 1998.

Hellebust, Lynn. *Think Tank Directory: A Guide to Nonprofit Public Policy Research Organizations.* Washington, DC: Government Research Service, 1996.

Hendin, Herbert. *Seduced by Death: Doctors, Patients, and Assisted Suicide.* New York: W. W. Norton, 1998.

Hennessee, Judith Adler. *Betty Friedan: Her Life.* New York: Random House, 1999.

Henson, Burt M. *Furman v. Georgia: The Death Penalty and the Constitution.* New York: Franklin Watts, 1996.

Hill, Robert A. *Marcus Garvey: Life and Lessons.* Irvine, CA: University of California Press, 1987.

Hoffer, Eric. *The True Believer.* New York: Harper and Row, 1951.

Hoffman, Abbie. *Revolution for the Hell of It.* New York: Pocket Books, 1970.

———. *Soon to Be a Major Motion Picture.* New York: Grove/Atlantic, 2000.

———. *Steal This Book.* 25th ed. New York: Four Walls Eight Windows, 1995.

Holsworth, Robert D. *Public Interest Liberalism and the Crisis of Affluence: Reflections on Nader, Environmentalism, and the Politics of a Sustainable Society.* Rochester, NY: Schenkman Books, 1981.

Horowitz, Daniel. *Betty Friedan and the Making of "The Feminine Mystique": The American Left, the Cold War, and Modern Feminism.* Amherst: University of Massachusetts Press, 1998.

Horton, Aimee Isgrig. *The Highlander Folk School: A History of Its Major Programs, 1932–1961.* Brooklyn: Carlson, 1989.

Horton, Myles, with Judith Kohl and Herbert Kohl. *The Long Haul: An Autobiography.* New York: Teachers College Press, 1998.

Horton, Myles, and Paolo Freire. *We Make the Road by Walking: Conversations on Education and Social Change.* Philadelphia: Temple University Press, 1990.

Horwitt, Sanford D. *Let Them Call Me Rebel: Saul Alinsky—His Life and Legacy.* New York: Alfred A. Knopf, 1989.

Howard, James R. *James R. Howard and the Farm Bureau.* Ames: Iowa State University Press, 1983.

Huckle, Patricia. *Tish Sommers, Activist, and the Founding of the Older Women's League.* Knoxville: University of Tennessee Press, 1991.

Hughes, Langston. *Fight for Freedom: The Story of the NAACP.* New York: W. W. Norton, 1962.

Hull, Mary. *Rosa Parks: Civil Rights Leader.* Broomall, PA: Chelsea House, 1994.

Humphry, Derek. *Final Exit: The Practicalities of Self-Deliverance and Assisted Suicide for the Dying.* Collingdale, PA: Diane Publishing, 1998.

INFACT. *INFACT Brings GE to Light: General Electric: Shaping Nuclear Weapons Policies for Profits.* Boston: INFACT, 1988.

———. *INFACT's 1998 People's Annual Report.* Boston: INFACT, 1999.

Ireland, Patricia. *What Women Want.* New York: Dutton, 1996.

Isserman, Maurice. *If I Had a Hammer . . . : The Death of the Old Left and the Birth of the New Left.* New York: Basic Books, 1987.

Isserman, Maurice, and Michael Kazin. *America Divided: The Civil War of the 1960s.* New York: Oxford University Press, 2000.

Izaak Walton League of America. *Annual Reports,* 1993–1998.

Jacobs, Ron. *The Way the Wind Blew: A History of the Weather Underground.* New York: Verso, 1997.

Jacobson, Michael F. *Marketing Madness: A Survival Guide for a Consumer Society.* Boulder, CO: Westview Press, 1995.

Jacobson, Michael F., and Sarah Fritschner. *The Fast-Food Guide: What's Good, What's Bad, and How to Tell the Difference.* New York: Workman Publishing, 1991.

Jaffe, Jerome H., ed. *Encyclopedia of Drugs and Alcohol.* New York: Macmillan, 1995.

James, Joy, ed. *The Angela Y. Davis Reader.* Cambridge, MA: Blackwell, 1998.

Jarvis, Howard. *I'm Mad as Hell.* New York: Times Books, 1979.

Jeansonne, Glen. *Gerald L. K. Smith: Minister of Hate.* New Haven: Yale University Press, 1988.

———. *Women of the Far Right: The Mothers' Movement and World War II.* Chicago: University of Chicago Press, 1996.

Jencks, Christopher. *The Homeless.* Cambridge, MA: Harvard University Press, 1994.

Jezer, Marty. *Abbie Hoffman: American Rebel.* Piscataway, NJ: Rutgers University Press, 1993.

Johanningsmeier, Edward P. *Forging American Communism: The Life of William Z. Foster.* Princeton, NJ: Princeton University Press, 1994.

Jones, J. Harry, Jr. *The Minutemen.* Garden City, NY: Doubleday, 1968.

Josephson, Judith Pinkerton. *Mother Jones: The Worker's Champion.* Minneapolis: Lerner Publishing Group, 1997.

Josephy, Alvin, Jr., and others. *Red Power: The American Indians' Fight for Freedom.* Lincoln: University of Nebraska Press, 1999.

Kamber, Victor, and others. *Giving Up on Democracy: Why Term Limits Are Bad for America.* Washington, DC: Regnery, 1995.

Kass, Leon R., and James Q. Wilson. *The Ethics of Human Cloning.* Washington, DC: AEI Press, 1998.

Katz, Jonathan. *Gay American History: Lesbians and Gay Men in the U.S.A. A Documentary.* New York: Harper and Row, 1985.

Kevorkian, Jack. *Prescription Medicide: The Goodness of Planned Death.* Buffalo, NY: Prometheus Books, 1991.

King, Dennis. *Lyndon LaRouche and the New American Fascism.* New York: Doubleday, 1989.

King, Martin Luther, Jr. *The Autobiography of Martin Luther King, Jr.* Edited by Clayborne Carson. New York: Warner Books, 1998.

Kleiman, Mark. *Against Excess: Drug Policy for Results.* New York: Basic Books, 1992.

Knobel, Dale T. *"America for the Americans": The Nativist Movement in the United States.* New York: Twayne, 1996.

Kollman, Ken. *Outside Lobbying: Public Opinion and Interest Group Strategies.* Princeton, NJ: Princeton University Press, 1998.

Kramer, Larry. *Reports from the Holocaust: The Story of an AIDS Activist.* New York: St. Martin's Press, 1994.

Kuhn, Maggie, with Christina Long and Laura Quinn: *No Stone Unturned: The Life and Times of Maggie Kuhn.* New York: Ballantine Books, 1991.

Laslett, John M., ed. *The United Mine Workers of America: A Model of Industrial Solidarity.* University Park: Pennsylvania State University Press, 1996.

Lear, Linda. *Rachel Carson: Witness for Nature.* New York: Henry Holt, 1997.

———, ed. *Lost Woods: The Discovered Writings of Rachel Carson.* Boston: Beacon Press, 1998.

Lee, Martha F. *Earth First! Environmental Apocalypse.* Syracuse, NY: Syracuse University Press, 1995.

———. *The Nation of Islam: An American Millenarian Movement.* Syracuse, NY: Syracuse University Press, 1996.

Leifermann, Henry P. *Crystal Lee: A Woman of Inheritance.* New York: Macmillan, 1975.

Lerner, Eric K., and Mary Ellen Hombs. *AIDS Crisis in America: A Reference Handbook.* 2nd ed. Santa Barbara: ABC-CLIO, 1998.

Levine, Susan. *Degrees of Equality: The American Association of University Women and the Challenge of Twentieth Century Feminism.* Philadelphia: Temple University Press, 1995.

Levy, Peter B. *The Civil Rights Movement.* Westport, CT: Greenwood Press, 1998.

Lewis, David Levering. *W.E.B. Du Bois: Biography*

of a Race, 1868–1919. New York: Henry Holt, 1993.

———. *W.E.B. Du Bois: The Fight for Equality and the American Century, 1919–1963*. New York: Henry Holt, 2000.

Lewis, John. *Walking with the Wind*. New York: Simon and Schuster, 1998.

Libby, Ronald T. *Eco-wars: Political Campaigns and Social Movements*. New York: Columbia University Press, 1998.

Library of Congress, Manuscript Division. *The Blackwell Family, Carrie Chapman Catt, and the National American Woman Suffrage Association*. Washington, DC: Library of Congress, Manuscript Division, 1985.

Lichtenstein, Nelson. *The Most Dangerous Man in Detroit: Walter Reuther and the Fate of American Labor*. New York: Basic Books, 1995.

Loeb, Paul Rogat. *Generation at the Crossroads: Apathy and Action on the American Campus*. New Brunswick, NJ: Rutgers University Press, 1994.

Loeper, John J. *Crusade for Kindness: Henry Bergh and the ASPCA*. New York: Atheneum Books for Young Readers, 1991.

Lunardini, Christine A. *The ABC-CLIO Companion to the American Peace Movement in the Twentieth Century*. Santa Barbara: ABC-CLIO, 1994.

———. *From Equal Suffrage to Equal Rights: Alice Paul and the National Woman's Party, 1910–1928*. New York: New York University Press, 1988.

Lynd, Staughton. *Living Inside Our Hope: A Steadfast Radical's Thoughts on Rebuilding the Movement*. Ithaca, NY: Cornell University Press, 1997.

Lynn, Barry. *Your Right to Religious Liberty: A Basic Guide to Religious Rights*. Carbondale: Southern Illinois University Press, 1995.

Lyon, Danny. *Memories of the Southern Civil Rights Movement*. Chapel Hill: University of North Carolina Press, 1992.

MacNair, Rachel. *Prolife Feminism—Yesterday and Today*. New York: Sulzburger and Graham, 1995.

Magida, Arthur J. *Prophet of Rage: A Life of Louis Farrakhan and His Nation*. New York: Basic Books, 1996.

Manis, Andrew M. *A Fire You Can't Put Out: The Civil Rights Life of Birmingham's Reverend Fred Shuttlesworth*. Tuscaloosa: University of Alabama Press, 1999.

Marcus, Sheldon. *Father Coughlin: The Tumultuous Life of the Priest of the Little Flower*. Boston: Little, Brown, 1973.

Marquez, Benjamin. *LULAC: The Evolution of a Mexican American Political Organization*. Austin: University of Texas Press, 1993.

Martin, William. *With God on Our Side: The Rise of the Religious Right in America*. New York: Broadway Books, 1996.

Mass, Lawrence D., ed. *We Must Love One Another or Die: The Life and Legacies of Larry Kramer*. New York: St. Martin's Press, 1997.

Massengill, Reed. *Portrait of a Racist*. New York: St. Martin's Press, 1994.

McCartney, Bill. *Sold Out: Becoming Man Enough to Make a Difference*. Nashville, TN: Word Publishing, 1997.

McDaniel, Melissa. *W.E.B. Du Bois: Scholar and Civil Rights Activist*. New York: Franklin Watts, 1999.

McFarland, Andrew S. *Common Cause: Lobbying in the Public Interest*. Chatham, NJ: Chatham House, 1984.

McGann, James G. *Think Tanks and Civil Societies: Catalysts for Ideas and Action*. Piscataway, NJ: Transaction, 2000.

McGlen, Nancy E., and Karen O'Connor. *Women, Politics, and American Society*. 2nd ed. Upper Saddle River, NJ: Prentice-Hall, 1998.

McKay, Emily Gantz. *The National Council of La Raza: The First Twenty-Five Years*. Washington, DC: The Council, 1993.

McNeal, Patricia F. *Harder than War: Catholic Peacemaking in Twentieth-Century America*. Trenton, NJ: Rutgers University Press, 1992.

McPhee, John. *Encounters with the Archdruid: Narratives about a Conservationist and Three of His Natural Enemies*. New York: Farrar, Straus and Giroux, 1971.

Means, Russell, with Marvin J. Wolf. *Where White Men Fear to Tread: The Autobiography of Russell Means*. New York: St. Martin's Press, 1995.

Meier, August. *CORE: A Study in the Civil Rights Movement, 1942–1968*. Champaign: University of Illinois Press, 1975.

Meigs, Cornelia L. *Jane Addams, Pioneer for Social Justice: A Biography*. Boston: Little, Brown, 1970.

Merchant, Carolyn. *Radical Ecology*. London: Routledge, 1992.

Milbrath, L. W. *Environmentalists: Vanguard for a New Society*. Albany: State University of New York Press, 1984.

Miles, John C. *Guardians of the Parks: A History*

of the National Parks and Conservation Association. Washington, DC: Taylor Francis, 1995.

Miller, Jim. *"Democracy Is in the Streets": From Port Huron to the Siege of Chicago*. New York: Simon and Schuster, 1987.

Miller, William. *Dorothy Day: A Biography*. New York: Harper and Row, 1982.

Mills, Kay. *This Little Light of Mine: The Life of Fannie Lou Hamer*. New York: Dutton, 1993.

Mintz, Frank P. *The Liberty Lobby and the American Right: Race, Conspiracy, and Culture*. Westport, CT: Greenwood Press, 1985.

Mooney, Patrick H., and Theo J. Majka. *Farmers' and Farm Workers' Movements: Social Protest in American Agriculture*. New York: Twayne, 1995.

Morris, Charles R. *The AARP: America's Most Powerful Lobby and the Clash of Generations*. New York: Random House, 1996.

Morris, David B. *Earth Warrior: Overboard with Paul Watson and the Sea Shepherd Conservation Society*. Golden, CO: Fulcrum Publishing, 1995.

Mott, Laurie. *Our Children at Risk: The Five Worst Environmental Threats to Their Health*. New York: Natural Resources Defense Council, 1997.

Mungazi, Dickson A. *Where He Stands: Albert Shanker of the American Federation of Teachers*. Westport, CT: Greenwood Publishing Group, 1995.

Myers, Walter Dean. *Malcolm X: A Fire Burning Brightly*. New York: HarperCollins, 2000.

Nader, Ralph. *Collision Course: The Truth about Airline Safety*. New York: McGraw-Hill Professional Publishing, 1995.

———. *The Menace of Atomic Energy*. New York: W.W. Norton, 1977.

———. *No Contest: How the Power Lawyers Are Perverting Justice in America*. New York: Random House, 1996.

———. *Who Runs Congress?* New York: Viking Penguin, 1979.

———. *Winning the Insurance Game: The Complete Consumer's Guide to Saving Money*. New York: Doubleday, 1993.

Naff, Alixa. *The Arab Americans*. Broomall, PA: Chelsea House, 1987.

National Civic League. *The Civic Index: The National Civic League Model for Improving Community Life*. Denver: National Civic League, 1998.

National Coalition Against Domestic Violence.

NCADV—Organizational Background. Denver: NCADV, 1994.

National Conference of State Legislatures. *1997 State Legislative Summary: Children, Youth and Family Issues*. Denver: NCSL, 1998.

National Taxpayers Union. *A Call to Action*. Alexandria, VA: NTU, 1989.

National Wildlife Federation. *Your Choices Count: National Wildlife Federation Citizen Action Guide*. Washington, DC: The Federation, 1990.

Natural Resources Defense Council. *Twenty-Five Years Defending the Environment: Natural Resources Defense Council, 1970–1995*. New York: NRDC, 1995.

Newkirk, Ingrid. *Free the Animals! The Inside Story of the U.S. Animal Liberation Front and Its Founder, "Valerie."* Chicago: Noble Press, 1992.

Newton, Huey P. *To Die for the People: The Writings of Huey P. Newton*. New York: Writers and Readers Publishing, 1995.

Null, Gary. *For Women Only! Your Guide to Health Empowerment*. New York: Seven Stories Press, 2000.

O'Connor, Karen. *No Neutral Ground? Abortion Politics in an Age of Absolutes*. Boulder, CO: Westview Press, 1996.

Odegard, Peter H. *Pressure Politics: The Story of the Anti-Saloon League*. New York: Hippocrene Books, 1967.

Owen, Marna. *Animal Rights: Yes or No?* Minneapolis: Lerner Publications, 1993.

Parks, Rosa, with Jim Haskins. *Rosa Parks: My Story*. New York: Penguin Putnam Books for Young Readers, 1992.

Patterson, Lillie. *A. Philip Randolph: Messenger for the Masses*. New York: Facts on File, 1996.

Pearson, Hugh. *The Shadow of the Panther: Huey Newton and the Price of Black Power in America*. Reading, MA: Addison Wesley Longman, 1995.

Pegram, Thomas R. *Battling Demon Rum: The Struggle for a Dry America, 1800–1933*. Chicago: Ivan R. Dee, 1998.

Peltier, Leonard. *Prison Writings: My Life Is My Sun Dance*. Edited by Harvey Arden. New York: St. Martin's, Press 1999.

Pencak, William. *For God and Country: The American Legion, 1919–1941*. Boston: Northeastern University Press, 1989.

Perlmutter, Nate, and Ruth Ann Perlmutter. *The Real Anti-Semitism in America*. New York: Morrow/Avon, 1982.

Peterson, Peter G. *Gray Dawn: How the Coming*

Age Wave Will Transform America—and the World. New York: Random House, 1999.

Pfeffer, Paula F. *A. Philip Randolph, Pioneer of the Civil Rights Movement*. Baton Rouge: Louisiana State University Press, 1990.

Piehl, Mel. *Breaking Bread: The Catholic Worker and the Origin of Catholic Radicalism in America*. Philadelphia: Temple University Press, 1982.

Polner, Murray, Jim O'Grady, and Anthony J. Lukas. *Disarmed and Dangerous: The Radical Lives and Times of Daniel and Philip Berrigan, Brothers in Religious Faith and Civil Disobedience*. Boulder, CO: Westview Press, 1998.

Powell, Lawrence A. *The Senior Rights Movement: Framing the Policy Debate in America*. New York: Twayne, 1996.

Pringle, Laurence. *The Environmental Movement: From Its Roots to the Challenges of a New Century*. New York: HarperCollins, 2000.

Rashke, Richard L. *The Killing of Karen Silkwood: The Story Behind the Kerr-McGee Plutonium Case*. Boston: Houghton Mifflin, 1981.

Ravitch, Frank S. *School Prayer and Discrimination: The Civil Rights of Religious Minorities and Dissenters*. Boston: Northeastern University Press, 1999.

Rawls, John. *Political Liberalism*. New York: Columbia University Press, 1993.

Reed, Ralph. *Active Faith: How Christians Are Changing the Soul of American Politics*. New York: The Free Press, 1996.

Rees, John, and Alan Brinkley. *Voices of Protest: Huey Long, Father Coughlin and the Great Depression*. New York: Alfred A. Knopf, 1982.

Regan, Tom. *The Case for Animal Rights*. Berkeley: University of California Press, 1983.

Rimmerman, Craig A. *The New Citizenship: Unconventional Politics, Activism, and Service*. Boulder, CO: Westview Press, 1997.

Risen, James, and Judy L. Thomas. *Wrath of Angels: The American Abortion War*. New York: Basic Books, 1998.

Roberts, Ron E. *John L. Lewis: Hard Labor and Wild Justice*. Dubuque, IA: Kendall/Hunt, 1994.

Robertson, Pat. *The End of the Age*. Nashville, TN: Word, 1995.

Roe, David. *Dynamos and Virgins*. New York: Random House, 1985.

Rogers, Kim Lacy. *Righteous Lives*. New York: New York University Press, 1993.

Rogers, Marion. *Acorn Days: The Environmental Defense Fund and How It Grew*. New York: EDF, 1990.

Rogers, Mary Beth. *Cold Anger: A Story of Faith and Power Politics*. Denton, TX: University of North Texas Press, 1990.

Romaine, Deborah S. *Roe v. Wade: Abortion and the Supreme Court*. San Diego: Lucent Books, 1998.

Roosevelt, Eleanor. *Courage in a Dangerous World: The Political Writings of Eleanor Roosevelt*. Edited by Allida M. Black. New York: Columbia University Press, 1999.

Rosen, Ruth. *The World Split Open: How the Modern Women's Movement Changed America*. New York: Viking, 2000.

Rothenberg, Lawrence S. *Linking Citizens to Government: Interest Group Politics at Common Cause*. Cambridge, England: Cambridge University Press, 1992.

Rowell, Andrew. *Green Backlash: Global Subversion of the Environmental Movement*. London: Routledge, 1996.

Rowell, Willis. *The National Farmers Organization: A Complete History*. Ames, IA: Sigler Printing and Publishing, 1993.

Rudwick, Elliot M. *W.E.B. Du Bois: Propagandist of the Negro Protest*. New York: Atheneum, 1972.

Rudy, Willis. *The Campus and a Nation in Crisis: From the American Revolution to Vietnam*. Madison, NJ: Fairleigh Dickinson University Press, 1996.

Rumer, Thomas A. *The American Legion: An Official History, 1919–1989*. New York: M. Evans and Co., 1990.

Rummel, Jack. *Malcolm X*. New York: Chelsea House, 1989.

Saloma, John, III. *Ominous Politics*. New York: Hill and Wang, 1984.

Salvatore, Nick. *Eugene V. Debs: Citizen and Socialist*. Champaign: University of Illinois Press, 1982.

Sampson, Robert J. *Crime in the Making: Pathways and Turning Points Through Life*. Cambridge, MA: Harvard University Press, 1993.

Sanger, Margaret. *Margaret Sanger: An Autobiography*. New York: W. W. Norton, 1938.

———. *The Margaret Sanger Papers: Collected Documents Series*. Bethesda, MD: University Publications of America, 1997.

———. *My Fight for Birth Control. Volume 4*. Elkins Park, IL: Franklin Book Co., 1959.

Schlafly, Phyllis. *A Choice, Not an Echo*. Alton, IL: Pere Marquette Press, 1964.

———. *First Reader*. Alton, IL: Pere Marquette Press, 1994.

Seale, Bobby. *Barbeque'n with Bobby*. Berkeley, CA: Ten Speed Press, 1988.

Sepp, Peter J. *By Popular Demand: How Citizen-Driven Ballot Measures Have Shaped Tax Policy for the Better*. Alexandria, VA: National Taxpayers Union Foundation, 1999.

Shaiko, Ronald G. *Voices and Echoes for the Environment: Public Interest Representation in the 1990s and Beyond*. New York: Columbia University Press, 1999.

Shields, Pete. *Guns Don't Die—People Do: The Pros, the Cons, the Facts*. New York: William Morrow, 1981.

Shorto, Russell. *Jane Fonda: Political Activist*. New York: Houghton Mifflin, 1992.

Sigler, Jay A. *Civil Rights in America: 1500 to the Present*. Detroit: Gale, 1998.

Silber, Norman Isaac. *Test and Protest*. New York: Holmes and Meier, 1983.

Singer, Peter Albert David. *Animal Liberation*. Rev. ed. New York: Morrow/Avon, 1991.

Singh, Robert. *The Farrakhan Phenomenon: Race, Reaction, and the Paranoid Style in American Politics*. Washington, DC: Georgetown University Press, 1997.

Sklar, Kathryn Kish. *Florence Kelley and the Nation's Work: The Rise of Women's Political Culture*. New Haven: Yale University Press, 1997.

Smith, Daniel A. *Tax Crusaders and the Politics of Direct Democracy*. New York: Routledge, 1998.

Smith, Gibbs M. *Joe Hill*. Layton, UT: Gibbs Smith, 1984.

Smith, Wesley J. *Forced Exit: The Slippery Slope from Assisted Suicide to Legalized Murder*. New York: Times Books, 1997.

Solinger, Rickie, ed. *Abortion Wars: A Half Century of Struggle, 1950–2000*. Berkeley: University of California Press, 1998.

Stefancic, Jean, and Richard Delgado. *No Mercy: How Conservative Think Tanks and Foundations Changed America's Social Agenda*. Philadelphia: Temple University Press, 1996.

Stein, Judith. *The World of Marcus Garvey: Race and Class in Modern Society*. Baton Rouge: Louisiana State University Press, 1986.

Steinem, Gloria. *Outrageous Acts and Everyday Rebellions*. New York: Henry Holt, 1995.

———. *Revolution from Within: A Book of Self Esteem*. New York: Little, Brown, 1992.

———. *Road to the Heart*. New York: Random House, 1998.

Stern, Kenneth S. *A Force upon the Plain: The American Militia Movement and the Politics of Hate*. Norman: University of Oklahoma Press, 1997.

———. *Loud Hawk: The United States Versus the American Indian Movement*. Norman: University of Oklahoma Press, 1994.

Stewart, Gail B. *Militias*. San Diego: Lucent Books, 1998.

Stock, Evelyn M. *The Citizen Lobbyist: Guide to Action in Albany*. Albany: League of Women Voters of New York State, 1993.

Storrs, Landon R.Y. *Civilizing Capitalism: The National Consumers' League, Women's Activism, and Labor Standards in the New Deal Era*. Chapel Hill: University of North Carolina Press, 2000.

Stuhler, Barbara. *For the Public Record: A Documentary History of the League of Women Voters*. Westport, CT: Greenwood Publishing Group, 1999.

Svonkin, Stuart. *Jews Against Prejudice: American Jews and the Fight for Civil Liberties*. New York: Columbia University Press, 1997.

Sweeney, John J. *America Needs a Raise: Fighting for Economic Security and Social Justice*. New York: Houghton Mifflin, 1996.

Thorne, Melvin J. *American Conservative Thought since World War II: The Core Ideas*. New York: Greenwood Press, 1990.

Tobias, Sheila. *Faces of Feminism: An Activist's Reflections on the Women's Movement*. Boulder, CO: Westview Press, 1997.

Tocqueville, Alexis de. *Democracy in America*. Edited by J. P. Mayer. Translated G. Lawrence. Garden City, NY: Anchor, 1969. (Originally published in 1838)

Tribe, Laurence H. *Abortion: The Clash of Absolutes*. New York: W. W. Norton, 1992.

Turner, Tom. *Sierra Club: One Hundred Years of Protecting Nature*. New York: Harry N. Abrams, 1993.

Uhler, Lewis K. *Setting Limits: Constitutional Control of Government*. Washington, DC: Regnery, 1989.

Unger, Irwin. *The Movement: A History of the American New Left, 1959–1972*. New York: Dodd, Mead, 1974.

U.S. House Committee on Internal Security. *The Symbionese Liberation Army: A Study for the Use of the Committee on Internal Security, House of Representatives*. Washington, DC: Federal Bureau of Investigation, February 18, 1974.

Utter, Glenn H. *Encyclopedia of Gun Control and Gun Rights*. Phoenix: Oryx Press, 1999.

BIBLIOGRAPHY

Van Vorris, Jacqueline. *Carrie Chapman Catt: A Public Life*. New York: Feminist Press of the City University of New York, 1987.

Viguerie, Richard A. *The Establishment vs. the People: Is a New Populist Revolt on the Way?* Washington, DC: Regnery, 1984.

———. *The New Right: We're Ready to Lead*. Falls Church, VA: Caroline House, 1980.

Voigt, William. *Born with Fists Doubled: Defending Outdoor America*. Iowa City: Izaak Walton League of America Endowment, 1992.

Vollers, Maryanne. *Ghosts of Mississippi*. Boston: Little, Brown, 1995.

Wade, Wyn Craig. *The Fiery Cross: The Ku Klux Klan in America*. New York: Simon and Schuster, 1987.

Wald, Kenneth D. *Religion and Politics in the United States*. 3rd ed. Washington, DC: Congressional Quarterly, 1996.

Walker, Samuel. *In Defense of American Liberties: A History of the ACLU*. New York: Oxford University Press, 1990.

Wall, Derek. *Earth First! and the Anti-Roads Movement: Radical Environmentalism and Comparative Social Movements*. New York: Routledge, 1999.

Wallace, Steven P. *The Senior Movement: References and Resources*. New York: Macmillan, 1992.

Watson, Justin. *The Christian Coalition: Dreams of Restoration, Demands for Recognition*. New York: St. Martin's Press, 1997.

Wattleton, Faye. *Life on the Line*. New York: Ballantine Publishing Group, 1996.

Wedin, Carolyn. *Inheritors of the Spirit: Mary White Ovington and the Founding of the NAACP*. New York: Wiley, 1998.

Wexler, Sanford. *The Civil Rights Movement: An Eyewitness History*. New York: Facts on File, 1993.

Weyrich, Paul, comp. *Future Twenty-One: Directions for America in the Twenty-First Century*. Old Greenwich, CT: David-Adair, 1984.

Whitman, Alden, ed. *American Reformers: An*

H. W. Wilson Biographical Dictionary. New York: H. W. Wilson, 1985.

Wilcox, Clyde. *Onward Christian Soldiers? The Religious Right in American Politics*. Boulder, CO: Westview Press, 1996.

Wilcox, Fred A. *Uncommon Martyrs: The Berrigans, the Catholic Left, and the Plowshares Movement*. Reading, MA: Addison-Wesley, 1991.

Wildavsky, Aaron B. *But Is It True? A Citizen's Guide to Environmental Health and Safety Issues*. Cambridge, MA: Harvard University Press, 1995.

Will, George F. *Restoration: Congress, Term Limits and the Recovery of Deliberative Democracy*. New York: The Free Press, 1993.

Wills, Garry. *A Necessary Evil: A History of American Distrust of Government*. New York: Simon and Schuster, 1999.

Winters, Paul A., ed. *The Civil Rights Movement*. San Diego: Greenhaven Press, 2000.

Wolf, Robert V. *Capital Punishment*. Philadelphia: Chelsea House, 1997.

Wuthnow, Robert, ed. *The Encyclopedia of Politics and Religion*. Washington, DC: Congressional Quarterly, 1998.

Yablonski, C., R. Hegblom, and A. Fulk. *Guide to Nonprofit Advocacy and Policy Groups*. Washington, DC: Capital Research Center, 1997.

Young, James P. *Reconsidering American Liberalism: The Troubled Odyssey of the Liberal Idea*. Boulder, CO: Westview Press, 1995.

Young, Louise M., and Ralph A. Young, Jr. *In the Public Interest: The League of Women Voters, 1920–1970*. Westport, CT: Greenwood Press, 1989.

Zakin, Susan. *Coyotes and Town Dogs*. New York: Viking, 1993.

Zaslowsky, Dyan. *These American Lands*. New York: Holt, 1986.

Zieger, Robert H. *John L. Lewis: Labor Leader*. Old Tappan, NJ: Macmillan, 1988.

Zimmerman, Michael E. *Contesting Earth's Future: Radical Ecology and Postmodernity*. Berkeley: University of California Press, 1994.

Index

About the Author

RICHARD S. HALSEY was dean of the School of Information Science and Policy, State University of New York at Albany, from 1980 until 1993. He has served as secretary of New York State Common Cause, executive director of the Citizens' Library Council of New York State, chair of the State Documents Committee of The New York State Historical Records Advisory Board and Committee for the New York State Library. Halsey's other publications include contributions on library information topics in *Academic American Encyclopedia, Funk & Wagnalls New Encyclopedia, New Book of Knowledge, Encarta*: *Classical Music Recordings for Home and Library* and *Halsey's Choice* in *CD Review Digest*.